Cricketers' Who's Who 2018

Foreword by
DARYL MITCHELL

Editor
BENJ MOOREHEAD

Compiled by
JO HARMAN
& BEN GARDNER

Design
JOE PROVIS & ROB WHITEHOUSE

The
Cricketers'
Who's Who
2018

This edition first published in the UK by Cricket Properties Ltd

© Cricket Properties Ltd 2018

ISBN: 978-1-909811-42-3

Published by Jellyfish Publishing
www.jellyfishsolutions.co.uk

Editor: *Benj Moorehead*; Research and editorial: *Jo Harman, Ben Gardner, Ben Page*
Design: *Joe Provis, Rob Whitehouse*; Images: *Getty Images unless stated*;
Print: *Jellyfish Print Solutions*

Acknowledgements
The publishers would like to thank the county clubs and the players for their assistance in helping to put together this book. Additional information has been gathered from espncricinfo.com and cricketarchive.com. Thanks also to Mike Vimpany for providing images.

CONTENTS

The
Cricketers'
Who's Who
2018

WISDEN CRICKET MONTHLY

THE INDEPENDENT VOICE OF CRICKET

SUBSCRIBE, SAVE, SIT BACK...

and enjoy words of Wisden all year round!

**QUOTE CWW2018
TO SAVE UP TO**

33%

ORDER NOW
QUOTING
CWW2018
0129 331 2094
wisdensubs.com

Openers

FOREWORD

By Daryl Mitchell

It is an honour to be asked to write the foreword to the 2018 edition of *The Cricketers' Who's Who*, a book in which I used to collect autographs as a kid and have occupied my own page since 2003.

The *Who's Who* continues to be much loved in county dressing rooms up and down the country, whether it's for a game of 'guess the cricketer' during a rain break or a quick check on an opposing player's stats to tee up a sledge for the next session of play. It's always amusing to look back at pictures of yourself when a fan asks you to sign an old edition at the back of the pavilion of some cricketing outpost such as Colwyn Bay or Horsham.

The book contains all the 420(ish) professional county cricketers whom I am tasked with representing following my election as chairman of the Professional Cricketers' Association in February 2017. My first year in the job has presented some enjoyable challenges and opened my eyes to a world off the field and closer to the boardroom.

There have never been more opportunities for players to earn a fantastic living and travel the world playing the sport they love, whether that's at international level or the numerous Twenty20 events that are popping up everywhere. However, that comes with the need to take responsibility for actions and be aware of the pitfalls that exist. The PCA do fantastic work with the players regarding education in a wide range of areas such as drink awareness, gambling, illicit drugs, driving safety, social media responsibilities and anti-corruption. As for all things, prevention is better than a cure.

The tinkering with the domestic structure has been prominent for as long as I can remember and the most recent changes, introduced at the beginning of last season, were very interesting. The overall feeling among the players is that they have been a success, even if reducing the amount of County Championship games to 14 has led to a lack of symmetry in the 10-team Division Two, which is not ideal. The players felt that playing the various competitions in blocks has improved the quality of practice and in turn the standards and the spectacle on show. Changing between formats only six times over the course of the season – as opposed to the 26 times in 2016 – makes all the difference.

Last summer was a fantastic year for cricket in this country, with England Women winning the World Cup as hosts and catching the imagination of the nation. The men's team had success too, although the Test side will want to pick themselves up after a very difficult Ashes in Australia over the winter.

Many congratulations to Essex for winning the County Championship for the first time in 25 years. In doing so immediately after winning promotion the previous season, they have gone some way to dispel the myth of the huge gap between the two divisions. Having been promoted six times – and relegated five times – in my time at Worcestershire, I can relate to what a special achievement it is to win Division Two and Division One in successive years.

We mustn't forget Nottinghamshire either, who picked up both one-day trophies and gained Championship promotion. It was a fitting way for Chris Read to finish his magnificent career.

At Worcestershire we certainly enjoyed our first season under new skipper Joe Leach. He must take a lot of credit for leading us to a home semi-final in the One-Day Cup and to the Division Two title. There were some special performances from the many homegrown players, as well as important contributions from our excellent overseas contingent of John Hastings, Nathan Lyon and Ravi Ashwin. The lads are looking forward to playing in Division One again and testing ourselves against the best teams in the country.

I wish everyone an enjoyable 2018 season – whichever team you play for or support.

Daryl Mitchell
March 2018

By Benj Moorehead

I t's been a long, hard winter: by day a grim struggle against the punishing cold, by night an Ashes inferno Down Under. But there's nothing like a whipping by Australia to breathe life into a new season. For the 400-odd county cricketers across these pages, the spring air is thick with opportunity. Test places are up for grabs.

They need only look at the catapulted careers of Liam Livingstone and Richard Gleeson to know that anything is possible. Three years ago Livingstone was a cricketer for Nantwich CC languishing in Lancashire's Second XI. Then he struck 350 from 138 balls in a T20 club match and by the end of the summer was part of the Lancashire side which won the T20 Blast. Now the 24-year-old is the county's captain and was in line for a Test debut in New Zealand as we went to print. Gleeson's tale is perhaps even more remarkable, that of a 28-year-old Minor Counties player transformed into the leader of the Northants attack which won the 2016 T20 Blast. In February, aged 30, he made his England Lions debut. Full international recognition is a real prospect.

These are stories to inspire English cricketers up and down the country. The door is open, and now is the time to deliver.

A fleet of young county batsmen are eyeing up a spot in England's shaky top order. Somewhere near the front is Worcestershire's Joe Clarke, a man "destined to play for England" according to Sussex allrounder Luke Wright, who told the *Cricketers' Who's Who* that he is the best young batsman he has seen. Sam Northeast will also be very close to selection if he can score first-division runs for Hampshire following his high-profile move from Kent.

Keep an eye on opener Alex Davies, who last summer became the first Lancashire wicketkeeper to pass 1,000 first-class runs in a season. In fact there are three Red Rose openers who have England ambitions, with Keaton Jennings signing from Durham over the winter and Haseeb Hameed – still only 21 – slowly recovering the form that brought him a Test debut in 2016. Luke Wells at Sussex, Rory Burns at Surrey, Essex duo Nick Browne and Dan Lawrence… the list goes on.

England haven't had a regular frontline spinner for more than three years now, and there are two twirlers in the West Country who are mounting a claim to follow Mason Crane into the Test arena. Jack Leach must be wondering what else he needs to do to make the grade, having followed up 68 first-class wickets in 2016 with another 53 last season – this after being forced to remodel his action the previous winter. His Somerset teammate Dom Bess, not yet 21, had 54 first-class wickets at 22.57 going into 2018. Even accounting for the fact that both play their cricket on those ragging pitches at Taunton, such figures will surely prove irresistible to the England selectors before long.

And who are the future heirs to James Anderson and Stuart Broad, daunting prospect though that is? The obvious candidate is Jamie Porter, capable at the age of 24 of leading the seam attack of county champions Essex. Further back, Ben Coad of Yorkshire (24) and Josh Tongue of Worcestershire (20) both produced outstanding maiden first-class seasons, with 53 and 47 wickets respectively. Middlesex's Tom Helm, who turns 24 in May, is also hotly tipped to play international cricket sooner rather than later, and can count Andy Flower among his many supporters.

And then there is Jofra Archer, who merits a chapter all his own. This time last year Archer was Hove's best-kept secret; now he is a global superstar, having been purchased for more than $1m by IPL franchise Rajasthan Royals after some stunning displays for Hobart Hurricanes in the 2017/18 Big Bash. It is easy to forget how good he has been for Sussex in red-ball cricket (to date 89 wickets at 26 and 833 runs at 38). Archer, born and raised in Barbados, has played for West Indies U19 but says he is intent on qualifying for England in 2022. These pages are full of glowing praise from his peers: "Effortless pace, and he is becoming more skilful and smarter with every game," says his former Sussex teammate Steve Magoffin. Or as Northants' Steven Crook succinctly puts it: "He's just very good at cricket." It will be fascinating to see how Archer goes this year at Sussex, where he will be tutored by arguably the finest coach on the circuit, Jason Gillespie.

Sussex have made the most eye-catching overseas signing of the winter, with leg-spinner Rashid Khan set to become the first Afghanistan player to play county cricket, along with his compatriot Mohammad Nabi at Leicestershire. Rashid, whom Gillespie coached at Big Bash champions Adelaide Strikers, is due to play in the first half of the T20 Blast. Nabi, also signed for the Blast, is one of three rabbits Leicestershire pulled out of the hat, with Pakistan seamers Mohammad Abbas and Sohail Khan to share the overseas berth at Grace Road this season. Among this year's influx of internationals, Aiden Markram, Duanne Olivier, Adam Zampa, Daniel Worrall, Joe Mennie, Doug Bracewell, Mitchell Marsh, Ishant Sharma and Billy Stanlake will also be appearing on the county scene for the first time.

It is 50 years since foreign players were allowed into county cricket without going through a residential qualification period – a license, we thought, to pick a greatest overseas XI designed to incite and delight in equal measure (see page 16). Jon Hotten has written a pen-portrait for our chosen few, each as silky as a Sangakkara cover drive (well, almost). Elsewhere in the features section, Paul Collingwood opens up to John Stern about the hurt and pain at his beloved Durham. For something lighter, try Marcus Berkmann's homage to cricketing trivia on page 24; can *you* name a team of Test cricketers whose fathers were vicars called Herbert?

Trivia is something that *The Cricketers' Who's Who* unashamedly indulges in. The signature of the book is, of course, our questionnaire, faithfully answered by the players of all 18 counties and England Women (with more than a little encouragement from their media whips, to whom we are hugely grateful). They offer a glimpse into the diversity of the characters on the county circuit, from the complete Brit Ruaidhri Smith (born in Scotland to an Irish mother and English father, raised in Wales) to the Scandinavian allrounder Martin Andersson ("my karaoke song of choice is Basshunter's 'Now You're Gone' in Swedish"). There's a stunning revelation from 17-year-old Derbyshire prodigy Hamidullah Qadri, born in Afghanistan, who says he learnt off-spin by watching YouTube. Who needs the coaching manual?

This year we asked the players: where is paradise? And, while it's true that Barbados was a popular choice, there were plenty of more revealing selections: the great lakes of Ontario, a workshop with tools, a peaceful coffee shop with a leather-bound book, Hogwarts, Wantage Road, Bournemouth beach, Glenbuchat in Aberdeenshire, the Cheshire Oaks Factory Outlet Centre, North Sweden (yes, Andersson again) and… the bottom of a pint.

Which brings us neatly to the response of Northants spinner Graeme White when we asked him for the best advice he has ever received: "You need a steak and a Guinness to fill out lad."

Enjoy the book and the season.

Benj Moorehead
March 2018

LAST MAN STANDING

He has won the Ashes home and away, captained England to World T20 glory, celebrated Championship titles. But Paul Collingwood goes into his 23rd season facing one of his toughest challenges yet: to save his beloved Durham from wreckage. John Stern *spoke to him as spring approached*

Once he was Brigadier Block but now the only appropriate moniker is General Custer. Paul Collingwood, 42 at the end of May, stands alone at the Riverside while north-eastern heroes have continued to desert Durham's sinking ship.

Five seasons ago Durham won the last of their three County Championship titles (achieved in the space of six summers). Only six of the 18 players who appeared in the 2013 triumph are at the club this season: Collingwood, Ben Stokes, Mark Wood, Chris Rushworth, Michael Richardson and former captain Will Smith, who was re-signed from Hampshire in the winter.

On October 3, 2016 Durham accepted relegation and a 48-point penalty for the following season in return for a £3.8m bail-out from the ECB. A year and a day later, it emerged that Durham-born batsman Jack Burnham, 20, would be banned for a year following a third failed drugs test (a situation that Collingwood describes as "pure stupidity").

The talent drain started with Scott Borthwick and Mark Stoneman leaving for Surrey in the winter of 2016 and continued at the end of last summer with 50-over captain Keaton Jennings and veteran seamer Graham Onions heading to Lancashire, while T20 skipper and England Lions allrounder Paul Coughlin has moved to Nottinghamshire.

Collingwood is hurting about the loss of those players. "I'm absolutely devastated," he says. "I get really upset by it. This is my 23rd season at Durham and I've never found an obvious reason to leave the place.

"In my eyes you get as equal an opportunity here as any other county to play for England. I can half-understand batsmen saying wickets aren't as good as you might get at The Oval but a bowler like Coughlin wanting to leave Durham is something I can't get my head around.

"I'd like to have seen players say they wanted to help get the club out of the second division. But all the T20 leagues around the world mean people are more used to going into different changing rooms now. Loyalty is not a word that can be used much these days. You've just got to get on with it."

Collingwood's fighting qualities are well known. It was after his 276-minute 40 at Cape Town in 2010 that the *Guardian*'s Mike Selvey was moved to call him "the Brigadier of Block" and, in the same report, the less-celebrated "Sultan of Stonewall".

Do Durham's dire straits suit his man-on-burning-deck instincts? "It probably does but I haven't got long left," says Collingwood, with a melancholic chuckle. "I would much prefer to be in a situation where we're fighting for promotion or at top of the first division rather than losing players."

He was full of bullish intent at the start of last season but reality has set in with all the biting chill of a wind blowing off the North Sea. Durham finished second-last in Division Two of the Championship, bottom of the North Group in the T20 Blast, and fifth of nine in the group stages of the One-Day Cup.

"You never go into the season without the ambition to win trophies," Collingwood says, "but we have to be realistic. We have lost five experienced players over the last two years

– guys we have built up to playing international cricket. That probably took four years so we're going to have to wait until the next generation come through now.

"We have some good youngsters who have shown potential but with young guys you don't get the consistency. You never know with Durham – if we can build that spirit early on and get things moving then anything can happen. But realistically we're building a team for four or five years down the line."

Collingwood won't be around then – at least on the field – but in 2017 he continued to defy the march of time. In late May he scored a Championship century against Glamorgan on his 41st birthday. Two months later he became the oldest man to make a T20 hundred, which was also Durham's first in the format. He finished the season as the seventh-highest run-scorer across both divisions of the Championship, with 1,087 runs at 49 and three centuries.

His winter has been no less busy. In September he was to be seen grinning in brightly coloured auto rickshaws as he and a group of other seasoned players from around the world brought international cricket back to Pakistan by representing an ICC World XI side. In November he was borrowing Mason Crane's whites to field for an over as England suffered an injury crisis during one of their Ashes warm-up matches. As the fielding coach, he was with the team for most of the five-month tour of Australia and New Zealand.

Collingwood, who last played for England seven years ago, is taking it one summer at a time, with a decision expected by mid-season as to whether his Durham career will continue into a 24th season.

Despite the high-profile exits, he is excited by those who are left such as Cameron Steel, who scored 899 Championship runs at 40 last year, and Matthew Potts, the 19-year-old fast bowler from Sunderland who was pulled out of the Academy to make his first-team debut against Kent last June. Potts finished with 14 wickets from his five matches. "I'd never seen him before," recalls Collingwood, "but he impressed straightaway. He looks the real deal and is very exciting."

The picture that the Durham skipper paints is one of a still-thriving north-eastern league scene with strapping young lads itching to restore some pride to a passionate, put-upon cricketing territory. The club have been passed over as a host for the new domestic T20 competition and hosting Test matches now appears almost a distant memory, though they are clinging to the top table with an allocation of one-day internationals from 2020-24.

"We have a great record of producing international cricketers and I'd like to think people would want to come to Durham because of that," Collingwood says. "We must be doing something right. We will have to build that brand back up of keeping players and having that pride of playing for Durham again.

"The leagues up here are still very strong and highly contested and there's a huge desire to play cricket for a living. The living proof is when these players come into our Academy or into the first team.

"Potts, for example, has some serious skills and a great attitude and a lot of that comes from playing league cricket. Playing against men from an early age has given them a kick-start, especially to their mentality."

Collingwood makes an interesting observation that players across the English game – especially those from private schools – who have not experienced the tougher environments of league cricket from an early age get a rude awakening when they graduate to the professional game. It's worth noting that the Durham Academy was one of the founder members of the North East Premier League.

"If you play club cricket from an early age you experience failure and you have to find a way to overcome it. It gives you mental strength. People who dominate from an early age and then experience failure find it really hard. I'm not saying it's black and white but it's an interesting debate."

Not long before he got picked for England, Collingwood won the Jack Ryder medal as the player of the season in Victoria's grade competition so he knows plenty about mixing it with unforgiving clubbies.

With 300 England caps to his name and almost 10,000 international runs, Collingwood has inarguably made the most of his talents. The question now, as captain and mentor, is whether he can help Durham's rookie remainers do the same.

THE GREATEST OVERSEAS XI?

Fifty years ago county cricket opened its doors to the world's greatest players by removing the need for residential qualification. To mark the half-century, the Cricketers' Who's Who dared to pick a dream team of overseas players and came up with a side which has no space for Sobers, Turner, Rice, Lara, Donald, Saqlain, Warne or Sangakkara (among other outrageously good cricketers). Of course we looked at the runs and the wickets, but just as important when picking our team was the degree to which a player became part of a county's genetics. Then we asked Jon Hotten to carry the selectors' can by writing a beautiful eulogy for each player

1 Barry Richards

Hampshire (1968-78)
First-class: 204 matches, 15,607 runs at 50.50, 46 wickets at 36.41, 264 catches
List A: 186 matches, 6,708 runs at 39.92, 6 wickets at 23.16, 82 catches

Perhaps uniquely among greats of the modern era, Richards' place at the game's highest table was laid by his county career. Denied all but four Tests – during which he averaged 72.57 – by South Africa's international ban, Richards instead made Hampshire his stage. He has been called "the world's most romanticised cricketer" and it's easy to see why. As an opening batsman he was a silken destroyer of attacks, in possession of brilliance so dazzling he would sometimes divide the ground into an imaginary clock face and hit a boundary to each part in turn. Nine of his 80 first-class hundreds were made before lunch. Richards could appear disinterested, but once roused – by quality of opposition or size of occasion – he might do anything, put the ball anywhere. During Hampshire's great era of overseas stars – Greenidge, Roberts, Marshall – few would argue that Bad Baz was the first among equals.

2 Chris Rogers

Derbyshire (2004 & 2008-10), Leicestershire (2005), Northamptonshire (2006-07), Middlesex (2011-14), Somerset (2016)
FC: 151 matches, 12,641 runs at 53.33, 133 catches
LA: 85 matches, 2,854 runs at 40.19, 44 catches

Rogers is an unlikely hero, a rugged and street-smart opener whose runs, rather than his style, took the eye; a batsman who belonged to county cricket rather than any one county. Born in Sydney, he first visited England at 19 to play club cricket in Devon, before a season at Derbyshire in 2004. By 2005 he'd hopped over to Grace Road, where he made 219 for Leicestershire against the touring Australians, sledged all the way by Matthew Hayden. He went back to Derby in 2008, and made 248, the county's highest individual score for 62 years, against Warwickshire. A move to Middlesex made him a beloved old-stager at HQ, and set him up for his successful Test comeback – he would hit 173 at Lord's for Australia in 2015. A final fling as Somerset's captain took them desperately close to a first Championship title, and left Rogers with twin hundreds in his last match, retiring as that rare thing: an Australian loved equally in England.

3 Viv Richards

Somerset (1974-86), Glamorgan (1990-93)
FC: 240 matches, 18,080 runs at 49.26, 105 wickets at 46.99, 207 catches
LA: 279 matches, 9,270 runs at 39.95, 148 wickets at 26.51, 124 catches

Imperious and regal, King Viv turned sleepy Taunton into a riotous carnival of county cricket, a totemic superstar who powered Somerset to two Gillette Cups, two B&H Trophies and the Sunday League title. Yet Richards was no helicoptered-in legend (despite arriving in a chopper to play for Rishton CC in 1987); his affinity for the county, and for English cricket,

ran bone-deep. He was 'discovered' by Len Creed, a bookmaker from Bath who watched the young Richards while on holiday in Antigua, and he served a qualifying period at Lansdown CC before making the first of his 14,698 first-class runs for the county in 1974. Richards' rise to global superstardom ran in tandem with his time at Somerset, and in tandem too with that of his flatmate and lifelong friend Ian Botham. Sadly, he departed in rancour before playing a handful of seasons with Glamorgan – where his final act was to lead the Welsh county to the Sunday League title in 1993 – but those golden days remain, an indelible part of summer in England.

4 Darren Lehmann

Yorkshire (1996-2007)
FC: 88 matches, 8,871 runs at 68.79, 61 wickets at 32.00, 35 catches
LA: 130 matches, 5,229 runs at 49.33, 79 wickets at 25.18, 41 catches

The position as Yorkshire's overseas professional is necessarily special, as for so long the county's rules prevented it. Thus, from Sachin Tendulkar's arrival as the first in 1992, it took a big player and big personality to step up. Lehmann, known universally as 'Boof', was the perfect fit, an uncomplicated yet brilliant left-hander who became so revered that the *Yorkshire Post* wrote of him: "The great man could probably break wind in these parts and draw a standing ovation." Lehmann was key to the 2001 side that brought the County Championship home for the first time since 1968, the celebration of which meant he went out to bat in a Sunday League fixture with champagne sloshing around in his helmet – he made 191 from 103 deliveries. It was just a part of a legend burnished by 26 first-class hundreds and almost 9,000 runs for the White Rose.

5 Clive Lloyd

Lancashire (1968-86)
FC: 219 matches, 12,764 runs at 44.94, 55 wickets at 32.89, 161 catches
LA: 273 matches, 8,522 runs at 41.16, 60 wickets at 26.35, 94 catches

Shaping West Indies into the world's greatest and most feared cricket team was simply the day job for the bespectacled, ursine colossus that is Clive Hubert Lloyd. At Lancashire his broad and legendarily weighty blade crashed down upon county attacks for season after season – Lloyd was as beloved at Old Trafford as anywhere in the Caribbean. He broke through in 1970, making 1,600 runs in the English summer and voted one of *Wisden*'s Five

Cricketers of the Year. His famous 1975 World Cup-winning century at Lord's was foretold by the crushing 126 that brought Lancashire the 1972 Gillette Cup, and Glamorgan's bowlers still awaken in cold sweats at the memory of the 201 not out that occupied just 120 minutes – then the fastest double hundred struck in first-class cricket – back in 1976. "It was a cricketing utopia for me," Lloyd reflected in 2004. "Those were some of the happiest days of my career."

6 Mike Procter (c)

Gloucestershire (1965-81)
FC: 259 matches, 14,441 runs at 36.19, 833 wickets at 19.56, 209 catches
LA: 223 matches, 5,631 runs at 28.29, 280 wickets at 18.78, 69 catches

So devastating were the South African's all-round talents that, during his fearsome 1970s peak, Gloucestershire were re-named 'Proctershire' by the fans. Like his friend Barry Richards, with whom he played a season in Gloucester's Second XI in 1965, Procter was exiled from the international game, and so the West Countrymen saw the best of him; a batsman brilliant enough to score six centuries in successive innings for Rhodesia and an opening bowler of high pace and deadly inswing famously

delivered off the 'wrong' foot. His feats were mighty: 109 not out from a team total of 135-3 in a Sunday League match; a hundred before lunch and a hat-trick against Leicestershire in the Championship, followed by another hat-trick – all lbw – against Yorkshire in the next game. He crowned it all with the Benson & Hedges Cup in 1977, by which time he'd added the captaincy to his bag of tricks.

7 Richard Hadlee

Nottinghamshire (1978-87)
FC: 148 matches, 5,854 runs at 38.76, 622 wickets at 14.51, 105 catches
LA: 160 matches, 2,951 runs at 28.65, 231 runs at 17.99, 58 catches

Has a bowler ever been more deadly, and more at home, than Richard Hadlee on Trent Bridge's slick green-top? Probably not, as the figures from his three most magical seasons show: 319 wickets at 13.67. Those years – 1981, 1984 and 1987 (the only three of his 10 terms at Notts that were undisturbed by either international calls or injury) – saw him voted the PCA Player of the Year on each occasion. In an era of county cricket when pace bowlers stalked the land, no pair carried quite the same threat as Hadlee and his late, great South African partner Clive Rice (pictured below). Their contribution to the Championship wins of 1981 and '87 was vast. Hadlee's threat didn't end with cherry in hand either – as a middle-order hitter he was good enough to make both a double-century and register a thousand runs, feats that bought him the famous 'double' in 1984.

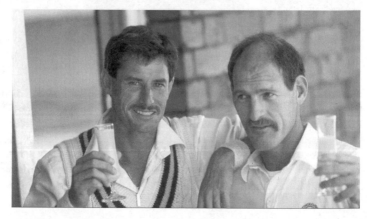

8 Farokh Engineer (wk)

Lancashire (1968-76)
FC: 175 matches, 5,942 runs at
26.64, 429 catches, 35 stumpings
LA: 154 matches, 2,843 runs at
22.74, 153 catches, 30 stumpings

Flamboyant and famous enough
to join Keith Miller and Denis
Compton in endorsing Brylcreem,
Engineer made his name by
keeping wicket to India's great
spin quartet of the 1960s and
early '70s, yet he would create a
life for himself in England, part
of the furniture at Old Trafford
and one of the great characters of
the county game. Immaculately
turned out, style was everything,
from his powerful, sometimes
quixotic, lower-order batting to
the supremely athletic glovework
that became his trademark. Although the Championship eluded them, it was a golden time
for Lancashire and Engineer, with four Gillette Cups and two Sunday League titles arriving
in quick and joyous succession.

9 Wasim Akram

Lancashire (1988-98), Hampshire (2003)
FC: 96 matches, 3,223 runs at 23.69, 394 wickets at 21.82, 23 catches
LA: 174 matches, 2,414 runs at 23.21, 270 wickets at 21.16, 34 catches

When asked who the best bowler he'd faced was, Brian Lara replied with a single word:
"Akram". The name would send chills through world cricket and the county game alike, as,
in 1988, Wasim began a decade-long reign of terror at Lancashire. "Straight away I thought
I'm going to make friends here," he said, and how right he was. He plucked out Graeme
Hick in the first over of his first big final, the B&H Cup in 1990, a herald for the successes

to come. For Lancashire he took 374 wickets in 91 first-class games at 21.65, evidence that Wasim played just as hard on those cold days in empty grounds as he would in the heat of Lord's finals. Throughout he was not just the best pace bowler in world cricket, but perhaps the greatest left-arm bowler of all time.

10 Mushtaq Ahmed

Somerset (1993-98), Surrey (2002), Sussex (2003-08)
FC: 149 matches, 3,035 runs at 17.44, 775 wickets at 25.84, 46 catches
LA: 155 matches, 821 runs at 12.07, 176 wickets at 28.18, 14 catches

The maestro from Multan had already spun his way into the heads of the world's great batsmen by the time he arrived at Sussex at the end of his Test career, and so electric would be his impact that, six years later, the south-coasters would have three Championship titles in the bag. The man they called Mushy was simply too good: the leading wicket-taker in the land for five years in a row from 2003, in all 478 wickets in 85 matches. Not to mention 289 wickets in 62 matches for Somerset in the mid-90s. But beyond the stats it was the artistry that turned him into a legend. Every variation in the leg-spinner's locker was at hand, and with age came a wisdom that saw him, post-retirement, become a hugely popular part of the England national team's coaching set-up before moving on to Pakistan's backroom, a hero in both lands.

11 Courtney Walsh

Gloucestershire (1984-98)
FC: 184 matches, 2,581 runs at 14.33, 869 wickets at 20.01, 52 catches
LA: 175 matches, 837 runs at 9.96, 243 wickets at 21.04, 29 catches

Look up 'indefatigable' in the dictionary and you'll find a picture of Courtney Walsh. Not content with more than 30,000 deliveries and 519 Test wickets, the master fast bowler from Jamaica would send down another 50,000 in the domestic first-class game. There was not a pro batsman of any merit that Courtney didn't account for at least once during his 11 years at Gloucestershire: all were familiar with his ability to switch from 80mph workhorse to 90mph steam train at the merest sniff of a breakthrough. In all, 1,112 wickets with white ball and red fell to him in county cricket, and as the man who saw most of them, Jack Russell, remarked: "In the early '80s batsmen used to run to get their pads on at Bristol. Once Courtney arrived, they used to look like ghosts they were so terrified."

12th man Bishan Bedi

Northamptonshire (1972-77)
FC: 110 matches, 1,002 runs at 11.13, 434 wickets at 20.89, 35 catches
LA: 53 matches, 173 runs at 6.92, 53 wickets at 28.03, 11 catches

By the time Bedi retired from first-class cricket in 1979, aged only 32, he had 1,560 wickets – more than any other Indian bowler. Throughout the decade, the man who had been a key component of India's symphonic spin quartet entranced the Wantage Road faithful with perhaps the most classically beautiful left-arm orthodox action of them all. Bedi's bowling was both an invitation and a trap, the flight and dip luring batsmen into fatal false shots. Coupled with his colourful gestures and forthright opinions, along with the patka he always wore, it ensured Bedi iconic status among the county's supporters. He could not quite contribute that longed-for first Championship title, Northants finishing runners-up in 1976, but Bedi was to help bring home the Gillette Cup at Lord's that same summer, when his innings-best 3-52 would have been even better had Lancashire's David Hughes not assailed his final over for 26.

THE IMPORTANCE OF BEING TRIVIAL

Marcus Berkmann *on the joy of picking a team of Test players whose fathers were vicars called Herbert, and other trifles*

A few months ago, I went to stay with my friend Julian in Lincolnshire. Julian used to be a senior civil servant, and he has a mind like a stiletto. We were watching the semi-final of the Champions Trophy on Sky Sports. Pakistan's exciting new fast bowler Rumman Raees came on to bowl.

I looked at Julian. I said the word "Raees" and then raised my eyebrow, as though to say: "What other cricketing relevance does that name have?"

It took him, at most, a second and a half to respond.

"The only Mohammad brother not to play Test cricket," he said. I congratulated him.

"Do you know anybody else who would have got that?" asked Julian, with a big beaming grin all over his face.

I thought a moment. "Only two people. Steven Lynch of ESPNcricinfo, and my friend Richard, who lives in Hampshire."

Later on, I emailed Richard to tell him of this conversation. He too used to be a senior civil servant, and he has a mind like a sabre. The following day he replied.

"By an astonishing coincidence," he wrote, "I was looking at the Mohammad family yesterday morning just before the start of the game. I'd searched 'Raees' on Cricinfo to find out more about Rumman Raees and of course one thing led to another. When I found a Mohammad Raees, who played a single first-class match in the early 1970s for Pakistan International Airlines, I got to wondering whether I could think of any other pairs of cricketers who shared their names in reverse. Unfortunately I didn't get very far because I was forced to start doing some work."

I'm imagining him in his huge office, drinking incredibly strong coffee and asking his secretary to take dictation, while actually trying to think of cricketers who share their names in reverse. His email continued:

"At a birthday lunch last Sunday, I profoundly impressed an Australian woman by knowing that Wally Grout's full name was Arthur Theodore Wallace Grout. I promise you, it just came up in conversation."

I have some very strange friends indeed.

Richard has sent me some wonderful emails over the years. He specialises in putting together cricket teams of players of the past with particular characteristics: all called Herbert, maybe, or Test players with fathers who were vicars, or, if he's really in the mood, Test players whose fathers were vicars called Herbert. When he was working in the Home Office in the early 2000s, they moved to a vast and splendid new building in Marsham Street, Westminster. To be precise, it is three connected buildings. The home secretary of the time, David Blunkett, decided to run a competition to name the building. Richard suggested they should be called Hobbs, Hammond and Hutton. As he explains: "One of the most serious mistakes Mr Blunkett made in his time as home secretary was to reject my suggestion and instead to name the buildings Peel, Fry and Seacole after some 'social reformers'."

Julian specialises in sending me fiendish cricket quiz questions, which he has put together while pottering around on CricketArchive when he really should be finishing his forthcoming paper on early Windsor armchairs. "Which England fast bowler in the 21st century took 10 wickets in an Ashes Test match and was never picked again? Only one man has carried his bat three times in three completed innings in Tests. Who?" Sometimes he gives me the answer before I start gnawing off the handle of my umbrella with my teeth, and sometimes he doesn't. (The answers are Andrew Caddick and Desmond Haynes.) Julian has analysed hundreds scored on Test debut by batting position, and concluded that you're best off batting at No.2 (23 out of 101) or No.6 (22 out of 101) but definitely not at Nos.9 or 11 (0 out of 101). Here he is on August 5, 2016: "What do Shane Warne, Darren Gough, Harbhajan Singh, Nuwan Zoysa, Stuart Broad and Rangana Herath have in common? Answer: each has taken a hat-trick as a bowler in Tests and also been one of the batsmen dismissed in another Test hat-trick: Warne by Harbhajan, Gough by Warne (right), Harbhajan by Broad, Zoysa by Mohammad Sami, Broad by Peter Siddle (previous page) and Herath by Abdul Razzaq." I'm guessing a lot of important work went undone on that day as well.

Psychiatrists might wonder why such intelligent men waste their valuable time on such rot and trivia, but I don't. Julian and Richard are, in their different ways, two of the happiest men I know. I occasionally wonder whether I should introduce them, but I worry that their meeting would cause a vast rip in the space-time continuum and bring the end of the universe as we know it. The risks wouldn't be just to me and my friendship with them both, but to all humankind.

Julian has recently made the acquaintance of Ms Fiona Crampin, granddaughter of Herbert Crampin, once a Grimsby trawler magnate and a keen cricket fan. All the Crampin Steam Fishing Company vessels, he has discovered, were named after cricketers with seven letters in their surnames. Over 25 years, from the 1930s to the 1950s, the Crampin trawlers were as follows: Pataudi, Bradman, Hammond, Statham, Trueman, Larwood, Jardine, Yardley, Barnett, Wellard, Padgett, Paynter, Leyland, Hendren, Gregory, Hassett, Pollard.

"A catholic selection, if a trifle odd," he tells me, "caused by the requirement for seven-letteredness, the reason for which I have never deduced. Ms Crampin, though a splendid woman in so many ways, is surprisingly ignorant of her grandfather's trawler-naming criteria." Richard theorised that maybe Crampin preferred seven-lettered names because both of his own names had seven letters. All I know is that I'd rather talk about drivel like this than do almost anything else in the world.

But let's face it: if you're reading this book the chances are that you know your own Julian or Richard. You may even be able to spot him from time to time in the mirror. My girlfriend, who regards me for much of the time with bemused pity, has been known to mention Obsessive-Compulsive Disorder, or OCD. But the point is that people with OCD do not gain any pleasure from their pernicketiness. For them, it's a terrible curse. If you're David Beckham, you have to have 23 cans of Diet Pepsi in the fridge and hoover the carpet in straight lines, or the world falls apart. For Julian, Richard and me, we gain unimaginable pleasure from all this. Julian it was who once noticed that Alec Stewart was born on 8.4.63 and had scored 8,463 Test runs. I don't know about you, but to me that single fact suggests that God might exist after all.

This article appeared in the 2017 winter edition of the Nightwatchman, *the Wisden Cricket Quarterly which specialises in long-form articles from an array of international authors. The 2018 spring edition was published in March*

LHB – Left-hand batsman

RHB – Right-hand batsman

LB – Leg-break bowler

LF – Left-arm fast bowler

LFM – Left-arm fast-medium bowler

LM – Left-arm medium bowler

LMF – Left-arm medium-fast bowler

MVP – Denotes a player's presence in the top 100 places of the 2017 Overall PCA MVP Rankings (the number next to 'MVP' denotes the player's specific placing)

OB – Off-break bowler

R – 1,000 or more first-class runs in an English season (the number next to 'R' denotes how many times the player has achieved this feat)

RF – Right-arm fast bowler

RFM – Right-arm fast-medium bowler

RM – Right-arm medium bowler

RMF – Right-arm medium-fast bowler

SLA – Slow left-arm orthodox bowler

SLC – Slow left-arm Chinaman bowler

W – 50 or more first-class wickets in an English season (the number next to 'W' denotes how many times the player has achieved this feat)

WK – Wicketkeeper

---

* – Not-out innings (e.g. 137*)

(s) – A competition has been shared between two or more winners

C&G – Cheltenham & Gloucester Trophy (English domestic 50-over competition, 2001-2006)

CB40 – Clydesdale Bank 40 (English domestic 40-over competition, 2010-2012)

CC1/CC2 – County Championship Division One/Division Two

MCCU – Marylebone Cricket Club University

Pro40 – NatWest Pro40 (English domestic 40-over competition, 2005-09)

RL50 – Royal London One-Day Cup (English domestic 50-over competition, 2014-18)

UCCE – University Centre of Cricketing Excellence

YB40 – Yorkshire Bank 40 (English domestic 40-over competition, 2013)

NOTES: The statistics given for a player's best batting and best bowling performance are limited to first-class cricket. If a field within a player's career statistics is left blank then the record for that particular statistic is incomplete, e.g. there is no record for how many balls a player has faced in first-class cricket. An '-' indicates that a particular statistic is inapplicable, e.g. a player has never bowled a ball in first-class cricket. All stats correct as of March 2, 2018

The
Teams

TEAM PROFILE

FORMED: 1870
HOME GROUND: The 3aaa County Ground, Derby
ONE-DAY NAME: Derbyshire Falcons
CAPTAIN: Billy Godleman (Championship and RL50), Gary Wilson (T20)
2017 RESULTS: CC2: 8/10; RL50: 7/9 North Group; T20: Quarter-finalists
HONOURS: Championship: 1936; Gillette/NatWest/C&G/FP Trophy: 1981; Benson & Hedges Cup: 1993; Sunday League: 1990

THE LOWDOWN

A modest 2017 peaked with a run to the T20 Blast quarter-finals, which paid immediate dividends on the appointment of John Wright as T20 coach. In the Championship, Derbyshire were hamstrung by form and fitness: promising paceman Will Davis and Hardus Viljoen, the South African Kolpak, managed only 10 games between them (38 wickets at 24.39). Wayne Madsen reserved his best for the Blast (526 runs), but three Championship wins were at least three more than they managed in 2016 and there were strong showings from emerging batsmen Alex Hughes and Luis Reece, in his first season since moving from Lancashire. Most exciting of all was off-spinner Hamidullah Qadri, who took 5-60 on his first-class debut at the age of 16. South Africa Test seamer Duanne Olivier, who is available for the first half of the season, will give the attack an extra edge alongside veteran West Indian Ravi Rampaul, while Kiwi left-arm spinner Mitchell Santner arrives in mid-summer for the Blast and remains until the end of the season. Shiv Thakor was sacked after he was found guilty of indecent exposure.

IN: Ravi Rampaul (Sur, Kolpak), Duanne Olivier (SA), Mitchell Santner (NZ)
OUT: Tom Taylor (Lei), Ben Cotton, Greg Cork, Rob Hemmings, Tom Milnes, Shiv Thakor, Tom Wood (all REL)

DIRECTOR OF CRICKET: KIM BARNETT

A batsman for Derbyshire between 1979 and 1998, Barnett captained the club for more than a decade and played four Tests. In 2016 his first act as director of cricket was to launch a review of the coaching structure, with former opener Steve Stubbings returning as first XI support coach and John Wright appointed as the T20 coach. A former New Zealand and Derbyshire batsman, Wright won the IPL with Mumbai Indians in 2013 and immediately guided the Falcons to the quarter-finals of the Blast.

COUNTY CHAMPIONSHIP AVERAGES 2017

	Mat	Inns	NO	Runs	HS	Ave	SR	100	50	4s	6s
GS Sandhu	1	2	1	55	46*	55.00	33.74	0	0	7	0
BD Cotton	2	4	3	50	32	50.00	90.90	0	0	10	0
AL Hughes	13	22	2	800	142	40.00	51.88	2	3	107	2
BA Godleman	12	22	2	799	156*	39.95	52.18	3	2	87	0
MJJ Critchley	5	8	1	266	102	38.00	64.40	1	1	41	0
BT Slater	8	15	2	490	74*	37.69	58.26	0	2	78	0
LM Reece	12	21	1	732	168	36.60	52.02	2	5	94	0
HR Hosein	4	7	2	166	52	33.20	43.56	0	1	17	0
SJ Thakor	6	11	1	328	132	32.80	61.53	1	0	52	0
GC Wilson	9	14	1	401	97	30.84	67.96	0	3	61	1
WL Madsen	13	22	0	667	121	30.31	56.28	1	5	105	4
HW Podmore	4	6	1	133	66*	26.60	57.57	0	1	12	4
TAI Taylor	6	10	1	183	69	20.33	41.87	0	1	24	0
D Smit	8	13	1	237	41	19.75	45.22	0	0	31	0
TP Milnes	3	5	0	96	53	19.20	52.17	0	1	12	0
RP Hemmings	1	1	0	19	19	19.00	73.07	0	0	3	0
C McKerr	2	3	1	33	17	16.50	38.37	0	0	5	0
WS Davis	5	7	2	64	25	12.80	69.56	0	0	11	1
BMAJ Mendis	7	12	1	132	27	12.00	61.39	0	0	18	1
Hamidullah Qadri	3	6	4	20	11*	10.00	35.08	0	0	3	0
AP Palladino	10	17	2	143	32	9.53	45.98	0	0	14	3
Imran Tahir	4	6	1	41	18*	8.20	59.42	0	0	6	0
GC Viljoen	5	8	1	36	19*	5.14	39.13	0	0	3	0

	Overs	Mdns	Runs	Wkts	BBI	BBM	Ave	Econ	SR	5w	10w
C McKerr	85.5	19	290	14	5/54	10/141	20.71	3.37	36.7	2	1
GC Viljoen	139.5	27	517	24	8/90	15/170	21.54	3.69	34.9	3	1
Hamidullah Qadri	101.3	22	288	10	5/60	6/76	28.80	2.83	60.9	1	0
GS Sandhu	21.3	2	87	3	3/60	3/87	29.00	4.04	43.0	0	0
WS Davis	103.5	13	410	14	4/60	7/123	29.28	3.94	44.5	0	0
BMAJ Mendis	252.0	24	908	30	6/204	8/283	30.26	3.60	50.4	1	0
Imran Tahir	123.1	16	407	13	5/76	7/199	31.30	3.30	56.8	2	0
MJJ Critchley	10.2	0	66	2	2/21	2/21	33.00	6.38	31.0	0	0
AP Palladino	254.4	56	818	24	4/36	6/105	34.08	3.21	63.6	0	0
TAI Taylor	144.0	30	548	16	4/67	6/125	34.25	3.80	54.0	0	0
WL Madsen	60.3	5	260	7	2/12	2/12	37.14	4.29	51.8	0	0
SJ Thakor	64.3	9	302	6	4/45	4/45	50.33	4.68	64.5	0	0
HW Podmore	85.3	12	310	6	2/44	3/95	51.66	3.62	85.5	0	0
LM Reece	127.3	26	473	8	3/38	4/79	59.12	3.70	95.6	0	0
TP Milnes	64.4	10	306	4	2/58	3/133	76.50	4.73	97.0	0	0
RP Hemmings	24.0	6	94	0	-	-	-	3.91	-	0	0
AL Hughes	33.0	8	121	0	-	-	-	3.66	-	0	0
BD Cotton	23.0	2	123	0	-	-	-	5.34	-	0	0

Catches/Stumpings:

21 Smit (inc 3st), 17 Wilson, 15 Hughes, 14 Madsen, 7 Godleman, Hosein, Reece, 3 Mendis, Palladino, Slater 2 Critchley, Davis, Milnes, Podmore, Qadri, Tahir, 1 Taylor, Thakor, Viljoen

Batting

	Mat	Inns	NO	Runs	HS	Ave	SR	100	50	4s	6s
AL Hughes	8	4	1	173	96*	57.66	102.36	0	1	14	5
D Smit	8	6	3	170	77*	56.66	99.41	0	1	14	3
BT Slater	8	7	1	312	82	52.00	85.47	0	3	39	2
WL Madsen	8	7	2	248	112	49.60	103.33	1	1	24	4
BA Godleman	8	7	0	289	95	41.28	78.10	0	2	35	1
SJ Thakor	8	7	0	280	130	40.00	99.29	1	1	26	4
MJJ Critchley	6	4	1	104	49	34.66	126.82	0	0	7	4
BMAJ Mendis	8	4	1	89	44*	29.66	96.73	0	0	8	2
GC Viljoen	5	3	2	6	6*	6.00	150.00	0	0	0	1
LM Reece	4	3	0	15	9	5.00	57.69	0	0	0	0
BD Cotton	8	1	0	2	2	2.00	28.57	0	0	0	0
GC Wilson	3	2	2	35	23*	-	175.00	0	0	5	0
TP Milnes	3	-	-	-	-	-	-	-	-	-	-
AP Palladino	2	-	-	-	-	-	-	-	-	-	-
TAI Taylor	1	-	-	-	-	-	-	-	-	-	-

Bowling

	Overs	Mdns	Runs	Wkts	BBI	Ave	Econ	SR	4w	5w
SJ Thakor	59.5	1	319	13	3/23	24.53	5.33	27.6	0	0
BMAJ Mendis	63.5	0	360	9	2/38	40.00	5.63	42.5	0	0
WL Madsen	11.2	1	65	2	2/26	32.50	5.73	34.0	0	0
BD Cotton	59.0	0	355	5	2/18	71.00	6.01	70.8	0	0
AP Palladino	13.0	0	85	0	-	-	6.53	-	0	0
AL Hughes	25.0	0	167	2	2/59	83.50	6.68	75.0	0	0
GC Viljoen	39.0	0	268	6	3/55	44.66	6.87	39.0	0	0
TAI Taylor	7.0	0	51	0	-	-	7.28	-	0	0
MJJ Critchley	24.0	0	180	3	1/23	60.00	7.50	48.0	0	0
LM Reece	6.0	0	48	0	-	-	8.00	-	0	0
TP Milnes	12.0	0	99	1	1/35	99.00	8.25	72.0	0	0

Catches/Stumpings:
8 Smit (inc 2st), 6 Hughes, 5 Madsen, 2 Godleman, Mendis, Thakor, 1 Milnes, Viljoen, Wilson (inc 1st)

	Mat	Inns	NO	Runs	HS	Ave	SR	100	50	4s	6s
WL Madsen	14	14	3	526	86*	47.81	145.30	0	4	61	8
LM Reece	14	14	2	433	97*	36.08	137.89	0	4	38	14
D Smit	14	9	5	141	42*	35.25	136.89	0	0	15	2
Imran Tahir	14	3	2	31	23	31.00	155.00	0	0	1	2
MJJ Critchley	12	11	2	245	72*	27.22	133.15	0	1	23	8
BA Godleman	14	14	0	270	70	19.28	144.38	0	2	31	7
GC Wilson	11	11	3	152	33*	19.00	152.00	0	0	19	5
GC Viljoen	14	8	5	56	20	18.66	133.33	0	0	4	2
AL Hughes	14	12	2	180	36*	18.00	125.87	0	0	14	7
TA Wood	2	2	0	33	24	16.50	106.45	0	0	5	0
MJ Henry	14	10	2	98	28	12.25	153.12	0	0	5	7
BT Slater	2	2	0	22	14	11.00	78.57	0	0	5	0
CAJ Brodrick	6	4	0	40	14	10.00	117.64	0	0	4	0
BD Cotton	8	1	1	30	30*	-	142.85	0	0	2	1
Hamidullah Qadri	1	-	-	-	-	-	-	-	-	-	-

Batting

	Overs	Mdns	Runs	Wkts	BBI	Ave	Econ	SR	4w	5w
WL Madsen	47.0	1	346	13	2/20	26.61	7.36	21.6	0	0
Imran Tahir	56.0	0	416	17	4/17	24.47	7.42	19.7	1	0
LM Reece	5.0	0	42	1	1/11	42.00	8.40	30.0	0	0
BD Cotton	21.4	0	183	9	2/14	20.33	8.44	14.4	0	0
GC Viljoen	50.3	0	460	14	3/28	32.85	9.10	21.6	0	0
AL Hughes	23.0	0	216	3	1/19	72.00	9.39	46.0	0	0
MJJ Critchley	18.0	0	172	7	3/32	24.57	9.55	15.4	0	0
MJ Henry	50.3	0	524	15	3/18	34.93	10.37	20.2	0	0
Hamidullah Qadri	1.0	0	12	0	-	-	12.00	-	0	0

Bowling

Catches/Stumpings:
10 Hughes, 9 Smit (inc 3st), 7 Madsen, Wilson, 6 Henry, Reece, 4 Godleman, 2 Brodrick, Critchley, Cotton, 1 Tahir, Viljoen

TEAM PROFILE

FORMED: 1882
HOME GROUND: Emirates Riverside
T20 BLAST NAME: Durham Jets
CAPTAIN: Paul Collingwood
(Championship), Tom Latham (RL50),
TBC (T20)
2017 RESULTS: CC2: 9/10; RL50: 5/9
North Group; T20: 9/9 North Group
HONOURS: Championship: (3) 2008,
2009, 2013; Gillette/NatWest/C&G/
FP Trophy: 2007; Pro40/National
League/CB40/YB40/RL50: 2014

THE LOWDOWN

A storm continues to blow over the north-east. It began with Championship relegation in 2016 and a whopping 48-point deduction in return for a £3.8 million bail-out from the ECB. Then the talent drain: first Mark Stoneman and Scott Borthwick a year ago, now Graham Onions, Keaton Jennings and Paul Coughlin have also moved on. Meanwhile batsman Jack Burnham is serving a one-year ban for using recreational drugs. But if you would pick a man to weather a storm it would be 41-year-old Paul Collingwood, who goes into his 23rd season with Durham after a summer in which he oozed defiance: 1,000 first-class runs for the first time since 2005, a maiden T20 hundred, and top of the 50-over averages. There were other bright spots in the form of young batsmen Cameron Steel and Graham Clark. Experienced Melburnian paceman Nathan Rimmington arrives on a British passport and ex-skipper Will Smith returns to Chester-le-Street. South Africa batsman Aiden Markram is due for the first month and is then replaced by Kiwi opener Tom Latham, who will act as the 50-over captain.

IN: Will Smith (Ham), Nathan Rimmington (Aus, UK passport), Aiden Markram (SA), Tom Latham (NZ); **OUT:** Paul Coughlin (Not), Keaton Jennings, Graham Onions (both Lan), Usman Arshad, Adam Hickey (both REL)

HEAD COACH: JON LEWIS

A solid opening batsman who made 16 first-class centuries with Essex and Durham, Lewis took over as head coach in June 2013 after Geoff Cook stepped down to recover from a heart attack, immediately leading the side to the County Championship title and then to victory in the One-Day Cup the following year. Lewis guided the club to their first T20 Finals Day in 2016.

COUNTY CHAMPIONSHIP AVERAGES 2017

Batting

	Mat	Inns	NO	Runs	HS	Ave	SR	100	50	4s	6s
BA Carse	2	3	2	91	61*	91.00	50.83	0	1	10	2
TWM Latham	4	7	1	382	124	63.66	52.90	2	1	44	2
PD Collingwood	14	24	2	1087	177	49.40	59.56	3	5	124	4
CT Steel	13	24	2	899	224	40.86	44.06	2	4	110	4
WJ Weighell	4	7	3	162	58	40.50	76.77	0	2	25	2
G Clark	12	21	0	769	109	36.61	62.26	1	6	101	10
P Coughlin	8	12	2	364	73*	36.40	65.23	0	3	40	3
MA Wood	5	8	2	195	72*	32.50	70.39	0	1	32	0
BJ McCarthy	5	6	2	129	39	32.25	46.40	0	0	14	0
MJ Richardson	10	16	1	460	82	30.66	51.68	0	4	53	0
SC Cook	7	14	1	348	89*	26.76	59.79	0	2	43	0
KK Jennings	11	21	2	490	102*	25.78	45.79	1	1	69	1
RD Pringle	13	22	4	459	71	25.50	45.85	0	3	65	2
JTA Burnham	7	11	2	223	93*	24.77	61.77	0	1	31	4
SW Poynter	9	14	1	269	65	20.69	62.85	0	1	38	0
MJ Potts	5	6	2	69	53*	17.25	46.00	0	1	6	0
C Rushworth	13	17	3	174	57	12.42	70.44	0	1	21	0
L Trevaskis	1	2	0	14	9	7.00	18.91	0	0	0	0
GT Main	2	3	1	13	13	6.50	48.14	0	0	3	0
G Onions	8	10	0	58	15	5.80	51.32	0	0	9	0
GHI Harding	1	1	0	0	0	0.00	0.00	0	0	0	0
BA Stokes	1	1	0	0	0	0.00	0.00	0	0	0	0

Bowling

	Overs	Mdns	Runs	Wkts	BBI	BBM	Ave	Econ	SR	5w	10w
KK Jennings	64.0	9	214	12	3/37	4/48	17.83	3.34	32.0	0	0
G Onions	237.0	48	725	32	6/62	8/107	22.65	3.05	44.4	1	0
C Rushworth	436.3	96	1217	47	5/52	8/111	25.89	2.78	55.7	1	0
BJ McCarthy	164.2	23	653	24	6/63	7/120	27.20	3.97	41.0	1	0
P Coughlin	208.1	31	804	27	5/49	10/133	29.77	3.86	46.2	2	1
MA Wood	123.0	17	389	13	5/54	5/54	29.92	3.16	56.7	1	0
MJ Potts	163.0	37	465	14	3/48	5/106	33.21	2.85	69.8	0	0
CT Steel	65.2	3	275	8	2/24	2/24	34.37	4.20	49.0	0	0
WJ Weighell	94.5	8	438	11	3/51	4/91	39.81	4.61	51.7	0	0
RD Pringle	197.5	41	688	15	4/73	4/73	45.86	3.47	79.1	0	0
GHI Harding	36.0	2	186	4	4/111	4/186	46.50	5.16	54.0	0	0
PD Collingwood	77.2	21	199	4	2/29	2/32	49.75	2.57	116.0	0	0
BA Carse	58.0	4	191	3	2/61	3/112	63.66	3.29	116.0	0	0
GT Main	43.0	3	219	3	2/58	3/105	73.00	5.09	86.0	0	0
L Trevaskis	26.0	3	126	1	1/69	1/126	126.00	4.84	156.0	0	0
SC Cook	1.0	0	16	0	-	-	-	16.00	-	0	0
BA Stokes	20.0	3	81	0	-	-	-	4.05	-	0	0

Catches/Stumpings:
30 Poynter, 23 Collingwood, 20 Richardson, 13 Jennings, 10 Clark, 9 Pringle, 5 Cook, Latham, Rushworth, 3 P Coughlin, Steel, 1 Burnham, Onions

Batting

	Mat	Inns	NO	Runs	HS	Ave	SR	100	50	4s	6s
PD Collingwood	8	7	4	224	73*	74.66	111.44	0	3	20	3
MJ Richardson	8	8	2	424	100*	70.66	89.07	1	4	32	7
KK Jennings	8	8	0	460	139	57.50	102.44	2	2	58	4
SC Cook	6	6	0	274	106	45.66	87.53	1	2	22	0
G Clark	8	8	1	275	114	39.28	87.85	1	1	26	3
CT Steel	7	6	1	132	77	26.40	72.92	0	1	13	1
SW Poynter	8	4	1	72	43	24.00	126.31	0	0	5	1
P Coughlin	8	7	2	99	22	19.80	128.57	0	0	11	3
RD Pringle	4	3	0	36	15	12.00	85.71	0	0	2	1
WJ Weighell	8	3	1	22	14	11.00	73.33	0	0	0	1
C Rushworth	8	2	2	45	28*	-	128.57	0	0	5	0
GHI Harding	5	2	2	20	18*	-	86.95	0	0	2	0
MA Wood	2	-	-	-	-	-	-	-	-	-	-

Bowling

	Overs	Mdns	Runs	Wkts	BBI	Ave	Econ	SR	4w	5w
PD Collingwood	62.0	2	304	8	3/42	38.00	4.90	46.5	0	0
C Rushworth	67.0	1	346	8	2/50	43.25	5.16	50.2	0	0
GHI Harding	47.0	0	251	4	2/52	62.75	5.34	70.5	0	0
MA Wood	17.5	1	96	5	3/62	19.20	5.38	21.4	0	0
P Coughlin	62.5	2	372	12	3/36	31.00	5.92	31.4	0	0
WJ Weighell	66.0	4	416	18	5/57	23.11	6.30	22.0	1	1
RD Pringle	5.0	0	38	1	1/24	38.00	7.60	30.0	0	0
KK Jennings	3.0	0	28	0	-	-	9.33	-	0	0
CT Steel	5.0	0	47	0	-	-	9.40	-	0	0

Catches/Stumpings:
6 Clark, Jennings, 5 Collingwood, Harding, 4 Poynter, Richardson, Rushworth, 3 P Coughlin, Weighell 2 Wood, 1 Cook, Pringle

Batting

	Mat	Inns	NO	Runs	HS	Ave	SR	100	50	4s	6s
P Coughlin	14	13	5	333	53	41.62	139.91	0	1	21	12
PD Collingwood	11	11	2	346	108*	38.44	140.08	1	1	25	13
SW Poynter	14	10	5	188	61*	37.60	134.28	0	1	12	6
MJ Richardson	13	12	4	261	53	32.62	122.53	0	1	20	4
U Arshad	9	5	3	56	27	28.00	105.66	0	0	3	1
TWM Latham	5	5	0	139	62	27.80	139.00	0	1	15	4
G Clark	14	14	0	272	71	19.42	134.65	0	2	32	8
CT Steel	6	6	0	93	37	15.50	125.67	0	0	11	1
JTA Burnham	12	9	1	123	53*	15.37	89.13	0	1	9	2
RD Pringle	14	9	0	106	25	11.77	117.77	0	0	9	0
GJ Harte	2	2	0	17	11	8.50	121.42	0	0	1	0
AJ Hickey	4	3	0	25	15	8.33	100.00	0	0	4	0
BA Carse	2	2	1	4	3	4.00	100.00	0	0	0	0
KK Jennings	4	4	0	13	5	3.25	54.16	0	0	2	0
C Rushworth	10	2	1	2	1*	2.00	33.33	0	0	0	0
BJ McCarthy	6	1	0	1	1	1.00	20.00	0	0	0	0
WJ Weighell	13	4	4	14	6*	-	140.00	0	0	0	1
L Trevaskis	1	1	1	13	13*	-	76.47	0	0	2	0

Bowling

	Overs	Mdns	Runs	Wkts	BBI	Ave	Econ	SR	4w	5w
JTA Burnham	0.1	0	0	0	-	-	0.00	-	0	0
AJ Hickey	3.0	0	11	1	1/11	11.00	3.66	18.0	0	0
KK Jennings	7.0	0	44	2	2/21	22.00	6.28	21.0	0	0
PD Collingwood	36.0	0	281	8	4/24	35.12	7.80	27.0	1	0
U Arshad	21.5	0	177	3	1/28	59.00	8.10	43.6	0	0
L Trevaskis	4.0	0	33	1	1/33	33.00	8.25	24.0	0	0
RD Pringle	32.0	0	268	11	3/30	24.36	8.37	17.4	0	0
BJ McCarthy	16.0	0	139	6	3/33	23.16	8.68	16.0	0	0
C Rushworth	26.0	0	238	3	1/14	79.33	9.15	52.0	0	0
WJ Weighell	37.3	0	350	9	3/28	38.88	9.33	25.0	0	0
P Coughlin	32.2	0	323	13	4/22	24.84	9.98	14.9	1	0
CT Steel	8.0	0	88	2	2/60	44.00	11.00	24.0	0	0
BA Carse	4.5	0	64	1	1/45	64.00	13.24	29.0	0	0

Catches/Stumpings:
9 Poynter (inc 3st), 7 Weighell, 5 Clark, Pringle, Richardson, 3 Burnham, Collingwood, Latham, Rushworth, 2 P Coughlin, Harte, Steel, 1 Arshad, Carse, Hickey, McCarthy

TEAM PROFILE

FORMED: 1876
HOME GROUND: The Cloudfm County Ground, Chelmsford
ONE-DAY NAME: Essex Eagles
CAPTAIN: Ryan ten Doeschate
2017 RESULTS: CC1: Winners; RL50: Semi-finalists; T20: 8/9 South Group
HONOURS: Championship: (7) 1979, 1983, 1984, 1986, 1991, 1992, 2017; Gillette/NatWest/C&G/FP Trophy: (3) 1985, 1997, 2008; Benson & Hedges Cup: (2) 1979, 1998; Pro40/National League/CB40/YB40/RL50: (2) 2005, 2006; Sunday League: (3) 1981, 1984, 1985

THE LOWDOWN

Ten victories, no defeats, a winning margin of 72 points, county champions: even the Chelmsford faithful will have found it hard to grumble about that. But you can already hear the cry: "Don't do a Middlesex!" That is the challenge for new coach Anthony McGrath. Jamie Porter and Simon Harmer took 147 of the 247 wickets but cannot be expected to repeat those miracles. Will Harmer's off-spin be as effective now that county batsmen have had a good look at him? In truth Essex are blessed with talent right through the team, with a fearsome top order of Cook, Browne, Lawrence, Westley, Bopara and ten Doeschate. They look primed for an assault on the One-Day Cup, winning seven out of nine last season and beaten only by Nottinghamshire's extraordinary chase of 371 in the semi-final. Allrounder Matt Coles is a potential match-winning addition, while Peter Siddle will hand the overseas baton to the returning Neil Wagner in May. Aussie leg-spinner Adam Zampa has been recruited for the T20 Blast.

IN: Matt Coles (Ken), Peter Siddle (Aus), Neil Wagner (NZ), Adam Zampa (Aus, T20)
OUT: Kishen Velani (REL)

HEAD COACH: ANTHONY MCGRATH

As assistant coach for the past two seasons, McGrath has helped deliver back-to-back titles in Division Two and Division One and now takes the reins after Chris Silverwood's appointment as England bowling coach. McGrath previously spent a year on Yorkshire's coaching staff following an 18-year playing career at Headingley in which he scored more than 23,000 runs and took 240 wickets in all formats. He played four Tests and 14 ODIs for England. Former Hampshire allrounder Dimitri Mascarenhas will be his assistant.

Batting

	Mat	Inns	NO	Runs	HS	Ave	SR	100	50	4s	6s
AN Cook	7	10	0	667	193	66.70	58.05	3	1	93	0
DW Lawrence	13	21	4	761	141*	44.76	45.95	3	3	94	4
Mohammad Amir	3	2	1	44	22*	44.00	88.00	0	0	8	0
NLJ Browne	14	22	0	952	221	43.27	45.09	1	5	128	2
T Westley	11	15	2	561	111	43.15	48.36	2	2	90	1
RN ten Doeschate	13	17	1	659	168*	41.18	61.18	1	4	86	4
RS Bopara	14	20	2	576	192	32.00	42.29	1	2	62	6
JS Foster	10	12	0	357	121	29.75	59.30	1	1	56	3
V Chopra	9	14	1	372	100*	28.61	55.19	1	1	42	7
PI Walter	5	5	2	76	32*	25.33	53.90	0	0	12	0
N Wagner	10	13	3	242	50	24.20	56.41	0	1	37	1
AJA Wheater	7	10	0	223	88	22.30	40.47	0	2	31	0
SR Harmer	14	18	2	260	64	16.25	43.62	0	2	35	0
Ashar Zaidi	2	2	0	29	23	14.50	54.71	0	0	3	1
AP Beard	3	4	3	11	4*	11.00	30.55	0	0	2	0
JA Porter	13	15	8	52	10*	7.42	28.26	0	0	7	0
MR Quinn	3	3	0	19	15	6.33	30.64	0	0	3	0
SJ Cook	4	4	3	0	0*	0.00	0.00	0	0	0	0

Bowling

	Overs	Mdns	Runs	Wkts	BBI	BBM	Ave	Econ	SR	5w	10w
Mohammad Amir	76.2	19	189	14	5/18	10/72	13.50	2.47	32.7	2	1
Ashar Zaidi	25.0	5	43	3	3/17	3/36	14.33	1.72	50.0	0	0
SJ Cook	99.4	24	286	18	5/18	7/102	15.88	2.86	33.2	2	0
JA Porter	399.0	89	1262	75	7/55	12/95	16.82	3.16	31.9	5	1
SR Harmer	521.2	121	1382	72	9/95	14/128	19.19	2.65	43.4	4	2
RN ten Doeschate	13.1	0	60	3	2/16	2/16	20.00	4.55	26.3	0	0
T Westley	21.3	5	72	3	1/6	1/6	24.00	3.34	43.0	0	0
N Wagner	316.4	54	1095	31	6/48	8/126	35.32	3.45	61.2	1	0
MR Quinn	61.5	13	221	6	3/66	3/79	36.83	3.57	61.8	0	0
AP Beard	67.0	10	241	6	3/47	5/92	40.16	3.59	67.0	0	0
RS Bopara	127.1	12	489	12	2/10	3/40	40.75	3.84	63.5	0	0
DW Lawrence	23.0	6	71	1	1/39	1/42	71.00	3.08	138.0	0	0
PI Walter	75.0	19	219	3	1/17	2/53	73.00	2.92	150.0	0	0

Catches/Stumpings:
49 Foster (inc 1st), 16 Wheater (inc 2st), 15 Chopra, 13 A Cook, 11 Harmer, 10 Lawrence, 8 ten Doeschate, 7 Bopara, 6 Browne, 5 Westley, 4 Wagner, 2 Zaidi, 1 Amir, Porter, Quinn

Batting

	Mat	Inns	NO	Runs	HS	Ave	SR	100	50	4s	6s
SR Harmer	9	4	3	85	44*	85.00	90.42	0	0	7	0
AN Cook	9	9	1	636	133	79.50	88.45	3	3	74	0
RS Bopara	8	8	2	329	92*	54.83	106.81	0	2	29	6
RN ten Doeschate	9	8	2	298	102*	49.66	115.95	2	0	22	7
V Chopra	9	9	0	334	124	37.11	76.95	1	1	37	4
T Westley	9	9	0	315	100	35.00	89.48	1	1	35	2
JS Foster	4	3	2	35	27*	35.00	145.83	0	0	3	0
DW Lawrence	2	2	0	66	34	33.00	85.71	0	0	5	1
Ashar Zaidi	9	9	1	195	72*	24.37	126.62	0	1	18	6
AJA Wheater	5	5	0	71	30	14.20	89.87	0	0	6	0
NLJ Browne	4	4	0	46	42	11.50	85.18	0	0	6	0
N Wagner	7	2	1	7	4	7.00	50.00	0	0	0	0
PI Walter	4	2	2	15	11*	-	166.66	0	0	0	1
MR Quinn	6	1	1	7	7*	-	116.66	0	0	1	0
JA Porter	5	1	1	0	0*	-	0.00	0	0	0	0

Bowling

	Overs	Mdns	Runs	Wkts	BBI	Ave	Econ	SR	4w	5w
T Westley	3.0	0	12	0	-	-	4.00	-	0	0
JA Porter	39.0	4	196	10	4/40	19.60	5.02	23.4	1	0
Ashar Zaidi	57.2	1	292	7	2/10	41.71	5.09	49.1	0	0
RS Bopara	55.0	0	288	9	3/34	32.00	5.23	36.6	0	0
MR Quinn	52.4	4	282	8	3/34	35.25	5.35	39.5	0	0
SR Harmer	74.2	2	418	10	3/56	41.80	5.62	44.6	0	0
PI Walter	26.4	0	155	7	4/37	22.14	5.81	22.8	1	0
N Wagner	57.2	7	353	14	4/41	25.21	6.15	24.5	2	0
RN ten Doeschate	23.0	0	144	4	2/29	36.00	6.26	34.5	0	0

Catches/Stumpings:
8 Wheater (inc 3st), 6 Foster, Harmer, 4 Bopara, Westley, 3 Chopra, A Cook, ten Doeschate, Zaidi, 2 Walter, 1 Lawrence, Quinn

www.essexcricket.org.uk / tel: 01245 252420

	Mat	Inns	NO	Runs	HS	Ave	SR	100	50	4s	6s
V Chopra	13	12	1	427	116	38.81	159.32	2	0	31	26
PI Walter	13	10	7	92	20*	30.66	127.77	0	0	7	3
AJA Wheater	6	6	1	139	50	27.80	156.17	0	1	14	6
RS Bopara	13	12	1	301	75	27.36	138.70	0	2	18	15
RN ten Doeschate	13	11	1	246	56	24.60	129.47	0	1	23	4
DW Lawrence	12	11	0	235	47	21.36	141.56	0	0	32	5
SR Harmer	13	5	3	39	21	19.50	125.80	0	0	4	1
T Westley	5	5	0	92	29	18.40	117.94	0	0	6	5
JS Foster	13	10	4	108	50	18.00	136.70	0	1	12	2
Ashar Zaidi	13	12	1	140	35	12.72	113.82	0	0	7	8
Tamim Iqbal	1	1	0	7	7	7.00	100.00	0	0	0	1
CJ Taylor	3	1	0	5	5	5.00	62.50	0	0	0	0
Mohammad Amir	13	4	1	6	5	2.00	75.00	0	0	1	0
MW Dixon	4	1	0	1	1	1.00	50.00	0	0	0	0
JA Porter	8	1	1	1	1*	-	100.00	0	0	0	0

Batting

	Overs	Mdns	Runs	Wkts	BBI	Ave	Econ	SR	4w	5w
Mohammad Amir	47.3	0	322	14	2/13	23.00	6.77	20.3	0	0
DW Lawrence	10.0	0	70	4	3/21	17.50	7.00	15.0	0	0
RS Bopara	45.0	0	335	13	4/19	25.76	7.44	20.7	1	0
SR Harmer	36.0	0	328	8	3/39	41.00	9.11	27.0	0	0
PI Walter	44.0	1	406	15	3/24	27.06	9.22	17.6	0	0
Ashar Zaidi	24.0	0	223	7	2/24	31.85	9.29	20.5	0	0
JA Porter	19.0	0	183	6	4/20	30.50	9.63	19.0	1	0
MW Dixon	9.0	0	92	3	2/49	30.66	10.22	18.0	0	0
RN ten Doeschate	4.0	0	43	1	1/10	43.00	10.75	24.0	0	0

Bowling

Catches/Stumpings:
12 Foster (inc 2st), 5 Walter, 4 ten Doeschate, Zaidi, 3 Bopara, Harmer, Porter, 2 Chopra, Westley, Wheater, 1 Amir, Lawrence

TEAM PROFILE

GLAMORGAN

FORMED: 1888
HOME GROUND: The SSE SWALEC, Cardiff
CAPTAIN: Michael Hogan (Championship), Colin Ingram (RL50 and T20)
2017 RESULTS: CC2: 7/10; RL50: 5/9 South Group; T20: Semi-finalists
HONOURS: Championship: (3) 1948, 1969, 1997; Pro40/National League/CB40/YB40/RL50: (2) 2002, 2004; Sunday League: 1993

THE LOWDOWN

Last year was just the second time Glamorgan had made it to T20 Finals Day – the first in 13 years – and only a narrow semi-final defeat to Birmingham Bears denied the county a shot at glory. That was the good news. In the Championship they were again woefully short of runs, with only the 22-year-old Nick Selman passing 700 for the season. Former captain Jacques Rudolph has retired and Will Bragg was forced to call time at the age of 31 due to illness. But Australian left-hander Shaun Marsh has signed for two years and forms a quartet of international cricketers upon whom much depends. South African Kolpak Colin Ingram – 'Kingram' to the locals – will lead the side in the shorter formats after another stunning season in limited-overs cricket, while the indefatigable Australian seamer Michael Hogan has taken on the Championship captaincy full time. Marchant de Lange, the South African quick, completes the set. But Glamorgan will need some of their Welsh protegés to kick on if they are to be a force this summer.

IN: Shaun Marsh (Aus)
OUT: Jacques Rudolph, Will Bragg (both RET)

HEAD COACH: ROBERT CROFT

Croft took over from Toby Radford after the 2015 season. Within his 23 years as a Glamorgan player the off-spinner played 21 Tests and 50 ODIs between 1996 and 2001. He was given an MBE in 2013 for services to cricket after finally hanging up his boots with a record of 903 appearances, 1,175 first-class wickets and 51 five-wicket hauls. His former teammate Matthew Maynard has been appointed as a batting consultant after ending his three-year spell as Somerset's director of cricket.

	Mat	Inns	NO	Runs	HS	Ave	SR	100	50	4s	6s
CB Cooke	12	21	5	695	113*	43.43	53.13	1	4	96	8
AG Salter	12	19	4	619	88	41.26	43.71	0	5	82	8
CA Ingram	12	20	2	672	155*	37.33	48.20	2	1	89	5
NJ Selman	14	26	2	872	142*	36.33	49.15	4	3	105	3
CAJ Meschede	6	8	0	290	87	36.25	67.59	0	1	38	4
KS Carlson	8	13	0	443	191	34.07	57.08	1	1	61	4
JA Rudolph	11	20	1	492	111	25.89	50.30	1	1	74	1
AHT Donald	11	20	1	487	66*	25.63	64.41	0	4	61	3
RAJ Smith	3	4	0	89	38	22.25	64.96	0	0	12	1
TN Cullen	2	4	0	84	42	21.00	45.40	0	0	7	1
CR Brown	2	4	0	83	35	20.75	43.68	0	0	16	0
GG Wagg	3	6	1	93	33*	18.60	36.47	0	0	9	0
LJ Carey	10	14	2	219	54	18.25	76.04	0	1	33	3
DL Lloyd	8	15	1	247	88	17.64	52.55	0	1	35	4
JR Murphy	4	6	0	97	27	16.16	40.08	0	0	12	0
M de Lange	11	17	1	254	39	15.87	72.98	0	0	29	8
MG Hogan	12	17	10	100	29*	14.28	72.46	0	0	15	1
WD Bragg	3	6	1	65	30	13.00	48.87	0	0	9	0
T van der Gugten	5	7	0	64	21	9.14	34.78	0	0	9	0
HW Podmore	2	4	1	21	10	7.00	30.43	0	0	2	0
AO Morgan	3	6	0	28	17	4.66	20.00	0	0	1	0

Batting

	Overs	Mdns	Runs	Wkts	BBI	BBM	Ave	Econ	SR	5w	10w
MG Hogan	370.4	84	1044	50	6/43	10/87	20.88	2.81	44.4	3	1
T van der Gugten	158.2	43	505	22	5/101	6/105	22.95	3.18	43.1	1	0
GG Wagg	60.0	10	206	7	2/14	4/67	29.42	3.43	51.4	0	0
LJ Carey	271.3	49	1051	35	4/85	5/103	30.02	3.87	46.5	0	0
RAJ Smith	69.4	6	302	9	3/64	5/123	33.55	4.33	46.4	0	0
CAJ Meschede	126.0	18	450	13	4/61	4/96	34.61	3.57	58.1	0	0
M de Lange	345.5	47	1315	34	5/95	6/135	38.67	3.80	61.0	1	0
HW Podmore	28.1	3	124	3	3/68	3/68	41.33	4.40	56.3	0	0
AG Salter	155.4	12	646	14	3/60	3/65	46.14	4.14	66.7	0	0
CA Ingram	37.1	0	155	2	1/6	1/17	77.50	4.17	111.5	0	0
DL Lloyd	69.0	7	320	4	2/37	2/37	80.00	4.63	103.5	0	0
CR Brown	4.0	0	14	0	-	-	-	3.50	-	0	0

Bowling

Catches/Stumpings:
39 Cooke, 15 Selman, 12 Donald, 9 Cullen (inc 1st), 5 de Lange, Ingram, Salter, 4 Carlson, Hogan, Lloyd, 3 Carey, Rudolph, 2 Bragg, Meschede, Wagg, 1 Morgan, Murphy, Podmore

GLAMORGAN

Batting

	Mat	Inns	NO	Runs	HS	Ave	SR	100	50	4s	6s
CA Ingram	8	8	0	564	142	70.50	104.44	3	2	31	29
WD Bragg	6	6	0	233	94	38.83	74.67	0	2	24	0
JA Rudolph	8	8	0	305	121	38.12	79.22	1	2	35	2
CB Cooke	8	8	1	253	62	36.14	104.97	0	2	20	8
AG Salter	5	5	2	81	29*	27.00	80.19	0	0	6	4
KS Carlson	8	8	0	206	63	25.75	100.00	0	1	19	3
T van der Gugten	4	2	1	20	11	20.00	66.66	0	0	2	0
M de Lange	8	8	4	79	24	19.75	112.85	0	0	6	3
DL Lloyd	8	8	0	127	48	15.87	64.14	0	0	16	1
CAJ Meschede	8	8	1	92	23	13.14	108.23	0	0	8	3
MG Hogan	7	4	2	13	5*	6.50	61.90	0	0	0	0
AHT Donald	5	5	0	20	10	4.00	64.51	0	0	1	0
AO Morgan	1	1	0	3	3	3.00	50.00	0	0	0	0
LJ Carey	4	1	1	9	9*	-	60.00	0	0	0	0

Bowling

	Overs	Mdns	Runs	Wkts	BBI	Ave	Econ	SR	4w	5w
M de Lange	73.2	4	405	18	5/49	22.50	5.52	24.4	0	1
MG Hogan	63.0	1	348	6	2/42	58.00	5.52	63.0	0	0
CAJ Meschede	64.0	0	372	4	2/53	93.00	5.81	96.0	0	0
KS Carlson	5.0	0	30	1	1/30	30.00	6.00	30.0	0	0
LJ Carey	30.0	0	183	3	1/21	61.00	6.10	60.0	0	0
CA Ingram	43.0	0	269	7	4/39	38.42	6.25	36.8	1	0
DL Lloyd	30.0	0	195	6	5/53	32.50	6.50	30.0	0	1
AO Morgan	2.0	0	14	0	-	-	7.00	-	0	0
T van der Gugten	35.4	0	253	4	1/47	63.25	7.09	53.5	0	0
AG Salter	17.0	0	125	0	-	-	7.35	-	0	0

Catches/Stumpings:
11 Cooke, 3 Ingram, 2 Bragg, de Lange, Hogan, Rudolph, 1 Carlson, Donald, Meschede

GLAMORGAN

	Mat	Inns	NO	Runs	HS	Ave	SR	100	50	4s	6s
GG Wagg	14	8	6	163	50	81.50	141.73	0	1	11	6
JA Rudolph	14	13	4	443	77*	49.22	129.15	0	4	43	8
CA Ingram	14	13	3	462	114	46.20	166.18	2	1	37	30
DA Miller	6	5	2	117	50	39.00	146.25	0	1	12	5
NJ Selman	4	3	0	99	66	33.00	128.57	0	1	9	0
AG Salter	14	5	2	83	37*	27.66	118.57	0	0	7	2
CB Cooke	14	10	2	172	49	21.50	131.29	0	0	14	6
AHT Donald	14	13	0	277	76	21.30	144.27	0	2	37	3
T van der Gugten	7	1	0	16	16	16.00	160.00	0	0	1	1
CAJ Meschede	12	6	3	34	14*	11.33	109.67	0	0	3	1
M de Lange	14	3	1	20	16	10.00	166.66	0	0	2	1
DL Lloyd	4	4	0	24	20	6.00	70.58	0	0	4	0
KS Carlson	5	2	0	3	3	1.50	42.85	0	0	0	0
MG Hogan	14	2	2	2	2*	-	100.00	0	0	0	0
LJ Carey	4	-	-	-	-	-	-	-	-	-	-

Batting

	Overs	Mdns	Runs	Wkts	BBI	Ave	Econ	SR	4w	5w
AG Salter	18.0	0	139	2	1/10	69.50	7.72	54.0	0	0
CA Ingram	40.0	0	315	9	2/27	35.00	7.87	26.6	0	0
CAJ Meschede	25.0	0	197	10	3/17	19.70	7.88	15.0	0	0
M de Lange	46.0	0	382	18	3/19	21.22	8.30	15.3	0	0
MG Hogan	46.5	0	390	20	5/17	19.50	8.32	14.0	0	1
LJ Carey	7.0	0	61	2	1/19	30.50	8.71	21.0	0	0
T van der Gugten	15.0	0	135	3	1/23	45.00	9.00	30.0	0	0
GG Wagg	37.2	0	341	9	2/12	37.88	9.13	24.8	0	0

Bowling

Catches/Stumpings:
9 Donald, 7 Cooke, 6 Hogan, Miller, 5 de Lange, Ingram, 3 Meschede, Salter, 2 Carlson, Rudolph, Selman, 1 Carey, van der Gugten, Wagg

TEAM PROFILE

FORMED: 1871
HOME GROUND: The Brightside Ground, Bristol
CAPTAIN: Chris Dent (Championship and RL50), TBC (T20)
2017 RESULTS: C2: 6/10; RL50: 7/9 South Group; T20: 9/9 South Group
HONOURS: Gillette/NatWest/C&G/FP Trophy: (5) 1973, 1999, 2000, 2003, 2004; Benson & Hedges Cup: (3) 1977, 1999, 2000; Pro40/National League/CB40/YB40/RL50: (2) 2000, 2015

THE LOWDOWN

Sixth in Division Two, seventh in their One-Day Cup section, bottom of their T20 Blast group: Gloucestershire's saving grace in 2017 was Alfred the Gorilla, who won the T20 Finals Day mascot race for the second year running. White-ball cricket is normally the county's strong suit but the batsmen were unable to back up a cast of savvy bowlers, among whom Benny Howell confirmed his status as one of the country's leading one-day performers with a Blast economy-rate of just 5.75 – the best in the competition. Liam Norwell was far and away Gloucestershire's best bowler in Championship cricket and will be supported by 26-year-old Australian seamer Daniel Worrall until July. Chris Dent, who captains the four-day and 50-over sides this summer, was alone in offering a steady flow of runs, although James Bracey, a 20-year-old Bristolian keeper-batsman, offered hope with 370 runs in six innings. Michael Klinger has retired from first-class cricket and his availability for the T20 Blast is in doubt after his wife was diagnosed with breast cancer. Jack Taylor will not bowl after receiving a ban for an illegal action – his third in five years.

IN: Ryan Higgins (Mid), Andrew Tye (Aus, T20), Daniel Worrall (Aus)
OUT: Brandon Gilmour, Patrick Grieshaber (both REL)

HEAD COACH: RICHARD DAWSON

Dawson was appointed in early 2015 after gaining some coaching experience with Yorkshire's Second XI and inspired Gloucestershire to win the One-Day Cup in his first season. A former Yorkshire and Gloucestershire off-spinner who played seven Tests, Dawson worked as a spin-bowling and one-day coach at Bristol following his retirement in 2011. Assistant coach Ian Harvey won six one-day trophies at the club between 1999 and 2003.

COUNTY CHAMPIONSHIP AVERAGES 2017

Batting

	Mat	Inns	NO	Runs	HS	Ave	SR	100	50	4s	6s
JR Bracey	4	6	1	370	156	74.00	55.63	1	2	47	3
BAC Howell	2	3	0	204	163	68.00	70.34	1	0	22	4
CDJ Dent	13	24	3	894	135*	42.57	46.65	2	7	111	4
CT Bancroft	11	21	4	685	206*	40.29	49.10	1	4	91	2
JMR Taylor	14	20	3	665	143	39.11	68.98	2	2	90	3
GH Roderick	8	12	1	400	96	36.36	55.40	0	4	48	2
DA Payne	10	11	5	203	54*	33.83	65.27	0	1	27	2
P Mustard	14	20	0	573	72	28.65	44.66	0	3	75	1
IA Cockbain	1	1	0	27	27	27.00	38.02	0	0	2	0
WA Tavaré	10	17	1	422	101	26.37	40.07	1	2	44	0
GT Hankins	11	17	1	387	79*	24.18	54.58	0	3	55	0
K Noema-Barnett	11	14	1	291	59	22.38	57.17	0	1	37	5
GL van Buuren	7	12	1	233	88*	21.18	45.41	0	2	30	2
TMJ Smith	2	3	1	31	14*	15.50	36.04	0	0	5	0
MD Taylor	5	7	3	55	36	13.75	35.71	0	0	5	0
CJ Liddle	5	7	3	54	21	13.50	37.24	0	0	8	0
LC Norwell	11	13	5	99	24	12.37	46.91	0	0	13	1
CN Miles	10	13	1	137	47	11.41	44.48	0	0	20	1
J Shaw	4	5	0	23	13	4.60	26.13	0	0	2	0
GS Drissell	1	1	0	0	0	0.00	0.00	0	0	0	0

Bowling

	Overs	Mdns	Runs	Wkts	BBI	BBM	Ave	Econ	SR	5w	10w
LC Norwell	321.0	66	1026	59	8/43	10/95	17.38	3.19	32.6	5	2
TMJ Smith	70.4	7	263	9	3/73	6/155	29.22	3.72	47.1	0	0
K Noema-Barnett	254.4	59	737	23	4/31	5/53	32.04	2.89	66.4	0	0
DA Payne	259.1	49	816	25	3/37	5/93	32.64	3.14	62.2	0	0
CN Miles	245.0	35	974	27	5/99	5/127	36.07	3.97	54.4	1	0
J Shaw	101.5	15	443	11	5/118	5/118	40.27	4.35	55.5	1	0
JMR Taylor	146.2	15	619	13	3/50	4/103	47.61	4.23	67.5	0	0
MD Taylor	127.0	19	492	10	3/80	3/80	49.20	3.87	76.2	0	0
CJ Liddle	119.1	23	438	8	2/46	3/90	54.75	3.67	89.3	0	0
CT Bancroft	7.0	0	67	1	1/67	1/67	67.00	9.57	42.0	0	0
GL van Buuren	114.3	23	342	5	2/28	2/69	68.40	2.98	137.4	0	0
BAC Howell	21.0	2	82	1	1/34	1/34	82.00	3.90	126.0	0	0
CDJ Dent	16.4	0	130	1	1/61	1/61	130.00	7.80	100.0	0	0
GT Hankins	2.1	0	13	0	-	-	-	6.00	-	0	0
WA Tavaré	8.0	1	52	0	-	-	-	6.50	-	0	0
GS Drissell	12.0	0	58	0	-	-	-	4.83	-	0	0
P Mustard	20.0	2	141	0	-	-	-	7.05	-	0	0

Catches/Stumpings:
24 Roderick (inc 1st), 21 Mustard, 20 Hankins, 14 Bancroft, 12 Dent, 10 J Taylor, 6 Bracey, Noema-Barnett, Tavaré, 4 Norwell, 3 van Buuren, 2 Miles, 1 Liddle, Payne

Batting

	Mat	Inns	NO	Runs	HS	Ave	SR	100	50	4s	6s
IA Cockbain	7	7	2	295	108*	59.00	88.85	1	1	20	7
M Klinger	7	7	0	369	134	52.71	78.01	1	2	38	8
JMR Taylor	7	7	0	302	68	43.14	131.30	0	4	29	12
BAC Howell	7	7	3	163	86*	40.75	98.78	0	1	12	4
GT Hankins	3	3	0	100	67	33.33	65.35	0	1	9	0
TMJ Smith	7	5	3	57	26*	28.50	89.06	0	0	4	0
P Mustard	7	7	0	180	90	25.71	67.92	0	1	19	2
GL van Buuren	4	3	0	61	51	20.33	56.48	0	1	7	0
CDJ Dent	6	6	0	113	43	18.83	72.90	0	0	10	0
MD Taylor	7	2	1	5	3	5.00	35.71	0	0	0	0
LC Norwell	6	5	0	19	16	3.80	95.00	0	0	1	1
CJ Liddle	6	4	2	6	3*	3.00	37.50	0	0	0	0
K Noema-Barnett	1	1	0	0	0	0.00	0.00	0	0	0	0
CN Miles	2	-	-	-	-	-	-	-	-	-	-

Bowling

	Overs	Mdns	Runs	Wkts	BBI	Ave	Econ	SR	4w	5w
LC Norwell	46.0	2	229	5	5/36	45.80	4.97	55.2	0	1
TMJ Smith	41.0	1	207	5	3/33	41.40	5.04	49.2	0	0
BAC Howell	66.2	1	352	13	3/40	27.07	5.30	30.6	0	0
CJ Liddle	51.0	0	272	18	5/36	15.11	5.33	17.0	1	2
JMR Taylor	47.0	0	264	2	1/53	132.00	5.61	141.0	0	0
GL van Buuren	20.0	1	114	1	1/52	114.00	5.70	120.0	0	0
CN Miles	11.0	0	65	0	-	-	5.90	-	0	0
MD Taylor	54.0	2	326	4	3/48	81.50	6.03	81.0	0	0
K Noema-Barnett	2.0	0	15	0	-	-	7.50	-	0	0

Catches/Stumpings:
7 Klinger, Mustard (inc 1st), 4 Dent, 2 Hankins, Howell, Miles, Noema-Barnett, Smith, J Taylor, 1 Cockbain, Norwell, M Taylor

GLOUCESTERSHIRE
COUNTY CRICKET CLUB

	Mat	Inns	NO	Runs	HS	Ave	SR	100	50	4s	6s	
CT Bancroft	6	6	1	149	51	29.80	134.23	0	1	12	4	
M Klinger	13	11	1	281	101*	28.10	137.07	1	1	21	14	
IA Cockbain	13	11	1	252	47*	25.20	127.27	0	0	22	8	
BAC Howell	12	10	0	235	34	23.50	115.19	0	0	14	6	
P Mustard	13	11	0	230	57	20.90	109.00	0	1	29	8	
JMR Taylor	13	11	3	140	31	17.50	116.66	0	0	6	6	
K Noema-Barnett	11	9	2	110	33	15.71	144.73	0	0	6	9	Batting
NLTC Perera	7	4	1	30	26*	10.00	142.85	0	0	0	2	
TMJ Smith	12	6	4	20	13*	10.00	58.82	0	0	0	0	
GL van Buuren	2	2	0	15	13	7.50	68.18	0	0	0	0	
DA Payne	13	4	2	13	6*	6.50	76.47	0	0	0	0	
GT Hankins	7	3	0	17	14	5.66	60.71	0	0	0	0	
MD Taylor	11	5	2	15	9*	5.00	71.42	0	0	1	0	
CN Miles	2	2	0	8	8	4.00	88.88	0	0	1	0	
CJ Liddle	7	1	0	0	0	0.00	0.00	0	0	0	0	
GH Roderick	1	-	-	-	-	-	-	-	-	-	-	

	Overs	Mdns	Runs	Wkts	BBI	Ave	Econ	SR	4w	5w	
BAC Howell	41.0	0	236	16	4/29	14.75	5.75	15.3	1	0	
CN Miles	8.0	0	55	3	3/25	18.33	6.87	16.0	0	0	
GL van Buuren	7.0	0	52	0	-	-	7.42	-	0	0	
DA Payne	39.4	1	298	17	3/13	17.52	7.51	14.0	0	0	Bowling
TMJ Smith	34.2	0	259	10	3/28	25.90	7.54	20.6	0	0	
NLTC Perera	17.5	0	138	10	3/31	13.80	7.73	10.7	0	0	
JMR Taylor	10.0	0	88	4	2/35	22.00	8.80	15.0	0	0	
K Noema-Barnett	8.2	0	76	1	1/34	76.00	9.12	50.0	0	0	
CJ Liddle	16.3	0	154	6	2/27	25.66	9.33	16.5	0	0	
MD Taylor	27.0	0	258	6	2/29	43.00	9.55	27.0	0	0	

Catches/Stumpings:
9 Mustard (inc 1st), 8 Howell, Klinger, 7 J Taylor, 6 Smith, 4 Noema-Barnett, 3 Cockbain, Payne, M Taylor, 2 Perera, 1 Bancroft, Hankins, Liddle, van Buuren

HAMPSHIRE
CRICKET

FORMED: 1863
HOME GROUND: The Ageas Bowl, Southampton
CAPTAIN: James Vince
2017 RESULTS: CC1: 5/8; RL50: 6/9 South Group; T20: Semi-finalists
HONOURS: Championship: (2) 1961, 1973; Gillette/NatWest/C&G/FP Trophy: (3) 1991, 2005, 2009; Benson & Hedges Cup: (2) 1988, 1992; Pro40/National League/CB40/YB40/ RL50: 2012; Sunday League: (3) 1975, 1978, 1986; T20 Cup: (2) 2010, 2012

THE LOWDOWN

Last summer Hampshire narrowly avoided Championship relegation for the third season running. They will need to churn out some wins at the batter-friendly Ageas Bowl to avoid another dice with the drop; five of their seven home games were drawn last year. And more runs too, with no batsman averaging 40 or above in 2017. The capture of Sam Northeast was a coup and a reminder of the pulling power of top-tier cricket, while the arrival of Hashim Amla for the first three months of the season will help cover for George Bailey, who will not return because of family commitments. Led by the South African Kolpak paceman Kyle Abbott, the bowling looks strong. Fidel Edwards is primed for his fourth season at the club and allrounder Ian Holland – a Victorian with a British passport – signed a two-year contract after impressing last summer. England spinner Mason Crane will want to improve on last year's haul of 16 wickets at 44.68. He was far more effective as part of a trio of Hampshire spinners who took the club to T20 Finals Day.

IN: Sam Northeast (Ken), Hashim Amla (SA)
OUT: Michael Carberry (Lei), Will Smith (Dur), George Bailey (Aus)

FIRST-TEAM COACH: CRAIG WHITE

White was appointed in November 2016 to replace Dale Benkenstein. The former England and Yorkshire allrounder has been on the Hampshire staff since 2012, taking up the roles of assistant and bowling coach, and took charge for six Championship matches at the end of the 2016 season before he was appointed first-team coach on a full-time basis. White had a distinguished 17-year playing career which included 30 Tests and 51 ODIs.

	Mat	Inns	NO	Runs	HS	Ave	SR	100	50	4s	6s
GJ Bailey	10	16	0	610	161	38.12	61.55	2	3	81	3
BJ Taylor	1	2	1	35	18	35.00	39.77	0	0	5	0
IG Holland	8	11	4	233	58*	33.28	43.30	0	2	26	0
JM Vince	12	19	0	626	147	32.94	55.15	2	1	94	2
JHK Adams	12	17	0	558	166	32.82	44.25	2	1	74	2
GK Berg	14	20	2	568	99*	31.55	74.83	0	2	67	14
KJ Abbott	14	18	4	418	97*	29.85	65.00	0	2	53	6
SM Ervine	14	21	1	572	203	28.60	51.53	1	2	63	1
MA Carberry	7	11	0	272	98	24.72	38.74	0	2	37	3
LD McManus	10	14	2	285	41*	23.75	50.62	0	0	38	3
RJW Topley	2	3	2	23	16	23.00	23.46	0	0	3	0
LA Dawson	10	16	0	334	75	20.87	40.68	0	2	42	2
RR Rossouw	8	13	0	253	99	19.46	64.54	0	1	40	1
TP Alsop	5	7	0	118	40	16.85	41.40	0	0	19	0
FS Organ	1	1	0	16	16	16.00	44.44	0	0	2	0
MET Salisbury	2	3	1	31	17*	15.50	35.22	0	0	3	1
MS Crane	7	8	3	66	29	13.20	40.99	0	0	8	1
JJ Weatherley	3	4	0	45	35	11.25	66.17	0	0	7	0
BTJ Wheal	4	4	1	31	18	10.33	24.80	0	0	4	0
FH Edwards	9	10	4	43	20	7.16	47.77	0	0	6	0
CM Dickinson	1	1	0	1	1	1.00	33.33	0	0	0	0

Batting

	Overs	Mdns	Runs	Wkts	BBI	BBM	Ave	Econ	SR	5w	10w
KJ Abbott	415.3	131	1092	60	7/41	9/105	18.20	2.62	41.5	4	0
IG Holland	133.0	38	351	19	4/16	6/39	18.47	2.63	42.0	0	0
FH Edwards	208.1	31	772	30	5/49	7/111	25.73	3.70	41.6	2	0
LA Dawson	333.2	87	809	31	4/22	8/129	26.09	2.42	64.5	0	0
GK Berg	391.5	103	987	37	4/28	7/45	26.67	2.51	63.5	0	0
BTJ Wheal	84.5	11	352	11	4/98	7/171	32.00	4.14	46.2	0	0
JM Vince	8.5	0	38	1	1/13	1/13	38.00	4.30	53.0	0	0
MET Salisbury	46.2	7	177	4	2/35	2/50	44.25	3.82	69.5	0	0
MS Crane	193.1	32	715	16	5/40	5/85	44.68	3.70	72.4	1	0
JJ Weatherley	15.0	3	55	1	1/46	1/46	55.00	3.66	90.0	0	0
SM Ervine	126.4	29	331	6	2/1	3/22	55.16	2.61	126.6	0	0
RJW Topley	44.2	6	178	2	1/56	2/143	89.00	4.01	133.0	0	0
BJ Taylor	40.0	1	180	2	2/180	2/180	90.00	4.50	120.0	0	0
JHK Adams	1.0	1	0	0	-	-	-	0.00	-	0	0
MA Carberry	2.0	1	1	0	-	-	-	0.50	-	0	0
GJ Bailey	2.0	0	9	0	-	-	-	4.50	-	0	0

Bowling

Catches/Stumpings:
31 McManus (inc 3st), 14 Adams, 13 Ervine, Vince, 9 Alsop, 7 Rossouw, 5 Bailey, Dawson, 3 Crane, 2 Berg, Carberry, 1 Abbott, Holland

HAMPSHIRE
CRICKET

Batting

	Mat	Inns	NO	Runs	HS	Ave	SR	100	50	4s	6s
GJ Bailey	6	6	2	312	145*	78.00	92.30	1	2	25	4
JM Vince	7	7	1	463	178	77.16	113.75	1	3	50	8
RR Rossouw	3	3	0	196	156	65.33	130.66	1	0	33	2
KJ Abbott	6	3	1	79	56	39.50	85.86	0	1	3	3
TP Alsop	7	7	1	203	112*	33.83	66.55	1	1	21	0
JHK Adams	2	2	0	58	36	29.00	109.43	0	0	9	0
LD McManus	7	5	2	85	33	28.33	86.73	0	0	7	2
LA Dawson	7	7	1	160	74	26.66	78.04	0	1	11	0
SM Ervine	7	6	1	112	33*	22.40	93.33	0	0	9	1
GK Berg	5	4	1	19	15	6.33	82.60	0	0	2	0
MS Crane	7	2	1	5	3	5.00	71.42	0	0	0	0
MA Carberry	3	3	0	9	9	3.00	47.36	0	0	2	0
IG Holland	2	1	1	11	11*	-	100.00	0	0	0	0
RJW Topley	5	1	1	0	0*	-	-	0	0	0	0
FH Edwards	2	-	-	-	-	-	-	-	-	-	-
CP Wood	1	-	-	-	-	-	-	-	-	-	-

Bowling

	Overs	Mdns	Runs	Wkts	BBI	Ave	Econ	SR	4w	5w
LA Dawson	68.0	3	303	9	3/30	33.66	4.45	45.3	0	0
CP Wood	5.3	0	30	0	-	-	5.45	-	0	0
GK Berg	46.0	1	253	7	3/44	36.14	5.50	39.4	0	0
SM Ervine	10.3	0	58	2	1/17	29.00	5.52	31.5	0	0
KJ Abbott	52.2	1	300	7	2/46	42.85	5.73	44.8	0	0
MS Crane	64.0	1	384	14	3/53	27.42	6.00	27.4	0	0
IG Holland	19.0	1	117	3	2/57	39.00	6.15	38.0	0	0
RJW Topley	45.3	3	300	9	4/68	33.33	6.59	30.3	1	0
FH Edwards	19.2	0	137	3	2/57	45.66	7.08	38.6	0	0

Catches/Stumpings:
11 McManus (inc 3st), 4 Dawson, Ervine, 3 Bailey, Berg, 2 Abbott, Carberry, Vince, 1 Alsop, Crane, Edwards, Topley, Wood

   www.ageasbowl.com / tel: 023 8047 2002

HAMPSHIRE
CRICKET

Batting

	Mat	Inns	NO	Runs	HS	Ave	SR	100	50	4s	6s
JM Vince	15	15	1	542	81	38.71	158.47	0	5	68	18
TP Alsop	10	10	2	267	64	33.37	120.27	0	1	27	3
MA Carberry	8	8	1	224	77	32.00	150.33	0	1	21	9
GJ Bailey	15	15	5	301	89*	30.10	125.94	0	1	28	6
RR Rossouw	10	10	1	255	60	28.33	137.09	0	1	29	6
LD McManus	10	8	2	128	59	21.33	134.73	0	1	6	8
CM Dickinson	5	5	0	102	51	20.40	152.23	0	1	16	2
Shahid Afridi	12	9	0	151	101	16.77	157.29	1	0	13	8
CP Wood	9	3	2	15	13*	15.00	55.55	0	0	1	0
GK Berg	14	8	3	72	31	14.40	122.03	0	0	3	1
SM Ervine	10	8	2	65	23*	10.83	87.83	0	0	4	1
LA Dawson	8	6	1	46	18	9.20	104.54	0	0	3	1
MS Crane	13	3	2	9	3*	9.00	56.25	0	0	0	0
JB Lintott	1	1	0	8	8	8.00	44.44	0	0	0	0
KJ Abbott	15	7	1	25	14	4.16	100.00	0	0	2	1
RJW Topley	7	3	1	1	1*	0.50	16.66	0	0	0	0
FH Edwards	1	1	1	8	8*	-	133.33	0	0	0	1
BTJ Wheal	1	1	1	2	2*	-	66.66	0	0	0	0
IG Holland	1	-	-	-	-	-	-				

	Overs	Mdns	Runs	Wkts	BBI	Ave	Econ	SR	4w	5w
MS Crane	47.0	0	312	18	3/15	17.33	6.63	15.6	0	0
Shahid Afridi	44.0	0	317	13	4/20	24.38	7.20	20.3	2	0
LA Dawson	32.0	2	237	14	3/28	16.92	7.40	13.7	0	0
JB Lintott	3.0	0	24	1	1/24	24.00	8.00	18.0	0	0
RJW Topley	24.0	0	193	7	3/23	27.57	8.04	20.5	0	0
IG Holland	4.0	0	33	1	1/33	33.00	8.25	24.0	0	0
FH Edwards	3.2	0	29	0	-	-	8.70	-	0	0
GK Berg	45.1	0	393	13	3/35	30.23	8.70	20.8	0	0
KJ Abbott	54.3	0	487	17	3/22	28.64	8.93	19.2	0	0
CP Wood	28.0	0	257	9	2/17	28.55	9.17	18.6	0	0
BTJ Wheal	4.0	0	45	1	1/45	45.00	11.25	24.0	0	0

Bowling

Catches/Stumpings:

12 Vince, 7 Rossouw, 6 Berg, McManus (inc 3st), 5 Afridi, Bailey, Carberry, Wood, 4 Abbott, Dickinson (inc 2st), Ervine, 3 Crane, 2 Alsop, Dawson, 1 Topley

TEAM PROFILE

FORMED: 1870
HOME GROUND: The Spitfire Ground, Canterbury
ONE-DAY NAME: Kent Spitfires
CAPTAIN: Sam Billings
2017 RESULTS: CC2: 5/10; RL50: 9/9 South Group; T20: 6/9 South Group
HONOURS: Championship: (7) 1906, 1909, 1910, 1913, 1970, 1977(s), 1978; Gillette/NatWest/C&G/FP Trophy: (2) 1967, 1974; Pro40/National League/CB40/RL50: 2001; Benson & Hedges Cup: (3) 1973, 1976, 1978; Sunday League: (4) 1972, 1973, 1976, 1995; T20 Cup: 2007

THE LOWDOWN

All change please – although the courtesies weren't obvious in the case of Sam Northeast, Kent's former captain and premier batsman, who joined Hampshire after being told that he would be reconsidered for the captaincy only if he signed a contract extension. Sam Billings will lead the side in all formats despite intermittent Championship appearances over the last two seasons due to England and IPL commitments. Paul Downton has filled the new role of director of cricket while outgoing CEO Jamie Clifford is replaced by operations manager Ben Green. It remains to be seen whether such profound change can shake Kent from their stupor of mediocrity which has left the county trophy-less for a decade and marooned in Division Two since 2010. Losing allrounder Matt Coles is a big blow and support is needed for the extraordinary Darren Stevens, who took 62 wickets at 18.08 last summer and turns 42 in April. The outstanding form of Joe Denly and emergence of Sean Dickson augur well, and South African batsman Heino Kuhn has been signed on a Kolpak deal to play in all formats (subject to a visa). Daniel Bell-Drummond will want to do justice to his potential after scoring no first-class hundreds in 2017.

IN: Heino Kuhn (SA, Kolpak)
OUT: Matt Coles (Ess), Sam Northeast (Ham), Adam Ball, Hugh Bernard, Charlie Hartley (all REL)

HEAD COACH: MATT WALKER

Walker was assistant coach to Jimmy Adams before his promotion ahead of the 2017 season, having previously worked with Essex and England Lions. As a left-handed batsman, he scored nearly 20,000 runs for Kent and Essex between 1992 and 2011, including 275 not out against Somerset in 1996 – the fourth-highest score by a Kent batsman. A year after being announced as assistant coach, former South Africa fast bowler Allan Donald is finally able to fulfil the role after being granted a work permit.

COUNTY CHAMPIONSHIP AVERAGES 2017

	Mat	Inns	NO	Runs	HS	Ave	SR	100	50	4s	6s
JL Denly	13	23	2	1165	227	55.47	62.23	4	5	145	18
SA Northeast	13	23	3	1017	173*	50.85	67.26	3	4	136	8
WD Parnell	2	3	1	100	51*	50.00	58.47	0	1	16	0
SW Billings	6	8	2	262	70*	43.66	78.20	0	1	45	1
Yasir Shah	3	4	1	131	48	43.66	55.27	0	0	17	1
DI Stevens	12	20	3	707	100	41.58	79.26	1	5	108	7
SR Dickson	12	21	0	804	318	38.28	52.44	1	4	86	4
JAR Harris	4	6	2	146	34	36.50	48.18	0	0	23	0
AP Rouse	10	16	2	491	95*	35.07	55.29	0	3	79	4
JC Tredwell	6	9	2	184	55	26.28	44.87	0	1	24	2
DJ Bell-Drummond	13	23	1	561	90	25.50	47.66	0	3	80	1
JJ Weatherley	5	8	0	190	36	23.75	39.74	0	0	29	0
MT Coles	11	16	2	304	56*	21.71	91.29	0	1	46	6
AF Milne	5	8	2	121	51	20.16	51.93	0	1	19	0
WRS Gidman	8	14	0	236	51	16.85	45.21	0	1	35	0
G Stewart	1	2	1	15	15*	15.00	45.45	0	0	3	0
ME Claydon	9	13	5	111	21*	13.87	71.61	0	0	18	2
Z Crawley	4	6	0	75	37	12.50	52.81	0	0	13	1
Imran Qayyum	3	5	1	40	39	10.00	43.47	0	0	6	0
CJ Haggett	3	5	0	35	21	7.00	25.00	0	0	3	0
MD Hunn	2	-	-	-	-	-	-	-	-	-	-

Batting

	Overs	Mdns	Runs	Wkts	BBI	BBM	Ave	Econ	SR	5w	10w
DI Stevens	395.4	102	1121	62	8/75	9/110	18.08	2.83	38.2	7	0
JAR Harris	114.2	25	400	19	4/56	7/140	21.05	3.49	36.1	0	0
WD Parnell	57.1	16	162	7	3/48	4/90	23.14	2.83	49.0	0	0
MD Hunn	46.5	7	202	7	3/90	4/112	28.85	4.31	40.1	0	0
JL Denly	66.3	11	228	7	2/49	2/49	32.57	3.42	57.0	0	0
Imran Qayyum	50.5	5	198	6	2/25	3/46	33.00	3.89	50.8	0	0
CJ Haggett	96.0	30	256	7	3/40	4/62	36.57	2.66	82.2	0	0
Yasir Shah	155.5	22	533	14	5/132	7/206	38.07	3.42	66.7	1	0
ME Claydon	241.5	45	884	23	5/54	7/129	38.43	3.65	63.0	1	0
MT Coles	335.0	60	1313	32	6/84	6/125	41.03	3.91	62.8	1	0
AF Milne	184.0	51	572	13	4/68	4/133	44.00	3.10	84.9	0	0
G Stewart	20.0	5	89	2	2/52	2/89	44.50	4.45	60.0	0	0
WRS Gidman	56.0	7	230	5	2/48	2/48	46.00	4.10	67.2	0	0
JC Tredwell	66.0	11	228	3	1/4	1/39	76.00	3.45	132.0	0	0
DJ Bell-Drummond	1.0	0	10	0	-	-	-	10.00	-	0	0

Bowling

Catches/Stumpings:
27 Rouse (inc 1st), 14 Gidman, 12 Billings, Coles, 10 Bell-Drummond, 9 Dickson, 8 Denly, 5 Northeast, Tredwell, 3 Crawley, 2 Qayyum, Stevens, 1 Claydon, Harris, Milne, Shah, Weatherley

Batting

	Mat	Inns	NO	Runs	HS	Ave	SR	100	50	4s	6s
DJ Bell-Drummond	8	8	1	443	138	63.28	87.37	2	2	35	3
SW Billings	2	2	0	93	69	46.50	87.73	0	1	3	3
DI Stevens	7	7	0	260	147	37.14	123.80	1	1	15	18
AJ Blake	8	8	1	252	116	36.00	158.49	1	1	31	7
SR Dickson	6	6	0	179	50	29.83	86.05	0	1	13	4
SA Northeast	8	8	0	223	55	27.87	71.24	0	2	14	6
WD Parnell	4	4	2	54	32	27.00	108.00	0	0	4	1
AP Rouse	6	5	3	51	24*	25.50	82.25	0	0	4	0
JL Denly	7	7	0	163	46	23.28	78.36	0	0	20	1
JC Tredwell	7	5	2	57	28	19.00	80.28	0	0	4	2
CJ Haggett	3	2	0	27	16	13.50	84.37	0	0	3	0
ME Claydon	4	2	0	25	19	12.50	108.69	0	0	2	1
MT Coles	6	6	0	60	26	10.00	113.20	0	0	5	4
JAR Harris	2	1	0	5	5	5.00	62.50	0	0	0	0
CF Hartley	4	3	1	6	5	3.00	35.29	0	0	0	0
Z Crawley	1	1	0	2	2	2.00	20.00	0	0	0	0
IAA Thomas	3	2	2	4	4*	-	50.00	0	0	1	0
AJ Ball	1	-	-	-	-	-	-	-	-	-	-
Imran Qayyum	1	-	-	-	-	-	-	-	-	-	-

Bowling

	Overs	Mdns	Runs	Wkts	BBI	Ave	Econ	SR	4w	5w
JC Tredwell	65.0	2	309	5	3/65	61.80	4.75	78.0	0	0
DI Stevens	61.0	4	331	6	2/37	55.16	5.42	61.0	0	0
JL Denly	25.0	1	140	4	3/20	35.00	5.60	37.5	0	0
MT Coles	49.1	3	278	8	4/57	34.75	5.65	36.8	1	0
AJ Ball	10.0	0	57	0	-	-	5.70	-	0	0
WD Parnell	31.0	4	184	5	3/33	36.80	5.93	37.2	0	0
CF Hartley	30.0	0	198	3	1/31	66.00	6.60	60.0	0	0
IAA Thomas	26.0	2	172	5	2/51	34.40	6.61	31.2	0	0
ME Claydon	30.5	0	215	4	2/51	53.75	6.97	46.2	0	0
CJ Haggett	26.0	0	202	5	2/59	40.40	7.76	31.2	0	0
JAR Harris	13.3	0	106	4	2/28	26.50	7.85	20.2	0	0
Imran Qayyum	10.0	0	79	2	2/79	39.50	7.90	30.0	0	0

Catches/Stumpings:
6 Bell-Drummond, 5 Billings, Denly, Rouse, Stevens, 3 Northeast, Tredwell, 2 Harris, 1 Coles, Dickson, Parnell, Thomas

NATWEST T20 BLAST AVERAGES 2017

	Mat	Inns	NO	Runs	HS	Ave	SR	100	50	4s	6s	
JL Denly	14	14	1	567	127	43.61	150.79	2	1	53	25	
DJ Bell-Drummond	14	14	2	462	90*	38.50	135.08	0	4	46	9	
SW Billings	14	14	3	361	74	32.81	148.55	0	3	30	14	
SA Northeast	14	13	2	345	60	31.36	137.45	0	4	32	11	
JDS Neesham	14	11	4	203	52	29.00	127.67	0	2	11	8	
JC Tredwell	8	4	3	22	8*	22.00	70.96	0	0	1	0	Batting
AF Milne	7	2	1	19	17*	19.00	126.66	0	0	0	1	
AJ Blake	14	11	4	116	27	16.57	111.53	0	0	8	2	
DI Stevens	14	8	0	113	19	14.12	124.17	0	0	9	3	
MT Coles	11	5	0	21	14	4.20	110.52	0	0	4	0	
Imran Qayyum	10	2	0	6	6	3.00	150.00	0	0	1	0	
CJ Haggett	7	3	3	8	6*	-	114.28	0	0	0	0	
ME Claydon	12	3	3	6	4*	-	54.54	0	0	0	0	
AJ Ball	1	-	-	-	-	-	-	-	-	-	-	

	Overs	Mdns	Runs	Wkts	BBI	Ave	Econ	SR	4w	5w	
AF Milne	25.5	1	187	15	5/11	12.46	7.23	10.3	0	1	
CJ Haggett	24.0	0	184	8	2/27	23.00	7.66	18.0	0	0	
JC Tredwell	27.0	0	216	4	1/18	54.00	8.00	40.5	0	0	Bowling
Imran Qayyum	33.0	0	274	7	2/19	39.14	8.30	28.2	0	0	
JL Denly	5.0	0	43	2	1/15	21.50	8.60	15.0	0	0	
DI Stevens	18.2	0	159	4	2/25	39.75	8.67	27.5	0	0	
ME Claydon	42.0	0	392	11	2/24	35.63	9.33	22.9	0	0	
MT Coles	38.0	1	356	8	4/32	44.50	9.36	28.5	1	0	
JDS Neesham	49.1	0	463	14	3/37	33.07	9.41	21.0	0	0	

Catches/Stumpings:

11 Blake, 9 Billings (inc 2st), 6 Bell-Drummond, 4 Neesham, Northeast, Qayyum, 3 Coles, 2 Claydon, Denly, Tredwell, 1 Haggett, Milne, Stevens

TEAM PROFILE

TM

Lancashire County Cricket Club

FORMED: 1864
HOME GROUND: Emirates Old Trafford, Manchester
ONE-DAY NAME: Lancashire Lightning
CAPTAIN: Liam Livingstone
2017 RESULTS: CC1: 2/8; RL50: 4/9 North Group; T20: 7/9 North Group
HONOURS: Championship: (9) 1897, 1904, 1926, 1927, 1928, 1930, 1934, 1950(s), 2011; Gillette/NatWest/C&G/FP Trophy: (7) 1970, 1971, 1972, 1985, 1990, 1996, 1998; Benson & Hedges Cup: (4) 1984, 1990, 1995, 1996; Pro40/National League/CB40/YB40/RL50: 1999; Sunday League: (4) 1969, 1970, 1989, 1998; T20 Cup: 2015

THE LOWDOWN

There are no prizes for the best of the rest but Lancashire looked a tough Championship outfit last summer. In Liam Livingstone, the new captain, the club has one of the most exciting talents in the country – although England are already all over him. Opener Alex Davies broke through with three Championship hundreds, becoming the first Lancashire wicketkeeper to pass 1,000 first-class runs in a season. Coupled with the arrival of Keaton Jennings, it means that Haseeb Hameed will face stiff competition for an opener's slot. Shiv Chanderpaul was as adhesive as ever and signed a one-year extension that will take him past his 44th birthday. Leg-spinner Matthew Parkinson looks to have supplanted Simon Kerrigan as the frontline spinner. The pace attack, so strong in recent seasons, is in transition. Zimbabwean Kyle Jarvis has left after cutting his Kolpak ties to return to international cricket and Ryan McLaren has gone back to South Africa. But those holes are neatly filled by Australian seamer Joe Mennie – a rare example of an overseas player who will stay from spring to autumn – and the veteran Graham Onions, recruited from Durham.

IN: Keaton Jennings, Graham Onions (both Dur), Joe Mennie (Aus), James Faulkner (Aus, T20)
OUT: Luke Procter (Nor), Kyle Jarvis (REL)

HEAD COACH: GLEN CHAPPLE

Chapple stepped into the breach at the beginning of last year following Ashley Giles's decision to return to his native Warwickshire. He took 1,373 wickets in 664 appearances during a 23-year playing career at Old Trafford which ended in 2016 and captained the club to the Championship title in 2011. Former Lancashire and England bowler Paul Allott has been appointed director of cricket, while Andrew Flintoff has joined the Lancashire board.

	Mat	Inns	NO	Runs	HS	Ave	SR	100	50	4s	6s
SC Kerrigan	2	2	1	79	59	79.00	59.39	0	1	10	0
S Chanderpaul	13	19	3	831	182	51.93	57.74	3	1	100	6
LS Livingstone	11	19	2	803	224	47.23	58.78	2	3	100	11
AL Davies	14	24	1	916	140*	39.82	55.51	3	3	142	3
R McLaren	14	19	1	602	107	33.44	45.57	1	2	76	1
DJ Vilas	14	22	2	662	244	33.10	61.63	1	2	76	4
SJ Croft	9	15	1	409	115	29.21	52.50	1	0	54	2
H Hameed	12	21	3	513	88	28.50	33.63	0	3	62	2
J Clark	11	14	1	364	140	28.00	57.68	1	0	55	4
JM Anderson	5	6	5	23	13*	23.00	47.91	0	0	3	0
TE Bailey	8	11	1	216	58	21.60	54.27	0	1	28	2
SD Parry	13	16	0	293	44	18.31	44.25	0	0	44	0
RP Jones	3	5	0	87	35	17.40	33.46	0	0	9	0
JC Buttler	4	6	0	103	49	17.16	59.19	0	0	12	3
LA Procter	4	6	0	71	24	11.83	40.34	0	0	8	0
KM Jarvis	9	11	2	106	30	11.77	61.27	0	0	15	2
MW Parkinson	5	6	3	20	13	6.66	22.22	0	0	2	0
S Mahmood	3	4	3	5	4*	5.00	16.12	0	0	0	0

Batting

	Overs	Mdns	Runs	Wkts	BBI	BBM	Ave	Econ	SR	5w	10w
S Mahmood	69.3	10	256	12	4/50	5/120	21.33	3.68	34.7	0	0
MW Parkinson	76.4	7	308	14	4/68	7/105	22.00	4.01	32.8	0	0
KM Jarvis	255.3	62	779	33	6/61	8/144	23.60	3.04	46.4	2	0
JM Anderson	162.3	46	373	15	4/20	6/109	24.86	2.29	65.0	0	0
R McLaren	379.1	87	1130	45	4/37	8/113	25.11	2.98	50.5	0	0
TE Bailey	217.2	48	629	25	5/44	10/98	25.16	2.89	52.1	2	1
LA Procter	46.0	6	160	6	3/43	3/43	26.66	3.47	46.0	0	0
SD Parry	322.3	68	777	25	5/45	6/101	31.08	2.40	77.4	1	0
J Clark	179.5	23	643	19	4/81	4/28	33.84	3.57	56.7	0	0
LS Livingstone	109.0	16	345	7	6/52	6/52	49.28	3.16	93.4	1	0
SC Kerrigan	83.0	14	287	5	2/35	4/136	57.40	3.45	99.6	0	0
H Hameed	4.0	1	9	0	-	-	-	2.25	-	0	0
SJ Croft	24.5	2	58	0	-	-	-	2.33	-	0	0

Bowling

Catches/Stumpings:
48 Davies (inc 6st), 13 Vilas, 12 Livingstone, 6 Croft, Hameed, McLaren, 5 Parry, 3 Anderson, Buttler, Chanderpaul, Jarvis, Jones, 1 Bailey, Kerrigan, Mahmood, Parkinson, Procter

Batting

	Mat	Inns	NO	Runs	HS	Ave	SR	100	50	4s	6s
J Clark	6	6	3	270	79*	90.00	143.61	0	2	20	11
DJ Vilas	8	8	1	408	108	58.28	113.64	2	2	46	2
SJ Croft	6	6	1	219	127	43.80	106.31	1	0	13	8
KR Brown	8	8	0	315	63	39.37	89.48	0	3	32	7
H Hameed	8	8	1	275	88	39.28	80.40	0	2	21	2
R McLaren	6	6	0	189	79	31.50	95.93	0	1	15	3
AL Davies	8	8	0	211	50	26.37	88.28	0	1	27	1
LS Livingstone	8	8	0	168	39	21.00	84.42	0	0	12	6
LA Procter	2	2	0	31	21	15.50	93.93	0	0	2	0
SD Parry	8	6	3	30	22*	10.00	150.00	0	0	4	0
TE Bailey	3	3	0	21	11	7.00	105.00	0	0	2	1
JM Anderson	8	2	2	5	5*	-	100.00	0	0	1	0
DJ Lamb	2	2	2	5	4*	-	83.33	0	0	0	0
KM Jarvis	5	1	1	4	4*	-	100.00	0	0	0	0
SC Kerrigan	2	1	1	2	2*	-	100.00	0	0	0	0

Bowling

	Overs	Mdns	Runs	Wkts	BBI	Ave	Econ	SR	4w	5w
JM Anderson	70.0	4	346	9	2/45	38.44	4.94	46.6	0	0
KM Jarvis	40.0	4	202	7	3/42	28.85	5.05	34.2	0	0
DJ Lamb	20.0	0	108	4	2/51	27.00	5.40	30.0	0	0
SD Parry	69.0	1	391	5	3/55	78.20	5.66	82.8	0	0
LS Livingstone	27.4	0	176	3	2/51	58.66	6.36	55.3	0	0
SC Kerrigan	14.2	1	95	5	3/60	19.00	6.62	17.2	0	0
J Clark	37.4	0	251	10	4/34	25.10	6.66	22.6	1	0
R McLaren	36.0	1	247	4	3/43	61.75	6.86	54.0	0	0
TE Bailey	20.2	0	147	2	1/44	73.50	7.22	61.0	0	0
SJ Croft	5.5	0	53	1	1/13	53.00	9.08	35.0	0	0
LA Procter	5.0	0	48	1	1/25	48.00	9.60	30.0	0	0

Catches/Stumpings:
10 Davies (inc 2st), 6 Parry, 5 Livingstone, 3 Anderson, Vilas, 2 Brown, Kerrigan, McLaren, 1 Croft, Hameed, Jarvis

	Mat	Inns	NO	Runs	HS	Ave	SR	100	50	4s	6s
JC Buttler	12	12	3	451	80*	50.11	144.55	0	5	33	15
R McLaren	11	10	5	228	77	45.60	149.01	0	1	21	8
LS Livingstone	12	12	0	345	61	28.75	136.36	0	1	28	15
KR Brown	10	10	0	221	61	22.10	126.28	0	1	21	5
DJ Lamb	1	1	0	22	22	22.00	122.22	0	0	0	1
SJ Croft	12	11	4	145	62	20.71	113.28	0	1	10	4
AM Lilley	12	9	0	177	38	19.66	158.03	0	0	23	6
DJ Vilas	12	12	1	209	40	19.00	120.80	0	0	13	5
TE Bailey	4	2	0	18	10	9.00	120.00	0	0	0	1
J Clark	11	8	2	53	17	8.83	112.76	0	0	3	2
SD Parry	12	5	2	19	15*	6.33	95.00	0	0	2	0
Junaid Khan	10	3	1	3	2	1.50	27.27	0	0	0	0
MW Parkinson	9	4	4	10	7*	-	111.11	0	0	1	0
KM Jarvis	1	-	-	-	-	-	-	-	-	-	-
RP Jones	2	-	-	-	-	-	-	-	-	-	-
S Mahmood	1	-	-	-	-	-	-	-	-	-	-

Batting

	Overs	Mdns	Runs	Wkts	BBI	Ave	Econ	SR	4w	5w
MW Parkinson	32.0	0	194	14	4/23	13.85	6.06	13.7	1	0
SJ Croft	15.1	0	113	2	1/12	56.50	7.45	45.5	0	0
SD Parry	39.0	0	291	6	2/27	48.50	7.46	39.0	0	0
DJ Lamb	4.0	0	30	3	3/30	10.00	7.50	8.0	0	0
LS Livingstone	6.3	0	50	3	2/11	16.66	7.69	13.0	0	0
AM Lilley	17.0	0	137	5	2/14	27.40	8.05	20.4	0	0
TE Bailey	13.0	0	105	4	2/28	26.25	8.07	19.5	0	0
Junaid Khan	38.0	0	316	13	3/28	24.30	8.31	17.5	0	0
KM Jarvis	4.0	0	35	0	-	-	8.75	-	0	0
J Clark	20.0	0	177	7	3/26	25.28	8.85	17.1	0	0
R McLaren	37.4	0	368	11	2/14	33.45	9.76	20.5	0	0
S Mahmood	1.0	0	14	0	-	-	14.00	-	0	0

Bowling

Catches/Stumpings:
11 Buttler (inc 5st), 9 Livingstone, 8 Croft, 6 Lilley, 3 Clark, Parry, 2 Khan, McLaren, Vilas,
1 Bailey, Parkinson

TEAM PROFILE

LEICESTERSHIRE
COUNTY CRICKET CLUB

FORMED: 1879
HOME GROUND: Fischer County Ground, Leicester
ONE-DAY NAME: Leicestershire Foxes
CAPTAIN: Michael Carberry
2017 RESULTS: CC2: 10/10; RL50: 6/9 North Group; T20: Quarter-finalists
HONOURS: Championship: (3) 1975, 1996, 1998; Benson & Hedges Cup: (3) 1972, 1975, 1985; Sunday League: (2) 1974, 1977; T20 Cup: (3) 2004, 2006, 2011

THE LOWDOWN

No wins, five draws, nine defeats: Leicestershire would have finished bottom of Division Two even if they had been spared a 16-point disciplinary deduction in April. Durham, who began the season with a 48-point handicap, finished 23 points above them. The hard-nosed Pierre de Bruyn resigned as head coach less than a year into the job, with the hot potato now in the hands of Leicester legend Paul Nixon. Rapid improvement is required in all disciplines. Mark Cosgrove aside, only one frontline batsman averaged above 30. Ben Raine led the attack heroically but now shoulders a heavy burden after the departure of Clint McKay. Michael Carberry, appointed captain in all formats, adds experience to the top order, though he has been short on form. The ray of light is the spirited 21-year-old slow left-armer Callum Parkinson. Leicestershire sprung a surprise by signing Pakistan seamers Mohammad Abbas (27) and Sohail Khan (33) to share the overseas spot, while also recruiting experienced Afghan allrounder Mohammad Nabi for the T20 Blast. Will Fazakerley retired aged 19 to pursue another career.

IN: Michael Carberry (Ham), Ateeq Javid (War), Tom Taylor (Der), Mohammad Abbas, Sohail Khan (both Pak), Mohammad Nabi (Afg, T20)
OUT: Clint McKay (REL), Will Fazakerley (RET)

HEAD COACH: PAUL NIXON

Leicestershire have gone back to the boot room by appointing Nixon, the former England wicketkeeper who has lived in Leicester for 30 years and won two Championship titles in the 1990s. "I think the guys just need a little bit of love," he said. Nixon has won the Caribbean Premier League twice as coach of Jamaica Tallawahs. His assistant John Sadler moves up from the second XI, while new bowling coach Matt Mason has been lured from his native Worcestershire.

www.leicestershireccc.co.uk / tel: 0116 2832 128

Batting

	Mat	Inns	NO	Runs	HS	Ave	SR	100	50	4s	6s
CF Parkinson	5	6	4	103	75	51.50	68.66	0	1	8	2
MJ Cosgrove	12	23	0	1112	188	48.34	67.47	2	6	165	5
LJ Hill	11	19	3	527	85*	32.93	45.98	0	2	58	0
CN Ackermann	12	22	3	618	118	32.52	51.37	2	1	85	5
ZJ Chappell	6	10	2	258	66	32.25	58.23	0	1	36	1
EJH Eckersley	14	26	2	716	158	29.83	64.10	1	3	96	2
TJ Wells	2	3	0	86	46	28.66	76.10	0	0	12	1
ML Pettini	7	12	1	303	110*	27.54	50.24	1	2	32	1
PJ Horton	10	19	0	504	71	26.52	47.63	0	2	71	0
CE Shreck	1	1	0	26	26	26.00	113.04	0	0	4	0
CJ McKay	11	18	4	347	66	24.78	73.20	0	1	46	7
BA Raine	9	17	4	301	57	23.15	61.93	0	2	36	6
NJ Dexter	8	15	2	300	114	23.07	49.66	1	0	44	2
RA Jones	2	4	2	45	23*	22.50	32.84	0	0	5	1
AM Ali	3	5	0	110	40	22.00	44.35	0	0	16	0
HE Dearden	10	19	0	401	87	21.10	36.85	0	2	49	0
ST Evans	1	2	0	37	29	18.50	33.94	0	0	5	0
A Harinath	2	4	0	68	26	17.00	44.73	0	0	8	0
MW Pillans	4	7	0	107	56	15.28	72.29	0	1	16	1
D Klein	9	14	3	138	26	12.54	71.50	0	0	18	1
CS Delport	1	2	0	21	20	10.50	47.72	0	0	3	1
RJ Sayer	3	5	0	39	31	7.80	37.14	0	0	3	1
MA Carberry	4	8	0	59	18	7.37	37.82	0	0	8	0
GT Griffiths	5	7	2	28	14*	5.60	27.45	0	0	3	0
WN Fazakerley	1	2	0	0	0	0.00	0.00	0	0	0	0
A Shahzad	1	-	-	-	-	-	-	-	-	-	-

Bowling

	Overs	Mdns	Runs	Wkts	BBI	BBM	Ave	Econ	SR	5w	10w
BA Raine	256.1	54	777	33	6/66	6/66	23.54	3.03	46.5	2	0
NJ Dexter	121.0	23	456	14	5/71	5/71	32.57	3.76	51.8	2	0
CF Parkinson	147.2	14	556	17	8/148	10/185	32.70	3.77	52.0	1	1
D Klein	206.0	21	958	28	6/80	7/124	34.21	4.65	44.1	2	0
MW Pillans	101.1	9	416	12	3/63	5/140	34.66	4.11	50.5	0	0
CJ McKay	315.3	97	809	22	4/35	6/121	36.77	2.56	86.0	0	0
RA Jones	58.0	5	228	5	2/50	3/142	45.60	3.93	69.6	0	0
AM Ali	6.0	0	46	1	1/10	1/31	46.00	7.66	36.0	0	0
HE Dearden	18.4	0	95	2	1/0	1/0	47.50	5.08	56.0	0	0
ZJ Chappell	114.5	13	514	9	4/108	4/124	57.11	4.47	76.5	0	0
TJ Wells	15.0	1	120	2	2/98	2/98	60.00	8.00	45.0	0	0
CN Ackermann	104.0	9	394	6	3/45	3/45	65.66	3.78	104.0	0	0
GT Griffiths	124.0	20	403	5	4/101	4/101	80.60	3.25	148.8	0	0
MJ Cosgrove	39.0	1	163	2	1/10	1/10	81.50	4.17	117.0	0	0
WN Fazakerley	12.0	2	83	1	1/83	1/83	83.00	6.91	72.0	0	0
CE Shreck	42.0	7	141	1	1/110	1/141	141.00	3.35	252.0	0	0
RJ Sayer	102.0	9	379	2	1/48	1/70	189.50	3.71	306.0	0	0
CS Delport	7.0	1	30	0	-	-	-	4.28	-	0	0
A Shahzad	25.0	1	104	0	-	-	-	4.16	-	0	0

Catches/Stumpings:

24 Hill (inc 2st), 16 Eckersley, 11 Dearden, 8 Horton, 5 Klein, 3 Parkinson, 2 Ackermann, Ali, Dexter, McKay, Sayer, 1 Carberry, Cosgrove, Evans, Jones, Pettini, Pillans, Raine, Shahzad, Wells

Batting

	Mat	Inns	NO	Runs	HS	Ave	SR	100	50	4s	6s
ML Pettini	8	7	0	294	159	42.00	101.73	1	1	36	1
MJ Cosgrove	8	7	0	277	80	39.57	107.78	0	3	29	4
EJH Eckersley	8	7	1	216	80	36.00	98.18	0	1	21	1
CS Delport	8	7	0	243	68	34.71	100.82	0	3	30	8
TJ Wells	8	7	2	157	67	31.40	96.31	0	1	9	6
LJ Hill	8	7	1	188	68*	31.33	92.15	0	1	24	1
D Klein	6	3	1	62	26	31.00	77.50	0	0	5	0
AM Ali	6	5	0	153	88	30.60	78.46	0	2	11	3
ZJ Chappell	6	5	2	82	59*	27.33	79.61	0	1	12	0
CJ McKay	4	2	0	49	35	24.50	89.09	0	0	2	2
RJ Sayer	5	4	0	67	25	16.75	94.36	0	0	4	3
CN Ackermann	1	1	0	15	15	15.00	53.57	0	0	1	0
CF Parkinson	1	1	0	3	3	3.00	37.50	0	0	0	0
JS Sykes	4	2	1	2	2	2.00	50.00	0	0	0	0
NJ Dexter	1	1	0	0	0	0.00	0.00	0	0	0	0
GT Griffiths	6	3	2	0	0*	0.00	0.00	0	0	0	0

Bowling

	Overs	Mdns	Runs	Wkts	BBI	Ave	Econ	SR	4w	5w
CJ McKay	30.4	2	132	2	2/28	66.00	4.30	92.0	0	0
CF Parkinson	9.0	0	44	1	1/44	44.00	4.88	54.0	0	0
D Klein	46.5	0	244	8	3/46	30.50	5.20	35.1	0	0
GT Griffiths	50.0	1	274	10	3/35	27.40	5.48	30.0	0	0
RJ Sayer	38.0	0	215	4	2/65	53.75	5.65	57.0	0	0
NJ Dexter	2.0	0	12	0	-	-	6.00	-	0	0
AM Ali	5.0	0	31	1	1/31	31.00	6.20	30.0	0	0
TJ Wells	64.4	0	401	10	3/44	40.10	6.20	38.8	0	0
JS Sykes	29.0	0	183	6	4/57	30.50	6.31	29.0	1	0
ZJ Chappell	49.0	0	314	4	2/44	78.50	6.40	73.5	0	0
CS Delport	11.0	0	80	1	1/20	80.00	7.27	66.0	0	0

Catches/Stumpings:
8 Hill (inc 1st), 3 Ali, Cosgrove, Eckersley, Griffiths, Pettini, 2 McKay, Sayer, Wells, 1 Delport

Batting

	Mat	Inns	NO	Runs	HS	Ave	SR	100	50	4s	6s
MJ Cosgrove	15	14	3	414	79	37.63	138.92	0	3	42	9
MW Pillans	15	10	7	107	34*	35.66	111.45	0	0	7	4
L Ronchi	15	14	1	429	63*	33.00	180.25	0	3	52	18
CN Ackermann	15	13	4	255	62*	28.33	115.90	0	2	26	5
CS Delport	15	14	1	339	109*	26.07	137.24	1	0	37	10
GT Griffiths	13	4	3	18	11	18.00	90.00	0	0	1	1
AM Ali	9	5	1	68	35*	17.00	95.77	0	0	3	1
CF Parkinson	15	5	4	15	8*	15.00	75.00	0	0	0	0
ML Pettini	3	3	1	27	16	13.50	81.81	0	0	1	0
EJH Eckersley	6	6	0	77	30	12.83	108.45	0	0	8	1
TJ Wells	15	12	1	139	31*	12.63	111.20	0	0	7	6
LJ Hill	12	8	1	76	17	10.85	88.37	0	0	2	3
CJ McKay	12	4	0	14	6	3.50	66.66	0	0	1	0
D Klein	5	1	0	3	3	3.00	75.00	0	0	0	0

Bowling

	Overs	Mdns	Runs	Wkts	BBI	Ave	Econ	SR	4w	5w
CS Delport	38.0	0	266	10	3/19	26.60	7.00	22.8	0	0
CJ McKay	43.0	1	328	23	5/11	14.26	7.62	11.2	0	1
AM Ali	12.0	0	93	4	2/22	23.25	7.75	18.0	0	0
CF Parkinson	47.0	0	377	15	3/20	25.13	8.02	18.8	0	0
CN Ackermann	20.0	0	164	6	3/21	27.33	8.20	20.0	0	0
D Klein	17.0	0	144	7	2/23	20.57	8.47	14.5	0	0
MW Pillans	53.5	0	470	17	3/24	27.64	8.73	19.0	0	0
GT Griffiths	38.5	0	355	8	2/29	44.37	9.14	29.1	0	0
TJ Wells	4.4	0	48	2	1/5	24.00	10.28	14.0	0	0

Catches/Stumpings:
12 Ronchi (inc 4st), Wells, 7 Ackermann, Hill, 4 Delport, McKay, 3 Ali, Griffiths, Parkinson,
2 Cosgrove, Eckersley, Klein, Pillans

MIDDLESEX

TEAM PROFILE

FORMED: 1864
HOME GROUND: Lord's Cricket Ground, London
CAPTAIN: Dawid Malan
2017 RESULTS: CC1: 7/8; RL50: 8/9 South Group; T20: 7/9 South Group
HONOURS: Championship: (13) 1903, 1920, 1921, 1947, 1949(s), 1976, 1977(s), 1980, 1982, 1985, 1990, 1993, 2016; Gillette/NatWest/C&G/FP Trophy: (4) 1977, 1980, 1984, 1998; Benson & Hedges Cup: (2) 1983, 1986; Sunday League: 1992; T20 Cup: 2008

THE LOWDOWN

County Championship winners in 2016, relegated in 2017. But a poor season deserves context: Middlesex finished just three points off fourth place. The winter has brought only one major change, with Dawid Malan appointed captain across all formats, though his England commitments will often leave the team in the hands of new vice-captain Sam Robson. What compounded last year's disappointment was the modest showings in white-ball cricket, a recurrent theme for a decade now. The hiring of specialist T20 coach Daniel Vettori has yet to reap dividends, with Brendon McCullum and Eoin Morgan both struggling for form last summer. Morgan, who last played a first-class match in July 2015, hopes to return to Championship action this summer. Middlesex could do with his runs; Nick Gubbins made 1,000 runs fewer than in 2016, while Nick Compton's travails continued. The pace attack is strong, although Steven Finn and Toby Roland-Jones are returning from winter injuries. Much is expected of 23-year-old fast bowler Tom Helm and 20-year-old batsman Max Holden, who earned the nickname of Mini Chef (think Alastair Cook) while on loan at Northants last year.

IN: (none)
OUT: Ryan Higgins (Glo)

HEAD COACH: RICHARD SCOTT

Scott goes into his ninth season as head coach under scrutiny, despite overseeing the Championship triumph in 2016. An immediate return to Division One is expected. Scott had an eight-year county career with Hampshire and Gloucestershire – as well as turning out for Middlesex Second XI, whom he coached for two seasons before his promotion to the top role in 2009. Former New Zealand spinner Daniel Vettori signed a three-year contract as the county's specialist T20 coach in December 2016.

Batting

	Mat	Inns	NO	Runs	HS	Ave	SR	100	50	4s	6s
SD Robson	11	20	0	785	159	39.25	57.04	2	4	115	0
AC Voges	9	14	3	402	92	36.54	44.46	0	3	47	0
DJ Malan	8	16	2	493	115	35.21	55.58	1	2	63	5
MDE Holden	1	1	0	35	35	35.00	35.35	0	0	6	0
PR Stirling	8	13	0	454	111	34.92	70.06	1	3	60	12
SS Eskinazi	14	25	2	793	179	34.47	56.16	2	4	109	8
JA Simpson	14	22	2	570	90	28.50	47.77	0	3	78	3
NRD Compton	11	19	2	446	120	26.23	38.41	1	0	51	0
NRT Gubbins	7	13	0	314	101	24.15	48.30	1	2	38	4
JEC Franklin	10	14	1	296	112	22.76	50.85	1	1	36	5
OP Rayner	11	15	2	274	52*	21.07	60.48	0	1	42	0
TS Roland-Jones	9	14	2	252	53	21.00	57.79	0	1	34	5
NA Sowter	1	2	0	37	37	18.50	148.00	0	0	6	1
RF Higgins	4	7	0	129	45	18.42	51.60	0	0	17	0
JAR Harris	6	10	1	110	19	12.22	36.78	0	0	12	3
TJ Murtagh	12	17	6	134	27	12.18	55.83	0	0	16	1
ST Finn	11	14	6	95	31*	11.87	47.97	0	0	17	0
TG Helm	5	7	1	65	28	10.83	44.52	0	0	11	0
RH Patel	2	4	2	12	7*	6.00	46.15	0	0	0	1

Bowling

	Overs	Mdns	Runs	Wkts	BBI	BBM	Ave	Econ	SR	5w	10w
DJ Malan	38.0	4	125	7	2/1	2/1	17.85	3.28	32.5	0	0
RH Patel	70.0	7	221	12	7/81	12/173	18.41	3.15	35.0	2	1
JEC Franklin	102.0	21	280	12	4/40	5/56	23.33	2.74	51.0	0	0
RF Higgins	98.0	24	281	12	4/75	5/79	23.41	2.86	49.0	0	0
NA Sowter	10.1	1	25	1	1/23	1/25	25.00	2.45	61.0	0	0
TJ Murtagh	372.0	93	995	36	6/63	6/79	27.63	2.67	62.0	1	0
ST Finn	287.2	45	1045	34	8/79	9/119	30.73	3.63	50.7	1	0
TS Roland-Jones	277.2	63	880	28	4/66	6/123	31.42	3.17	59.4	0	0
TG Helm	167.5	30	602	19	5/59	7/140	31.68	3.58	53.0	1	0
JAR Harris	154.5	32	490	15	4/119	4/138	32.66	3.16	61.9	0	0
OP Rayner	265.3	62	778	20	4/35	5/62	38.90	2.93	79.6	0	0
PR Stirling	57.0	8	165	4	2/70	3/101	41.25	2.89	85.5	0	0
AC Voges	17.0	0	80	1	1/15	1/15	80.00	4.70	102.0	0	0
NRD Compton	1.0	0	2	0	-	-	-	2.00	-	0	0
NRT Gubbins	1.0	0	4	0	-	-	-	4.00	-	0	0
JA Simpson	2.0	0	21	0	-	-	-	10.50	-	0	0

Catches/Stumpings:

54 Simpson (inc 1st), 15 Rayner, 12 Voges, 11 Eskinazi, 10 Robson, 6 Finn, 5 Compton, 4 Franklin, Malan, Stirling, 2 Helm, Murtagh, Roland-Jones, 1 Harris, Patel

Batting

	Mat	Inns	NO	Runs	HS	Ave	SR	100	50	4s	6s
PR Stirling	2	2	0	97	71	48.50	118.29	0	1	13	2
ST Finn	4	3	2	45	21*	45.00	80.35	0	0	3	2
JA Simpson	7	7	1	224	82*	37.33	92.94	0	2	24	1
AC Voges	7	7	0	247	81	35.28	76.94	0	1	25	0
NRT Gubbins	7	7	0	225	114	32.14	78.94	1	1	24	1
JEC Franklin	7	7	0	220	69	31.42	82.08	0	2	10	6
DJ Malan	7	7	0	155	50	22.14	78.68	0	1	24	0
RH Patel	6	5	3	39	18	19.50	75.00	0	0	2	1
TS Roland-Jones	7	6	0	116	65	19.33	70.30	0	1	11	1
RF Higgins	7	7	1	94	48*	15.66	85.45	0	0	7	3
JK Fuller	3	3	1	31	16	15.50	79.48	0	0	1	1
NRD Compton	4	4	0	53	37	13.25	49.07	0	0	6	0
TG Helm	7	6	2	50	25	12.50	74.62	0	0	5	0
SD Robson	1	1	0	12	12	12.00	133.33	0	0	2	0
OP Rayner	1	1	0	8	8	8.00	61.53	0	0	0	0

Bowling

	Overs	Mdns	Runs	Wkts	BBI	Ave	Econ	SR	4w	5w
RH Patel	44.0	2	173	6	2/39	28.83	3.93	44.0	0	0
TS Roland-Jones	51.0	7	201	11	4/10	18.27	3.94	27.8	1	0
TG Helm	53.0	7	264	7	2/42	37.71	4.98	45.4	0	0
RF Higgins	19.4	0	100	5	3/32	20.00	5.08	23.6	0	0
OP Rayner	9.0	0	48	0	-	-	5.33	-	0	0
ST Finn	29.0	1	160	4	4/39	40.00	5.51	43.5	1	0
JK Fuller	19.5	0	118	0	-	-	5.94	-	0	0
DJ Malan	12.4	0	76	3	2/39	25.33	6.00	25.3	0	0
JEC Franklin	15.0	0	97	3	2/26	32.33	6.46	30.0	0	0

Catches/Stumpings:
12 Simpson (1st), 6 Voges, 4 Helm, 2 Gubbins, Higgins, 1 Compton, Finn, Franklin, Malan, Roland-Jones

	Mat	Inns	NO	Runs	HS	Ave	SR	100	50	4s	6s
AC Voges	3	3	1	110	58*	55.00	152.77	0	1	11	0
SS Eskinazi	5	5	1	165	57*	41.25	133.06	0	1	15	3
GFB Scott	6	6	2	121	38*	30.25	103.41	0	0	6	4
RF Higgins	14	14	4	251	68*	25.10	160.89	0	1	20	12
BB McCullum	9	9	0	220	88	24.44	149.65	0	2	22	14
EJG Morgan	14	14	0	319	59	22.78	129.67	0	1	24	15
DJ Malan	6	6	0	132	41	22.00	132.00	0	0	16	4
JA Simpson	14	14	1	268	51	20.61	127.61	0	1	23	9
TG Southee	13	11	6	94	64*	18.80	159.32	0	1	3	7
PR Stirling	10	10	0	184	44	18.40	133.33	0	0	16	9
JEC Franklin	13	13	2	155	38	14.09	118.32	0	0	7	9
NA Sowter	14	5	2	32	12	10.66	133.33	0	0	5	0
NRT Gubbins	4	4	0	28	21	7.00	80.00	0	0	2	1
TS Roland-Jones	4	4	1	18	8	6.00	75.00	0	0	1	0
HW Podmore	1	1	0	6	6	6.00	50.00	0	0	0	0
TG Helm	12	4	3	4	4	4.00	133.33	0	0	0	0
TE Barber	2	1	0	0	0	0.00	0.00	0	0	0	0
ST Finn	10	1	1	4	4*	-	133.33	0	0	1	0

Batting

	Overs	Mdns	Runs	Wkts	BBI	Ave	Econ	SR	4w	5w
PR Stirling	13.0	0	85	5	2/16	17.00	6.53	15.6	0	0
TG Southee	45.0	0	337	15	3/9	22.46	7.48	18.0	0	0
TG Helm	39.1	0	302	19	5/11	15.89	7.71	12.3	0	1
DJ Malan	5.0	0	39	1	1/23	39.00	7.80	30.0	0	0
NA Sowter	44.0	0	351	14	4/23	25.07	7.97	18.8	1	0
ST Finn	34.0	1	278	16	4/24	17.37	8.17	12.7	1	0
RF Higgins	22.0	0	182	6	2/13	30.33	8.27	22.0	0	0
HW Podmore	2.3	0	22	0	-	-	8.80	-	0	0
TE Barber	7.0	0	69	1	1/32	69.00	9.85	42.0	0	0
TS Roland-Jones	16.0	0	169	7	4/39	24.14	10.56	13.7	1	0
GFB Scott	2.0	0	22	1	1/22	22.00	11.00	12.0	0	0
JEC Franklin	8.5	0	109	3	3/19	36.33	12.33	17.6	0	0

Bowling

Catches/Stumpings:

9 Morgan, 8 Simpson, 7 Southee, 6 Higgins, Malan, 5 Franklin, McCullum, Sowter, 3 Stirling, 2 Finn, Scott, 1 Eskinazi, Gubbins, Helm, Podmore, Roland-Jones, Voges

TEAM PROFILE

FORMED: 1878
HOME GROUND: County Ground, Northampton
ONE-DAY NAME: Northamptonshire Steelbacks
CAPTAIN: Alex Wakely
2017 RESULTS: CC2: 3/10; RL50: 8/9 North Group; T20: 6/9 North Group
HONOURS: Gillette/NatWest/C&G/FP Trophy: (2) 1976, 1992; Benson & Hedges Cup: 1980; T20 Cup: (2) 2013, 2016

THE LOWDOWN

Northants won nine Championship games in 2017 – and still missed out on promotion. Ultimately they were separated from second-placed Nottinghamshire by the five-point penalty incurred for a slow over-rate at, ironically, Trent Bridge. This should not cloud a hugely encouraging Championship campaign. Five seamers took more than 30 wickets at an average in the low-20s. Runs were also spread evenly. The T20 campaign was a failure by the county's high standards, the Steelbacks falling one victory short of making the quarter-finals. The club have signed two established cricketers in Ben Hutton and Luke Procter, and Sri Lankan spinner Seekkuge Prasanna returns for the T20 Blast. Kiwi allrounder Doug Bracewell will cover for Rory Kleinveldt until May. Ben Duckett's misdemeanour on the Lions' winter tour seem to have frozen his England prospects, which is to Northants' gain, although he will miss the start of the season with a finger injury. The effervescent Muhammad Azharullah has departed after four seasons in which he has been a key member of two T20-winning sides.

IN: Brett Hutton (Not), Luke Procter (Lan), Doug Bracewell (NZ), Seekkuge Prasanna (SL, T20), Ricardo Vasconcelos (SA, Portugese passport)
OUT: Muhammad Azharullah (REL), David Murphy (RET)

HEAD COACH: DAVID RIPLEY

A Northamptonshire stalwart, Ripley led the club to their maiden T20 title in 2013 – their first trophy in two decades – and repeated the trick in 2016. In a 17-year playing career Ripley scored over 10,000 runs for the county with more than 1,000 dismissals as a wicketkeeper. After retiring in 2001, he became Northants Second XI coach before his promotion in 2012. David Sales, the former captain who scored more than 22,000 runs for Northants, has been appointed batting coach.

	Mat	Inns	NO	Runs	HS	Ave	SR	100	50	4s	6s
LA Procter	2	4	0	235	94	58.75	54.65	0	3	23	2
RE Levi	10	19	3	734	115	45.87	90.28	2	3	100	12
BM Duckett	11	19	0	799	193	42.05	76.82	3	3	123	0
MDE Holden	9	16	0	629	153	39.31	49.37	2	2	78	1
RI Newton	13	24	0	894	108	37.25	55.94	1	10	116	2
AG Wakely	13	24	3	658	112	31.33	52.85	1	2	70	4
AM Rossington	8	13	1	358	112	29.83	66.05	1	2	43	2
JJ Cobb	10	18	4	410	96	29.28	60.83	0	1	49	5
SC Kerrigan	4	5	1	98	62	24.50	54.74	0	1	12	1
GG White	3	4	0	88	47	22.00	65.67	0	0	13	1
RK Kleinveldt	12	19	1	394	86	21.88	98.99	0	1	46	14
RI Keogh	12	22	3	408	105*	21.47	44.59	1	1	41	1
NL Buck	8	13	3	201	43	20.10	55.21	0	0	30	5
SP Crook	5	8	1	128	30	18.28	66.66	0	0	16	0
Azharullah	7	10	5	73	23	14.60	63.47	0	0	11	0
RJ Gleeson	7	9	4	63	25	12.60	42.56	0	0	10	0
CF Hughes	3	6	0	60	21	10.00	60.60	0	0	10	0
D Murphy	5	7	0	67	30	9.57	46.85	0	0	10	0
A Sheikh	1	1	0	7	7	7.00	43.75	0	0	1	0
BW Sanderson	10	16	5	72	16*	6.54	52.55	0	0	10	1
A Carter	1	2	0	11	8	5.50	50.00	0	0	1	0

Batting

	Overs	Mdns	Runs	Wkts	BBI	BBM	Ave	Econ	SR	5w	10w
A Carter	22.0	5	90	5	3/51	5/90	18.00	4.09	26.4	0	0
RJ Gleeson	222.2	44	745	40	5/46	8/131	18.62	3.35	33.3	3	0
NL Buck	222.4	37	770	36	6/34	7/91	21.38	3.45	37.1	3	0
BW Sanderson	334.1	93	860	40	5/39	9/83	21.50	2.57	50.1	2	0
Azharullah	192.0	36	677	31	5/63	8/136	21.83	3.52	37.1	2	0
RK Kleinveldt	350.1	68	1153	50	9/65	13/98	23.06	3.29	42.0	2	1
SC Kerrigan	120.4	24	389	12	4/62	4/68	32.41	3.22	60.3	0	0
A Sheikh	8.0	1	36	1	1/36	1/36	36.00	4.50	48.0	0	0
BM Duckett	9.0	0	41	1	1/21	1/32	41.00	4.55	54.0	0	0
RI Keogh	112.1	17	461	9	3/44	3/44	51.22	4.10	74.7	0	0
MDE Holden	33.0	2	159	3	2/59	3/94	53.00	4.81	66.0	0	0
RI Newton	9.0	0	82	1	1/82	1/82	82.00	9.11	54.0	0	0
SP Crook	74.4	6	333	4	2/35	3/51	83.25	4.45	112.0	0	0
GG White	72.0	9	305	3	2/40	2/40	101.66	4.23	144.0	0	0
JJ Cobb	32.0	0	113	1	1/42	1/106	113.00	3.53	192.0	0	0
LA Procter	31.0	3	138	1	1/67	1/86	138.00	4.45	186.0	0	0
CF Hughes	2.0	0	16	0	-	-	-	8.00	-	0	0
AM Rossington	12.0	1	48	0	-	-	-	4.00	-	0	0
AG Wakely	9.2	0	75	0	-	-	-	8.03	-	0	0

Bowling

Catches/Stumpings:
21 Rossington (inc 2st), 16 Duckett, 15 Murphy (inc 3st), 14 Wakely, 12 Levi, 8 Kleinveldt,
5 Keogh, 4 Buck, Holden, 3 Cobb, Hughes, Sanderson, 2 Crook, Kerrigan, Procter,
1 Azharullah, Gleeson, Murphy, Newton

Batting

	Mat	Inns	NO	Runs	HS	Ave	SR	100	50	4s	6s
RE Levi	7	6	1	305	109	61.00	108.15	1	3	37	4
AM Rossington	8	6	2	213	69	53.25	129.87	0	2	26	4
AG Wakely	6	6	1	247	109*	49.40	86.66	1	1	24	1
RI Newton	6	6	1	226	107	45.20	88.97	1	1	25	1
RI Keogh	5	5	1	177	69*	44.25	86.34	0	2	12	2
RK Kleinveldt	2	1	0	31	31	31.00	79.48	0	0	3	1
SP Crook	7	4	1	83	48	27.66	86.45	0	0	5	0
BW Sanderson	4	3	2	25	19*	25.00	62.50	0	0	2	0
JJ Cobb	6	6	0	129	56	21.50	87.16	0	1	16	5
BM Duckett	5	5	1	86	56*	21.50	98.85	0	1	13	0
GG White	8	5	0	59	40	11.80	98.33	0	0	4	4
RJ Gleeson	6	3	1	6	6*	3.00	46.15	0	0	0	0
Azharullah	8	2	1	2	2	2.00	28.57	0	0	0	0
NL Buck	5	1	0	1	1	1.00	50.00	0	0	0	0
MDE Holden	2	1	1	23	23*	-	62.16	0	0	3	0
MA Richardson	1	1	1	1	1*	-	33.33	0	0	0	0
SA Zaib	2	-	-	-	-	-	-	-	-	-	-

Bowling

	Overs	Mdns	Runs	Wkts	BBI	Ave	Econ	SR	4w	5w
BW Sanderson	40.0	4	201	8	3/36	25.12	5.02	30.0	0	0
GG White	55.0	0	280	5	2/37	56.00	5.09	66.0	0	0
Azharullah	52.4	2	303	7	3/55	43.28	5.75	45.1	0	0
JJ Cobb	20.0	0	121	0	-	-	6.05	-	0	0
RI Keogh	19.0	1	116	1	1/52	116.00	6.10	114.0	0	0
SP Crook	24.0	0	155	1	1/36	155.00	6.45	144.0	0	0
RK Kleinveldt	9.0	0	61	1	1/61	61.00	6.77	54.0	0	0
RJ Gleeson	31.0	0	213	4	2/56	53.25	6.87	46.5	0	0
MA Richardson	2.0	0	15	0	-	-	7.50	-	0	0
NL Buck	22.0	1	172	2	1/69	86.00	7.81	66.0	0	0

Catches/Stumpings:
4 Rossington, Wakely, 3 White, 1 Cobb, Crook, Duckett, Gleeson, Keogh, Newton

www.northantscricket.com / tel: 01604 514455

	Mat	Inns	NO	Runs	HS	Ave	SR	100	50	4s	6s
RE Levi	9	8	0	375	88	46.87	166.66	0	3	40	21
BM Duckett	12	11	1	297	92*	29.70	129.69	0	3	34	4
AG Wakely	12	11	2	258	52	28.66	121.69	0	1	16	7
AM Rossington	12	11	0	308	67	28.00	161.25	0	1	46	9
SP Crook	12	10	5	129	34*	25.80	150.00	0	0	12	4
RI Keogh	12	10	3	178	41*	25.42	117.88	0	0	15	1
JJ Cobb	6	5	0	113	48	22.60	111.88	0	0	10	4
BW Sanderson	10	4	3	20	12*	20.00	117.64	0	0	1	1
RI Newton	1	1	0	8	8	8.00	88.88	0	0	0	0
RJ Gleeson	12	3	2	7	4*	7.00	100.00	0	0	0	0
RK Kleinveldt	12	8	2	35	13	5.83	100.00	0	0	0	2
SA Zaib	5	2	0	7	6	3.50	50.00	0	0	0	0
Azharullah	5	1	1	2	2*	-	66.66	0	0	0	0
GG White	4	1	1	0	0*	-	-	0	0	0	0
NL Buck	3	-	-	-	-	-	-	-	-	-	-
T Shamsi	5	-	-	-	-	-	-	-	-	-	-

	Overs	Mdns	Runs	Wkts	BBI	Ave	Econ	SR	4w	5w
T Shamsi	14.1	0	92	4	2/20	23.00	6.49	21.2	0	0
RJ Gleeson	42.3	0	331	10	3/12	33.10	7.78	25.5	0	0
RK Kleinveldt	43.0	1	341	14	3/16	24.35	7.93	18.4	0	0
Azharullah	20.0	0	181	7	2/36	25.85	9.05	17.1	0	0
NL Buck	12.0	0	110	4	2/41	27.50	9.16	18.0	0	0
GG White	11.0	0	101	3	2/30	33.66	9.18	22.0	0	0
RI Keogh	22.0	0	206	6	2/27	34.33	9.36	22.0	0	0
SA Zaib	8.0	0	76	0	-	-	9.50	-	0	0
BW Sanderson	30.1	0	303	7	2/26	43.28	10.04	25.8	0	0
SP Crook	10.0	0	106	0	-	-	10.60	-	0	0
JJ Cobb	6.0	0	66	1	1/16	66.00	11.00	36.0	0	0

Catches/Stumpings:
10 Rossington (inc 1st), 5 Crook, Wakely, 4 Cobb, 3 Duckett, 2 Gleeson, Keogh, Kleinveldt, Zaib, 1 Azharullah, Levi, White

TEAM PROFILE

NOTTINGHAMSHIRE
COUNTY CRICKET CLUB

FORMED: 1841
HOME GROUND: Trent Bridge, Nottingham
ONE-DAY NAME: Notts Outlaws
CAPTAIN: Steven Mullaney (Championship and RL50), Dan Christian (T20)
2017 RESULTS: CC2: 2/10; RL50: Winners; T20: Winners
HONOURS: County Championship: (6) 1907, 1929, 1981, 1987, 2005, 2010; Gillette/NatWest/C&G/FP Trophy: 1987; Pro40/National League/CB40/YB40/RL50: (2) 2013, 2017; Benson & Hedges Cup: 1989; Sunday League: 1991; T20 Cup: 2017

THE LOWDOWN

The biggest challenge for Notts will be to return from seventh heaven onto terra firma after a season which brought both limited-overs trophies and Championship promotion. Their white-ball campaigns were catapulted by a devastating top order – particularly in 50-over cricket, where there were eight hundreds by six batsmen. By contrast it was the bowlers who fired in the Championship, with seven taking 16 wickets or more at less than 30. The common thread across all formats was a depth in resources – as well as golden summers for Samit Patel and Riki Wessels. Wicketkeeper Tom Moores, son of head coach Peter, has big boots to fill following the retirement of Chris Read, who is succeeded as captain by Steven Mullaney, with Dan Christian continuing as T20 skipper. Alex Hales has signed a deal to play white-ball cricket only. Chris Nash replaces Michael Lumb, forced to retire last season due to injury, and Paul Coughlin fills the allrounder's spot vacated by Brett Hutton. Kiwi spinner Ish Sodhi plays in the Blast and his compatriot Ross Taylor is available until late June. Luke Fletcher has been cleared to bowl after a horrific head injury suffered last July.

IN: Paul Coughlin (Dur), Chris Nash (Sus), Ross Taylor (NZ), Dan Christian (Aus, T20), Ish Sodhi (NZ, T20); **OUT:** Brett Hutton (Nor), Brendan Taylor (Zim, REL), Chris Read (RET)

HEAD COACH: PETER MOORES

Moores replaced the long-serving Mick Newell – now the director of cricket – as head coach in 2016 and immediately led the club to one of the best seasons in their history. Moores had two spells as England head coach and won the Championship with Sussex in 2003 and Lancashire in 2011. Paul Franks is his deputy, with South African Ant Botha the assistant coach. The retired Chris Read is taking on a part-time coaching role.

	Mat	Inns	NO	Runs	HS	Ave	SR	100	50	4s	6s
SR Patel	14	19	2	906	257*	53.29	68.74	2	2	114	9
WT Root	2	3	0	150	132	50.00	66.37	1	0	18	0
JL Pattinson	5	5	1	197	89*	49.25	65.88	0	2	32	2
MH Wessels	14	18	1	823	202*	48.41	69.27	3	2	109	14
AD Hales	7	9	0	424	218	47.11	81.85	1	1	68	3
SCJ Broad	5	5	1	171	57	42.75	91.93	0	3	22	5
SJ Mullaney	11	15	0	620	168	41.33	56.51	1	4	94	3
CMW Read	14	18	2	622	124	38.87	66.24	1	3	83	7
JT Ball	7	9	4	174	43	34.80	92.55	0	0	26	5
L Wood	6	9	3	199	44	33.16	65.24	0	0	28	1
M Carter	1	1	0	33	33	33.00	61.11	0	0	4	0
MJ Lumb	8	9	0	292	117	32.44	51.40	1	0	40	0
GP Smith	3	5	2	91	60*	30.33	69.46	0	1	12	1
CA Pujara	8	12	0	333	112	27.75	46.50	1	1	41	0
BRM Taylor	4	5	0	123	61	24.60	45.89	0	1	18	0
JD Libby	14	20	1	464	109	24.42	41.80	1	0	50	0
LJ Fletcher	9	10	2	139	92	17.37	46.48	0	1	19	0
BA Hutton	9	13	0	210	61	16.15	43.93	0	1	26	0
HF Gurney	11	12	5	60	42*	8.57	53.09	0	0	10	0
TJ Moores	1	2	0	1	1	0.50	4.76	0	0	0	0
MHA Footitt	1	-	-	-	-	-	-	-	-	-	-

Batting

	Overs	Mdns	Runs	Wkts	BBI	BBM	Ave	Econ	SR	5w	10w
WT Root	7.2	1	29	3	3/29	3/29	9.66	3.95	14.6	0	0
JL Pattinson	139.3	34	386	32	5/29	8/71	12.06	2.76	26.1	2	0
SJ Mullaney	177.0	58	486	25	5/32	7/46	19.44	2.74	42.4	1	0
SCJ Broad	122.1	23	334	16	3/40	5/78	20.87	2.73	45.8	0	0
LJ Fletcher	252.3	48	808	36	4/35	5/68	22.44	3.20	42.0	0	0
MHA Footitt	27.2	4	95	4	2/46	4/95	23.75	3.47	41.0	0	0
JT Ball	183.2	39	675	27	3/36	6/116	25.00	3.68	40.7	0	0
BA Hutton	289.2	64	995	37	5/52	10/126	26.89	3.43	46.9	2	1
L Wood	130.2	15	512	18	4/31	8/83	28.44	3.92	43.4	0	0
SR Patel	223.0	55	682	19	3/17	3/17	35.89	3.05	70.4	0	0
HF Gurney	288.0	48	985	27	3/55	5/130	36.48	3.42	64.0	0	0
M Carter	25.0	3	161	4	4/106	4/161	40.25	6.44	37.5	0	0
MJ Lumb	2.0	0	5	0	-	-	-	2.50	-	0	0
MH Wessels	5.0	0	15	0	-	-	-	3.00	-	0	0
CA Pujara	5.0	0	17	0	-	-	-	3.40	-	0	0
JD Libby	10.0	0	41	0	-	-	-	4.10	-	0	0

Bowling

Catches/Stumpings:
53 Read, 21 Wessels, 15 Mullaney, 7 Pujara, 6 Hutton, Patel, Taylor, 5 Smith, 4 Broad, Libby, 2 Fletcher, Lumb, Wood, 1 Ball, Carter, Gurney

OUTLAWS

Batting

	Mat	Inns	NO	Runs	HS	Ave	SR	100	50	4s	6s
AD Hales	7	7	1	434	187*	72.33	105.85	2	1	50	9
SR Patel	11	10	2	539	122*	67.37	94.23	2	3	56	7
WT Root	9	7	3	259	107*	64.75	92.17	1	1	20	3
SJ Mullaney	8	7	1	378	111	63.00	113.17	1	3	33	14
BRM Taylor	9	8	1	376	154	53.71	106.81	1	3	43	6
MJ Lumb	11	10	0	311	104	31.10	91.47	1	1	31	10
MH Wessels	11	10	0	302	81	30.20	90.96	0	2	33	8
CMW Read	11	8	2	143	61	23.83	111.71	0	2	16	2
SCJ Broad	11	4	1	42	20*	14.00	140.00	0	0	4	0
JL Pattinson	10	6	3	34	10	11.33	109.67	0	0	3	0
JT Ball	6	2	0	4	4	2.00	80.00	0	0	1	0
LJ Fletcher	5	1	1	3	3*	-	150.00	0	0	0	0
HF Gurney	11	3	3	2	1*	-	66.66	0	0	0	0
L Wood	1	-	-	-	-	-	-	-	-	-	-

Bowling

	Overs	Mdns	Runs	Wkts	BBI	Ave	Econ	SR	4w	5w
L Wood	3.0	0	13	0	-	-	4.33	-	0	0
SCJ Broad	85.5	0	470	10	2/48	47.00	5.47	51.5	0	0
WT Root	7.4	0	42	0	-	-	5.47	-	0	0
JL Pattinson	83.0	0	475	13	4/42	36.53	5.72	38.3	1	0
SR Patel	77.0	0	497	9	3/51	55.22	6.45	51.3	0	0
LJ Fletcher	29.0	0	188	4	1/17	47.00	6.48	43.5	0	0
JT Ball	45.0	0	295	5	2/42	59.00	6.55	54.0	0	0
SJ Mullaney	47.4	0	313	8	3/66	39.12	6.56	35.7	0	0
HF Gurney	80.1	3	535	13	3/29	41.15	6.67	37.0	0	0

Catches/Stumpings:
12 Read, 5 Patel, Wessels, 4 Mullaney, 2 Ball, Broad, Lumb, Pattinson, Taylor, 1 Gurney, Root

OUTLAWS

	Mat	Inns	NO	Runs	HS	Ave	SR	100	50	4s	6s
WT Root	10	4	3	78	37	78.00	130.00	0	0	6	0
MH Wessels	16	16	3	559	110	43.00	151.49	1	1	53	28
SR Patel	16	14	4	405	77*	40.50	146.20	0	3	39	15
DT Christian	16	14	4	356	73	35.60	153.44	0	1	25	20
BRM Taylor	14	13	3	351	67*	35.10	124.46	0	2	38	5
AD Hales	16	16	1	507	101	33.80	204.43	1	3	78	20
SJ Mullaney	16	11	4	173	46	24.71	158.71	0	0	15	8
TJ Moores	16	13	3	191	57	19.10	144.69	0	1	17	11
MJ Lumb	2	2	0	17	16	8.50	113.33	0	0	2	1
IS Sodhi	16	5	1	20	15*	5.00	117.64	0	0	0	1
JT Ball	14	2	1	5	4	5.00	125.00	0	0	1	0
L Wood	6	2	1	1	1*	1.00	50.00	0	0	0	0
LJ Fletcher	2	1	1	11	11*	-	183.33	0	0	0	1
HF Gurney	16	1	1	0	0*	-	-	0	0	0	0

Batting

	Overs	Mdns	Runs	Wkts	BBI	Ave	Econ	SR	4w	5w
SR Patel	60.0	0	437	16	3/26	27.31	7.28	22.5	0	0
SJ Mullaney	40.0	0	350	8	3/22	43.75	8.75	30.0	0	0
JT Ball	48.4	1	428	22	3/27	19.45	8.79	13.2	0	0
HF Gurney	56.1	0	500	21	4/17	23.80	8.90	16.0	1	0
DT Christian	26.5	0	259	11	3/18	23.54	9.65	14.6	0	0
IS Sodhi	47.0	0	463	15	3/39	30.86	9.85	18.8	0	0
LJ Fletcher	4.1	0	43	1	1/43	43.00	10.32	25.0	0	0
L Wood	13.0	0	146	5	2/15	29.20	11.23	15.6	0	0
WT Root	1.0	0	17	0	-	-	17.00	-	0	0

Bowling

Catches/Stumpings:
13 Moores (inc 1st), 9 Christian, 8 Patel, Wessels, 7 Hales, 5 Taylor, 4 Ball, Gurney, Mullaney, 3 Lumb, 2 Wood, 1 Root, Sodhi

SOMERSET
CRICKET CLUB

FORMED: 1875
HOME GROUND: The Cooper Associates County Ground, Taunton
CAPTAIN: Tom Abell (Championship and RL50), Lewis Gregory (T20)
2017 RESULTS: CC1: 6/8; RL50: Quarter-finalists; T20: Quarter-finalists
HONOURS: Gillette/NatWest/C&G/FP Trophy: (3) 1979, 1983, 2001; Benson & Hedges Cup: (2) 1981, 1982; Sunday League: 1979; T20 Cup: 2005

THE LOWDOWN

Never a dull season at Taunton. In 2016 Somerset were brilliant but finished with glum faces after another Championship near-miss; in 2017 they struggled but came up smiling after out-spinning Middlesex in a relegation shootout. Their best shot at a first trophy in 13 years appears to be in the short formats, having suffered two narrow defeats to eventual champions Nottinghamshire in the quarter-finals last season. Runs were the problem in 2017, epitomised by the travails of 24-year-old captain Tom Abell, who dropped himself from a Championship match in July. With Jim Allenby moving on, Abell now has the 50-over captaincy on his plate too. Lewis Gregory is the new T20 skipper and will be able to call on powerful Kiwi allrounder Corey Anderson, who returns for another Blast campaign. Somerset are likely to see less of England's Craig Overton but hopefully more of his injury-prone twin brother Jamie. Especially at Taunton, their greatest weapon is spin: the Leach-Bess axis with the red ball, Waller-van der Merwe with white. Overseas signing Cameron Bancroft, the Aussie opener, has the task of replacing Dean Elgar, who was outstanding in Championship and 50-over cricket last summer.

IN: Cameron Bancroft (Aus), Corey Anderson (Som, T20)
OUT: Jim Allenby, Ryan Davies, Michael Leask (all REL)

HEAD COACH: JASON KERR

A new management structure is in place after director of cricket Matthew Maynard left following three rollercoaster seasons. Jason Kerr, the former Somerset allrounder, has been promoted from bowling to head coach, while Andy Hurry is Maynard's replacement. Hurry had a successful spell as coach between 2006-13 before taking charge of the ECB's England Development Programme over the last three years. Andy Nash stepped down after a decade as chairman to be replaced by committee member Charles Clark.

Batting

	Mat	Inns	NO	Runs	HS	Ave	SR	100	50	4s	6s
D Elgar	6	12	1	517	158	47.00	50.19	2	2	67	3
SM Davies	14	24	2	775	142	35.22	54.30	2	3	93	1
AJ Hose	3	6	0	194	68	32.33	51.73	0	2	27	1
JC Hildreth	14	26	1	756	109	30.24	65.79	2	2	94	1
ME Trescothick	14	27	2	714	119*	28.56	51.40	2	1	107	2
EJ Byrom	8	15	0	401	56	26.73	42.61	0	1	57	0
TB Abell	13	25	3	572	96	26.00	49.26	0	4	83	2
L Gregory	7	12	0	299	137	24.91	47.31	1	0	35	1
TD Groenewald	10	14	8	146	41*	24.33	52.70	0	0	11	7
PD Trego	8	12	0	257	68	21.41	53.43	0	2	29	1
DM Bess	9	14	4	198	55	19.80	55.46	0	1	28	1
TD Rouse	3	5	0	83	69	16.60	49.11	0	1	6	0
C Overton	13	21	3	287	44*	15.94	49.31	0	0	29	6
MJ Leach	14	21	5	237	52	14.81	40.93	0	1	31	3
JH Davey	3	5	1	58	47	14.50	51.32	0	0	6	1
GA Bartlett	4	8	1	100	28	14.28	55.86	0	0	16	2
J Allenby	2	2	0	28	19	14.00	56.00	0	0	4	0
J Overton	5	8	1	92	37	13.14	89.32	0	0	8	4
RE van der Merwe	3	5	0	33	24	6.60	67.34	0	0	2	1
PA van Meekeren	1	2	1	1	1*	1.00	10.00	0	0	0	0

Bowling

	Overs	Mdns	Runs	Wkts	BBI	BBM	Ave	Econ	SR	5w	10w
D Elgar	1.0	0	4	1	1/4	1/4	4.00	4.00	6.0	0	0
RE van der Merwe	68.4	17	189	11	4/22	5/40	17.18	2.75	37.4	0	0
C Overton	373.5	106	1030	46	5/47	9/134	22.39	2.75	48.7	2	0
L Gregory	176.3	49	484	21	5/74	5/85	23.04	2.74	50.4	1	0
DM Bess	265.5	62	843	36	7/117	10/162	23.41	3.17	44.3	3	1
TD Groenewald	243.4	71	646	26	5/58	5/65	24.84	2.65	56.2	1	0
MJ Leach	520.1	150	1315	51	6/78	9/111	25.78	2.52	61.1	4	0
J Overton	103.0	22	312	12	3/30	3/67	26.00	3.02	51.5	0	0
PA van Meekeren	34.0	9	132	4	4/60	4/132	33.00	3.88	51.0	0	0
PD Trego	79.5	13	265	7	5/67	5/68	37.85	3.31	68.4	1	0
TB Abell	27.0	6	96	2	2/71	2/71	48.00	3.55	81.0	0	0
JH Davey	75.0	17	186	3	2/33	2/73	62.00	2.48	150.0	0	0
TD Rouse	1.0	0	1	0	-	-	-	1.00	-	0	0
J Allenby	14.0	6	25	0	-	-	-	1.78	-	0	0

Catches/Stumpings:
46 S Davies (inc 7st), 21 Trescothick, 12 Abell, Hildreth, 9 C Overton, 5 Allenby, Bess, 4 Leach, 3 Bartlett, Elgar, 2 Byrom, Davey, van der Merwe, 1 Groenewald, Gregory, Hose, J Overton, Rouse, Trego, van Meekeren

SOMERSET
CRICKET CLUB

Batting

	Mat	Inns	NO	Runs	HS	Ave	SR	100	50	4s	6s
D Elgar	6	6	1	519	131*	103.80	98.85	1	5	40	12
RE van der Merwe	8	7	3	280	165*	70.00	133.97	1	0	33	7
L Gregory	4	3	2	57	26	57.00	114.00	0	0	8	0
AJ Hose	8	7	1	330	101*	55.00	105.76	1	2	28	7
J Allenby	8	8	1	377	144*	53.85	87.26	1	2	38	7
JG Myburgh	3	3	0	120	57	40.00	193.54	0	1	20	4
PD Trego	8	8	0	313	135	39.12	110.60	1	2	31	11
TD Groenewald	6	3	2	31	17	31.00	86.11	0	0	2	1
JC Hildreth	7	7	1	175	64	29.16	106.06	0	2	17	4
J Overton	4	4	0	100	40	25.00	142.85	0	0	4	8
C Overton	8	4	1	46	22	15.33	102.22	0	0	4	1
SM Davies	6	6	0	28	20	4.66	63.63	0	0	3	0
JH Davey	5	1	0	2	2	2.00	25.00	0	0	0	0
RC Davies	2	1	0	0	0	0.00	0.00	0	0	0	0
MTC Waller	4	1	1	0	0*	-	-	0	0	0	0
PA van Meekeren	1	-	-	-	-	-	-	-	-	-	-

Bowling

	Overs	Mdns	Runs	Wkts	BBi	Ave	Econ	SR	4w	5w
MTC Waller	22.5	1	121	4	3/37	30.25	5.29	34.2	0	0
TD Groenewald	56.0	1	336	5	2/48	67.20	6.00	67.2	0	0
RE van der Merwe	64.0	1	385	11	3/21	35.00	6.01	34.9	0	0
C Overton	63.0	7	385	16	3/21	24.06	6.11	23.6	0	0
J Allenby	22.0	0	141	1	1/37	141.00	6.40	132.0	0	0
JH Davey	35.0	1	230	7	2/26	32.85	6.57	30.0	0	0
PA van Meekeren	4.0	0	28	1	1/28	28.00	7.00	24.0	0	0
J Overton	31.0	2	226	9	4/64	25.11	7.29	20.6	1	0
L Gregory	31.0	1	245	8	4/60	30.62	7.90	23.2	1	0
PD Trego	3.0	0	26	0	-	-	8.66	-	0	0
JG Myburgh	3.0	0	28	0	-	-	9.33	-	0	0
D Elgar	1.0	0	13	1	1/13	13.00	13.00	6.0	0	0

Catches/Stumpings:
7 S Davies (inc 1st), 6 van der Merwe, 5 Hildreth, Hose, C Overton, 3 Allenby, Elgar,
J Overton, 2 R Davies, Davey, Trego, Waller, 1 Gregory

SOMERSET
CRICKET CLUB

	Mat	Inns	NO	Runs	HS	Ave	SR	100	50	4s	6s
CJ Anderson	4	4	2	142	81	71.00	184.41	0	1	8	11
JG Myburgh	9	9	1	290	87	36.25	171.59	0	3	28	14
C Overton	14	8	4	141	35*	35.25	135.57	0	0	6	6
JC Hildreth	14	12	2	293	63	29.30	147.97	0	1	26	9
PD Trego	10	9	2	199	84*	28.42	119.87	0	1	22	4
RE van der Merwe	14	12	5	179	36	25.57	140.94	0	0	15	7
D Elgar	2	2	0	49	25	24.50	113.95	0	0	4	1
AJ Hose	5	4	0	93	59	23.25	143.07	0	1	12	2
MTC Waller	14	6	5	23	17	23.00	85.18	0	0	1	0
SM Davies	12	11	0	214	62	19.45	156.20	0	2	25	8
L Gregory	14	12	0	203	43	16.91	158.59	0	0	30	5
J Allenby	13	11	0	156	37	14.18	105.40	0	0	16	3
MA Leask	5	3	0	19	13	6.33	90.47	0	0	1	1
T Banton	2	1	0	4	4	4.00	57.14	0	0	0	0
TB Abell	3	2	0	6	5	3.00	46.15	0	0	0	0
PA van Meekeren	5	2	0	2	1	1.00	50.00	0	0	0	0
TD Groenewald	11	4	0	1	1	0.25	9.09	0	0	0	0
JH Davey	3	2	2	22	12*	-	157.14	0	0	3	0

Batting

	Overs	Mdns	Runs	Wkts	BBI	Ave	Econ	SR	4w	5w
CJ Anderson	1.0	0	6	0	-	-	6.00	-	0	0
RE van der Merwe	53.0	0	392	15	3/13	26.13	7.39	21.2	0	0
MA Leask	3.0	0	23	1	1/11	23.00	7.66	18.0	0	0
MTC Waller	49.0	0	379	16	2/13	23.68	7.73	18.3	0	0
C Overton	48.0	0	410	15	3/17	27.33	8.54	19.2	0	0
PA van Meekeren	13.2	0	117	2	1/23	58.50	8.77	40.0	0	0
TD Groenewald	31.2	0	281	11	2/26	25.54	8.96	17.0	0	0
L Gregory	41.2	0	409	12	2/42	34.08	9.89	20.6	0	0
J Allenby	4.0	0	44	0	-	-	11.00	-	0	0
JH Davey	7.0	0	104	3	2/37	34.66	14.85	14.0	0	0

Bowling

Catches/Stumpings:
12 Waller, 7 C Overton, van der Merwe, 6 S Davies (inc 4st), 5 Gregory, 4 Allenby, 3 Trego, van Meekeren, 2 Elgar, Groenewald, Hildreth, 1 Banton (inc 1st), Hose, Leask, Myburgh

TEAM PROFILE

SURREY
COUNTY CRICKET CLUB

FORMED: 1845
GROUND: The Kia Oval, London
CAPTAIN: Rory Burns (Championship and RL50),
Jade Dernbach (T20)
2017 RESULTS: CC1: 3/8; RL50: Runners-up; T20:
Quarter-finalists
HONOURS: Championship: (19) 1890, 1891, 1892,
1894, 1895, 1899, 1914, 1950, 1952, 1953, 1954, 1955,
1956, 1957, 1958, 1971, 1999, 2000, 2002; Gillette/
NatWest/C&G/FP Trophy: 1982; Benson & Hedges
Cup: (3) 1974, 1997, 2001; Pro40/National League/
CB40/YB40/RL50: (2) 2003, 2011; Sunday League:
1996; T20 Cup: 2003

THE LOWDOWN

The present Surrey squad is stronger than it has been for years but the pressure is growing
to produce a trophy. And now they are without Kumar Sangakkara, who in three seasons
at The Oval made 4,391 runs (19 centuries) across all formats and had an immeasurable
influence on the county's young guns. Surrey are also hampered by increasing international
call-ups, with Tom Curran now part of England's plans and his younger brother Sam not
far behind. Rory Burns has taken over the four-day and 50-over captaincy from Gareth
Batty, still going strong at 40, while Jade Dernbach is the new T20 skipper. Last year's
Championship campaign was a draw fest – 10 of them in all – and testament to a struggling
bowling attack. The burden is eased by the return of Rikki Clarke, part of a swap deal in
which Dom Sibley went to Warwickshire last August, and overseas signing Mitchell Marsh.
Surrey are well-equipped for another assault on the short formats – if they can overcome the
psychological trauma of losing the last three Lord's finals. No one has a more frightening T20
opening pair than Jason Roy and Aaron Finch, who returns on a two-year contract.

IN: Mitchell Marsh (Aus), Aaron Finch (Aus, T20)
OUT: Ravi Rampaul (WI, Der), Kumar Sangakkara (SL, RET)

HEAD COACH: MICHAEL DI VENUTO

A prolific batsman for Sussex, Derbyshire and Durham from 1999-
2012, Di Venuto took over from Graham Ford before the 2016 season,
having been Australia's batting coach for three years. Former
England batsman Vikram Solanki is his new deputy, with Stuart
Barnes departing after five years at the club. Chris Taylor, the former
Gloucestershire batsman and England fielding coach, has joined as
fielding consultant.

COUNTY CHAMPIONSHIP AVERAGES 2017

	Mat	Inns	NO	Runs	HS	Ave	SR	100	50	4s	6s
KC Sangakkara	10	16	2	1491	200	106.50	68.30	8	2	174	14
MD Stoneman	12	19	0	1156	197	60.84	66.62	4	4	168	4
RJ Burns	14	22	1	1041	219*	49.57	48.41	1	8	135	2
JJ Roy	5	7	1	257	87	42.83	78.35	0	2	25	8
BT Foakes	14	20	4	680	110	42.50	52.42	1	4	93	2
AJ Finch	1	1	0	39	39	39.00	43.33	0	0	3	1
OJ Pope	5	8	2	226	100*	37.66	57.36	1	1	33	1
DP Sibley	7	12	2	330	69	33.00	40.54	0	4	41	2
R Patel	4	6	0	170	81	28.33	43.36	0	1	19	1
TK Curran	9	11	2	247	53	27.44	53.00	0	1	37	1
SM Curran	13	17	1	423	90	26.43	55.07	0	4	66	3
SG Borthwick	12	19	1	446	108*	24.77	38.95	1	1	54	0
R Clarke	6	7	0	157	50	22.42	50.80	0	1	20	5
GJ Batty	12	14	4	175	33	17.50	48.34	0	0	25	3
SC Meaker	9	13	3	174	49	17.40	41.72	0	0	21	0
A Virdi	3	4	1	18	8*	6.00	40.90	0	0	4	0
FOE van den Bergh	1	1	0	5	5	5.00	20.00	0	0	0	0
JW Dernbach	5	5	1	17	8*	4.25	45.94	0	0	0	1
ZS Ansari	1	1	0	3	3	3.00	8.57	0	0	0	0
R Rampaul	2	4	2	4	3	2.00	26.66	0	0	0	0
MHA Footitt	7	8	1	7	4	1.00	20.58	0	0	1	0
C McKerr	2	1	0	1	1	1.00	5.88	0	0	0	0

Batting

	Overs	Mdns	Runs	Wkts	BBI	BBM	Ave	Econ	SR	5w	10w
R Clarke	166.2	52	436	22	7/55	9/83	19.81	2.62	45.3	1	0
MHA Footitt	178.3	25	686	23	6/14	8/118	29.82	3.84	46.5	2	0
GJ Batty	308.1	64	857	25	3/70	5/124	34.28	2.78	73.9	0	0
TK Curran	256.3	50	832	24	4/69	8/210	34.66	3.24	64.1	0	0
FOE van den Bergh	57.0	13	145	4	3/84	4/145	36.25	2.54	85.5	0	0
SC Meaker	215.3	33	869	21	4/92	4/106	41.38	4.03	61.5	0	0
JW Dernbach	140.3	32	433	10	3/51	3/51	43.30	3.08	84.3	0	0
A Virdi	88.0	13	271	6	3/82	3/82	45.16	3.07	88.0	0	0
SM Curran	339.5	60	1179	25	3/74	4/126	47.16	3.46	81.5	0	0
DP Sibley	6.4	0	50	1	1/50	1/50	50.00	7.50	40.0	0	0
R Patel	42.0	8	128	2	1/11	1/28	64.00	3.04	126.0	0	0
R Rampaul	62.0	15	193	3	1/47	2/120	64.33	3.11	124.0	0	0
SG Borthwick	77.1	1	347	4	1/22	1/22	86.75	4.49	115.7	0	0
C McKerr	25.0	1	102	1	1/102	1/102	102.00	4.08	150.0	0	0
ZS Ansari	27.0	5	88	0	-	-	-	3.25	-	0	0

Bowling

Catches/Stumpings:
31 Foakes (inc 2st), 21 Borthwick, 7 Burns, Clarke, 6 Sangakkara, 4 S Curran, Stoneman,
3 T Curran, Meaker, Sibley, 2 Footitt, Patel, Pope

SURREY
COUNTY CRICKET CLUB

Batting

	Mat	Inns	NO	Runs	HS	Ave	SR	100	50	4s	6s
BT Foakes	10	8	3	482	92	96.40	105.47	0	6	44	3
KC Sangakkara	9	9	2	545	124*	77.85	96.97	2	3	52	8
MD Stoneman	10	10	1	456	144*	50.66	102.01	1	4	55	2
JJ Roy	4	4	0	160	92	40.00	102.56	0	1	23	1
RJ Burns	9	9	3	192	67*	32.00	72.72	0	1	16	0
OJ Pope	5	4	0	118	55	29.50	106.30	0	1	9	3
SG Borthwick	9	7	0	171	45	24.42	70.37	0	0	16	1
DP Sibley	4	4	0	79	37	19.75	71.17	0	0	10	0
SM Curran	10	7	0	124	39	17.71	95.38	0	0	13	2
GJ Batty	10	7	4	46	14	15.33	97.87	0	0	3	2
TK Curran	10	7	2	74	33	14.80	112.12	0	0	8	0
JW Dernbach	6	2	0	15	10	7.50	136.36	0	0	0	1
R Rampaul	9	3	1	3	2	1.50	37.50	0	0	0	0
SC Meaker	5	2	2	9	6*	-	45.00	0	0	0	0

Bowling

	Overs	Mdns	Runs	Wkts	BBI	Ave	Econ	SR	4w	5w
GJ Batty	75.0	0	362	9	5/40	40.22	4.82	50.0	0	1
JW Dernbach	55.5	1	277	15	4/31	18.46	4.96	22.3	1	0
SC Meaker	40.4	2	222	6	4/37	37.00	5.45	40.6	1	0
SM Curran	89.3	0	498	20	3/43	24.90	5.56	26.8	0	0
R Rampaul	79.0	2	444	18	4/40	24.66	5.62	26.3	2	0
TK Curran	81.3	3	482	9	2/45	53.55	5.91	54.3	0	0
SG Borthwick	37.0	0	234	2	1/37	117.00	6.32	111.0	0	0

Catches/Stumpings:
19 Foakes, 9 Burns, 4 S Curran, T Curran, Meaker, Sangakkara, 3 Stoneman, 2 Dernbach,
Pope, Rampaul, 1 Batty, Sibley

NATWEST T20 BLAST AVERAGES 2017

SURREY
COUNTY CRICKET CLUB

	Mat	Inns	NO	Runs	HS	Ave	SR	100	50	4s	6s
AJ Finch	13	13	1	489	114*	40.75	166.89	1	2	49	25
MC Henriques	7	7	1	187	48*	31.16	109.35	0	0	15	3
KC Sangakkara	4	4	0	120	70	30.00	146.34	0	1	9	5
TK Curran	10	9	5	119	51*	29.75	132.22	0	1	6	4
JJ Roy	12	12	0	350	78	29.16	159.09	0	4	41	13
KP Pietersen	2	2	0	56	52	28.00	127.27	0	1	1	5
OJ Pope	13	13	3	253	46	25.30	124.63	0	0	27	2
DP Sibley	6	6	0	141	61	23.50	121.55	0	1	9	5
BT Foakes	5	4	1	53	15	17.66	110.41	0	0	5	0
MD Stoneman	5	4	0	55	34	13.75	117.02	0	0	9	0
R Clarke	6	5	1	46	16*	11.50	121.05	0	0	4	1
SM Curran	13	12	0	122	39	10.16	112.96	0	0	8	4
SC Meaker	8	5	2	18	6	6.00	94.73	0	0	2	0
RJ Burns	4	4	0	22	7	5.50	73.33	0	0	2	0
GJ Batty	11	5	2	9	7*	3.00	69.23	0	0	1	0
R Rampaul	4	1	0	0	0	0.00	0.00	0	0	0	0
SG Borthwick	7	4	4	33	16*	-	86.84	0	0	2	0
JW Dernbach	13	2	2	1	1*	-	33.33	0	0	0	0

Batting

	Overs	Mdns	Runs	Wkts	BBI	Ave	Econ	SR	4w	5w
GJ Batty	35.0	1	249	14	4/14	17.78	7.11	15.0	2	0
TK Curran	36.0	2	281	12	3/28	23.41	7.80	18.0	0	0
R Clarke	22.2	0	179	10	4/16	17.90	8.01	13.4	1	0
SM Curran	45.0	1	374	13	4/13	28.76	8.31	20.7	1	0
SC Meaker	21.0	0	175	6	2/27	29.16	8.33	21.0	0	0
JW Dernbach	48.2	0	415	16	3/29	25.93	8.58	18.1	0	0
DP Sibley	9.0	0	86	0	-	-	9.55	-	0	0
MC Henriques	8.0	0	79	2	1/16	39.50	9.87	24.0	0	0
SG Borthwick	9.3	0	98	2	1/19	49.00	10.31	28.5	0	0
R Rampaul	15.1	0	161	4	2/41	40.25	10.61	22.7	0	0

Bowling

Catches/Stumpings:
7 Finch, 5 Borthwick, Stoneman, 4 Batty, Clarke, T Curran, Meaker, Roy, 3 Foakes, Henriques, Pope, Sangakkara (inc 1st), Sibley, 2 Burns, S Curran

TEAM PROFILE

FORMED: 1839
HOME GROUND: The 1st Central County Ground, Hove
ONE-DAY NAME: Sussex Sharks
CAPTAIN: Ben Brown
2017 RESULTS: CC2: 4/10; RL50: 4/9 South Group; T20: 5/9 South Group
HONOURS: Championship: (3) 2003, 2006, 2007; Gillette/NatWest/C&G/FP Trophy: (5) 1963, 1964, 1978, 1986, 2006; Pro40/National League/CB40/YB40/RL50: (2) 2008, 2009; Sunday League: 1982; T20 Cup: 2009

THE LOWDOWN

After a season of mid-table finishes, Sussex are starting afresh with new coach Jason Gillespie, who may have been the signing of the winter. Chris Nash and Steve Magoffin – two of Hove's most recognisable faces over the last decade – have moved to other counties. Both will be missed, especially the 38-year-old Magoffin, who took 334 first-class wickets at 20.72 in six seasons on the south coast, though injury blighted the last of them. A big burden rests on Chris Jordan and 23-year-old allrounder Jofra Archer, an overnight T20 superstar who was also Sussex's leading wicket-taker in the Championship last summer. Ishant Sharma adds support in the opening two months ahead of India's Test series later in the summer. The spin options look bare, with Danny Briggs struggling to fulfil his early promise. England prospect Luke Wells and Kolpak signing Stiaan van Zyl both passed 1,000 Championship runs in 2017 but the rest of the top order were inconsistent. The T20 campaign was hindered by the misfiring Ross Taylor, and much is expected of Afghanistan leg-spinner Rashid Khan, part of the Adelaide Strikers side which won the 2017/18 Big Bash under Gillespie. Rashid is available for the first half of the Blast.

IN: Ishant Sharma (Ind), Rashid Khan (Afg, T20)
OUT: Steve Magoffin (Wor), Chris Nash (Not)

HEAD COACH: JASON GILLESPIE

CEO Rob Andrew could hardly have done any better with a replacement for Mark Davis, who left by mutual consent in October. In five seasons at Headingley, Gillespie led Yorkshire to Championship promotion and then back-to-back titles in 2014 and 2015. And he now has some T20 silverware after coaching Adelaide Strikers to the Big Bash trophy over the winter. The former Australia fast bowler took 402 international wickets and was an integral part of the all-conquering team of the late 1990s and early 2000s.

	Mat	Inns	NO	Runs	HS	Ave	SR	100	50	4s	6s
LWP Wells	12	22	2	1292	258	64.60	64.76	4	4	185	15
VD Philander	5	7	3	211	73*	52.75	62.79	0	2	28	1
S van Zyl	13	22	1	1023	166*	48.71	51.69	2	4	145	2
MGK Burgess	6	10	1	434	146	48.22	59.04	1	2	57	4
JC Archer	13	20	6	638	81*	45.57	88.00	0	5	72	21
BC Brown	8	14	1	483	90	37.15	82.00	0	5	70	3
LJ Wright	12	21	1	742	118	37.10	72.81	1	4	109	8
CJ Jordan	11	17	3	438	147	31.28	60.58	1	2	53	4
CD Nash	12	21	0	578	118	27.52	60.58	1	3	84	4
D Wiese	10	15	0	404	66	26.93	66.12	0	2	55	7
PD Salt	2	4	0	100	72	25.00	65.78	0	1	13	0
WAT Beer	1	1	0	25	25	25.00	28.40	0	0	1	0
AJ Robson	4	8	1	169	72	24.14	57.48	0	1	28	0
HZ Finch	11	20	2	405	82	22.50	58.10	0	3	59	0
AP Barton	1	2	1	18	13*	18.00	31.03	0	0	3	0
DR Briggs	8	12	5	116	27	16.57	46.03	0	0	14	0
OE Robinson	4	8	1	116	41*	16.57	84.67	0	0	17	2
DMW Rawlins	4	8	0	121	55	15.12	36.55	0	1	20	1
A Sakande	3	3	2	14	7*	14.00	60.86	0	0	2	0
GHS Garton	2	4	0	43	18	10.75	79.62	0	0	5	2
SG Whittingham	5	8	2	43	22	7.16	48.86	0	0	6	1
LJ Evans	4	8	0	48	19	6.00	42.10	0	0	8	0
SJ Magoffin	2	2	1	5	5	5.00	33.33	0	0	1	0
A Shahzad	1	2	0	6	5	3.00	19.35	0	0	0	0

Batting

	Overs	Mdns	Runs	Wkts	BBI	BBM	Ave	Econ	SR	5w	10w
SJ Magoffin	27.0	10	69	5	5/51	5/51	13.80	2.55	32.4	1	0
OE Robinson	149.3	30	412	19	5/69	7/94	21.68	2.75	47.2	1	0
WAT Beer	27.3	1	88	4	2/35	4/88	22.00	3.20	41.2	0	0
JC Archer	475.1	91	1543	61	7/67	11/137	25.29	3.24	46.7	4	1
VD Philander	121.3	29	429	16	4/39	6/99	26.81	3.53	45.5	0	0
GHS Garton	56.0	0	262	9	3/20	5/109	29.11	4.67	37.3	0	0
A Sakande	51.4	8	212	7	2/53	3/91	30.28	4.10	44.2	0	0
A Shahzad	48.0	6	187	6	3/91	6/187	31.16	3.89	48.0	0	0
CJ Jordan	353.5	57	1182	36	5/46	8/128	32.83	3.34	58.9	1	0
SG Whittingham	105.5	12	494	15	5/80	5/118	32.93	4.66	42.3	1	0
S van Zyl	116.1	24	368	10	2/25	3/59	36.80	3.16	69.7	0	0
D Wiese	248.3	44	834	22	4/63	5/78	37.90	3.35	67.7	0	0
DR Briggs	218.1	36	677	14	3/40	4/104	48.35	3.10	93.5	0	0
DMW Rawlins	39.0	1	154	1	1/46	1/46	154.00	3.94	234.0	0	0
HZ Finch	1.0	0	2	0	-	-	-	2.00	-	0	0
CD Nash	24.0	6	66	0	-	-	-	2.75	-	0	0
AP Barton	11.0	0	81	0	-	-	-	7.36	-	0	0

Bowling

Catches/Stumpings:
23 Brown, 18 Burgess, 14 Finch, 13 Jordan, 12 Nash, 9 Archer, 6 van Zyl, Wright, 5 Briggs, 4 Evans, Wells, 3 Robson, Wiese, 2 Garton, Robinson, 1 Philander, Salt, Whittingham

SUSSEX SHARKS

Batting

	Mat	Inns	NO	Runs	HS	Ave	SR	100	50	4s	6s
LJ Evans	7	6	1	289	134*	57.80	120.41	1	0	18	18
CD Nash	7	7	1	278	82	46.33	91.44	0	2	32	4
HZ Finch	7	7	1	217	80	36.16	77.50	0	2	17	1
LJ Wright	7	7	0	245	84	35.00	81.12	0	2	27	5
S van Zyl	7	6	0	203	96	33.83	90.22	0	2	15	4
BC Brown	4	2	0	62	60	31.00	110.71	0	1	7	1
JC Archer	7	5	1	84	45	21.00	144.82	0	0	7	4
D Wiese	7	6	2	72	35*	18.00	120.00	0	0	3	4
MGK Burgess	3	3	0	39	23	13.00	73.58	0	0	2	1
DR Briggs	7	4	2	25	9*	12.50	119.04	0	0	3	0
JE Taylor	5	2	1	8	7	8.00	114.28	0	0	1	0
WAT Beer	3	2	0	15	10	7.50	107.14	0	0	1	1
GHS Garton	4	1	1	7	7*	-	175.00	0	0	1	0
A Shahzad	2	1	1	3	3*	-	100.00	0	0	0	0

Bowling

	Overs	Mdns	Runs	Wkts	BBI	Ave	Econ	SR	4w	5w
WAT Beer	26.0	0	139	3	2/51	46.33	5.34	52.0	0	0
JC Archer	63.4	5	341	9	3/54	37.88	5.35	42.4	0	0
DR Briggs	60.0	1	323	9	3/53	35.88	5.38	40.0	0	0
S van Zyl	22.0	0	119	0	-	-	5.40	-	0	0
D Wiese	61.1	2	336	11	4/29	30.54	5.49	33.3	1	0
GHS Garton	32.0	1	201	4	2/34	50.25	6.28	48.0	0	0
JE Taylor	43.0	2	278	6	3/65	46.33	6.46	43.0	0	0
A Shahzad	19.0	0	152	2	2/88	76.00	8.00	57.0	0	0
CD Nash	2.0	0	16	0	-	-	8.00	-	0	0

Catches/Stumpings:
5 Briggs, Burgess, 4 Archer, 3 Brown, Wright, 2 Evans, Garton, 1 Shahzad, J Taylor, van Zyl, Wiese

www.sussexcricket.co.uk / tel: 0844 264 0202

SUSSEX SHARKS

Batting

	Mat	Inns	NO	Runs	HS	Ave	SR	100	50	4s	6s
CD Nash	14	13	2	520	73*	47.27	141.68	0	6	55	19
LJ Evans	14	11	3	214	47*	26.75	121.59	0	0	12	8
S van Zyl	9	8	1	170	52	24.28	161.90	0	1	19	6
LJ Wright	10	10	0	235	101	23.50	153.59	1	1	16	15
CJ Jordan	14	7	5	45	24*	22.50	140.62	0	0	4	1
BC Brown	14	10	1	185	49	20.55	119.35	0	0	19	1
LRPL Taylor	13	12	3	177	47*	19.66	112.73	0	0	12	7
D Wiese	14	8	3	78	28	15.60	116.41	0	0	3	5
JC Archer	14	6	3	42	22	14.00	113.51	0	0	5	0
WAT Beer	9	2	1	12	12*	12.00	200.00	0	0	0	1
PD Salt	1	1	1	28	28*	-	133.33	0	0	3	1
DR Briggs	14	2	2	1	1*	-	100.00	0	0	0	0
GHS Garton	10	-	-	-	-	-	-	-	-	-	-
TS Mills	4	-	-	-	-	-	-	-	-	-	-

Bowling

	Overs	Mdns	Runs	Wkts	BBI	Ave	Econ	SR	4w	5w
TS Mills	15.0	0	96	5	3/20	19.20	6.40	18.0	0	0
DR Briggs	44.0	0	308	13	2/12	23.69	7.00	20.3	0	0
CJ Jordan	41.5	0	327	16	3/17	20.43	7.81	15.6	0	0
JC Archer	43.5	0	366	14	4/18	26.14	8.34	18.7	1	0
D Wiese	29.4	0	267	9	2/16	29.66	9.00	19.7	0	0
WAT Beer	20.0	0	181	7	3/36	25.85	9.05	17.1	0	0
GHS Garton	25.0	0	227	7	3/35	32.42	9.08	21.4	0	0
CD Nash	1.0	0	14	0	-	-	14.00	-	0	0

Catches/Stumpings:
13 Brown, 5 Evans, Jordan, Nash, 4 Archer, 3 van Zyl, Wiese, 2 Beer, Garton, Wright, 1 Mills, R Taylor

TEAM PROFILE

FORMED: 1882
HOME GROUND: Edgbaston Stadium, Birmingham
T20 BLAST NAME: Birmingham Bears
CAPTAIN: Jeetan Patel (Championship and RL50), Grant Elliott (T20)
2017 RESULTS: CC1: 8/8; RL50: 9/9 North Group; T20: Runners-up
HONOURS: Championship: (7) 1911, 1951, 1972, 1994, 1995, 2004, 2012; Gillette/NatWest/C&G/FP Trophy: (5) 1966, 1968, 1989, 1993, 1995; Benson & Hedges Cup: (2) 1994, 2002; Pro40/National League/CB40/YB40/RL50: (2) 2010, 2016; Sunday League: (3) 1980, 1994, 1997; T20 Cup: 2014

THE LOWDOWN

Even victory in the T20 final would not have saved Warwickshire's season. They finished bottom of Division One in the County Championship and their One-Day Cup group, which in total produced just three wins. There were nine defeats in the Championship, five by an innings. Of the frontline batsmen, only Jonathan Trott held his own. Ian Bell resigned the captaincy shortly after he was dropped from the T20 side. Young Sam Hain was excellent in the short formats but suffered against the red ball. With the exception of Jeetan Patel – now the four-day and 50-over captain – and Keith Barker, none of Warwickshire's usual suspects showed up. They were grateful to uncover another wicket-taking Ryan Sidebottom – this one a 28-year-old Australian with a UK passport. But the emphasis now is on youth, reflected in the signings of vice-captain Dom Sibley (22) and Adam Hose (25) last summer, and Will Rhodes (23) over the winter. Ed Pollock (22) and Aaron Thomason (20) both shone in T20 cricket. Colin de Grandhomme returns for another Blast campaign under the captaincy of seasoned Kiwi compatriot Grant Elliott.

IN: Will Rhodes (Yor), Colin de Grandhomme (NZ, T20)
OUT: Ateeq Javid (Lei), Mark Adair, William Porterfield (both REL)

SPORT DIRECTOR: ASHLEY GILES

A veteran of 54 Tests and 62 ODIs, Giles replaced Dougie Brown in 2016 to begin a second spell in charge of the club where he spent his entire playing career. As director of cricket, Giles helped Warwickshire win the CB40 in 2010 and the Championship title in 2012 before a brief spell as England's limited-overs coach. Graeme Welch returns to Edgbaston to replace Alan Richardson as bowling coach, and former captain Ian Westwood has become development coach just five months after retiring.

	Mat	Inns	NO	Runs	HS	Ave	SR	100	50	4s	6s
OP Stone	1	2	1	39	32	39.00	43.82	0	0	7	0
IJL Trott	14	26	0	967	175	37.19	50.84	3	5	119	4
IJ Westwood	4	7	0	253	153	36.14	54.17	1	1	34	2
KHD Barker	12	22	4	536	70*	29.77	50.70	0	6	80	0
DP Sibley	6	12	1	310	92*	28.18	43.47	0	3	39	1
JS Patel	13	24	2	608	100	27.63	72.64	1	2	82	6
IR Bell	13	24	1	596	99	25.91	57.86	0	5	90	2
CR Woakes	2	4	0	100	53	25.00	50.76	0	1	21	0
MJ Lamb	7	14	0	329	71	23.50	37.60	0	2	49	0
ARI Umeed	8	14	0	325	113	23.21	31.98	1	0	31	0
TR Ambrose	13	24	1	513	104	22.30	45.19	1	2	65	1
R Clarke	8	14	0	265	83	18.92	43.94	0	2	33	4
CJC Wright	8	16	3	241	41	18.53	52.27	0	0	38	1
AT Thomson	2	4	0	70	26	17.50	40.22	0	0	12	0
SR Hain	8	14	0	216	58	15.42	46.65	0	1	27	0
WTS Porterfield	5	9	0	137	45	15.22	37.32	0	0	18	0
L Banks	2	4	0	57	29	14.25	37.25	0	0	10	0
WB Rankin	5	9	4	61	21*	12.20	29.46	0	0	10	0
A Javid	1	2	0	22	14	11.00	25.00	0	0	1	0
AJ Mellor	3	6	0	59	18	9.83	31.72	0	0	9	0
GT Thornton	2	3	1	19	10	9.50	27.94	0	0	2	0
OJ Hannon-Dalby	4	7	2	44	12	8.80	28.75	0	0	8	0
HJH Brookes	1	2	0	15	11	7.50	34.09	0	0	2	0
GD Panayi	2	3	0	17	16	5.66	29.31	0	0	3	0
RN Sidebottom	6	12	5	26	13	3.71	23.85	0	0	5	0
Sukhjit Singh	4	7	2	18	16*	3.60	18.55	0	0	2	0

Batting

	Overs	Mdns	Runs	Wkts	BBI	BBM	Ave	Econ	SR	5w	10w
MJ Lamb	20.0	4	66	3	1/19	1/19	22.00	3.30	40.0	0	0
RN Sidebottom	129.5	28	510	23	4/29	6/70	22.17	3.92	33.8	0	0
CR Woakes	44.0	7	159	7	3/38	5/95	22.71	3.61	37.7	0	0
OJ Hannon-Dalby	89.1	22	269	11	4/29	6/62	24.45	3.01	48.6	0	0
JS Patel	482.0	149	1222	41	6/50	8/111	29.80	2.53	70.5	1	0
Sukhjit Singh	122.4	13	400	13	6/144	6/144	30.76	3.26	56.6	2	0
GT Thornton	36.2	4	138	4	4/34	4/42	34.50	3.79	54.5	0	0
WB Rankin	114.2	13	423	12	3/48	4/89	35.25	3.69	57.1	0	0
GD Panayi	38.3	7	141	4	3/41	3/75	35.25	3.66	57.7	0	0
ARI Umeed	14.0	0	73	2	1/19	1/19	36.50	5.21	42.0	0	0
KHD Barker	301.0	59	950	26	3/21	5/128	36.53	3.15	69.4	0	0
R Clarke	199.0	41	615	15	3/29	5/119	41.00	3.09	79.6	0	0
CJC Wright	199.3	37	694	16	5/113	5/113	43.37	3.47	74.8	1	0
OP Stone	17.0	3	70	1	1/70	1/70	70.00	4.11	102.0	0	0
IJL Trott	36.0	4	111	1	1/48	1/48	111.00	3.08	216.0	0	0
AT Thomson	3.0	2	1	0	-	-	-	0.33	-	0	0
A Javid	4.0	0	15	0	-	-	-	3.75	-	0	0
DP Sibley	2.0	0	17	0	-	-	-	8.50	-	0	0
HJH Brookes	11.0	1	43	0	-	-	-	3.90	-	0	0

Bowling

Catches/Stumpings:
28 Ambrose (inc 3st), 10 Trott, 9 Bell, Patel, Umeed, 6 Clarke, 4 Hain, Sibley, 3 Lamb, Mellor, Porterfield, 2 Barker, Wright, 1 Banks, Rankin, Singh, Thomson, Westwood

Batting

	Mat	Inns	NO	Runs	HS	Ave	SR	100	50	4s	6s
SR Hain	8	8	1	456	109	65.14	94.60	2	2	53	0
IR Bell	8	7	0	410	104	58.57	94.90	1	3	40	6
R Clarke	8	7	2	257	84*	51.40	135.97	0	2	23	12
IJL Trott	8	7	0	308	104	44.00	93.90	1	2	37	3
TR Ambrose	8	7	0	297	83	42.42	97.69	0	2	29	2
WTS Porterfield	3	3	1	67	63*	33.50	83.75	0	1	6	0
AD Thomason	8	7	2	105	28	21.00	92.92	0	0	7	2
A Javid	4	3	1	38	28	19.00	80.85	0	0	2	1
KHD Barker	6	4	1	56	34	18.66	101.81	0	0	6	0
OJ Hannon-Dalby	5	4	2	27	17*	13.50	103.84	0	0	2	1
MJ Lamb	2	2	0	14	12	7.00	56.00	0	0	2	0
GT Thornton	4	1	0	7	7	7.00	116.66	0	0	1	0
JS Patel	8	4	0	21	15	5.25	123.52	0	0	2	0
JE Poysden	3	2	0	0	0	0.00	0.00	0	0	0	0
CJC Wright	2	1	1	10	10*	-	58.82	0	0	0	0
MR Adair	3	1	1	0	0*	-	0.00	0	0	0	0

Bowling

	Overs	Mdns	Runs	Wkts	BBI	Ave	Econ	SR	4w	5w
JS Patel	68.5	1	353	10	3/48	35.30	5.12	41.3	0	0
R Clarke	72.0	4	413	8	2/18	51.62	5.73	54.0	0	0
A Javid	27.0	0	164	2	2/57	82.00	6.07	81.0	0	0
KHD Barker	53.4	1	353	10	3/63	35.30	6.57	32.2	0	0
JE Poysden	21.0	0	139	3	2/57	46.33	6.61	42.0	0	0
MR Adair	16.0	0	107	0	-	-	6.68	-	0	0
CJC Wright	11.0	0	75	1	1/35	75.00	6.81	66.0	0	0
GT Thornton	26.0	0	185	8	4/42	23.12	7.11	19.5	1	0
OJ Hannon-Dalby	37.4	0	316	7	3/24	45.14	8.38	32.2	0	0
MJ Lamb	1.0	0	9	0	-	-	9.00	-	0	0
AD Thomason	16.0	0	147	4	4/64	36.75	9.18	24.0	1	0

Catches/Stumpings:
8 Ambrose, 7 Hain, 5 Hannon-Dalby, 4 Patel, Thomason, 2 Clarke, Porterfield, 1 Adair, Barker, Bell, Lamb, Thornton, Trott, Wright

Batting

	Mat	Inns	NO	Runs	HS	Ave	SR	100	50	4s	6s
GD Elliott	16	14	4	332	59*	33.20	134.41	0	1	30	7
SR Hain	16	15	1	458	82*	32.71	134.70	0	3	48	11
DP Sibley	7	7	1	191	53	31.83	121.65	0	2	16	5
EJ Pollock	9	9	0	283	66	31.44	174.69	0	3	26	18
C de Grandhomme	16	15	3	322	65*	26.83	170.37	0	1	27	17
IR Bell	12	11	1	251	75*	25.10	117.28	0	2	29	3
AJ Hose	8	8	0	200	76	25.00	158.73	0	1	17	12
AD Thomason	15	12	4	200	42	25.00	149.25	0	0	9	11
KHD Barker	6	4	1	67	35	22.33	152.27	0	0	4	4
WTS Porterfield	7	7	0	149	35	21.28	130.70	0	0	8	6
WB Rankin	9	3	2	14	12	14.00	107.69	0	0	1	1
AJ Mellor	8	5	2	28	18*	9.33	93.33	0	0	1	1
JS Patel	16	7	3	36	10	9.00	128.57	0	0	2	1
TR Ambrose	8	3	1	16	15	8.00	64.00	0	0	1	0
CR Woakes	2	2	1	6	4*	6.00	100.00	0	0	0	0
R Clarke	3	2	2	34	24*	-	103.03	0	0	2	0
OJ Hannon-Dalby	8	1	1	9	9*	-	180.00	0	0	0	1
OP Stone	7	2	2	8	8*	-	400.00	0	0	0	1
A Javid	1	-	-	-	-	-	-	-	-	-	-
JE Poysden	2	-	-	-	-	-	-	-	-	-	-

Bowling

	Overs	Mdns	Runs	Wkts	BBI	Ave	Econ	SR	4w	5w
R Clarke	8.0	0	53	3	3/20	17.66	6.62	16.0	0	0
JS Patel	64.0	0	437	20	4/22	21.85	6.82	19.2	1	0
JE Poysden	8.0	0	56	3	2/28	18.66	7.00	16.0	0	0
DP Sibley	16.0	0	125	1	1/20	125.00	7.81	96.0	0	0
GD Elliott	42.0	0	344	12	4/37	28.66	8.19	21.0	1	0
WB Rankin	31.0	0	265	10	3/26	26.50	8.54	18.6	0	0
OJ Hannon-Dalby	28.0	0	241	14	3/33	17.21	8.60	12.0	0	0
KHD Barker	22.0	0	193	7	3/33	27.57	8.77	18.8	0	0
CR Woakes	7.4	0	69	6	3/29	11.50	9.00	7.6	0	0
A Javid	2.0	0	18	0	-	-	9.00	-	0	0
OP Stone	28.0	0	262	9	3/29	29.11	9.35	18.6	0	0
AD Thomason	26.0	0	252	10	3/33	25.20	9.69	15.6	0	0
C de Grandhomme	35.1	0	348	5	2/29	69.60	9.89	42.2	0	0

Catches/Stumpings:

13 Hain, 9 de Grandhomme, 8 Elliott, 7 Bell, Patel, 6 Ambrose, 5 Thomason, 4 Mellor, Porterfield, Sibley, 3 Pollock, 1 Hannon-Dalby, Hose, Poysden, Stone

TEAM PROFILE

FORMED: 1865

HOME GROUND: County Ground, Worcester

ONE-DAY NAME: Worcestershire Rapids

CAPTAIN: Joe Leach

2017 RESULTS: CC2: Winners; RL50: Semi-finalists; T20: 8/9 North Group

HONOURS: Championship: (5) 1964, 1965, 1974, 1988, 1989; Gillette/NatWest/C&G/FP Trophy: 1994; Benson & Hedges Cup: 1991; Pro40/National League/CB40/YB40/RL50: 2007; Sunday League: (3) 1971, 1987, 1988

THE LOWDOWN

Last October everything was rosy for Worcestershire. The county had stormed to promotion with a team of homegrown cricketers sprinkled with a puff of overseas magic. Daryl Mitchell responded to losing the captaincy with seven Championship hundreds, his successor Joe Leach produced another outstanding season with the ball and allrounder Brett D'Oliveira enjoyed his best season yet. Youth blossomed: Joe Clarke (21) impressed again; fast bowler Josh Tongue (20) took 47 wickets at 25.78 in his first full season; Ed Barnard (22) emerged as a genuine allrounder. Yet by Christmas one of their young players had been charged with rape and their coach had been sacked. An internal investigation judged Steve Rhodes to have failed to report Alex Hepburn's initial arrest, thus ending his three-decade association with the club. But Worcestershire's on-field resources remain strong. Veteran Aussie seamer Steve Magoffin fills the hole created by John Hastings' retirement from first-class and 50-over cricket, while his compatriot Travis Head will bolster the batting in all formats. Beware the yo-yo effect; Worcestershire have been promoted and relegated in successive seasons on four occasions since the two-division split.

IN: Steve Magoffin (Sus), Travis Head (Aus)
OUT: (none)

HEAD COACH: KEVIN SHARP

Worcestershire's Second XI batting coach since 2014, Sharp was chosen ahead of some high-profile candidates to replace Steve Rhodes in December, an appointment which the club said "reflects the desire for continuity". A Leeds-born former Yorkshire batsman (1976-90), Sharp worked with some of Headingley's batting prodigies in the 2000s and assisted briefly with England's Test team last summer. Former Pears paceman Alan Richardson has returned to New Road as bowling coach, while ex-spinner Matt Rawnsley replaces outgoing CEO Tom Scott.

Batting

	Mat	Inns	NO	Runs	HS	Ave	SR	100	50	4s	6s
DKH Mitchell	14	26	3	1266	161	55.04	61.90	7	3	159	6
T Kohler-Cadmore	4	5	0	242	102	48.40	60.80	1	1	31	2
JM Clarke	14	26	5	920	142	43.80	71.15	2	3	129	2
R Ashwin	4	6	1	214	82	42.80	74.04	0	1	22	2
MM Ali	3	5	0	208	63	41.60	83.53	0	3	24	2
EG Barnard	14	20	4	580	75	36.25	65.46	0	5	70	6
BL D'Oliveira	14	25	0	891	150	35.64	57.07	3	3	113	6
OB Cox	14	21	1	675	124	33.75	66.96	1	3	96	6
GH Rhodes	8	15	2	379	52	29.15	41.24	0	2	48	0
JD Shantry	6	8	4	94	30*	23.50	82.45	0	0	13	1
RA Whiteley	5	9	1	170	53	21.25	45.57	0	1	20	4
J Leach	14	19	2	347	57*	20.41	88.07	0	2	46	6
JW Hastings	6	8	1	139	51	19.85	70.20	0	1	17	2
TC Fell	13	23	1	323	47	14.68	47.08	0	0	47	0
JC Tongue	14	18	3	138	41	9.20	41.56	0	0	17	0
NM Lyon	4	5	3	15	6*	7.50	65.21	0	0	3	0
PR Brown	4	5	3	12	5*	6.00	22.64	0	0	1	0

Bowling

	Overs	Mdns	Runs	Wkts	BBI	BBM	Ave	Econ	SR	5w	10w
J Leach	397.5	73	1338	69	5/32	10/122	19.39	3.36	34.5	4	1
EG Barnard	321.3	48	1187	47	4/23	7/149	25.25	3.69	41.0	0	0
JC Tongue	333.4	46	1212	47	6/97	6/97	25.78	3.63	42.5	2	0
JD Shantry	100.3	19	310	11	3/54	5/104	28.18	3.08	54.8	0	0
R Ashwin	184.2	29	583	20	5/68	8/162	29.15	3.16	55.3	2	0
PR Brown	42.4	4	199	6	2/15	3/70	33.16	4.66	42.6	0	0
JW Hastings	161.1	41	550	16	3/44	5/124	34.37	3.41	60.4	0	0
DKH Mitchell	7.4	0	37	1	1/16	1/29	37.00	4.82	46.0	0	0
MM Ali	41.0	4	166	3	2/104	3/152	55.33	4.04	82.0	0	0
NM Lyon	131.4	21	403	6	3/94	3/119	67.16	3.06	131.6	0	0
GH Rhodes	38.0	7	202	3	1/12	1/12	67.33	5.31	76.0	0	0
RA Whiteley	2.0	0	20	0	-	-	-	10.00	-	0	0
BL D'Oliveira	60.0	0	271	0	-	-	-	4.51	-	0	0

Catches/Stumpings:
43 Cox (inc 1st), 21 Mitchell, 10 D'Oliveira, 9 Clarke, 8 Barnard, 7 Fell, Leach, 6 Whiteley, 5 Hastings, Rhodes, 4 Kohler-Cadmore, 3 Shantry, 2 Ali, Ashwin, Lyon, Tongue, 1 Brown

Batting

	Mat	Inns	NO	Runs	HS	Ave	SR	100	50	4s	6s
EG Barnard	9	7	4	112	42*	37.33	134.93	0	0	11	3
T Kohler-Cadmore	8	8	0	290	118	36.25	100.34	1	1	30	11
DKH Mitchell	7	7	0	250	75	35.71	93.63	0	3	23	1
RA Whiteley	9	9	3	210	55	35.00	122.80	0	1	17	11
MM Ali	6	6	0	186	90	31.00	102.19	0	1	28	4
OB Cox	9	9	0	277	82	30.77	96.85	0	1	28	4
JM Clarke	8	8	0	245	56	30.62	90.07	0	1	29	2
BL D'Oliveira	9	9	1	222	73*	27.75	94.06	0	2	18	4
JW Hastings	8	7	2	133	36	26.60	138.54	0	0	6	10
J Leach	9	8	2	102	41	17.00	102.00	0	0	12	0
TC Fell	6	5	0	83	39	16.60	83.00	0	0	8	1
JC Tongue	4	3	2	12	11*	12.00	66.66	0	0	1	0
JD Shantry	6	1	1	12	12*	-	133.33	0	0	2	0
NM Lyon	1	-	-	-	-	-	-	-	-	-	-

Bowling

	Overs	Mdns	Runs	Wkts	BBI	Ave	Econ	SR	4w	5w
BL D'Oliveira	63.0	0	305	7	2/34	43.57	4.84	54.0	0	0
JD Shantry	49.0	2	271	6	3/64	45.16	5.53	49.0	0	0
DKH Mitchell	36.0	0	201	8	3/38	25.12	5.58	27.0	0	0
MM Ali	56.0	0	313	5	2/49	62.60	5.58	67.2	0	0
NM Lyon	5.0	0	31	1	1/31	31.00	6.20	30.0	0	0
EG Barnard	49.0	0	314	7	3/37	44.85	6.40	42.0	0	0
JW Hastings	73.2	3	473	11	3/50	43.00	6.45	40.0	0	0
J Leach	74.0	2	497	12	4/66	41.41	6.71	37.0	1	0
JC Tongue	23.3	0	162	4	2/46	40.50	6.89	35.2	0	0

Catches/Stumpings:
11 Cox (inc 2st), 6 Barnard, Kohler-Cadmore, 5 Whiteley, 4 D'Oliveira, 3 Mitchell, Shantry, 2 Hastings, 1 Ali, Clarke, Fell, Leach, Lyon

	Mat	Inns	NO	Runs	HS	Ave	SR	100	50	4s	6s
JM Clarke	13	13	1	381	124*	31.75	183.17	1	2	45	19
DKH Mitchell	12	11	3	208	36*	26.00	114.91	0	0	18	2
JW Hastings	9	9	2	179	51	25.57	179.00	0	1	17	12
OB Cox	13	13	1	297	51	24.75	116.47	0	1	29	4
RA Whiteley	13	13	1	276	65	23.00	137.31	0	1	17	18
EG Barnard	12	10	4	122	34*	20.33	152.50	0	0	16	3
BL D'Oliveira	13	12	2	201	52	20.10	108.06	0	1	13	3
MJ Santner	13	12	0	239	38	19.91	120.10	0	0	14	13
GH Rhodes	6	4	2	27	17*	13.50	103.84	0	0	2	0
A Hepburn	5	3	1	25	10	12.50	89.28	0	0	3	0
J Leach	13	9	1	47	24	5.87	94.00	0	0	5	1
PR Brown	6	2	0	0	0	0.00	0.00	0	0	0	0
JD Shantry	6	2	2	11	9*	-	157.14	0	0	0	1
JC Tongue	5	2	2	3	2*	-	150.00	0	0	0	0
GLS Scrimshaw	4	1	1	1	1*	-	50.00	0	0	0	0

Batting

	Overs	Mdns	Runs	Wkts	BBI	Ave	Econ	SR	4w	5w
MJ Santner	51.0	0	339	13	3/16	26.07	6.64	23.5	0	0
BL D'Oliveira	34.0	0	232	11	2/19	21.09	6.82	18.5	0	0
DKH Mitchell	30.0	0	228	5	1/10	45.60	7.60	36.0	0	0
A Hepburn	12.3	0	108	6	5/24	18.00	8.64	12.5	0	1
JC Tongue	14.0	0	122	3	2/32	40.66	8.71	28.0	0	0
GLS Scrimshaw	10.0	0	90	3	1/20	30.00	9.00	20.0	0	0
JW Hastings	31.5	0	333	8	3/31	41.62	10.46	23.8	0	0
JD Shantry	16.3	0	173	2	1/29	86.50	10.48	49.5	0	0
PR Brown	12.0	0	127	1	1/22	127.00	10.58	72.0	0	0
GH Rhodes	3.0	0	34	0	-	-	11.33	-	0	0
J Leach	28.3	0	324	6	2/33	54.00	11.36	28.5	0	0
EG Barnard	7.1	0	99	1	1/38	99.00	13.81	43.0	0	0

Bowling

Catches/Stumpings:
11 Cox (inc 7st), 9 Santner, 4 Clarke, Leach, 3 Barnard, Brown, D'Oliveira, Mitchell, Whiteley, 2 Hepburn, Rhodes, Tongue

THE YORKSHIRE
COUNTY CRICKET CLUB

FORMED: 1863
HOME GROUND: Headingley Carnegie, Leeds
ONE-DAY NAME: Yorkshire Vikings
CAPTAIN: Gary Ballance
2017 RESULTS: CC1: 4/8; RL50: Quarter-finalists; T20: 5/9 North Group
HONOURS: County Championship: (33) 1893, 1896, 1898, 1900, 1901, 1902, 1905, 1908, 1912, 1919, 1922, 1923, 1924, 1925, 1931, 1932, 1933, 1935, 1937, 1938, 1939, 1946, 1949, 1959, 1960, 1962, 1963, 1966, 1967, 1968, 2001, 2014, 2015; Gillette/ NatWest/C&G/FP Trophy: (3) 1965, 1969, 2002; Benson & Hedges Cup: 1987; Sunday League: 1983

THE LOWDOWN

The pressure is on Yorkshire after two barren years since back-to-back Championships. Finishing 100 points behind champions Essex – whom they lost to by 376 runs at Chelmsford – will have hurt, and the threat of relegation hung over Headingley until the final match. The batting decline was sharp: after Gary Ballance (951 runs at 67.92), no one managed more than Adam Lyth's 555 runs. Having Cheteshwar Pujara and Kane Williamson share the overseas spot will help this summer. The four-day bowling unit seems to be creaking: Steve Patterson and Tim Bresnan are into their mid-30s, Jack Brooks is looking for his mojo, Adil Rashid has put his red-ball career on ice and Ryan Sidebottom has retired after taking 281 first-class wickets at 21.46 since re-joining Yorkshire in 2011. The onus is on the county's crop of young talent to follow in the footsteps of 24-year-old Ben Coad, who claimed 50 Championship scalps in his first full season. And what about a first limited-overs trophy since 2002? The signing of Australia's towering 23-year-old quick Billy Stanlake for the T20 Blast – bolstering an attack which should also feature Bresnan, David Willey and spin twins Rashid and Azeem Rafiq – will further raise expectations among the ever-demanding White Rose faithful.

IN: Cheteshwar Pujara (Ind), Kane Williamson (NZ), Billy Stanlake (Aus, T20)
OUT: Will Rhodes (War), Ryan Sidebottom (RET)

HEAD COACH: ANDREW GALE

Jason Gillespie was always going to be a hard act to follow and Gale experienced a challenging first season after making the immediate transition from captain to coach in 2017. He knows better than anyone that he will need to deliver this summer, having spent a 14-year career at Yorkshire – eight of them as skipper – with more than 8,000 first-class runs and 20 centuries. "Andrew's appointment was a long-term measure," said director of cricket Martyn Moxon. "The change that needs to happen is the mindset of our players."

COUNTY CHAMPIONSHIP AVERAGES 2017

Batting

	Mat	Inns	NO	Runs	HS	Ave	SR	100	50	4s	6s
SE Marsh	2	3	1	225	125*	112.50	49.23	1	1	35	0
GS Ballance	12	18	4	951	203*	67.92	51.82	3	4	127	3
PSP Handscomb	9	14	1	441	101*	33.92	59.51	1	2	62	1
LE Plunkett	2	3	0	92	39	30.66	92.00	0	0	13	3
JA Leaning	10	15	0	454	118	30.26	42.11	1	2	55	5
A Lyth	13	23	1	555	100	25.22	47.59	1	2	68	6
T Kohler-Cadmore	3	6	0	151	78	25.16	47.18	0	1	21	2
AZ Lees	14	25	3	531	102	24.13	46.29	1	2	75	3
AJ Hodd	12	19	1	428	59	23.77	60.28	0	4	61	2
AU Rashid	7	10	1	211	65	23.44	50.72	0	1	31	0
MD Fisher	2	4	0	86	37	21.50	34.81	0	0	12	0
JA Brooks	8	11	2	178	109*	19.77	54.76	1	0	17	5
RJ Sidebottom	8	11	8	57	12*	19.00	26.02	0	0	9	0
TT Bresnan	11	15	0	284	61	18.93	41.58	0	1	42	1
SA Patterson	9	13	4	165	44*	18.33	38.91	0	0	24	0
HC Brook	4	6	0	82	38	13.66	41.41	0	0	11	0
DJ Willey	2	2	0	27	19	13.50	46.55	0	0	2	0
K Carver	2	4	0	48	20	12.00	28.07	0	0	7	0
BO Coad	12	16	5	128	28	11.63	54.93	0	0	17	2
JE Root	2	3	1	22	12*	11.00	37.93	0	0	2	0
MJ Waite	1	2	0	22	18	11.00	41.50	0	0	4	0
KC Brathwaite	2	4	0	40	18	10.00	25.31	0	0	4	0
Azeem Rafiq	5	7	0	54	17	7.71	45.37	0	0	8	0
JM Bairstow	2	2	0	8	7	4.00	27.58	0	0	1	0
J Shaw	1	2	0	3	3	1.50	21.42	0	0	0	0

Bowling

	Overs	Mdns	Runs	Wkts	BBI	BBM	Ave	Econ	SR	5w	10w
RJ Sidebottom	186.4	43	518	25	5/56	8/115	20.72	2.77	44.8	1	0
BO Coad	356.4	93	1043	50	6/25	10/102	20.86	2.92	42.8	4	1
LE Plunkett	43.0	11	136	6	4/73	4/83	22.66	3.16	43.0	0	0
MJ Waite	16.0	0	70	3	2/41	3/70	23.33	4.37	32.0	0	0
MD Fisher	60.3	11	195	8	5/54	5/89	24.37	3.22	45.3	1	0
K Carver	35.2	4	118	4	2/10	2/59	29.50	3.33	53.0	0	0
SA Patterson	280.2	72	754	23	4/46	5/73	32.78	2.68	73.1	0	0
TT Bresnan	240.0	49	887	27	4/53	7/126	32.85	3.69	53.3	0	0
DJ Willey	60.0	15	148	4	2/20	2/62	37.00	2.46	90.0	0	0
JA Brooks	205.0	24	865	23	5/113	5/113	37.60	4.21	53.4	1	0
AU Rashid	108.0	10	500	10	3/94	3/31	50.00	4.62	64.8	0	0
JE Root	13.4	0	53	1	1/22	1/22	53.00	3.87	82.0	0	0
A Lyth	39.3	2	127	2	2/45	2/45	63.50	3.21	118.5	0	0
HC Brook	19.0	4	65	1	1/54	1/65	65.00	3.42	114.0	0	0
Azeem Rafiq	107.0	13	393	5	3/128	3/128	78.60	3.67	128.4	0	0
JA Leaning	6.0	0	26	0	-	-	-	4.33	-	0	0
J Shaw	16.0	3	59	0	-	-	-	3.68	-	0	0

Catches/Stumpings:
39 Hodd, 19 Lyth, 8 Bresnan, 7 Bairstow, Handscomb, Lees, 5 Leaning, Patterson, 3 Ballance, 2 Brooks, Carver, Sidebottom, 1 Brathwaite, Brook, Coad, Kohler-Cadmore, Marsh

Batting

	Mat	Inns	NO	Runs	HS	Ave	SR	100	50	4s	6s
GS Ballance	9	9	2	483	152*	69.00	105.00	1	3	45	7
PSP Handscomb	9	9	1	504	140	63.00	109.56	1	3	43	10
JE Root	5	5	1	241	83	60.25	84.56	0	3	20	1
MD Fisher	7	5	4	54	36*	54.00	114.89	0	0	3	2
JM Bairstow	5	5	0	268	174	53.60	115.51	1	0	24	10
MJ Waite	7	6	1	185	71	37.00	97.88	0	1	17	2
A Lyth	9	9	0	304	75	33.77	95.89	0	3	40	4
Azeem Rafiq	9	5	2	78	52*	26.00	127.86	0	1	4	3
AU Rashid	5	3	1	49	41	24.50	108.88	0	0	5	0
JA Leaning	4	4	0	96	42	24.00	69.06	0	0	5	1
TT Bresnan	8	7	1	138	65	23.00	80.70	0	1	9	4
AZ Lees	4	4	0	77	26	19.25	81.05	0	0	7	3
WMH Rhodes	1	1	0	10	10	10.00	125.00	0	0	2	0
LE Plunkett	4	2	1	9	6	9.00	81.81	0	0	1	0
SA Patterson	2	1	0	5	5	5.00	100.00	0	0	1	0
DJ Willey	4	2	0	2	1	1.00	25.00	0	0	0	0
K Carver	3	1	1	2	2*	-	100.00	0	0	0	0
BO Coad	4	1	1	0	0*	-	0.00	0	0	0	0

Bowling

	Overs	Mdns	Runs	Wkts	BBI	Ave	Econ	SR	4w	5w
K Carver	24.0	1	113	5	3/24	22.60	4.70	28.8	0	0
AU Rashid	44.0	1	214	6	2/34	35.66	4.86	44.0	0	0
LE Plunkett	30.3	2	150	2	1/22	75.00	4.91	91.5	0	0
A Lyth	8.0	0	43	0	-	-	5.37	-	0	0
TT Bresnan	63.0	3	356	9	3/22	39.55	5.65	42.0	0	0
Azeem Rafiq	70.3	0	408	18	4/47	22.66	5.78	23.5	1	0
DJ Willey	24.5	1	155	6	2/22	25.83	6.24	24.8	0	0
JE Root	3.0	0	19	0	-	-	6.33	-	0	0
BO Coad	30.0	1	195	8	4/63	24.37	6.50	22.5	1	0
MJ Waite	42.3	1	284	10	4/65	28.40	6.68	25.5	1	0
MD Fisher	47.0	0	317	6	2/73	52.83	6.74	47.0	0	0
SA Patterson	14.0	0	100	3	3/67	33.33	7.14	28.0	0	0

Catches/Stumpings:
10 Handscomb (inc 1st), Lyth, 6 Bairstow (inc 1st), 5 Leaning, Rafiq, 4 Bresnan, 3 Fisher, Plunkett, 2 Ballance, Rhodes, 1 Carver, Coad, Lees, Rashid, Root

NATWEST T20 BLAST AVERAGES 2017

	Mat	Inns	NO	Runs	HS	Ave	SR	100	50	4s	6s
A Lyth	12	12	0	535	161	44.58	164.61	1	4	56	22
AU Rashid	12	5	4	44	26*	44.00	146.66	0	0	4	1
SE Marsh	11	11	4	289	60*	41.28	127.31	0	2	27	4
DJ Willey	12	12	1	446	118	40.54	168.30	1	1	34	26
JA Leaning	11	9	3	161	32*	26.83	150.46	0	0	10	9
T Kohler-Cadmore	11	11	0	286	75	26.00	156.28	0	1	28	19
TT Bresnan	12	10	5	105	24	21.00	140.00	0	0	9	4
AZ Lees	2	2	0	40	29	20.00	121.21	0	0	4	2
PSP Handscomb	7	6	0	97	31	16.16	146.96	0	0	6	6
Sarfraz Ahmed	5	4	0	53	42	13.25	108.16	0	0	3	3
Azeem Rafiq	12	2	1	4	3*	4.00	66.66	0	0	0	0
LE Plunkett	4	2	2	10	7*	-	100.00	0	0	1	0
MD Fisher	3	1	1	6	6*	-	100.00	0	0	1	0
MJ Waite	2	1	1	1	1*	-	100.00	0	0	0	0
GS Ballance	1	-	-	-	-	-	-	-	-	-	-
K Carver	1	-	-	-	-	-	-	-	-	-	-
BO Coad	2	-	-	-	-	-	-	-	-	-	-
SA Patterson	12	-	-	-	-	-	-	-	-	-	-

Batting

	Overs	Mdns	Runs	Wkts	BBI	Ave	Econ	SR	4w	5w
AU Rashid	48.0	0	341	15	4/19	22.73	7.10	19.2	1	0
SA Patterson	41.5	0	339	14	3/37	24.21	8.10	17.9	0	0
Azeem Rafiq	44.0	0	368	17	5/19	21.64	8.36	15.5	0	1
TT Bresnan	39.3	2	338	17	6/19	19.88	8.55	13.9	0	1
DJ Willey	37.0	0	349	11	2/23	31.72	9.43	20.1	0	0
MD Fisher	5.0	0	48	0	-	-	9.60	-	0	0
BO Coad	3.0	0	32	0	-	-	10.66	-	0	0
LE Plunkett	10.0	0	114	4	3/42	28.50	11.40	15.0	0	0
MJ Waite	1.0	0	16	1	1/16	16.00	16.00	6.0	0	0
K Carver	2.0	0	47	0	-	-	23.50	-	0	0

Bowling

Catches/Stumpings:
8 Kohler-Cadmore, Leaning, 7 Lyth, 6 Handscomb (inc 3st), Rashid, Willey, 4 Ahmed (inc 1st),
3 Bresnan, Plunkett, Rafiq, 2 Carver, Coad, 1 Ballance, Fisher, Marsh, Waite

The
Players

MOHAMMAD ABBAS RHB / RMF / R0 / W0

FULL NAME: Mohammad Abbas
BORN: March 10, 1990, Sialkot, Punjab
SQUAD NO: 26
TEAMS: Pakistan, Leicestershire, Khan Research Laboratories, Multan Sultans, Pakistan Television, Sialkot
ROLE: Bowler
DEBUT: Test: 2017; First-class: 2009; List A: 2009; T20: 2013

BEST BATTING: 40 Khan Research Laboratories vs Karachi Whites, Karachi, 2016
BEST BOWLING: 8-46 Khan Research Laboratories vs Karachi Whites, Karachi, 2016

NOTES: Leicestershire have signed the right-arm seam bowler as their overseas player for the first Championship match of the season and then from June onwards, with compatriot Sohail Khan filling the gap. Abbas' career has progressed rapidly in the past few years. He made his first-class debut in 2009 but until the start of 2014 had taken just 74 wickets at an average of 35.45, working in a leather factory, as a welder, and as a helper in a law firm to support his cricket career. Since 2014 he has claimed 230 wickets at 16.43 apiece. In the 2016 Quaid-e-Azam Trophy, which immediately preceded his Test debut, he took 71 wickets in 10 games at an average of 12.74, and he struck with his second Test delivery, West Indian Kraigg Brathwaite edging behind. His maiden Test five-for followed in the same series to set up a third-Test victory which secured a 2-1 series win. His figures of 4-57 in the final of the most recent Quaid-e-Azam trophy helped Sui Northern Gas Pipelines Ltd secure the title. Leicestershire head coach Paul Nixon said: "We have been looking for a quality fast bowler as our overseas professional and Mohammad Abbas ticks all of the boxes"

Batting	Mat	Inns	NO	Runs	HS	Ave	SR	100	50	Ct	St
Tests	5	8	5	11	4	3.66	8.94	0	0	1	0
First-class	69	102	38	463	40	7.23	30.20	0	0	20	0
List A	47	28	12	124	15*	7.75	51.23	0	0	11	0
T20s	12	3	1	7	7*	3.50	116.66	0	0	3	0

Bowling	Mat	Balls	Runs	Wkts	BBI	BBM	Ave	Econ	SR	5w	10
Tests	5	1211	491	23	5/46	6/77	21.34	2.43	52.6	1	0
First-class	69	13709	6401	304	8/46	14/93	21.05	2.80	45.0	24	7
List A	47	2238	1756	63	4/31	4/31	27.87	4.70	35.5	0	0
T20s	12	234	338	8	2/18	2/18	42.25	8.66	29.2	0	0

KYLE ABBOTT

RHB / RFM / R0 / W1 / MVP3

FULL NAME: Kyle John Abbott
BORN: June 18, 1987, Empangeni, KwaZulu-Natal, South Africa
SQUAD NO: 87
NICKNAME: Jimmy
EDUCATION: Kearsney College, KwaZulu-Natal
TEAMS: South Africa, Hampshire, Dolphins, Kings XI Punjab, KwaZulu-Natal, Middlesex, Warriors, Worcestershire
ROLE: Bowler
DEBUT: Test: 2013; ODI: 2013; T20I: 2013; First-class: 2009; List A: 2009; T20: 2011

BEST BATTING: 97* Hampshire vs Lancashire, Old Trafford, 2017
BEST BOWLING: 8-45 Dolphins vs Cape Cobras, Cape Town, 2013

TWITTER: @Kyle_Abbott87
NOTES: A well-built South African fast bowler, Abbott interrupted his international career to sign a four-year Kolpak deal with Hampshire in January 2017 and had an immediate impact with 60 Championship wickets at 18.20 to help save the county from relegation. He took 17 wickets in the T20 Blast. His Test debut figures of 7-29 are the second-best for South Africa, behind only Lance Klusener's 8-64 at Eden Gardens in 1996. He previously played for Hampshire as an overseas player in 2014, impressing with 36 wickets at 20.33

Batting	Mat	Inns	NO	Runs	HS	Ave	SR	100	50	Ct	St
Tests	11	14	0	95	17	6.78	28.10	0	0	4	0
ODIs	28	13	4	76	23	8.44	60.31	0	0	7	0
T20Is	21	6	4	23	9*	11.50	115.00	0	0	7	0
First-class	85	117	21	1762	97*	18.35	46.79	0	6	17	0
List A	94	44	18	470	56	18.07	88.18	0	1	26	0
T20s	112	38	21	171	16*	10.05	103.01	0	0	29	0
Bowling	Mat	Balls	Runs	Wkts	BBI	BBM	Ave	Econ	SR	5w	10
Tests	11	2081	886	39	7/29	9/68	22.71	2.55	53.3	3	0
ODIs	28	1303	1051	34	4/21	4/21	30.91	4.83	38.3	0	0
T20Is	21	436	579	26	3/20	3/20	22.26	7.96	16.7	0	0
First-class	85	15311	6911	319	8/45	12/96	21.66	2.70	47.9	20	2
List A	94	4217	3627	121	4/21	4/21	29.97	5.16	34.8	0	0
T20s	112	2340	3158	106	5/14	5/14	29.79	8.09	22.0	1	0

TOM ABELL

RHB / RM / RO / WO

SOMERSET

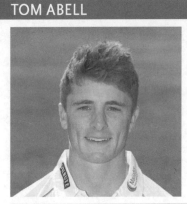

FULL NAME: Thomas Benjamin Abell
BORN: March 5, 1994, Taunton
SQUAD NO: 28
HEIGHT: 5ft 11in
NICKNAME: Tabes
EDUCATION: Taunton School; Exeter University
TEAMS: Somerset
ROLE: Batsman
DEBUT: First-class: 2014; List A: 2015; T20: 2016

BEST BATTING: 135 Somerset vs Lancashire, Old Trafford, 2016
BEST BOWLING: 2-71 Somerset vs Surrey, The Oval, 2017

BEST ADVICE EVER RECEIVED? Don't try and be anyone else – be the best possible version of you
'ROY OF THE ROVERS' MOMENT? Avoiding relegation last season was a special effort, but on a personal level it would be making my debut for Somerset
BEST THING ABOUT YOUR HOME GROUND? Taunton is an intimate ground – therefore you really feel the support we get
YOUNG OPPOSING PLAYER WHO HAS IMPRESSED YOU? Jamie Porter (Ess) – led the Essex attack and performed all season
WHERE IS PARADISE? The Maldives
CRICKETING HERO? Brian Lara for his flair
NON-CRICKETING HERO? Jonny Wilkinson – I love rugby and loved everything he was about
UNUSUAL OBJECT AT HOME? A pogo stick
TWITTER: @tomabell1

Batting	Mat	Inns	NO	Runs	HS	Ave	SR	100	50	Ct	St
First-class	45	81	8	2172	135	29.75	47.95	3	13	33	0
List A	12	10	1	343	106	38.11	70.86	1	1	4	0
T20s	4	3	0	13	7	4.33	56.52	0	0	0	0

Bowling	Mat	Balls	Runs	Wkts	BBI	BBM	Ave	Econ	SR	5w	10
First-class	45	208	129	3	2/71	2/71	43.00	3.72	69.3	0	0
List A	12	-	-	-	-	-	-	-	-	-	-
T20s	4	-	-	-	-	-	-	-	-	-	-

COLIN ACKERMANN RHB / OB / R0 / W0

FULL NAME: Colin Niel Ackermann
BORN: April 4, 1991, George, Cape Province, South Africa
SQUAD NO: 48
HEIGHT: 6ft 1in
NICKNAME: Ackers
EDUCATION: Grey High School, Port Elizabeth; University of South Africa
TEAMS: Leicestershire, Eastern Province, Warriors
ROLE: Batsman
DEBUT: First-class: 2010; List A: 2010; T20: 2011

LEICESTERSHIRE

BEST BATTING: 187* Warriors vs Knights, Kimberley, 2017
BEST BOWLING: 3-45 Leicestershire vs Northamptonshire, Northampton, 2017

WHAT GOT YOU INTO CRICKET? My dad played a bit and by the age of three I had a bat in my hands
BEST ADVICE EVER RECEIVED? Watch the ball
'ROY OF THE ROVERS' MOMENT? Walking on to the field at Centurion for the 2016 T20 Challenge final in South Africa
BEST THING ABOUT YOUR HOME GROUND? Grace Road has the best net facilities on the county circuit
BEST OPPOSING PLAYER IN COUNTY CRICKET? Samit Patel (Not)
YOUNG OPPOSING PLAYER WHO HAS IMPRESSED YOU? Josh Tongue (Wor)
IF YOU WEREN'T A CRICKETER? I'd be involved in property
WHERE IS PARADISE? Anywhere in Italy
CRICKETING HERO? Jacques Kallis
TWITTER: @ackers38

Batting	Mat	Inns	NO	Runs	HS	Ave	SR	100	50	Ct	St
First-class	88	155	15	5684	187*	40.60	48.67	13	35	70	0
List A	63	57	11	1453	92	31.58	73.38	0	10	45	0
T20s	68	64	10	1521	79*	28.16	114.53	0	9	39	0

Bowling	Mat	Balls	Runs	Wkts	BBI	BBM	Ave	Econ	SR	5w	10
First-class	88	3446	1767	39	3/45	4/54	45.30	3.07	88.3	0	0
List A	63	1683	1250	36	4/48	4/48	34.72	4.45	46.7	0	0
T20s	68	750	876	26	3/21	3/21	33.69	7.00	28.8	0	0

JIMMY ADAMS · LHB / LM / R5 / W0

HAMPSHIRE

FULL NAME: James Henry Kenneth Adams
BORN: September 23, 1980, Winchester, Hampshire
SQUAD NO: 4
HEIGHT: 6ft 1in
NICKNAME: Bison
EDUCATION: Twyford School, Hampshire; Sherborne School, Dorset; Loughborough University
TEAMS: Hampshire, Auckland, England Lions
ROLE: Batsman
DEBUT: First-class: 2002; List A: 2002; T20: 2005

BEST BATTING: 262* Hampshire vs Nottingham, Nottingham, 2006
BEST BOWLING: 2-16 Hampshire vs Durham, Chester-le-Street, 2004
COUNTY CAP: 2006; BENEFIT: 2015

WHAT GOT YOU INTO CRICKET? Playing with my dad and my brothers in the garden, and watching Robin Smith on the telly
FAMILY TIES? My dad played a bit for Kent Schoolboys and my brothers played Hampshire age-group until they decided to pursue other things
STRANGEST THING SEEN IN A GAME? James Tomlinson taking a one-handed catch at fine-leg while holding a half-eaten banana in his other hand
'ROY OF THE ROVERS' MOMENT? Winning at Lord's in the 2009 one-day final. (I wish I'd also been able to enjoy batting with Robin Smith on my debut but I was too busy bricking myself)
HOW WOULD YOUR TEAMMATES DESCRIBE YOU IN THREE WORDS? Indecisive, steady, hungry
BEST OPPOSING PLAYER IN COUNTY CRICKET? Tough one… can't decide (see above)
NON-CRICKETING HEROES? Rorschach, Wolverine, Jimmy Page, Keith Moon
SURPRISING FACT? My brother is/was a far better cricketer than me – he just fancied doing something else
TWITTER: @Jhkadams

Batting	Mat	Inns	NO	Runs	HS	Ave	SR	100	50	Ct	St
First-class	218	383	28	13371	262*	37.66		23	72	173	0
List A	116	110	13	3890	131	40.10	86.17	2	29	47	0
T20s	135	124	14	2643	101*	24.02	123.44	2	9	36	0

Bowling	Mat	Balls	Runs	Wkts	BBI	BBM	Ave	Econ	SR	5w	10
First-class	218	1069	718	13	2/16		55.23	4.02	82.2	0	0
List A	116	79	105	1	1/34	1/34	105.00	7.97	79.0	0	0
T20s	135	36	60	0	-	-	-	10.00	-	0	0

FULL NAME: Aadil Masud Ali
BORN: December 29, 1994, Leicester
SQUAD NO: 14
HEIGHT: 6ft
NICKNAME: Dil
EDUCATION: Lancaster School, Leicester;
Wyggeston and Queen Elizabeth I College,
Leicester
TEAMS: Leicestershire
ROLE: Batsman
DEBUT: First-class: 2015; List A: 2015; T20:
2015

LEICESTERSHIRE

BEST BATTING: 80 Leicestershire vs Gloucestershire, Leicester, 2015
BEST BOWLING: 1-10 Leicestershire vs Worcestershire, Worcester, 2017

WHAT FIRST GOT YOU INTO CRICKET? One day my dad's team were a player short so I was made to field. And watching Sachin Tendulkar
FAMILY TIES? My dad came over 25 years ago to play as an overseas player and then settled down. Biggest cricket badger around
BEST ADVICE EVER RECEIVED? See ball, hit ball
'ROY OF THE ROVERS' MOMENT? Making my first-class debut
BEST THING ABOUT YOUR HOME GROUND? The Stench and Benno Stand
BEST OPPOSING PLAYER IN COUNTY CRICKET? Ravi Bopara (Ess)
YOUNG OPPOSING PLAYER WHO HAS IMPRESSED YOU? Haseeb Hameed (Lan)
– composure
IF YOU WEREN'T A CRICKETER? I'd be a striker for Arsenal
SURPRISING FACT ABOUT YOU? I dropped out of Cambridge to live the dream
WHERE IS PARADISE? Home
NON-CRICKETING HERO? My dad – he's been there for me through thick and thin
TWITTER: @aadil_ali94

Batting	Mat	Inns	NO	Runs	HS	Ave	SR	100	50	Ct	St
First-class	15	25	1	639	80	26.62	39.08	0	3	6	0
List A	15	13	0	308	88	23.69	73.33	0	3	8	0
T20s	11	7	1	98	35*	16.33	103.15	0	0	4	0

Bowling	Mat	Balls	Runs	Wkts	BBI	BBM	Ave	Econ	SR	5w	10
First-class	15	78	86	1	1/10	1/31	86.00	6.61	78.0	0	0
List A	15	102	93	1	1/31	1/31	93.00	5.47	102.0	0	0
T20s	11	72	93	4	2/22	2/22	23.25	7.75	18.0	0	0

MOEEN ALI

LHB / OB / R2 / W0

WORCESTERSHIRE

FULL NAME: Moeen Munir Ali
BORN: June 18, 1987, Birmingham
SQUAD NO: 8
HEIGHT: 6ft
NICKNAME: Brother Mo
EDUCATION: Moseley School, Birmingham
TEAMS: England, Worcestershire, Duronto Rajshahi, Matabeleland Tuskers, Moors Sports Club, Warwickshire
ROLE: Allrounder
DEBUT: Test: 2014; ODI: 2014; T20I: 2014; First-class: 2005; List A: 2006; T20: 2007

BEST BATTING: 250 Worcestershire vs Glamorgan, Worcester, 2013
BEST BOWLING: 6-29 Worcestershire vs Lancashire, Old Trafford, 2012
COUNTY CAP: 2007 (Worcestershire)

FAMILY TIES? My cousin Kabir played for England and my brother Kadeer played for Worcestershire, Gloucestershire and Leicestershire
'ROY OF THE ROVERS' MOMENT? Playing for England
CRICKETING HEROES? Saeed Anwar and Brian Lara
NON-CRICKETING HEROES? Muhammad Ali
IF YOU WEREN'T A CRICKETER? I'd be working in a chippy

Batting	Mat	Inns	NO	Runs	HS	Ave	SR	100	50	Ct	St
Tests	49	83	8	2467	155*	32.89	52.37	5	12	27	0
ODIs	70	60	10	1423	128	28.46	105.64	3	5	23	0
T20Is	22	19	5	202	72*	14.42	112.84	0	1	6	0
First-class	178	302	27	10378	250	37.73	54.85	19	65	105	0
List A	181	166	12	4570	158	29.67	102.37	10	20	55	0
T20s	109	103	8	2139	90	22.51	128.85	0	11	33	0

Bowling	Mat	Balls	Runs	Wkts	BBI	BBM	Ave	Econ	SR	5w	10
Tests	49	8834	5352	133	6/53	10/112	40.24	3.63	66.4	4	1
ODIs	70	3287	2787	56	3/32	3/32	49.76	5.08	58.6	0	0
T20Is	22	312	400	14	2/21	2/21	28.57	7.69	22.2	0	0
First-class	178	20584	12149	295	6/29	12/96	41.18	3.54	69.7	9	2
List A	181	6056	5395	117	3/28	3/28	46.11	5.34	51.7	0	0
T20s	109	1502	1849	69	5/34	5/34	26.79	7.38	21.7	1	0

TOM ALSOP

LHB / WK / R0 / W0

FULL NAME: Thomas Philip Alsop
BORN: November 27, 1995, High Wycombe, Buckinghamshire
SQUAD NO: 9
HEIGHT: 5ft 11in
NICKNAME: Deeney, Alsop, Sloppy, T
EDUCATION: Lavington School; The John Bentley School, Wiltshire
TEAMS: Hampshire, England Lions
ROLE: Batsman
DEBUT: First-class: 2014; List A: 2014; T20: 2016

HAMPSHIRE

BEST BATTING: 117 Hampshire vs Surrey, The Oval, 2016
BEST BOWLING: 2-59 Hampshire vs Yorkshire, Headingley, 2016

FAMILY TIES? Dad played for Merchant Taylors' School and my older brother Owen played for Wiltshire CCC and was in the Hampshire Academy. My little (not so little) brother plays for Wiltshire age-groups
BEST ADVICE EVER RECEIVED? Stay in the present
'ROY OF THE ROVERS' MOMENT? Receiving my England Lions cap
BEST OPPOSING PLAYER IN COUNTY CRICKET? James Hildreth (Som)
YOUNG OPPOSING PLAYER WHO HAS IMPRESSED YOU? Sam Cook (Ess) – has really good skill and control with the ball
IF YOU WEREN'T A CRICKETER? I'd be doing something in the car or watch industry
SURPRISING FACT ABOUT YOU? I played hockey to a reasonable standard
SURPRISING FACT ABOUT A TEAMMATE? Jimmy Adams has a huge bromance with James Hildreth
WHERE IS PARADISE? Rome
CRICKETING HERO? Shikhar Dhawan – if only I was half as good as him!
NON-CRICKETING HERO? My mother – she's the head of an NHS intensive care unit saving lives (I've got huge respect for anyone within the NHS)
UNUSUAL OBJECT AT HOME? A watch-winder

Batting	Mat	Inns	NO	Runs	HS	Ave	SR	100	50	Ct	St
First-class	25	42	0	1085	117	25.83	48.72	1	8	24	0
List A	33	33	2	866	116	27.93	71.21	2	4	16	0
T20s	18	17	2	410	85	27.33	119.18	0	2	5	0

Bowling	Mat	Balls	Runs	Wkts	BBI	BBM	Ave	Econ	SR	5w	10
First-class	25	60	66	2	2/59	2/59	33.00	6.60	30.0	0	0
List A	33	-	-	-	-	-	-	-	-	-	-
T20s	18	-	-	-	-	-	-	-	-	-	-

TIM AMBROSE

RHB / WK / RO / WO

WARWICKSHIRE

FULL NAME: Timothy Raymond Ambrose
BORN: December 1, 1982, Newcastle, New South Wales, Australia
SQUAD NO: 11
HEIGHT: 5ft 7in
NICKNAME: Amby, Shambrose
EDUCATION: Merewether Selective High, NSW; Training and Further Education College, NSW
TEAMS: England, Warwickshire, Sussex
ROLE: Wicketkeeper
DEBUT: Test: 2008; ODI: 2008; T20I: 2008; First-class: 2001; List A: 2001; T20: 2003

BEST BATTING: 251* Warwickshire vs Worcestershire, Worcester, 2007
BEST BOWLING: 1-0 Warwickshire vs Middlesex, Lord's, 2016
COUNTY CAP: 2003 (Sussex); 2007 (Warwickshire); **BENEFIT:** 2016 (Warwickshire)

FAMILY TIES? My father played for Nelson Bay CC in Australia
'ROY OF THE ROVERS' MOMENT? County Championship wins in 2003 and 2012 and T20 win in 2014. Anytime playing for England
CRICKETING HEROES? Ian Healy for his attention to detail in wicketkeeping. Steve Waugh and Sachin Tendulkar for mental strength and concentration
NON-CRICKETING HEROES? Michael Jordan for his ability to deliver under pressure
SURPRISING FACT? I have a three-year-old Puggle named Frank
TWITTER: @timambrose2016

Batting	Mat	Inns	NO	Runs	HS	Ave	SR	100	50	Ct	St
Tests	11	16	1	447	102	29.80	46.41	1	3	31	0
ODIs	5	5	1	10	6	2.50	29.41	0	0	3	0
T20Is	1	-	-	-	-	-	-	-	-	1	1
First-class	224	342	32	10284	251*	33.17	51.85	16	62	581	40
List A	170	139	20	3883	135	32.63	79.13	3	22	164	32
T20s	92	61	17	1076	77	24.45	111.96	0	3	55	23

Bowling	Mat	Balls	Runs	Wkts	BBI	BBM	Ave	Econ	SR	5w	10
Tests	11	-	-	-	-	-	-	-	-	-	-
ODIs	5	-	-	-	-	-	-	-	-	-	-
T20Is	1	-	-	-	-	-	-	-	-	-	-
First-class	224	17	1	1	1/0	1/0	1.00	0.35	17.0	0	0
List A	170	-	-	-	-	-	-	-	-	-	-
T20s	92	-	-	-	-	-	-	-	-	-	-

HASHIM AMLA

RHB / OB / R0 / W0

FULL NAME: Hashim Mahomed Amla
BORN: March 31, 1983, Durban, South Africa
SQUAD NO: TBC
TEAMS: South Africa, Hampshire, Cape Cobras, Derbyshire, Dolphins, Essex, Kings XI Punjab, KwaZulu-Natal, Nottinghamshire, Surrey, Trinbago Knight Riders
ROLE: Batsman
DEBUT: Test: 2004; ODI: 2008; T20I: 2009; First-class: 1999; List A: 2002; T20: 2004

BEST BATTING: 311* South Africa vs England, The Oval, 2012
BEST BOWLING: 1-10 South Africa A vs India A, Kimbereley, 2002

TWITTER: @amlahash
NOTES: Hampshire have signed the immensely experienced South African as an overseas player for the first three months of the season. "Hashim is a world-class player," said director of cricket Giles White. "He is someone we have admired from a distance and it will be great to have him around. I spoke to him about opening the batting. He normally bats at three for South Africa but he is very comfortable opening." Hampshire will be Amla's fifth county, having previously had spells at Essex, Notts, Surrey and Derbyshire. The 35-year-old sits third on South Africa's all-time list of Test run-scorers behind Jacques Kallis and Graeme Smith and his tally of 26 ODI hundreds is bettered by only four batsmen in the history of the game

Batting	Mat	Inns	NO	Runs	HS	Ave	SR	100	50	Ct	St
Tests	113	193	14	8786	311*	49.08	50.61	28	38	99	0
ODIs	164	161	11	7535	159	50.23	88.90	26	35	81	0
T20Is	43	43	6	1277	97*	34.51	132.60	0	8	19	0
First-class	220	363	29	16716	311*	50.04		50	81	174	0
List A	222	216	13	9276	159	45.69		29	47	101	0
T20s	132	131	14	4049	104*	34.60	130.06	2	27	34	0

Bowling	Mat	Balls	Runs	Wkts	BBI	BBM	Ave	Econ	SR	5w	10
Tests	113	54	37	0	-	-	-	4.11	-	0	0
ODIs	164	-	-	-	-	-	-	-	-	-	-
T20Is	43	-	-	-	-	-	-	-	-	-	-
First-class	220	393	277	1	1/10		277.00	4.22	393.0	0	0
List A	222	16	28	0	-	-	-	10.50	-	0	0
T20s	132	2	5	0	-	-	-	15.00	-	0	0

COREY ANDERSON

LHB / LMF / RO / WO

SOMERSET

FULL NAME: Corey James Anderson
BORN: December 13, 1990, Christchurch, Canterbury
SQUAD NO: 78
TEAMS: New Zealand, Somerset, Canterbury, Delhi Daredevils, Mumbai Indians, Northern Districts
ROLE: Allrounder
DEBUT: Test: 2013; ODI: 2013; T20I: 2012; First-class: 2007; List A: 2007; T20: 2009

BEST BATTING: 167 Northern Districts vs Otago, Hamilton, 2012
BEST BOWLING: 5-22 Canterbury vs Northern Districts, Hamilton, 2009

TWITTER: @coreyanderson78
NOTES: The Kiwi allrounder is returning for a second spell at Somerset, having played four T20 matches for the county last season, which included hitting 81 from 45 balls against Surrey on debut. Anderson is set to be available throughout the T20 Blast, hoping to help Somerset win the title for the first time since 2005. "I believe that continuity throughout this competition is going to be key in achieving success and therefore it was crucial for us to be able to bring in a high-quality player who would be available for the duration of the tournament," said director of cricket Andy Hurry. "His all-round ability will have a huge impact on our performances." Anderson will be aiming to show the form which saw him hit a 36-ball hundred against West Indies in 2014, then the fastest hundred in the ODI history

Batting	Mat	Inns	NO	Runs	HS	Ave	SR	100	50	Ct	St
Tests	13	22	1	683	116	32.52	56.86	1	4	7	0
ODIs	49	45	5	1109	131*	27.72	108.72	1	4	11	0
T20Is	29	22	3	432	94*	22.73	137.57	0	2	18	0
First-class	50	85	10	2727	167	36.36	58.20	4	12	38	0
List A	81	75	8	1933	131*	28.85	101.62	1	11	28	0
T20s	100	85	18	1768	95*	26.38	138.23	0	7	47	0

Bowling	Mat	Balls	Runs	Wkts	BBI	BBM	Ave	Econ	SR	5w	10
Tests	13	1302	659	16	3/47	4/69	41.18	3.03	81.3	0	0
ODIs	49	1485	1502	60	5/63	5/63	25.03	6.06	24.7	1	0
T20Is	29	360	495	14	2/17	2/17	35.35	8.25	25.7	0	0
First-class	50	3129	1663	40	5/22	7/60	41.57	3.18	78.2	1	0
List A	81	1683	1668	67	5/26	5/26	24.89	5.94	25.1	2	0
T20s	100	683	997	27	2/17	2/17	36.92	8.75	25.2	0	0

JAMES ANDERSON LHB / RFM / R0 / W3

FULL NAME: James Michael Anderson
BORN: July 30, 1982, Burnley, Lancashire
SQUAD NO: 9
HEIGHT: 6ft 2in
NICKNAME: Jimmy, Jimbo, Jimbob
EDUCATION: St Theodore's Roman Catholic High School, Burnley
TEAMS: England, Lancashire, Auckland
ROLE: Bowler
DEBUT: Test: 2003; ODI: 2002; T20I: 2007; First-class: 2002; List A: 2000; T20: 2004

LANCASHIRE

BEST BATTING: 81 England vs India, Trent Bridge, 2014
BEST BOWLING: 7-42 England vs West Indies, Lord's, 2017
COUNTY CAP: 2003; **BENEFIT:** 2012

FAMILY TIES? My dad played for Burnley CC
'ROY OF THE ROVERS' MOMENT? Ashes wins, County Championship winners' medal
CRICKETING HEROES? Allan Donald, Peter Martin, Glen Chapple
NON-CRICKETING HEROES? Ian Wright, Steve Davis (ex-Burnley FC), Boris Becker
IF YOU WEREN'T A CRICKETER? I'd be busking with my recorder
SURPRISING FACT? I can peel a potato in 2.4 seconds. I have a personality. I'm allergic to mushrooms
TWITTER: @jimmy9

Batting	Mat	Inns	NO	Runs	HS	Ave	SR	100	50	Ct	St
Tests	134	186	73	1128	81	9.98	40.50	0	1	84	0
ODIs	194	79	43	273	28	7.58	48.66	0	0	53	0
T20Is	19	4	3	1	1*	1.00	50.00	0	0	3	0
First-class	222	283	111	1730	81	10.05		0	1	132	0
List A	255	102	62	371	28	9.27		0	0	65	0
T20s	44	10	6	23	16	5.75	88.46	0	0	8	0

Bowling	Mat	Balls	Runs	Wkts	BBI	BBM	Ave	Econ	SR	5w	10
Tests	134	29600	14333	523	7/42	11/71	27.40	2.90	56.5	25	3
ODIs	194	9584	7861	269	5/23	5/23	29.22	4.92	35.6	2	0
T20Is	19	422	552	18	3/23	3/23	30.66	7.84	23.4	0	0
First-class	222	45168	22009	859	7/42	11/71	25.62	2.92	52.5	43	6
List A	255	12414	10003	352	5/23	5/23	28.41	4.83	35.2	2	0
T20s	44	933	1318	41	3/23	3/23	32.14	8.47	22.7	0	0

MARTIN ANDERSSON

RHB / RM / RO / WO

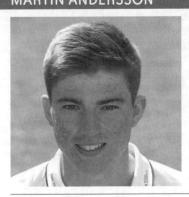

FULL NAME: Martin Kristoffer Andersson
BORN: September 6, 1996, Reading
SQUAD NO: 24
HEIGHT: 6ft 1in
NICKNAME: Tino, Pasty
EDUCATION: Reading Blue Coat School;
University of Leeds
TEAMS: Middlesex
ROLE: Allrounder
DEBUT: First-class: 2017

BEST BATTING: 12 Leeds/Bradford MCCU vs Yorkshire, Headingley, 2017

WHAT GOT YOU INTO CRICKET? The 2005 Ashes
BEST ADVICE EVER RECEIVED? Just do it
'ROY OF THE ROVERS' MOMENT? Hitting a six off the penultimate ball to win the Second XI
T20 final in 2016
BEST THING ABOUT YOUR HOME GROUND? The unbelievable match teas
BEST OPPOSING PLAYER IN COUNTY CRICKET? Darren Stevens (Ken)
YOUNG OPPOSING PLAYER WHO HAS IMPRESSED YOU? Jamie Porter (Ess)
IF YOU WEREN'T A CRICKETER? I'd be a UFC fighter
SURPRISING FACT ABOUT YOU? My karaoke song of choice is Basshunter's 'Now You're
Gone' in Swedish. I have 90% of my middle finger left – the other 10% was left in a door
frame in a building at school
WHERE IS PARADISE? North Sweden
CRICKETING HERO? Hashim Amla
NON-CRICKETING HERO? Neil Armstrong
UNUSUAL OBJECT AT HOME? A didgeridoo
TWITTER: @MartinAnderss11

Batting	Mat	Inns	NO	Runs	HS	Ave	SR	100	50	Ct	St
First-class	2	4	0	16	12	4.00	30.18	0	0	4	0

Bowling	Mat	Balls	Runs	Wkts	BBI	BBM	Ave	Econ	SR	5w	10
First-class	2	-	-	-	-	-	-	-	-	-	-

JOFRA ARCHER

RHB / RFM / R0 / W1 / MVP9

FULL NAME: Jofra Chioke Archer
BORN: April 1, 1995, Bridgetown, Barbados
SQUAD NO: 22
HEIGHT: 6ft 2in
NICKNAME: Regi
EDUCATION: Christ Church Foundation School, Barbados
TEAMS: Sussex, Hobart Hurricanes, Rajasthan Royals
ROLE: Allrounder
DEBUT: First-class: 2016; List A: 2016; T20: 2016

SUSSEX

BEST BATTING: 81* Sussex vs Northamptonshire, Northampton, 2017
BEST BOWLING: 7-67 Sussex vs Kent, Hove, 2017

WHAT GOT YOU INTO CRICKET? I've been playing for as long as I can remember
BEST ADVICE EVER RECEIVED? Be the best in your own way
'ROY OF THE ROVERS' MOMENT? Dismissing Eoin Morgan in a televised T20 match against Middlesex in 2017
BEST THING ABOUT YOUR HOME GROUND? The slope at Hove gives that extra push to fast bowlers
BEST OPPOSING PLAYER IN COUNTY CRICKET? Riki Wessels (Not)
YOUNG OPPOSING PLAYER WHO HAS IMPRESSED YOU? Ed Barnard (Wor)
IF YOU WEREN'T A CRICKETER? I'd be a Nat Geo Wild presenter
SURPRISING FACT ABOUT YOU? I'm ambidextrous
SURPRISING FACT ABOUT A TEAMMATE? One of them is afraid of clowns
WHERE IS PARADISE? Barbados
CRICKETING HERO? Don't have one
NON-CRICKETING HERO? My parents
TWITTER: @craig_arch

Batting	Mat	Inns	NO	Runs	HS	Ave	SR	100	50	Ct	St
First-class	20	28	6	833	81*	37.86	77.48	0	6	13	0
List A	10	8	2	130	45	21.66	115.04	0	0	4	0
T20s	41	22	13	195	36	21.66	143.38	0	0	13	0

Bowling	Mat	Balls	Runs	Wkts	BBI	BBM	Ave	Econ	SR	5w	10
First-class	20	4310	2321	89	7/67	11/137	26.07	3.23	48.4	4	1
List A	10	557	477	16	5/42	5/42	29.81	5.13	34.8	1	0
T20s	41	883	1164	50	4/18	4/18	23.28	7.90	17.6	0	0

GUS ATKINSON

RHB / **RM** / **RO** / **WO**

SURREY

FULL NAME: Angus Alexander Patrick Atkinson
BORN: January 19, 1998, Chelsea, Middlesex
SQUAD NO: 37
HEIGHT: 6ft 1in
NICKNAME: Gus
EDUCATION: Northcote Lodge, London; Bradfield College, Berkshire
TEAMS: Surrey
ROLE: Bowler

WHAT GOT YOU INTO CRICKET? My father
BEST ADVICE EVER RECEIVED? Always back your ability
'ROY OF THE ROVERS' MOMENT? Taking 6-64 for Surrey Second XI against Middlesex Second XI at Richmond last season
BEST THING ABOUT YOUR HOME GROUND? Its history and location
BEST OPPOSING PLAYER IN COUNTY CRICKET? Samit Patel (Not)
YOUNG OPPOSING PLAYER WHO HAS IMPRESSED YOU? Tom Lace (Mid) – he has the ability to score runs in all formats of the game
IF YOU WEREN'T A CRICKETER? I'd be a student
SURPRISING FACT ABOUT YOU? I had a rugby trial for Harlequins aged 13
WHERE IS PARADISE? Turks and Caicos Islands in the Caribbean
CRICKETING HERO? Andrew Flintoff for the way he could change a game
NON-CRICKETING HERO? Lionel Messi for his modesty despite being one of the greatest footballers of all time
TWITTER: @gus_atkinson1

TOM BAILEY

RHB / RFM / R0 / W0

FULL NAME: Thomas Ernest Bailey
BORN: April 21, 1991, Preston, Lancashire
SQUAD NO: 8
HEIGHT: 6ft 4in
NICKNAME: Jebby, Bails
EDUCATION: Myerscough College, Lancashire
TEAMS: Lancashire
ROLE: Bowler
DEBUT: First-class: 2012; List A: 2014; T20: 2015

LANCASHIRE

BEST BATTING: 58 Lancashire vs Middlesex, Southport, 2017
BEST BOWLING: 5-12 Lancashire vs Leicestershire, Leicester, 2015

FAMILY TIES? My dad played for a local side and I used to watch him every weekend as a kid
BEST ADVICE EVER RECEIVED? You're only young once
'ROY OF THE ROVERS' MOMENT? Winning the T20 Blast with Lancashire in 2015
BEST THING ABOUT YOUR HOME GROUND? Good wicket for both batsmen and bowlers
YOUNG OPPOSING PLAYER WHO HAS IMPRESSED YOU? Jason Roy (Sur)
IF YOU WEREN'T A CRICKETER? I'd be a nuclear scientist
SURPRISING FACT? I'm actually really smart
WHERE IS PARADISE? Dubai
CRICKETING HERO? Steve Harmison – bowled fast and won the Ashes for England in 2005
NON-CRICKETING HERO? Tom Webster
TWITTER: @TomBaildog

Batting	Mat	Inns	NO	Runs	HS	Ave	SR	100	50	Ct	St
First-class	31	42	9	596	58	18.06	48.33	0	2	3	0
List A	10	6	3	33	11	11.00	82.50	0	0	1	0
T20s	13	4	1	18	10	6.00	112.50	0	0	6	0

Bowling	Mat	Balls	Runs	Wkts	BBI	BBM	Ave	Econ	SR	5w	10
First-class	31	5331	2758	90	5/12	10/98	30.64	3.10	59.2	5	1
List A	10	451	437	12	3/31	3/31	36.41	5.81	37.5	0	0
T20s	13	216	351	11	2/24	2/24	31.90	9.75	19.6	0	0

JONNY BAIRSTOW

RHB / WK / R3 / W0

YORKSHIRE

FULL NAME: Jonathan Marc Bairstow
BORN: September 26, 1989, Bradford
SQUAD NO: 21
NICKNAME: Bluey
EDUCATION: St Peter's School, York; Leeds Metropolitan University
TEAMS: England, Yorkshire, Peshawar Zalmi
ROLE: Batsman/wicketkeeper
DEBUT: Test: 2012; ODI: 2011; T20I: 2011; First-class: 2009; List A: 2009; T20: 2010

BEST BATTING: 246 Yorkshire vs Hampshire, Headingley, 2016
COUNTY CAP: 2011

FAMILY TIES? My father David played for Yorkshire and England
CRICKETING HERO? Sachin Tendulkar
NON-CRICKETING HEROES? Jonny Wilkinson and Steve Irwin
IF YOU WEREN'T A CRICKETER? I'd be a rugby player
SURPRISING FACT? I played football for the Leeds United Academy for seven years
TWITTER: @jbairstow21

Batting	Mat	Inns	NO	Runs	HS	Ave	SR	100	50	Ct	St
Tests	50	86	6	3130	167*	39.12	55.23	4	17	129	8
ODIs	39	35	8	1190	141*	44.07	91.89	2	6	19	2
T20Is	23	18	5	329	60*	25.30	120.07	0	2	23	0
First-class	158	256	32	10413	246	46.48		22	55	406	19
List A	106	96	14	3109	174	37.91	98.04	5	16	69	8
T20s	92	80	16	1582	102*	24.71	125.25	1	6	56	10
Bowling	Mat	Balls	Runs	Wkts	BBI	BBM	Ave	Econ	SR	5w	10
Tests	50	-	-	-	-	-	-	-	-	-	-
ODIs	39	-	-	-	-	-	-	-	-	-	-
T20Is	23	-	-	-	-	-	-	-	-	-	-
First-class	158	6	1	0	-	-	-	1.00	-	0	0
List A	106	-	-	-	-	-	-	-	-	-	-
T20s	92	-	-	-	-	-	-	-	-	-	-

JAKE BALL

RHB / RFM / R0 / W1 / MVP77

FULL NAME: Jacob Timothy Ball
BORN: March 14, 1991, Mansfield, Nottinghamshire
SQUAD NO: 28
HEIGHT: 6ft 3in
NICKNAME: Yak
EDUCATION: Meden School, Mansfield
TEAMS: England, Nottinghamshire
ROLE: Bowler
DEBUT: Test: 2016; ODI: 2016; First-class: 2011; List A: 2009; T20: 2011

NOTTINGHAMSHIRE

BEST BATTING: 49* Nottinghamshire vs Warwickshire, Trent Bridge, 2015
BEST BOWLING: 6-49 Nottinghamshire vs Sussex, Trent Bridge, 2015

FAMILY TIES? My uncle Bruce French played for England. My older brother Jonathan has played Minor Counties for Lincolnshire
HOW WOULD YOUR TEAMMATES DESCRIBE YOU IN THREE WORDS? Funny and laid-back
SUPERSTITIONS? Always turn the same way at the end of my mark
NON-CRICKETING HERO? David Beckham – for everything he did on and off the field
IF YOU WEREN'T A CRICKETER? I'd be working in property
SURPRISING FACT? I was a batter till the age of 15
TWITTER: @Jakeball30

Batting	Mat	Inns	NO	Runs	HS	Ave	SR	100	50	Ct	St
Tests	4	8	0	67	31	8.37	53.60	0	0	1	0
ODIs	17	5	1	37	28	9.25	94.87	0	0	4	0
First-class	46	69	10	767	49*	13.00	77.00	0	0	6	0
List A	79	29	12	163	28	9.58	108.66	0	0	15	0
T20s	52	11	8	25	8*	8.33	96.15	0	0	13	0

Bowling	Mat	Balls	Runs	Wkts	BBI	BBM	Ave	Econ	SR	5w	10
Tests	4	612	343	3	1/47	1/47	114.33	3.36	204.0	0	0
ODIs	17	917	951	21	5/51	5/51	45.28	6.22	43.6	1	0
First-class	46	6819	3907	145	6/49	9/67	26.94	3.43	47.0	4	0
List A	79	3292	3206	90	5/51	5/51	35.62	5.84	36.5	1	0
T20s	52	1045	1480	61	3/27	3/27	24.26	8.49	17.1	0	0

GARY BALLANCE

LHB / LB / R3 / W0 / MVP42

FULL NAME: Gary Simon Ballance
BORN: November 22, 1989, Zimbabwe
SQUAD NO: 19
NICKNAME: Gazza, Gaz
EDUCATION: Peterhouse School, Marondera, Zimbabwe; Harrow School, London
TEAMS: England, Yorkshire, Derbyshire, Mid West Rhinos
ROLE: Batsman
DEBUT: Test: 2014; ODI: 2013; First-class: 2008; List A: 2006; T20: 2010

BEST BATTING: 210 Mid West Rhinos vs Southern Rocks, Masvingo, 2011
COUNTY CAP: 2012 (Yorkshire)

NOTES: A close family friend of former Zimbabwe skipper David Houghton, Ballance signed for Derbyshire at 16 before joining the Yorkshire Academy in 2008. He played for Zimbabwe U19 at the World Cup in 2006 before qualifying to play for England. Made his ODI debut in 2013 before making his Test bow at Sydney in the 2013/14 Ashes. He had an exceptional summer in Test cricket in 2014, hitting three centuries to cement his place at No.3. Lost his Test place during the 2015 Ashes but was recalled in 2016, only to be jettisoned again after struggling in Bangladesh later that year. Recalled in 2017 but did not play a Test in the Ashes and was left out of the subsequent tour of New Zealand. Made captain of Yorkshire across all formats in 2017 and led from the front, with 951 runs at 67.93 in the Championship and 483 runs at 69 in the One-Day Cup

Batting	Mat	Inns	NO	Runs	HS	Ave	SR	100	50	Ct	St
Tests	23	42	2	1498	156	37.45	47.16	4	7	22	0
ODIs	16	15	1	297	79	21.21	67.04	0	2	8	0
First-class	133	215	22	9362	210	48.50	51.35	32	44	112	0
List A	97	91	14	3819	152*	49.59	88.34	7	23	41	0
T20s	70	62	8	1322	68	24.48	119.96	0	5	40	0

Bowling	Mat	Balls	Runs	Wkts	BBI	BBM	Ave	Econ	SR	5w	10
Tests	23	12	5	0	-	-	-	2.50	-	0	0
ODIs	16	-	-	-	-	-	-	-	-	-	-
First-class	133	162	154	0	-	-	-	5.70	-	0	0
List A	97	-	-	-	-	-	-	-	-	-	-
T20s	70	-	-	-	-	-	-	-	-	-	-

CAMERON BANCROFT

RHB / WK / R0 / W0

FULL NAME: Cameron Timothy Bancroft
BORN: November 19, 1992, Perth, Australia
SQUAD NO: 4
HEIGHT: 5ft 10in
EDUCATION: Aquinas College, Perth
TEAMS: Australia, Somerset, Gloucestershire, Perth Scorchers, Western Australia
ROLE: Batsman/wicketkeeper
DEBUT: Test: 2017; T20I: 2016; First-class: 2013; List A: 2011; T20: 2014

SOMERSET

BEST BATTING: 228* Western Australia vs South Australia, Perth, 2017
BEST BOWLING: 1-67 Gloucestershire vs Sussex, Hove, 2017

TWITTER: @cbancroft4
NOTES: An opening batsman who can keep wicket, Bancroft averaged 47 in the 2014/15 Sheffield Shield and scored a double hundred in the final game of the season. After making another double in October 2017, he was selected for his Test debut against England at Brisbane the following month, scoring an unbeaten 82 in the second innings. Played all five Ashes Tests but failed to make it to fifty again. Joined Gloucestershire for the first two months of the 2016 season and found the going tough but was stronger for the county last summer, scoring 685 Championship runs at 40.29. Somerset have signed him as an overseas player for four-day and 50-over cricket. "Cameron has the appetite and the temperament for scoring big hundreds," said director of cricket Andy Hurry. "He really values the price of his wicket, is mentally tough and highly driven to succeed"

Batting	Mat	Inns	NO	Runs	HS	Ave	SR	100	50	Ct	St
Tests	5	8	1	179	82*	25.57	39.86	0	1	5	0
T20Is	1	1	1	0	0*	-	-	0	0	1	0
First-class	73	133	11	4687	228*	38.41	42.98	11	18	95	1
List A	41	39	5	1224	176	36.00	77.81	1	9	35	1
T20s	25	20	5	502	75*	33.46	128.71	0	4	12	4

Bowling	Mat	Balls	Runs	Wkts	BBI	BBM	Ave	Econ	SR	5w	10
Tests	5	-	-	-	-	-	-	-	-	-	-
T20Is	1	-	-	-	-	-	-	-	-	-	-
First-class	73	48	67	1	1/67	1/67	67.00	8.37	48.0	0	0
List A	41	-	-	-	-	-	-	-	-	-	-
T20s	25	-	-	-	-	-	-	-	-	-	-

LIAM BANKS

RHB / RM / RO / WO

WARWICKSHIRE

FULL NAME: Liam Banks
BORN: March 27, 1999, Stoke-on-Trent
SQUAD NO: 8
HEIGHT: 5ft 11in
NICKNAME: Banksy
EDUCATION: Newcastle-under-Lyme School and Sixth Form College
TEAMS: Warwickshire
ROLE: Batsman
DEBUT: First-class: 2017

BEST BATTING: 29 Warwickshire vs Yorkshire, Headingley, 2017

WHAT GOT YOU INTO CRICKET? Living close to the cricket club
STRANGEST THING SEEN IN A GAME? A cow on a cricket field
'ROY OF THE ROVERS' MOMENT? Scoring a hundred after my grandad died
HOW WOULD YOUR TEAMMATES DESCRIBE YOU IN THREE WORDS? Leader, honest, fun
CRICKETING HEROES? Joe Root, Ricky Ponting
IF YOU WEREN'T A CRICKETER? I'd be a cricket coach or a labour worker
SURPRISING FACT? I love animals and fishing
UNUSUAL OBJECT AT HOME? A piece of rock from Lanzarote

Batting	Mat	Inns	NO	Runs	HS	Ave	SR	100	50	Ct	St
First-class	2	4	0	57	29	14.25	37.25	0	0	1	0

Bowling	Mat	Balls	Runs	Wkts	BBI	BBM	Ave	Econ	SR	5w	10
First-class	2	-	-	-	-	-	-	-	-	-	-

TOM BANTON

RHB / WK / R0 / W0

FULL NAME: Thomas Banton
BORN: November 11, 1998, Chiltern, Buckinghamshire
SQUAD NO: 18
HEIGHT: 6ft 2in
NICKNAME: Bants
EDUCATION: King's College, Taunton
TEAMS: Somerset
ROLE: Wicketkeeper/batsman
DEBUT: T20: 2017

WHAT GOT YOU INTO CRICKET? My dad
BEST ADVICE EVER RECEIVED? Play your natural game
'ROY OF THE ROVERS' MOMENT? Making my Somerset debut
BEST THING ABOUT YOUR HOME GROUND? The support we get from the local fans
YOUNG OPPOSING PLAYER WHO HAS IMPRESSED YOU? Harry Brook (Yor) – he puts so much effort into his training
IF YOU WEREN'T A CRICKETER? I'd be working in London in currency exchange
SURPRISING FACT ABOUT YOU? I love playing hockey
SURPRISING FACT ABOUT A TEAMMATE? Eddie Byrom is a vegan
WHERE IS PARADISE? Cape Town
CRICKETING HERO? Virat Kohli – for the way he keeps it so simple
NON-CRICKETING HERO? Fernando Torres – I wanted to have my hair exactly like his when I was younger
TWITTER: @tombanton18

Batting	Mat	Inns	NO	Runs	HS	Ave	SR	100	50	Ct	St
T20s	2	1	0	4	4	4.00	57.14	0	0	0	1
Bowling	Mat	Balls	Runs	Wkts	BBI	BBM	Ave	Econ	SR	5w	10
T20s	2	-	-	-	-	-	-	-	-	-	-

TOM BARBER

RHB / LFM / R0 / W0

MIDDLESEX

FULL NAME: Thomas Edward Barber
BORN: August 8, 1995, Poole, Dorset
SQUAD NO: 25
HEIGHT: 6ft 3in
NICKNAME: Barbs
EDUCATION: Bournemouth Grammar School
TEAMS: Middlesex, Hampshire
ROLE: Bowler
DEBUT: List A: 2014; T20: 2017

BEST ADVICE EVER RECEIVED? Hit the top of off stump
'ROY OF THE ROVERS' MOMENT? Dismissing Kane Williamson and Anthony McGrath in consecutive balls for Hampshire against Yorkshire in 2014
BEST THING ABOUT YOUR HOME GROUND? It's Lord's – need I say any more?
YOUNG OPPOSING PLAYER WHO HAS IMPRESSED YOU? George Scrimshaw (Wor)
SURPRISING FACT ABOUT YOU? I broke the record for the fastest ball bowled in the Vicon testing at Loughborough – 89.6mph
WHERE IS PARADISE? Bournemouth beach
CRICKETING HERO? Andrew Flintoff and Brett Lee – watching these two inspired me to become a fast bowler
NON-CRICKETING HERO? My parents – for all the support they give me
TWITTER: @Tom_Barber20

Batting	Mat	Inns	NO	Runs	HS	Ave	SR	100	50	Ct	St
List A	2	1	0	0	0	0.00	0.00	0	0	0	0
T20s	2	1	0	0	0	0.00	0.00	0	0	0	0

Bowling	Mat	Balls	Runs	Wkts	BBI	BBM	Ave	Econ	SR	5w	10
List A	2	48	50	2	2/22	2/22	25.00	6.25	24.0	0	0
T20s	2	42	69	1	1/32	1/32	69.00	9.85	42.0	0	0

KEITH BARKER

LHB / LFM / R0 / W3 / MVP47

FULL NAME: Keith Hubert Douglas Barker
BORN: October 21, 1986, Manchester
SQUAD NO: 13
HEIGHT: 6ft 2in
NICKNAME: Barks, Barky, Barksy
EDUCATION: Moorhead High School,
Accrington; Preston College
TEAMS: Warwickshire
ROLE: Allrounder
DEBUT: First-class: 2009; List A: 2009; T20:
2009

WARWICKSHIRE

BEST BATTING: 125 Warwickshire vs Surrey, Guildford, 2013
BEST BOWLING: 6-40 Warwickshire vs Somerset, Taunton, 2012
COUNTY CAP: 2013

FAMILY TIES? Father, godfather and brothers all played various levels of cricket
BEST ADVICE EVER RECEIVED? It's only a game
YOUNG OPPOSING PLAYER WHO HAS IMPRESSED YOU? Tom and Sam Curran (Sur) – very good cricketers and I'm sure there is a lot more to come from both of them
IF YOU WEREN'T A CRICKETER? I'd be Xaro Xhoan Daxos (Game of Thrones)
SURPRISING FACT ABOUT YOU? I never scored a hundred for the Enfield CC first team
SURPRISING FACT ABOUT A TEAMMATE? Chris Wright wears short shorts
WHERE IS PARADISE? Barbados
CRICKETING HERO? My father
NON-CRICKETING HERO? Lewis Hamilton – confident in his ability and backs himself in any situation

Batting	Mat	Inns	NO	Runs	HS	Ave	SR	100	50	Ct	St
First-class	102	136	23	3336	125	29.52	58.53	6	15	32	0
List A	55	37	9	496	56	17.71	90.18	0	1	12	0
T20s	65	35	7	383	46	13.67	111.01	0	0	17	0

Bowling	Mat	Balls	Runs	Wkts	BBI	BBM	Ave	Econ	SR	5w	10
First-class	102	16881	8440	318	6/40	10/70	26.54	2.99	53.0	12	1
List A	55	2036	1992	63	4/33	4/33	31.61	5.87	32.3	0	0
T20s	65	1206	1588	69	4/19	4/19	23.01	7.90	17.4	0	0

WORCESTERSHIRE

ED BARNARD

RHB / RFM / R0 / W0 / MVP33

FULL NAME: Edward George Barnard
BORN: November 20, 1995, Shrewsbury
SQUAD NO: 30
HEIGHT: 6ft
NICKNAME: Test-tube, Barndoor, Earthworm Jim
EDUCATION: Meole Brace School, Shrewsbury; Shrewsbury School
TEAMS: Worcestershire
ROLE: Bowler
DEBUT: First-class: 2015; List A: 2015; T20: 2015

BEST BATTING: 75 Worcestershire vs Durham, Worcester, 2017
BEST BOWLING: 4-23 Worcestershire vs Gloucestershire, Worcester, 2016

FAMILY TIES? Dad (Andy) played for Shropshire; brother (Mike) played for Shropshire and first-class cricket for Oxford MCCU; brother (Steve) played for Shropshire
'ROY OF THE ROVERS' MOMENT? Beating India in the last over of the 2014 U19 World Cup quarter-final at Dubai
BEST THING ABOUT YOUR HOME GROUND? The view
BEST OPPOSING PLAYER IN COUNTY CRICKET? Wayne Madsen (Der)
YOUNG OPPOSING PLAYER WHO HAS IMPRESSED YOU? Jofra Archer (Sus)
IF YOU WEREN'T A CRICKETER? I'd be a struggling student
WHERE IS PARADISE? Anywhere in Perth on a Sunday afternoon
CRICKETING HERO? Andrew Flintoff in the 2005 Ashes
NON-CRICKETING HERO? Alan Shearer
TWITTER: @EdBarn95

Batting	Mat	Inns	NO	Runs	HS	Ave	SR	100	50	Ct	St
First-class	33	45	10	1083	75	30.94	60.00	0	7	15	0
List A	24	17	5	280	51	23.33	105.66	0	1	14	0
T20s	36	19	7	160	34*	13.33	130.08	0	0	16	0

Bowling	Mat	Balls	Runs	Wkts	BBI	BBM	Ave	Econ	SR	5w	10
First-class	33	4824	2955	94	4/23	7/149	31.43	3.67	51.3	0	0
List A	24	984	972	28	3/37	3/37	34.71	5.92	35.1	0	0
T20s	36	428	658	14	2/18	2/18	47.00	9.22	30.5	0	0

GEORGE BARTLETT

RHB / OB / R0 / W0

FULL NAME: George Anthony Bartlett
BORN: March 14, 1998, Frimley, Surrey
SQUAD NO: 14
EDUCATION: Millfield School, Somerset
TEAMS: Somerset
ROLE: Batsman
DEBUT: First-class: 2017

SOMERSET

BEST BATTING: 28 Somerset vs Surrey, The Oval, 2017

TWITTER: @georgebartlett9
NOTES: A batsman who bowls off-spin, Bartlett is a product of the Somerset Academy and signed a contract with the club in October 2016. In early 2017 he made 179 for England U19 against India U19 in a four-day match at Nagpur, taking Nasser Hussain's record for the highest score by an England U19 batsman overseas. Bartlett made his debut for Somerset Second XI in 2014 and featured in the 2016 U19 World Cup. He made a hundred in the U19 Test against Sri Lanka in 2016 and earned a senior contract on the back of consistent performances for Somerset seconds. He made his first-class debut last summer but has yet to play senior white-ball cricket

Batting	Mat	Inns	NO	Runs	HS	Ave	SR	100	50	Ct	St
First-class	4	8	1	100	28	14.28	55.86	0	0	3	0

Bowling	Mat	Balls	Runs	Wkts	BBI	BBM	Ave	Econ	SR	5w	10
First-class	4	-	-	-	-	-	-	-	-	-	-

GARETH BATTY

RHB / OB / RO / W2 / MVP54

FULL NAME: Gareth Jon Batty
BORN: October 13, 1977, Bradford
SQUAD NO: 13
HEIGHT: 5ft 11in
NICKNAME: Bats, Stuta
EDUCATION: Bingley Grammar School
TEAMS: England, Surrey, Worcestershire, Yorkshire
ROLE: Bowler
DEBUT: Test: 2003; ODI: 2002; T20I: 2009; First-class: 1997; List A: 1998; T20: 2003

BEST BATTING: 133 Worcestershire vs Surrey, The Oval, 2004
BEST BOWLING: 8-68 Surrey vs Essex, Chelmsford, 2014
COUNTY CAP: 2011 (Surrey); **BENEFIT:** 2017 (Surrey)

FAMILY TIES? Dad played for Yorkshire seconds, brother Jeremy played for Yorkshire and Somerset
CRICKETING HEROES? Vic Richards, Joel Garner
NON-CRICKETING HEROES? Winston Churchill and Maggie Thatcher – people who had the courage to make decisions
IF YOU WEREN'T A CRICKETER? I'd be a fireman
SURPRISING FACT? This is my 22nd year as a pro
UNUSUAL OBJECT AT HOME? A carrier pigeon
TWITTER: @Garethbatty2017

Batting	Mat	Inns	NO	Runs	HS	Ave	SR	100	50	Ct	St
Tests	9	12	2	149	38	14.90	25.68	0	0	3	0
ODIs	10	8	2	30	17	5.00	41.09	0	0	4	0
T20Is	1	1	0	4	4	4.00	57.14	0	0	0	0
First-class	253	374	64	7276	133	23.47		3	30	161	0
List A	257	191	41	2325	83*	15.50		0	5	81	0
T20s	144	85	29	604	87	10.78	103.07	0	1	42	0

Bowling	Mat	Balls	Runs	Wkts	BBI	BBM	Ave	Econ	SR	5w	10
Tests	9	1714	914	15	3/55	5/153	60.93	3.19	114.2	0	0
ODIs	10	440	366	5	2/40	2/40	73.20	4.99	88.00	0	0
T20Is	1	18	17	0	-	-	-	5.66	-	0	0
First-class	253	44776	21678	656	8/68	10/113	33.04	2.90	68.2	26	3
List A	257	10035	7712	241	5/35	5/35	32.00	4.61	41.6	3	0
T20s	144	2545	3102	113	4/13	4/13	27.45	7.31	22.5	0	0

AARON BEARD

LHB / RMF / R0 / W0

FULL NAME: Aaron Paul Beard
BORN: October 15, 1997, Chelmsford
SQUAD NO: 14
HEIGHT: 5ft 11in
NICKNAME: Beardo, AB
EDUCATION: The Boswells School, Chelmsford; Great Baddow High School, Chelmsford
TEAMS: Essex
ROLE: Bowler
DEBUT: First-class: 2016

ESSEX

BEST BATTING: 58* Essex vs Durham MCCU, Chelmsford, 2017
BEST BOWLING: 4-62 Essex vs Sri Lankans, Chelmsford, 2016

WHAT GOT YOU INTO CRICKET? My dad and uncle both played and I used to go along and watch
BEST ADVICE EVER RECEIVED? Play straight, be great
'ROY OF THE ROVERS' MOMENT? Taking 4-62 against Sri Lanka on my first-class debut in 2016
BEST THING ABOUT YOUR HOME GROUND? The fans
BEST OPPOSING PLAYER IN COUNTY CRICKET? Joe Root (Yor)
YOUNG OPPOSING PLAYER WHO HAS IMPRESSED YOU? Mason Crane (Ham)
IF YOU WEREN'T A CRICKETER? I'd be in the building industry
SURPRISING FACT ABOUT YOU? When playing golf I putt right-handed and play the rest of my shots left-handed
WHERE IS PARADISE? Cape Town
CRICKETING HEROES? Tom Westley and Nick Browne
NON-CRICKETING HERO? David Beckham
TWITTER: @aaronbeard_14

Batting	Mat	Inns	NO	Runs	HS	Ave	SR	100	50	Ct	St
First-class	8	7	5	79	58*	39.50	60.30	0	1	1	0

Bowling	Mat	Balls	Runs	Wkts	BBI	BBM	Ave	Econ	SR	5w	10
First-class	8	1130	704	16	4/62	5/81	44.00	3.73	70.6	0	0

WILL BEER

RHB / LB / RO / WO

FULL NAME: William Andrew Thomas Beer
BORN: October 8, 1988, Crawley, Sussex
SQUAD NO: 18
HEIGHT: 5ft 9.5in
NICKNAME: Beery
EDUCATION: Reigate Grammar School; Collyer's Sixth Form College, Horsham
TEAMS: Sussex
ROLE: Bowler
DEBUT: First-class: 2008; List A: 2009; T20: 2008

BEST BATTING: 39 Sussex vs Middlesex, Lord's, 2013
BEST BOWLING: 6-29 Sussex vs South Africa A, Arundel, 2017

WHAT GOT YOU INTO CRICKET? Regularly dismissing Chris Nash at Horsham CC when I was aged seven
FAMILY TIES? My dad played for Sussex Second XI and Horsham
'ROY OF THE ROVERS' MOMENT? Taking 8-38 (including a hat-trick) and scoring 46* for Sussex U13
BEST OPPOSING PLAYER IN COUNTY CRICKET? Chris Nash (Not)
YOUNG OPPOSING PLAYER WHO HAS IMPRESSED YOU? Mason Crane (Ham) – a fellow leg-spinner who has made his England debut at such a young age
IF YOU WEREN'T A CRICKETER? I'd be running a one-stop building contractor business
SURPRISING FACT ABOUT YOU? I backed Don Cossack for the 2016 Cheltenham Gold Cup
SURPRISING FACT ABOUT A TEAMMATE? Laurie Evans never leaves the dressing room without checking his hair
WHERE IS PARADISE? Harbour Lights nightclub, Barbados
CRICKETING HERO? Shane Warne
TWITTER: @willbeer18

Batting	Mat	Inns	NO	Runs	HS	Ave	SR	100	50	Ct	St
First-class	14	16	3	288	39	22.15	31.44	0	0	5	0
List A	53	32	9	349	45*	15.17	83.29	0	0	10	0
T20s	99	52	17	328	37	9.37	127.62	0	0	21	0

Bowling	Mat	Balls	Runs	Wkts	BBI	BBM	Ave	Econ	SR	5w	10
First-class	14	1607	898	29	6/29	11/91	30.96	3.35	55.4	2	1
List A	53	2226	1919	47	3/27	3/27	40.82	5.17	47.3	0	0
T20s	99	1764	2162	77	3/14	3/14	28.07	7.35	22.9	0	0

IAN BELL

RHB / RM / R4 / W0 / MVP58

FULL NAME: Ian Ronald Bell
BORN: April 11, 1982, Walsgrave, Coventry
SQUAD NO: 4
HEIGHT: 5ft 10in
NICKNAME: Belly
EDUCATION: Princethorpe College, Rugby
TEAMS: England, Warwickshire, Perth Scorchers
ROLE: Batsman
DEBUT: Test: 2004; ODI: 2004; T20I: 2006; First-class: 1999; List A: 1999; T20: 2003

BEST BATTING: 262* Warwickshire vs Sussex, Horsham, 2004
BEST BOWLING: 4-4 Warwickshire vs Middlesex, Lord's, 2004
COUNTY CAP: 2001; **BENEFIT:** 2011

'ROY OF THE ROVERS' MOMENT? Winning the County Championship with Warwickshire and Ashes victories
CRICKETING HEROES? Ricky Ponting, Dominic Ostler, Jeetan Patel
NON-CRICKETING HEROES? Gary Shaw, Gordon Cowans
IF YOU WEREN'T A CRICKETER? I'd be sitting at the Holte End watching the Villa
SURPRISING FACT? I have an honorary doctorate at Coventry University
TWITTER: @Ian_Bell

Batting	Mat	Inns	NO	Runs	HS	Ave	SR	100	50	Ct	St
Tests	118	205	24	7727	235	42.69	49.46	22	46	100	0
ODIs	161	157	14	5416	141	37.87	77.16	4	35	54	0
T20Is	8	8	1	188	60*	26.85	115.33	0	1	4	0
First-class	292	492	51	19129	262*	43.37		51	101	220	0
List A	310	296	30	10904	158	40.99		12	79	107	0
T20s	89	85	10	2115	90	28.20	121.48	0	13	33	0

Bowling	Mat	Balls	Runs	Wkts	BBI	BBM	Ave	Econ	SR	5w	10
Tests	118	108	76	1	1/33	1/33	76.00	4.22	108.0	0	0
ODIs	161	88	88	6	3/9	3/9	14.66	6.00	14.6	0	0
T20Is	8	-	-	-	-	-	-	-	-	-	-
First-class	292	2875	1615	47	4/4	6/45	34.36	3.37	61.1	0	0
List A	310	1290	1138	33	5/41	5/41	34.48	5.29	39.0	1	0
T20s	89	132	186	3	1/12	1/12	62.00	8.45	44.0	0	0

DANIEL BELL-DRUMMOND RHB/RM/R1/W0/MVP44

KENT

FULL NAME: Daniel James Bell-Drummond
BORN: August 4, 1993, Lewisham, London
SQUAD NO: 23
HEIGHT: 5ft 11in
NICKNAME: DBD, Deebz
EDUCATION: Millfield School, Somerset; Anglia Ruskin University
TEAMS: Kent, England Lions
ROLE: Batsman
DEBUT: First-class: 2011; List A: 2011; T20: 2011

BEST BATTING: 206* Kent vs Loughborough MCCU, Canterbury, 2016
COUNTY CAP: 2015

FAMILY TIES? My father got me into cricket. I've always really enjoyed spending time at my local club Catford Wanderers CC
'ROY OF THE ROVERS' MOMENT? Making my first-class debut
YOUNG OPPOSING PLAYER WHO HAS IMPRESSED YOU? Tom Helm (Mid)
CRICKETING HEROES? Brian Lara, Kevin Pietersen, Chris Gayle, Marcus Trescothick
NON-CRICKETING HEROES? Nelson Mandela, Muhammad Ali, Thierry Henry
IF YOU WEREN'T A CRICKETER? I'd be a musician
TWITTER: @deebzz23

Batting	Mat	Inns	NO	Runs	HS	Ave	SR	100	50	Ct	St
First-class	82	138	12	4385	206*	34.80	49.98	9	23	37	0
List A	71	70	7	2604	171*	41.33	79.95	5	17	26	0
T20s	60	60	4	1557	112*	27.80	130.51	1	10	17	0

Bowling	Mat	Balls	Runs	Wkts	BBI	BBM	Ave	Econ	SR	5w	10
First-class	82	47	64	0	-	-	-	8.17	-	0	0
List A	71	12	15	0	-	-	-	7.50	-	0	0
T20s	60	-	-	-	-	-	-	-	-	-	-

GARETH BERG RHB / RMF / R0 / W0 / MVP20

FULL NAME: Gareth Kyle Berg
BORN: January 18, 1981, Cape Town, South Africa
SQUAD NO: 13
HEIGHT: 6ft
NICKNAME: Ice, Bergy, Ford
EDUCATION: South African College School, Cape Town
TEAMS: Italy, Hampshire, Middlesex
ROLE: Allrounder
DEBUT: First-class: 2008; List A: 2008; T20: 2009

BEST BATTING: 130* Middlesex vs Leicestershire, Leicester, 2011
BEST BOWLING: 6-56 Hampshire vs Yorkshire, Southampton, 2016
COUNTY CAP: 2010 (Middlesex)

BEST ADVICE EVER RECEIVED? Hit the ball, hit the stumps
'ROY OF THE ROVERS' MOMENT? Every day I wake up I cherish the fact that I've made it to first-class cricket
BEST THING ABOUT YOUR HOME GROUND? That someone's dream to build this amazing stadium gives us the opportunity to play in his playground
BEST OPPOSING PLAYER IN COUNTY CRICKET? Marcus Trescothick (Som)
YOUNG OPPOSING PLAYER WHO HAS IMPRESSED YOU? Jamie Porter (Ess)
IF YOU WEREN'T A CRICKETER? I'd be a professional pianist
SURPRISING FACT ABOUT YOU? I'm Batman
WHERE IS PARADISE? Home with my kids and my beautiful fiancée
CRICKETING HERO? I've never had a hero
TWITTER: @Bergy646

Batting	Mat	Inns	NO	Runs	HS	Ave	SR	100	50	Ct	St
First-class	112	170	20	4510	130*	30.06	66.44	2	25	60	0
List A	81	61	10	1151	75	22.56	89.85	0	5	30	0
T20s	80	61	21	987	90	24.67	127.51	0	3	21	0

Bowling	Mat	Balls	Runs	Wkts	BBI	BBM	Ave	Econ	SR	5w	10
First-class	112	14830	7403	239	6/56	7/45	30.97	2.99	62.0	4	0
List A	81	2549	2280	64	4/24	4/24	35.62	5.36	39.8	0	0
T20s	80	1417	1845	68	4/20	4/20	27.13	7.81	20.8	0	0

DOM BESS

RHB / OB / R0 / W0

SOMERSET

FULL NAME: Dominic Mark Bess
BORN: July 22, 1997, Exeter, Devon
SQUAD NO: 22
HEIGHT: 5ft 11in
NICKNAME: Calf, Bessy
EDUCATION: Blundell's School, Tiverton, Devon
TEAMS: Somerset, England Lions
ROLE: Bowler
DEBUT: First-class: 2016; T20: 2016

BEST BATTING: 55 Somerset vs Surrey, Taunton, 2017
BEST BOWLING: 7-117 Somerset vs Hampshire, Taunton, 2017

WHAT GOT YOU INTO CRICKET? Playing with my grandad in his garden
'ROY OF THE ROVERS' MOMENT? Beating Middlesex at Taunton last year to keep ourselves in Division One
BEST THING ABOUT YOUR HOME GROUND? The fans – always out in good numbers and cheering us on. Or the pitches – they have spun and kept me in a job!
YOUNG OPPOSING PLAYER WHO HAS IMPRESSED YOU? Adam Hose (War) – very good batman against red and white ball. Hits it very cleanly
IF YOU WEREN'T A CRICKETER? I'd be working for my old man as an electrician
SURPRISING FACT ABOUT YOU? My head is abnormally square and flat
SURPRISING FACT ABOUT A TEAMMATE? George Bartlett doesn't know his alphabet
WHERE IS PARADISE? New York
CRICKETING HERO? Graeme Swann
NON-CRICKETING HERO? Jonny Wilkinson
TWITTER: @DomBess99

Batting	Mat	Inns	NO	Runs	HS	Ave	SR	100	50	Ct	St
First-class	13	21	4	320	55	18.82	50.31	0	1	10	0
T20s	1	1	0	1	1	1.00	50.00	0	0	0	0

Bowling	Mat	Balls	Runs	Wkts	BBI	BBM	Ave	Econ	SR	5w	10
First-class	13	2368	1219	54	7/117	10/162	22.57	3.08	43.8	6	1
T20s	1	24	31	1	1/31	1/31	31.00	7.75	24.0	0	0

SAM BILLINGS

RHB / WK / R0 / W0

FULL NAME: Samuel William Billings
BORN: June 15, 1991, Pembury, Kent
SQUAD NO: 7
HEIGHT: 6ft
NICKNAME: Bilbo, Skittles
EDUCATION: Haileybury and Imperial College, Hertfordshire; Loughborough University
TEAMS: England, Kent, Delhi Daredevils, Sydney Sixers
ROLE: Batsman/wicketkeeper
DEBUT: ODI: 2015; T20I: 2015; First-class: 2011; List A: 2011; T20: 2011

KENT

BEST BATTING: 171 Kent vs Gloucestershire, Bristol, 2016
COUNTY CAP: 2015

'ROY OF THE ROVERS' MOMENT? Making my England debut
CRICKETING HEROES? Adam Gilchrist and Sachin Tendulkar – both phenomenal players. One is the best-ever in my opinion and the other single-handedly changed the role of the wicketkeeper
NON-CRICKETING HEROES? Lewis Hamilton, David Beckham and Cristiano Ronaldo – all unbelievable athletes who have excelled in their fields
IF YOU WEREN'T A CRICKETER? I'd be working for the family business or in the City. I'm very driven – if I want something I'll work tirelessly to get it
TWITTER: @sambillings

Batting	Mat	Inns	NO	Runs	HS	Ave	SR	100	50	Ct	St
ODIs	13	10	0	248	62	24.80	93.23	0	2	10	0
T20Is	17	15	0	205	53	13.66	134.86	0	1	11	1
First-class	53	75	7	2271	171	33.39	60.96	3	11	137	9
List A	77	69	12	2444	175	42.87	107.80	5	17	70	7
T20s	132	125	15	2441	78*	22.19	128.06	0	12	77	10

Bowling	Mat	Balls	Runs	Wkts	BBI	BBM	Ave	Econ	SR	5w	10
ODIs	13	-	-	-	-	-	-	-	-	-	-
T20Is	17	-	-	-	-	-	-	-	-	-	-
First-class	53	1	4	0	-	-	-	24.00	-	0	0
List A	77	-	-	-	-	-	-	-	-	-	-
T20s	132	-	-	-	-	-	-	-	-	-	-

ALEX BLAKE

KENT

FULL NAME: Alexander James Blake
BORN: January 25, 1989, Farnborough, Kent
SQUAD NO: 10
HEIGHT: 6ft 2in
NICKNAME: Blakey, Butler, TS
EDUCATION: Hayes Secondary School, Kent; Leeds Metropolitan University
TEAMS: Kent
ROLE: Batsman
DEBUT: First-class: 2008; List A: 2007; T20: 2010

BEST BATTING: 105* Kent vs Yorkshire, Headingley, 2010
BEST BOWLING: 2-9 Kent vs Pakistanis, Canterbury, 2010

WHAT GOT YOU INTO CRICKET? Watching my dad play club cricket for Bromley Town CC on Saturdays
'ROY OF THE ROVERS' MOMENT? My one and only first-class hundred!
BEST THING ABOUT YOUR HOME GROUND? That it's so picturesque. It even has a tree on it
BEST OPPOSING PLAYER IN COUNTY CRICKET? Colin Ingram (Gla)
YOUNG OPPOSING PLAYER WHO HAS IMPRESSED YOU? Jofra Archer (Sus) – very skilful and deceptively quick
IF YOU WEREN'T A CRICKETER? I'd be a trader
SURPRISING FACT ABOUT YOU? I can name every player's squad number in county cricket (give or take)
SURPRISING FACT ABOUT A TEAMMATE? Adam Riley is an avid trainspotter
WHERE IS PARADISE? Las Vegas
CRICKETING HERO? As a fellow left-hander, I hugely admired Graham Thorpe as I was growing up
NON-CRICKETING HERO? Harry Kane – bangs in the goals for the mighty Spurs
TWITTER: @aj_blake10

Batting	Mat	Inns	NO	Runs	HS	Ave	SR	100	50	Ct	St
First-class	38	60	6	1343	105*	24.87	57.78	1	6	23	0
List A	86	72	16	1598	116	28.53	95.63	1	9	42	0
T20s	92	80	22	1236	71*	21.31	130.65	0	5	50	0

Bowling	Mat	Balls	Runs	Wkts	BBI	BBM	Ave	Econ	SR	5w	10
First-class	38	204	129	3	2/9	2/9	43.00	3.79	68.0	0	0
List A	86	84	74	3	2/13	2/13	24.66	5.28	28.0	0	0
T20s	92	-	-	-	-	-	-	-	-	-	-

JACK BLATHERWICK   RHB / RFM / RO / WO

FULL NAME: Jack Morgan Blatherwick
BORN: June 4, 1998, Nottingham
SQUAD NO: 80
HEIGHT: 6ft 3in
NICKNAME: Blathers
EDUCATION: Holgate Academy, Hucknall;
Central College, Nottingham
TEAMS: Nottinghamshire, England U19
ROLE: Bowler

NOTTINGHAMSHIRE

WHAT GOT YOU INTO CRICKET? My family. And Andrew Flintoff in 2005
BEST ADVICE EVER RECEIVED? Be yourself, don't follow the crowd
BEST THING ABOUT YOUR HOME GROUND? The fans – they always bring a great
atmosphere and make you feel they're behind you with every ball
BEST OPPOSING PLAYER IN COUNTY CRICKET? Jofra Archer (Sus)
YOUNG OPPOSING PLAYER WHO HAS IMPRESSED YOU? Harry Brook (Yor) – bowling at him
is like bowling at a wall
SURPRISING FACT ABOUT A TEAMMATE? Luke Wood gets through three cans of hairspray
every month
WHERE IS PARADISE? The Maldives
CRICKETING HERO? Andrew Flintoff – for his whole persona. Always up for the fight
TWITTER: @BlatherwickJM
NOTES: The fast bowler has been a regular fixture in the Notts Second XI and England
Under-19s over the past couple of seasons and also toured Barbados with the
Nottinghamshire first team in early 2016. "I'll be starting with the seconds and trying to take
as many wickets as I can and then hopefully at the back end of the season I can put myself
in contention for a first-team spot," said Blatherwick

JOSH BOHANNON

RHB / RMF / R0 / W0

FULL NAME: Joshua James Bohannon
BORN: April 9, 1997, Bolton, Lancashire
SQUAD NO: 20
HEIGHT: 5ft 9in
NICKNAME: Bo'ey
EDUCATION: Harper Green High School, Bolton
TEAMS: Lancashire
ROLE: Allrounder

WHAT GOT YOU INTO CRICKET? I started watching my brother play for a local team and then began playing there myself
BEST ADVICE EVER RECEIVED? Train hard, play hard
'ROY OF THE ROVERS' MOMENT? Signing my first professional contract with Lancashire ahead of the 2018 season
BEST THING ABOUT YOUR HOME GROUND? Everything! Old Trafford is the best ground in the country
IF YOU WEREN'T A CRICKETER? That's a very good question
SURPRISING FACT ABOUT YOU? I played junior cricket alongside Haseeb Hameed at Farnworth Social Circle CC (Bolton League)
WHERE IS PARADISE? Little Bay Beach, Sydney (I spent the winter in Sydney playing grade cricket for Randwick Petersham)
CRICKETING HERO? Joe Root – for the way he goes about his batting, his captaincy, and the game in general
NON-CRICKETING HERO? My dad – he's an inspiration to me
TWITTER: @joshbo97

RAVI BOPARA

RHB / RM / R1 / W0 / MVP19

FULL NAME: Ravinder Singh Bopara
BORN: May 4, 1985, Forest Gate, London
SQUAD NO: 25
HEIGHT: 5ft 10in
NICKNAME: Puppy
EDUCATION: Brampton Manor, London
TEAMS: England, Essex, Auckland, Chittagong Kings, Dhaka Dynamites, Gloucestershire, Karachi Kings, Kings XI Punjab, Sunrisers Hyderabad, Sydney Sixers
ROLE: Allrounder
DEBUT: Test: 2007; ODI: 2007; T20I: 2008; First-class: 2002; List A: 2002; T20: 2003

ESSEX

BEST BATTING: 229 Essex vs Northamptonshire, Chelmsford, 2007
BEST BOWLING: 5-49 Essex vs Derbyshire, Chelmsford, 2016
COUNTY CAP: 2005 (Essex); **BENEFIT:** 2015 (Essex)

FAMILY TIES? My brother played Essex age-group cricket
'ROY OF THE ROVERS' MOMENT? Scoring 201* against Leicestershire in a one-day match, playing in the IPL, and scoring three centuries in a row for England
CRICKETING HEROES? Sachin Tendulkar
NON-CRICKETING HEROES? My dad, my son, my family
SURPRISING FACT? I have a fast-food business
TWITTER: @ravibopara

Batting	Mat	Inns	NO	Runs	HS	Ave	SR	100	50	Ct	St
Tests	13	19	1	575	143	31.94	52.89	3	0	6	0
ODIs	120	109	21	2695	101*	30.62	77.84	1	14	35	0
T20Is	38	35	10	711	65*	28.44	118.69	0	3	7	0
First-class	196	318	34	11475	229	40.40	51.40	27	48	100	0
List A	306	285	55	9265	201*	40.28		14	55	99	0
T20s	280	259	50	5721	105*	27.37	119.23	1	31	93	0

Bowling	Mat	Balls	Runs	Wkts	BBI	BBM	Ave	Econ	SR	5w	10
Tests	13	434	290	1	1/39	1/39	290.00	4.00	434.0	0	0
ODIs	120	1860	1523	40	4/38	4/38	38.07	4.91	46.5	0	0
T20Is	38	322	387	16	4/10	4/10	24.18	7.21	20.1	0	0
First-class	196	14476	8803	239	5/49	7/23	36.83	3.64	60.5	3	0
List A	306	7345	6467	229	5/63	5/63	28.24	5.28	32.0	1	0
T20s	280	3826	4725	191	6/16	6/16	24.73	7.40	20.0	1	0

SCOTT BORTHWICK

LHB / LB / R3 / W0

SURREY

FULL NAME: Scott George Borthwick
BORN: April 19, 1990, Sunderland, County Durham
SQUAD NO: 6
HEIGHT: 5ft 10in
NICKNAME: Badger
EDUCATION: Farringdon Community Sports College, Sunderland
TEAMS: England, Surrey, Chilaw Marians, Durham, Wellington
ROLE: Allrounder
DEBUT: Test: 2014; ODI: 2011; T20I: 2011; First-class 2009; List A: 2009; T20: 2008

BEST BATTING: 216 Durham vs Middlesex, Chester-le-Street, 2014
BEST BOWLING: 6-70 Durham vs Surrey, The Oval, 2013

WHAT GOT YOU INTO CRICKET? Watching my dad slog a few on a Saturday afternoon
STRANGEST THING SEEN IN A GAME? Steve Harmison bowling a bouncer at Tony Frost and hitting him on the head and his glasses falling to me at short-leg
'ROY OF THE ROVERS' MOMENT? Scoring a first-class double hundred
CRICKETING HEROES? Shane Warne, Graham Thorpe
NON-CRICKETING HERO? Niall Quinn
IF YOU WEREN'T A CRICKETER? Naturally I'd be playing for Sunderland FC
SURPRISING FACT? I know Only Fools And Horses word for word
UNUSUAL OBJECT AT HOME? A snooker cue
TWITTER: @Borthwick16

Batting	Mat	Inns	NO	Runs	HS	Ave	SR	100	50	Ct	St
Tests	1	2	0	5	4	2.50	26.31	0	0	2	0
ODIs	2	2	0	18	15	9.00	112.50	0	0	0	0
T20Is	1	1	0	14	14	14.00	87.50	0	0	1	0
First-class	141	238	23	7756	216	36.07	54.14	16	41	185	0
List A	95	70	10	1304	87	21.73	78.17	0	7	30	0
T20s	87	48	17	541	62	17.45	96.26	0	1	38	0

Bowling	Mat	Balls	Runs	Wkts	BBI	BBM	Ave	Econ	SR	5w	10
Tests	1	78	82	4	3/33	4/82	20.50	6.30	19.5	0	0
ODIs	2	54	72	0	-	-	-	8.00	-	0	0
T20Is	1	24	15	1	1/15	1/15	15.00	3.75	24.0	0	0
First-class	141	11484	7582	200	6/70	8/84	37.91	3.96	57.4	3	0
List A	95	2672	2690	65	5/38	5/38	41.38	6.04	41.1	1	0
T20s	87	1088	1457	63	4/18	4/18	23.12	8.03	17.2	0	0

DOUG BRACEWELL

RHB / RFM / R0 / W0

FULL NAME: Douglas Andrew John Bracewell
BORN: September 28, 1990, Tauranga, Bay of Plenty, New Zealand
SQUAD NO: TBC
TEAMS: New Zealand, Northamptonshire, Central Districts, Delhi Daredevils
ROLE: Bowler
DEBUT: Test: 2011; ODI: 2011; T20I: 2011; First-class: 2008; List A: 2008; T20: 2010

BEST BATTING: 105 Central Districts vs Queenstown, Queenstown, 2015
BEST BOWLING: 7-35 Central Districts vs Canterbury, Rangiora, 2013

TWITTER: @DougBracewell
NOTES: Northamptonshire have signed Bracewell as their overseas player for the start of the season, with South African allrounder Rory Kleinveldt set to replace him for the beginning of the One-Day Cup campaign. A bowling allrounder, Bracewell comes from a family steeped in cricketing tradition. His father Brendon played six Tests for New Zealand, while his uncle John was a mainstay of the national side for many years before later coaching Gloucestershire, the Black Caps and most recently Ireland. Doug claimed a five-for on Test debut against Zimbabwe in 2011 before taking nine wickets during a famous win over Australia in Hobart in just his third match. "He will give us the additional firepower we need alongside an already high-quality attacking unit," said Northants head coach David Ripley

Batting	Mat	Inns	NO	Runs	HS	Ave	SR	100	50	Ct	St
Tests	27	45	4	568	47	13.85	46.36	0	0	10	0
ODIs	16	9	2	79	30	11.28	58.51	0	0	3	0
T20Is	17	9	5	77	21*	19.25	135.08	0	0	5	0
First-class	82	125	18	2914	105	27.23	57.50	2	15	40	0
List A	63	46	9	846	80	22.86	90.19	0	4	17	0
T20s	50	33	14	525	37	27.63	146.64	0	0	16	0

Bowling	Mat	Balls	Runs	Wkts	BBI	BBM	Ave	Econ	SR	5w	10
Tests	27	4984	2796	72	6/40	9/60	38.83	3.36	69.2	2	0
ODIs	16	794	667	22	4/55	4/55	30.31	5.04	36.0	0	0
T20Is	17	274	418	19	3/25	3/25	22.00	9.15	14.4	0	0
First-class	82	14898	8513	253	7/35	9/60	33.64	3.42	58.8	8	0
List A	63	2807	2390	82	4/43	4/43	29.14	5.10	34.2	0	0
T20s	50	845	1228	55	3/21	3/21	22.32	8.71	15.3	0	0

JAMES BRACEY

LHB / WK / R0 / W0

FULL NAME: James Robert Bracey
BORN: May 3, 1997, Bristol
SQUAD NO: TBC
HEIGHT: 6ft 1in
NICKNAME: Bob, Brace, Dagger
EDUCATION: The Ridings High School, Bristol; SGS Filton College; Loughborough University
TEAMS: Gloucestershire
ROLE: Wicketkeeper/batsman
DEBUT: First-class: 2016

BEST BATTING: 156 Gloucestershire vs Glamorgan, Cardiff, 2017

WHAT GOT YOU INTO CRICKET? My local cricket club is outside my back gate
FAMILY TIES? My older brother Sam has played first-class cricket for Cardiff MCCU
BEST ADVICE EVER RECEIVED? Make the most of every opportunity
'ROY OF THE ROVERS' MOMENT? Winning the National Schools T20 region with SGS Filton College. I scored 115 not out as we beat Millfield in the regional final – the first time the college had ever beaten Millfield
BEST THING ABOUT YOUR HOME GROUND? The new flats at one end and the new stands enhance the atmosphere
BEST OPPOSING PLAYER IN COUNTY CRICKET? Steve Magoffin (Wor)
YOUNG OPPOSING PLAYER WHO HAS IMPRESSED YOU? Sam Cook (Ess) – good young seamer who took crucial wickets in the Championship for 2017 champions Essex
IF YOU WEREN'T A CRICKETER? I'd be an elite sport psychologist
SURPRISING FACT ABOUT YOU? I was probably the only child ever who did not like Ketchup or baked beans
WHERE IS PARADISE? Barbados
CRICKETING HERO? Alastair Cook – for his temperament and sheer runs
NON-CRICKETING HERO? Rickie Lambert – Bristol Rovers legend
TWITTER: @bobbybracey114

Batting	Mat	Inns	NO	Runs	HS	Ave	SR	100	50	Ct	St
First-class	7	10	1	463	156	51.44	52.08	1	3	6	0

Bowling	Mat	Balls	Runs	Wkts	BBI	BBM	Ave	Econ	SR	5w	10
First-class	7	-	-	-	-	-	-	-	-	-	-

TIM BRESNAN
RHB / RFM / R0 / W0 / MVP35

FULL NAME: Timothy Thomas Bresnan
BORN: February 28, 1985, Pontefract, Yorkshire
SQUAD NO: 16
HEIGHT: 6ft
NICKNAME: Brez, Brezzylad
EDUCATION: Castleford High School, West Yorkshire; New College Pontefract
TEAMS: England, Yorkshire, Hobart Hurricanes, Perth Scorchers
ROLE: Allrounder
DEBUT: Test: 2009; ODI: 2006; T20I: 2006; First-class: 2003; List A: 2001; T20: 2003

YORKSHIRE

BEST BATTING: 169* Yorkshire vs Durham, Chester-le-Street, 2015
BEST BOWLING: 5-36 Yorkshire vs Nottinghamshire, Scarborough, 2016
COUNTY CAP: 2006; **BENEFIT:** 2014

'ROY OF THE ROVERS' MOMENT? The MCG on Boxing Day in the 2010/11 Ashes, with 96,000 people in the ground at 11am singing the national anthem
CRICKETING HEROES? Shaun Pollock, Jacques Kallis – great allrounders who played the game in the right way
NON-CRICKETING HEROES? Anyone in the armed forces – fighting to protect our rights and way of life while endangering themselves
IF YOU WEREN'T A CRICKETER? I'd be a builder
SURPRISING FACT? I'm a fully qualified scuba-diver
TWITTER: @timbresnan

Batting	Mat	Inns	NO	Runs	HS	Ave	SR	100	50	Ct	St
Tests	23	26	4	575	91	26.13	39.43	0	3	8	0
ODIs	85	64	20	871	80	19.79	90.25	0	1	20	0
T20Is	34	22	9	216	47*	16.61	127.05	0	0	10	0
First-class	182	242	38	6071	169*	29.75	47.81	6	31	92	0
List A	266	192	52	2964	95*	21.17	90.33	0	9	70	0
T20s	153	111	45	1412	51	21.39	131.34	0	1	53	0

Bowling	Mat	Balls	Runs	Wkts	BBI	BBM	Ave	Econ	SR	5w	10
Tests	23	4674	2357	72	5/48	8/141	32.73	3.02	64.9	1	0
ODIs	85	4221	3813	109	5/48	5/48	34.98	5.42	38.7	1	0
T20Is	34	663	887	24	3/10	3/10	36.95	8.02	27.6	0	0
First-class	182	30677	15861	511	5/36	8/51	31.03	3.10	60.0	8	0
List A	266	11732	10197	302	5/48	5/48	33.76	5.21	38.8	1	0
T20s	153	2981	3948	153	6/19	6/19	25.80	7.94	19.4	1	0

DANNY BRIGGS

RHB / SLA / RO / WO

SUSSEX

FULL NAME: Danny Richard Briggs
BORN: April 30, 1991, Newport, Isle of Wight
SQUAD NO: 21
HEIGHT: 6ft 2in
NICKNAME: Briggsy
EDUCATION: Carisbrooke High School
TEAMS: England, Sussex, Hampshire
ROLE: Bowler
DEBUT: ODI: 2012; T20I: 2012; First-class: 2009; List A: 2009; T20: 2010

BEST BATTING: 120* Sussex vs South Africa A, Arundel, 2017
BEST BOWLING: 6-45 England Lions vs Windward Islands, Roseau, 2011
COUNTY CAP: 2012 (Hampshire)

'ROY OF THE ROVERS' MOMENT? Winning the one-day double with Hampshire in 2012
BEST THING ABOUT YOUR HOME GROUND? The local fans
BEST OPPOSING PLAYER IN COUNTY CRICKET? Shivnarine Chanderpaul (Lan)
YOUNG OPPOSING PLAYER WHO HAS IMPRESSED YOU? Sam Curran (Sur) – seems to have a lot of skill and does well under pressure
IF YOU WEREN'T A CRICKETER? I'd be a golfer
WHERE IS PARADISE? Barbados
CRICKETING HERO? Daniel Vettori – he made it to the top of his field in all three formats. Always seems to be a step ahead
TWITTER: @DannyBriggs19

Batting	Mat	Inns	NO	Runs	HS	Ave	SR	100	50	Ct	St
ODIs	1	-	-	-	-	-	-	-	-	0	0
T20Is	7	1	1	0	0*	-	-	0	0	1	0
First-class	89	108	28	1420	120*	17.75		1	1	31	0
List A	82	39	17	278	25	12.63	94.88	0	0	27	0
T20s	127	25	17	78	13	9.75	109.85	0	0	21	0

Bowling	Mat	Balls	Runs	Wkts	BBI	BBM	Ave	Econ	SR	5w	10
ODIs	1	60	39	2	2/39	2/39	19.50	3.90	30.0	0	0
T20Is	7	108	199	5	2/25	2/25	39.80	11.05	21.6	0	0
First-class	89	16057	8103	233	6/45	9/96	34.77	3.02	68.9	8	0
List A	82	3638	3130	86	4/32	4/32	36.39	5.16	42.3	0	0
T20s	127	2587	3107	146	5/19	5/19	21.28	7.20	17.7	1	0

STUART BROAD

LHB / RFM / R0 / W0

FULL NAME: Stuart Christopher John Broad
BORN: June 24, 1986, Nottingham
SQUAD NO: 8
HEIGHT: 6ft 5in
NICKNAME: Broady
EDUCATION: Oakham School, Rutland
TEAMS: England, Nottinghamshire, Hobart Hurricanes, Kings XI Punjab, Leicestershire
ROLE: Bowler
DEBUT: Test: 2007; ODI: 2006; T20I: 2006; First-class: 2005; List A: 2005; T20: 2006

NOTTINGHAMSHIRE

BEST BATTING: 169 England vs Pakistan, Lord's, 2010
BEST BOWLING: 8-15 England vs Australia, Trent Bridge, 2015
COUNTY CAP: 2007 (Leicestershire)

FAMILY TIES? My father Chris played for England, Nottinghamshire and Gloucestershire and is now an ICC match official
SUPERSTITIONS? Three warm-up balls before I bowl a new spell
CRICKETING HEROES? Glenn McGrath, Shaun Pollock
NON-CRICKETING HEROES? Brian Clough, Lewis Hamilton
IF YOU WEREN'T A CRICKETER? I'd be a traffic warden
SURPRISING FACT? I often dream in French
TWITTER: @StuartBroad8

Batting	Mat	Inns	NO	Runs	HS	Ave	SR	100	50	Ct	St
Tests	114	164	21	2956	169	20.67	65.99	1	12	36	0
ODIs	121	68	25	529	45*	12.30	74.61	0	0	27	0
T20Is	56	26	10	118	18*	7.37	100.00	0	0	21	0
First-class	185	253	37	4679	169	21.66	64.11	1	24	65	0
List A	151	80	28	620	45*	11.92	75.88	0	0	32	0
T20s	85	32	12	152	18*	7.60	102.01	0	0	26	0

Bowling	Mat	Balls	Runs	Wkts	BBI	BBM	Ave	Econ	SR	5w	10
Tests	114	23533	11706	399	8/15	11/121	29.33	2.98	58.9	15	2
ODIs	121	6109	5364	178	5/23	5/23	30.13	5.26	34.3	1	0
T20Is	56	1173	1491	65	4/24	4/24	22.93	7.62	18.0	0	0
First-class	185	35393	18259	654	8/15	11/121	27.91	3.09	54.1	26	3
List A	151	7496	6591	216	5/23	5/23	30.51	5.27	34.7	1	0
T20s	85	1788	2144	100	4/24	4/24	21.44	7.19	17.8	0	0

CALLUM BRODRICK

DERBYSHIRE

FULL NAME: Callum Ashley James Brodrick
BORN: January 24, 1998, Burton-upon-Trent, Staffordshire
SQUAD NO: 19
EDUCATION: John Taylor High School, Barton-under-Needwood, Staffordshire
TEAMS: Derbyshire
ROLE: Batsman
DEBUT: First-class: 2017; T20: 2017

BEST BATTING: 52 Derbyshire vs West Indians, Derby, 2017

TWITTER: @callumbrodrick
NOTES: A promising young batsman, Brodrick signed his first professional contract in September 2017. The Derbyshire Academy graduate made his first-team debut last summer, going on to make six T20 appeareances as well as his first-class debut against West Indies, a match in which he top-scored with 52. Development coach Mal Loye said: "Callum is a talented local lad who has worked incredibly hard over the last 18 months and has demonstrated a real hunger to learn and improve his game. He has been rewarded with opportunities in the first team this summer and he has impressed all with his attitude, work ethic and ability. We look forward to seeing Callum continue his development"

Batting	Mat	Inns	NO	Runs	HS	Ave	SR	100	50	Ct	St
First-class	1	1	0	52	52	52.00	57.14	0	1	1	0
T20s	6	4	0	40	14	10.00	117.64	0	0	2	0

Bowling	Mat	Balls	Runs	Wkts	BBI	BBM	Ave	Econ	SR	5w	10
First-class	1	-	-	-	-	-	-	-	-	-	-
T20s	6	-	-	-	-	-	-	-	-	-	-

HARRY BROOK

RHB / RMF / RO / WO

FULL NAME: Harry Cherrington Brook
BORN: February 22, 1999, Keighley, Yorkshire
SQUAD NO: 88
HEIGHT: 6ft
NICKNAME: Brooky
EDUCATION: Sedbergh School, Cumbria
TEAMS: Yorkshire
ROLE: Batsman
DEBUT: First-class: 2016; List A: 2017

YORKSHIRE

BEST BATTING: 38 Yorkshire vs Middlesex, Lord's 2017
BEST BOWLING: 1-54 Yorkshire vs Somerset, Scarborough, 2017

BEST ADVICE EVER RECEIVED? What will be will be
'ROY OF THE ROVERS' MOMENT? My first-class debut for Yorkshire against Pakistan A at Headingley in 2016
BEST THING ABOUT YOUR HOME GROUND? The players and the people
YOUNG OPPOSING PLAYER WHO HAS IMPRESSED YOU? Prithvi Shaw (India U19) – he scored lots of runs against us when India U19 toured in 2017
SURPRISING FACT ABOUT YOU? I love Tinder
WHERE IS PARADISE? Home
CRICKETING HERO? Jacques Kallis – the best all-round player
NON-CRICKETING HERO? Tommy Shelby (Peaky Blinders)
TWITTER: @harry_brook88

Batting	Mat	Inns	NO	Runs	HS	Ave	SR	100	50	Ct	St
First-class	5	7	0	82	38	11.71	41.20	0	0	1	0
List A	1	-	-	-	-	-	-	-	-	0	0

Bowling	Mat	Balls	Runs	Wkts	BBI	BBM	Ave	Econ	SR	5w	10
First-class	5	114	65	1	1/54	1/65	65.00	3.42	114.0	0	0
List A	1	-	-	-	-	-	-	-	-	-	-

HENRY BROOKES

RHB / RMF / R0 / W0

WARWICKSHIRE

FULL NAME: Henry James Hamilton Brookes
BORN: August 21, 1999, Solihull, Warwickshire
SQUAD NO: 10
HEIGHT: 6ft 4in
NICKNAME: Brookesy
EDUCATION: Tudor Grange Academy, Solihull
TEAMS: Warwickshire
ROLE: Bowler
DEBUT: First-class: 2017

BEST BATTING: 15 Warwickshire vs Essex, Edgbaston, 2017

WHAT GOT YOU INTO CRICKET? My father
FAMILY TIES? My two brothers Ben and Ethan have both played age-group cricket for Warwickshire
BEST ADVICE EVER RECEIVED? Play late and straight
'ROY OF THE ROVERS' MOMENT? My County Championship debut for Warwickshire in 2017
BEST THING ABOUT YOUR HOME GROUND? The changing rooms are so spacious
BEST OPPOSING PLAYER IN COUNTY CRICKET? Alastair Cook (Ess)
YOUNG OPPOSING PLAYER WHO HAS IMPRESSED YOU? Jofra Archer (Sus) – his bowling looks effortless
IF YOU WEREN'T A CRICKETER? I'd be an engineer
SURPRISING FACT ABOUT YOU? I am a good cook
SURPRISING FACT ABOUT A TEAMMATE? I wouldn't have a clue!
WHERE IS PARADISE? The Maldives
CRICKETING HERO? Ian Botham – he was always so entertaining to watch with his aggressive brand of cricket
NON-CRICKETING HERO? My grandad
TWITTER: @BrookesHenry

Batting	Mat	Inns	NO	Runs	HS	Ave	SR	100	50	Ct	St
First-class	1	2	0	15	11	7.50	34.09	0	0	0	0

Bowling	Mat	Balls	Runs	Wkts	BBI	BBM	Ave	Econ	SR	5w	10
First-class	1	66	43	0	-	-	-	3.90	-	0	0

JACK BROOKS

RHB / RFM / R0 / W3

YORKSHIRE

FULL NAME: Jack Alexander Brooks
BORN: June 4, 1984, Oxford
SQUAD NO: 70
HEIGHT: 6ft 2in
NICKNAME: Animal, Ferret, SuBo, Headband Warrior, King of Oxford, Therapist
EDUCATION: Wheatley Park School, South Oxfordshire
TEAMS: Yorkshire, England Lions, Northamptonshire
ROLE: Bowler
DEBUT: First-class: 2009; List A: 2009; T20: 2010

BEST BATTING: 109* Yorkshire vs Lancashire, Old Trafford, 2017
BEST BOWLING: 6-65 Yorkshire vs Middlesex, Lord's, 2016
COUNTY CAP: 2012 (Northamptonshire); 2013 (Yorkshire)

'ROY OF THE ROVERS' MOMENT? My first-class debut against Australia in 2009 – I had been a clubbie just a year earlier
BEST THING ABOUT YOUR HOME GROUND? It seams around under cloud at Headingley. And we get decent support when we're winning
BEST OPPOSING PLAYER IN COUNTY CRICKET? Marcus Trescothick (Som)
YOUNG OPPOSING PLAYER WHO HAS IMPRESSED YOU? Jamie Porter (Ess) – for his consistency
IF YOU WEREN'T A CRICKETER? I'd be the village idiot
SURPRISING FACT ABOUT YOU? I breed ferrets
SURPRISING FACT ABOUT A TEAMMATE? Steve Patterson has a degree in Moaning
WHERE IS PARADISE? Oxfordshire
CRICKETING HEROES? Dennis Lillee, Curtly Ambrose, Allan Donald, Darren Gough, Jason Gillespie
NON-CRICKETING HERO? Miguel Ángel Jiménez
TWITTER: @brooksyferret

Batting	Mat	Inns	NO	Runs	HS	Ave	SR	100	50	Ct	St
First-class	106	123	46	1306	109*	16.96	54.59	1	3	28	0
List A	36	15	5	49	10	4.90	52.12	0	0	4	0
T20s	46	10	6	59	33*	14.75	134.09	0	0	9	0

Bowling	Mat	Balls	Runs	Wkts	BBI	BBM	Ave	Econ	SR	5w	10
First-class	106	18000	10439	383	6/65	9/84	27.25	3.47	46.9	14	0
List A	36	1584	1276	37	3/30	3/30	34.48	4.83	42.8	0	0
T20s	46	822	1014	38	5/21	5/21	26.68	7.40	21.6	1	0

BEN BROWN

SUSSEX

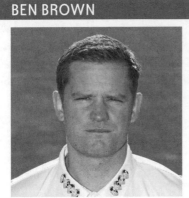

FULL NAME: Ben Christopher Brown
BORN: November 23, 1988, Crawley, Sussex
SQUAD NO: 26
HEIGHT: 5ft 8in
NICKNAME: Brownie, Goblin
EDUCATION: Ardingly College
TEAMS: Sussex
ROLE: Wicketkeeper/batsman
DEBUT: First-class: 2007; List A: 2007; T20: 2008

BEST BATTING: 163 Sussex vs Durham, Hove, 2014
BEST BOWLING: 1-48 Sussex vs Essex, Colchester, 2016
COUNTY CAP: 2014

WHAT GOT YOU INTO CRICKET? The local village culture was all about playing cricket and everyone played after school and on weekends
BEST THING ABOUT YOUR HOME GROUND? The people and staff – from gateman to caterers, everyone knows each other so it's a very warm atmosphere
BEST OPPOSING PLAYER IN COUNTY CRICKET? Chris Nash (Not)
IF YOU WEREN'T A CRICKETER? I'd possibly be a journalist, assuming I failed to make it at Chelsea FC
SURPRISING FACT ABOUT YOU? I don't like cheese
SURPRISING FACT ABOUT A TEAMMATE? William Beer goes out with my cousin
WHERE IS PARADISE? The Bay Hotel, Cape Town. Or mum and dad's for a Sunday roast
CRICKETING HERO? Adam Gilchrist – moved the role of wicketkeeper/batsman into a new era
NON-CRICKETING HERO? Gianfranco Zola
TWITTER: @Ben_brown26

Batting	Mat	Inns	NO	Runs	HS	Ave	SR	100	50	Ct	St
First-class	110	170	26	5464	163	37.94	62.63	13	29	289	15
List A	58	43	10	782	62	23.69	91.56	0	5	55	10
T20s	74	61	8	797	68	15.03	111.62	0	1	36	7

Bowling	Mat	Balls	Runs	Wkts	BBI	BBM	Ave	Econ	SR	5w	10
First-class	110	90	93	1	1/48	1/48	93.00	6.20	90.0	0	0
List A	58	-	-	-	-	-	-	-	-	-	-
T20s	74	-	-	-	-	-	-	-	-	-	-

CONNOR BROWN — RHB / OB / R0 / W0

FULL NAME: Connor Rhys Brown
BORN: April 28, 1997, Caerphilly, Wales
SQUAD NO: 28
HEIGHT: 6ft
NICKNAME: Browntown, Browny
EDUCATION: Y Pant Comprehensive School, Llantrisant; Cardiff Metropolitan University
TEAMS: Glamorgan
ROLE: Batsman
DEBUT: First-class: 2017

GLAMORGAN

BEST BATTING: 35 Glamorgan vs Gloucestershire, Cardiff, 2017

BEST ADVICE EVER RECEIVED? Back your ability no matter what
'ROY OF THE ROVERS' MOMENT? Making my first-class debut for Glamorgan at Cardiff in 2017
BEST THING ABOUT YOUR HOME GROUND? It's in Cardiff – the best city in the world
BEST OPPOSING PLAYER IN COUNTY CRICKET? Darren Stevens (Ken)
YOUNG OPPOSING PLAYER WHO HAS IMPRESSED YOU? Mason Crane (Ham) – he's still very young and it was a great achievement to make the Ashes squad
IF YOU WEREN'T A CRICKETER? I'd be a golfer
SURPRISING FACT ABOUT YOU? I do a fantastic homemade lasagne
SURPRISING FACT ABOUT A TEAMMATE? Owen Morgan bowls inswingers and calls himself a spinner
WHERE IS PARADISE? Barbados
CRICKETING HERO? AB de Villiers – for his ability to change a game and step up when his team needs him. Mitchell Starc – because he is very quick and very hostile
TWITTER: @connorbrown_97

Batting	Mat	Inns	NO	Runs	HS	Ave	SR	100	50	Ct	St
First-class	4	7	0	154	35	22.00	35.98	0	0	0	0

Bowling	Mat	Balls	Runs	Wkts	BBI	BBM	Ave	Econ	SR	5w	10
First-class	4	24	14	0	-	-	-	3.50	-	0	0

KARL BROWN

RHB / RM / RO / WO

LANCASHIRE

FULL NAME: Karl Robert Brown
BORN: May 17, 1988, Bolton, Lancashire
SQUAD NO: 14
HEIGHT: 5ft 10in
NICKNAME: Browny, Charlie
EDUCATION: Hesketh Fletcher CofE High School, Greater Manchester
TEAMS: Lancashire, Moors Sports Club
ROLE: Batsman
DEBUT: First-class: 2006; List A: 2007; T20: 2011

BEST BATTING: 132 Lancashire vs Glamorgan, Old Trafford, 2015
BEST BOWLING: 2-30 Lancashire vs Nottinghamshire, Trent Bridge, 2009
COUNTY CAP: 2015

FAMILY TIES? My dad played league cricket for Atherton CC and was the professional for Clifton CC
'ROY OF THE ROVERS' MOMENT? Scoring my maiden first-class and one-day hundreds and playing for England U19
CRICKETING HEROES? Andrew Flintoff, Stuart Law
NON-CRICKETING HEROES? Kevin Davies, Lionel Messi, Ronnie O'Sullivan, Phil Taylor, Sergio García
SURPRISING FACT? I played football for Wigan Athletic
TWITTER: @karlos173

Batting	Mat	Inns	NO	Runs	HS	Ave	SR	100	50	Ct	St
First-class	83	136	6	3505	132	26.96	46.46	2	22	51	0
List A	76	72	11	2331	129	38.21	83.63	2	14	21	0
T20s	84	81	9	1984	69	27.55	126.69	0	14	26	0

Bowling	Mat	Balls	Runs	Wkts	BBI	BBM	Ave	Econ	SR	5w	10
First-class	83	90	65	2	2/30	2/37	32.50	4.33	45.0	0	0
List A	76	6	17	0	-	-	-	17.00	-	0	0
T20s	84	-	-	-	-	-	-	-	-	-	-

PAT BROWN

RHB / RMF / R0 / W0

FULL NAME: Patrick Rhys Brown
BORN: August 23, 1998, Peterborough, Cambridgeshire
SQUAD NO: 36
HEIGHT: 6ft 2in
NICKNAME: Browny, Brownfish
EDUCATION: Bourne Grammar School, Lincolnshire; University of Worcester
TEAMS: Worcestershire
ROLE: Allrounder
DEBUT: First-class: 2017; T20: 2017

BEST BATTING: 5* Worcestershire vs Sussex, Worcester, 2017
BEST BOWLING: 2-15 Worcestershire vs Gloucestershire, Worcester, 2017

WHAT GOT YOU INTO CRICKET? My dad took me to a training session at a local club and I never looked back from there
BEST ADVICE EVER RECEIVED? You don't become a professional cricketer when you're 15 – keep working hard for your dream and when your chance comes, grab it with both hands
'ROY OF THE ROVERS' MOMENT? Beating Birmingham Bears in the T20 Blast at Edgbaston live on Sky – despite dropping a catch!
BEST THING ABOUT YOUR HOME GROUND? The view from the Graeme Hick Pavilion looking out towards the cathedral
BEST OPPOSING PLAYER IN COUNTY CRICKET? Wayne Madsen (Der)
YOUNG OPPOSING PLAYER WHO HAS IMPRESSED YOU? Liam Banks (War) – never felt like I can get on top of him when I've bowled at him. Always seems in control
SURPRISING FACT ABOUT YOU? I'm not as grumpy as I seem when I am bowling
CRICKETING HERO? Brett Lee – he offers a fantastic technical framework for bowling fast
NON-CRICKETING HERO? Steven Gerrard – fantastic leader, always gave 100 per cent, and lived for the pivotal moments
TWITTER: @patbrowny6

Batting	Mat	Inns	NO	Runs	HS	Ave	SR	100	50	Ct	St
First-class	4	5	3	12	5*	6.00	22.64	0	0	1	0
T20s	6	2	0	0	0	0.00	0.00	0	0	3	0

Bowling	Mat	Balls	Runs	Wkts	BBI	BBM	Ave	Econ	SR	5w	10
First-class	4	256	199	6	2/15	3/70	33.16	4.66	42.6	0	0
T20s	6	72	127	1	1/22	1/22	127.00	10.58	72.0	0	0

NICK BROWNE

LHB / LB / R3 / W0

FULL NAME: Nicholas Laurence Joseph Browne
BORN: March 24, 1991, Leytonstone, Essex
SQUAD NO: 10
HEIGHT: 6ft 3in
NICKNAME: Brownie, Orse
EDUCATION: Trinity Catholic High School, London
TEAMS: Essex
ROLE: Batsman
DEBUT: First-class: 2013; List A: 2015; T20: 2015

BEST BATTING: 255 Essex vs Derbyshire, Chelmsford, 2016
COUNTY CAP: 2015

WHAT GOT YOU INTO CRICKET? I was practically born into South Woodford Cricket Club, where there weren't enough hours in the day for me to play cricket
STRANGEST THING SEEN IN A GAME? When a certain ex-England left-arm spinner lay stretched out on all fours without even noticing that the ball had flown passed him towards the boundary
'ROY OF THE ROVERS' MOMENT? Scoring my maiden first-class hundred. I was lucky enough to have my family there at the ground, and to see my mother and father so emotional was a moment I'll never forget
CRICKETING HEROES? Alastair Cook, Graham Gooch, Marcus Trescothick
TWITTER: @NickBrowne4

Batting	Mat	Inns	NO	Runs	HS	Ave	SR	100	50	Ct	St
First-class	64	104	9	4257	255	44.81	50.69	13	17	48	0
List A	21	18	0	557	99	30.94	89.83	0	3	7	0
T20s	14	12	2	165	38	16.50	114.58	0	0	6	0

Bowling	Mat	Balls	Runs	Wkts	BBI	BBM	Ave	Econ	SR	5w	10
First-class	64	262	171	0	-	-	-	3.91	-	0	0
List A	21	-	-	-	-	-	-	-	-	-	-
T20s	14	-	-	-	-	-	-	-	-	-	-

NATHAN BUCK

RHB / RFM / R0 / W0

FULL NAME: Nathan Liam Buck
BORN: April 26, 1991, Leicester
SQUAD NO: 11
HEIGHT: 6ft 3in
NICKNAME: Bucky, Top Bag
EDUCATION: Ashby Grammar School, Ashby-de-la-Zouch
TEAMS: Northamptonshire, England Lions, Lancashire, Leicestershire
ROLE: Bowler
DEBUT: First-class: 2009; List A: 2009; T20: 2010

BEST BATTING: 43 Northamptonshire vs Derbyshire, Derby, 2017
BEST BOWLING: 6-34 Northamptonshire vs Durham, Chester-le-Street, 2017
COUNTY CAP: 2011 (Leicestershire)

WHAT GOT YOU INTO CRICKET? My older brother Mitchell played, so I joined in with him at the age of 12 and it went from there
BEST ADVICE EVER RECEIVED? Always get off 'em
BEST THING ABOUT YOUR HOME GROUND? The lunches
YOUNG OPPOSING PLAYER WHO HAS IMPRESSED YOU? Max Holden (Mid)
SURPRISING FACT ABOUT YOU? I got seven A stars and three As in my GCSEs
SURPRISING FACT ABOUT A TEAMMATE? Josh Cobb's teeth are real
WHERE IS PARADISE? Somewhere without bowling boots
NON-CRICKETING HERO? Ronald McDonald
UNUSUAL OBJECT AT HOME? A grip cone beside my bed
TWITTER: @nathanbuck17

Batting	Mat	Inns	NO	Runs	HS	Ave	SR	100	50	Ct	St
First-class	74	102	29	923	43	12.64		0	0	15	0
List A	47	20	8	92	21	7.66	61.33	0	0	10	0
T20s	35	7	5	19	8*	9.50	79.16	0	0	5	0

Bowling	Mat	Balls	Runs	Wkts	BBI	BBM	Ave	Econ	SR	5w	10
First-class	74	11760	6902	194	6/34	7/79	35.57	3.52	60.6	7	0
List A	47	1873	1958	53	4/39	4/39	36.94	6.27	35.3	0	0
T20s	35	735	1039	45	4/26	4/26	23.08	8.48	16.3	0	0

GLAMORGAN

FULL NAME: Kieran Andrew Bull
BORN: April 5, 1995, Haverfordwest, Pembrokeshire
SQUAD NO: 11
HEIGHT: 6ft 1in
NICKNAME: Bully
EDUCATION: Queen Elizabeth High School, Haverfordwest; Cardiff Metropolitan University
TEAMS: Glamorgan
ROLE: Bowler
DEBUT: First-class: 2014; List A: 2015

BEST BATTING: 31 Glamorgan vs Gloucestershire, Swansea, 2015
BEST BOWLING: 4-62 Glamorgan vs Kent, Canterbury, 2014

WHAT GOT YOU INTO CRICKET? Watching my brother play at our local club
STRANGEST THING SEEN IN A GAME? Play suspended due to a helicopter landing on the field
'ROY OF THE ROVERS' MOMENT? Making my first-class debut at Canterbury
YOUNG OPPOSING PLAYER WHO HAS IMPRESSED YOU? Jake Libby (Not)
CRICKETING HEROES? Darren Gough, Graeme Swann
NON-CRICKETING HEROES? Steven Gerrard, Ron Burgundy
SURPRISING FACT? I set off an alarm every time I walk into a shop due to the metal screw in my back. Aged 10 I moved to Spain to take up a place in a tennis academy and lived there for two years, representing Spain at age-group level. I was also ball boy for Rafael Nadal
UNUSUAL OBJECT AT HOME? A singing fish on the wall
TWITTER: @Kieran_Bull89

Batting	Mat	Inns	NO	Runs	HS	Ave	SR	100	50	Ct	St
First-class	7	10	3	69	31	9.85	23.15	0	0	1	0
List A	2	-	-	-	-	-	-	-	-	0	0

Bowling	Mat	Balls	Runs	Wkts	BBI	BBM	Ave	Econ	SR	5w	10
First-class	7	744	483	9	4/62	4/62	53.66	3.89	82.6	0	0
List A	2	52	48	1	1/40	1/40	48.00	5.53	52.0	0	0

MICHAEL BURGESS

RHB / WK / RO / WO

FULL NAME: Michael Gregory Kerran Burgess
BORN: July 8, 1994, Epsom
SQUAD NO: 5
HEIGHT: 6ft 1in
NICKNAME: Burge
EDUCATION: Cranleigh School; Loughborough University
TEAMS: Sussex, Leicestershire
ROLE: Wicketkeeper/batsman
DEBUT: First-class: 2014; List A: 2015; T20: 2016

BEST BATTING: 146 Sussex vs Nottinghamshire, Hove, 2017

BEST ADVICE EVER RECEIVED? Bat your own way
BEST THING ABOUT YOUR HOME GROUND? Picturesque location by the seafront
BEST OPPOSING PLAYER IN COUNTY CRICKET? Darren Stevens (Ken)
YOUNG OPPOSING PLAYER WHO HAS IMPRESSED YOU? Dominic Sibley (Sur) – he likes making big scores
IF YOU WEREN'T A CRICKETER? I'd be a teacher
SURPRISING FACT ABOUT YOU? I have unusually hairy legs for someone with no hair anywhere else
SURPRISING FACT ABOUT A TEAMMATE? Stuart Whittingham has a missing abdominal
WHERE IS PARADISE? The Alps
CRICKETING HERO? Brendon McCullum – he has always played aggressively and entertained
NON-CRICKETING HERO? Ian Poulter – always rises to the occasion for the Ryder Cup
TWITTER: @mgkburgess

Batting	Mat	Inns	NO	Runs	HS	Ave	SR	100	50	Ct	St
First-class	13	18	2	777	146	48.56	64.21	1	4	23	0
List A	10	10	0	184	49	18.40	88.46	0	0	6	0
T20s	1	-	-	-	-	-	-	-	-	0	0

Bowling	Mat	Balls	Runs	Wkts	BBI	BBM	Ave	Econ	SR	5w	10
First-class	13	-	-	-	-	-	-	-	-	-	-
List A	10	-	-	-	-	-	-	-	-	-	-
T20s	1	-	-	-	-	-	-	-	-	-	-

RORY BURNS — LHB / RM / WK / R4 / W0 / MVP96

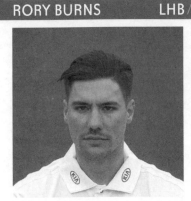

FULL NAME: Rory Joseph Burns
BORN: August 26, 1990, Epsom, Surrey
SQUAD NO: 17
HEIGHT: 5ft 10in
NICKNAME: Fong, The Cat (goalkeeper)
EDUCATION: Whitgift School; City of London Freemen's; Cardiff Metropolitan University
TEAMS: Surrey
ROLE: Batsman
DEBUT: First-class: 2011; List A: 2012; T20: 2012

BEST BATTING: 219* Surrey vs Hampshire, The Oval, 2017
BEST BOWLING: 1-18 Surrey vs Middlesex, Lord's, 2013
COUNTY CAP: 2014

BEST ADVICE EVER RECEIVED? Watch the ball
'ROY OF THE ROVERS' MOMENT? Being off the field for only 30 mins during the whole of the Championship game against Hampshire last year, when I was captaining the side
BEST THING ABOUT YOUR HOME GROUND? The history. From FA Cups to the Ashes, The Oval has had it all
BEST OPPOSING PLAYER IN COUNTY CRICKET? Dom Sibley (War)
IF YOU WEREN'T A CRICKETER? I'd be a digital marketer
SURPRISING FACT ABOUT YOU? I love Smartwater
SURPRISING FACT ABOUT A TEAMMATE? Matthew Dunn labels his socks left and right and always wears them the wrong way round
CRICKETING HERO? Kumar Sangakkara – The King
NON-CRICKETING HERO? Chris and Christine Burns, for raising me and my brothers
UNUSUAL OBJECT AT HOME? A strong whisky collection
TWITTER: @roryburns17

Batting	Mat	Inns	NO	Runs	HS	Ave	SR	100	50	Ct	St
First-class	92	160	13	6199	219*	42.17	48.96	11	35	82	0
List A	41	40	6	1254	95	36.88	85.89	0	10	23	0
T20s	31	27	3	276	46*	11.50	103.37	0	0	9	1

Bowling	Mat	Balls	Runs	Wkts	BBI	BBM	Ave	Econ	SR	5w	10
First-class	92	180	127	2	1/18	1/18	63.50	4.23	90.0	0	0
List A	41	-	-	-	-	-	-	-	-	-	-
T20s	31	-	-	-	-	-	-	-	-	-	-

JOS BUTTLER

RHB / WK / R0 / W0

LANCASHIRE

FULL NAME: Joseph Charles Buttler
BORN: September 8, 1990, Taunton
SQUAD NO: 6
NICKNAME: Jose
EDUCATION: King's College, Taunton
TEAMS: England, Lancashire, Melbourne Renegades, Mumbai Indians, Somerset
ROLE: Wicketkeeper/batsman
DEBUT: Test: 2014; ODI: 2012; T20I: 2011; First-class: 2009; List A: 2009; T20: 2009

BEST BATTING: 144 Somerset vs Hampshire, Southampton, 2013
COUNTY CAP: 2013 (Somerset)

TWITTER: @josbuttler
NOTES: Signed for Lancashire in September 2013 to pursue more opportunities as a keeper after sharing duties with Craig Kieswetter at Somerset. Called up for England's limited-overs squads in 2012 and usurped Matt Prior as England's No.1 Test wicketkeeper in 2014, scoring 85 on Test debut against India at Southampton. Lost his place to Jonny Bairstow following a poor Ashes series, returned to the Test side on the 2016/17 tour of India but again couldn't hold on to his spot. Has three of England's four fastest ODI hundreds, including the quickest of all: a 46-ball whirlwind against Pakistan at Dubai in 2015. Plays very little Championship cricket but was Lancashire's leading run-scorer in the T20 Blast last summer. Has played for Mumbai Indians and was signed by Rajasthan Royals for the 2018 IPL

Batting	Mat	Inns	NO	Runs	HS	Ave	SR	100	50	Ct	St
Tests	18	30	5	784	85	31.36	55.52	0	6	54	0
ODIs	106	90	18	2787	129	38.70	118.04	5	15	137	19
T20Is	61	53	11	1069	73*	25.45	134.29	0	5	22	3
First-class	81	126	12	3593	144	31.51	58.77	4	20	168	2
List A	176	150	38	4953	129	44.22	119.29	7	31	189	24
T20s	213	192	38	4357	81	28.29	142.80	0	26	114	23

Bowling	Mat	Balls	Runs	Wkts	BBI	BBM	Ave	Econ	SR	5w	10
Tests	18	-	-	-	-	-	-	-	-	-	-
ODIs	106	-	-	-	-	-	-	-	-	-	-
T20Is	61	-	-	-	-	-	-	-	-	-	-
First-class	81	12	11	0	-	-	-	5.50	-	0	0
List A	176	-	-	-	-	-	-	-	-	-	-
T20s	213	-	-	-	-	-	-	-	-	-	-

EDDIE BYROM

LHB / OB / R0 / W0

SOMERSET

FULL NAME: Edward James Byrom
BORN: June 17, 1997, Harare, Zimbabwe
SQUAD NO: 97
HEIGHT: 6ft
NICKNAME: Ed
EDUCATION: King's College, Taunton
TEAMS: Somerset, Rising Stars
ROLE: Batsman
DEBUT: First-class: 2017

BEST BATTING: 152 Rising Stars vs Tuskers, Kwekwe, 2017

BEST ADVICE EVER RECEIVED? You're entitled to nothing – you have to work for everything you want
'ROY OF THE ROVERS' MOMENT? Beating Middlesex in the County Championship to stay in Division One at the end of last season
BEST THING ABOUT YOUR HOME GROUND? The supporters – they always turn up in great numbers. And the church in the background
YOUNG OPPOSING PLAYER WHO HAS IMPRESSED YOU? Liam Livingstone (Lan) – he has a great presence when he walks out to bat
IF YOU WEREN'T A CRICKETER? I'd be a Formula 1 driver for sure
SURPRISING FACT ABOUT YOU? I play the guitar
SURPRISING FACT ABOUT A TEAMMATE? Tom Banton cannot play a sweep shot, only a reverse sweep
WHERE IS PARADISE? Somewhere that's chilled-out and sunny
CRICKETING HERO? Brian Lara. Whenever West Indies were playing I would watch him bat and as soon as he got out I would change the channel. He was always a cut above
NON-CRICKETING HERO? Gary Vaynerchuk and Tony Robbins for their life-coaching advice. I listen to their podcasts all the time
TWITTER: @EddieByrom

Batting	Mat	Inns	NO	Runs	HS	Ave	SR	100	50	Ct	St
First-class	11	21	0	606	152	28.85	43.16	1	1	5	0

Bowling	Mat	Balls	Runs	Wkts	BBI	BBM	Ave	Econ	SR	5w	10
First-class	11	-	-	-	-	-	-	-	-	-	-

MICHAEL CARBERRY

LHB / OB / R4 / W0

FULL NAME: Michael Alexander Carberry
BORN: September 29, 1980, Croydon, Surrey
SQUAD NO: 15
HEIGHT: 5ft 11in
NICKNAME: Carbs
EDUCATION: St John Rigby College, Wigan
TEAMS: England, Leicestershire, Hampshire, Kent, Perth Scorchers, Surrey
ROLE: Batsman
DEBUT: Test: 2010; ODI: 2013; T20I: 2014; First-class: 2001; List A: 1999; T20: 2003

BEST BATTING: 300* Hampshire vs Yorkshire, Southampton, 2011
BEST BOWLING: 2-85 Hampshire vs Durham, Chester-le-Street, 2006
COUNTY CAP: 2006 (Hampshire)

TWITTER: @carbs646
NOTES: The 37-year-old opener joined Leicestershire in September 2017 after more than a decade at Hampshire. He will captain his new club in all three formats. Carberry made his Test debut against Bangladesh in 2010, scoring 30 and 34. It was three years until his next chance, when he was drafted in for the doomed tour of Australia in 2013/14. He was England's second-highest run-scorer overall in the series with 281 but hasn't played a Test since. Scored 300* against Yorkshire in Southampton 2011. Helped Hampshire to the T20-CB40 double in 2012. Hit over 1,000 first-class runs in 2015. Having survived a blood clot on the lung in 2010, Carberry was diagnosed with a cancerous tumour midway through the 2016 season but he returned to action last summer, albeit short of form

Batting	Mat	Inns	NO	Runs	HS	Ave	SR	100	50	Ct	St
Tests	6	12	0	345	60	28.75	41.31	0	1	7	0
ODIs	6	6	0	114	63	19.00	63.33	0	1	2	0
T20Is	1	1	0	7	7	7.00	100.00	0	0	1	0
First-class	204	357	25	13675	300*	41.18	50.95	35	66	93	0
List A	171	160	16	4659	150*	32.35		6	34	62	0
T20s	146	137	17	3720	100*	31.00	124.41	1	29	48	0

Bowling	Mat	Balls	Runs	Wkts	BBI	BBM	Ave	Econ	SR	5w	10
Tests	6	-	-	-	-	-	-	-	-	-	-
ODIs	6	6	12	0	-	-	-	12.00	-	0	0
T20Is	1	-	-	-	-	-	-	-	-	-	-
First-class	204	1565	1074	17	2/85	2/85	63.17	4.11	92.0	0	0
List A	171	322	297	11	3/37	3/37	27.00	5.53	29.2	0	0
T20s	146	18	19	1	1/16	1/16	19.00	6.33	18.0	0	0

LUKAS CAREY

RHB / RFM / R0 / W0

GLAMORGAN

FULL NAME: Lukas John Carey
BORN: July 17, 1997, Carmarthen, Wales
SQUAD NO: 17
EDUCATION: Pontarddulais Comprehensive
School, Swansea; Gower College Swansea
TEAMS: Glamorgan
ROLE: Bowler
DEBUT: First-class: 2016; List A: 2017; T20:
2017

BEST BATTING: 54 Glamorgan vs Worcestershire, Worcester, 2017
BEST BOWLING: 4-85 Glamorgan vs Northamptonshire, Northampton, 2017

TWITTER: @LukasCarey
NOTES: Hailing from Robert Croft's club Pontarddulais, Carey made a promising start to
his Glamorgan career in August 2016, picking up seven wickets against Northants with his
skiddy fast-medium seamers. Last year was a breakthrough season, with Carey taking 35
wickets at 30.03 in 10 Championship matches, as well as making his maiden first-class half-
century. Another graduate from Glamorgan's Academy, he joins Aneurin Donald and Kiran
Carlson in the ranks of talented local products looking to reinvigorate the Welsh club

Batting	Mat	Inns	NO	Runs	HS	Ave	SR	100	50	Ct	St
First-class	14	19	3	231	54	14.43	72.18	0	1	4	0
List A	4	1	1	9	9*	-	60.00	0	0	0	0
T20s	4	-	-	-	-	-	-	-	-	1	0

Bowling	Mat	Balls	Runs	Wkts	BBI	BBM	Ave	Econ	SR	5w	10
First-class	14	2185	1390	48	4/85	7/151	28.95	3.81	45.5	0	0
List A	4	180	183	3	1/21	1/21	61.00	6.10	60.0	0	0
T20s	4	42	61	2	1/19	1/19	30.50	8.71	21.0	0	0

KIRAN CARLSON

RHB / OB / R0 / W0

FULL NAME: Kiran Shah Carlson
BORN: May 16, 1998, Cardiff
SQUAD NO: 5
HEIGHT: 5ft 8in
NICKNAME: Peter Dinklage
EDUCATION: Whitchurch High School, Cardiff; Cardiff University
TEAMS: Glamorgan
ROLE: Allrounder
DEBUT: First-class: 2016; List A: 2016; T20: 2017

GLAMORGAN

BEST BATTING: 191 Glamorgan vs Gloucestershire, Cardiff, 2017
BEST BOWLING: 5-28 Glamorgan vs Northamptonshire, Northampton, 2016

WHAT GOT YOU INTO CRICKET? Playing catch with my dad
BEST ADVICE EVER RECEIVED? Relax and enjoy yourself
'ROY OF THE ROVERS' MOMENT? Playing on T20 Finals Day in 2017
BEST THING ABOUT YOUR HOME GROUND? The atmosphere at Cardiff for a Friday night T20 match
YOUNG OPPOSING PLAYER WHO HAS IMPRESSED YOU? Josh Tongue (Wor) – bowls quick
IF YOU WEREN'T A CRICKETER? I'd be a student
SURPRISING FACT ABOUT YOU? I'm half-Indian
SURPRISING FACT ABOUT A TEAMMATE? Andrew Salter won a competition for the biggest nose in west Wales when he was 13
WHERE IS PARADISE? On an Australian beach with a barbacue
CRICKETING HERO? Sachin Tendulkar
NON-CRICKETING HERO? My old man – he's selfless and gives everything without wanting anything in return
TWITTER: @kiran_carlson

Batting	Mat	Inns	NO	Runs	HS	Ave	SR	100	50	Ct	St
First-class	13	22	1	696	191	33.14	55.59	2	2	5	0
List A	9	9	0	223	63	24.77	99.55	0	1	2	0
T20s	5	2	0	3	3	1.50	42.85	0	0	2	0

Bowling	Mat	Balls	Runs	Wkts	BBI	BBM	Ave	Econ	SR	5w	10
First-class	13	270	178	6	5/28	5/78	29.66	3.95	45.0	1	0
List A	9	30	30	1	1/30	1/30	30.00	6.00	30.0	0	0
T20s	5	-	-	-	-	-	-	-	-	-	-

BRYDON CARSE

RHB / RFM / R0 / W0

DURHAM

FULL NAME: Brydon Alexander Carse
BORN: July 31, 1995, Port Elizabeth, South Africa
SQUAD NO: 99
HEIGHT: 6ft 2in
NICKNAME: Cheesy
EDUCATION: Pearson High School, Port Elizabeth
TEAMS: Durham, Eastern Province
ROLE: Bowler
DEBUT: First-class: 2016; T20: 2014

BEST BATTING: 61* Durham vs Sussex, Chester-le-Street, 2017
BEST BOWLING: 3-38 Durham vs Lancashire, Chester-le-Street, 2016

FAMILY TIES? My dad James played for Northamptonshire, Rhodesia, Eastern Province, Border and Western Province
BEST ADVICE EVER RECEIVED? Watch the ball
'ROY OF THE ROVERS' MOMENT? Making my first-class debut for Durham in 2016
BEST THING ABOUT YOUR HOME GROUND? It's always red hot
BEST OPPOSING PLAYER IN COUNTY CRICKET? Chris Woakes (War)
YOUNG OPPOSING PLAYER WHO HAS IMPRESSED YOU? Jofra Archer (Sus) – he bowls with pace
IF YOU WEREN'T A CRICKETER? I'd be the head of sport at a school
SURPRISING FACT ABOUT YOU? I can play the euphonium
WHERE IS PARADISE? Portugal
CRICKETING HERO? Jacques Kallis – the greatest allrounder
NON-CRICKETING HERO? James Bond – the greatest agent
UNUSUAL OBJECT AT HOME? Buddha ornaments
TWITTER: @CarseBrydon

Batting	Mat	Inns	NO	Runs	HS	Ave	SR	100	50	Ct	St
First-class	11	11	4	267	61*	38.14	50.85	0	1	2	0
T20s	3	3	1	5	3	2.50	83.33	0	0	1	0

Bowling	Mat	Balls	Runs	Wkts	BBI	BBM	Ave	Econ	SR	5w	10
First-class	11	1298	798	20	3/38	4/86	39.90	3.68	64.9	0	0
T20s	3	47	75	2	1/11	1/11	37.50	9.57	23.5	0	0

MATT CARTER

RHB / OB / RO / WO

FULL NAME: Matthew Carter
BORN: May 26, 1996, Lincoln
SQUAD NO: 20
HEIGHT: 6ft 6in
NICKNAME: Carts
EDUCATION: Branston Community Academy, Lincolnshire
TEAMS: Nottinghamshire
ROLE: Bowler
DEBUT: First-class: 2015

NOTTINGHAMSHIRE

BEST BATTING: 33 Nottinghamshire vs Sussex, Hove, 2017
BEST BOWLING: 7-56 Nottinghamshire vs Somerset, Taunton, 2015

FAMILY TIES? My dad and oldest brother played at village level. My brother Andrew played for Notts, Derby and Hampshire before retiring in 2016
BEST ADVICE EVER RECEIVED? If it's to be, it's up to me
'ROY OF THE ROVERS' MOMENT? Taking seven wickets in the first innings on my first-class debut
BEST THING ABOUT YOUR HOME GROUND? The atmosphere on T20 nights
BEST OPPOSING PLAYER IN COUNTY CRICKET? Gary Ballance (Yor)
YOUNG OPPOSING PLAYER WHO HAS IMPRESSED YOU? Josh Tongue (Wor) – what an entrance onto the first-class circuit
IF YOU WEREN'T A CRICKETER? I'd be doing a lot of shooting (see below)
SURPRISING FACT ABOUT YOU? Any chance I get, whether for an hour or a full day, it's spent with the dog in the middle of a field shooting. I've had a lot of swimming achievements but now I'm scared of swimming
WHERE IS PARADISE? Home
CRICKETING HERO? Andrew Flintoff in the 2005 Ashes
UNUSUAL OBJECT AT HOME? A cabinet full of guns

Batting	Mat	Inns	NO	Runs	HS	Ave	SR	100	50	Ct	St
First-class	5	8	1	64	33	9.14	48.12	0	0	4	0

Bowling	Mat	Balls	Runs	Wkts	BBI	BBM	Ave	Econ	SR	5w	10
First-class	5	904	672	17	7/56	10/195	39.52	4.46	53.1	1	1

KARL CARVER

LHB / SLA / R0 / W0

FULL NAME: Karl Carver
BORN: March 26, 1996, Northallerton, Yorkshire
SQUAD NO: 29
HEIGHT: 5ft 11in
NICKNAME: Keith, Carves , Curly
EDUCATION: Thirsk School and Sixth Form College, North Yorkshire
TEAMS: Yorkshire
ROLE: Bowler
DEBUT: First-class: 2014; List A: 2015; T20: 2015

BEST BATTING: 20 Yorkshire vs Somerset, Taunton, 2017
BEST BOWLING: 4-106 Yorkshire vs MCC, Abu Dhabi, 2016

WHAT GOT YOU INTO CRICKET? Watching my grandad and dad play every week
STRANGEST THING SEEN IN A GAME? Our fine-leg fielder at Sheriff Hutton Bridge having his lunch stolen and his coffee knocked over by a bird
'ROY OF THE ROVERS' MOMENT? Making my full debuts in all formats for my home county Yorkshire. Getting the wicket of Kumar Sangakkara on my List A debut against Surrey in 2015
SUPERSTITIONS? Wearing my sunglasses when bowling. Often bat in a long-sleeved shirt
HOW WOULD YOUR TEAMMATES DESCRIBE YOU IN THREE WORDS? Quiet, team-man, smiley
CRICKETING HERO? Joe Root – because even though he's the best player in the world he's a nice guy too
SURPRISING FACT? I went on tour to India in February 2016 and ended up playing for Hong Kong in a T20 because they were short on numbers
TWITTER: @Carver_Karl

Batting	Mat	Inns	NO	Runs	HS	Ave	SR	100	50	Ct	St
First-class	7	11	4	107	20	15.28	36.02	0	0	4	0
List A	13	3	3	49	35*	-	76.56	0	0	2	0
T20s	9	2	1	2	2	2.00	50.00	0	0	5	0

Bowling	Mat	Balls	Runs	Wkts	BBI	BBM	Ave	Econ	SR	5w	10
First-class	7	946	543	18	4/106	6/194	30.16	3.44	52.5	0	0
List A	13	390	309	12	3/5	3/5	25.75	4.75	32.5	0	0
T20s	9	108	179	6	3/40	3/40	29.83	9.94	18.0	0	0

SHIVNARINE CHANDERPAUL

LHB / LB / R1 / W0

FULL NAME: Shivnarine Chanderpaul
BORN: August 16, 1974, Unity Village, Demerara, Guyana
SQUAD NO: 11
NICKNAME: Shiv, Tiger
EDUCATION: Gibson School, Guyana; Cove and John High School, Guyana
TEAMS: West Indies, Lancashire, Derbyshire, Durham, Guyana, Khulna Royal Bengals, Royal Challengers Bangalore, Sylhet Royals, Uva Next, Warwickshire
ROLE: Batsman
DEBUT: Test: 1994; ODI: 1994; T20I: 2006; First-class 1992; List A: 1992; T20: 2006

BEST BATTING: 303* Guyana vs Jamaica, Kingston, 1996
BEST BOWLING: 4-48 Guyana vs Leeward Islands, Basseterre, 1993
COUNTY CAP: 2010 (Lancashire); 2014 (Derbyshire)

NOTES: The middle-order left-hander is West Indies' most capped Test cricketer and sits at No.8 on the all-time Test run-scorers list. He played eight matches for Lancashire as an overseas player in 2010, in which he scored two hundreds and five fifties. Having retired from international cricket, he rejoined Lancashire in 2017 at the age of 42 as a Kolpak player and last summer made 831 Championship runs at 51.94 with three hundreds. He has represented four county sides and scored well over 4,500 Championship runs

Batting	Mat	Inns	NO	Runs	HS	Ave	SR	100	50	Ct	St
Tests	164	280	49	11867	203*	51.37	43.31	30	66	66	0
ODIs	268	251	40	8778	150	41.60	70.74	11	59	73	0
T20Is	22	22	5	343	41	20.17	98.84	0	0	7	0
First-class	377	613	108	27288	303*	54.03		77	142	192	0
List A	423	394	74	13439	150	41.99		13	98	118	0
T20s	81	78	11	1576	87*	23.52	105.77	0	8	24	0
Bowling	Mat	Balls	Runs	Wkts	BBI	BBM	Ave	Econ	SR	5w	10
Tests	164	1740	883	9	1/2	1/2	98.11	3.04	193.3	0	0
ODIs	268	740	636	14	3/18	3/18	45.42	5.15	52.8	0	0
T20Is	22	-	-	-	-	-	-	-	-	-	-
First-class	377	4812	2532	60	4/48	5/54	42.20	3.15	80.2	0	0
List A	423	1681	1388	56	4/22	4/22	24.78	4.95	30.0	0	0
T20s	81	-	-	-	-	-	-	-	-	-	-

ZAK CHAPPELL

RHB / RFM / R0 / W0

LEICESTERSHIRE

FULL NAME: Zachariah John Chappell
BORN: August 21, 1996, Grantham, Lincolnshire
SQUAD NO: 32
HEIGHT: 6ft 6in
NICKNAME: Chappy, Chappelly
EDUCATION: Stamford School, Lincolnshire
TEAMS: Leicestershire
ROLE: Bowler
DEBUT: First-class: 2015; List A: 2015; T20: 2015

BEST BATTING: 96 Leicestershire vs Derbyshire, Derby, 2015
BEST BOWLING: 4-108 Leicestershire vs Derbyshire, Derby, 2017

BEST ADVICE EVER RECEIVED? Play across, be a boss
'ROY OF THE ROVERS' MOMENT? Scoring 96 on my Championship debut batting at No.10
BEST THING ABOUT YOUR HOME GROUND? The big hill (which can also be the worst thing about the ground)
BEST OPPOSING PLAYER IN COUNTY CRICKET? Jofra Archer (Sus)
IF YOU WEREN'T A CRICKETER? I'd be a nutritionist
SURPRISING FACT ABOUT YOU? I can walk on my hands
CRICKETING HERO? Brett Lee – he bowled rockets
NON-CRICKETING HERO? Muhammad Ali
TWITTER: @ZakkChappell

Batting	Mat	Inns	NO	Runs	HS	Ave	SR	100	50	Ct	St
First-class	10	16	2	387	96	27.64	59.26	0	2	0	0
List A	8	7	3	114	59*	28.50	66.27	0	1	0	0
T20s	1	-	-	-	-	-	-	-	-	0	0

Bowling	Mat	Balls	Runs	Wkts	BBI	BBM	Ave	Econ	SR	5w	10
First-class	10	1081	771	15	4/108	4/124	51.40	4.27	72.0	0	0
List A	8	359	367	5	2/44	2/44	73.40	6.13	71.8	0	0
T20s	1	12	25	0	-	-	-	12.50	-	0	0

VARUN CHOPRA — RHB / LB / R3 / W0 / MVP55

FULL NAME: Varun Chopra
BORN: June 21, 1987, Barking, Essex
SQUAD NO: 6
HEIGHT: 6ft 1in
NICKNAME: Tiddles, Chops
EDUCATION: Ilford County High School
TEAMS: Essex, Tamil Union Cricket and Athletic Club, Warwickshire
ROLE: Batsman
DEBUT: First-class: 2006; List A: 2006; T20: 2006

ESSEX

BEST BATTING: 233* Tamil Union vs Sinhalese Sports Club, Colombo, 2012
COUNTY CAP: 2012 (Warwickshire)

WHAT GOT YOU INTO CRICKET? Dad taking me to Joe Hussain's Ilford Cricket School
BEST ADVICE EVER RECEIVED? It's not how, it's how many
'ROY OF THE ROVERS' MOMENT? Winning the T20 competition in 2014 off the last ball in front of a packed house at Edgbaston
BEST THING ABOUT YOUR HOME GROUND? The crowd
BEST OPPOSING PLAYER IN COUNTY CRICKET? Samit Patel (Not)
IF YOU WEREN'T A CRICKETER? I'd be an architect
SURPRISING FACT ABOUT YOU? I love a chin-up
SURPRISING FACT ABOUT A TEAMMATE? James Foster has never bought a round
WHERE IS PARADISE? The Maldives
CRICKETING HERO? Sachin Tendulkar
NON-CRICKETING HERO? Roger Federer
UNUSUAL OBJECT AT HOME? A chin-up bar
TWITTER: @vchops06

Batting	Mat	Inns	NO	Runs	HS	Ave	SR	100	50	Ct	St
First-class	179	292	20	9776	233*	35.94	50.92	20	49	213	0
List A	100	97	6	3840	124	42.19	74.79	8	25	36	0
T20s	92	89	11	2251	116	28.85	117.42	2	14	20	0

Bowling	Mat	Balls	Runs	Wkts	BBI	BBM	Ave	Econ	SR	5w	10
First-class	179	204	128	0	-	-	-	3.76	-	0	0
List A	100	18	18	0	-	-	-	6.00	-	0	0
T20s	92	-	-	-	-	-	-	-	-	-	-

NOTTINGHAMSHIRE

FULL NAME: Daniel Trevor Christian
BORN: May 4, 1983, Sydney, Australia
SQUAD NO: 54
HEIGHT: 6ft
EDUCATION: St Gregory's College, Sydney
TEAMS: Australia, Nottinghamshire, Brisbane
Heat, Deccan Chargers, Gloucestershire,
Hampshire, Hobart Hurricanes, Middlesex,
New South Wales, Royal Challengers
Bangalore, South Australia, Victoria
ROLE: Allrounder
DEBUT: ODI: 2012; T20I: 2010; First-class:
2008; List A: 2006; T20: 2006

BEST BATTING: 131* South Australia vs New South Wales, Adelaide, 2011
BEST BOWLING: 5-24 South Australia vs Western Australia, Perth, 2010
COUNTY CAP: 2013 (Gloucestershire)

TWITTER: @danchristian54
NOTES: A veteran of the IPL and the Big Bash, the Australian allrounder captained
Nottinghamshire to nine straight wins in the 2016 T20 Blast before leading the club to the
holy grail last summer, weighing in with 356 runs and 11 wickets. This will be his fourth
consecutive summer at Trent Bridge, and his new contract will take him into a fifth in 2019.
He has also played for Hampshire, Gloucestershire and Middlesex. He last played for
Australia in 2014, struggling to cement a regular place in either of the limited-overs sides

Batting	Mat	Inns	NO	Runs	HS	Ave	SR	100	50	Ct	St
ODIs	19	18	5	273	39	21.00	88.92	0	0	10	0
T20Is	16	7	3	27	9	6.75	96.42	0	0	5	0
First-class	81	138	17	3657	131*	30.22	53.31	5	15	89	0
List A	119	108	21	2844	117	32.68	101.64	2	14	43	0
T20s	227	193	44	3308	129	22.20	135.07	1	11	88	0

Bowling	Mat	Balls	Runs	Wkts	BBI	BBM	Ave	Econ	SR	5w	10
ODIs	19	727	595	20	5/31	5/31	29.75	4.91	36.3	1	0
T20Is	16	213	317	11	3/27	3/27	28.81	8.92	19.3	0	0
First-class	81	10181	5601	160	5/24	9/87	35.00	3.30	63.6	3	0
List A	119	3896	3585	107	6/48	6/48	33.50	5.52	36.4	3	0
T20s	227	3568	4932	172	5/14	5/14	28.67	8.29	20.7	2	0

GRAHAM CLARK

RHB / RM / R0 / W0 / MVP80

FULL NAME: Graham Clark
BORN: March 16, 1993, Whitehaven, Cumbria
SQUAD NO: 7
HEIGHT: 6ft 1in
NICKNAME: Sparky, Schnoz
EDUCATION: St Benedict's Catholic High School, Whitehaven
TEAMS: Durham
ROLE: Batsman
DEBUT: First-class: 2015; List A: 2015; T20: 2015

DURHAM

BEST BATTING: 109 Durham vs Glamorgan, Chester-le-Street, 2017

FAMILY TIES? My older brother Jordan plays for Lancashire, while both my eldest brother Darren and my dad have represented Cumbria at Minor Counties level. My dad is a Level 3 coach and my mam is a Level 2 coach
'ROY OF THE ROVERS' MOMENT? Scoring my maiden first-class hundred in the County Championship in 2017
BEST THING ABOUT YOUR HOME GROUND? On a nice day there aren't many better settings than Chester-le-Street, especially with Lumley Castle in the background
BEST OPPOSING PLAYER IN COUNTY CRICKET? Sam Northeast (Ham)
YOUNG OPPOSING PLAYER WHO HAS IMPRESSED YOU? Jofra Archer (Sus) – bowls at a good pace, takes a lot of wickets and gets through a lot of overs
SURPRISING FACT ABOUT YOU? I started out as a wicketkeeper, then bowled leg-spin for years and I'm now trying my hand at medium-pace
SURPRISING FACT ABOUT A TEAMMATE? James Weighell has gone three seasons without buying a round
WHERE IS PARADISE? The Auld Dubliner, Dublin
TWITTER: @GrahamClark16

Batting	Mat	Inns	NO	Runs	HS	Ave	SR	100	50	Ct	St
First-class	18	33	0	1004	109	30.42	56.81	1	8	12	0
List A	18	18	1	445	114	26.17	87.94	1	1	6	0
T20s	23	23	2	457	91*	21.76	136.01	0	3	7	0

Bowling	Mat	Balls	Runs	Wkts	BBI	BBM	Ave	Econ	SR	5w	10
First-class	18	-	-	-	-	-	-	-	-	-	-
List A	18	-	-	-	-	-	-	-	-	-	-
T20s	23	12	21	0	-	-	-	10.50	-	0	0

JORDAN CLARK

RHB / RM / R0 / W0 / MVP74

FULL NAME: Jordan Clark
BORN: October 14, 1990, Whitehaven, Cumbria
SQUAD NO: 16
HEIGHT: 6ft 4in
NICKNAME: Clarky
EDUCATION: Sedbergh School, Cumbria
TEAMS: Lancashire
ROLE: Allounder
DEBUT: First-class: 2015; List A: 2010; T20: 2011

BEST BATTING: 140 Lancashire vs Surrey, The Oval, 2017
BEST BOWLING: 4-81 Lancashire vs Warwickshire, Edgbaston, 2017

FAMILY TIES? My younger brother Graham plays for Durham. My older brother Darren has played Minor Counties with Cumberland and together with dad won the National Village Cup with Cleator CC in 2013
'ROY OF THE ROVERS' MOMENT? Taking four wickets in eight balls in the T20 quarter-final against Glamorgan in 2014, or my maiden first-class hundred against Surrey in 2017
YOUNG OPPOSING PLAYER WHO HAS IMPRESSED YOU? Jamie Porter (Ess)
IF YOU WEREN'T A CRICKETER? I'd be a plumber
SURPRISING FACT ABOUT YOU? I once split a testicle when pole dancing
SURPRISING FACT ABOUT A TEAMMATE? Tom Bailey gets a tattoo of every country he visits
CRICKETING HERO? Andrew Flintoff – inspirational in the 2005 Ashes when I was growing up
NON-CRICKETING HERO? Karl Pilkington – I love his outlook on life
TWITTER: @Clarksy16

Batting	Mat	Inns	NO	Runs	HS	Ave	SR	100	50	Ct	St
First-class	31	43	4	1078	140	27.64	54.94	1	4	4	0
List A	38	28	7	686	79*	32.66	102.23	0	3	5	0
T20s	58	41	14	501	44	18.55	129.12	0	0	18	0

Bowling	Mat	Balls	Runs	Wkts	BBI	BBM	Ave	Econ	SR	5w	10
First-class	31	3411	1998	52	4/81	6/159	38.42	3.51	65.5	0	0
List A	38	1036	1068	29	4/34	4/34	36.82	6.18	35.7	0	0
T20s	58	678	998	37	4/22	4/22	26.97	8.83	18.3	0	0

JOE CLARKE

RHB / WK / R1 / W0 / MVP41

FULL NAME: Joseph Michael Clarke
BORN: May 26, 1996, Shrewsbury, Shropshire
SQUAD NO: 33
HEIGHT: 5ft 11in
NICKNAME: Clarkey
EDUCATION: Llanfyllin High School, Powys
TEAMS: Worcestershire, England Lions
ROLE: Batsman
DEBUT: First-class: 2015; List A: 2015; T20: 2015

BEST BATTING: 194 Worcestershire vs Derbyshire, Worcester, 2016

WHAT GOT YOU INTO CRICKET? My older brother Ollie and the 2005 Ashes
BEST ADVICE EVER RECEIVED? Watch the ball
'ROY OF THE ROVERS' MOMENT? Beating India in the quarter-final of the U19 World Cup
BEST THING ABOUT YOUR HOME GROUND? The cathedral – the view from the changing rooms every morning is top-drawer
BEST OPPOSING PLAYER IN COUNTY CRICKET? Jack Taylor (Glo)
IF YOU WEREN'T A CRICKETER? I'd be a model
SURPRISING FACT ABOUT YOU? I can speak (some) Welsh
WHERE IS PARADISE? Dunsborough, Western Australia
CRICKETING HERO? Adam Gilchrist – he inspired me to play cricket
NON-CRICKETING HERO? Cristiano Ronaldo
TWITTER: @joeclarke10

Batting	Mat	Inns	NO	Runs	HS	Ave	SR	100	50	Ct	St
First-class	47	79	7	2983	194	41.43	61.61	9	13	21	0
List A	35	34	4	855	131*	28.50	84.90	1	4	17	2
T20s	27	26	2	624	124*	26.00	152.19	1	3	6	0

Bowling	Mat	Balls	Runs	Wkts	BBI	BBM	Ave	Econ	SR	5w	10
First-class	47	12	22	0	-	-	-	11.00	-	0	0
List A	35	-	-	-	-	-	-	-	-	-	-
T20s	27	-	-	-	-	-	-	-	-	-	-

RIKKI CLARKE

RHB / RMF / R1 / W0 / MVP13

FULL NAME: Rikki Clarke
BORN: September 29, 1981, Orsett, Essex
SQUAD NO: 81
HEIGHT: 6ft 4in
NICKNAME: Clarkey, Crouchy, Rock
EDUCATION: Broadwater Secondary;
Godalming College
TEAMS: England, Surrey, Derbyshire,
Warwickshire
ROLE: Allrounder
DEBUT: Test: 2003; ODI: 2003; First-class:
2002; List A: 2001; T20: 2003

BEST BATTING: 214 Surrey vs Somerset, Guildford, 2006
BEST BOWLING: 7-55 Surrey vs Somerset, The Oval, 2017
COUNTY CAP: 2005 (Surrey); 2011 (Warwickshire)

BEST ADVICE EVER RECEIVED? It's your career: do it your way
'ROY OF THE ROVERS' MOMENT? Becoming the joint world-record holder for most catches
by an outfielder in a first-class innings (seven, Lancashire v Warwickshire, 2011)
BEST THING ABOUT YOUR HOME GROUND? That it really is home
BEST OPPOSING PLAYER IN COUNTY CRICKET? Established international cricketers aside,
I'd say Liam Livingstone (Lan)
YOUNG OPPOSING PLAYER WHO HAS IMPRESSED YOU? Ed Pollock (War)
SURPRISING FACT ABOUT YOU? I am named after Ricky Villa, who scored the winning goal
for Spurs in the FA Cup final in 1981 – the year I was born
TWITTER: @rikkiclarke81

Batting	Mat	Inns	NO	Runs	HS	Ave	SR	100	50	Ct	St
Tests	2	3	0	96	55	32.00	37.94	0	1	1	0
ODIs	20	13	0	144	39	11.07	62.06	0	0	11	0
First-class	225	341	39	9926	214	32.86		16	52	337	0
List A	221	182	26	4019	98*	25.76		0	21	100	0
T20s	146	131	35	2010	79*	20.93	119.64	0	5	70	0

Bowling	Mat	Balls	Runs	Wkts	BBI	BBM	Ave	Econ	SR	5w	10
Tests	2	174	60	4	2/7	3/11	15.00	2.06	43.5	0	0
ODIs	20	469	415	11	2/28	2/28	37.72	5.30	42.6	0	0
First-class	225	23944	13447	413	7/55	9/83	32.55	3.36	57.9	4	0
List A	221	5912	5332	137	5/26	5/26	38.91	5.41	43.1	1	0
T20s	146	1877	2273	96	4/16	4/16	23.67	7.26	19.5	0	0

MITCHELL CLAYDON

LHB / RMF / RO / W2

FULL NAME: Mitchell Eric Claydon
BORN: November 25, 1982, Fairfield, New South Wales, Australia
SQUAD NO: 8
HEIGHT: 6ft 3in
NICKNAME: Ellen, Precious, Lips
EDUCATION: Westfield Sports High School, Sydney
TEAMS: Kent, Canterbury, Central Districts, Durham, Yorkshire
ROLE: Bowler
DEBUT: First-class: 2005; List A: 2006; T20: 2006

BEST BATTING: 77 Kent vs Leicestershire, Leicester, 2014
BEST BOWLING: 6-104 Durham vs Somerset, Taunton, 2011
COUNTY CAP: 2016 (Kent)

'ROY OF THE ROVERS' MOMENT? Winning three County Championship titles with Durham and being voted as the players' Player of the Year at Kent in 2014
CRICKETING HERO? Ricky Ponting
NON-CRICKETING HERO? Tiger Woods
IF YOU WEREN'T A CRICKETER? I'd be a policeman
SURPRISING FACT? I'm a magician, a keen surfer and I love to play a prank or two
TWITTER: @mitchellclaydon

Batting	Mat	Inns	NO	Runs	HS	Ave	SR	100	50	Ct	St
First-class	101	128	28	1556	77	15.56	60.52	0	4	11	0
List A	99	46	13	264	19	8.00	83.54	0	0	7	0
T20s	134	45	26	181	19	9.52	90.04	0	0	26	0

Bowling	Mat	Balls	Runs	Wkts	BBI	BBM	Ave	Econ	SR	5w	10
First-class	101	15171	9102	278	6/104	9/151	32.74	3.59	54.5	8	0
List A	99	4295	3947	128	5/31	5/31	30.83	5.51	33.5	1	0
T20s	134	2761	3844	150	5/26	5/26	25.62	8.35	18.4	2	0

BEN COAD

RHB / RFM / R0 / W1 / MVP48

FULL NAME: Benjamin Oliver Coad
BORN: January 10, 1994, Harrogate, Yorkshire
SQUAD NO: 10
HEIGHT: 6ft 3in
NICKNAME: Coady, Hench
EDUCATION: Thirsk School and Sixth Form College, North Yorkshire
TEAMS: Yorkshire
ROLE: Bowler
DEBUT: First-class: 2016; List A: 2013; T20: 2015

BEST BATTING: 28 Yorkshire vs Essex, Scarborough, 2017
BEST BOWLING: 6-25 Yorkshire vs Lancashire, Headingley, 2017

FAMILY TIES? My brothers played representative cricket at junior levels. My dad played Minor Counties cricket for Suffolk
'ROY OF THE ROVERS' MOMENT? My second T20 game in 2015, playing against Warwickshire at home in front of a very good crowd and managing to take two wickets and winning the game against the defending champions
SUPERSTITIONS? When playing at Headingley I touch the White Rose on the stairs as I walk out
SURPRISING FACT? I'm a Newcastle United fan
TWITTER: @bencoad10

Batting	Mat	Inns	NO	Runs	HS	Ave	SR	100	50	Ct	St
First-class	15	18	6	146	28	12.16	52.89	0	0	1	0
List A	11	4	4	3	2*	-	23.07	0	0	4	0
T20s	7	2	1	3	2*	3.00	60.00	0	0	5	0

Bowling	Mat	Balls	Runs	Wkts	BBI	BBM	Ave	Econ	SR	5w	10
First-class	15	2638	1246	55	6/25	10/102	22.65	2.83	47.9	4	1
List A	11	440	477	11	4/63	4/63	43.36	6.50	40.0	0	0
T20s	7	109	186	6	2/24	2/24	31.00	10.23	18.1	0	0

JOSH COBB · RHB / OB / R0 / W0

FULL NAME: Joshua James Cobb
BORN: August 17, 1990, Leicester
SQUAD NO: 4
HEIGHT: 6ft
NICKNAME: Cobby, Tuck Shop, Lord
EDUCATION: Oakham School, Rutland
TEAMS: Northamptonshire, Barisal Bulls, Central Districts, Dhaka Gladiators, Leicestershire, Prime Doleshwar Sporting Club, Sylhet Superstars
ROLE: Batsman
DEBUT: First-class: 2007; List A: 2008; T20: 2008

BEST BATTING: 148* Leicestershire vs Middlesex, Lord's, 2008
BEST BOWLING: 2-11 Leicestershire vs Gloucestershire, Leicester, 2011

FAMILY TIES? My dad Russell played for Leicestershire
BEST ADVICE EVER RECEIVED? Listen to everything and take what you need
'ROY OF THE ROVERS' MOMENT? Being Man of the Match in two T20-winning finals
BEST THING ABOUT YOUR HOME GROUND? Friday night T20s – the atmosphere is fantastic
BEST OPPOSING PLAYER IN COUNTY CRICKET? Riki Wessels (Not)
YOUNG OPPOSING PLAYER WHO HAS IMPRESSED YOU? Max Holden (Mid)
IF YOU WEREN'T A CRICKETER? At Oakham I was a member of the debating society and took an active interest in historical and modern British politics, so most likely I would be involved in local politics and government. I take a number of book and papers with me to away games which keep me busy during rain delays, much to the dismay of my teammates
SURPRISING FACT ABOUT YOU? I was once a childhood model for Next… where did it all go wrong?
CRICKETING HERO? Brad Hodge – serious player, fun to be around, and still going strong at 43
TWITTER: @Cobby24

Batting	Mat	Inns	NO	Runs	HS	Ave	SR	100	50	Ct	St
First-class	113	193	22	4503	148*	26.33	48.73	3	26	50	0
List A	83	79	6	2705	137	37.05	93.40	6	16	25	0
T20s	122	115	12	2463	84	23.91	131.64	0	13	61	0

Bowling	Mat	Balls	Runs	Wkts	BBI	BBM	Ave	Econ	SR	5w	10
First-class	113	2466	1449	17	2/11	2/11	85.23	3.52	145.0	0	0
List A	83	1566	1534	31	3/34	3/34	49.48	5.87	50.5	0	0
T20s	122	1107	1525	53	4/22	4/22	28.77	8.26	20.8	0	0

IAN COCKBAIN RHB / RM / R0 / W0

GLOUCESTERSHIRE

FULL NAME: Ian Andrew Cockbain
BORN: February 17, 1987, Liverpool
SQUAD NO: 28
HEIGHT: 6ft
NICKNAME: Coey, Bird's Nest
EDUCATION: Maghull High School, Sefton;
Liverpool John Moores University
TEAMS: Gloucestershire
ROLE: Batsman
DEBUT: First-class: 2011; List A: 2011; T20:
2011

BEST BATTING: 151* Gloucestershire vs Surrey, Bristol, 2014
BEST BOWLING: 1-23 Gloucestershire vs Durham MCCU, Bristol, 2016
COUNTY CAP: 2011

FAMILY TIES? My dad Ian played for Lancashire
BEST THING ABOUT YOUR HOME GROUND? The new flats create an amazing atmosphere
YOUNG OPPOSING PLAYER WHO HAS IMPRESSED YOU? Jamie Porter (Ess) – manages to
take wickets and be a nice bloke at the same time
IF YOU WEREN'T A CRICKETER? I'd be working as an independent financial advisor with my
old man for Ian Cockbain Wealth Management
WHERE IS PARADISE? A secluded beach surrounded by forests and some perfect waves
CRICKETING HERO? Andrew Flintoff – a fellow Lancastrian. I loved the way he went about
the game
NON-CRICKETING HERO? Roger Federer – he has awesome presence, and the way he
moves and plays is pure genius
UNUSUAL OBJECT AT HOME? Some spiritual stones my partner places around our home

Batting	Mat	Inns	NO	Runs	HS	Ave	SR	100	50	Ct	St
First-class	50	85	6	2382	151*	30.15	42.85	4	13	34	0
List A	59	52	10	1331	108*	31.69	88.26	1	8	38	0
T20s	84	78	13	2026	91*	31.16	125.99	0	12	41	0

Bowling	Mat	Balls	Runs	Wkts	BBI	BBM	Ave	Econ	SR	5w	10
First-class	50	47	44	1	1/23	1/23	44.00	5.61	47.0	0	0
List A	59	-	-	-	-	-	-	-	-	-	-
T20s	84	-	-	-	-	-	-	-	-	-	-

MATT COLES

LHB / RFM / R0 / W2 / MVP83

FULL NAME: Matthew Thomas Coles
BORN: May 26, 1990, Maidstone, Kent
SQUAD NO: 1
HEIGHT: 6ft 3in
NICKNAME: Colesy
EDUCATION: Maplesden Noakes School, Maidstone; MidKent College
TEAMS: Essex, Dhaka Dynamites, England Lions, Hampshire, Kent
ROLE: Allrounder
DEBUT: First-class: 2009; List A: 2009; T20: 2010

ESSEX

BEST BATTING: 103* Kent vs Yorkshire, Headingley, 2012
BEST BOWLING: 6-51 Kent vs Northamptonshire, Northampton, 2012
COUNTY CAP: 2012 (Kent)

WHAT GOT YOU INTO CRICKET? Playing six-a-side indoor cricket when I was five
BEST ADVICE EVER RECEIVED? Play with a smile on your face
'ROY OF THE ROVERS' MOMENT? Taking 100 wickets for Kent across all formats in 2015
BEST THING ABOUT YOUR HOME GROUND? I have a new home now, so we'll have to wait and see
IF YOU WEREN'T A CRICKETER? I'd be a gardener
SURPRISING FACT ABOUT YOU? I took two white-ball hat-tricks for Kent – the first in a 50-over game against Nottinghamshire at Trent Bridge in 2015 and the second in a T20 match against Middlesex at Richmond in 2017
SURPRISING FACT ABOUT A TEAMMATE? I'm still getting to know them!
WHERE IS PARADISE? In front of a plate of roast lamb
CRICKETING HERO? Andrew Flintoff
TWITTER: @MattColes_90

Batting	Mat	Inns	NO	Runs	HS	Ave	SR	100	50	Ct	St
First-class	106	140	18	2461	103*	20.17	68.91	1	12	56	0
List A	72	42	5	525	100	14.18	112.17	1	1	28	0
T20s	84	58	9	476	54	9.71	135.22	0	1	28	0

Bowling	Mat	Balls	Runs	Wkts	BBI	BBM	Ave	Econ	SR	5w	10
First-class	106	16216	9770	334	6/51	10/98	29.25	3.61	48.5	11	2
List A	72	2907	2737	121	6/32	6/32	22.61	5.64	24.0	2	0
T20s	84	1673	2464	81	4/27	4/27	30.41	8.83	20.6	0	0

PAUL COLLINGWOOD   RHB / RM / R3 / W0 / MVP12

FULL NAME: Paul David Collingwood
BORN: May 26, 1976, Shotley Bridge, County Durham
SQUAD NO: 5
HEIGHT: 5ft 11in
NICKNAME: Colly, Weed, Wobbles
EDUCATION: Blackfyne Comprehensive School; Derwentside College, Consett
TEAMS: England, Durham, Delhi Daredevils, Impi, Perth Scorchers, Rajasthan Royals
ROLE: Allrounder
DEBUT: Test: 2003; ODI: 2001; T20I: 2005; First-class: 1996; List A: 1995; T20: 2005

BEST BATTING: 206 England vs Australia, Adelaide, 2006
BEST BOWLING: 5-52 Durham vs Somerset, Grangefield Road, 2005
BENEFIT: 2007

FAMILY TIES? My dad and brother played for Shotley Bridge
'ROY OF THE ROVERS' MOMENT? Playing for England, winning the World T20 and the three Ashes wins
SUPERSTITIONS? A little jig as I walk out to bat, but it's getting harder as it involves squatting three times!
NON-CRICKETING HEROES? Luke Donald
TWITTER: @Colly622

Batting	Mat	Inns	NO	Runs	HS	Ave	SR	100	50	Ct	St
Tests	68	115	10	4259	206	40.56	46.44	10	20	96	0
ODIs	197	181	37	5092	120*	35.36	76.98	5	26	108	0
T20Is	36	33	2	583	79	18.80	127.01	0	3	15	0
First-class	294	506	52	16594	206	36.55		35	85	340	0
List A	425	398	73	11221	132	34.52		10	65	206	0
T20s	136	119	14	2221	108*	21.15	122.57	1	8	44	0

Bowling	Mat	Balls	Runs	Wkts	BBI	BBM	Ave	Econ	SR	5w	10
Tests	68	1905	1018	17	3/23	3/35	59.88	3.20	112.0	0	0
ODIs	197	5186	4294	111	6/31	6/31	38.68	4.96	46.7	1	0
T20Is	36	234	347	16	4/22	4/22	21.68	8.89	14.6	0	0
First-class	294	12346	6269	159	5/52	8/98	39.42	3.04	77.6	2	0
List A	425	11332	9104	272	6/31	6/31	33.47	4.82	41.6	1	0
T20s	136	1600	1921	89	5/6	5/6	21.58	7.20	17.9	2	0

NICK COMPTON

RHB / OB / R6 / W0

FULL NAME: Nicholas Richard Denis Compton
BORN: June 26, 1983, Durban, South Africa
SQUAD NO: 3
HEIGHT: 6ft 2in
NICKNAME: Compdog, Compo
EDUCATION: Hilton College, KwaZulu-Natal; Harrow School, London; Durham University
TEAMS: England, Middlesex, Somerset, Mashonaland Eagles, Worcestershire
ROLE: Batsman
DEBUT: Test: 2012; First-class: 2004; List A: 2001; T20: 2004

BEST BATTING: 254* Somerset vs Durham, Chester-le-Street, 2011
BEST BOWLING: 1-1 Somerset vs Hampshire, Southampton, 2010
COUNTY CAP: 2006 (Middlesex); 2011 (Somerset)

FAMILY TIES? My dad Richard played club cricket in Durban. Grandfather played a bit of cricket and football in England during the 1940s and 1950s. He had a cool hairstyle
'ROY OF THE ROVERS' MOMENT? Winning an away Test series in India with England for the first time in 28 years
IF YOU WEREN'T A CRICKETER? I would be a world-famous travel photographer exploring India and other indigenous countries and cultures
SURPRISING FACT? I broke my arm when I was five, which is why I give the impression that I am carrying large Persian carpets under my arm
CRICKETING HEROES? Jacques Kallis – consistency and a master of his emotions. Brian Lara – arrogance and the best to watch. Jos Buttler – for his large shnozz. James Taylor – had more strengths as a cricketer than anyone I know
TWITTER: @thecompdog

Batting	Mat	Inns	NO	Runs	HS	Ave	SR	100	50	Ct	St
Tests	16	30	3	775	117	28.70	36.04	2	2	7	0
First-class	194	338	37	12168	254*	40.42	46.52	27	59	98	0
List A	118	108	20	3098	131	35.20	78.05	6	19	47	0
T20s	87	74	7	1318	78	19.67	114.21	0	7	31	0

Bowling	Mat	Balls	Runs	Wkts	BBI	BBM	Ave	Econ	SR	5w	10
Tests	16	-	-	-	-	-	-	-	-	-	-
First-class	194	182	229	3	1/1	1/1	76.33	7.54	60.6	0	0
List A	118	61	53	1	1/0	1/0	53.00	5.21	61.0	0	0
T20s	87	-	-	-	-	-	-	-	-	-	-

ESSEX

ALASTAIR COOK LHB / RM / R7 / W0 / MVP50

FULL NAME: Alastair Nathan Cook
BORN: December 25, 1984, Gloucester
SQUAD NO: 26
HEIGHT: 6ft 2in
NICKNAME: Cookie, Chef
EDUCATION: Bedford School
TEAMS: England, Essex
ROLE: Batsman
DEBUT: Test: 2006; ODI: 2006; T20I: 2007;
First-class: 2003; List A: 2003; T20: 2005

BEST BATTING: 294 England vs India, Edgbaston, 2011
BEST BOWLING: 3-13 Essex vs Northamptonshire, Chelmsford, 2005
COUNTY CAP: 2005; BENEFIT: 2014

FAMILY TIES? Dad played for the local club side and was a very good opening bat, while my mum made the teas. My brothers played for Maldon Cricket Club
'ROY OF THE ROVERS' MOMENT? Ashes wins home and away, becoming the world No.1 Test team, Essex winning the 50-over competition, making my England debut
CRICKETING HEROES? Graham Gooch – I watched him playing for Essex at the County Ground
IF YOU WEREN'T A CRICKETER? I'd be a farmer

Batting	Mat	Inns	NO	Runs	HS	Ave	SR	100	50	Ct	St
Tests	152	275	16	12005	294	46.35	47.05	32	55	156	0
ODIs	92	92	4	3204	137	36.40	77.13	5	19	36	0
T20Is	4	4	0	61	26	15.25	112.96	0	0	1	0
First-class	273	484	36	21540	294	48.08	50.85	61	101	281	0
List A	159	157	11	5840	137	40.00	79.89	12	34	66	0
T20s	32	30	2	892	100*	31.85	127.61	1	5	13	0
Bowling	Mat	Balls	Runs	Wkts	BBI	BBM	Ave	Econ	SR	5w	10
Tests	152	18	7	1	1/6	1/6	7.00	2.33	18.0	0	0
ODIs	92	-	-	-	-	-	-	-	-	-	-
T20Is	4	-	-	-	-	-	-	-	-	-	-
First-class	273	282	211	7	3/13	3/13	30.14	4.48	40.2	0	0
List A	159	18	10	0	-	-	-	3.33	-	0	0
T20s	32	-	-	-	-	-	-	-	-	-	-

SAM COOK

RHB / RFM / R0 / W0

FULL NAME: Samuel James Cook
BORN: August 4, 1997, Chelmsford, Essex
SQUAD NO: 16
HEIGHT: 6ft 2in
NICKNAME: Cookie
EDUCATION: Great Baddow High School, Chelmsford; Loughborough University
TEAMS: Essex
ROLE: Bowler
DEBUT: First-class: 2016

ESSEX

BEST BATTING: 3 Loughborough MCCU vs Leicestershire, Leicester, 2017
BEST BOWLING: 5-18 Essex vs Hampshire, Southampton, 2017

WHAT GOT YOU INTO CRICKET? The 2005 Ashes
BEST ADVICE EVER RECEIVED? Back your ability
'ROY OF THE ROVERS' MOMENT? Winning the County Championship in my first season – that was unexpected!
BEST THING ABOUT YOUR HOME GROUND? The atmosphere and the crowd – there's not many grounds which have the same buzz as a full house at Chelmsford
BEST OPPOSING PLAYER IN COUNTY CRICKET? Kyle Abbott (Ham)
YOUNG OPPOSING PLAYER WHO HAS IMPRESSED YOU? James Bracey (Glo) – very impressive that he has scored such a volume of runs in such a short space of time
IF YOU WEREN'T A CRICKETER? I'd be running a dog kennel
SURPRISING FACT ABOUT YOU? I don't like cheese
SURPRISING FACT ABOUT A TEAMMATE? Me and Aaron Beard have played for the same club team since we were 11
WHERE IS PARADISE? Mauritius
CRICKETING HERO? Glenn McGrath – for his consistency and skill
NON-CRICKETING HERO? Alex Ferguson – for the success he achieved with one team
UNUSUAL OBJECT AT HOME? DJ decks
TWITTER: @samcook09

Batting	Mat	Inns	NO	Runs	HS	Ave	SR	100	50	Ct	St
First-class	9	8	4	4	3	1.00	10.52	0	0	0	0

Bowling	Mat	Balls	Runs	Wkts	BBI	BBM	Ave	Econ	SR	5w	10
First-class	9	1385	711	26	5/18	7/102	27.34	3.08	53.2	2	0

CHRIS COOKE

RHB / WK / R0 / W0 / MVP84

GLAMORGAN

FULL NAME: Christopher Barry Cooke
BORN: May 30, 1986, Johannesburg, South Africa
SQUAD NO: 46
HEIGHT: 5ft 11in
NICKNAME: Chris Jelly, Dough, Beans, Minty, Shapeless, Cookie
EDUCATION: Bishops School, Cape Town; University of Cape Town
TEAMS: Glamorgan, Western Province
ROLE: Batsman/wicketkeeper
DEBUT: First-class: 2009; List A: 2009; T20: 2011

BEST BATTING: 171 Glamorgan vs Kent, Canterbury, 2014

WHAT GOT YOU INTO CRICKET? I grew up watching my old man and two big brothers playing cricket – and must have copied them as they were both keeper-batters
BEST ADVICE EVER RECEIVED? The quicker you learn, the quicker you'll be on the team sheet. Think small under pressure
'ROY OF THE ROVERS' MOMENT? The 2013 one-day final at Lord's
BEST THING ABOUT YOUR HOME GROUND? The Y Mochyn Du pub
BEST OPPOSING PLAYER IN COUNTY CRICKET? Darren Stevens (Ken)
YOUNG OPPOSING PLAYER WHO HAS IMPRESSED YOU? Josh Tongue (Wor)
SURPRISING FACT ABOUT YOU? I'm allergic to shellfish, I'm a decent leggie, and I have to have the volume on an even number
WHERE IS PARADISE? Cape Town
CRICKETING HERO? Hylton Ackerman
NON-CRICKETING HERO? Nelson Mandela
UNUSUAL OBJECT AT HOME? A couple of Puggles
TWITTER: @Cooky_24

Batting	Mat	Inns	NO	Runs	HS	Ave	SR	100	50	Ct	St
First-class	63	107	15	3504	171	38.08	52.65	4	23	82	1
List A	72	66	9	2102	137*	36.87	100.67	2	13	37	2
T20s	79	65	13	1225	65*	23.55	139.20	0	3	44	2

Bowling	Mat	Balls	Runs	Wkts	BBI	BBM	Ave	Econ	SR	5w	10
First-class	63	-	-	-	-	-	-	-	-	-	-
List A	72	-	-	-	-	-	-	-	-	-	-
T20s	79	-	-	-	-	-	-	-	-	-	-

FULL NAME: Mark James Cosgrove
BORN: June 14, 1984, Adelaide, Australia
SQUAD NO: 55
HEIGHT: 5ft 9in
NICKNAME: Cozzie
EDUCATION: Trinity College, Adelaide
TEAMS: Australia, Leicestershire, Glamorgan, Hobart Hurricanes, South Australia, Sydney Sixers, Sydney Thunder, Tasmania
ROLE: Batsman
DEBUT: ODI: 2006; First-class: 2002; List A: 2002; T20: 2006

LEICESTERSHIRE

BEST BATTING: 233 Glamorgan vs Derbyshire, Derby, 2006
BEST BOWLING: 3-3 South Australia vs Tasmania, Adelaide, 2007
COUNTY CAP: 2006 (Glamorgan)

WHAT GOT YOU INTO CRICKET? Playing in the backyard
'ROY OF THE ROVERS' MOMENT? Receiving the Man of the Match award in my first ODI for Australia
SUPERSTITIONS? Listening to music before I go out to bat
IF YOU WEREN'T A CRICKETER? I'd be an Aussie rules player
SURPRISING FACT? I grew up at the same club as Darren Lehmann, Ryan Harris and Graham Manou
CRICKETING HERO? Brian Lara
NON-CRICKETING HERO? Steven Gerrard
UNUSUAL OBJECT AT HOME? A swimming pool
TWITTER: @Cozzie99

Batting	Mat	Inns	NO	Runs	HS	Ave	SR	100	50	Ct	St
ODIs	3	3	0	112	74	37.33	96.55	0	1	0	0
First-class	194	346	19	13839	233	42.32	63.16	35	78	125	0
List A	145	139	4	4320	121	32.00	88.65	4	34	45	0
T20s	113	109	9	2540	89	25.40	123.00	0	13	23	0

Bowling	Mat	Balls	Runs	Wkts	BBI	BBM	Ave	Econ	SR	5w	10
ODIs	3	30	13	1	1/1	1/1	13.00	2.60	30.0	0	0
First-class	194	4186	2349	52	3/3	3/3	45.17	3.36	80.5	0	0
List A	145	1067	1141	18	2/21	2/21	63.38	6.41	59.2	0	0
T20s	113	197	320	10	2/11	2/11	32.00	9.74	19.7	0	0

JOSH COUGHLIN LHB / RM / R0 / W0

FULL NAME: Josh Coughlin
BORN: September 29, 1997, Sunderland
SQUAD NO: 29
HEIGHT: 6ft 4in
NICKNAME: Coggers
EDUCATION: St Robert of Newminster
Catholic School, Sunderland
TEAMS: Durham
ROLE: Allrounder
DEBUT: First-class: 2016

BEST BOWLING: 1-10 Durham v Sri Lanka A, Chester-le-Street, 2016

WHAT GOT YOU INTO CRICKET? My brother
FAMILY TIES? My gran's brother played Minor Counties, and my older brother Paul plays for Nottinghamshire
BEST ADVICE EVER RECEIVED? Be yourself and give it everything
'ROY OF THE ROVERS' MOMENT? Winning the Second XI Championship at the Riverside in 2016
BEST THING ABOUT YOUR HOME GROUND? The facilities – there's always somewhere to practise
BEST OPPOSING PLAYER IN COUNTY CRICKET? Joe Root (Yor)
YOUNG OPPOSING PLAYER WHO HAS IMPRESSED YOU? Max Holden (Mid) – scored runs while on loan at Northants last year
IF YOU WEREN'T A CRICKETER? I'd be a university student
WHERE IS PARADISE? Florida
CRICKETING HERO? Andrew Flintoff – great cricketer on the pitch and a good man off it
NON-CRICKETING HERO? My parents
UNUSUAL OBJECT AT HOME? Nerf guns

Batting	Mat	Inns	NO	Runs	HS	Ave	SR	100	50	Ct	St
First-class	1	1	0	0	0	0.00	0.00	0	0	0	0

Bowling	Mat	Balls	Runs	Wkts	BBI	BBM	Ave	Econ	SR	5w	10
First-class	1	156	45	2	1/10	2/45	22.50	1.73	78.0	0	0

PAUL COUGHLIN RHB / RFM / R0 / W0 / MVP27

FULL NAME: Paul Coughlin
BORN: October 23, 1992, Sunderland
SQUAD NO: 29
HEIGHT: 6ft 2in
NICKNAME: Coggers
EDUCATION: St Robert of Newminster Catholic School, Sunderland
TEAMS: Nottinghamshire, Durham, England Lions
ROLE: Allrounder
DEBUT: First-class: 2012; List A: 2012; T20: 2014

NOTTINGHAMSHIRE

BEST BATTING: 85 Durham vs Lancashire, Chester-le-Street, 2014
BEST BOWLING: 5-49 Durham vs Northamptonshire, Chester-le-Street, 2017

WHAT GOT YOU INTO CRICKET? Playing in my uncle's homemade net in his back garden
FAMILY TIES? A different uncle, Tommy Harland, played for Durham as a Minor County. My younger brother Josh is currently at Durham
STRANGEST THING SEEN IN A GAME? A fielder placed directly behind the bowler's arm
'ROY OF THE ROVERS' MOMENT? Winning the One-Day Cup at Lord's in 2014
CRICKETING HERO? Andrew Flintoff – amazing to watch. Kept the crowd entertained in all aspects of the game
SURPRISING FACT? I started out aiming to be a wicketkeeper. Then tried myself as a batter. Ended up being more of a bowler
TWITTER: @Coughlin92

Batting	Mat	Inns	NO	Runs	HS	Ave	SR	100	50	Ct	St
First-class	32	51	7	1168	85	26.54	57.08	0	7	13	0
List A	23	15	3	154	22	12.83	98.71	0	0	4	0
T20s	30	19	7	420	53	35.00	141.41	0	1	6	0

Bowling	Mat	Balls	Runs	Wkts	BBI	BBM	Ave	Econ	SR	5w	10
First-class	32	3951	2244	75	5/49	10/133	29.92	3.40	52.6	2	1
List A	23	845	788	16	3/36	3/36	49.25	5.59	52.8	0	0
T20s	30	493	768	34	5/42	5/42	22.58	9.34	14.5	1	0

BEN COX

RHB / WK / R0 / W0 / MVP40

WORCESTERSHIRE

FULL NAME: Oliver Benjamin Cox
BORN: February 2, 1992, Wordsley, Stourbridge, Worcestershire
SQUAD NO: 10
HEIGHT: 5ft 10in
NICKNAME: Cocko, Cockballs, Coxy, Benji
EDUCATION: Bromsgrove School, Worcestershire
TEAMS: Worcestershire
ROLE: Wicketkeeper
DEBUT: First-class: 2009; List A: 2010; T20: 2010

BEST BATTING: 124 Worcestershire vs Gloucestershire, Cheltenham, 2017

FAMILY TIES? My old man was a wicketkeeper at Belbroughton CC and had pretty decent hands (so I'm told). He was fearless going up to the stumps for the quick bowlers – it must run in the family!
BEST ADVICE EVER RECEIVED? Work harder than those you are competing with and success will take care of itself
'ROY OF THE ROVERS' MOMENT? My first-class debut in 2009 – I left school to play against the Somerset of Langer and Trescothick and then had to be back in the classroom on Monday morning
BEST THING ABOUT YOUR HOME GROUND? The cakes in the ladies' pavilion
BEST OPPOSING PLAYER IN COUNTY CRICKET? Samit Patel (Not)
YOUNG OPPOSING PLAYER WHO HAS IMPRESSED YOU? Olly Stone (War) – bowls rockets
SURPRISING FACT ABOUT YOU? I had an England U18 rugby trial with Jonathan Joseph, Owen Farrell and George Ford
SURPRISING FACT ABOUT A TEAMMATE? Two of them use sprinkle to cover up thin patches of hair
TWITTER: @bencox10

Batting	Mat	Inns	NO	Runs	HS	Ave	SR	100	50	Ct	St
First-class	89	143	21	3609	124	29.58	62.58	3	21	232	12
List A	57	42	5	737	82	19.91	94.12	0	1	51	8
T20s	71	61	27	970	59*	28.52	130.02	0	2	26	19

Bowling	Mat	Balls	Runs	Wkts	BBI	BBM	Ave	Econ	SR	5w	10
First-class	89	-	-	-	-	-	-	-	-	-	-
List A	57	-	-	-	-	-	-	-	-	-	-
T20s	71	-	-	-	-	-	-	-	-	-	-

MASON CRANE

RHB / LB / R0 / W0 / MVP93

FULL NAME: Mason Sidney Crane
BORN: February 18, 1997, Shoreham-by-Sea, Sussex
SQUAD NO: 32
HEIGHT: 5ft 9in
EDUCATION: Lancing College, West Sussex
TEAMS: England, Hampshire, New South Wales
ROLE: Bowler
DEBUT: Test: 2018; T20I: 2017; First-class: 2015; List A: 2015; T20: 2015

BEST BATTING: 29 Hampshire vs Somerset, Taunton, 2017
BEST BOWLING: 5-35 Hampshire vs Warwickshire, Southampton, 2015

WHAT GOT YOU INTO CRICKET? The 2005 Ashes
BEST ADVICE EVER RECEIVED? Never leave a birdie putt short
BEST THING ABOUT YOUR HOME GROUND? Everything – it's awesome!
IF YOU WEREN'T A CRICKETER? I'd be wishing I tried harder at school
SURPRISING FACT ABOUT YOU? To walk back to my mark I always go past the stumps the same side I'm bowling and always turn left at my mark
WHERE IS PARADISE? Home
CRICKETING HERO? Shane Warne
UNUSUAL OBJECT AT HOME? Two tortoises
TWITTER: @masoncrane32

Batting	Mat	Inns	NO	Runs	HS	Ave	SR	100	50	Ct	St
Tests	1	2	0	6	4	3.00	54.54	0	0	0	0
T20Is	2	-	-	-	-	-	-	-	-	0	0
First-class	32	45	17	321	29	11.46	34.59	0	0	9	0
List A	22	9	5	38	16*	9.50	65.51	0	0	9	0
T20s	20	5	4	11	3*	11.00	52.38	0	0	4	0

Bowling	Mat	Balls	Runs	Wkts	BBI	BBM	Ave	Econ	SR	5w	10
Tests	1	288	193	1	1/193	1/193	193.00	4.02	288.0	0	0
T20Is	2	48	62	1	1/38	1/38	62.00	7.75	48.0	0	0
First-class	32	5563	3607	77	5/35	6/89	46.84	3.89	72.2	2	0
List A	22	1093	1126	38	4/30	4/30	29.63	6.18	28.7	0	0
T20s	20	420	512	22	3/15	3/15	23.27	7.31	19.0	0	0

KENT

FULL NAME: Zak Crawley
BORN: February 3, 1998, Bromley, Kent
SQUAD NO: 16
HEIGHT: 6ft 5in
NICKNAME: Creepy, Orangutan
EDUCATION: Tonbridge School, Kent
TEAMS: Kent
ROLE: Batsman
DEBUT: First-class: 2017; List A: 2017

BEST BATTING: 62 Kent vs West Indians, Canterbury, 2017

WHAT GOT YOU INTO CRICKET? I got given pads and a bat at the age of about four and so played in the garden with my dad
FAMILY TIES? Dad played a bit at school. My great uncle was a good club cricketer
HOW WOULD YOUR TEAMMATES DESCRIBE YOU IN THREE WORDS? Tall, argumentative, infallible
BEST OPPOSING PLAYER IN COUNTY CRICKET? Joe Root (Yor)
YOUNG OPPOSING PLAYER WHO HAS IMPRESSED YOU? Sam Curran (Sur)
CRICKETING HEROES? Viv Richards – batted the way we all want to bat. Ricky Ponting – he was the one I most enjoyed watching
NON-CRICKETING HERO? Tiger Woods – greatest champion of all time. Just knew how to get over the line. Most mentally tough sportsman ever
IF YOU WEREN'T A CRICKETER? I'd be a golfer
SURPRISING FACT? I used to eat 50 apples a week before the age of 12
TWITTER: @zakcrawley

Batting	Mat	Inns	NO	Runs	HS	Ave	SR	100	50	Ct	St
First-class	5	7	0	137	62	19.57	50.18	0	1	4	0
List A	10	10	1	269	99*	29.88	61.41	0	2	5	0

Bowling	Mat	Balls	Runs	Wkts	BBI	BBM	Ave	Econ	SR	5w	10
First-class	5	-	-	-	-	-	-	-	-	-	-
List A	10	-	-	-	-	-	-	-	-	-	-

MATT CRITCHLEY

RHB / LB / RO / WO

FULL NAME: Matthew James John Critchley
BORN: August 13, 1996, Preston, Lancashire
SQUAD NO: 20
HEIGHT: 6ft 2in
NICKNAME: Critch
EDUCATION: St Michael's CofE High School, Chorley; Cardinal Newman College, Preston; University of Derby
TEAMS: Derbyshire, England Lions
ROLE: Allrounder
DEBUT: First-class: 2015; List A: 2015; T20: 2016

BEST BATTING: 137* Derbyshire vs Northamptonshire, Derby, 2015
BEST BOWLING: 3-50 Derbyshire vs Lancashire, Southport, 2015

'ROY OF THE ROVERS' MOMENT? Scoring a hundred in my first home game for Derbyshire in 2015
BEST THING ABOUT YOUR HOME GROUND? Edwin the dressing-room attendant – absolute legend of a bloke
BEST OPPOSING PLAYER IN COUNTY CRICKET? Joe Root (Yor)
YOUNG OPPOSING PLAYER WHO HAS IMPRESSED YOU? Joe Clarke (Wor)
IF YOU WEREN'T A CRICKETER? I'd be a student
SURPRISING FACT ABOUT A TEAMMATE? Alex Hughes reached the X Factor bootcamp
WHERE IS PARADISE? Coogee Beach, New South Wales
CRICKETING HERO? Shane Warne – arguably the best bowler ever
NON-CRICKETING HERO? Steven Gerrard
TWITTER: @mattcritchley96

Batting	Mat	Inns	NO	Runs	HS	Ave	SR	100	50	Ct	St
First-class	18	28	4	775	137*	32.29	60.59	2	2	7	0
List A	21	13	3	203	49	20.30	116.00	0	0	3	0
T20s	24	16	4	276	72*	23.00	133.98	0	1	5	0

Bowling	Mat	Balls	Runs	Wkts	BBI	BBM	Ave	Econ	SR	5w	10
First-class	18	1253	1068	10	3/50	3/50	106.80	5.11	125.3	0	0
List A	21	738	828	15	4/48	4/48	55.20	6.73	49.2	0	0
T20s	24	335	431	18	3/32	3/32	23.94	7.71	18.6	0	0

STEVEN CROFT

RHB / RMF / OB / R0 / W0

LANCASHIRE

FULL NAME: Steven John Croft
BORN: October 11, 1984, Blackpool
SQUAD NO: 15
HEIGHT: 5ft 11in
NICKNAME: Crofty
EDUCATION: Highfield High School, Blackpool; Myerscough College, Lancashire
TEAMS: Lancashire, Auckland, Northern Districts
ROLE: Allrounder
DEBUT: First-class: 2005; List A: 2003; T20: 2006

BEST BATTING: 156 Lancashire vs Northamptonshire, Old Trafford, 2014
BEST BOWLING: 6-41 Lancashire vs Worcestershire, Old Trafford, 2012
COUNTY CAP: 2010

WHAT GOT YOU INTO CRICKET? Living in Sri Lanka as an eight-year-old (there was nothing else to do)
'ROY OF THE ROVERS' MOMENT? Hitting a six off the last ball of the match to beat Leicestershire in 2006 in my second T20 appearance
BEST THING ABOUT YOUR HOME GROUND? The mix of modernity and tradition
BEST OPPOSING PLAYER IN COUNTY CRICKET? Marcus Trescothick (Som)
YOUNG OPPOSING PLAYER WHO HAS IMPRESSED YOU? Sam Curran (Sur) – with both bat and ball
IF YOU WEREN'T A CRICKETER? I'd be involved with the armed forces
SURPRISING FACT ABOUT A TEAMMATE? Simon Kerrigan can smile
WHERE IS PARADISE? Home with family
CRICKETING HERO? Andrew Flintoff – he was from around my area and played in the same league as me
TWITTER: @Stevenjcroft

Batting	Mat	Inns	NO	Runs	HS	Ave	SR	100	50	Ct	St
First-class	156	244	22	7367	156	33.18	50.76	12	42	162	0
List A	142	127	22	3668	127	34.93		2	28	71	0
T20s	160	150	36	3521	94*	30.88	122.81	0	21	95	0

Bowling	Mat	Balls	Runs	Wkts	BBI	BBM	Ave	Econ	SR	5w	10
First-class	156	5171	2903	71	6/41	9/105	40.88	3.36	72.8	1	0
List A	142	2583	2350	60	4/24	4/24	39.16	5.45	43.0	0	0
T20s	160	1474	1842	63	3/6	3/6	29.23	7.49	23.3	0	0

STEVEN CROOK

RHB / RFM / R0 / W0 /

FULL NAME: Steven Paul Crook
BORN: May 28, 1983, Adelaide, Australia
SQUAD NO: 25
HEIGHT: 5ft 11in
NICKNAME: Crooky
EDUCATION: Rostrevor College, Adelaide;
University of South Australia
TEAMS: Northamptonshire, Lancashire,
Middlesex, Sheikh Jamal Dhanmondi Club
ROLE: Allrounder
DEBUT: First-class: 2003; List A: 2003;
T20: 2004

BEST BATTING: 145 Northamptonshire vs Worcestershire, Worcester, 2016
BEST BOWLING: 5-48 Middlesex vs Lancashire, Lord's, 2012
COUNTY CAP: 2013 (Northamptonshire)

WHAT GOT YOU INTO CRICKET? Watching my dad play in Adelaide
FAMILY TIES? My older brother Andrew played for South Australia, Lancashire and
Northamptonshire. I only ever got hand-me-downs
'ROY OF THE ROVERS' MOMENT? Winning the T20 Blast with Northants in 2013
BEST THING ABOUT YOUR HOME GROUND? The fans really get behind us – especially on a
T20 night
BEST OPPOSING PLAYER IN COUNTY CRICKET? Riki Wessels (Not)
YOUNG OPPOSING PLAYER WHO HAS IMPRESSED YOU? Jofra Archer (Sus) – he's just very
good at cricket
IF YOU WEREN'T A CRICKETER? I'd be a failed musician
SURPRISING FACT ABOUT YOU? I starred (briefly) in Neighbours
CRICKETING HERO? Shoaib Akhtar – fast
NON-CRICKETING HERO? Jim Morrison – the coolest guy in history
TWITTER: @stevecrook25

Batting	Mat	Inns	NO	Runs	HS	Ave	SR	100	50	Ct	St
First-class	101	135	19	3682	145	31.74	76.74	5	19	33	0
List A	88	64	8	1198	100	21.39	101.18	1	5	18	0
T20s	122	91	25	1260	63	19.09	132.07	0	3	36	0

Bowling	Mat	Balls	Runs	Wkts	BBI	BBM	Ave	Econ	SR	5w	10
First-class	101	12142	7976	195	5/48	7/95	40.90	3.94	62.2	3	0
List A	88	2965	2853	82	5/36	5/36	34.79	5.77	36.1	1	0
T20s	122	1513	2116	73	3/19	3/19	28.98	8.39	20.7	0	0

GLAMORGAN

FULL NAME: Thomas Nicholas Cullen
BORN: January 4, 1992, Perth, Australia
SQUAD NO: 54
HEIGHT: 5ft 10in
NICKNAME: TC, Culley
EDUCATION: Cardiff Metropolitan University
TEAMS: Glamorgan
ROLE: Wicketkeeper
DEBUT: First-class: 2015

BEST BATTING: 42 Glamorgan vs Sussex, Colwyn Bay, 2017

WHAT GOT YOU INTO CRICKET? Growing up in Australia, cricket was everywhere
BEST ADVICE EVER RECEIVED? Nothing worth experiencing comes easy
'ROY OF THE ROVERS' MOMENT? Winning the University Challenge final at Lord's with Cardiff MCCU, then getting a call from Robert Croft the next morning (when I had a bit of a sore head) telling me to race back to Cardiff to travel with Glamorgan and make my debut. Two days later I was receiving my Glamorgan cap from Michael Hogan
BEST THING ABOUT YOUR HOME GROUND? It's in the heart of Cardiff
BEST OPPOSING PLAYER IN COUNTY CRICKET? Paul Collingwood (Dur) – much as I wanted him to get out, it was a pleasure watching him bat on my debut
IF YOU WEREN'T A CRICKETER? I'd be doing something with my degree
SURPRISING FACT ABOUT YOU? When I was younger I wanted to be a fighter pilot
SURPRISING FACT ABOUT A TEAMMATE? Connor Brown has a lot of stories and will make a great grandad one day
CRICKETING HERO? I loved watching Ricky Ponting and Adam Gilchrist come to play at the WACA every year
NON-CRICKETING HERO? My mum, who sadly passed away three years ago. She gave me the confidence to pursue my dreams. I try to honour her by giving everything to cricket
TWITTER: @thomascullen186

Batting	Mat	Inns	NO	Runs	HS	Ave	SR	100	50	Ct	St
First-class	6	9	0	154	42	17.11	34.76	0	0	13	1

Bowling	Mat	Balls	Runs	Wkts	BBI	BBM	Ave	Econ	SR	5w	10
First-class	6	-	-	-	-	-	-	-	-	-	-

SAM CURRAN

LHB / LFM / R0 / W0 / MVP21

FULL NAME: Samuel Matthew Curran
BORN: June 3, 1998, Northampton
SQUAD NO: 58
HEIGHT: 5ft 11in
NICKNAME: Junior, Sammy
EDUCATION: Wellington College, Berkshire
TEAMS: Surrey, England Lions
ROLE: Allrounder
DEBUT: First-class: 2015; List A: 2015; T20: 2015

SURREY

BEST BATTING: 96 Surrey vs Lancashire, The Oval, 2016
BEST BOWLING: 7-58 Surrey vs Durham, Chester-le-Street, 2016

FAMILY TIES? My father Kevin played for Zimbabwe, Gloucestershire and Northamptonshire and my brother Tom plays for Surrey. We have always been a competitive family
BEST ADVICE EVER RECEIVED? Enjoy it
BEST THING ABOUT YOUR HOME GROUND? Big crowds, great atmosphere
YOUNG OPPOSING PLAYER WHO HAS IMPRESSED YOU? Dan Lawrence (Ess) – scores lots of runs
SURPRISING FACT ABOUT YOU? I always put my right shoe on first
SURPRISING FACT ABOUT A TEAMMATE? Freddie van den Bergh is a scratch golfer
WHERE IS PARADISE? Cape Town
CRICKETING HERO? Brian Lara and Brett Lee – geniuses with bat and ball
NON-CRICKETING HERO? Conor McGregor
UNUSUAL OBJECT AT HOME? A big wooden hippo
TWITTER: @CurranSM

Batting	Mat	Inns	NO	Runs	HS	Ave	SR	100	50	Ct	St
First-class	34	51	7	1277	96	29.02	57.52	0	10	10	0
List A	37	24	4	466	57	23.30	90.13	0	1	13	0
T20s	43	34	5	449	50	15.48	118.15	0	1	11	0

Bowling	Mat	Balls	Runs	Wkts	BBI	BBM	Ave	Econ	SR	5w	10
First-class	34	4820	2814	86	7/58	8/120	32.72	3.50	56.0	4	0
List A	37	1650	1491	47	4/32	4/32	31.72	5.42	35.1	0	0
T20s	43	816	1138	40	4/13	4/13	28.45	8.36	20.4	0	0

TOM CURRAN

RHB / RFM / R0 / W1 / MVP61

FULL NAME: Thomas Kevin Curran
BORN: March 12, 1995, Cape Town, South Africa
SQUAD NO: 59
HEIGHT: 6ft
NICKNAME: TC
EDUCATION: Wellington College, Berkshire
TEAMS: England, Surrey
ROLE: Bowler
DEBUT: Test: 2017; ODI: 2017; T20I: 2017; First-class: 2014; List A: 2013; T20: 2014

BEST BATTING: 60 Surrey vs Leicestershire, Leicester, 2015
BEST BOWLING: 7-20 Surrey vs Gloucestershire, The Oval, 2015

FAMILY TIES? My father Kevin played for Northants and Zimbabwe and my brother Sam also plays for Surrey
CRICKETING HEROES? Hamilton Masakadza – he smashes it
IF YOU WEREN'T A CRICKETER? I would be fishing or playing the guitar in a bar somewhere exotic
SURPRISING FACT? I have a degree in Law
UNUSUAL OBJECT AT HOME? A harp
TWITTER: @_TC59

Batting	Mat	Inns	NO	Runs	HS	Ave	SR	100	50	Ct	St
Tests	2	3	1	66	39	33.00	55.00	0	0	0	0
ODIs	5	3	2	46	35	46.00	109.52	0	0	2	0
T20Is	6	3	2	8	6	8.00	133.33	0	0	1	0
First-class	53	72	10	1128	60	18.19	50.04	0	5	20	0
List A	57	39	14	458	44	18.32	96.82	0	0	19	0
T20s	51	29	10	362	51*	19.05	128.36	0	1	18	0

Bowling	Mat	Balls	Runs	Wkts	BBI	BBM	Ave	Econ	SR	5w	10
Tests	2	396	200	2	1/65	1/82	100.00	3.03	198.0	0	0
ODIs	5	242	225	8	5/35	5/35	28.12	5.57	30.2	1	0
T20Is	6	126	195	7	3/33	3/33	27.85	9.28	18.0	0	0
First-class	53	9449	5183	173	7/20	10/176	29.95	3.29	54.6	6	1
List A	57	2549	2317	86	5/16	5/16	26.94	5.45	29.6	3	0
T20s	51	1047	1440	53	4/35	4/35	27.16	8.25	19.7	0	0

OLIVER CURRILL

RHB / RMF / RO / WO

FULL NAME: Oliver Charles Currill
BORN: February 27, 1997, Banbury, Oxfordshire
SQUAD NO: TBC
HEIGHT: 6ft 4in
NICKNAME: Nurrell
EDUCATION: Chipping Campden Academy
TEAMS: Gloucestershire
ROLE: Bowler
DEBUT: First-class: 2017

GLOUCESTERSHIRE

WHAT GOT YOU INTO CRICKET? My dad and playing in the back garden
BEST ADVICE EVER RECEIVED? Be selective with the advice you use (from Gloucestershire assistant Academy coach Steve Cashmore)
'ROY OF THE ROVERS' MOMENT? Taking a hat-trick while bowling off-spin in the Great Tew six-a-side tournament in Oxfordshire
BEST THING ABOUT YOUR HOME GROUND? Boston Tea Party café on Gloucester Road
BEST OPPOSING PLAYER IN COUNTY CRICKET? Marcus Trescothick (Som)
YOUNG OPPOSING PLAYER WHO HAS IMPRESSED YOU? Graham Clark (Dur)
IF YOU WEREN'T A CRICKETER? I'd be a professional goalkeeper
SURPRISING FACT ABOUT A TEAMMATE? George Hankins has no earlobes
WHERE IS PARADISE? Old Trafford
CRICKETING HERO? Shaun Pollock – he's the player I aspire to become like
NON-CRICKETING HERO? Sir Alex Ferguson

Batting	Mat	Inns	NO	Runs	HS	Ave	SR	100	50	Ct	St
First-class	1	-	-	-	-	-	-	-	-	0	0

Bowling	Mat	Balls	Runs	Wkts	BBI	BBM	Ave	Econ	SR	5w	10
First-class	1	90	83	0	-	-	-	5.53	-	0	0

JOSH DAVEY

RHB / RMF / R0 / W0

SOMERSET

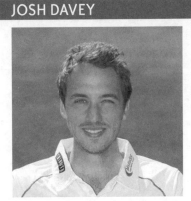

FULL NAME: Joshua Henry Davey
BORN: August 3, 1990, Aberdeen, Scotland
SQUAD NO: 38
EDUCATION: Culford School
TEAMS: Scotland, Somerset, Middlesex
ROLE: Allrounder
DEBUT: ODI: 2010; T20I: 2012; First-class: 2010; List A: 2010; T20: 2010

BEST BATTING: 72 Middlesex vs Oxford MCCU, Oxford, 2010
BEST BOWLING: 4-53 Scotland vs Afghanistan, Abu Dhabi, 2013

TWITTER: @JoshDavey38
NOTES: After four years at Middlesex, Davey was released at the end of 2013 and excelled for Somerset Second XI in 2014, which led to a full contract at the county. The seam-bowling allrounder hit an unbeaten 48 and took 3-41 for Scotland against Ireland at Edinburgh in the 2011 Tri-Nation Tournament to help his country to a five-wicket win. Took 5-9 for Scotland against Afghanistan at Ayr in 2010. In January 2015, against the same opponents, he took 6-28 and scored 53*. He played for Scotland in the 2015 World Cup, finishing as his team's highest wicket-taker. Has been a peripheral figure for Somerset over the last few seasons, although he did play 11 matches across all formats in 2017

Batting	Mat	Inns	NO	Runs	HS	Ave	SR	100	50	Ct	St
ODIs	29	26	5	471	64	22.42	65.87	0	2	9	0
T20Is	14	7	2	55	24	11.00	127.90	0	0	9	0
First-class	15	25	2	420	72	18.26	42.51	0	3	8	0
List A	72	60	11	1132	91	23.10	65.66	0	5	23	0
T20s	35	20	9	173	24	15.72	124.46	0	0	21	0

Bowling	Mat	Balls	Runs	Wkts	BBI	BBM	Ave	Econ	SR	5w	10
ODIs	29	1199	1014	47	6/28	6/28	21.57	5.07	25.5	2	0
T20Is	14	298	422	14	4/34	4/34	30.14	8.49	21.2	0	0
First-class	15	1527	775	25	4/53	6/79	31.00	3.04	61.0	0	0
List A	72	2531	2314	88	6/28	6/28	26.29	5.48	28.7	2	0
T20s	35	520	780	28	4/34	4/34	27.85	9.00	18.5	0	0

ALEX DAVIES

RHB / WK / R1 / W0 / MVP39

FULL NAME: Alexander Luke Davies
BORN: August 23, 1994, Darwen, Lancashire
SQUAD NO: 17
HEIGHT: 5ft 8in
NICKNAME: Davo, Chikwambo, Little Boy
EDUCATION: Queen Elizabeth's Grammar School, Blackburn
TEAMS: Lancashire, England Lions
ROLE: Wicketkeeper
DEBUT: First-class: 2012; List A: 2011; T20: 2014

LANCASHIRE

BEST BATTING: 140* Lancashire vs Essex, Chelmsford, 2017

FAMILY TIES? Dad played club cricket all his life
'ROY OF THE ROVERS' MOMENT? Winning the T20 Blast with Lancashire in 2015
HOW WOULD YOUR TEAMMATES DESCRIBE YOU IN THREE WORDS? Little-man syndrome
CRICKETING HEROES? Sachin Tendulkar – timed the ball amazingly. Adam Gilchrist – first high-quality, aggressive batsman-keeper. AB de Villiers – 360-degree gameplay
NON-CRICKETING HEROES? Alan Shearer, David Beckham, grandad
SURPRISING FACT? Despite being a wicketkeeper, I can bowl with both arms
TWITTER: @aldavies23

Batting	Mat	Inns	NO	Runs	HS	Ave	SR	100	50	Ct	St
First-class	50	75	4	2546	140*	35.85	54.36	3	16	135	14
List A	24	21	3	591	73*	32.83	96.72	0	4	24	5
T20s	25	23	2	274	47	13.04	129.24	0	0	19	4

Bowling	Mat	Balls	Runs	Wkts	BBI	BBM	Ave	Econ	SR	5w	10
First-class	50	-	-	-	-	-	-	-	-	-	-
List A	24	-	-	-	-	-	-	-	-	-	-
T20s	25	-	-	-	-	-	-	-	-	-	-

STEVEN DAVIES

LHB / WK / R6 / W0 / MVP36

SOMERSET

FULL NAME: Steven Michael Davies
BORN: June 17, 1986, Bromsgrove, Worcestershire
SQUAD NO: 11
HEIGHT: 5ft 11in
NICKNAME: Dave
EDUCATION: King Charles High School, Kidderminster
TEAMS: England, Somerset, Surrey, Worcestershire
ROLE: Batsman/wicketkeeper
DEBUT: ODI: 2009; T20I: 2009; First-class: 2005; List A: 2003; T20: 2006

BEST BATTING: 200* Surrey vs Glamorgan, Cardiff, 2015
COUNTY CAP: 2011 (Surrey)

'ROY OF THE ROVERS' MOMENT? My double hundred against Glamorgan in 2015
SUPERSTITIONS? My area in the dressing room must be tidy and I always shadow shots in the mirror before batting
HOW WOULD YOUR TEAMMATES DESCRIBE YOU IN THREE WORDS? Laid-back, calm, loyal
BEST OPPOSING PLAYER IN COUNTY CRICKET? Tom Curran (Sur)
CRICKETING HERO? Adam Gilchrist
NON-CRICKETING HERO? Roger Federer
IF YOU WEREN'T A CRICKETER? I'd be a professional tennis player
SURPRISING FACT? I'm a session harp player
TWITTER: @SteveDavies43

Batting	Mat	Inns	NO	Runs	HS	Ave	SR	100	50	Ct	St
ODIs	8	8	0	244	87	30.50	105.62	0	1	8	0
T20Is	5	5	0	102	33	20.40	124.39	0	0	2	1
First-class	196	323	32	11653	200*	40.04	61.66	23	53	446	27
List A	176	165	14	5487	127*	36.33		9	34	137	42
T20s	128	119	8	2431	99*	21.90	142.24	0	14	57	22

Bowling	Mat	Balls	Runs	Wkts	BBI	BBM	Ave	Econ	SR	5w	10
ODIs	8	-	-	-	-	-	-	-	-	-	-
T20Is	5	-	-	-	-	-	-	-	-	-	-
First-class	196	-	-	-	-	-	-	-	-	-	-
List A	176	-	-	-	-	-	-	-	-	-	-
T20s	128	-	-	-	-	-	-	-	-	-	-

WILL DAVIS

RHB / RFM / RO / WO

FULL NAME: William Samuel Davis
BORN: March 6, 1996, Stafford
SQUAD NO: 44
HEIGHT: 6ft 2in
NICKNAME: Thumb, Spaceman
EDUCATION: Stafford Grammar School
TEAMS: Derbyshire
ROLE: Bowler
DEBUT: First-class: 2015; List A: 2016

DERBYSHIRE

BEST BATTING: 25 Derbyshire vs Sussex, Hove, 2017
BEST BOWLING: 7-146 Derbyshire vs Glamorgan, Colwyn Bay, 2016

STRANGEST THING SEEN IN A GAME? Greg Cork's field placements
'ROY OF THE ROVERS' MOMENT? Taking my maiden five-wicket haul in first-class cricket against Glamorgan at Colwyn Bay in 2016
SUPERSTITIONS? I have to turn at the end of my bowling mark before running in
HOW WOULD YOUR TEAMMATES DESCRIBE YOU IN THREE WORDS? Switched-on, clever, spaceman
CRICKETING HERO? Andrew Flintoff
NON-CRICKETING HERO? Cristiano Ronaldo
IF YOU WEREN'T A CRICKETER? I'd be a professional gamer
UNUSUAL OBJECT AT HOME? Slendertone
TWITTER: @W_Davis44

Batting	Mat	Inns	NO	Runs	HS	Ave	SR	100	50	Ct	St
First-class	12	16	4	106	25	8.83	58.88	0	0	2	0
List A	1	-	-	-	-	-	-	-	-	-	-

Bowling	Mat	Balls	Runs	Wkts	BBI	BBM	Ave	Econ	SR	5w	10
First-class	12	1777	1224	38	7/146	8/204	32.21	4.13	46.7	1	0
List A	1	-	-	-	-	-	-	-	-	-	-

LIAM DAWSON

RHB / SLA / R1 / W0 / MVP24

HAMPSHIRE

FULL NAME: Liam Andrew Dawson
BORN: March 1, 1990, Swindon
SQUAD NO: 8
HEIGHT: 5ft 8in
NICKNAME: Daws, Lemmy, Chav, Stomper
EDUCATION: The John Bentley School, Wiltshire
TEAMS: England, Hampshire, Essex, Mountaineers, Rangpur Riders
ROLE: Allrounder
DEBUT: Test: 2016; ODI: 2016; T20I: 2016; First-class: 2007; List A: 2007; T20: 2008

BEST BATTING: 169 Hampshire vs Somerset, Southampton, 2011
BEST BOWLING: 7-51 Mountaineers vs Mashonaland Eagles, Mutare Sports Club, 2011
COUNTY CAP: 2013 (Hampshire)

WHAT GOT YOU INTO CRICKET? Watching my dad play for Goatacre CC
FAMILY TIES? My brother Brad has played Minor Counties for Wiltshire
STRANGEST THING SEEN IN A GAME? Benny Howell
'ROY OF THE ROVERS' MOMENT? My England debut in 2016
HOW WOULD YOUR TEAMMATES DESCRIBE YOU IN THREE WORDS? Stubborn, chav, argumentative
BEST OPPOSING PLAYER IN COUNTY CRICKET? Mark Wood (Dur)
CRICKETING HERO? Shane Warne
IF YOU WEREN'T A CRICKETER? I'd be an umpire
TWITTER: @daws128

Batting	Mat	Inns	NO	Runs	HS	Ave	SR	100	50	Ct	St
Tests	3	6	2	84	66*	21.00	42.63	0	1	2	0
ODIs	1	1	0	10	10	10.00	76.92	0	0	0	0
T20Is	6	2	1	17	10	17.00	212.50	0	0	2	0
First-class	131	215	23	6279	169	32.70	48.16	8	34	132	0
List A	141	116	21	3082	113*	32.44	93.42	2	16	66	0
T20s	112	78	22	971	76*	17.33	110.59	0	1	51	0

Bowling	Mat	Balls	Runs	Wkts	BBI	BBM	Ave	Econ	SR	5w	10
Tests	3	526	298	7	2/34	4/101	42.57	3.39	75.1	0	0
ODIs	1	48	70	2	2/70	2/70	35.00	8.75	24.0	0	0
T20Is	6	120	152	5	3/27	3/27	30.40	7.60	24.0	0	0
First-class	131	11863	6005	169	7/51	8/129	35.53	3.03	70.1	3	0
List A	141	5186	4191	122	6/47	6/47	34.35	4.84	42.5	1	0
T20s	112	1696	2070	84	5/17	5/17	24.64	7.32	20.1	1	0

COLIN DE GRANDHOMME RHB / RMF / R0 / W0

FULL NAME: Colin de Grandhomme
BORN: July 22, 1986, Harare, Zimbabwe
SQUAD NO: 77
TEAMS: New Zealand, Warwickshire, Auckland, Manicaland, Midlands, Nagenahira Nagas
ROLE: Allrounder
DEBUT: Test: 2016; ODI: 2012; T20I: 2012; First-class: 2005; List A: 2004; T20: 2007

WARWICKSHIRE

BEST BATTING: 144* Auckland vs Otago, Auckland, 2016
BEST BOWLING: 6-24 Auckland vs Wellington, Auckland, 2014

NOTES: Warwickshire have re-signed the seam-bowling allrounder for the duration of the T20 Blast. De Grandhomme plundered 322 runs from 16 games as Warwickshire made it to the final last year, although he will be looking to improve on his return of five wickets at 69.60. He made his New Zealand debut in 2012 against his native Zimbabwe but had to wait until the 2016 home series against Pakistan for his maiden Test match, taking 6-41 in Christchurch. In December 2017 he scored the second-fastest Test century by a New Zealander (71 balls). "I absolutely loved my time with the Bears last season," said de Grandhomme. "We played some excellent T20 cricket and came very close to winning the T20 Blast on Finals Day. We've got a young squad with plenty of firepower and I believe that we have every chance of going one step further in 2018"

Batting	Mat	Inns	NO	Runs	HS	Ave	SR	100	50	Ct	St
Tests	8	12	1	391	105	35.54	98.98	1	2	8	0
ODIs	16	13	5	357	74*	44.62	109.84	0	1	3	0
T20Is	19	17	7	162	41*	16.20	151.40	0	0	9	0
First-class	92	151	19	4749	144*	35.97	71.95	11	28	94	0
List A	117	106	15	2431	151	26.71		2	7	50	0
T20s	141	126	31	2314	72*	24.35	167.80	0	7	62	0

Bowling	Mat	Balls	Runs	Wkts	BBI	BBM	Ave	Econ	SR	5w	10
Tests	8	1217	522	20	6/41	7/64	26.10	2.57	60.8	1	0
ODIs	16	528	482	9	2/40	2/40	53.55	5.47	58.6	0	0
T20Is	19	197	305	7	2/22	2/22	43.57	9.28	28.1	0	0
First-class	92	9255	4310	147	6/24	7/64	29.31	2.79	62.9	2	0
List A	117	3080	2727	61	4/37	4/37	44.70	5.31	50.4	0	0
T20s	141	1216	1873	54	3/4	3/4	34.68	9.24	22.5	0	0

MARCHANT DE LANGE   RHB / RF / R0 / W0 / MVP25

FULL NAME: Marchant de Lange
BORN: October 13, 1990, Tzaneen, Transvaal, South Africa
SQUAD NO: 90
HEIGHT: 6ft 7in
NICKNAME: Shanna
TEAMS: South Africa, Glamorgan, Barbados Tridents, Easterns, Free State, Guyana Amazon Warriors, Knights, Kolkata Knight Riders, Mumbai Indians, Titans
ROLE: Bowler
DEBUT: Test: 2011; ODI: 2012; T20I: 2012; First-class: 2010; List A: 2010; T20: 2011

BEST BATTING: 65 Knights vs Lions, Kimberley, 2016
BEST BOWLING: 7-23 Knights vs Titans, Centurion, 2016

BEST ADVICE EVER RECEIVED? To bowl top of off
'ROY OF THE ROVERS' MOMENT? Taking seven wickets on my Test debut
YOUNG OPPOSING PLAYER WHO HAS IMPRESSED YOU? Jamie Porter (Ess) – consistent and skilful in four-day cricket
IF YOU WEREN'T A CRICKETER? I'd be a MotoGP rider or Formula 1 driver
SURPRISING FACT ABOUT YOU? I love art and building
WHERE IS PARADISE? Santorini
CRICKETING HERO? Dale Steyn or Brett Lee – both very passionate
NON-CRICKETING HERO? Valentino Rossi – the best-ever MotoGP rider

Batting	Mat	Inns	NO	Runs	HS	Ave	SR	100	50	Ct	St
Tests	2	2	0	9	9	4.50	47.36	0	0	1	0
ODIs	4	-	-	-	-	-	-	-	-	0	0
T20Is	6	-	-	-	-	-	-	-	-	1	0
First-class	69	91	11	1163	65	14.53	70.06	0	1	31	0
List A	76	53	16	513	53	13.86	96.79	0	1	18	0
T20s	75	27	13	159	27*	11.35	133.61	0	0	14	0

Bowling	Mat	Balls	Runs	Wkts	BBI	BBM	Ave	Econ	SR	5w	10
Tests	2	448	277	9	7/81	8/126	30.77	3.70	49.7	1	0
ODIs	4	209	198	10	4/46	4/46	19.80	5.68	20.9	0	0
T20Is	6	140	228	7	2/26	2/26	32.57	9.77	20.0	0	0
First-class	69	12749	7633	256	7/23	11/62	29.81	3.59	49.8	10	2
List A	76	3787	3372	134	5/49	5/49	25.16	5.34	28.2	4	0
T20s	75	1519	2160	86	4/23	4/23	25.11	8.53	17.6	0	0

HARRY DEARDEN

LHB / OB / R0 / W0

FULL NAME: Harry Edward Dearden
BORN: May 7, 1997, Bury, Lancashire
SQUAD NO: 5
HEIGHT: 5ft 8in
NICKNAME: H, Haz, Deards
EDUCATION: Tottington High School, Bury; Bury College
TEAMS: Leicestershire
ROLE: Batsman
DEBUT: First-class: 2016

BEST BATTING: 87 Leicestershire vs Glamorgan, Leicester, 2017
BEST BOWLING: 1-0 Leicestershire vs Kent, Leicester, 2017

WHAT GOT YOU INTO CRICKET? The 2005 Ashes. I still have the box set at home and get it out from time to time
FAMILY TIES? Dad played for the Lancashire Cricket Board and still plays cricket now
'ROY OF THE ROVERS' MOMENT? My first-class debut for Leicestershire in 2016
STRANGEST THING SEEN IN A GAME? It happened during a T20 on a wet Friday night for my club team. The ball was pretty soggy before an opposition batter hit it out the ground. We gave a replacement ball to the umpire, who proceeded to wipe it along the wet outfield, claiming the substitute ball had to be in the exact same state as the lost one. Madness
BEST OPPOSING PLAYER IN COUNTY CRICKET? Tim Bresnan (Yor)
SURPRISING FACT? I was on a Channel 4 roadshow for the 2001 Ashes series, having a split-screen with Shane Warne
CRICKETING HEROES? Brian Lara, Alastair Cook, Shane Warne
NON-CRICKETING HEROES? Paul Scholes, Roy Keane
TWITTER: @HarryDearden97

Batting	Mat	Inns	NO	Runs	HS	Ave	SR	100	50	Ct	St
First-class	13	25	0	481	87	19.24	38.11	0	2	14	0

Bowling	Mat	Balls	Runs	Wkts	BBI	BBM	Ave	Econ	SR	5w	10
First-class	13	112	95	2	1/0	1/0	47.50	5.08	56.0	0	0

CAMERON DELPORT

LHB / RMF / RO / WO

FULL NAME: Cameron Scott Delport
BORN: May 12, 1989, Durban, South Africa
SQUAD NO: 24
HEIGHT: 5ft 10in
NICKNAME: Camo, Delpo, Goose
EDUCATION: Kloof Senior School, Durban;
Westville Boys' High School, Durban
TEAMS: Leicestershire, Dolphins, KwaZulu-Natal, Lahore Qalandars, Sydney Thunder, Trinidad and Tobago Red Steel
ROLE: Allrounder
DEBUT: First-class: 2009; List A: 2009; T20: 2010

BEST BATTING: 163 KwaZulu-Natal vs Northerns, Centurion, 2011
BEST BOWLING: 2-10 KwaZulu-Natal vs Northern Cape, Chatsworth, 2016

WHAT GOT YOU INTO CRICKET? My uncle, my dad – in fact pretty much the whole family
BEST ADVICE EVER RECEIVED? See ball, hit ball
'ROY OF THE ROVERS' MOMENT? In general terms, playing and sharing dressing rooms with international cricketers in various T20 tournaments around the world – getting their advice and hearing about how their careers have been shaped through good and bad times
BEST THING ABOUT YOUR HOME GROUND? I have many home grounds at the moment! As long as they are batter-friendly then I am happy
BEST OPPOSING PLAYER IN COUNTY CRICKET? Alex Hales (Not)
YOUNG OPPOSING PLAYER WHO HAS IMPRESSED YOU? The Parkinson twins, Matt (Lan) and Callum (Lei). They're both fearless, passionate and want to learn
IF YOU WEREN'T A CRICKETER? I'd be a surfer-traveller-businessman
SURPRISING FACT ABOUT YOU? I am a great BBQ chef and entertainer
NON-CRICKETING HERO? Kelly Slater – amazing pro surfer and an amazing man
TWITTER: @Cam12Delport

Batting	Mat	Inns	NO	Runs	HS	Ave	SR	100	50	Ct	St
First-class	61	106	6	3206	163	32.06	88.29	3	19	36	0
List A	102	92	6	2591	169*	30.12	106.71	2	15	35	0
T20s	139	132	10	3224	109*	26.42	138.54	3	17	53	0

Bowling	Mat	Balls	Runs	Wkts	BBI	BBM	Ave	Econ	SR	5w	10
First-class	61	1183	723	14	2/10	2/10	51.64	3.66	84.5	0	0
List A	102	1495	1485	37	4/42	4/42	40.13	5.95	40.4	0	0
T20s	139	955	1219	48	4/17	4/17	25.39	7.65	19.8	0	0

RHB / LB / R4 / W0 / MVP14

FULL NAME: Joseph Liam Denly
BORN: March 16, 1986, Canterbury, Kent
SQUAD NO: 6
HEIGHT: 6ft
NICKNAME: JD, Denners, No Pants
EDUCATION: Chaucer Technology School, Canterbury
TEAMS: England, Kent, Barisal Burners, Brothers Union, Karachi Kings, Middlesex
ROLE: Batsman
DEBUT: ODI: 2009; T20I: 2009; First-class: 2004; List A: 2004; T20: 2004

KENT

BEST BATTING: 227 Kent vs Worcestershire, Worcester, 2017
BEST BOWLING: 3-43 Kent vs Surrey, The Oval, 2011
COUNTY CAP: 2008 (Kent); 2012 (Middlesex)

TWITTER: @joed1986
NOTES: Fluent batsman who many thought would play more than just nine ODIs and five T20Is for England after making an impressive start to his career. Came up through the Kent ranks and re-joined the county in 2015 after an unsuccessful spell at Middlesex. Made one Championship hundred in 2016 and was outstanding in the shorter formats, hitting 428 runs at 61.14 in the One-Day Cup as well as three T20 Blast fifties. He surpassed those heights last summer, scoring well over 1,000 Championship runs as well as being the leading run-scorer in the T20 Blast (567 runs). Appointed Kent's vice-captain ahead of the 2018 campaign

Batting	Mat	Inns	NO	Runs	HS	Ave	SR	100	50	Ct	St
ODIs	9	9	0	268	67	29.77	65.52	0	2	5	0
T20Is	5	5	0	20	14	4.00	68.96	0	0	1	0
First-class	173	299	21	10032	227	36.08	56.50	23	51	75	0 -
List A	140	134	12	4176	115	34.22	74.95	6	21	47	0
T20s	169	165	13	4183	127	27.51	120.68	3	24	64	0

Bowling	Mat	Balls	Runs	Wkts	BBI	BBM	Ave	Econ	SR	5w	10
ODIs	9	-	-	-	-	-	-	-	-	-	-
T20Is	5	6	9	1	1/9	1/9	9.00	9.00	6.0	0	0
First-class	173	3301	1869	39	3/43	6/114	47.92	3.39	84.6	0	0
List A	140	866	667	32	4/35	4/35	20.84	4.62	27.0	0	0
T20s	169	102	142	4	1/9	1/9	35.50	8.35	25.5	0	0

CHRIS DENT

LHB / SLA / R3 / W0

GLOUCESTERSHIRE

FULL NAME: Christopher David James Dent
BORN: January 20, 1991, Bristol
SQUAD NO: 15
HEIGHT: 5ft 10in
NICKNAME: Denty, Maggot
EDUCATION: Backwell School, North Somerset; Filton College, Bristol
TEAMS: Gloucestershire
ROLE: Batsman
DEBUT: First-class: 2010; List A: 2009; T20: 2010

BEST BATTING: 268 Gloucestershire vs Glamorgan, Bristol, 2015
BEST BOWLING: 2-21 Gloucestershire vs Sussex, Hove, 2016
COUNTY CAP: 2010

WHAT GOT YOU INTO CRICKET? Watching my dad play at Cleeve CC
BEST ADVICE EVER RECEIVED? Straight and late till 28
'ROY OF THE ROVERS' MOMENT? Winning the One-Day Cup final against Surrey in 2015
BEST THING ABOUT YOUR HOME GROUND? The filing cabinet in the shower. Why would you have a filing cabinet in the shower? So that you can file and shower at the same time
BEST OPPOSING PLAYER IN COUNTY CRICKET? Jofra Archer (Sus)
YOUNG OPPOSING PLAYER WHO HAS IMPRESSED YOU? Josh Tongue (Wor)
IF YOU WEREN'T A CRICKETER? I'd be working on a till
SURPRISING FACT ABOUT YOU? I once scored nine goals in a football match
SURPRISING FACT ABOUT A TEAMMATE? George Hankins has no abs
WHERE IS PARADISE? Walt Disney World in Florida with the kids
CRICKETING HERO? Brian Lara
NON-CRICKETING HERO? Michael Jordan – I loved the Chicago Bulls and the Space Jam film
TWITTER: @cdent15

Batting	Mat	Inns	NO	Runs	HS	Ave	SR	100	50	Ct	St
First-class	114	202	19	6991	268	38.20	52.65	13	43	137	0
List A	55	50	4	1334	151*	29.00	93.15	3	2	19	0
T20s	49	43	7	725	63*	20.13	116.37	0	3	17	0

Bowling	Mat	Balls	Runs	Wkts	BBI	BBM	Ave	Econ	SR	5w	10
First-class	114	1182	793	8	2/21	2/21	99.12	4.02	147.7	0	0
List A	55	438	412	12	4/43	4/43	34.33	5.64	36.5	0	0
T20s	49	120	168	5	1/4	1/4	33.60	8.40	24.0	0	0

JADE DERNBACH

RHB / RFM / R0 / W1

FULL NAME: Jade Winston Dernbach
BORN: March 3, 1986, Johannesburg, South Africa
SQUAD NO: 16
HEIGHT: 6ft 2in
NICKNAME: Dirtbag, DJ Douche
EDUCATION: St John the Baptist School, Woking
TEAMS: England, Surrey, Melbourne Stars, Wellington
ROLE: Bowler
DEBUT: ODI: 2011; T20I: 2011; First-class: 2003; List A: 2005; T20: 2005

BEST BATTING: 56* Surrey vs Northamptonshire, Northampton, 2011
BEST BOWLING: 6-47 Surrey vs Leicestershire, Leicester, 2010
COUNTY CAP: 2011

WHAT GOT YOU INTO CRICKET? It chose me
'ROY OF THE ROVERS' MOMENT? Winning the C&G Trophy. Promotion to Division One of the Championship. My England debut
HOW WOULD YOUR TEAMMATES DESCRIBE YOU IN THREE WORDS? Charismatic, attractive, high-end
CRICKETING HERO? Allan Donald – because he bowled fast
NON-CRICKETING HERO? David Beckham – he is high-end
IF YOU WEREN'T A CRICKETER? I would be Harvey Specter's understudy
SURPRISING FACT? I am the 17th-best pick-up-sticks player in Surrey
UNUSUAL OBJECT AT HOME? The Great Gatsby
TWITTER: @Jwd_16

Batting	Mat	Inns	NO	Runs	HS	Ave	SR	100	50	Ct	St
ODIs	24	8	1	19	5	2.71	48.71	0	0	5	0
T20Is	34	7	2	24	12	4.80	114.28	0	0	8	0
First-class	103	126	45	742	56*	9.16		0	1	15	0
List A	138	49	19	228	31	7.60	82.60	0	0	28	0
T20s	131	31	14	142	24*	8.35	111.81	0	0	27	0

Bowling	Mat	Balls	Runs	Wkts	BBI	BBM	Ave	Econ	SR	5w	10
ODIs	24	1234	1308	31	4/45	4/45	42.19	6.35	39.8	0	0
T20Is	34	702	1020	39	4/22	4/22	26.15	8.71	18.0	0	0
First-class	103	16507	9210	279	6/47	9/138	33.01	3.34	59.1	10	0
List A	138	5978	5859	222	6/35	6/35	26.39	5.88	26.9	3	0
T20s	131	2667	3764	146	4/22	4/22	25.78	8.46	18.2	0	0

NEIL DEXTER

RHB / RM / RO / WO

LEICESTERSHIRE

FULL NAME: Neil John Dexter
BORN: August 21, 1984, Johannesburg, South Africa
SQUAD NO: 17
HEIGHT: 5ft 11in
NICKNAME: Dexy, Dex, Sexy Dexy
EDUCATION: Northwood School, Durban; University of South Africa
TEAMS: Leicestershire, Essex, Kent, Middlesex
ROLE: Allrounder
DEBUT: First-class: 2005; List A: 2005; T20: 2006

BEST BATTING: 163* Middlesex vs Northamptonshire, Northampton, 2014
BEST BOWLING: 6-63 Middlesex vs Lancashire, Lord's, 2014
COUNTY CAP: 2010 (Middlesex)

'ROY OF THE ROVERS' MOMENT? Taking six wickets against Lancashire and reaching my PB with the bat against Northants in 2014
CRICKETING HEROES? Brett Lee – fast and aggressive but played the game in the right spirit. AB de Villiers – the best player in the world in all formats and very humble
NON-CRICKETING HEROES? My family, as they are my number-one fans
IF YOU WEREN'T A CRICKETER? I'd probably be a scientist
TWITTER: @dexy214

Batting	Mat	Inns	NO	Runs	HS	Ave	SR	100	50	Ct	St
First-class	141	237	27	7290	163*	34.71	51.33	17	34	88	0
List A	101	84	19	1949	135*	29.98	81.41	2	8	26	0
T20s	117	94	15	1550	73	19.62	109.92	0	2	44	0

Bowling	Mat	Balls	Runs	Wkts	BBI	BBM	Ave	Econ	SR	5w	10
First-class	141	9334	4891	148	6/63	6/47	33.04	3.14	63.0	6	0
List A	101	2305	2156	42	4/22	4/22	51.33	5.61	54.8	0	0
T20s	117	1415	1775	64	4/21	4/21	27.73	7.52	22.1	0	0

CALVIN DICKINSON

RHB / WK / R0 / W0

FULL NAME: Calvin Miles Dickinson
BORN: November 3, 1996, Durban, South Africa
SQUAD NO: 21
HEIGHT: 5ft 9in
NICKNAME: Calv
EDUCATION: St Edward's School, Oxford
TEAMS: Hampshire
ROLE: Wicketkeeper/batsman
DEBUT: First-class: 2016; List A: 2018; T20: 2017

BEST BATTING: 99 Hampshire vs South Africa A, Southampton, 2017

WHAT GOT YOU INTO CRICKET? Watching my dad play from a young age
BEST ADVICE EVER RECEIVED? Back your ability
'ROY OF THE ROVERS' MOMENT? Playing for Hampshire on T20 Finals Day in 2017
BEST THING ABOUT YOUR HOME GROUND? The facilities at the Ageas Bowl help me get the most out of my practice
BEST OPPOSING PLAYER IN COUNTY CRICKET? Colin Ingram (Gla)
YOUNG OPPOSING PLAYER WHO HAS IMPRESSED YOU? Ethan Bamber (Mid 2nd XI) – he bowled really well against us in a second XI game last year
WHERE IS PARADISE? Durban
CRICKETING HERO? AB de Villiers
NON-CRICKETING HERO? My dad – he inspires me with how hard he works
TWITTER: @dickinson1996

Batting	Mat	Inns	NO	Runs	HS	Ave	SR	100	50	Ct	St
First-class	4	6	0	211	99	35.16	83.07	0	2	4	0
List A	6	5	0	45	21	9.00	63.38	0	0	4	0
T20s	5	5	0	102	51	20.40	152.23	0	1	2	2

Bowling	Mat	Balls	Runs	Wkts	BBI	BBM	Ave	Econ	SR	5w	10
First-class	4	-	-	-	-	-	-	-	-	-	-
List A	6	-	-	-	-	-	-	-	-	-	-
T20s	5	-	-	-	-	-	-	-	-	-	-

SEAN DICKSON

RHB / RM / R0 / W0

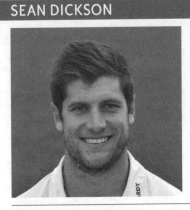

FULL NAME: Sean Robert Dickson
BORN: September 2, 1991, Johannesburg, South Africa
SQUAD NO: 58
HEIGHT: 5ft 10in
NICKNAME: Dicko
EDUCATION: King Edward VII School, Johannesburg; University of Pretoria
TEAMS: Kent, Northerns
ROLE: Batsman
DEBUT: First-class: 2013; List A: 2013; T20: 2014

BEST BATTING: 318 Kent vs Northamptonshire, Beckenham, 2017
BEST BOWLING: 1-15 Northerns vs Griqualand West, Centurion, 2015

WHAT GOT YOU INTO CRICKET? Just the interest in playing an incredible sport. Also going to watch live games and watching on the telly
FAMILY TIES? They are unbelievably dedicated spectators
CRICKETING HERO? Hashim Amla
IF YOU WEREN'T A CRICKETER? I'd be a big-shot CEO
SURPRISING FACT? I am an unbelievable dancer
UNUSUAL OBJECT AT HOME? A book
TWITTER: @Seano_146

Batting	Mat	Inns	NO	Runs	HS	Ave	SR	100	50	Ct	St
First-class	41	66	6	2275	318	37.91	51.18	4	11	21	0
List A	29	28	1	783	99	29.00	73.10	0	6	9	0
T20s	4	4	0	114	53	28.50	139.02	0	1	1	0

Bowling	Mat	Balls	Runs	Wkts	BBI	BBM	Ave	Econ	SR	5w	10
First-class	41	72	44	2	1/15	2/40	22.00	3.66	36.0	0	0
List A	29	-	-	-	-	-	-	-	-	-	-
T20s	4	6	9	1	1/9	1/9	9.00	9.00	6.0	0	0

FULL NAME: Matthew William Dixon
BORN: June 12, 1992, Perth, Australia
SQUAD NO: 30
HEIGHT: 6ft 3in
NICKNAME: Dicko
EDUCATION: Servite College, Perth;
University of Hertfordshire
TEAMS: Essex, Western Australia, Perth
Scorchers
ROLE: Bowler
DEBUT: First-class: 2011; List A 2010; T20:
2014

ESSEX

BEST BATTING: 22 Western Australia vs Queensland, Perth, 2011
BEST BOWLING: 5-124 Essex vs Kent, Canterbury, 2016

FAMILY TIES? My dad was my first coach and a player until his mid-20s
BEST ADVICE EVER RECEIVED? Always have fun
'ROY OF THE ROVERS' MOMENT? My first five-for in first-class cricket against Kent in 2016
BEST THING ABOUT YOUR HOME GROUND? The atmosphere on T20 nights
YOUNG OPPOSING PLAYER WHO HAS IMPRESSED YOU? Jofra Archer (Sus)
SURPRISING FACT ABOUT YOU? I have been a Type 1 diabetic for 16 years
WHERE IS PARADISE? Eagle Bay, Western Australia
CRICKETING HERO? Brett Lee – he always tried to bowl as fast as possible
NON-CRICKETING HERO? My mum and dad
TWITTER: @mattyd_30

Batting	Mat	Inns	NO	Runs	HS	Ave	SR	100	50	Ct	St
First-class	12	12	3	68	22	7.55	37.98	0	0	1	0
List A	11	5	2	17	12	5.66	68.00	0	0	1	0
T20s	9	3	0	2	1	0.66	20.00	0	0	0	0

Bowling	Mat	Balls	Runs	Wkts	BBI	BBM	Ave	Econ	SR	5w	10
First-class	12	1588	1124	27	5/124	6/189	41.62	4.24	58.8	1	0
List A	11	492	470	7	3/40	3/40	67.14	5.73	70.2	0	0
T20s	9	174	259	10	3/32	3/32	25.90	8.93	17.4	0	0

ANEURIN DONALD

RHB / OB / R1 / W0

GLAMORGAN

FULL NAME: Aneurin Henry Thomas Donald
BORN: December 20, 1996, Swansea
SQUAD NO: 12
HEIGHT: 6ft 3in
NICKNAME: Sir Don, The Don
EDUCATION: Pontarddulais Comprehensive School, Swansea; Gower College Swansea
TEAMS: Glamorgan
ROLE: Batsman
DEBUT: First-class: 2014; List A: 2015; T20: 2015

BEST BATTING: 234 Glamorgan vs Derbyshire, Colwyn Bay, 2016

FAMILY TIES? My grand-uncle, Bernard Hedges, scored the first one-day century for Glamorgan. My brother Gafyn played Wales age-group cricket and plays in the Welsh Premier League for Pontarddulais CC
CRICKETING HEROES? Kevin Pietersen, Jos Buttler
SURPRISING FACT? When I used to net with my brother and father on a Saturday morning, rugby international Leigh Halfpenny would be there every week practising his goal-kicking. I never had the courage to ask him to feed the bowling machine
TWITTER: @AneurinDonald12

Batting	Mat	Inns	NO	Runs	HS	Ave	SR	100	50	Ct	St
First-class	35	64	3	1989	234	32.60	71.70	2	13	29	0
List A	17	14	0	178	53	12.71	77.39	0	1	7	0
T20s	30	26	3	518	76	22.52	135.24	0	4	16	0
Bowling	Mat	Balls	Runs	Wkts	BBI	BBM	Ave	Econ	SR	5w	10
First-class	35	-	-	-	-	-	-	-	-	-	-
List A	17	-	-	-	-	-	-	-	-	-	-
T20s	30	-	-	-	-	-	-	-	-	-	-

GEORGE DRISSELL

RHB / OB / R0 / W0

FULL NAME: George Samuel Drissell
BORN: January 20, 1999, Bristol
SQUAD NO: TBC
HEIGHT: 6ft 2in
NICKNAME: Dris, Lemon, Lethal
EDUCATION: Bedminster Down Secondary School; SGS Filton College
TEAMS: Gloucestershire
ROLE: Allrounder
DEBUT: First-class: 2017

GLOUCESTERSHIRE

WHAT GOT YOU INTO CRICKET? My friends persuaded me to join a cricket club
BEST ADVICE EVER RECEIVED? Enjoy it
'ROY OF THE ROVERS' MOMENT? My first-team Gloucestershire debut against Northamptonshire at Wantage Road in the 2017 County Championship
BEST THING ABOUT YOUR HOME GROUND? When the stands are put up and it's a full house on a Twenty20 night
BEST OPPOSING PLAYER IN COUNTY CRICKET? Joe Root (Yor)
IF YOU WEREN'T A CRICKETER? I'd be a professional footballer
SURPRISING FACT ABOUT YOU? I'm a big fan of Bristol City FC. My club is Bedminster CC (Bristol) but I also played football for Bedminster Cricketers FC
SURPRISING FACT ABOUT A TEAMMATE? Miles Hammond has six toes
WHERE IS PARADISE? Ashton Gate (home of Bristol City)
CRICKETING HERO? Graeme Swann – the best England spinner of all time
TWITTER: @GeorgeDrissell

Batting	Mat	Inns	NO	Runs	HS	Ave	SR	100	50	Ct	St
First-class	1	1	0	0	0	0.00	0.00	0	0	0	0

Bowling	Mat	Balls	Runs	Wkts	BBI	BBM	Ave	Econ	SR	5w	10
First-class	1	72	58	0	-	-	-	4.83	-	0	0

BEN DUCKETT — LHB / OB / WK / R2 / W0 / MVP81

NORTHAMPTONSHIRE

FULL NAME: Ben Matthew Duckett
BORN: October 17, 1994, Farnborough, Kent
SQUAD NO: 17
HEIGHT: 5ft 9in
NICKNAME: Ducky, Toilet
EDUCATION: Millfield School, Somerset; Winchester House School; Stowe School
TEAMS: England, Northamptonshire, Islamabad United
ROLE: Batsman
DEBUT: Test: 2016; ODI: 2016; First-class: 2013; List A: 2013; T20: 2012

BEST BATTING: 282* Northamptonshire vs Sussex, Northampton, 2016
BEST BOWLING: 1-21 Northamptonshire vs Kent, Beckenham, 2017

FAMILY TIES? My dad (Graham) was on the Surrey staff and my grandad was an umpire
BEST ADVICE EVER RECEIVED? Don't get beaten up about cricket, just enjoy it
'ROY OF THE ROVERS' MOMENT? Receiving my Test cap in Bangladesh or winning the PCA's Player of the Year award
BEST THING ABOUT YOUR HOME GROUND? Small ground, great one-day wickets
BEST OPPOSING PLAYER IN COUNTY CRICKET? Joe Leach (Wor)
YOUNG OPPOSING PLAYER WHO HAS IMPRESSED YOU? Dan Lawrence (Ess) – he's scored so many hundreds at such a young age
SURPRISING FACT ABOUT YOU? I have a tattoo of a duck with the number 17 and a cricket bat on one side of my bottom
TWITTER: @benduckett1

Batting	Mat	Inns	NO	Runs	HS	Ave	SR	100	50	Ct	St
Tests	4	7	0	110	56	15.71	57.89	0	1	1	0
ODIs	3	3	0	123	63	41.00	80.92	0	2	0	0
First-class	62	104	6	4094	282*	41.77	71.66	13	19	53	3
List A	53	49	6	1916	220*	44.55	103.23	3	13	28	3
T20s	59	54	14	1203	92*	30.07	129.07	0	6	22	1

Bowling	Mat	Balls	Runs	Wkts	BBI	BBM	Ave	Econ	SR	5w	10
Tests	4	-	-	-	-	-	-	-	-	-	-
ODIs	3	-	-	-	-	-	-	-	-	-	-
First-class	62	59	49	1	1/21	1/32	49.00	4.98	59.0	0	0
List A	53	-	-	-	-	-	-	-	-	-	-
T20s	59	-	-	-	-	-	-	-	-	-	-

MATT DUNN

LHB / RFM / R0 / W0

FULL NAME: Matthew Peter Dunn
BORN: May 5, 1992, Egham, Surrey
SQUAD NO: 4
HEIGHT: 6ft 1in
NICKNAME: Dunny
EDUCATION: Bishopsgate School; Bearwood College, Wokingham
TEAMS: Surrey
ROLE: Bowler
DEBUT: First-class: 2010; List A: 2011; T20: 2013

SURREY

BEST BATTING: 31* Surrey vs Kent, Guildford, 2014
BEST BOWLING: 5-48 Surrey vs Gloucestershire, The Oval, 2014

WHAT GOT YOU INTO CRICKET? Playing in the back garden with my brother
BEST ADVICE EVER RECEIVED? Keep it simple
'ROY OF THE ROVERS' MOMENT? Taking five wickets on debut for Surrey in 2011
BEST THING ABOUT YOUR HOME GROUND? The history of The Oval
BEST OPPOSING PLAYER IN COUNTY CRICKET? Marcus Trescothick (Som)
YOUNG OPPOSING PLAYER WHO HAS IMPRESSED YOU? Lewis McManus (Ham)
IF YOU WEREN'T A CRICKETER? I'd be a barista
SURPRISING FACT ABOUT YOU? I lived in Norway when I was younger, and I can breakdance. And I absolutely love coffee
WHERE IS PARADISE? A peaceful coffee shop with a leather-bound book
CRICKETING HERO? Brett Lee – fast
NON-CRICKETING HERO? Usain Bolt – fast

Batting	Mat	Inns	NO	Runs	HS	Ave	SR	100	50	Ct	St
First-class	34	35	17	133	31*	7.38	20.62	0	0	5	0
List A	1	-	-	-	-	-	-	-	-	1	0
T20s	16	2	0	3	2	1.50	60.00	0	0	4	0

Bowling	Mat	Balls	Runs	Wkts	BBI	BBM	Ave	Econ	SR	5w	10
First-class	34	5062	3405	96	5/48	6/84	35.46	4.03	52.7	3	0
List A	1	36	32	2	2/32	2/32	16.00	5.33	18.0	0	0
T20s	16	300	450	22	3/8	3/8	20.45	9.00	13.6	0	0

WORCESTERSHIRE

FULL NAME: Brett Louis D'Oliveira
BORN: February 28, 1992, Worcester
SQUAD NO: 15
HEIGHT: 5ft 9in
NICKNAME: Dolly
EDUCATION: Blessed Edward Oldcorne Catholic College; Worcester Sixth Form College
TEAMS: Worcestershire, England Lions
ROLE: Allrounder
DEBUT: First-class: 2012; List A: 2011; T20: 2012

BEST BATTING: 202* Worcestershire vs Glamorgan, Cardiff, 2016
BEST BOWLING: 5-48 Worcestershire vs Durham, Chester-le-Street, 2015
COUNTY CAP: 2012

WHAT GOT YOU INTO CRICKET? Watching it live
FAMILY TIES? My grandad Basil played for England and Worcestershire and also went on to coach Worcestershire. My dad Damian played for Worcestershire and went on to be assistant coach and Academy director
'ROY OF THE ROVERS' MOMENT? Signing my first contract for Worcestershire
BEST THING ABOUT YOUR HOME GROUND? The cathedral in the background
IF YOU WEREN'T A CRICKETER? I'd be a cricket coach
SURPRISING FACT ABOUT YOU? I've got a coaching qualification in basketball
SURPRISING FACT ABOUT A TEAMMATE? There are rumours that Joe Leach puts sprinkles in his hair
WHERE IS PARADISE? Cape Town
CRICKETING HERO? Shane Warne – for his passion and outstanding skills
NON-CRICKETING HERO? Nelson Mandela – for changing the world
TWITTER: @Bdolly09

Batting	Mat	Inns	NO	Runs	HS	Ave	SR	100	50	Ct	St
First-class	41	72	2	2189	202*	31.27	54.82	6	5	23	0
List A	45	35	9	515	73*	19.80	83.06	0	2	17	0
T20s	63	44	16	751	62*	26.82	124.13	0	3	14	0

Bowling	Mat	Balls	Runs	Wkts	BBI	BBM	Ave	Econ	SR	5w	10
First-class	41	3042	1773	33	5/48	7/133	53.72	3.49	92.1	1	0
List A	45	1610	1393	31	3/35	3/35	44.93	5.19	51.9	0	0
T20s	63	858	1075	32	3/20	3/20	33.59	7.51	26.8	0	0

FULL NAME: Edmund James Holden Eckersley
BORN: August 9, 1989, Oxford
SQUAD NO: 33
HEIGHT: 5ft 11in
NICKNAME: Eckers
EDUCATION: St Benedict's School, Ealing
TEAMS: Leicestershire, Mountaineers
ROLE: Batsman/wicketkeeper
DEBUT: First-class: 2011; List A: 2008; T20: 2011

BEST BATTING: 158 Leicestershire vs Derbyshire, Derby, 2017
BEST BOWLING: 2-29 Leicestershire vs Lancashire, Old Trafford, 2013
COUNTY CAP: 2013

WHAT GOT YOU INTO CRICKET? Junior cricket at Ealing CC, my home club
'ROY OF THE ROVERS' MOMENT? Every morning in warm-up football
BEST OPPOSING PLAYER IN COUNTY CRICKET? Samit Patel (Not)
YOUNG OPPOSING PLAYER WHO HAS IMPRESSED YOU? Joe Clarke (Wor)
IF YOU WEREN'T A CRICKETER? I'd be more intelligent
SURPRISING FACT ABOUT YOU? I can play TV theme tunes on the piano
SURPRISING FACT ABOUT A TEAMMATE? Zak Chappell doesn't know the name of the ocean between the UK and America
WHERE IS PARADISE? Palm Beach, Sydney
CRICKETING HERO? Alec Stewart – he wanted to be a frontline batsman and a wicketkeeper and he was the best when I was a kid
NON-CRICKETING HERO? David Attenborough
TWITTER: @nedeckersley

Batting	Mat	Inns	NO	Runs	HS	Ave	SR	100	50	Ct	St
First-class	101	181	12	5559	158	32.89	51.18	14	17	149	3
List A	38	36	4	896	108	28.00	87.15	1	4	21	1
T20s	55	49	9	607	43	15.17	108.58	0	0	18	3

Bowling	Mat	Balls	Runs	Wkts	BBI	BBM	Ave	Econ	SR	5w	10
First-class	101	88	67	2	2/29	2/29	33.50	4.56	44.0	0	0
List A	38	-	-	-	-	-	-	-	-	-	-
T20s	55	-	-	-	-	-	-	-	-	-	-

HAMPSHIRE

FULL NAME: Fidel Henderson Edwards
BORN: February 6, 1982, Gays, Barbados
SQUAD NO: 82
HEIGHT: 5ft 4in
NICKNAME: Castro
TEAMS: West Indies, Hampshire, Barbados,
Deccan Chargers, Dolphins, Rajasthan
Royals, St Lucia Zouks, Sydney Thunder,
Sylhet Superstars, Trinidad and Tobago Red
Steel
ROLE: Bowler
DEBUT: Test: 2003; ODI: 2003; T20I: 2007;
First-class: 2001; List A: 2003; T20: 2007

BEST BATTING: 40 Barbados vs Jamaica, Bridgetown, 2008
BEST BOWLING: 7-87 West Indies vs New Zealand, Napier, 2008

TWITTER: @EdwardsFidel
NOTES: The slingy Barbadian fast bowler was drafted into Hampshire's squad late in the
2015 season and took a remarkable 45 wickets in eight games to help his county stave
off relegation from Division One of the Championship. Made just two Championship
appearances in 2016 after breaking his ankle playing football. Came back to collect 30
Championship wickets in nine matches last summer before signing a one-year contract
extension. Edwards took five wickets on Test debut after playing just one match for
Barbados and being spotted in the nets by Brian Lara. Played the last of his 55 Tests in 2012

Batting	Mat	Inns	NO	Runs	HS	Ave	SR	100	50	Ct	St
Tests	55	88	28	394	30	6.56	28.20	0	0	10	0
ODIs	50	22	14	73	13	9.12	45.62	0	0	4	0
T20Is	20	4	2	10	7*	5.00	111.11	0	0	5	0
First-class	107	153	56	682	40	7.03		0	0	19	0
List A	87	36	20	138	21*	8.62		0	0	11	0
T20s	90	28	13	95	11*	6.33	86.36	0	0	12	0

Bowling	Mat	Balls	Runs	Wkts	BBI	BBM	Ave	Econ	SR	5w	10
Tests	55	9602	6249	165	7/87	8/132	37.87	3.90	58.1	12	0
ODIs	50	2138	1812	60	6/22	6/22	30.20	5.08	35.6	2	0
T20Is	20	360	497	16	3/23	3/23	31.06	8.28	22.5	0	0
First-class	107	17003	10955	350	7/87	10/83	31.30	3.86	48.5	21	2
List A	87	3870	3316	111	6/22	6/22	29.87	5.14	34.8	3	0
T20s	90	1798	2276	84	5/22	5/22	27.09	7.59	21.4	1	0

GRANT ELLIOTT

RHB / RM / RO / WO

FULL NAME: Grant David Elliott
BORN: March 21, 1979, Johannesburg, South Africa
SQUAD NO: 88
TEAMS: New Zealand, Warwickshire, Chittagong Vikings, Gauteng, Griqualand West, Leicestershire, St Lucia Zouks, Surrey, Transvaal, Wellington
ROLE: Allrounder
DEBUT: Test: 2008; ODI: 2008; T20I: 2009; First-class: 1997; List A: 1999; T20: 2006

BEST BATTING: 196* Wellington vs Auckland, Wellington, 2008
BEST BOWLING: 5-33 Wellington vs Northern Districts, Whangarei, 2014

TWITTER: @grantelliottnz
NOTES: A veteran allrounder who represented New Zealand 104 times between 2008 and 2016, most notably playing a key part in the side which reached the 2015 World Cup final. In the semi-final he was Man of the Match for his 84 not out against South Africa, and he top-scored with 83 in a losing cause against Australia in the final. Elliott made his Test debut in 2008 but played only four more thereafter. Effectively ended his international career by signing for Warwickshire on a Kolpak deal in March 2017 and had an instant impact after taking over from Ian Bell as captain of the T20 side, leading the Bears to the final. He will keep the role for this summer's campaign

Batting	Mat	Inns	NO	Runs	HS	Ave	SR	100	50	Ct	St
Tests	5	9	1	86	25	10.75	26.70	0	0	2	0
ODIs	83	69	11	1976	115	34.06	81.78	2	11	17	0
T20Is	17	15	4	171	27	15.54	108.91	0	0	4	0
First-class	83	134	7	3883	196*	30.57		8	20	46	0
List A	211	183	30	5126	115	33.50		7	28	70	0
T20s	136	117	27	2129	70	23.65	129.18	0	8	49	0

Bowling	Mat	Balls	Runs	Wkts	BBI	BBM	Ave	Econ	SR	5w	10
Tests	5	282	140	4	2/8	2/8	35.00	2.97	70.5	0	0
ODIs	83	1302	1179	39	4/31	4/31	30.23	5.43	33.3	0	0
T20Is	17	192	235	14	4/22	4/22	16.78	7.34	13.7	0	0
First-class	83	7216	3378	92	5/33	5/39	36.71	2.80	78.4	1	0
List A	211	4827	4337	130	5/34	5/34	33.36	5.39	37.1	1	0
T20s	136	1714	2310	93	4/15	4/15	24.83	8.08	18.4	0	0

SEAN ERVINE

LHB / RM / R1 / W0

FULL NAME: Sean Michael Ervine
BORN: December 6, 1982, Harare, Zimbabwe
SQUAD NO: 7
HEIGHT: 6ft 2in
NICKNAME: Slug, Lion, Siuc
EDUCATION: Lomagundi College, Zimbabwe
TEAMS: Zimbabwe, Hampshire, Duronto Rajshahi, Matabeleland Tuskers, Midlands, Mountaineers, Southern Rocks, Western Australia
ROLE: Allrounder
DEBUT: Test: 2003; ODI: 2001; First-class: 2001; List A: 2001; T20: 2005

BEST BATTING: 237* Hampshire vs Somerset, Southampton, 2010
BEST BOWLING: 6-82 Midlands vs Mashonaland, Kwekwe, 2003
COUNTY CAP: 2005; **BENEFIT:** 2016

FAMILY TIES? My father Rory played first-class cricket in Zimbabwe and my brother Craig plays for the current Zimbabwe team
BEST THING ABOUT YOUR HOME GROUND? It's beautiful to look at it. Big yet great value for runs
BEST OPPOSING PLAYER IN COUNTY CRICKET? Jofra Archer (Sus)
YOUNG OPPOSING PLAYER WHO HAS IMPRESSED YOU? Jamie Porter (Ess) – very accurate, fast enough, seams it both ways
SURPRISING FACT ABOUT A TEAMMATE? If Kyle Abbott is not on a cricket field then he's fishing
WHERE IS PARADISE? Cruising on the Zambezi
CRICKETING HERO? Andy Flower, who I idolised at school. As a teammate he helped me realise the professional standard required for international level
TWITTER: @Sean_Ervine

Batting	Mat	Inns	NO	Runs	HS	Ave	SR	100	50	Ct	St
Tests	5	8	0	261	86	32.62	55.41	0	3	7	0
ODIs	42	34	7	698	100	25.85	85.53	1	2	5	0
First-class	225	351	42	11256	237*	36.42		22	56	194	0
List A	251	221	30	5716	167*	29.92		7	27	77	0
T20s	184	167	35	3082	82	23.34	128.20	0	10	59	0

Bowling	Mat	Balls	Runs	Wkts	BBI	BBM	Ave	Econ	SR	5w	10
Tests	5	570	388	9	4/146	4/146	43.11	4.08	63.3	0	0
ODIs	42	1649	1561	41	3/29	3/29	38.07	5.67	40.2	0	0
First-class	225	20344	11836	280	6/82	9/127	42.27	3.49	72.6	5	0
List A	251	7564	7087	206	5/50	5/50	34.40	5.62	36.7	2	0
T20s	184	1404	2074	68	4/12	4/12	30.50	8.86	20.6	0	0

STEVIE ESKINAZI RHB / WK / R0 / W0

FULL NAME: Stephen Sean Eskinazi
BORN: March 28, 1994, Johannesburg, South Africa
SQUAD NO: 28
HEIGHT: 6ft 2in
NICKNAME: Eski, Esk
EDUCATION: Christ Church Grammar School, Perth; University of Western Australia; University of Hertfordshire
TEAMS: Middlesex
ROLE: Batsman/wicketkeeper
DEBUT: First-class: 2015; T20: 2016

BEST BATTING: 179 Middlesex vs Warwickshire, Edgbaston, 2017

WHAT GOT YOU INTO CRICKET? My parents put a bat in my crib the minute I came home
FAMILY TIES? My dad played a good standard of club cricket in South Africa. My brother Greg played for the first XI at school and my cousin Marc was an extremely talented middle-order batsman and medium-pacer
'ROY OF THE ROVERS' MOMENT? Winning the County Championship in 2016
STRANGEST THING SEEN IN A GAME? A couple run onto the field during a first-class game and stop in the middle of the pitch to kiss. Tim Murtagh then gave the bloke the ball and he bowled it – after drinking half a bottle of vodka. And I once saw Nathan Sowter take a catch in the slips – that was incredible
SUPERSTITIONS? I always walk out to bat with the same routine: jog on, six back-kicks, three side-to-sides (on each side), a squat, and finally a look up at the sky
IF YOU WEREN'T A CRICKETER? I'd be finishing my Commerce degree at uni and playing hockey at the highest level I could
SURPRISING FACT? I could have four passports (if that was legal)
CRICKETING HEROES? Kane Williamson, James Taylor, Jacques Kallis, Ricky Ponting
UNUSUAL OBJECT AT HOME? Chin-up bar, dumbells and protein powder
TWITTER: @seskinazi

Batting	Mat	Inns	NO	Runs	HS	Ave	SR	100	50	Ct	St
First-class	25	44	3	1472	179	35.90	53.82	4	6	16	0
T20s	6	6	1	194	57*	38.80	128.47	0	1	1	0
Bowling	Mat	Balls	Runs	Wkts	BBI	BBM	Ave	Econ	SR	5w	10
First-class	25	-	-	-	-	-	-	-	-	-	-
T20s	6	-	-	-	-	-	-	-	-	-	-

LAURIE EVANS

RHB / RM / RO / WO

FULL NAME: Laurie John Evans
BORN: October 12, 1987, Lambeth, London
SQUAD NO: 32
HEIGHT: 6ft
NICKNAME: Loz
EDUCATION: Whitgift School; The John Fisher School, Purley; Durham University
TEAMS: Sussex, Northamptonshire, Surrey, Warwickshire
ROLE: Batsman
DEBUT: First-class: 2007; List A: 2009; T20: 2009

BEST BATTING: 213* Warwickshire vs Sussex, Edgbaston, 2015
BEST BOWLING: 1-29 Warwickshire vs Sussex, Edgbaston, 2015

WHAT GOT YOU INTO CRICKET? It was something to do outside the rugby season
'ROY OF THE ROVERS' MOMENT? Winning all three domestic competitions with Warwickshire in 2014
BEST THING ABOUT YOUR HOME GROUND? There's no better place to be than by the sea in the summer
BEST OPPOSING PLAYER IN COUNTY CRICKET? Ben Stokes (Dur)
IF YOU WEREN'T A CRICKETER? I'd be a rugby player (my brother plays professional rugby for Nottingham)
SURPRISING FACT ABOUT A TEAMMATE? Luke Wright has a crush on me
WHERE IS PARADISE? A golf course
CRICKETING HERO? Brian Lara
NON-CRICKETING HERO? Jonny Wilkinson
TWITTER: @laurieevans32

Batting	Mat	Inns	NO	Runs	HS	Ave	SR	100	50	Ct	St
First-class	58	100	6	2974	213*	31.63	45.27	5	16	48	0
List A	44	39	9	1008	134*	33.60	103.91	1	2	19	0
T20s	78	66	15	1214	69*	23.80	125.93	0	6	34	0

Bowling	Mat	Balls	Runs	Wkts	BBI	BBM	Ave	Econ	SR	5w	10
First-class	58	354	259	2	1/29	1/29	129.50	4.38	177.0	0	0
List A	44	36	53	0	-	-	-	8.83	-	0	0
T20s	78	22	35	1	1/5	1/5	35.00	9.54	22.0	0	0

SAM EVANS

RHB / RO / WO

FULL NAME: Samuel Thomes Evans
BORN: December 20, 1997, Leicester
SQUAD NO: 21
HEIGHT: 5ft 8in
NICKNAME: Smevs
EDUCATION: Lancaster Boys School, Leicester; Wyggeston QE I College; Loughborough University
TEAMS: Leicestershire
ROLE: Batsman
DEBUT: First-class: 2017

BEST BATTING: 114 Loughborough MCCU vs Northamptonshire, Northampton, 2017

WHAT GOT YOU INTO CRICKET? Playing cricket in the garden with my dad
BEST ADVICE EVER RECEIVED? You'll have more bad days than good so enjoy the good ones
'ROY OF THE ROVERS' MOMENT? Making my first-class debut in 2017
BEST THING ABOUT YOUR HOME GROUND? The lovely food
BEST OPPOSING PLAYER IN COUNTY CRICKET? Jeetan Patel (War)
YOUNG OPPOSING PLAYER WHO HAS IMPRESSED YOU? Sam Cook (Ess) – consistent and skilful bowler
IF YOU WEREN'T A CRICKETER? I'd be a student
SURPRISING FACT ABOUT YOU? I go to Loughborough University and am one of the few who is not studying Sports Science
CRICKETING HERO? Ricky Ponting – he made batting look elegant and easy
NON-CRICKETING HERO? Jamie Vardy – for his tenacity and desire. He started at the bottom and made it to the top
TWITTER: @SamEvans97

Batting	Mat	Inns	NO	Runs	HS	Ave	SR	100	50	Ct	St
First-class	3	4	0	163	114	40.75	53.97	1	0	1	0

Bowling	Mat	Balls	Runs	Wkts	BBI	BBM	Ave	Econ	SR	5w	10
First-class	3	30	21	0	-	-	-	4.20	-	0	0

JAMES FAULKNER

LANCASHIRE

FULL NAME: James Peter Faulkner
BORN: April 29, 1990, Launceston, Tasmania, Australia
SQUAD NO: 44
HEIGHT: 6ft 1in
TEAMS: Australia, Lancashire, Gujarat Lions, Kings XI Punjab, Melbourne Stars, Pune Warriors, Rajasthan Royals, Tasmania
ROLE: Allrounder
DEBUT: Test: 2013; ODI: 2013; T20I: 2012; First-class: 2008; List A: 2008; T20: 2009

BEST BATTING: 121 Lancashire vs Surrey, The Oval, 2015
BEST BOWLING: 5-5 Tasmania vs South Australia, Hobart, 2010

TWITTER: @JamesFaulkner44

NOTES: A left-arm seam-bowling allrounder, Faulkner was Man of the Match in the 2015 World Cup final against New Zealand, taking 3-36, and was the first Australian to take a five-for in T20Is, claiming 5-27 against Pakistan at the 2016 World T20. With the bat he made an ODI hundred against India in Bangalore and also scored an unbeaten 69 from 47 balls against England at Brisbane in 2013, contributing 55 to a last-wicket partnership of 57 as he helped snatch a final-over one-wicket win. His sole Test appearance was in the final game of the 2013 Ashes. He played a starring role in Lancashire's 2015 T20 title win, scoring 302 runs and taking 25 wickets, and last December he signed a two-year T20 contract with the club

Batting	Mat	Inns	NO	Runs	HS	Ave	SR	100	50	Ct	St
Tests	1	2	0	45	23	22.50	104.65	0	0	0	0
ODIs	69	52	22	1032	116	34.40	104.24	1	4	21	0
T20Is	24	18	7	159	41*	14.45	115.21	0	0	11	0
First-class	63	95	12	2566	121	30.91	50.91	2	15	26	0
List A	121	94	30	1936	116	30.25	91.45	1	10	34	0
T20s	159	121	52	1565	73	22.68	122.55	0	1	52	0

Bowling	Mat	Balls	Runs	Wkts	BBI	BBM	Ave	Econ	SR	5w	10
Tests	1	166	98	6	4/51	6/98	16.33	3.54	27.6	0	0
ODIs	69	3211	2962	96	4/32	4/32	30.85	5.53	33.4	0	0
T20Is	24	515	684	36	5/27	5/27	19.00	7.96	14.3	1	0
First-class	63	9776	4759	192	5/5	8/97	24.78	2.92	50.9	5	0
List A	121	5719	5102	168	4/20	4/20	30.36	5.35	34.0	0	0
T20s	159	3226	4274	176	5/16	5/16	24.28	7.94	18.3	3	0

TOM FELL

RHB / OB / R1 / W0

FULL NAME: Thomas Charles Fell
BORN: October 17, 1993, Hillingdon, Middlesex
SQUAD NO: 29
HEIGHT: 6ft
NICKNAME: Lord, Feltch
EDUCATION: Tettenhall College, Wolverhampton; Oakham School, Rutland; Oxford Brookes University
TEAMS: Worcestershire
ROLE: Batsman
DEBUT: First-class: 2013; List A: 2013

BEST BATTING: 171 Worcestershire vs Middlesex, Worcester, 2015
COUNTY CAP: 2013

FAMILY TIES? My dad got a blue at Cambridge University and played in the same team as Mike Atherton
'ROY OF THE ROVERS' MOMENT? Beating Surrey by 27 runs at New Road at the end of the 2014 season to secure Championship promotion. Alexei Kervezee's direct hit won us the game
BEST THING ABOUT YOUR HOME GROUND? Great views and just one of the nicest grounds in the country
YOUNG OPPOSING PLAYER WHO HAS IMPRESSED YOU? Tom Kohler-Cadmore (Yor) – hits the ball cleaner than anyone I have seen
IF YOU WEREN'T A CRICKETER? I'd go skiing in the winter, play a lot of golf, and go on holiday in the summer
WHERE IS PARADISE? The wine farms in Stellenbosch, South Africa
NON-CRICKETING HERO? Tiger Woods – he is the reason I love golf

Batting	Mat	Inns	NO	Runs	HS	Ave	SR	100	50	Ct	St
First-class	60	102	5	3020	171	31.13	50.82	5	12	49	0
List A	32	31	4	1033	116*	38.25	81.59	1	9	8	0

Bowling	Mat	Balls	Runs	Wkts	BBI	BBM	Ave	Econ	SR	5w	10
First-class	60	20	17	0	-	-	-	5.10	-	0	0
List A	32	-	-	-	-	-	-	-	-	-	-

AARON FINCH

RHB / SLA / R0 / W0

FULL NAME: Aaron James Finch
BORN: November 17, 1986, Colac, Victoria, Australia
SQUAD NO: 15
HEIGHT: 5ft 8in
TEAMS: Australia, Surrey, Auckland, Delhi Daredevils, Gujarat Lions, Melbourne Renegades, Mumbai Indians, Pune Warriors, Rajasthan Royals, Ruhuna Royals, Sunrisers Hyderabad, Victoria, Yorkshire
ROLE: Batsman
DEBUT: ODI: 2013; T20I: 2011; First-class: 2007; List A: 2007; T20: 2009

BEST BATTING: 288* Cricket Australia XI vs New Zealanders, Sydney, 2015
BEST BOWLING: 1-0 Victoria vs Western Australia, Perth, 2013

TWITTER: @AaronFinch5
NOTES: Short-format specialist opener for Australia who returns to Surrey for his third consecutive summer at the county after signing a two-year contract to play T20 cricket until the end of the 2019 season. A powerful hitter with a simple technique, Finch hit three fifties in six T20 appearances for Surrey in 2016 and was the county's leading run-scorer last summer (489 runs, including one hundred). A former Australia T20 captain, Finch became the fastest batsman to score 10 ODI hundreds for Australia (83 innings) earlier this year

Batting	Mat	Inns	NO	Runs	HS	Ave	SR	100	50	Ct	St
ODIs	88	84	1	3200	148	38.55	90.09	10	18	43	0
T20Is	36	36	6	1206	156	40.20	151.69	1	7	10	0
First-class	72	119	6	4232	288*	37.45	62.87	7	27	67	0
List A	165	161	6	5957	154	38.43	88.63	14	36	69	0
T20s	210	206	20	6427	156	34.55	139.38	3	47	87	0

Bowling	Mat	Balls	Runs	Wkts	BBi	BBM	Ave	Econ	SR	5w	10
ODIs	88	152	130	2	1/2	1/2	65.00	5.13	76.0	0	0
T20Is	36	12	27	0	-	-	-	13.50	-	0	0
First-class	72	452	310	5	1/0	1/0	62.00	4.11	90.4	0	0
List A	165	347	311	7	2/44	2/44	44.42	5.37	49.5	0	0
T20s	210	221	340	7	1/9	1/9	48.57	9.23	31.5	0	0

HARRY FINCH

RHB / RM / RO / WO

FULL NAME: Harry Zacariah Finch
BORN: February 10, 1995, Hastings, Sussex
SQUAD NO: 6
HEIGHT: 5ft 9in
NICKNAME: Chozza, Finchy
EDUCATION: St Richard's Catholic College, Bexhill; Eastbourne College
TEAMS: Sussex
ROLE: Batsman
DEBUT: First-class: 2013; List A: 2013; T20: 2014

BEST BATTING: 135* Sussex vs Leeds/Bradford MCCU, Hove, 2016
BEST BOWLING: 1-9 Sussex vs Leeds/Bradford MCCU, Hove, 2016

BEST ADVICE EVER RECEIVED? Be the best version of yourself
'ROY OF THE ROVERS' MOMENT? Watching Laurie Evans score a brilliant unbeaten 134 when we chased 332 against Kent in a 50-over game in 2017
BEST THING ABOUT YOUR HOME GROUND? The outfield – brilliant to play football on
BEST OPPOSING PLAYER IN COUNTY CRICKET? Samit Patel (Not)
YOUNG OPPOSING PLAYER WHO HAS IMPRESSED YOU? Sam Curran (Sur) – can be a match-winner with bat and ball
IF YOU WEREN'T A CRICKETER? I'd be trying to be a professional footballer
SURPRISING FACT ABOUT YOU? I don't like chocolate bourbons
SURPRISING FACT ABOUT A TEAMMATE? George Garton can smile
WHERE IS PARADISE? Cape Town
CRICKETING HEROES? Jacques Kallis, Andrew Flintoff, Ricky Ponting, AB de Villiers – they all have dominated the game in their own way
NON-CRICKETING HERO? Roger Federer – unbelievable consistency and temperament
TWITTER: @hfinch72

Batting	Mat	Inns	NO	Runs	HS	Ave	SR	100	50	Ct	St
First-class	24	38	5	926	135*	28.06	52.52	2	5	25	0
List A	19	18	3	655	92*	43.66	79.78	0	6	2	0
T20s	17	12	3	138	35*	15.33	102.22	0	0	3	0

Bowling	Mat	Balls	Runs	Wkts	BBI	BBM	Ave	Econ	SR	5w	10
First-class	24	156	109	2	1/9	1/9	54.50	4.19	78.0	0	0
List A	19	16	24	0	-	-	-	9.00	-	0	0
T20s	17	-	-	-	-	-	-	-	-	-	-

STEVEN FINN — RHB / RFM / R0 / W2 / MVP63

MIDDLESEX

FULL NAME: Steven Thomas Finn
BORN: April 4, 1989, Watford, Hertfordshire
SQUAD NO: 9
HEIGHT: 6ft 7in
NICKNAME: Finny, Cyril, Finndog
EDUCATION: Parmiter's School, Watford
TEAMS: England, Middlesex, Islamabad United, Otago
ROLE: Bowler
DEBUT: Test: 2010; ODI: 2011; T20I: 2011; First-class: 2005; List A: 2007; T20: 2008

BEST BATTING: 56 England vs New Zealand, Dunedin, 2013
BEST BOWLING: 9-37 Middlesex vs Worcestershire, Worcester, 2010
COUNTY CAP: 2009

FAMILY TIES? My father, Terry, played Minor Counties cricket and my grandad played club cricket
'ROY OF THE ROVERS' MOMENT? My Test debut, my first Test five-for and winning the Ashes in Australia in 2010/11
CRICKETING HERO? Glenn McGrath – the best seam bowler in the world as I was growing up
NON-CRICKETING HERO? Tony Soprano
TWITTER: @finnysteve

Batting	Mat	Inns	NO	Runs	HS	Ave	SR	100	50	Ct	St
Tests	36	47	22	279	56	11.16	30.96	0	1	8	0
ODIs	69	30	13	136	35	8.00	60.98	0	0	15	0
T20Is	21	3	3	14	8*	-	73.68	0	0	6	0
First-class	145	176	59	1061	56	9.06	37.25	0	1	47	0
List A	134	51	21	314	42*	10.46	60.97	0	0	26	0
T20s	78	13	10	49	8*	16.33	87.50	0	0	18	0

Bowling	Mat	Balls	Runs	Wkts	BBI	BBM	Ave	Econ	SR	5w	10
Tests	36	6412	3800	125	6/79	9/187	30.40	3.55	51.2	5	0
ODIs	69	3550	2996	102	5/33	5/33	29.37	5.06	34.8	2	0
T20Is	21	480	583	27	3/16	3/16	21.59	7.28	17.7	0	0
First-class	145	25998	14986	522	9/37	14/106	28.70	3.45	49.8	13	1
List A	134	6331	5390	188	5/33	5/33	28.67	5.10	33.6	3	0
T20s	78	1640	2032	94	4/24	4/24	21.61	7.43	17.4	0	0

MATTHEW FISHER

RHB / RFM / RO / WO

FULL NAME: Matthew David Fisher
BORN: November 9, 1997, York
SQUAD NO: 7
HEIGHT: 6ft 2in
NICKNAME: Fish, Nemo, Pup
EDUCATION: Easingwold School, North Yorkshire
TEAMS: Yorkshire
ROLE: Bowler
DEBUT: First-class: 2015; List A: 2013; T20: 2015

BEST BATTING: 37 Yorkshire vs Warwickshire, Headingley, 2017
BEST BOWLING: 5-54 Yorkshire vs Warwickshire, Headingley, 2017

WHAT GOT YOU INTO CRICKET? Playing with my brothers at our local club. And the 2005 Ashes
BEST ADVICE EVER RECEIVED? Always work hard
'ROY OF THE ROVERS' MOMENT? Taking 5-22 against Derbyshire at Headingley on my T20 Blast debut for Yorkshire in 2015
BEST THING ABOUT YOUR HOME GROUND? The Dickie Bird Players' Balcony – all paid for by Dickie. Legend of Yorkshire cricket
BEST OPPOSING PLAYER IN COUNTY CRICKET? Mark Stoneman or Ben Foakes (both Sur)
YOUNG OPPOSING PLAYER WHO HAS IMPRESSED YOU? Ollie Pope (Sur) – he has a great temperament and is a very modern player
SURPRISING FACT ABOUT YOU? I'm deaf in one ear
SURPRISING FACT ABOUT A TEAMMATE? Alex Lees is a very good magician
CRICKETING HERO? Andrew Flintoff – he played at his best when under pressure
NON-CRICKETING HERO? My dad – he taught me values and morals
TWITTER: @9M_Fisher

Batting	Mat	Inns	NO	Runs	HS	Ave	SR	100	50	Ct	St
First-class	5	6	1	86	37	17.20	33.85	0	0	1	0
List A	21	10	7	116	36*	38.66	94.30	0	0	5	0
T20s	16	2	2	6	6*	-	85.71	0	0	6	0

Bowling	Mat	Balls	Runs	Wkts	BBI	BBM	Ave	Econ	SR	5w	10
First-class	5	806	438	13	5/54	5/89	33.69	3.26	62.0	1	0
List A	21	797	771	18	3/32	3/32	42.83	5.80	44.2	0	0
T20s	16	275	410	16	5/22	5/22	25.62	8.94	17.1	1	0

LUKE FLETCHER

NOTTINGHAMSHIRE

FULL NAME: Luke Jack Fletcher
BORN: September 18, 1988, Nottingham
SQUAD NO: 19
HEIGHT: 6ft 7in
NICKNAME: Fletch
EDUCATION: Henry Mellish Comprehensive School, Nottingham
TEAMS: Nottinghamshire, Derbyshire, Surrey, Wellington
ROLE: Bowler
DEBUT: First-class: 2008; List A: 2008; T20: 2009

BEST BATTING: 92 Nottinghamshire vs Hampshire, Southampton, 2009
BEST BOWLING: 5-52 Nottinghamshire vs Warwickshire, Trent Bridge, 2013
COUNTY CAP: 2014 (Nottinghamshire)

BEST ADVICE EVER RECEIVED? Enjoy yourself and get stuck in
BEST THING ABOUT YOUR HOME GROUND? The atmosphere on Friday nights for T20 matches
YOUNG OPPOSING PLAYER WHO HAS IMPRESSED YOU? Jamie Porter (Ess) – he's a very consistent bowler
IF YOU WEREN'T A CRICKETER? I applied for the police before I signed for Notts but I'd like to be a bowling coach one day
SURPRISING FACT ABOUT YOU? My previous job was as a chef at Hooters
SURPRISING FACT ABOUT A TEAMMATE? Samit Patel puts Vaseline on his eyebrows every time he goes out to bat
WHERE IS PARADISE? Home with my family
CRICKETING HERO? Andrew Flintoff – for what he did in the 2005 Ashes
NON-CRICKETING HERO? Ronnie O'Sullivan
TWITTER: @fletcherluke

Batting	Mat	Inns	NO	Runs	HS	Ave	SR	100	50	Ct	St
First-class	91	129	26	1516	92	14.71	49.80	0	4	22	0
List A	59	27	11	224	40*	14.00	97.39	0	0	9	0
T20s	56	17	9	47	11*	5.87	92.15	0	0	9	0

Bowling	Mat	Balls	Runs	Wkts	BBI	BBM	Ave	Econ	SR	5w	10
First-class	91	15675	7751	270	5/52	9/108	28.70	2.96	58.0	3	0
List A	59	2373	2243	55	4/44	4/44	40.78	5.67	43.1	0	0
T20s	56	1157	1512	61	4/30	4/30	24.78	7.84	18.9	0	0

BEN FOAKES

RHB / WK / R0 / W0 / MVP68

FULL NAME: Benjamin Thomas Foakes
BORN: February 15, 1993, Colchester, Essex
SQUAD NO: 7
HEIGHT: 6ft 2in
NICKNAME: Foakesey
EDUCATION: Tendring Technology College, Essex
TEAMS: Surrey, England Lions, Essex
ROLE: Wicketkeeper/batsman
DEBUT: First-class: 2011; List A: 2013; T20: 2014

BEST BATTING: 141* Surrey vs Hampshire, Southampton, 2016
COUNTY CAP: 2016 (Surrey)

WHAT GOT YOU INTO CRICKET? Growing up in a small town there wasn't a lot to do so I got involved with all the local sports clubs
FAMILY TIES? My brother plays in the East Anglian Premier League for Frinton-on-Sea
'ROY OF THE ROVERS' MOMENT? The quarter-final of 2015 One-Day Cup: taking a skyer off Matt Coles to send us into the semis after his incredible innings and an amazing game. The emotion and joy as the team came together was quite something
SUPERSTITIONS? I touch my belly button and top and bottom lip between each ball
CRICKETING HERO? James Foster – he made me want to become keeper when I first started watching Essex play as a kid
IF YOU WEREN'T A CRICKETER? I'd be exploring Asia
SURPRISING FACT? After I had a car crash a tooth was glued back together. It came unstuck while I was batting and was dangling, so I had to tear it out at lunch and proceeded to bat with no front teeth
UNUSUAL OBJECT AT HOME? A record player

Batting	Mat	Inns	NO	Runs	HS	Ave	SR	100	50	Ct	St
First-class	78	119	24	3928	141*	41.34	53.65	8	20	137	14
List A	52	44	7	1224	92	33.08	89.21	0	11	63	6
T20s	41	29	7	400	49	18.18	112.04	0	0	22	3

Bowling	Mat	Balls	Runs	Wkts	BBI	BBM	Ave	Econ	SR	5w	10
First-class	78	6	6	0	-	-	-	6.00	-	0	0
List A	52	-	-	-	-	-	-	-	-	-	-
T20s	41	-	-	-	-	-	-	-	-	-	-

MARK FOOTITT

NOTTINGHAMSHIRE

FULL NAME: Mark Harold Alan Footitt
BORN: November 25, 1985, Nottingham
SQUAD NO: 7
HEIGHT: 6ft 2in
NICKNAME: Footy
EDUCATION: Carlton Le Willows School, Gedling; West Nottinghamshire College
TEAMS: Nottinghamshire, Derbyshire, Surrey
ROLE: Bowler
DEBUT: First-class: 2005; List A: 2002; T20: 2005

BEST BATTING: 34 Derbyshire vs Leicestershire, Leicester, 2015
BEST BOWLING: 7-62 Surrey vs Lancashire, The Oval, 2016
COUNTY CAP: 2014 (Derbyshire)

WHAT GOT YOU INTO CRICKET? Watching my dad and grandad playing for the local team
BEST ADVICE EVER RECEIVED? Be yourself and work hard
'ROY OF THE ROVERS' MOMENT? Getting a seven-for for Surrey against Lancashire in 2016
BEST THING ABOUT YOUR HOME GROUND? Its history
IF YOU WEREN'T A CRICKETER? I'd be a plumber
SURPRISING FACT ABOUT YOU? I started bowling right-arm then changed to left-arm
WHERE IS PARADISE? At home with my wife and child
CRICKETING HERO? Brett Lee
NON-CRICKETING HERO? Stone Cold Steve Austin – "coz Stone Cold said so!"
UNUSUAL OBJECT AT HOME? Harry Potter wands
TWITTER: @footitt_mark

Batting	Mat	Inns	NO	Runs	HS	Ave	SR	100	50	Ct	St
First-class	92	117	35	640	34	7.80	60.66	0	0	24	0
List A	36	10	4	28	11*	4.66	68.29	0	0	6	0
T20s	14	3	2	2	2*	2.00	66.66	0	0	1	0

Bowling	Mat	Balls	Runs	Wkts	BBI	BBM	Ave	Econ	SR	5w	10
First-class	92	15089	8894	345	7/62		25.77	3.53	43.7	21	1
List A	36	1331	1387	47	5/28	5/28	29.51	6.25	28.3	2	0
T20s	14	240	431	12	3/22	3/22	35.91	10.77	20.0	0	0

JAMES FOSTER

RHB / WK / R1 / W0

FULL NAME: James Savin Foster
BORN: April 15, 1980, Whipps Cross, Leytonstone, Essex
SQUAD NO: 7
HEIGHT: 6ft 1in
NICKNAME: Fozzy, Chief, Chiefton
EDUCATION: Forest School, Walthamstow, London; Durham University
TEAMS: England, Essex, Northern Districts
ROLE: Wicketkeeper
DEBUT: Test: 2001; ODI: 2001; T20I: 2009; First-class: 2000; List A: 2000; T20: 2003

BEST BATTING: 212 Essex vs Leicestershire, Chelmsford, 2004
BEST BOWLING: 1-122 Essex vs Northamptonshire, Northampton, 2008
COUNTY CAP: 2001; BENEFIT: 2011

STRANGEST THING SEEN IN A GAME? Australia keeper Peter Nevill getting hit in the head with a cricket bat while standing back
'ROY OF THE ROVERS' MOMENT? Standing up to a seamer and catching an edge off a full toss
CRICKETING HEROES? Nasser Hussain, Jack Russell
NON-CRICKETING HEROES? Paul Archer (architect)
IF YOU WEREN'T A CRICKETER? I'd be an architect
TWITTER: @JamesFoster07

Batting	Mat	Inns	NO	Runs	HS	Ave	SR	100	50	Ct	St
Tests	7	12	3	226	48	25.11	34.55	0	0	17	1
ODIs	11	6	3	41	13	13.66	57.74	0	0	13	7
T20Is	5	5	2	37	14*	12.33	115.62	0	0	3	3
First-class	283	418	52	13533	212	36.97		23	69	823	60
List A	223	164	46	3357	83*	28.44		0	16	246	65
T20s	177	140	40	2158	65*	21.58	140.40	0	7	79	46

Bowling	Mat	Balls	Runs	Wkts	BBI	BBM	Ave	Econ	SR	5w	10
Tests	7	-	-	-	-	-	-	-	-	-	-
ODIs	11	-	-	-	-	-	-	-	-	-	-
T20Is	5	-	-	-	-	-	-	-	-	-	-
First-class	283	84	128	1	1/122	1/122	128.00	9.14	84.0	0	0
List A	223	-	-	-	-	-	-	-	-	-	-
T20s	177	-	-	-	-	-	-	-	-	-	-

JAMES FRANKLIN

LHB / LM / RO / WO

MIDDLESEX

FULL NAME: James Edward Charles Franklin
BORN: November 7, 1980, Wellington, New Zealand
SQUAD NO: 74
HEIGHT: 6ft 4in
NICKNAME: Franky, Tank
TEAMS: New Zealand, Middlesex, Adelaide Strikers, Barbados Tridents, Essex, Glamorgan, Gloucestershire, Guyana Amazon Warriors, Mumbai Indians, North Island, Nottinghamshire, Wellington
ROLE: Allrounder
DEBUT: Test: 2001; ODI: 2001; T20I: 2006; First-class: 1998; List A: 1999; T20: 2004

BEST BATTING: 219 Wellington vs Auckland, Auckland, 2008
BEST BOWLING: 7-14 Gloucestershire vs Derbyshire, Bristol, 2010
COUNTY CAP: 2006 (Glamorgan); 2014 (Nottinghamshire); 2015 (Middlesex)

FAMILY TIES? My aunt, Jean Coulston, represented New Zealand in the 1950s
'ROY OF THE ROVERS' MOMENT? Nothing beats being involved in a team that wins trophies – like Middlesex in 2016!
CRICKETING HERO? Wasim Akram – a genius
NON-CRICKETING HERO? Mike Horn – an explorer who has some incredible stories
IF YOU WEREN'T A CRICKETER? I'd be working for NASA on their next space programme
SURPRISING FACT? I can wiggle my ears
TWITTER: @jecfranklin

Batting	Mat	Inns	NO	Runs	HS	Ave	SR	100	50	Ct	St
Tests	31	46	7	808	122*	20.71	37.35	1	2	12	0
ODIs	110	80	27	1270	98*	23.96	76.92	0	4	26	0
T20Is	38	31	8	463	60	20.13	118.41	0	2	13	0
First-class	206	321	46	9780	219	35.56		22	44	107	0
List A	283	236	63	5632	133*	32.55		4	33	88	0
T20s	227	205	50	4301	90	27.74	124.70	0	15	78	0

Bowling	Mat	Balls	Runs	Wkts	BBI	BBM	Ave	Econ	SR	5w	10
Tests	31	4767	2786	82	6/119	7/117	33.97	3.50	58.1	3	0
ODIs	110	3848	3354	81	5/42	5/42	41.40	5.22	47.5	1	0
T20Is	38	327	417	20	4/15	4/15	20.85	7.65	16.3	0	0
First-class	206	25509	13503	479	7/14	10/71	28.18	3.17	53.2	14	1
List A	283	9353	7707	226	5/42	5/42	34.10	4.94	41.3	2	0
T20s	227	2380	3341	110	5/21	5/21	30.37	8.42	21.6	1	0

JAMES FULLER

RHB / RFM / RO / WO

FULL NAME: James Kerr Fuller
BORN: January 24, 1990, Cape Town, South Africa
SQUAD NO: 26
HEIGHT: 6ft 2in
NICKNAME: Fuller, Foz
EDUCATION: Westlake Boys High School, Auckland; University of Otago
TEAMS: Middlesex, Auckland, Gloucestershire, Otago
ROLE: Bowler
DEBUT: First-class: 2010; List A: 2011; T20: 2011

MIDDLESEX

BEST BATTING: 93 Middlesex vs Somerset, Taunton, 2016
BEST BOWLING: 6-24 Otago vs Wellington, Dunedin, 2013
COUNTY CAP: 2011 (Gloucestershire)

WHAT GOT YOU INTO CRICKET? Watching the Black Caps play Australia on telly
'ROY OF THE ROVERS' MOMENT? The glorious Glosters winning the 2015 one-day trophy
BEST THING ABOUT YOUR HOME GROUND? The food – lamb cutlets for lunch… wow
BEST OPPOSING PLAYER IN COUNTY CRICKET? Liam Norwell (Glo)
YOUNG OPPOSING PLAYER WHO HAS IMPRESSED YOU? Sam Curran (Sur)
IF YOU WEREN'T A CRICKETER? I'd be a scientist
SURPRISING FACT ABOUT YOU? I have held my breath for over three minutes and 30 seconds
SURPRISING FACT ABOUT A TEAMMATE? Olly Rayner can rattle off all 84 spells that are used in the Harry Potter books
WHERE IS PARADISE? Hauraki Gulf, New Zealand. Line in the water
NON-CRICKETING HERO? Louis Zamperini – teenage Olympian, highly skilled bombardier and surviving POW. If you haven't read the book Unbroken, then I highly recommend it
TWITTER: @James_Fuller246

Batting	Mat	Inns	NO	Runs	HS	Ave	SR	100	50	Ct	St
First-class	41	48	5	859	93	19.97	66.90	0	4	17	0
List A	52	41	14	597	45	22.11	98.02	0	0	15	0
T20s	62	31	11	323	36	16.15	142.92	0	0	25	0

Bowling	Mat	Balls	Runs	Wkts	BBI	BBM	Ave	Econ	SR	5w	10
First-class	41	6494	3817	113	6/24	10/79	33.77	3.52	57.4	5	1
List A	52	2161	2082	70	6/35	6/35	29.74	5.78	30.8	1	0
T20s	62	1285	1770	79	4/24	4/24	22.40	8.26	16.2	0	0

GEORGE GARTON

LHB / LF / RO / WO

SUSSEX

FULL NAME: George Henry Simmons Garton
BORN: April 15, 1997, Brighton
SQUAD NO: 15
EDUCATION: Hurstpierpoint College, West Sussex
TEAMS: Sussex, England Lions
ROLE: Bowler
DEBUT: First-class: 2016; List A: 2016; T20: 2016

BEST BATTING: 18* Sussex vs Glamorgan, Cardiff, 2016
BEST BOWLING: 3-20 Sussex vs Durham, Chester-le-Street, 2017

TWITTER: @george_garton
NOTES: A left-arm seamer with pace and nip who made enough of an impression in his debut season for Sussex to receive a call-up to the England Lions one-day side, culminating in a four-wicket burst against Sri Lanka A in July 2016. Garton was already well known to the ECB's top brass, having represented England U19 with distinction, and despite his inexperience at professional level, there is much expected of him as the search for an English left-arm seamer of true international standard continues

Batting	Mat	Inns	NO	Runs	HS	Ave	SR	100	50	Ct	St
First-class	9	10	2	79	18*	9.87	50.96	0	0	3	0
List A	15	5	2	20	7*	6.66	90.90	0	0	7	0
T20s	12	1	1	2	2*	-	100.00	0	0	3	0

Bowling	Mat	Balls	Runs	Wkts	BBI	BBM	Ave	Econ	SR	5w	10
First-class	9	1225	839	23	3/20	5/109	36.47	4.10	53.2	0	0
List A	15	642	690	20	4/43	4/43	34.50	6.44	32.1	0	0
T20s	12	186	272	11	4/16	4/16	24.72	8.77	16.9	0	0

WILL GIDMAN

LHB / RMF / R1 / W2

FULL NAME: William Robert Simon Gidman
BORN: February 14, 1985, High Wycombe, Buckinghamshire
SQUAD NO: 42
HEIGHT: 6ft 2in
NICKNAME: Giddo, Willow
EDUCATION: Wycliffe College, Gloucestershire; Berkshire College of Agriculture, Maidenhead
TEAMS: Kent, Nottinghamshire, Durham, Gloucestershire
ROLE: Allrounder
DEBUT: First-class: 2007; List A: 2003; T20: 2011

KENT

BEST BATTING: 143 Gloucestershire vs Leicestershire, Bristol, 2013
BEST BOWLING: 6-15 Gloucestershire vs Leicestershire, Bristol, 2013
COUNTY CAP: 2011 (Nottinghamshire)

WHAT GOT YOU INTO CRICKET? School, garden games with my brother, and watching it on TV
FAMILY TIES? My brother Alex played for Gloucestershire and Worcestershire and has recently became second XI coach at New Road. My sister Charlotte is a high-class umpire
'ROY OF THE ROVERS' MOMENT? Not on the pitch, but being on the balcony when England won the Ashes in 2015 was very special
HOW WOULD YOUR TEAMMATES DESCRIBE YOU IN THREE WORDS? Posh, poor banter
NON-CRICKETING HEROES? Jonny Wilkinson and Muhammad Ali – both changed attitudes
IF YOU WEREN'T A CRICKETER? I'd be running a highly successful law firm!
SURPRISING FACT? I went to an agricultural college and studied sport
TWITTER: @wgiddo

Batting	Mat	Inns	NO	Runs	HS	Ave	SR	100	50	Ct	St
First-class	78	121	21	3646	143	36.46	50.28	5	21	36	0
List A	66	47	9	945	94	24.86	108.77	0	4	18	0
T20s	15	14	6	186	40*	23.25	108.77	0	0	3	0

Bowling	Mat	Balls	Runs	Wkts	BBI	BBM	Ave	Econ	SR	5w	10
First-class	78	10407	5053	212	6/15	10/43	23.83	2.91	49.0	9	1
List A	66	2411	1813	61	4/20	4/20	29.72	4.51	39.5	0	0
T20s	15	156	228	6	2/23	2/23	38.00	8.76	26.0	0	0

ALFIE GLEADALL RHB / RMF / RO / WO

FULL NAME: Alfie Frank Gleadall
BORN: May 28, 2000, Chesterfield
SQUAD NO: 17
EDUCATION: Westfield Sports College, Sheffield
TEAMS: Derbyshire
ROLE: Bowler
DEBUT: List A: 2017

NOTES: Gleadall signed a two-year professional contract with Derbyshire in June 2017. The right-arm pace bowler was a regular in the second XI last summer and made his first-team debut in the tour fixture against South Africa A in May. Development coach Mal Loye said: "Alfie is a talented local lad who has come through the Cricket Derbyshire Academy and has shown great promise as a young fast bowler. He has a very good attitude towards his own game and has made great progress, which has been highlighted in his performances for the Academy and second XI this season. He has already been around the first-team squad and we feel there are opportunities for a fast bowler to come through, and he's certainly impressed us so far"

Batting	Mat	Inns	NO	Runs	HS	Ave	SR	100	50	Ct	St
List A	1	-	-	-	-	-	-	-	-	0	0

Bowling	Mat	Balls	Runs	Wkts	BBI	BBM	Ave	Econ	SR	5w	10
List A	1	18	22	0	-	-	-	7.33	-	0	0

RICHARD GLEESON — RHB / RFM / R0 / W0 / MVP95

FULL NAME: Richard James Gleeson
BORN: December 2, 1987, Blackpool, Lancashire
SQUAD NO: 33
HEIGHT: 6ft 3in
NICKNAME: Gleese
EDUCATION: Baines High School, Lancashire; University of Cumbria
TEAMS: Northamptonshire, England Lions, Rangpur Riders
ROLE: Bowler
DEBUT: First-class: 2015; List A: 2016; T20: 2016

NORTHAMPTONSHIRE

BEST BATTING: 31 Northamptonshire vs Gloucestershire, Bristol, 2016
BEST BOWLING: 5-46 Northamptonshire vs Gloucestershire, Northampton, 2017

FAMILY TIES? My father ran the bar at our local cricket club, sister ran the kitchen, brother-in-law was the first XI captain
BEST ADVICE EVER RECEIVED? Just enjoy it maaaate (Steven Crook)
'ROY OF THE ROVERS' MOMENT? Becoming a pro at the age of 28
BEST THING ABOUT YOUR HOME GROUND? The recovery pool on the morning of a match (providing it's warm)
IF YOU WEREN'T A CRICKETER? I'd be on MasterChef
SURPRISING FACT ABOUT YOU? I am a published poet
SURPRISING FACT ABOUT A TEAMMATE? Adam Rossington is a butcher and wears a butcher's hat
WHERE IS PARADISE? Blackpool
CRICKETING HERO? Allan Donald – loved the way he got fired up
NON-CRICKETING HERO? Steven Gerrard
UNUSUAL OBJECT AT HOME? A Buddha head
TWITTER: @RicGleeson

Batting	Mat	Inns	NO	Runs	HS	Ave	SR	100	50	Ct	St
First-class	17	19	7	172	31	14.33	34.19	0	0	4	0
List A	15	8	3	18	6*	3.60	37.50	0	0	3	0
T20s	25	7	3	21	7*	5.25	95.45	0	0	4	0

Bowling	Mat	Balls	Runs	Wkts	BBI	BBM	Ave	Econ	SR	5w	10
First-class	17	2696	1505	59	5/46	8/131	25.50	3.34	45.6	3	0
List A	15	559	545	18	5/47	5/47	30.27	5.84	31.0	1	0
T20s	25	517	608	27	3/12	3/12	22.51	7.05	19.1	0	0

BILLY GODLEMAN LHB / LB / R1 / W0 / MVP86

DERBYSHIRE

FULL NAME: Billy Ashley Godleman
BORN: February 11, 1989, Camden, London
SQUAD NO: 1
HEIGHT: 6ft 2in
NICKNAME: G, Chief
EDUCATION: Islington Green School, London
TEAMS: Derbyshire, Essex, Middlesex
ROLE: Batsman
DEBUT: First-class: 2005; List A: 2007; T20: 2006

BEST BATTING: 204 Derbyshire vs Worcestershire, Derby, 2016

WHAT GOT YOU INTO CRICKET? Watching my dad play on a Saturday
BEST ADVICE EVER RECEIVED? Break your innings down into shorter, more manageable chunks of time
'ROY OF THE ROVERS' MOMENT? Winning the T20 final vs Kent in 2008 with Middlesex
BEST THING ABOUT YOUR HOME GROUND? It's got a great deck
SURPRISING FACT ABOUT YOU? I don't engage on social media
SURPRISING FACT ABOUT A TEAMMATE? My close friend Tony Palladino wears a Batman skin under his whites – very apt as he has delivered many superhuman spells over the years
WHERE IS PARADISE? At home with my family
CRICKETING HERO? I admire Hashim Amla. He stands for something more than cricket. He shares his experience and inside knowledge with other players. And he scores runs consistently in all competitions. Top bloke. Also Ed Smith – a brilliant and inspirational thinker on cricket and beyond, and a very nice man
NON-CRICKETING HERO? My mum and dad

Batting	Mat	Inns	NO	Runs	HS	Ave	SR	100	50	Ct	St
First-class	127	226	11	7009	204	32.60	45.26	15	33	87	0
List A	52	50	6	1517	109*	34.47	72.58	1	8	20	0
T20s	56	52	2	892	70	17.84	116.60	0	5	24	0

Bowling	Mat	Balls	Runs	Wkts	BBI	BBM	Ave	Econ	SR	5w	10
First-class	127	30	35	0	-	-	-	7.00	-	0	0
List A	52	-	-	-	-	-	-	-	-	-	-
T20s	56	-	-	-	-	-	-	-	-	-	-

BEN GREEN

RHB / RFM / R0 / W0

FULL NAME: Benjamin George Frederick Green
BORN: September 28, 1997, Exeter, Devon
SQUAD NO: 54
EDUCATION: Exeter School
TEAMS: Somerset
ROLE: Allrounder
DEBUT: T20: 2016

SOMERSET

NOTES: Seam-bowling allrounder who signed a three-year contract with Somerset in August 2016. Made his Somerset debut in the T20 Blast against Hampshire in 2016 but did not play any first-team cricket last summer after suffering a back injury. A product of the Devon age-group system, Green joined the Somerset Academy in 2013 but continued to play club cricket for Exeter CC, where he was a strong performer in junior and men's cricket. He has represented England at U15, U17 and U19 level. He made his Somerset Second XI debut in 2014, claiming 3-18 and has been a regular in the side over the last three seasons. "I am happy that I got so much cricket in after my back injury in 2016," said Green. "This was a massive positive to have played as much as I have. I felt like I bowled quite nicely at the start of the season and found some rhythm and bowled with good control. I scored some good runs and got a hundred and a few nice starts, but overall I would have liked to kick on a bit more"

Batting	Mat	Inns	NO	Runs	HS	Ave	SR	100	50	Ct	St
T20s	1	1	1	12	12*	-	92.30	0	0	0	0

Bowling	Mat	Balls	Runs	Wkts	BBI	BBM	Ave	Econ	SR	5w	10
T20s	1	12	12	0	-	-	-	6.00	-	0	0

CALLUM GREGORY   RHB / RMF / R0 / W0

GLOUCESTERSHIRE

FULL NAME: Callum James William Gregory
BORN: February 14, 1997, Reading, Berkshire
SQUAD NO: TBC
HEIGHT: 6ft 2in
NICKNAME: Greggers
EDUCATION: Maiden Erlegh School, Reading
TEAMS: Gloucestershire
ROLE: Bowler

WHAT GOT YOU INTO CRICKET? Playing in the back garden with my older brother
BEST ADVICE EVER RECEIVED? Back yourself
'ROY OF THE ROVERS' MOMENT? Year 7 in the County Cup final – we were chasing 70 to win and I made 51 of them
BEST THING ABOUT YOUR HOME GROUND? The atmosphere for the Twenty20 matches
YOUNG OPPOSING PLAYER WHO HAS IMPRESSED YOU? Adam Hose (War) – he hit me for the biggest six I have ever seen
IF YOU WEREN'T A CRICKETER? I'd be a golf caddy
WHERE IS PARADISE? The Caribbean
TWITTER: @callumgregory97
NOTES: Gregory is a fast bowler from Reading who has come up through Gloucestershire's Academy but is yet to make his senior debut in any format. He was a regular for the second XI throughout the 2017 season as part of the county's Academy Plus Programme, which is designed to ease the jump between the Academy and the professional squad. Prior to last summer he was part of a group of players selected for the Tom Maynard Academy, spending nine days in Spain overseen by then Somerset director of cricket Matt Maynard

LEWIS GREGORY

RHB / RFM / R0 / W0 / MVP49

FULL NAME: Lewis Gregory
BORN: May 24, 1992, Plymouth
SQUAD NO: 24
HEIGHT: 6ft
NICKNAME: Mowgli
EDUCATION: Hele's School, Plymouth
TEAMS: Somerset
ROLE: Allrounder
DEBUT: First-class: 2011; List A: 2010; T20: 2011

BEST BATTING: 137 Somerset vs Middlesex, Lord's, 2017
BEST BOWLING: 6-47 Somerset vs Northamptonshire, Northampton, 2014

WHAT GOT YOU INTO CRICKET? Saw it on TV and gave it a go
STRANGEST THING SEEN IN A GAME? Ryan Davies going out in a 50-over game to bat in the wrong shirt
'ROY OF THE ROVERS' MOMENT? Taking my maiden first-class five-wicket haul at Lord's and scoring my maiden first-class hundred at the same ground
BEST OPPOSING PLAYER IN COUNTY CRICKET? Jeetan Patel (War)
CRICKETING HEROES? Jacques Kallis, Michael Vaughan
NON-CRICKETING HEROES? Tiger Woods, Jonny Wilkinson
SURPRISING FACT? I'm a black belt in taekwondo
TWITTER: @Lewisgregory23

Batting	Mat	Inns	NO	Runs	HS	Ave	SR	100	50	Ct	St
First-class	59	83	9	1531	137	20.68	52.43	1	4	23	0
List A	51	34	4	631	105*	21.03	92.25	1	2	20	0
T20s	61	44	11	613	43	18.57	130.14	0	0	22	0

Bowling	Mat	Balls	Runs	Wkts	BBI	BBM	Ave	Econ	SR	5w	10
First-class	59	8310	4766	167	6/47	11/122	28.53	3.44	49.7	9	1
List A	51	1821	1888	73	4/23	4/23	25.86	6.22	24.9	0	0
T20s	61	1021	1473	57	4/15	4/15	25.84	8.65	17.9	0	0

LEICESTERSHIRE

GAVIN GRIFFITHS

RHB / RFM / R0 / W0

FULL NAME: Gavin Timothy Griffiths
BORN: November 19, 1993, Ormskirk, Lancashire
SQUAD NO: 93
HEIGHT: 6ft 2in
NICKNAME: Gavlar
EDUCATION: St Michael's CofE High School, Chorley; St Mary's College, Crosby
TEAMS: Leicestershire, Hampshire, Lancashire
ROLE: Bowler
DEBUT: First-class: 2017; List A: 2014; T20: 2015

BEST BATTING: 14* Leicestershire vs Kent, Leicester, 2017
BEST BOWLING: 4-101 Leicestershire vs Gloucestershire, Bristol, 2017

WHAT GOT YOU INTO CRICKET? My grandad
BEST ADVICE EVER RECEIVED? Don't compare yourself to others
'ROY OF THE ROVERS' MOMENT? Winning T20 Finals Day with Lancashire in 2015
BEST THING ABOUT YOUR HOME GROUND? Jon Stew's cricket teas
BEST OPPOSING PLAYER IN COUNTY CRICKET? Samit Patel (Not)
YOUNG OPPOSING PLAYER WHO HAS IMPRESSED YOU? Matt Potts (Dur) – swung the ball both ways at decent pace last year
IF YOU WEREN'T A CRICKETER? I'd be an umpire
SURPRISING FACT ABOUT YOU? I have played chess for England
SURPRISING FACT ABOUT A TEAMMATE? Zak Chappell has played Call of Duty on the Xbox professionally
CRICKETING HERO? Andrew Flintoff and Allan Donald
TWITTER: @Gavvlar

Batting	Mat	Inns	NO	Runs	HS	Ave	SR	100	50	Ct	St
First-class	6	8	3	37	14*	7.40	29.60	0	0	0	0
List A	11	5	4	7	5*	7.00	35.00	0	0	8	0
T20s	20	6	5	24	11	24.00	88.88	0	0	5	0

Bowling	Mat	Balls	Runs	Wkts	BBI	BBM	Ave	Econ	SR	5w	10
First-class	6	834	434	8	4/101	4/101	54.25	3.12	104.2	0	0
List A	11	526	454	14	3/35	3/35	32.42	5.17	37.5	0	0
T20s	20	342	500	15	3/33	3/33	33.33	8.77	22.8	0	0

TIM GROENEWALD RHB / RFM / R0 / W0 / MVP94

FULL NAME: Timothy Duncan Groenewald
BORN: January 10, 1984, Pietermaritzburg, South Africa
SQUAD NO: 5
HEIGHT: 6ft
NICKNAME: TimmyG, Groeners
EDUCATION: Maritzburg College; University of South Africa
TEAMS: Somerset, Derbyshire, Warwickshire
ROLE: Bowler
DEBUT: First-class: 2006; List A: 2006; T20: 2006

SOMERSET

BEST BATTING: 78 Warwickshire vs Bangladesh A, Edgbaston, 2008
BEST BOWLING: 6-50 Derbyshire vs Surrey, Whitgift School, 2009
COUNTY CAP: 2011 (Derbyshire), 2016 (Somerset)

WHAT GOT YOU INTO CRICKET? Dad bought me a cricket set aged four and I've never wanted to do anything else since
STRANGEST THING SEEN IN A GAME? A batsman caught at short-leg when the ball went straight into the fielder's pocket
'ROY OF THE ROVERS' MOMENT? Together with Jack Leach knocking off the required 31 runs for Somerset to beat Surrey in the Championship when we were nine down – the crowd were incredible, as were the celebrations
HOW WOULD YOUR TEAMMATES DESCRIBE YOU IN THREE WORDS? Bad cricket watcher
CRICKETING HEROES? Hansie Cronje, Jonty Rhodes, Allan Donald
NON-CRICKETING HEROES? My boys, Jamie and Hayden
IF YOU WEREN'T A CRICKETER? I'd be a coffee-shop owner, one with a great vibe where people love coming!
SURPRISING FACT? I grow Bonsai trees
TWITTER: @timmyg12

Batting	Mat	Inns	NO	Runs	HS	Ave	SR	100	50	Ct	St
First-class	124	176	58	2184	78	18.50	51.21	0	6	40	0
List A	99	57	22	701	57	20.02	110.74	0	2	25	0
T20s	103	42	17	384	41	15.36	126.73	0	0	29	0

Bowling	Mat	Balls	Runs	Wkts	BBI	BBM	Ave	Econ	SR	5w	10
First-class	124	20992	10804	362	6/50	9/136	29.84	3.08	57.9	15	0
List A	99	3886	3600	107	4/22	4/22	33.64	5.55	36.3	0	0
T20s	103	1855	2535	87	4/21	4/21	29.13	8.19	21.3	0	0

NICK GUBBINS

LHB / LB / R1 / W0

MIDDLESEX

FULL NAME: Nicholas Richard Trail Gubbins
BORN: December 31, 1993, Richmond, Surrey
SQUAD NO: 18
HEIGHT: 6ft 1in
NICKNAME: Gubbs, Gubbo
EDUCATION: Radley College, Oxfordshire; University of Leeds
TEAMS: Middlesex, England Lions
ROLE: Batsman
DEBUT: First-class: 2013; List A: 2014; T20: 2015

BEST BATTING: 201* Middlesex vs Lancashire, Lord's, 2016
COUNTY CAP: 2016

WHAT GOT YOU INTO CRICKET? Watching my dad play for Singapore Cricket Club from the boundary
FAMILY TIES? My dad played one ODI for Singapore
'ROY OF THE ROVERS' MOMENT? Winning the County Championship in front of our home crowd at Lord's for the first time in 23 years in 2016
BEST THING ABOUT YOUR HOME GROUND? It's Lord's
YOUNG OPPOSING PLAYER WHO HAS IMPRESSED YOU? Jofra Archer (Sus) – you do the maths
IF YOU WEREN'T A CRICKETER? A seedy bloke with no direction in life
SURPRISING FACT ABOUT YOU? I've never lost a game of FIFA playing a 4-2-3-1 formation
SURPRISING FACT ABOUT A TEAMMATE? Tom Helm has a hidden gut/shelf. #dairymilk
WHERE IS PARADISE? Shepherd's Bush, London
CRICKETING HERO? Marcus Trescothick – I used to get his GM bats when I was younger and I always tried to mimic him in the back garden
TWITTER: @ngubbins18

Batting	Mat	Inns	NO	Runs	HS	Ave	SR	100	50	Ct	St
First-class	47	82	2	2825	201*	35.31	48.11	5	20	20	0
List A	26	26	0	872	141	33.53	87.55	2	4	5	0
T20s	21	19	0	268	46	14.10	118.58	0	0	8	0

Bowling	Mat	Balls	Runs	Wkts	BBI	BBM	Ave	Econ	SR	5w	10
First-class	47	66	52	0	-	-	-	4.72	-	0	0
List A	26	-	-	-	-	-	-	-	-	-	-
T20s	21	-	-	-	-	-	-	-	-	-	-

BROOKE GUEST

RHB / WK / R0 / W0

FULL NAME: Brooke David Guest
BORN: May 14, 1997, Whitworth Park, Manchester
SQUAD NO: 29
EDUCATION: Kent Street Senior High School, Perth; Murdoch University, Perth
TEAMS: Lancashire, Australia U19
ROLE: Wicketkeeper

NOTES: Born in Manchester, Guest moved to Australia as a young boy and made his Australia U19 debut in 2016. He has also captained Western Australia U19. Committed his future to England after returning to the UK in 2016 to play for Lancashire, where he turned out for the second XI, and for Sale CC in the Cheshire County Cricket League. His 803 runs at 53.53, including two hundreds, were more than anyone else in the division. The wicketkeeper faces stiff competition for a place in the Lancashire first team, with England's Jos Buttler and the in-form Alex Davies blocking his path. Guest did not make a senior appearance last summer but did help Lancashire's second team reach T20 Finals Day and win the three-day Championship title. He scored 395 runs from nine three-day matches with three fifties, including a best of 96 not out, and claimed 21 catches behind the stumps

HARRY GURNEY

RHB / LFM / R0 / W0 / MVP87

FULL NAME: Harry Frederick Gurney
BORN: October 20, 1986, Nottingham
SQUAD NO: 11
HEIGHT: 6ft 3in
NICKNAME: Gramps
EDUCATION: Garendon High School, Loughborough; Loughborough Grammar School; University of Leeds
TEAMS: England, Nottinghamshire, Leicestershire
ROLE: Bowler
DEBUT: ODI: 2014; T20I: 2014; First-class: 2007; List A: 2009; T20: 2009

BEST BATTING: 42* Nottinghamshire vs Sussex, Hove, 2017
BEST BOWLING: 6-61 Nottinghamshire vs Durham, Chester-le-Street, 2016

BEST ADVICE EVER RECEIVED? Bowl as fast as you can at the top of off
BEST THING ABOUT YOUR HOME GROUND? The crowds on T20 Friday nights
YOUNG OPPOSING PLAYER WHO HAS IMPRESSED YOU? Mason Crane (Ham) – leg-spin is such a difficult art and he is only going to get better and better
SURPRISING FACT ABOUT YOU? I own a third of a pub company
SURPRISING FACT ABOUT A TEAMMATE? Steven Mullaney has a fascination with wind socks
WHERE IS PARADISE? St Anton, Austria
CRICKETING HERO? Simon Kerrigan – he is an inspiration to all lower-order batters
NON-CRICKETING HERO? Elon Musk – in addition to his success in business, he is determined to change the world
UNUSUAL OBJECT AT HOME? My name-board from the old scoreboard at Trent Bridge
TWITTER: @gurneyhf

Batting	Mat	Inns	NO	Runs	HS	Ave	SR	100	50	Ct	St
ODIs	10	6	4	15	6*	7.50	45.45	0	0	1	0
T20Is	2	-	-	-	-	-	-	-	-	0	0
First-class	92	115	53	351	42*	5.66	38.40	0	0	11	0
List A	88	26	16	58	13*	5.80	49.57	0	0	7	0
T20s	99	10	8	12	5*	6.00	92.30	0	0	13	0

Bowling	Mat	Balls	Runs	Wkts	BBI	BBM	Ave	Econ	SR	5w	10
ODIs	10	455	432	11	4/55	4/55	39.27	5.69	41.3	0	0
T20Is	2	48	55	3	2/26	2/26	18.33	6.87	16.0	0	0
First-class	92	14956	8335	268	6/61	9/136	31.10	3.34	55.8	6	0
List A	88	3676	3568	104	5/24	5/24	34.30	5.82	35.3	3	0
T20s	99	2065	2681	114	4/17	4/17	23.51	7.78	18.1	0	0

CALUM HAGGETT

LHB / RM / RO / WO

FULL NAME: Calum John Haggett
BORN: October 30, 1990, Taunton
SQUAD NO: 25
HEIGHT: 6ft 3in
NICKNAME: Hagg
EDUCATION: Crispin School, Somerset; Millfield School
TEAMS: Kent, Somerset
ROLE: Bowler
DEBUT: First-class: 2013; List A: 2013; T20: 2011

KENT

BEST BATTING: 80 Kent vs Surrey, The Oval, 2015
BEST BOWLING: 4-15 Kent vs Derbyshire, Derby, 2016

WHAT GOT YOU INTO CRICKET? I lived next to a cricket club
FAMILY TIES? My father played village cricket and my brother played for Somerset seconds
'ROY OF THE ROVERS' MOMENT? Making my first-class debut
HOW WOULD YOUR TEAMMATES DESCRIBE YOU IN THREE WORDS? Tidy, stubborn, unique
CRICKETING HEROES? Chris March and Phil Hunt from Ashcott and Shapwick CC. They showed me what to do after the game
NON-CRICKETING HEROES? Mother Teresa, Nelson Mandela, Gandhi
IF YOU WEREN'T A CRICKETER? I'd be a twitcher
SURPRISING FACT? I have a webbed toe

Batting	Mat	Inns	NO	Runs	HS	Ave	SR	100	50	Ct	St
First-class	38	50	13	873	80	23.59	40.00	0	2	9	0
List A	27	18	2	273	45	17.06	73.98	0	0	10	0
T20s	19	10	6	35	11	8.75	102.94	0	0	4	0

Bowling	Mat	Balls	Runs	Wkts	BBI	BBM	Ave	Econ	SR	5w	10
First-class	38	5710	2923	83	4/15	7/97	35.21	3.07	68.7	0	0
List A	27	1182	1102	33	4/59	4/59	33.39	5.59	35.8	0	0
T20s	19	318	475	15	2/12	2/12	31.66	8.96	21.2	0	0

SAM HAIN

RHB / RM / R0 / W0 / MVP64

FULL NAME: Samuel Robert Hain
BORN: July 16, 1995, Hong Kong
SQUAD NO: 16
HEIGHT: 6ft
NICKNAME: Ched, Hainy
EDUCATION: The Southport School, Queensland, Australia
TEAMS: Warwickshire, England Lions
ROLE: Batsman
DEBUT: First-class: 2014; List A: 2013; T20: 2016

BEST BATTING: 208 Warwickshire vs Northamptonshire, Edgbaston, 2014

WHAT GOT YOU INTO CRICKET? The battles with the brothers in the backyard. Always ended in tears
'ROY OF THE ROVERS' MOMENT? Winning the One-Day Cup at Lord's in 2016
BEST THING ABOUT YOUR HOME GROUND? What's not to love? It's got everything you'd want for your home ground
BEST OPPOSING PLAYER IN COUNTY CRICKET? Varun Chopra (Ess)
IF YOU WEREN'T A CRICKETER? I'd be opening a coffeehouse on the Gold Coast with my best mate
WHERE IS PARADISE? Any sunny afternoon on the first tee at Royal Pines on the Gold Coast
NON-CRICKETING HERO? Bryson DeChambeau – I've tried to copy his golf swing
TWITTER: @Sammiehain

Batting	Mat	Inns	NO	Runs	HS	Ave	SR	100	50	Ct	St
First-class	47	74	6	2139	208	31.45	49.01	7	7	37	0
List A	23	23	2	1166	109	55.52	85.54	4	6	11	0
T20s	29	27	2	829	92*	33.16	128.12	0	5	22	0

Bowling	Mat	Balls	Runs	Wkts	BBI	BBM	Ave	Econ	SR	5w	10
First-class	47	42	31	0	-	-	-	4.42	-	0	0
List A	23	-	-	-	-	-	-	-	-	-	-
T20s	29	-	-	-	-	-	-	-	-	-	-

TOM HAINES

LHB / RM / RO / WO

FULL NAME: Thomas Jacob Haines
BORN: October 28, 1998, Crawley, West Sussex
SQUAD NO: 20
HEIGHT: 5ft 11in
NICKNAME: Hainus
EDUCATION: Hurstpierpoint College
TEAMS: Sussex
ROLE: Allrounder
DEBUT: First-class: 2016

SUSSEX

BEST BATTING: 11 Sussex vs Kent, Hove, 2016

BEST ADVICE EVER RECEIVED? Watch the ball
'ROY OF THE ROVERS' MOMENT? The 2014 Bunbury Festival
BEST THING ABOUT YOUR HOME GROUND? The atmosphere
BEST OPPOSING PLAYER IN COUNTY CRICKET? Marcus Trescothick (Som)
YOUNG OPPOSING PLAYER WHO HAS IMPRESSED YOU? Ollie Pope (Sur)
IF YOU WEREN'T A CRICKETER? I'd be a footballer
WHERE IS PARADISE? Hope Cove, Devon
CRICKETING HERO? Marcus Trescothick
NON-CRICKETING HERO? Jan Vertonghen
TWITTER: @tomhaines
NOTES: Haines is a 19-year-old left-handed opening batsman from Crawley who has come through the Sussex Academy. He also bowls medium-pace. Haines signed a one-year professional contract last October after playing for the second XI throughout 2017, scoring two hundreds and helping the side win the T20 competition. Haines made his first-class debut in 2016 at the age of 17. Sussex director of cricket Keith Greenfield said: "Tom has been a standout batsman through our youth and academy cricket. He is a very exciting talent for us to progress over the years to come"

Batting	Mat	Inns	NO	Runs	HS	Ave	SR	100	50	Ct	St
First-class	2	3	0	12	11	4.00	27.27	0	0	1	0

Bowling	Mat	Balls	Runs	Wkts	BBI	BBM	Ave	Econ	SR	5w	10
First-class	2	24	8	0	-	-	-	2.00	-	0	0

ALEX HALES

RHB / RM / R3 / W0 / MVP34

NOTTINGHAMSHIRE

FULL NAME: Alexander Daniel Hales
BORN: January 3, 1989, Hillingdon, Middlesex
SQUAD NO: 10
HEIGHT: 6ft 5in
NICKNAME: Baz
EDUCATION: Chesham High School, Buckinghamshire
TEAMS: England, Nottinghamshire, Adelaide Strikers, Hobart Hurricanes, Melbourne Renegades, Worcestershire
ROLE: Batsman
DEBUT: Test: 2015; ODI: 2014; T20I: 2011; First-class: 2008; List A: 2008; T20: 2009

BEST BATTING: 236 Nottinghamshire vs Yorkshire, Trent Bridge, 2015
BEST BOWLING: 2-63 Nottinghamshire vs Yorkshire, Trent Bridge, 2009
COUNTY CAP: 2011 (Nottinghamshire)

WHAT GOT YOU INTO CRICKET? Living in the bungalow at Denham CC
HOW WOULD YOUR TEAMMATES DESCRIBE YOU IN THREE WORDS? Annoying, entertaining, grubby
YOUNG OPPOSING PLAYER WHO HAS IMPRESSED YOU? Joe Clarke (Wor)
CRICKETING HEROES? Marcus Trescothick, Jacques Kallis, Dominic Cork
TWITTER: @AlexHales1
NOTES: Signed a deal in February to play only white-ball cricket for Notts until the end of 2019

Batting	Mat	Inns	NO	Runs	HS	Ave	SR	100	50	Ct	St
Tests	11	21	0	573	94	27.28	43.84	0	5	8	0
ODIs	58	56	2	1957	171	36.24	95.46	5	11	21	0
T20Is	52	52	6	1456	116*	31.65	136.32	1	7	27	0
First-class	107	182	6	6655	236	37.81	59.06	13	38	84	0
List A	157	153	5	5670	187*	38.31	99.77	16	28	54	0
T20s	170	169	10	4617	116*	29.03	143.74	2	30	69	0
Bowling	Mat	Balls	Runs	Wkts	BBI	BBM	Ave	Econ	SR	5w	10
Tests	11	18	2	0	-	-	-	0.66	-	0	0
ODIs	58	-	-	-	-	-	-	-	-	-	-
T20Is	52	-	-	-	-	-	-	-	-	-	-
First-class	107	311	173	3	2/63	2/63	57.66	3.33	103.6	0	0
List A	157	4	10	0	-	-	-	15.00	-	0	0
T20s	170	3	7	0	-	-	-	14.00	-	0	0

HASEEB HAMEED

RHB / LB / R1 / W0

FULL NAME: Haseeb Hameed
BORN: January 17, 1997, Bolton, Lancashire
SQUAD NO: 23
HEIGHT: 6ft 2in
NICKNAME: Has
EDUCATION: Bolton School
TEAMS: England, Lancashire
ROLE: Batsman
DEBUT: Test: 2016; First-class: 2015; List A: 2017

LANCASHIRE

BEST BATTING: 122 Lancashire vs Nottinghamshire, Trent Bridge, 2015
COUNTY CAP: 2016

TWITTER: @HaseebHameed97
NOTES: Tipped as one of the hottest batting prospects in England, Hameed exceeded his reputation in 2016 by making more than 1,000 Championship runs in his first full season at Old Trafford – at 19 years of age becoming the youngest batsman to achieve the feat for Lancashire – and looking immediately at ease when scoring a fifty on his Test debut against India in Rajkot later that year. In August 2014 he hit 389 runs in five matches for England U19 against South Africa U19, an international record for a batsman in a youth bilateral one-day series. Impressed in four Championship matches for Lancashire in 2015. Struggled for form last year (no hundreds) but there were encouraging signs towards the end of the summer as he fights to win back his Test place

Batting	Mat	Inns	NO	Runs	HS	Ave	SR	100	50	Ct	St
Tests	3	6	1	219	82	43.80	34.21	0	2	4	0
First-class	42	73	8	2396	122	36.86	36.62	4	14	24	0
List A	8	8	1	275	88	39.28	80.40	0	2	1	0
Bowling	Mat	Balls	Runs	Wkts	BBI	BBM	Ave	Econ	SR	5w	10
Tests	3	-	-	-	-	-	-	-	-	-	-
First-class	42	42	21	0	-	-	-	3.00	-	0	0
List A	8	-	-	-	-	-	-	-	-	-	-

MILES HAMMOND   GLOUCESTERSHIRE

FULL NAME: Miles Arthur Halhead Hammond
BORN: January 11, 1996, Cheltenham, Gloucestershire
SQUAD NO: 88
HEIGHT: 6ft
NICKNAME: Hammo, Wally, Cryles
EDUCATION: St Edward's School, Oxford; University of the Arts London
TEAMS: Gloucestershire
ROLE: Bowler
DEBUT: First-class: 2013; List A: 2013; T20: 2013

BEST BATTING: 30 Gloucestershire vs Glamorgan, Swansea, 2015
BEST BOWLING: 1-96 Gloucestershire vs Glamorgan, Bristol, 2013

WHAT GOT YOU INTO CRICKET? Dad throwing balls at me when I was two
STRANGEST THING SEEN IN A GAME? An umpire being hit on the backside by a wild throw from a fielder
'ROY OF THE ROVERS' MOMENT? Beating Yorkshire at Headingley on my Gloucestershire debut
SUPERSTITIONS? Left sock has to be inside out and I wear my house key around my neck
HOW WOULD YOUR TEAMMATES DESCRIBE YOU IN THREE WORDS? A space cadet
CRICKETING HEROES? Walter Hammond, Marcus Trescothick, Moeen Ali
NON-CRICKETING HEROES? Jonny Wilkinson, Dan Bilzerian
IF YOU WEREN'T A CRICKETER? I'd be an architect
UNUSUAL OBJECT AT HOME? A solar illuminating glass cube
TWITTER: @hammo125

Batting	Mat	Inns	NO	Runs	HS	Ave	SR	100	50	Ct	St
First-class	3	3	0	34	30	11.33	38.63	0	0	1	0
List A	3	1	0	0	0	0.00	0.00	0	0	0	0
T20s	2	-	-	-	-	-	-	-	-	0	0

Bowling	Mat	Balls	Runs	Wkts	BBI	BBM	Ave	Econ	SR	5w	10
First-class	3	294	196	1	1/96	1/155	196.00	4.00	294.0	0	0
List A	3	114	97	5	2/18	2/18	19.40	5.10	22.8	0	0
T20s	2	12	17	0	-	-	-	8.50	-	0	0

GLOUCESTERSHIRE

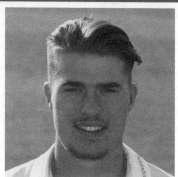

FULL NAME: George Thomas Hankins
BORN: January 4, 1997, Bath
SQUAD NO: 21
HEIGHT: 6ft 1in
NICKNAME: Hanks, Hanko
EDUCATION: Kingswood School, Bath; Millfield School, Somerset
TEAMS: Gloucestershire
ROLE: Batsman
DEBUT: First-class: 2016; List A: 2017; T20: 2017

BEST BATTING: 116 Gloucestershire vs Northamptonshire, Northampton, 2016

WHAT GOT YOU INTO CRICKET? Watching my uncle on Saturdays
BEST ADVICE EVER RECEIVED? See it, hit it
'ROY OF THE ROVERS' MOMENT? Taking 7-9 against Clifton School in Year 8
BEST THING ABOUT YOUR HOME GROUND? It's very close to the Boston Tea Party café
YOUNG OPPOSING PLAYER WHO HAS IMPRESSED YOU? Dan Lawrence (Ess)
IF YOU WEREN'T A CRICKETER? I'd be a lawyer
SURPRISING FACT ABOUT YOU? I have no earlobes
WHERE IS PARADISE? Kendleshire Golf Club, south Gloucestershire
CRICKETING HERO? Joe Root
NON-CRICKETING HERO? Justin Bieber
TWITTER: @hankins1997

Batting	Mat	Inns	NO	Runs	HS	Ave	SR	100	50	Ct	St
First-class	22	35	1	862	116	25.35	52.85	1	5	26	0
List A	3	3	0	100	67	33.33	65.35	0	1	2	0
T20s	7	3	0	17	14	5.66	60.71	0	0	1	0

Bowling	Mat	Balls	Runs	Wkts	BBI	BBM	Ave	Econ	SR	5w	10
First-class	22	13	13	0	-	-	-	6.00	-	0	0
List A	3	-	-	-	-	-	-	-	-	-	-
T20s	7	-	-	-	-	-	-	-	-	-	-

OLIVER HANNON-DALBY · LHB / RMF / RO / WO

WARWICKSHIRE

FULL NAME: Oliver James Hannon-Dalby
BORN: June 20, 1989, Halifax, Yorkshire
SQUAD NO: 20
HEIGHT: 6ft 8in
NICKNAME: Owl Face, Owl Head, André Schürrle, OHD
EDUCATION: Brooksbank School; Leeds Metropolitan University
TEAMS: Warwickshire, Yorkshire
ROLE: Bowler
DEBUT: First-class: 2008; List A: 2011; T20: 2012

BEST BATTING: 40 Warwickshire vs Somerset, Taunton, 2014
BEST BOWLING: 5-68 Yorkshire vs Somerset, Headingley, 2010

FAMILY TIES? My whole family either play or support local cricket in the Halifax League
BEST ADVICE EVER RECEIVED? Work hard to be a good cricketer, work even harder to be a good bloke
'ROY OF THE ROVERS' MOMENT? Blocking out for a draw at Taunton with a broken arm in 2013
YOUNG OPPOSING PLAYER WHO HAS IMPRESSED YOU? George Garton (Sus) – he has serious pace
SURPRISING FACT ABOUT YOU? I've won a ballroom dancing competition
SURPRISING FACT ABOUT A TEAMMATE? Josh Poysden has to nap at 3pm every day otherwise he gets cranky
WHERE IS PARADISE? Anywhere with my dog, girlfriend, sun and a golf course
CRICKETING HERO? James Anderson – wish I could do what he does with the ball
NON-CRICKETING HERO? My dog Toby – he's my life coach
UNUSUAL OBJECT AT HOME? A furminator
TWITTER: @OHD_20

Batting	Mat	Inns	NO	Runs	HS	Ave	SR	100	50	Ct	St
First-class	53	61	23	265	40	6.97	24.02	0	0	5	0
List A	35	12	7	77	21*	15.40	101.31	0	0	10	0
T20s	45	9	5	36	9*	9.00	83.72	0	0	7	0

Bowling	Mat	Balls	Runs	Wkts	BBI	BBM	Ave	Econ	SR	5w	10
First-class	53	7303	4097	109	5/68	7/122	37.58	3.36	67.0	2	0
List A	35	1567	1625	51	5/27	5/27	31.86	6.22	30.7	1	0
T20s	45	940	1350	57	4/29	4/29	23.68	8.61	16.4	0	0

GEORGE HARDING

RHB / SLA / R0 / W0

FULL NAME: George Harvey Idris Harding
BORN: October 12, 1996, Poole, Dorset
SQUAD NO: 39
HEIGHT: 6ft 6in
EDUCATION: Brine Leas High School, Nantwich; Myerscough College, Preston
TEAMS: Durham
ROLE: Bowler
DEBUT: First-class: 2017; List A: 2017

DURHAM

BEST BOWLING: 4-111 Durham vs Glamorgan, Swansea, 2017

WHAT GOT YOU INTO CRICKET? The 2005 Ashes
BEST ADVICE EVER RECEIVED? You can only do your best
BEST THING ABOUT YOUR HOME GROUND? The castle in the background
BEST OPPOSING PLAYER IN COUNTY CRICKET? Graham Onions (Lan)
YOUNG OPPOSING PLAYER WHO HAS IMPRESSED YOU? Sam Curran (Sur) – he's able to adapt to all forms of the game
IF YOU WEREN'T A CRICKETER? I'd be a lorry driver
SURPRISING FACT ABOUT YOU? I'm a big Chester FC fan
SURPRISING FACT ABOUT A TEAMMATE? Stuart Poynter has a dog called Wayne
WHERE IS PARADISE? Bickerton, Cheshire
CRICKETING HERO? Andrew Flintoff (2005 Ashes)
NON-CRICKETING HERO? Lewis Jones – inspirational speaker about oats and chocolate pillows
TWITTER: @gharding96

Batting	Mat	Inns	NO	Runs	HS	Ave	SR	100	50	Ct	St
First-class	1	1	0	0	0	0.00	0.00	0	0	0	0
List A	5	2	2	20	18*	-	86.95	0	0	5	0

Bowling	Mat	Balls	Runs	Wkts	BBI	BBM	Ave	Econ	SR	5w	10
First-class	1	216	186	4	4/111	4/186	46.50	5.16	54.0	0	0
List A	5	282	251	4	2/52	2/52	62.75	5.34	70.5	0	0

ARUN HARINATH

LHB / OB / RO / WO

SURREY

FULL NAME: Arun Harinath
BORN: April 3, 1987, Sutton, Surrey
SQUAD NO: 10
HEIGHT: 5ft 11in
NICKNAME: Baron
EDUCATION: Tiffin School, Kingston-upon-Thames; Loughborough University
TEAMS: Surrey, Leicestershire
ROLE: Batsman
DEBUT: First-class: 2007; List A: 2009

BEST BATTING: 154 Surrey vs Derbyshire, Derby, 2013
BEST BOWLING: 2-1 Surrey vs Middlesex, Lord's, 2013

FAMILY TIES? My dad played club cricket in Sri Lanka and my brother Muhunthan has also played for Surrey
BEST ADVICE EVER RECEIVED? Work hard but don't take it too seriously. I'm still trying to follow that!
'ROY OF THE ROVERS' MOMENT? Scoring my maiden first-class hundred for Surrey against Middlesex at The Oval in 2012
BEST OPPOSING PLAYER IN COUNTY CRICKET? Ben Stokes (Dur)
YOUNG OPPOSING PLAYER WHO HAS IMPRESSED YOU? Craig Overton (Som)
SURPRISING FACT ABOUT YOU? I have two university degrees
SURPRISING FACT ABOUT A TEAMMATE? Rory Burns plays the saxophone
WHERE IS PARADISE? The Maldives
CRICKETING HERO? My former teammate Kumar Sangakkara – a great player and person
NON-CRICKETING HERO? Dalai Lama
UNUSUAL OBJECT AT HOME? An enormous ornamental owl sitting on our balcony to scare the pigeons away
TWITTER: @arunharinath

Batting	Mat	Inns	NO	Runs	HS	Ave	SR	100	50	Ct	St
First-class	72	126	6	3797	154	31.64	44.43	6	21	19	0
List A	7	7	2	108	52	21.60	78.83	0	1	1	0
Bowling	Mat	Balls	Runs	Wkts	BBI	BBM	Ave	Econ	SR	5w	10
First-class	72	351	195	5	2/1	2/1	39.00	3.33	70.2	0	0
List A	7	18	16	0	-	-	-	5.33	-	0	0

SIMON HARMER

RHB / OB / R0 / W1 / MVP6

FULL NAME: Simon Ross Harmer
BORN: February 10, 1989, Pretoria, South Africa
SQUAD NO: 11
EDUCATION: Nelson Mandela Metropolitan University, Port Elizabeth
TEAMS: South Africa, Essex, Border, Eastern Province, Warriors
ROLE: Bowler
DEBUT: Test: 2015; First-class: 2009; List A: 2010; T20: 2011

ESSEX

BEST BATTING: 100* Eastern Province vs Border, East London, 2011
BEST BOWLING: 9-95 Essex vs Middlesex, Chelmsford, 2017

TWITTER: @SimonHarmerRSA
NOTES: Essex were delighted to sign a proven Test off-spinner on a Kolpak deal ahead of the 2017 season but could not have envisaged the impact he would make: 72 Championship wickets to help the county to the title. Harmer has signed an extension to his contract which will keep him at Chelmsford until the end of the 2019 season. He played five Tests for South Africa but decided his future is best served in county cricket after falling down the national pecking order. He took seven wickets on Test debut against West Indies at Newlands in 2015 and claimed 10 in two matches on South Africa's tour of India later that year

Batting	Mat	Inns	NO	Runs	HS	Ave	SR	100	50	Ct	St
Tests	5	6	1	58	13	11.60	33.33	0	0	1	0
First-class	106	162	34	3216	100*	25.12	47.77	1	19	100	0
List A	68	57	16	859	44*	20.95	97.72	0	0	46	0
T20s	54	32	14	465	43	25.83	129.88	0	0	17	0

Bowling	Mat	Balls	Runs	Wkts	BBI	BBM	Ave	Econ	SR	5w	10
Tests	5	1148	588	20	4/61	7/153	29.40	3.07	57.4	0	0
First-class	106	24988	12585	421	9/95	14/128	29.89	3.02	59.3	18	4
List A	68	3234	2723	67	4/42	4/42	40.64	5.05	48.2	0	0
T20s	54	1040	1266	34	3/28	3/28	37.23	7.30	30.5	0	0

JAMES HARRIS

RHB / RMF / R0 / W2

FULL NAME: James Alexander Russell Harris
BORN: May 16, 1990, Morriston, Swansea
SQUAD NO: 5
HEIGHT: 6ft 1in
NICKNAME: Bones, Jimmy, Harry, Lance
EDUCATION: Pontarddulais Comprehensive School, Swansea; Gorseinon College, Swansea
TEAMS: Middlesex, England Lions, Glamorgan, Kent
ROLE: Bowler
DEBUT: First-class: 2007; List A: 2007; T20: 2008

BEST BATTING: 87* Glamorgan vs Nottinghamshire, Swansea, 2007
BEST BOWLING: 9-34 Middlesex vs Durham, Lord's, 2015
COUNTY CAP: 2010 (Glamorgan); 2015 (Middlesex)

FAMILY TIES? My father played for British Universities
STRANGEST THING SEEN IN A GAME? A drunk couple running onto the field before lunch in a first-class game at The Parks vs Oxford MCCU. They had a long snog on the square, he bowled a ball, and then they strolled off
'ROY OF THE ROVERS' MOMENT? Taking a nine-for at Lord's in 2015, bowling from the Nursery End towards the old Pavilion
NON-CRICKETING HEROES? Eddy Merckx – really into my road cycling and he's easily the greatest ever to throw his leg over a bike. Alberto Contador – for the way he turns around to look at his rivals, stands up on the pedals, and swaggers off up the mountain
SURPRISING FACT? On my days off I tend to spend my time clad in Lycra riding around the roads on one of my bikes
UNUSUAL OBJECT AT HOME? Road bike battery charger
TWITTER: @James_Harris9

Batting	Mat	Inns	NO	Runs	HS	Ave	SR	100	50	Ct	St
First-class	121	170	37	2811	87*	21.13		0	12	34	0
List A	58	35	8	300	32	11.11	65.78	0	0	14	0
T20s	48	23	10	138	18	10.61	111.29	0	0	5	0

Bowling	Mat	Balls	Runs	Wkts	BBI	BBM	Ave	Econ	SR	5w	10
First-class	121	21132	11728	401	9/34	13/103	29.24	3.32	52.6	12	2
List A	58	2380	2279	79	4/38	4/38	28.84	5.74	30.1	0	0
T20s	48	872	1301	41	4/23	4/23	31.73	8.95	21.2	0	0

ASHER HART

RHB / RM / RO / WO

FULL NAME: Asher Hale-Bopp Joseph Arthur Hart
BORN: March 30, 1997, Carlisle, Cumbria
SQUAD NO: 28
HEIGHT: 6ft
EDUCATION: Ullswater Community College, Cumbria
TEAMS: Hampshire
ROLE: Allrounder
DEBUT: First-class: 2017; List A: 2018

BEST BATTING: 36 Hampshire vs South Africa A, Southampton, 2017
BEST BOWLING: 3-17 Hampshire vs Cardiff MCCU, Southampton, 2017

WHAT GOT YOU INTO CRICKET? The 2005 Ashes
BEST ADVICE EVER RECEIVED? Always put Jelly Beans in your pic 'n' mix because they don't take up much space
'ROY OF THE ROVERS' MOMENT? Making my first-class debut
BEST THING ABOUT YOUR HOME GROUND? The stands around the Ageas Bowl – they create an atmosphere which is nothing like I have experienced before
BEST OPPOSING PLAYER IN COUNTY CRICKET? Jamie Porter (Ess)
YOUNG OPPOSING PLAYER WHO HAS IMPRESSED YOU? Jofra Archer (Sus) – makes it look so easy
IF YOU WEREN'T A CRICKETER? I'd be a school teacher or in the marketing business
SURPRISING FACT ABOUT YOU? I played football for Carlisle United when I was younger
WHERE IS PARADISE? Barbados
CRICKETING HERO? Ben Stokes
NON-CRICKETING HERO? Tom Hardy
TWITTER: @asher_hart

Batting	Mat	Inns	NO	Runs	HS	Ave	SR	100	50	Ct	St
First-class	2	4	1	44	36	14.66	30.55	0	0	1	0
List A	5	5	0	58	21	11.60	40.27	0	0	2	0
Bowling	Mat	Balls	Runs	Wkts	BBI	BBM	Ave	Econ	SR	5w	10
First-class	2	263	111	5	3/17	4/37	22.20	2.53	52.6	0	0
List A	5	144	144	3	2/34	2/34	48.00	6.00	48.0	0	0

GARETH HARTE

RHB / RM / R0 / W0

FULL NAME: Gareth Jason Harte
BORN: March 15, 1993, Johannesburg, South Africa
SQUAD NO: 93
HEIGHT: 5ft 9in
NICKNAME: Gaz
EDUCATION: King Edward VII School, Johannesburg
TEAMS: Durham
ROLE: Batsman
DEBUT: T20: 2017

'ROY OF THE ROVERS' MOMENT? Making my debut for Durham in the T20 Blast at Old Trafford in 2017
BEST THING ABOUT YOUR HOME GROUND? The facilities are great and there is everything I need to improve my game
BEST OPPOSING PLAYER IN COUNTY CRICKET? Samit Patel (Not)
YOUNG OPPOSING PLAYER WHO HAS IMPRESSED YOU? Sam Curran (Sur) – he swings the new ball and always picks up important wickets
IF YOU WEREN'T A CRICKETER? I'd be a motorbike rider
SURPRISING FACT ABOUT YOU? I'm the best player of FIFA in the whole Durham squad
SURPRISING FACT ABOUT A TEAMMATE? Brydon Carse uses girls' deodorant
WHERE IS PARADISE? Cape Town
CRICKETING HERO? Ricky Ponting – he was a ruthless cricketer who always performed when his team needed him the most
NON-CRICKETING HERO? Conor McGregor – his story of coming from nothing to become a world superstar in such a small amount of time is inspiring. I admire his work ethic and self-belief
TWITTER: @HarteGareth

Batting	Mat	Inns	NO	Runs	HS	Ave	SR	100	50	Ct	St
T20s	2	2	0	17	11	8.50	121.42	0	0	2	0
Bowling	Mat	Balls	Runs	Wkts	BBI	BBM	Ave	Econ	SR	5w	10
T20s	2	-	-	-	-	-	-	-	-	-	-

TRAVIS HEAD

LHB / OB / R0 / W0

FULL NAME: Travis Michael Head
BORN: December 29, 1993, Adelaide, Australia
SQUAD NO: 62
TEAMS: Australia, Worcestershire, Adelaide Strikers, Delhi Daredevils, Royal Challengers Bangalore, South Australia, Yorkshire
ROLE: Batsman
DEBUT: ODI: 2016; T20I: 2016; First-class: 2012; List A: 2013; T20: 2013

WORCESTERSHIRE

BEST BATTING: 192 South Australia vs Tasmania, Adelaide, 2016
BEST BOWLING: 3-42 South Australia vs New South Wales, Adelaide, 2015

TWITTER: @travishead34
NOTES: Worcestershire have signed Head as their main overseas player for the season and he will be available in all competitions – although he is expected to miss some Championship action when Australia take on England in an ODI series and one-off T20I in June. The Australian top-order batsman, who is also an effective off-spinner in T20 cricket, played nine matches across all formats for Yorkshire in 2016 and was due to return to Headingley last summer, only for international commitments to scupper the deal. He has enjoyed a strong start to 2018, having captained Adelaide Strikers to victory in the Big Bash League and top-scored with 96 in the fourth ODI against England in January. "He is ambitious to play Test cricket and Cricket Australia have encouraged him and other young players to play cricket this summer," said Worcestershire vice-chairman Tim Curtis. "He is hungry to do well and play all types of cricket"

Batting	Mat	Inns	NO	Runs	HS	Ave	SR	100	50	Ct	St
ODIs	34	31	2	1064	128	36.68	87.71	1	7	11	0
T20Is	10	10	2	210	48*	26.25	131.25	0	0	3	0
First-class	60	111	3	3819	192	35.36	63.55	6	26	24	0
List A	69	65	3	2295	202	37.01	94.75	4	11	22	0
T20s	59	58	10	1516	101*	31.58	136.94	1	8	19	0

Bowling	Mat	Balls	Runs	Wkts	BBI	BBM	Ave	Econ	SR	5w	10
ODIs	34	765	737	12	2/22	2/22	61.41	5.78	63.7	0	0
T20Is	10	24	39	1	1/16	1/16	39.00	9.75	24.0	0	0
First-class	60	2708	1846	31	3/42	4/64	59.54	4.09	87.3	0	0
List A	69	1044	1020	16	2/9	2/9	63.75	5.86	65.2	0	0
T20s	59	295	428	16	3/16	3/16	26.75	8.70	18.4	0	0

TOM HELM

RHB / RFM / R0 / W0

MIDDLESEX

FULL NAME: Thomas George Helm
BORN: May 7, 1994, Aylesbury, Buckinghamshire
SQUAD NO: 7
HEIGHT: 6ft 4in
NICKNAME: Ched, Helmet, Helmy
EDUCATION: The Misbourne School, Buckinghamshire
TEAMS: Middlesex, England Lions, Glamorgan
ROLE: Bowler
DEBUT: First-class: 2013; List A: 2013; T20: 2016

BEST BATTING: 28 Middlesex vs Somerset, Lord's, 2017
BEST BOWLING: 5-59 Middlesex vs Warwickshire, Edgbaston, 2017

FAMILY TIES? My brother Sam plays Minor Counties for Buckinghamshire
BEST ADVICE EVER RECEIVED? Don't bowl it in the slot
'ROY OF THE ROVERS' MOMENT? Bowling the final over of a T20 match at Lord's and defending five runs
BEST THING ABOUT YOUR HOME GROUND? The Lord's lunches
BEST OPPOSING PLAYER IN COUNTY CRICKET? Jamie Porter (Ess)
YOUNG OPPOSING PLAYER WHO HAS IMPRESSED YOU? Josh Tongue (Wor)
IF YOU WEREN'T A CRICKETER? I'd be controlling the midfield at Stamford Bridge
SURPRISING FACT ABOUT YOU? I am addicted to chocolate
SURPRISING FACT ABOUT A TEAMMATE? Stevie Eskinazi has the biggest nose in county cricket
WHERE IS PARADISE? Edgware, north London
CRICKETING HERO? James Anderson
NON-CRICKETING HERO? Stephen Curry (NBA)
TWITTER: @tomhelm7

Batting	Mat	Inns	NO	Runs	HS	Ave	SR	100	50	Ct	St
First-class	17	24	5	241	28	12.68	40.77	0	0	6	0
List A	18	12	6	90	25	15.00	75.63	0	0	7	0
T20s	13	4	3	4	4	4.00	133.33	0	0	1	0

Bowling	Mat	Balls	Runs	Wkts	BBI	BBM	Ave	Econ	SR	5w	10
First-class	17	2593	1457	47	5/59	7/140	31.00	3.37	55.1	1	0
List A	18	702	556	21	5/33	5/33	26.47	4.75	33.4	1	0
T20s	13	259	331	20	5/11	5/11	16.55	7.66	12.9	1	0

RYAN HIGGINS

RHB / OB / R0 / W0

FULL NAME: Ryan Francis Higgins
BORN: January 6, 1995, Harare, Zimbabwe
SQUAD NO: 29
HEIGHT: 6ft 3in
NICKNAME: Mad Bri, Brian, Higgo, Matchstick
EDUCATION: Peterhouse School, Marondera, Zimbabwe; Bradfield College, Reading
TEAMS: Gloucestershire, Middlesex
ROLE: Allrounder
DEBUT: First-class: 2017; List A: 2014; T20: 2014

BEST BATTING: 45 Middlesex vs Warwickshire, Edgbaston, 2017
BEST BOWLING: 4-75 Middlesex vs Warwickshire, Lord's, 2017

WHAT GOT YOU INTO CRICKET? My grandad
BEST ADVICE EVER RECEIVED? Be positive
BEST THING ABOUT YOUR HOME GROUND? The dressing room
BEST OPPOSING PLAYER IN COUNTY CRICKET? Steve Eskinazi (Mid)
YOUNG OPPOSING PLAYER WHO HAS IMPRESSED YOU? Max Holden (Mid) – a very composed batsman
SURPRISING FACT ABOUT A TEAMMATE? My former Middlesex teammate Nathan Sowter is actually a great bloke
WHERE IS PARADISE? New Zealand
CRICKETING HERO? Michael Hussey
NON-CRICKETING HERO? My mum and dad
UNUSUAL OBJECT AT HOME? A colourful giraffe
TWITTER: @ryanhiggins21

Batting	Mat	Inns	NO	Runs	HS	Ave	SR	100	50	Ct	St
First-class	4	7	0	129	45	18.42	51.60	0	0	0	0
List A	17	16	2	241	48*	17.21	79.27	0	0	3	0
T20s	36	33	10	530	68*	23.04	132.83	0	2	10	0

Bowling	Mat	Balls	Runs	Wkts	BBI	BBM	Ave	Econ	SR	5w	10
First-class	4	588	281	12	4/75	5/79	23.41	2.86	49.0	0	0
List A	17	208	197	6	3/32	3/32	32.83	5.68	34.6	0	0
T20s	36	216	280	13	5/13	5/13	21.53	7.77	16.6	1	0

JAMES HILDRETH RHB / RM / R6 / W0 / MVP52

FULL NAME: James Charles Hildreth
BORN: September 9, 1984, Milton Keynes, Buckinghamshire
SQUAD NO: 25
HEIGHT: 5ft 10in
NICKNAME: Hildy, Hildz
EDUCATION: Millfield School, Somerset
TEAMS: Somerset, England Lions
ROLE: Batsman
DEBUT: First-class: 2003; List A: 2003; T20: 2004

BEST BATTING: 303* Somerset vs Warwickshire, Taunton, 2009
BEST BOWLING: 2-39 Somerset vs Hampshire, Taunton, 2009
COUNTY CAP: 2007

'ROY OF THE ROVERS' MOMENT? Winning the T20 in 2005, captaining England Lions and captaining Somerset
CRICKETING HERO? Ricky Ponting
IF YOU WEREN'T A CRICKETER? I'd be travelling or I'd be on a beach somewhere
SURPRISING FACT? I'm a big MK Dons fan
TWITTER: @dreth25

Batting	Mat	Inns	NO	Runs	HS	Ave	SR	100	50	Ct	St
First-class	234	382	28	15338	303*	43.32		41	68	193	0
List A	193	180	34	4886	151	33.46		6	21	73	0
T20s	163	151	28	2956	107*	24.03	121.89	1	12	61	0

Bowling	Mat	Balls	Runs	Wkts	BBI	BBM	Ave	Econ	SR	5w	10
First-class	234	576	492	6	2/39	2/39	82.00	5.12	96.0	0	0
List A	193	150	185	6	2/26	2/26	30.83	7.40	25.0	0	0
T20s	163	169	247	10	3/24	3/24	24.70	8.76	16.9	0	0

LEWIS HILL

RHB / WK / RO / WO

FULL NAME: Lewis John Hill
BORN: October 5, 1990, Leicester
SQUAD NO: 23
HEIGHT: 5ft 8in
NICKNAME: Lew Show, Lew, Hilly
EDUCATION: Hastings High School, Hinckley;
John Cleveland College, Hinckley
TEAMS: Leicestershire
ROLE: Wicketkeeper
DEBUT: First-class: 2015; List A: 2012; T20:
2015

BEST BATTING: 126 Leicestershire vs Surrey, The Oval, 2015

WHAT GOT YOU INTO CRICKET? Friends played it when we were nine years old, so I joined in at their club
FAMILY TIES? My dad and brother both play for Lutterworth CC
'ROY OF THE ROVERS' MOMENT? Scoring my maiden first-class century at The Oval and having Kumar Sangakkara and Kevin Pietersen shake my hand at the end of the day
BEST OPPOSING PLAYER IN COUNTY CRICKET? Alex Davies (Lan)
YOUNG OPPOSING PLAYER WHO HAS IMPRESSED YOU? Josh Tongue (Wor)
IF YOU WEREN'T A CRICKETER? I'd be working for my dad in the family sports engineering business
SURPRISING FACT ABOUT YOU? I was targeted by armed robbers twice while working at my local newsagents
WHERE IS PARADISE? The Maldives
CRICKETING HERO? Karl Smith, Craig Wilson and Nathan Welham of Lutterworth CC
TWITTER: @lhjill23

Batting	Mat	Inns	NO	Runs	HS	Ave	SR	100	50	Ct	St
First-class	24	44	5	986	126	25.28	49.72	1	3	39	2
List A	30	27	2	583	86	23.32	87.93	0	3	15	2
T20s	24	16	4	263	31*	21.91	127.66	0	0	10	0

Bowling	Mat	Balls	Runs	Wkts	BBI	BBM	Ave	Econ	SR	5w	10
First-class	24	12	6	0	-	-	-	3.00	-	0	0
List A	30	-	-	-	-	-	-	-	-	-	-
T20s	24	-	-	-	-	-	-	-	-	-	-

ANDY HODD

RHB / WK / R0 / W0

FULL NAME: Andrew John Hodd
BORN: January 12, 1984, Chichester, West Sussex
SQUAD NO: 4
HEIGHT: 6ft
NICKNAME: Hoddfather
EDUCATION: Bexhill High School, East Sussex; Bexhill College; Loughborough University
TEAMS: Yorkshire, Surrey, Sussex
ROLE: Wicketkeeper
DEBUT: First-class: 2003; List A: 2002; T20: 2005

BEST BATTING: 123 Sussex vs Yorkshire, Hove, 2007
COUNTY CAP: 2016 (Yorkshire)

WHAT GOT YOU INTO CRICKET? Dad throwing balls at me in the back garden and mum dragging me to my local club
FAMILY TIES? I come from a long line of enthusiastic club cricketers
SUPERSTITIONS? No! I've been working meticulously on my mental strength – and my mind game is on point!
CRICKETING HEROES? My old man for possessing the finest forward D in the business. Brendon McCullum and Adam Gilchrist as fellow wicketkeepers
NON-CRICKETING HEROES? My wife – for putting up with me. Also Giles from Gogglebox
IF YOU WEREN'T A CRICKETER? I'd be the manager of a successful paper merchants
TWITTER: @Hoddfather

Batting	Mat	Inns	NO	Runs	HS	Ave	SR	100	50	Ct	St
First-class	111	157	25	3634	123	27.53	47.49	4	21	266	23
List A	71	54	13	916	91	22.34		0	2	69	16
T20s	73	42	8	400	70	11.76	104.16	0	1	31	16

Bowling	Mat	Balls	Runs	Wkts	BBI	BBM	Ave	Econ	SR	5w	10
First-class	111	16	21	0	-	-	-	7.87	-	0	0
List A	71	-	-	-	-	-	-	-	-	-	-
T20s	73	-	-	-	-	-	-	-	-	-	-

MICHAEL HOGAN RHB / RFM / R0 / W3 / MVP32

FULL NAME: Michael Garry Hogan
BORN: May 31, 1981, Newcastle, Australia
SQUAD NO: 31
HEIGHT: 6ft 5in
NICKNAME: Hulk, Hoges
TEAMS: Glamorgan, Hobart Hurricanes, Western Australia
ROLE: Bowler
DEBUT: First-class: 2009; List A: 2009; T20: 2010

BEST BATTING: 57 Glamorgan vs Lancashire, Colwyn Bay, 2015
BEST BOWLING: 7-92 Glamorgan vs Gloucestershire, Bristol, 2013
COUNTY CAP: 2013

BEST ADVICE EVER RECEIVED? If the grass looks greener on the other side, there's probably more shit there
'ROY OF THE ROVERS' MOMENT? Defending three when I was bowling the final over in a T20 game against Kent a few years ago
BEST THING ABOUT YOUR HOME GROUND? The Friday night T20 atmosphere
YOUNG OPPOSING PLAYER WHO HAS IMPRESSED YOU? Dan Lawrence (Ess) – looks like he has a big future
SURPRISING FACT ABOUT YOU? I'm very boring
SURPRISING FACT ABOUT A TEAMMATE? Marchant de Lange drinks two litres of Coke every day
WHERE IS PARADISE? Fiji
CRICKETING HERO? Glenn McGrath – genius
NON-CRICKETING HERO? Roger Federer – still getting it done at 36
TWITTER: @hoges31

Batting	Mat	Inns	NO	Runs	HS	Ave	SR	100	50	Ct	St
First-class	131	185	71	1852	57	16.24	83.99	0	2	68	0
List A	64	24	14	154	27	15.40	79.79	0	0	23	0
T20s	79	15	9	50	13	8.33	102.04	0	0	34	0

Bowling	Mat	Balls	Runs	Wkts	BBI	BBM	Ave	Econ	SR	5w	10
First-class	131	27464	12364	503	7/92	10/87	24.58	2.70	54.6	20	2
List A	64	3304	2784	99	5/44	5/44	28.12	5.05	33.3	1	0
T20s	79	1618	2032	91	5/17	5/17	22.32	7.53	17.7	1	0

MIDDLESEX

FULL NAME: Max David Edward Holden
BORN: December 18, 1997, Cambridge
SQUAD NO: 4
HEIGHT: 6ft 1in
NICKNAME: Texas, Pepsi, Little Chef, Derick
EDUCATION: Sawston Village College, Cambridge; Hills Road Sixth Form College, Cambridge
TEAMS: Middlesex, Northamptonshire
ROLE: Batsman
DEBUT: First-class: 2017; List A: 2017

BEST BATTING: 153 Northamptonshire vs Kent, Beckenham, 2017
BEST BOWLING: 2-59 Northamptonshire vs Kent, Beckenham, 2017

WHAT GOT YOU INTO CRICKET? I joined a local club with friends
BEST ADVICE EVER RECEIVED? Keep things simple and watch the ball
'ROY OF THE ROVERS' MOMENT? Hitting a six off the last ball to win a game for Cambridge St Giles U10
BEST THING ABOUT YOUR HOME GROUND? It's Lord's
BEST OPPOSING PLAYER IN COUNTY CRICKET? Ben Duckett (Nor)
YOUNG OPPOSING PLAYER WHO HAS IMPRESSED YOU? Ollie Pope (Sur) – he's got every shot in the book
IF YOU WEREN'T A CRICKETER? I'd be playing up front for Arsenal, or I'd be training to become a zookeeper
WHERE IS PARADISE? Finchley Indoor School, London
CRICKETING HERO? Brian Lara
NON-CRICKETING HERO? Thierry Henry – a goal machine. I have modelled my game on him for the pre-match football warm-up
UNUSUAL OBJECT AT HOME? A Venus flytrap
TWITTER: @maxholden_4

Batting	Mat	Inns	NO	Runs	HS	Ave	SR	100	50	Ct	St
First-class	11	19	1	758	153	42.11	48.62	2	3	5	0
List A	3	2	1	78	55	78.00	84.78	0	1	0	0

Bowling	Mat	Balls	Runs	Wkts	BBI	BBM	Ave	Econ	SR	5w	10
First-class	11	258	203	4	2/59	3/94	50.75	4.72	64.5	0	0
List A	3	-	-	-	-	-	-	-	-	-	-

IAN HOLLAND

RHB / RMF / R0 / W0

FULL NAME: Ian Gabriel Holland
BORN: October 3, 1990, Wisconsin, USA
SQUAD NO: 22
HEIGHT: 6ft
NICKNAME: Dutchy
EDUCATION: Ringwood Secondary College, Melbourne
TEAMS: Hampshire, Victoria
ROLE: Allrounder
DEBUT: First-class: 2016; List A: 2017; T20: 2017

BEST BATTING: 58* Hampshire vs Surrey, The Oval, 2017
BEST BOWLING: 4-16 Hampshire vs Somerset, Southampton, 2017

WHAT GOT YOU INTO CRICKET? Playing with my siblings and cousins in the back yard
BEST ADVICE EVER RECEIVED? Be who you are
'ROY OF THE ROVERS' MOMENT? Channelling my inner Jimmy Adams against Warwickshire in the last game of the 2017 season when we blocked out for a draw to stay in Division One
BEST THING ABOUT YOUR HOME GROUND? That it has a golf course
YOUNG OPPOSING PLAYER WHO HAS IMPRESSED YOU? Jofra Archer – good pace and swing
IF YOU WEREN'T A CRICKETER? I'd be an armchair expert
SURPRISING FACT ABOUT YOU? I was born in Wisconsin
SURPRISING FACT ABOUT A TEAMMATE? Kyle Abbott could easily be the next Bear Grylls
WHERE IS PARADISE? Surfing on the Portuguese coast
CRICKETING HERO? Jacques Kallis – the ultimate allrounder
NON-CRICKETING HERO? Roger Federer – he is the pinnacle of a professional athlete in every respect
TWITTER: @IanHolland22

Batting	Mat	Inns	NO	Runs	HS	Ave	SR	100	50	Ct	St
First-class	10	14	4	258	58*	25.80	41.54	0	2	1	0
List A	2	1	1	11	11*	-	100.00	0	0	0	0
T20s	1	-	-	-	-	-	-	-	-	0	0
Bowling	Mat	Balls	Runs	Wkts	BBI	BBM	Ave	Econ	SR	5w	10
First-class	10	1002	429	20	4/16	6/39	21.45	2.56	50.1	0	0
List A	2	114	117	3	2/57	2/57	39.00	6.15	38.0	0	0
T20s	1	24	33	1	1/33	1/33	33.00	8.25	24.0	0	0

PAUL HORTON

LEICESTERSHIRE

FULL NAME: Paul James Horton
BORN: September 20, 1982, Sydney, Australia
SQUAD NO: 2
HEIGHT: 5ft 10in
NICKNAME: Horts, Torts, Aussie, Custard
EDUCATION: Colo High School, Sydney; St Margaret's High School, Liverpool
TEAMS: Leicestershire, Lancashire, Matabeleland Tuskers
ROLE: Batsman
DEBUT: First-class: 2003; List A: 2003; T20: 2005

BEST BATTING: 209 Matabeleland Tuskers vs Southern Rocks, Masvingo, 2011
BEST BOWLING: 2-6 Leicestershire vs Sussex, Leicester, 2016
COUNTY CAP: 2007 (Lancashire)

STRANGEST THING SEEN IN A GAME? A team refuse to take the field because they weren't being paid enough
'ROY OF THE ROVERS' MOMENT? Nothing can top winning the County Championship in 2011 with Lancashire. Back-to-back Logan Cup trophies with Matabeleland Tuskers in 2010/11 and 2011/12 was also special
BEST OPPOSING PLAYER IN COUNTY CRICKET? Ben Stokes (Dur)
YOUNG OPPOSING PLAYER WHO HAS IMPRESSED YOU? Alex Davies (Lan)
CRICKETING HEROES? Mark Waugh, Dean Jones, Brian Lara
NON-CRICKETING HEROES? Roger Federer, Robbie Fowler
SURPRISING FACT? I was a left-handed batsman as a kid. And I was once detained as an illegal immigrant
UNUSUAL OBJECT AT HOME? My French bulldog is pretty unusual at times
TWITTER: @PJHorton20

Batting	Mat	Inns	NO	Runs	HS	Ave	SR	100	50	Ct	St
First-class	191	324	24	10964	209	36.54	48.34	23	59	185	1
List A	107	98	13	2584	111*	30.40		2	13	42	0
T20s	82	76	14	1477	71*	23.82	108.52	0	5	32	0

Bowling	Mat	Balls	Runs	Wkts	BBI	BBM	Ave	Econ	SR	5w	10
First-class	191	118	80	2	2/6	2/6	40.00	4.06	59.0	0	0
List A	107	12	7	1	1/7	1/7	7.00	3.50	12.0	0	0
T20s	82	-	-	-	-	-	-	-	-	-	-

ADAM HOSE

RHB / RM / R0 / W0

FULL NAME: Adam John Hose
BORN: October 25, 1992, Newport, Isle of Wight
SQUAD NO: 21
HEIGHT: 6ft 5in
NICKNAME: Pipe
EDUCATION: Carisbrooke School, Newport
TEAMS: Warwickshire, Somerset
ROLE: Batsman
DEBUT: First-class: 2016; List A: 2015; T20: 2015

BEST BATTING: 68 Somerset vs Yorkshire, Taunton, 2017

WHAT GOT YOU INTO CRICKET? My dad. Ever since I can remember I was down at my home club (Ventnor CC) on the Isle of Wight, watching and pestering all the players to throw me balls
BEST ADVICE EVER RECEIVED? Watch it and hit it
'ROY OF THE ROVERS' MOMENT? My first win in Somerset colours
BEST THING ABOUT YOUR HOME GROUND? The unique bowl of Ventnor CC
BEST OPPOSING PLAYER IN COUNTY CRICKET? Jamie Porter (Ess) – so consistent
SURPRISING FACT ABOUT YOU? Travelling, dogs and live music are a few of my favourite things
WHERE IS PARADISE? South-east Asia
CRICKETING HERO? Kevin Pietersen – loved the way he dominated
NON-CRICKETING HERO? My grandad – so wise
TWITTER: @adamhose21

Batting	Mat	Inns	NO	Runs	HS	Ave	SR	100	50	Ct	St
First-class	4	8	0	212	68	26.50	48.40	0	2	1	0
List A	20	18	1	593	101*	34.88	91.51	1	3	12	0
T20s	15	14	0	317	76	22.64	150.95	0	2	2	0

Bowling	Mat	Balls	Runs	Wkts	BBI	BBM	Ave	Econ	SR	5w	10
First-class	4	-	-	-	-	-	-	-	-	-	-
List A	20	-	-	-	-	-	-	-	-	-	-
T20s	15	-	-	-	-	-	-	-	-	-	-

HARVEY HOSEIN

RHB / WK / R0 / W0

DERBYSHIRE

FULL NAME: Harvey Richard Hosein
BORN: August 12, 1996, Chesterfield, Derbyshire
SQUAD NO: 16
HEIGHT: 5ft 11in
NICKNAME: Harv
EDUCATION: Denstone College, Staffordshire
TEAMS: Derbyshire
ROLE: Wicketkeeper
DEBUT: First-class: 2014; List A: 2016; T20: 2016

BEST BATTING: 108 Derbyshire vs Worcestershire, Worcester, 2016

WHAT GOT YOU INTO CRICKET? My school
BEST ADVICE EVER RECEIVED? Enjoy every moment
'ROY OF THE ROVERS' MOMENT? Scoring my maiden first-class century against Worcestershire in 2016 and taking a world-record 11 catches on my first-class debut at The Oval in 2014
BEST THING ABOUT YOUR HOME GROUND? The new changing rooms offer a good viewpoint while waiting to bat
YOUNG OPPOSING PLAYER WHO HAS IMPRESSED YOU? Tom Curran (Sur)
SURPRISING FACT ABOUT YOU? I played county-level tennis when I was younger
SURPRISING FACT ABOUT A TEAMMATE? Wayne Madsen was an international hockey player for South Africa before coming to England to play cricket
WHERE IS PARADISE? Barbados
CRICKETING HERO? AB de Villiers – fantastic all-round player and entertaining to watch
NON-CRICKETING HERO? Roger Federer

Batting	Mat	Inns	NO	Runs	HS	Ave	SR	100	50	Ct	St
First-class	23	36	8	883	108	31.53	42.69	1	6	63	1
List A	4	2	1	42	40	42.00	110.52	0	0	1	1
T20s	5	2	2	0	0*	-	-	0	0	7	0

Bowling	Mat	Balls	Runs	Wkts	BBI	BBM	Ave	Econ	SR	5w	10
First-class	23	-	-	-	-	-	-	-	-	-	-
List A	4	-	-	-	-	-	-	-	-	-	-
T20s	5	-	-	-	-	-	-	-	-	-	-

BENNY HOWELL — RHB / RM / R0 / W0 / MVP65

FULL NAME: Benny Alexander Cameron Howell
BORN: October 5, 1988, Bordeaux, France
SQUAD NO: 13
HEIGHT: 6ft
NICKNAME: Novak, Trowell, Growler
EDUCATION: The Oratory School, Reading
TEAMS: Gloucestershire, Hampshire, Khulna Titans, Unicorns
ROLE: Allrounder
DEBUT: First-class: 2011; List A: 2010; T20: 2011

BEST BATTING: 163 Gloucestershire vs Glamorgan, Cardiff, 2017
BEST BOWLING: 5-57 Gloucestershire vs Leicestershire, Leicester, 2013
COUNTY CAP: 2012 (Gloucestershire)

FAMILY TIES? My dad Jonathan played for Warwickshire for a season
'ROY OF THE ROVERS' MOMENT? Winning league promotion with Goatacre CC (Wiltshire) – there was a pitch invasion after we won the deciding match in the last over
BEST THING ABOUT YOUR HOME GROUND? The Cheltenham Festival – great crowds
BEST OPPOSING PLAYER IN COUNTY CRICKET? Rilee Rossouw (Ham)
IF YOU WEREN'T A CRICKETER? I'd be playing Major League Baseball
SURPRISING FACT ABOUT YOU? I speak Spanish
SURPRISING FACT ABOUT A TEAMMATE? Jack Taylor will be my brother-in-law
WHERE IS PARADISE? Mornington Peninsula, Victoria, Australia
CRICKETING HERO? Michael Klinger – the ultimate professional and extremely humble. He never gave up on his dream to play for Australia
NON-CRICKETING HERO? Tom Brady – told he wasn't good enough but has now won five Super Bowl rings
TWITTER: @bennyhowell510

Batting	Mat	Inns	NO	Runs	HS	Ave	SR	100	50	Ct	St
First-class	62	96	12	2316	163	27.57	53.62	2	11	31	0
List A	70	57	12	1624	122	36.08	90.02	1	9	22	0
T20s	90	74	23	1172	57	22.98	118.62	0	3	32	0

Bowling	Mat	Balls	Runs	Wkts	BBI	BBM	Ave	Econ	SR	5w	10
First-class	62	5703	2838	85	5/57	8/96	33.38	2.98	67.0	1	0
List A	70	2343	1969	59	3/37	3/37	33.37	5.04	39.7	0	0
T20s	90	1530	1758	92	4/26	4/26	19.10	6.89	16.6	0	0

ALEX HUGHES RHB / RM / R0 / W0 / MVP88

DERBYSHIRE

FULL NAME: Alex Lloyd Hughes
BORN: September 29, 1991, Wordsley, Staffordshire
SQUAD NO: 18
HEIGHT: 5ft 10in
NICKNAME: Yozza, Barry Horse, Jude Law
EDUCATION: Ounsdale High School, Wolverhampton; University of Worcester
TEAMS: Derbyshire
ROLE: Allrounder
DEBUT: First-class: 2013; List A: 2012; T20: 2011

BEST BATTING: 142 Derbyshire vs Gloucestershire, Bristol, 2017
BEST BOWLING: 4-46 Derbyshire vs Glamorgan, Derby, 2014

'ROY OF THE ROVERS' MOMENT? Playing in the same team as Shiv Chanderpaul
HOW WOULD YOUR TEAMMATES DESCRIBE YOU IN THREE WORDS? Rapper, entrepreneur, motivator
CRICKETING HEROES? Mike Brearley, Dimi Mascarenhas, Mark Ealham
IF YOU WEREN'T A CRICKETER? I'd be an Uber driver or stuntman
SURPRISING FACT? I got to The X Factor bootcamp in 2012
UNUSUAL OBJECT AT HOME? A samurai sword
TWITTER: @Yozza18

Batting	Mat	Inns	NO	Runs	HS	Ave	SR	100	50	Ct	St
First-class	44	74	9	1962	142	30.18	47.94	4	7	32	0
List A	48	30	6	581	96*	24.20	88.16	0	2	20	0
T20s	54	43	8	533	43*	15.22	116.63	0	0	23	0
Bowling	Mat	Balls	Runs	Wkts	BBI	BBM	Ave	Econ	SR	5w	10
First-class	44	2301	1241	22	4/46	4/75	56.40	3.23	104.5	0	0
List A	48	1541	1383	31	3/31	3/31	44.61	5.38	49.7	0	0
T20s	54	791	1096	22	3/23	3/23	49.81	8.31	35.9	0	0

MATT HUNN

RHB / RFM / R0 / W0

FULL NAME: Matthew David Hunn
BORN: March 22, 1994, Colchester, Essex
SQUAD NO: 14
HEIGHT: 6ft 5in
NICKNAME: Hunny
EDUCATION: St Joseph's College, Ipswich
TEAMS: Kent
ROLE: Bowler
DEBUT: First-class: 2013; List A: 2015; T20: 2015

KENT

BEST BATTING: 32* Kent vs Gloucestershire, Canterbury, 2016
BEST BOWLING: 5-99 Kent vs Australians, Canterbury, 2015

WHAT GOT YOU INTO CRICKET? My dad
STRANGEST THING SEEN IN A GAME? Someone set up a tent and get into it during a professional game
'ROY OF THE ROVERS' MOMENT? Signing my first contract and making my debut, and taking five wickets against Australia in 2015
SURPRISING FACT ABOUT YOU? I hold a 24-hour indoor rowing Guinness world record with my school
WHERE IS PARADISE? On a beach
CRICKETING HERO? Andrew Flintoff
NON-CRICKETING HERO? Nelson Mandela
TWITTER: @matthunn10

Batting	Mat	Inns	NO	Runs	HS	Ave	SR	100	50	Ct	St
First-class	19	16	11	94	32*	18.80	34.81	0	0	8	0
List A	7	4	3	7	5*	7.00	43.75	0	0	2	0
T20s	2	-	-	-	-	-	-	-	-	1	0

Bowling	Mat	Balls	Runs	Wkts	BBI	BBM	Ave	Econ	SR	5w	10
First-class	19	2643	1647	46	5/99	6/125	35.80	3.73	57.4	1	0
List A	7	288	258	6	2/31	2/31	43.00	5.37	48.0	0	0
T20s	2	42	65	4	3/30	3/30	16.25	9.28	10.5	0	0

LIAM HURT

RHB / RMF / RO / WO

LANCASHIRE

FULL NAME: Liam Jack Hurt
BORN: March 15, 1994, Preston, Lancashire
SQUAD NO: 22
HEIGHT: 6ft 3in
NICKNAME: Hurty
EDUCATION: Balshaw's CofE High School, Leyland, Lancashire
TEAMS: Lancashire, Leicestershire
ROLE: Bowler
DEBUT: List A: 2015

WHAT GOT YOU INTO CRICKET? Playing in the garden with my grandparents always watching
BEST ADVICE EVER RECEIVED? You will play at your best when you are enjoying it most
BEST THING ABOUT YOUR HOME GROUND? The history of Old Trafford and the ground's facilities
BEST OPPOSING PLAYER IN COUNTY CRICKET? Alastair Cook (Ess)
IF YOU WEREN'T A CRICKETER? I'd be a plumber
WHERE IS PARADISE? The Caribbean
CRICKETING HERO? Andrew Flintoff – he is the first player I remember watching when I was a youngster
TWITTER: @LiamHurt
NOTES: The Preston seamer has signed his first professional contract with his home county. First represented the Lancashire Academy in 2011 but left the club in 2015 and went on trial for a number of teams. His only senior appearance is his List A debut for Leicestershire in 2015. Returned to Lancashire last summer and took 19 wickets for the second XI in all formats, as well as making handy runs down the order. He also helped his club side in Manchester, Clifton CC, reach T20 Club Finals Day

Batting	Mat	Inns	NO	Runs	HS	Ave	SR	100	50	Ct	St
List A	1	1	0	15	15	15.00	68.18	0	0	1	0

Bowling	Mat	Balls	Runs	Wkts	BBI	BBM	Ave	Econ	SR	5w	10
List A	1	48	59	2	2/59	2/59	29.50	7.37	24.0	0	0

BRETT HUTTON

RHB / RMF / R0 / W0

FULL NAME: Brett Alan Hutton
BORN: February 6, 1993, Doncaster, Yorkshire
SQUAD NO: 16
HEIGHT: 6ft 3in
NICKNAME: Bert
EDUCATION: Worksop College, Nottinghamshire
TEAMS: Northamptonshire, Nottinghamshire
ROLE: Bowler
DEBUT: First-class: 2011; List A: 2011; T20: 2016

BEST BATTING: 74 Nottinghamshire vs Durham, Trent Bridge, 2016
BEST BOWLING: 5-29 Nottinghamshire vs Durham, Trent Bridge, 2015

'ROY OF THE ROVERS' MOMENT? Making my County Championship debut for Nottinghamshire in 2013
BEST THING ABOUT YOUR HOME GROUND? The crowd
YOUNG OPPOSING PLAYER WHO HAS IMPRESSED YOU? Josh Tongue (Wor) – he's got a nice action
IF YOU WEREN'T A CRICKETER? I'd be a rubbish collector
SURPRISING FACT ABOUT YOU? I have a stamp collection
SURPRISING FACT ABOUT A TEAMMATE? Won't name names, but one of my teammates has crashed his car more times than years he has been driving
WHERE IS PARADISE? Augusta
CRICKETING HERO? Paul Franks – he had a very good career. I played club cricket with him from a young age, watching him and learning
NON-CRICKETING HERO? Tiger Woods – he was the best at his sport for such a long time
TWITTER: @BrettAH26

Batting	Mat	Inns	NO	Runs	HS	Ave	SR	100	50	Ct	St
First-class	33	51	6	970	74	21.55	44.23	0	4	16	0
List A	9	6	3	66	33*	22.00	88.00	0	0	3	0
T20s	1	1	1	4	4*	-	133.33	0	0	0	0

Bowling	Mat	Balls	Runs	Wkts	BBI	BBM	Ave	Econ	SR	5w	10
First-class	33	5208	3133	106	5/29	10/106	29.55	3.60	49.1	4	2
List A	9	414	438	9	3/72	3/72	48.66	6.34	46.0	0	0
T20s	1	12	24	1	1/24	1/24	24.00	12.00	12.0	0	0

GLAMORGAN

FULL NAME: Colin Alexander Ingram
BORN: July 3, 1985, Port Elizabeth, South Africa
SQUAD NO: 41
HEIGHT: 5ft 10in
NICKNAME: Bozie, Stingray, Farmer
EDUCATION: Woodbridge College, Eastern Cape, South Africa
TEAMS: South Africa, Glamorgan, Adelaide Strikers, Delhi Daredevils, Eastern Province, Free State, Somerset, Warriors
ROLE: Allrounder
DEBUT: ODI: 2010; T20I: 2010; First-class: 2004; List A: 2005; T20: 2007

BEST BATTING: 190 Eastern Province vs KwaZulu-Natal, Port Elizabeth, 2009
BEST BOWLING: 4-16 Eastern Province vs Boland, Port Elizabeth, 2006

BEST ADVICE EVER RECEIVED? Hit them high, make them fly, there ain't no fielders in the sky… sixes!
BEST THING ABOUT YOUR HOME GROUND? The Welsh singing at the SWALEC reminds me of my other home ground, St George's Park (Eastern Province), where the band plays
BEST OPPOSING PLAYER IN COUNTY CRICKET? Joe Denly (Ken) – always gets runs against us. I like watching him bat even if it's from cover
IF YOU WEREN'T A CRICKETER? Anything outdoors – growing up on a farm makes you that way
SURPRISING FACT ABOUT YOU? I do a bit of home brewing
SURPRISING FACT ABOUT A TEAMMATE? Andy Salter wants to start a business taking portable Jacuzzis to events with a Land Rover. He's going to call it Salty Tubs
WHERE IS PARADISE? A calm stretch of water where I can cast a line in peace… but if my wife is reading this, then a holiday in Mauritius!
TWITTER: @CAIngram41

Batting	Mat	Inns	NO	Runs	HS	Ave	SR	100	50	Ct	St
ODIs	31	29	3	843	124	32.42	82.32	3	3	12	0
T20Is	9	9	1	210	78	26.25	129.62	0	1	2	0
First-class	111	195	17	6641	190	37.30		14	30	75	0
List A	178	170	17	7182	142	46.94	89.73	18	45	62	0
T20s	167	163	19	4223	114	29.32	136.88	3	25	53	0

Bowling	Mat	Balls	Runs	Wkts	BBI	BBM	Ave	Econ	SR	5w	10
ODIs	31	6	17	0	-	-	-	17.00	-	0	0
T20Is	9	-	-	-	-	-	-	-	-	-	-
First-class	111	3516	2132	50	4/16	5/50	42.64	3.63	70.3	0	0
List A	178	1244	1124	36	4/39	4/39	31.22	5.42	34.5	0	0
T20s	167	764	970	31	4/32	4/32	31.29	7.61	24.6	0	0

WILL JACKS

RHB / OB / R0 / W0

FULL NAME: William George Jacks
BORN: November 21, 1998, Chertsey, Surrey
SQUAD NO: 9
HEIGHT: 6ft 1in
NICKNAME: Jacksy
EDUCATION: St George's College, Weybridge
TEAMS: Surrey, England U19
ROLE: Allrounder

SURREY

BEST ADVICE EVER RECEIVED? It doesn't matter what others think of you
'ROY OF THE ROVERS' MOMENT? Scoring a hundred for England U19 against India U19 in the youth Test at Worcester last season
BEST THING ABOUT YOUR HOME GROUND? The history of The Oval – so many great players and so many great matches over the years
YOUNG OPPOSING PLAYER WHO HAS IMPRESSED YOU? Max Holden (Mid)
IF YOU WEREN'T A CRICKETER? I'd probably be unemployed
SURPRISING FACT ABOUT A TEAMMATE? Amar Virdi had a full beard at the age of 14
WHERE IS PARADISE? St Lucia
CRICKETING HERO? Kevin Pietersen – he is always enjoyable to watch
NON-CRICKETING HERO? LeBron James – he's just incredible and inspires so many people
TWITTER: @Wjacks9

FULL NAME: Ateeq Javid
BORN: October 15, 1991, Birmingham
SQUAD NO: 99
HEIGHT: 5ft 7in
NICKNAME: King AJ
EDUCATION: Aston Manor Academy, Birmingham
TEAMS: Leicestershire, Warwickshire
ROLE: Allrounder
DEBUT: First-class: 2009; List A: 2011; T20: 2013

BEST BATTING: 133 Warwickshire vs Somerset, Edgbaston, 2013
BEST BOWLING: 1-1 Warwickshire vs Lancashire, Old Trafford, 2014

WHAT GOT YOU INTO CRICKET? While growing up all the kids used to play on streets so I joined in
FAMILY TIES? They just love it
'ROY OF THE ROVERS' MOMENT? Celebrating winning the T20 Blast with Warwickshire in 2014
HOW WOULD YOUR TEAMMATES DESCRIBE YOU IN THREE WORDS? Hard-working, smart, intelligent
IF YOU WEREN'T A CRICKETER? I'd be a businessman
SURPRISING FACT? I hate going to parties
CRICKETING HERO? Sachin Tendulkar
NON-CRICKETING HERO? Muhammad Ali
TWITTER: @ateeqjavid

Batting	Mat	Inns	NO	Runs	HS	Ave	SR	100	50	Ct	St
First-class	32	51	6	1090	133	24.22	35.76	2	3	16	0
List A	40	32	12	578	43	28.90	86.52	0	0	6	0
T20s	53	35	15	449	51*	22.45	118.78	0	1	10	0

Bowling	Mat	Balls	Runs	Wkts	BBI	BBM	Ave	Econ	SR	5w	10
First-class	32	600	355	3	1/1	1/1	118.33	3.55	200.0	0	0
List A	40	1182	1136	24	4/42	4/42	47.33	5.76	49.2	0	0
T20s	53	687	836	30	4/17	4/17	27.86	7.30	22.9	0	0

KEATON JENNINGS

LHB / RM / R1 / W0 / MVP78

FULL NAME: Keaton Kent Jennings
BORN: June 19, 1992, Johannesburg, South Africa
SQUAD NO: 1
HEIGHT: 6ft 4in
EDUCATION: King Edward VII School; University of South Africa
TEAMS: England, Lancashire, Durham, Gauteng
ROLE: Batsman
DEBUT: Test: 2016; First-class: 2011; List A: 2012; T20: 2014

BEST BATTING: 221* Durham vs Yorkshire, Chester-le-Street, 2016
BEST BOWLING: 3-37 Durham vs Sussex, Chester-le-Street, 2017

FAMILY TIES? My brother Dylan, uncle Kenneth and father Ray have all played first-class cricket
CRICKETING HERO? Mike Hussey – I really enjoyed the way he went about playing the game
IF YOU WEREN'T A CRICKETER? I'd be working in some sort of accountancy job
TWITTER: @JetJennings
NOTES: Following a prolific 2016 season, Jennings found it tougher going last year and has moved to Old Trafford, along with his ex-Durham teammate Graham Onions, in a bid to regain the opening spot in the Test team which he surrendered last summer. Captained Durham in the One-Day Cup in 2017

Batting	Mat	Inns	NO	Runs	HS	Ave	SR	100	50	Ct	St
Tests	6	12	0	294	112	24.50	42.91	1	1	3	0
First-class	96	173	10	5472	221*	33.57	46.01	14	20	62	0
List A	47	46	11	1432	139	40.91	82.48	3	9	13	0
T20s	34	22	7	363	88	24.20	119.80	0	1	7	0

Bowling	Mat	Balls	Runs	Wkts	BBI	BBM	Ave	Econ	SR	5w	10
Tests	6	36	22	0	-	-	-	3.66	-	0	0
First-class	96	1364	750	28	3/37	4/48	26.78	3.29	48.7	0	0
List A	47	408	434	3	1/9	1/9	144.66	6.38	136.0	0	0
T20s	34	498	612	21	4/37	4/37	29.14	7.37	23.7	0	0

RICHARD JONES

RHB / RMF / RO / WO

LEICESTERSHIRE

FULL NAME: Richard Alan Jones
BORN: November 6, 1986, Stourbridge, Worcestershire
SQUAD NO: 25
HEIGHT: 6ft 2in
NICKNAME: Dick, Jonah, Jonesy
EDUCATION: Manchester Metropolitan University
TEAMS: Leicestershire, Matabeleland Tuskers, Warwickshire, Worcestershire
ROLE: Bowler
DEBUT: First-class: 2007; List A: 2008; T20: 2010

BEST BATTING: 62 Matabeleland Tuskers vs Southern Rocks, Bulawayo, 2012
BEST BOWLING: 7-115 Worcestershire vs Sussex, Hove, 2010
COUNTY CAP: 2007 (Worcestershire)

WHAT GOT YOU INTO CRICKET? When I was nine my best mate started going to nets at a local school and told me how much he enjoyed it. I was sick of him being loads better than me at football, so I decided to get my own back. My whole career has been an attempt to poke fun at my best mate's woeful off-spinners
FAMILY TIES? My dad played for Old Hill CC as a kid, but turned into one of their most loyal bar-frequenting members
'ROY OF THE ROVERS' MOMENT? Taking eight wickets in a day for Worcestershire vs Surrey on the same day that my nephew Noah was born
IF YOU WEREN'T A CRICKETER? I'd be an anthropologist
CRICKETING HEROES? Growing up as a Worcestershire fan, Graeme Hick. To get the chance to play with him was brilliant
NON-CRICKETING HEROES? The work of Professor Tim Noakes has been a huge influence on me
TWITTER: @richardjones441

Batting	Mat	Inns	NO	Runs	HS	Ave	SR	100	50	Ct	St
First-class	58	89	17	895	62	12.43	39.90	0	2	21	0
List A	13	7	3	49	26	12.25	106.52	0	0	2	0
T20s	9	2	1	14	9	14.00	77.77	0	0	7	0

Bowling	Mat	Balls	Runs	Wkts	BBI	BBM	Ave	Econ	SR	5w	10
First-class	58	7766	5276	162	7/115	8/105	32.56	4.07	47.9	5	0
List A	13	453	554	5	1/25	1/25	110.80	7.33	90.6	0	0
T20s	9	126	230	9	5/34	5/34	25.55	10.95	14.0	1	0

ROB JONES

RHB / LB / RO / WO

FULL NAME: Robert Peter Jones
BORN: November 3, 1995, Warrington, Cheshire
SQUAD NO: 12
HEIGHT: 5ft 11in
NICKNAME: Jonesy
EDUCATION: Bridgewater High School, Warrington
TEAMS: Lancashire
ROLE: Batsman
DEBUT: First-class: 2016; T20: 2017

LANCASHIRE

BEST BATTING: 106* Lancashire vs Middlesex, Old Trafford, 2016

WHAT GOT YOU INTO CRICKET? Playing cricket with my dad in the garage
BEST ADVICE EVER RECEIVED? Train as hard as you can
'ROY OF THE ROVERS' MOMENT? Hitting my maiden first-class century against Middlesex at Old Trafford in 2016
BEST THING ABOUT YOUR HOME GROUND? The incredible facilities we have in the Players and Media Centre with a pool, gym, changing rooms etc
WHERE IS PARADISE? Abersoch, north Wales
CRICKETING HERO? Jos Buttler – he's just an incredible player
NON-CRICKETING HERO? David Attenborough
TWITTER: @robpeterjones

Batting	Mat	Inns	NO	Runs	HS	Ave	SR	100	50	Ct	St
First-class	7	12	2	299	106*	29.90	32.85	1	0	6	0
T20s	2	-	-	-	-	-	-	-	-	0	0

Bowling	Mat	Balls	Runs	Wkts	BBI	BBM	Ave	Econ	SR	5w	10
First-class	7	-	-	-	-	-	-	-	-	-	-
T20s	2	-	-	-	-	-	-	-	-	-	-

CHRIS JORDAN

RHB / RFM / R0 / W1 / MVP73

SUSSEX

FULL NAME: Christopher James Jordan
BORN: October 4, 1988, Christ Church, Barbados
SQUAD NO: 8
HEIGHT: 6ft 2in
NICKNAME: CJ
EDUCATION: Combermere School, Barbados; Dulwich College
TEAMS: England, Sussex, Adelaide Strikers, Barbados, Northern Districts, Peshawar Zalmi, Royal Challengers Bangalore, Surrey
ROLE: Allrounder
DEBUT: Test: 2014; ODI: 2013; T20I: 2014; First-class: 2007; List A: 2007; T20: 2008

BEST BATTING: 147 Sussex vs Nottinghamshire, Hove, 2017
BEST BOWLING: 7-43 Barbados vs Combined Campuses and Colleges, Bridgetown, 2013
COUNTY CAP: 2014 (Sussex)

TWITTER: @ChrisJordan94
NOTES: Born in Barbados, Jordan is eligible to represent England through his grandmother. An allrounder known for his brilliant close catching, Jordan is a regular member of England's T20 side but hasn't played an ODI for more than a year and his last Test was in May 2015. Released by Surrey after the 2012 season, Jordan took 61 first-class wickets in his first summer at Hove. Injury restricted his appearances in 2015 and 2016 but he was a key figure in Championship and T20 cricket last summer, scoring a first-class best of 147 against Notts at Hove. Won the 2016/17 Pakistan Super League with Peshawar Zalmi. Re-signed by Sunrisers Hyderabad for the 2018 IPL

Batting	Mat	Inns	NO	Runs	HS	Ave	SR	100	50	Ct	St
Tests	8	11	1	180	35	18.00	56.25	0	0	14	0
ODIs	31	21	7	169	38*	12.07	89.89	0	0	19	0
T20Is	30	20	9	163	27*	14.81	117.26	0	0	13	0
First-class	94	129	21	2700	147	25.00		2	12	114	0
List A	72	50	12	560	55	14.73		0	1	42	0
T20s	113	74	33	751	45*	18.31	122.11	0	0	65	0

Bowling	Mat	Balls	Runs	Wkts	BBI	BBM	Ave	Econ	SR	5w	10
Tests	8	1530	752	21	4/18	7/50	35.80	2.94	72.8	0	0
ODIs	31	1532	1521	43	5/29	5/29	35.37	5.95	35.6	1	0
T20Is	30	648	948	34	4/28	4/28	27.88	8.77	19.0	0	0
First-class	94	15973	9160	284	7/43	9/58	32.25	3.44	56.2	9	0
List A	72	3298	3144	109	5/28	5/28	28.84	5.71	30.2	2	0
T20s	113	2210	3109	116	4/11	4/11	26.80	8.44	19.0	0	0

FULL NAME: Robert Ian Keogh
BORN: October 21, 1991, Dunstable, Bedfordshire
SQUAD NO: 14
HEIGHT: 6ft 2in
NICKNAME: Keezy, Key Dog, Chav
EDUCATION: Queensbury Upper School, Dunstable; Dunstable College
TEAMS: Northamptonshire
ROLE: Allrounder
DEBUT: First-class: 2012; List A: 2010; T20: 2011

NORTHAMPTONSHIRE

BEST BATTING: 221 Northamptonshire vs Hampshire, Southampton, 2013
BEST BOWLING: 9-52 Northamptonshire vs Glamorgan, Northampton, 2016

WHAT GOT YOU INTO CRICKET? My dad played for Dunstable Town CC and I'd go along to watch and play with the other kids
'ROY OF THE ROVERS' MOMENT? Hitting the winning runs in the T20 Blast final against Durham in 2016 and celebrating with the boys in the middle
BEST THING ABOUT YOUR HOME GROUND? It's five minutes from my house
YOUNG OPPOSING PLAYER WHO HAS IMPRESSED YOU? Sam Curran (Sur)
IF YOU WEREN'T A CRICKETER? I'd be a terrible second-hand car salesman
SURPRISING FACT ABOUT A TEAMMATE? Nathan Buck has the worst gags on the county circuit
WHERE IS PARADISE? Barbados
CRICKETING HERO? Ricky Ponting – just loved watching him bat
NON-CRICKETING HERO? David Beckham
TWITTER: @RobKeogh91

Batting	Mat	Inns	NO	Runs	HS	Ave	SR	100	50	Ct	St
First-class	59	97	8	2704	221	30.38	51.24	7	7	16	0
List A	33	30	3	821	134	30.40	88.56	1	7	6	0
T20s	47	25	6	348	41*	18.31	117.17	0	0	23	0

Bowling	Mat	Balls	Runs	Wkts	BBI	BBM	Ave	Econ	SR	5w	10
First-class	59	4419	2593	65	9/52	13/125	39.89	3.52	67.9	1	1
List A	33	630	603	2	1/49	1/49	301.50	5.74	315.0	0	0
T20s	47	180	267	6	2/27	2/27	44.50	8.90	30.0	0	0

SIMON KERRIGAN

RHB / SLA / R0 / W2

FULL NAME: Simon Christopher Kerrigan
BORN: May 10, 1989, Preston, Lancashire
SQUAD NO: 10
HEIGHT: 5ft 9in
NICKNAME: Kegs, Kegsy, Kegger, Bish
EDUCATION: Corpus Christi High School, Lancashire; Preston College; Edge Hill University, Ormskirk
TEAMS: England, Lancashire, Northamptonshire
ROLE: Bowler
DEBUT: Test: 2013; First-class: 2010; List A: 2011; T20: 2010

BEST BATTING: 62* Lancashire vs Hampshire, Southport, 2013
BEST BOWLING: 9-51 Lancashire vs Hampshire, Liverpool, 2011
COUNTY CAP: 2013 (Lancashire)

WHAT GOT YOU INTO CRICKET? Watching it on TV
'ROY OF THE ROVERS' MOMENT? Taking nine wickets in an innings against Hampshire when Lancashire won the Championship in 2011
BEST THING ABOUT YOUR HOME GROUND? Good wicket and training facilities. It's got a massive history as well
YOUNG OPPOSING PLAYER WHO HAS IMPRESSED YOU? Sam Curran (Sur)
IF YOU WEREN'T A CRICKETER? I'd be a dog-walker
WHERE IS PARADISE? Somewhere sunny
CRICKETING HERO? Andrew Flintoff – he used to live two minutes away from me. Lancashire and England legend
NON-CRICKETING HERO? Alan Shearer
TWITTER: @Kegs10

Batting	Mat	Inns	NO	Runs	HS	Ave	SR	100	50	Ct	St
Tests	1	1	1	1	1*	-	8.33	0	0	0	0
First-class	104	122	42	1058	62*	13.22	37.73	0	3	36	0
List A	35	15	6	53	30	3.33	50.84	0	0	11	0
T20s	24	4	4	9	4*	-	180.00	0	0	11	0

Bowling	Mat	Balls	Runs	Wkts	BBI	BBM	Ave	Econ	SR	5w	10
Tests	1	48	53	0	-	-	-	6.62	-	0	0
First-class	104	20644	9844	322	9/51	12/192	30.57	2.86	64.1	13	3
List A	35	1456	1302	28	3/21	3/21	46.50	5.36	52.0	0	0
T20s	24	516	595	20	3/17	3/17	29.75	6.91	25.8	0	0

RASHID KHAN

RHB / LB / RO / WO

FULL NAME: Rashid Khan Arman
BORN: September 20, 1998, Nangarhar, Afghanistan
SQUAD NO: 1
TEAMS: Afghanistan, Sussex, Adelaide Strikers, Guyana Amazon Warriors, Quetta Gladiators, Sunrisers Hyderabad
ROLE: Bowler
DEBUT: ODI: 2015; T20I: 2015; First-class: 2016; List A: 2015; T20: 2015

SUSSEX

BEST BATTING: 52 Afghanistan vs England Lions, Abu Dhabi, 2016
BEST BOWLING: 8-74 Afghanistan vs England Lions, Abu Dhabi, 2016

NOTES: The teenage leg-spinner is set to become the first Afghan to play county cricket having been signed by Sussex to play the first half of the T20 Blast, subject to international clearance and visa approval. In January, Rashid was named the ICC Associate Cricketer of the Year after sensational returns for his country in limited-overs cricket. At the time of writing his T20 economy-rate of 5.80 is the lowest of any bowler to have taken 100 career wickets. Rashid will be reunited with Jason Gillespie, Sussex's new head coach who worked with him in the Big Bash League for Adelaide Strikers. "His form for Afghanistan and the T20 teams he has played for over the last couple of years has been phenomenal," said Gillespie. "I have worked closely with Rash at the Adelaide Strikers in the BBL and have been incredibly impressed with his attitude, work ethic and team-first mentality"

Batting	Mat	Inns	NO	Runs	HS	Ave	SR	100	50	Ct	St
ODIs	37	28	4	545	60*	22.70	99.81	0	2	12	0
T20Is	29	11	5	100	33	16.66	129.87	0	0	8	0
First-class	4	4	1	125	52	41.66	74.85	0	1	0	0
List A	38	28	4	545	60*	22.70	99.81	0	2	12	0
T20s	91	34	15	209	33	11.00	128.22	0	0	27	0

Bowling	Mat	Balls	Runs	Wkts	BBI	BBM	Ave	Econ	SR	5w	10
ODIs	37	1791	1141	86	7/18	7/18	13.26	3.82	20.8	3	0
T20Is	29	660	645	47	5/3	5/3	13.72	5.86	14.0	1	0
First-class	4	1179	527	35	8/74	12/122	15.05	2.68	33.6	4	1
List A	38	1839	1184	87	7/18	7/18	13.60	3.86	21.1	3	0
T20s	91	2112	2045	135	5/3	5/3	15.14	5.80	15.6	1	0

SOHAIL KHAN

RHB / RFM / R0 / W0

FULL NAME: Sohail Khan
BORN: March 6, 1984, Malakand, North-West Frontier Province, Pakistan
SQUAD NO: 19
TEAMS: Pakistan, Leicestershire, Karachi Dolphins, Karachi Kings, Lahore Qalandars, Sind, Sui Southern Gas Corporation
ROLE: Bowler
DEBUT: Test: 2009; ODI: 2008; T20I: 2008; First-class: 2007; List A: 2008; T20: 2008

BEST BATTING: 65 Pakistan vs Australia, Melbourne, 2016
BEST BOWLING: 9-109 Sui Southern Gas Corporation vs Water and Power Development Authority, Karachi, 2007

NOTES: An experienced right-arm seamer, Sohail will share Leicestershire's overseas duties with his compatriot Mohammad Abbas and is expected to be available from late April to mid-June. He impressed on Pakistan's tour of England in 2016, taking seven wickets at Edgbaston in his first Test match for five years and then returning match figures of 6-118 at The Oval. He has since slipped out of the international reckoning but will bring a wealth of experience to Leicestershire's attack. "Sohail Khan has a superb record in both red- and white-ball cricket," said Leicestershire's new head coach Paul Nixon. "He has good experience in English conditions and really stood out on the last tour when Pakistan played here. Sohail's bowling will be ideally suited to early-season conditions here"

Batting	Mat	Inns	NO	Runs	HS	Ave	SR	100	50	Ct	St
Tests	9	12	2	252	65	25.20	76.82	0	1	2	0
ODIs	13	6	1	25	7	5.00	49.01	0	0	3	0
T20Is	5	1	1	1	1*	-	100.00	0	0	0	0
First-class	96	128	30	1482	65	15.12	62.53	0	3	24	0
List A	74	52	12	489	39	12.22	90.72	0	0	13	0
T20s	68	37	19	302	45*	16.77	139.81	0	0	11	0

Bowling	Mat	Balls	Runs	Wkts	BBI	BBM	Ave	Econ	SR	5w	10
Tests	9	1828	1125	27	5/68	7/207	41.66	3.69	67.7	2	0
ODIs	13	666	597	19	5/55	5/55	31.42	5.37	35.0	1	0
T20Is	5	90	123	5	2/13	2/13	24.60	8.20	18.0	0	0
First-class	96	18033	10529	432	9/109	16/189	24.37	3.50	41.7	34	7
List A	74	3655	3212	132	6/44	6/44	24.33	5.27	27.6	6	0
T20s	68	1455	1862	87	5/23	5/23	21.40	7.67	16.7	1	0

FEROZE KHUSHI

RHB / OB / R0 / W0

FULL NAME: Feroze Isa Nazir Khushi
BORN: June 23, 1999, Whipps Cross, Essex
SQUAD NO: 23
HEIGHT: 6ft 1in
NICKNAME: Fink
EDUCATION: Kelmscott School, Walthamstow, London
TEAMS: Essex
ROLE: Batsman

ESSEX

WHAT GOT YOU INTO CRICKET? My father introduced me to cricket at the age of three

BEST ADVICE EVER RECEIVED? Work hard and be dedicated

'ROY OF THE ROVERS' MOMENT? When I hit six sixes in the last over of a school match when we needed 30 runs to win

BEST THING ABOUT YOUR HOME GROUND? Chelmsford has a good batting track, a fast outfield and short boundaries. And there is a great atmosphere for the T20 games

YOUNG OPPOSING PLAYER WHO HAS IMPRESSED YOU? Sam Curran (Sur) – he bowls at a good pace, executes his plans consistently and mixes up his varierty of deliveries really well

IF YOU WEREN'T A CRICKETER? I'd be a professional footballer

SURPRISING FACT ABOUT YOU? I went to the same school as Fabrice Muamba

CRICKETING HERO? Shahid Afridi – with his explosive batting, he can destroy the opposition and win matches on his own

NON-CRICKETING HERO? Cristiano Ronaldo – he works very hard at his game and is a great role model of professionalism on and off the field

NOTES: Khushi is a right-handed batsman who signed a professional contract with Essex in October 2017 after a number of impressive performances for Essex Second XI last summer, including an unbeaten 101 against Middlesex Second XI at Colchester in August

BEN KITT

RHB / RMF / RO / WO

NOTTINGHAMSHIRE

FULL NAME: Ben Michael Kitt
BORN: January 18, 1995, Plymouth, Devon
SQUAD NO: 17
HEIGHT: 6ft 3in
NICKNAME: Kitty, BK, Doggers
EDUCATION: Saltash.net Community School, Cornwall; Central College Nottingham
TEAMS: Nottinghamshire
ROLE: Bowler

WHAT GOT YOU INTO CRICKET? My grandad made me a bat in his shed when I was two

FAMILY TIES? Pretty much everyone in my family has played for clubs in Cornwall and some of them for the county

STRANGEST THING SEEN IN A GAME? Once at Falmouth CC (Cornwall) we had to lie on the floor for a few minutes as there was a massive swarm of bees flying over the ground. The only reason I was on the floor was because I thought it was part of the warm-up

'ROY OF THE ROVERS' MOMENT? Winning the Second XI Championship in 2015

SUPERSTITIONS? I always hold the ball the same way round when I bowl and I always turn the same way at the top of my mark

HOW WOULD YOUR TEAMMATES DESCRIBE YOU IN THREE WORDS? Aggressive, fun, helpful

CRICKETING HERO? Andrew Flintoff when I was a kid, Jake Ball now

NON-CRICKETING HERO? Cristiano Ronaldo

IF YOU WEREN'T A CRICKETER? I'd be a footballer or masseur

SURPRISING FACT? I play darts for about 12 hours a week

UNUSUAL OBJECT AT HOME? Three cuddly toys from my sister

TWITTER: @benkitt18

DIETER KLEIN

RHB / LFM / R0 / W0

FULL NAME: Dieter Klein
BORN: October 31, 1988, Lichtenburg, North West Province, South Africa
SQUAD NO: 77
HEIGHT: 5ft 9in
NICKNAME: Diets
EDUCATION: Hoërskool Lichtenberg, South Africa
TEAMS: Leicestershire, Lions, North West
ROLE: Bowler
DEBUT: First-class: 2008; List A: 2008; T20: 2013

BEST BATTING: 66 North West vs Border, East London, 2014
BEST BOWLING: 8-72 North West vs Northerns, Potchefstroom, 2014

WHAT GOT YOU INTO CRICKET? I always had a love for all sports, but something had to give and eventually cricket won through
BEST ADVICE EVER RECEIVED? Nothing comes for free. What you put in is what you get out. Anything is possible
BEST THING ABOUT YOUR HOME GROUND? Our very own Barmy Army
IF YOU WEREN'T A CRICKETER? I'd be a pilot
STRANGEST THING SEEN IN A GAME? During a club game one of the players went in to bat with his mobile in his pocket. He was batting very poorly and one of his teammates called him on his mobile and asked if they could bring him a pair of glasses
WHERE IS PARADISE? On a beach
CRICKETING HERO? Jacques Kallis – very controlled and good at all aspects of the game
NON-CRICKETING HERO? My brother – just a hero. Nothing gets him down. One hell of a fighter

Batting	Mat	Inns	NO	Runs	HS	Ave	SR	100	50	Ct	St
First-class	53	76	15	1066	66	17.47	75.81	0	4	17	0
List A	24	11	3	102	26	12.75	72.85	0	0	1	0
T20s	13	7	3	49	16	12.25	106.52	0	0	3	0

Bowling	Mat	Balls	Runs	Wkts	BBI	BBM	Ave	Econ	SR	5w	10
First-class	53	8015	5172	191	8/72	10/125	27.07	3.87	41.9	10	1
List A	24	1131	888	36	5/35	5/35	24.66	4.71	31.4	1	0
T20s	13	226	274	13	3/27	3/27	21.07	7.27	17.3	0	0

RORY KLEINVELDT

RHB / RFM / R0 / W2 / MVP31

FULL NAME: Rory Keith Kleinveldt
BORN: March 15, 1983, Cape Town, South Africa
SQUAD NO: 6
NICKNAME: Rors
TEAMS: South Africa, Northamptonshire, Cape Cobras, Hampshire, Western Province
ROLE: Allrounder
DEBUT: Test: 2012; ODI: 2013; T20I: 2008; First-class: 2002; List A: 2002; T20: 2004

BEST BATTING: 115* Western Province vs KwaZulu-Natal, Chatsworth, 2005
BEST BOWLING: 9-65 Northamptonshire vs Nottinghamshire, Northampton, 2017

TWITTER: @RoryK_9
NOTES: A powerful, fast-bowling allrounder, Kleinveldt has played four Tests, 10 ODIs and six T20Is for South Africa but hasn't represented his country since 2013. Took over 50 Championship wickets in 2015, his first season as Northants' overseas player, and was the county's leading wicket-taker (15) in the victorious 2016 T20 Blast campaign. Took most wickets for Northants in the Championship (50) and the T20 Blast (14) last summer. This season he will join up with the county in mid-May, with New Zealand's Doug Bracewell covering for the opening weeks

Batting	Mat	Inns	NO	Runs	HS	Ave	SR	100	50	Ct	St
Tests	4	5	2	27	17*	9.00	44.26	0	0	2	0
ODIs	10	7	0	105	43	15.00	84.67	0	0	4	0
T20Is	6	3	2	25	22	25.00	250.00	0	0	1	0
First-class	143	200	23	3564	115*	20.13	74.84	1	16	70	0
List A	161	105	22	1699	128	20.46	115.03	1	3	26	0
T20s	138	92	29	814	46	12.92	148.00	0	0	27	0

Bowling	Mat	Balls	Runs	Wkts	BBI	BBM	Ave	Econ	SR	5w	10
Tests	4	667	422	10	3/65	4/97	42.20	3.79	66.7	0	0
ODIs	10	513	448	12	4/22	4/22	37.33	5.23	42.7	0	0
T20Is	6	122	173	9	3/18	3/18	19.22	8.50	13.5	0	0
First-class	143	24181	12204	436	9/65	13/98	27.99	3.02	55.4	20	2
List A	161	7384	5855	182	4/22	4/22	32.17	4.75	40.5	0	0
T20s	138	2791	3560	130	3/14	3/14	27.38	7.65	21.4	0	0

MICHAEL KLINGER

RHB / R1 / W0

FULL NAME: Michael Klinger
BORN: July 4, 1980, Melbourne, Australia
SQUAD NO: 2
HEIGHT: 5ft 11in
NICKNAME: Maxy
EDUCATION: Deakin University, Victoria
TEAMS: Australia, Gloucestershire, Adelaide Strikers, Kochi Tuskers Kerala, Perth Scorchers, South Australia, Victoria, Western Australia, Worcestershire
ROLE: Batsman
DEBUT: T20I: 2017; First-class: 1999; List A: 1999; T20: 2006

BEST BATTING: 255 South Australia vs Western Australia, Adelaide, 2008
COUNTY CAP: 2012 (Worcestershire); 2013 (Gloucestershire)

BEST ADVICE EVER RECEIVED? If you want to be number one then train like you are number two
'ROY OF THE ROVERS' MOMENT? Winning the 50-over competition with Gloucestershire in 2015
BEST THING ABOUT YOUR HOME GROUND? The support from the fans
BEST OPPOSING PLAYER IN COUNTY CRICKET? Colin Ingram (Gla) – fearless player but equally consistent
SURPRISING FACT ABOUT YOU? I used to have an afro
CRICKETING HERO? Ricky Ponting – great to watch
NON-CRICKETING HERO? My wife – takes great care of our kids while I'm away playing cricket
TWITTER: @maxyklinger
NOTES: Klinger announced his retirement from first-class cricket in March 2018 but was still due to play for Gloucestershire in this summer's T20 Blast competition

Batting	Mat	Inns	NO	Runs	HS	Ave	SR	100	50	Ct	St
T20Is	3	3	0	143	62	47.66	127.67	0	1	2	0
First-class	182	321	33	11320	255	39.30	45.91	30	49	178	0
List A	177	174	23	7449	166*	49.33		18	44	72	0
T20s	166	161	23	4997	126*	36.21	125.58	7	29	61	0

Bowling	Mat	Balls	Runs	Wkts	BBI	BBM	Ave	Econ	SR	5w	10
T20Is	3	-	-	-	-	-	-	-	-	-	-
First-class	182	6	3	0	-	-	-	3.00	-	0	0
List A	177	-	-	-	-	-	-	-	-	-	-
T20s	166	-	-	-	-	-	-	-	-	-	-

YORKSHIRE

FULL NAME: Tom Kohler-Cadmore
BORN: August 19, 1994, Chatham, Kent
SQUAD NO: 32
HEIGHT: 6ft 2in
NICKNAME: Pepsi, Herbert, Brother Bilo
EDUCATION: Malvern College, Worcestershire
TEAMS: Yorkshire, Worcestershire
ROLE: Batsman
DEBUT: First-class: 2014; List A: 2013; T20: 2014

BEST BATTING: 169 Worcestershire vs Gloucestershire, Worcester, 2016

BEST ADVICE EVER RECEIVED? In cricket: hit the sightscreen. In life: never eat yellow snow
BEST THING ABOUT YOUR HOME GROUND? My dad works there – he does the washing so I don't have to
BEST OPPOSING PLAYER IN COUNTY CRICKET? Wayne Madsen (Der)
YOUNG OPPOSING PLAYER WHO HAS IMPRESSED YOU? Josh Tongue (Wor) – he's not as boring as he looks
IF YOU WEREN'T A CRICKETER? I'd be an underwater fireman
SURPRISING FACT ABOUT YOU? I've been called the songbird of my generation by people who have heard me sing
SURPRISING FACT ABOUT A TEAMMATE? Ben Coad only eats chicken nuggets. I've never seen someone take down 20 nuggets so quickly and easily and come back for more
WHERE IS PARADISE? A McDonald's with Ben Coad
CRICKETING HERO? Dwayne Leverock – because of that one-handed screamer
UNUSUAL OBJECT AT HOME? A samurai sword signed by Randy Jackson
TWITTER: @tomkcadmore

Batting	Mat	Inns	NO	Runs	HS	Ave	SR	100	50	Ct	St
First-class	40	66	4	1914	169	30.87	54.51	4	10	48	0
List A	31	30	0	817	119	27.23	82.02	2	2	11	0
T20s	49	49	2	1201	127	25.55	142.46	1	6	31	0
Bowling	Mat	Balls	Runs	Wkts	BBI	BBM	Ave	Econ	SR	5w	10
First-class	40	-	-	-	-	-	-	-	-	-	-
List A	31	-	-	-	-	-	-	-	-	-	-
T20s	49	-	-	-	-	-	-	-	-	-	-

FULL NAME: Heino Gunther Kuhn
BORN: April 1, 1984, Piet Retief, South Africa
SQUAD NO: TBC
TEAMS: South Africa, Kent, Northerns, Titans
ROLE: Batsman/wicketkeeper
DEBUT: Test: 2017; T20I: 2009; First-class: 2005; List A: 2005; T20: 2007

BEST BATTING: 244* Titans vs Lions, Benoni, 2015

TWITTER: @HeinoKuhn

NOTES: Kent have signed the South African opening batsman on a Kolpak deal, subject to him obtaining a visa. Kuhn made his Test debut during the Proteas' tour of England last summer, playing all four matches but scoring only 113 runs at an average of 14.12. He subsequently lost his place to Aiden Markram – who he may come up against in Division Two of the Championship this season, with Markram turning out in for Durham – and has decided to pursue his career in England. He has had a decorated career in South African domestic cricket, winning three successive T20 titles with reigning champions Titans, as well as lifting four-day and one-day trophies with Northerns. Also a competent wicketkeeper, Kuhn will be available for Kent in all three competitions. "We believe Heino can complement our talented batsmen across the three formats and serve as a mentor to those coming through the ranks," said Kent director of cricket Paul Downton

Batting	Mat	Inns	NO	Runs	HS	Ave	SR	100	50	Ct	St
Tests	4	8	0	113	34	14.12	38.04	0	0	1	0
T20Is	7	6	2	49	29	12.25	116.66	0	0	5	0
First-class	142	247	24	9698	244*	43.48		23	46	335	18
List A	150	136	12	3795	141*	30.60	86.66	8	20	168	22
T20s	81	66	10	1403	83*	25.05	124.15	0	7	43	6

Bowling	Mat	Balls	Runs	Wkts	BBI	BBM	Ave	Econ	SR	5w	10
Tests	4	-	-	-	-	-	-	-	-	-	-
T20Is	7	-	-	-	-	-	-	-	-	-	-
First-class	142	6	12	0	-	-	-	12.00	-	0	0
List A	150	-	-	-	-	-	-	-	-	-	-
T20s	81	-	-	-	-	-	-	-	-	-	-

TOM LACE

RHB / WK / R0 / W0

MIDDLESEX

FULL NAME: Thomas Cresswell Lace
BORN: May 27, 1998, Hammersmith
SQUAD NO: 27
HEIGHT: 5ft 9in
NICKNAME: Lacey
EDUCATION: Millfield School; Royal Holloway, University of London
TEAMS: Middlesex
ROLE: Wicketkeeper/batsman

WHAT GOT YOU INTO CRICKET? The 2005 Ashes
BEST ADVICE EVER RECEIVED? Be interested and interesting
'ROY OF THE ROVERS' MOMENT? Signing for Middlesex
BEST THING ABOUT YOUR HOME GROUND? It's Lord's
YOUNG OPPOSING PLAYER WHO HAS IMPRESSED YOU? Dom Bess (Som)
SURPRISING FACT ABOUT YOU? I love Chelsea
SURPRISING FACT ABOUT A TEAMMATE? Max Holden has never scored in a game of warm-up football
WHERE IS PARADISE? St Lucia
CRICKETING HERO? Andrew Flintoff
NON-CRICKETING HERO? Frank Lampard
TWITTER: @tom_lace
NOTES: Lace is a 19-year-old wicketkeeper-batsman who has been part of the Middlesex set-up since he was 10. He made his Middlesex Second XI debut against Worcestershire as a 16-year-old in April 2015 and has since appeared regularly for the seconds, making 56 appearances. He scored his maiden second XI hundred in August 2016 against Worcestershire. Lace signed a three-year summer contract with the county this winter. Managing director of cricket Angus Fraser said: "Tom thoroughly deserves this opportunity. He has the knack of scoring important runs when conditions are far from ideal, which is a good sign moving forward"

DANNY LAMB

RHB / RFM / RO / WO

FULL NAME: Daniel John Lamb
BORN: September 7, 1995, Preston, Lancashire
SQUAD NO: 26
HEIGHT: 6ft 4in
NICKNAME: Lamby, Frank the Tank, The Shermanator
EDUCATION: St Michael's CofE High School, Chorley; Cardinal Newman College, Preston; Edgehill University
TEAMS: Lancashire
ROLE: Allrounder
DEBUT: List A: 2017; T20: 2017

LANCASHIRE

WHAT GOT YOU INTO CRICKET? Playing with my dad in the garden of the local cricket club
FAMILY TIES? My younger sister Emma plays for Lancashire and we have played together regularly for Bramhall in the Cheshire Premier League
'ROY OF THE ROVERS' MOMENT? Making my Lancashire debut in 2017
BEST THING ABOUT YOUR HOME GROUND? The dressing rooms are unreal
YOUNG OPPOSING PLAYER WHO HAS IMPRESSED YOU? Sam Curran (Sur) – very talented allrounder
IF YOU WEREN'T A CRICKETER? I'd be trying to be a professional footballer
SURPRISING FACT? I was Blackburn Rovers FC Academy goalkeeper from U9 to U16 level
WHERE IS PARADISE? Sydney
CRICKETING HERO? Andrew Flintoff – I grew up wanting to be like him
NON-CRICKETING HERO? Conor McGregor
TWITTER: @lamby236

Batting	Mat	Inns	NO	Runs	HS	Ave	SR	100	50	Ct	St
List A	2	2	2	5	4*	-	83.33	0	0	0	0
T20s	1	1	0	22	22	22.00	122.22	0	0	0	0
Bowling	Mat	Balls	Runs	Wkts	BBI	BBM	Ave	Econ	SR	5w	10
List A	2	120	108	4	2/51	2/51	27.00	5.40	30.0	0	0
T20s	1	24	30	3	3/30	3/30	10.00	7.50	8.0	0	0

MATT LAMB

RHB / RM / RO / WO

FULL NAME: Matthew Lamb
BORN: July 19, 1996, Wolverhampton, Staffordshire
SQUAD NO: 7
HEIGHT: 6ft 3in
NICKNAME: Lamby
EDUCATION: North Bromsgrove High School, Worcestershire
TEAMS: Warwickshire
ROLE: Batsman
DEBUT: First-class: 2016; List A: 2017

BEST BATTING: 71 Warwickshire vs Middlesex, Lord's, 2017
BEST BOWLING: 1-19 Warwickshire vs Somerset, Edgbaston, 2017

FAMILY TIES? My grandad and dad didn't have any interest in cricket. It was my brother who was the only one who played and subsequently got me involved
'ROY OF THE ROVERS' MOMENT? Scoring 200 and 167 in one game for Warwickshire Second XI
HOW WOULD YOUR TEAMMATES DESCRIBE YOU IN THREE WORDS? Quiet, unassuming, chilled
CRICKETING HERO? Andrew Flintoff – I loved the way he could make things happen from nowhere
NON-CRICKETING HEROES? Steve Bull, Jonny Wilkinson
IF YOU WEREN'T A CRICKETER? I'd be a professional surfer or a plumber
SURPRISING FACT? I was about to quit cricket until I was luckily selected for a second XI game against Worcestershire in September 2015 and managed to score 142
TWITTER: @Lamb_Matt

Batting	Mat	Inns	NO	Runs	HS	Ave	SR	100	50	Ct	St
First-class	8	16	0	331	71	20.68	37.27	0	2	3	0
List A	2	2	0	14	12	7.00	56.00	0	0	1	0
Bowling	Mat	Balls	Runs	Wkts	BBI	BBM	Ave	Econ	SR	5w	10
First-class	8	120	66	3	1/19	1/19	22.00	3.30	40.0	0	0
List A	2	6	9	0	-	-	-	9.00	-	0	0

TOM LATHAM

LHB / RM / WK / R0 / W0

FULL NAME: Thomas William Maxwell Latham
BORN: April 2, 1992, Christchurch, New Zealand
SQUAD NO: 48
HEIGHT: 5ft 6in
NICKNAME: Tommy
EDUCATION: Lincoln University, Christchurch
TEAMS: New Zealand, Durham, Scotland, Canterbury, Kent
ROLE: Batsman/wicketkeeper
DEBUT: Test: 2014; ODI: 2012; T20I: 2012; First-class: 2010; List A: 2011; T20: 2012

BEST BATTING: 261 Canterbury vs Central Districs, Napier, 2014
BEST BOWLING: 1-7 New Zealanders vs Cricket Australia XI, Sydney, 2015

FAMILY TIES? My father Rod played cricket for New Zealand in the 1990s
'ROY OF THE ROVERS' MOMENT? Making my debut for New Zealand in all three forms
BEST PLAYER IN COUNTY CRICKET? Jeetan Patel (War)
HOW WOULD YOUR TEAMMATES DESCRIBE YOU IN THREE WORDS? Hard-working, team-first, easy-going
CRICKETING HEROES? Mike Hussey – fellow left-hand top-order batter, always enjoyed the way he played and how he loves cricket so much. Brendon McCullum – admired how he went out and smashed the ball everywhere
IF YOU WEREN'T A CRICKETER? I'd be a builder
TWITTER: @tomlatham2

Batting	Mat	Inns	NO	Runs	HS	Ave	SR	100	50	Ct	St
Tests	34	62	2	2295	177	38.25	46.48	6	13	35	0
ODIs	71	69	8	2053	137	33.65	81.59	4	10	47	5
T20Is	13	10	0	163	39	16.30	103.82	0	0	6	0
First-class	87	153	11	5883	261	41.42	50.55	12	37	106	1
List A	130	121	13	3772	137	34.92	83.28	6	19	97	10
T20s	59	50	2	1192	82	24.83	129.00	0	6	22	2

Bowling	Mat	Balls	Runs	Wkts	BBI	BBM	Ave	Econ	SR	5w	10
Tests	34	-	-	-	-	-	-	-	-	-	-
ODIs	71	-	-	-	-	-	-	-	-	-	-
T20Is	13	-	-	-	-	-	-	-	-	-	-
First-class	87	26	18	1	1/7	1/7	18.00	4.15	26.0	0	0
List A	130	-	-	-	-	-	-	-	-	-	-
T20s	59	-	-	-	-	-	-	-	-	-	-

GLAMORGAN

FULL NAME: Jeremy Lloyd Lawlor
BORN: November 4, 1995, Cardiff
SQUAD NO: 6
HEIGHT: 6ft
NICKNAME: Jez, King
EDUCATION: The Cathedral School, Llandaff;
Cardiff Metropolitan University
TEAMS: Glamorgan
ROLE: Batsman
DEBUT: First-class: 2015

BEST BATTING: 81 Cardiff MCCU vs Hampshire, Southampton, 2016
BEST BOWLING: 1-26 Cardiff MCCU vs Glamorgan, Cardiff, 2017

WHAT GOT YOU INTO CRICKET? My dad taking me down to St Fagans CC
FAMILY TIES? My dad Peter played for Glamorgan
BEST THING ABOUT YOUR HOME GROUND? The food
BEST OPPOSING PLAYER IN COUNTY CRICKET? Jake Ball (Not)
YOUNG OPPOSING PLAYER WHO HAS IMPRESSED YOU? Mason Crane (Ham)
IF YOU WEREN'T A CRICKETER? I'd be working in the City
SURPRISING FACT ABOUT YOU? I was the inter-house chess champion at school
WHERE IS PARADISE? Australia
CRICKETING HERO? Sachin Tendulkar
NON-CRICKETING HERO? Conor McGregor

Batting	Mat	Inns	NO	Runs	HS	Ave	SR	100	50	Ct	St
First-class	6	8	2	261	81	43.50	47.02	0	3	3	0

Bowling	Mat	Balls	Runs	Wkts	BBI	BBM	Ave	Econ	SR	5w	10
First-class	6	264	154	3	1/26	2/79	51.33	3.50	88.0	0	0

DAN LAWRENCE

RHB / LB / R1 / W0 / MVP89

FULL NAME: Daniel William Lawrence
BORN: July 12, 1997, Whipps Cross, Essex
SQUAD NO: 28
EDUCATION: Trinity Catholic High School, London
TEAMS: Essex, England Lions
ROLE: Batsman
DEBUT: First-class: 2015; List A: 2016; T20: 2015

ESSEX

BEST BATTING: 161 Essex vs Surrey, The Oval, 2015
BEST BOWLING: 1-0 England Lions vs South Africa A, Canterbury, 2017

FAMILY TIES? My dad is the groundsman at Chingford Cricket Club. My great uncle played for England
CRICKETING HEROES? Ricky Ponting, Graeme Smith, AB de Villiers
NON-CRICKETING HEROES? Martin Luther King, David Beckham
TWITTER: @Lawrenc28Daniel

Batting	Mat	Inns	NO	Runs	HS	Ave	SR	100	50	Ct	St
First-class	40	62	7	2359	161	42.89	53.56	7	10	32	0
List A	11	9	0	159	35	17.66	79.89	0	0	5	0
T20s	28	24	3	467	47	22.23	129.00	0	0	7	0

Bowling	Mat	Balls	Runs	Wkts	BBI	BBM	Ave	Econ	SR	5w	10
First-class	40	324	214	7	1/0	2/8	30.57	3.96	46.2	0	0
List A	11	276	255	6	3/35	3/35	42.50	5.54	46.0	0	0
T20s	28	216	255	14	3/21	3/21	18.21	7.08	15.4	0	0

JACK LEACH — LHB / SLA / RO / W2 / MVP53

SOMERSET

FULL NAME: Matthew Jack Leach
BORN: June 22, 1991, Taunton, Somerset
SQUAD NO: 17
HEIGHT: 6ft
NICKNAME: Nut, Nutter
EDUCATION: Bishop Fox's Community School; Richard Huish College; Cardiff Metropolitan University
TEAMS: Somerset, England Lions
ROLE: Bowler
DEBUT: First-class: 2012; List A: 2012

BEST BATTING: 52 Somerset vs Lancashire, Old Trafford, 2017
BEST BOWLING: 7-106 Somerset vs Warwickshire, Taunton, 2015

WHAT GOT YOU INTO CRICKET? Watching Somerset from a young age
STRANGEST THING SEEN IN A GAME? Marcus Trescothick offering some banter
'ROY OF THE ROVERS' MOMENT? Being involved in a last-wicket partnership with Tim Groenewald to beat Surrey in the County Championship
HOW WOULD YOUR TEAMMATES DESCRIBE YOU IN THREE WORDS? What a nut
BEST OPPOSING PLAYER IN COUNTY CRICKET? Jeetan Patel (War)
CRICKETING HERO? It pains me to say this but it used to be Marcus Trescothick! Now it's Jos Buttler – I like how he keeps his nut down and gets on with it
NON-CRICKETING HERO? Terry Tibbs from Fonejacker
IF YOU WEREN'T A CRICKETER? I'd work at Sainsbury's
SURPRISING FACT? I wrote a letter to Marcus Trescothick asking for advice when I was about 10 years old. He sent me a long reply and I still have the letter. What a man
TWITTER: @jackleach1991

Batting	Mat	Inns	NO	Runs	HS	Ave	SR	100	50	Ct	St
First-class	54	70	18	625	52	12.01	34.64	0	1	17	0
List A	16	5	2	22	18	7.33	44.00	0	0	9	0

Bowling	Mat	Balls	Runs	Wkts	BBI	BBM	Ave	Econ	SR	5w	10
First-class	54	10791	4801	185	7/106	11/180	25.95	2.66	58.3	13	1
List A	16	824	641	21	3/7	3/7	30.52	4.66	39.2	0	0

FULL NAME: Joseph Leach
BORN: October 30, 1990, Stafford
SQUAD NO: 23
HEIGHT: 6ft
NICKNAME: Leachy, Lusty SSSB
EDUCATION: Shrewsbury School; University of Leeds
TEAMS: Worcestershire
ROLE: Allrounder
DEBUT: First-class: 2012; List A: 2012; T20: 2013

WORCESTERSHIRE

BEST BATTING: 114 Worcestershire vs Gloucestershire, Cheltenham, 2013
BEST BOWLING: 6-73 Worcestershire vs Warwickshire, Edgbaston, 2015
COUNTY CAP: 2012

WHAT GOT YOU INTO CRICKET? My grandfather throwing balls at me in the back garden
FAMILY TIES? My brother Steve has played for Oxford MCCU and is captain of Shropshire CCC
'ROY OF THE ROVERS' MOMENT? Taking a hat-trick with the first three balls of our one-day game with Northants in 2015. But it was bitter-sweet – we still managed to lose the game
BEST THING ABOUT YOUR HOME GROUND? The view is one of the best in the world
BEST OPPOSING PLAYER IN COUNTY CRICKET? Wayne Madsen (Der)
YOUNG OPPOSING PLAYER WHO HAS IMPRESSED YOU? Jofra Archer (Sus) – proper bowler
SURPRISING FACT ABOUT YOU? I studied French at university
SURPRISING FACT ABOUT A TEAMMATE? If Josh Tongue runs fast enough he takes off like Dumbo
NON-CRICKETING HERO? Nuno Espírito Santo – taking Wolves to the Premier League
UNUSUAL OBJECT AT HOME? A garden gnome painted in Wolves colours and with Steve Bull's name on the back
TWITTER: @joeleach230

Batting	Mat	Inns	NO	Runs	HS	Ave	SR	100	50	Ct	St
First-class	70	102	12	2386	114	26.51	64.31	2	16	20	0
List A	31	25	7	490	63	27.22	103.15	0	1	8	0
T20s	51	32	8	260	24	10.83	114.03	0	0	10	0

Bowling	Mat	Balls	Runs	Wkts	BBI	BBM	Ave	Econ	SR	5w	10
First-class	70	10746	6472	246	6/73	10/122	26.30	3.61	43.6	12	1
List A	31	1398	1404	36	4/30	4/30	39.00	6.02	38.8	0	0
T20s	51	825	1296	52	5/33	5/33	24.92	9.42	15.8	1	0

JACK LEANING

RHB / RMF / R0 / W0

FULL NAME: Jack Andrew Leaning
BORN: October 18, 1993, Bristol
SQUAD NO: 34
HEIGHT: 6ft
EDUCATION: Archbishop Holgate's School, York; York College
TEAMS: Yorkshire
ROLE: Batsman
DEBUT: First-class: 2013; List A: 2012; T20: 2013

BEST BATTING: 123 Yorkshire vs Somerset, Taunton, 2015
BEST BOWLING: 2-30 Yorkshire vs MCC, Abu Dhabi, 2016
COUNTY CAP: 2016

TWITTER: @JackLeaning1
NOTES: Son of former York City goalkeeper Andy, Leaning wrote himself into the Yorkshire record books when he hit an unbeaten 164 for the county's U14 side against Cheshire. He was Yorkshire's Academy Player of the Year in 2012 and made his List A debut in the same season. He made his first-class debut in 2013 against Surrey at Headingley and played 10 Championship matches in 2014, top-scoring with 99. Made his maiden Championship century in 2015 and added two more as he compiled 922 runs. Struggled in 2016, with just 233 runs in 15 Championship innings, but improved last summer (454 runs at 30.27)

Batting	Mat	Inns	NO	Runs	HS	Ave	SR	100	50	Ct	St
First-class	51	79	8	2269	123	31.95	44.39	4	11	39	0
List A	40	35	6	919	131*	31.68	82.27	2	4	18	0
T20s	41	37	10	785	64	29.07	137.47	0	2	18	0

Bowling	Mat	Balls	Runs	Wkts	BBI	BBM	Ave	Econ	SR	5w	10
First-class	51	340	270	3	2/30	2/30	90.00	4.76	113.3	0	0
List A	40	255	236	9	5/22	5/22	26.22	5.55	28.3	1	0
T20s	41	12	30	0	-	-	-	15.00	-	0	0

FULL NAME: Alexander Zak Lees
BORN: April 14, 1993, Halifax, Yorkshire
SQUAD NO: 14
HEIGHT: 6ft 3in
NICKNAME: Leesy
EDUCATION: Holy Trinity Senior School, Halifax
TEAMS: Yorkshire, England Lions
ROLE: Batsman
DEBUT: First-class: 2010; List A: 2011; T20: 2013

YORKSHIRE

BEST BATTING: 275* Yorkshire vs Derbyshire, Chesterfield, 2013
BEST BOWLING: 2-51 Yorkshire vs Middlesex, Lord's, 2016
COUNTY CAP: 2014

'ROY OF THE ROVERS' MOMENT? My 275 not out against Derbyshire in 2013
CRICKETING HEROES? Brian Lara and Matthew Hayden
IF YOU WEREN'T A CRICKETER? I'd be a policeman
SURPRISING FACT? I do a bit of magic on the side
TWITTER: @aleesy14
NOTES: Yorkshire's leading run-scorer in the Championship in 2016 (1,165 runs) and captained the side in limited-overs cricket that summer before handing over to Gary Ballance. Found it tougher last summer, with 514 Championship runs at 24.14, and could not cement a place in the T20 or 50-over sides

Batting	Mat	Inns	NO	Runs	HS	Ave	SR	100	50	Ct	St
First-class	85	144	12	4785	275*	36.25	48.44	12	22	62	0
List A	46	42	2	1172	102	29.30	73.34	1	8	16	0
T20s	37	36	2	857	67*	25.20	121.90	0	4	12	0
Bowling	Mat	Balls	Runs	Wkts	BBI	BBM	Ave	Econ	SR	5w	10
First-class	85	54	77	2	2/51	2/51	38.50	8.55	27.0	0	0
List A	46	-	-	-	-	-	-	-	-	-	-
T20s	37	-	-	-	-	-	-	-	-	-	-

TOBY LESTER

LHB / LFM / R0 / W0

FULL NAME: Toby James Lester
BORN: April 5, 1993, Blackpool
SQUAD NO: 5
HEIGHT: 6ft 4 in
NICKNAME: Tobs
EDUCATION: Baines High School, Blackpool; Rossall School, Lancashire; Loughborough University
TEAMS: Lancashire
ROLE: Bowler
DEBUT: First-class: 2012

BEST BATTING: 2* Loughborough MCCU vs Sussex, Hove, 2014
BEST BOWLING: 3-50 Lancashire vs Essex, Old Trafford, 2015

WHAT GOT YOU INTO CRICKET? Playing cricket in the back garden with my brothers
'ROY OF THE ROVERS' MOMENT? Making my debut for Lancashire and taking my first wicket
BEST THING ABOUT YOUR HOME GROUND? Being able to walk out onto the pitch and know how many unbelievable players have played there
WHERE IS PARADISE? Sydney
CRICKETING HERO? Andrew Flintoff
NON-CRICKETING HERO? Will Ferrell
TWITTER: @lobylester
NOTES: Left-arm pace bowler who made his first-class debut for Loughborough MCCU in 2014. Lester impressed with his performances for Lancashire Second XI in 2015, earning him a first call-up to the senior side for two matches and a Championship debut against Essex at Old Trafford. Played two more Championship matches in 2016 without taking a wicket and didn't feature at all last summer

Batting	Mat	Inns	NO	Runs	HS	Ave	SR	100	50	Ct	St
First-class	10	11	7	6	2*	1.50	9.37	0	0	2	0

Bowling	Mat	Balls	Runs	Wkts	BBI	BBM	Ave	Econ	SR	5w	10
First-class	10	1278	821	9	3/50	3/73	91.22	3.85	142.0	0	0

RICHARD LEVI

RHB / RM / R0 / W0 / MVP38

FULL NAME: Richard Ernst Levi
BORN: January 14, 1988, Johannesburg, South Africa
SQUAD NO: 88
HEIGHT: 6ft
NICKNAME: Bear
EDUCATION: Wynberg Boys' High School, Cape Town; University of South Africa
TEAMS: South Africa, Northamptonshire, Cape Cobras, Mumbai Indians, Somerset, Western Province
ROLE: Batsman
DEBUT: T20I: 2012; First-class: 2006; List A: 2005; T20: 2008

BEST BATTING: 168 Northamptonshire vs Essex, Northampton, 2015

'ROY OF THE ROVERS' MOMENT? Making my debuts for my province, South Africa and Northamptonshire
BEST THING ABOUT YOUR HOME GROUND? The support of the crowd
YOUNG OPPOSING PLAYER WHO HAS IMPRESSED YOU? Max Holden (Mid) – he has unbelievable gnashers
IF YOU WEREN'T A CRICKETER? I'd be a lumberjack
SURPRISING FACT ABOUT YOU? I like chalk
SURPRISING FACT ABOUT A TEAMMATE? Adam Rossington is a teetotaller
WHERE IS PARADISE? At the bottom of a pint
CRICKETING HERO? Gary Kirsten – he worked hard to achieve what he did and still does to this day
NON-CRICKETING HEROES? Roger Federer – for his longevity. Also my old man – he did everything for me, no questions asked
TWITTER: @RichardLevi88

Batting	Mat	Inns	NO	Runs	HS	Ave	SR	100	50	Ct	St
T20Is	13	13	2	236	117*	21.45	141.31	1	1	4	0
First-class	88	144	15	5012	168	38.85	68.62	10	29	69	0
List A	127	119	6	4285	166	37.92	106.06	8	27	40	0
T20s	189	180	11	4837	117*	28.62	144.56	3	32	51	0
Bowling	Mat	Balls	Runs	Wkts	BBI	BBM	Ave	Econ	SR	5w	10
T20Is	13	-	-	-	-	-	-	-	-	-	-
First-class	88	-	-	-	-	-	-	-	-	-	-
List A	127	-	-	-	-	-	-	-	-	-	-
T20s	189	-	-	-	-	-	-	-	-	-	-

JAKE LIBBY

RHB / OB / R0 / W0

NOTTINGHAMSHIRE

FULL NAME: Jacob Daniel Libby
BORN: January 3, 1993, Plymouth, Devon
SQUAD NO: 2
HEIGHT: 5ft 8in
NICKNAME: Libs
EDUCATION: Plymouth College; Truro College, Cornwall; Cardiff Metropolitan University
TEAMS: Nottinghamshire, Northamptonshire
ROLE: Batsman
DEBUT: First-class: 2014

BEST BATTING: 144 Nottinghamshire vs Durham, Chester-le-Street, 2016
BEST BOWLING: 1-13 Northamptonshire vs Leicestershire, Leicester, 2016

WHAT GOT YOU INTO CRICKET? My dad played for Looe CC and I played with him after his games on a Saturday
FAMILY TIES? My brother plays and captains Callington CC in the Cornish Premier League
BEST ADVICE EVER RECEIVED? Be relentless
'ROY OF THE ROVERS' MOMENT? My maiden first-class hundred on my Championship debut at Trent Bridge in 2014
BEST THING ABOUT YOUR HOME GROUND? The history
YOUNG OPPOSING PLAYER WHO HAS IMPRESSED YOU? Ben Duckett (Nor)
IF YOU WEREN'T A CRICKETER? I'd be a pilot
SURPRISING FACT ABOUT YOU? I played the lead role in all the school plays
SURPRISING FACT ABOUT A TEAMMATE? Luke Wood thinks he's a model
WHERE IS PARADISE? The east coast of Tasmania
CRICKETING HERO? Marcus Trescothick – I grew up watching him at Taunton
NON-CRICKETING HERO? Tiger Woods – he was relentless
UNUSUAL OBJECT AT HOME? A giant Minion teddy
TWITTER: @JakeLibby1

Batting	Mat	Inns	NO	Runs	HS	Ave	SR	100	50	Ct	St
First-class	36	59	4	1723	144	31.32	41.22	4	6	10	0

Bowling	Mat	Balls	Runs	Wkts	BBI	BBM	Ave	Econ	SR	5w	10
First-class	36	365	224	3	1/13	1/22	74.66	3.68	121.6	0	0

CHRIS LIDDLE

RHB / LMF / R0 / W0

FULL NAME: Christopher John Liddle
BORN: February 1, 1984, Middlesbrough, Yorkshire
SQUAD NO: 23
HEIGHT: 6ft 4in
NICKNAME: Lids
EDUCATION: Nunthorpe Comprehensive, Middlesborough; Teeside Tertiary College
TEAMS: Gloucestershire, Dhaka Gladiators, Leicestershire, Sussex
ROLE: Bowler
DEBUT: First-class: 2005; List A: 2006; T20: 2008

GLOUCESTERSHIRE

BEST BATTING: 53 Sussex vs Worcestershire, Hove, 2007
BEST BOWLING: 3-42 Leicestershire vs Somerset, Leicester, 2006

WHAT GOT YOU INTO CRICKET? My primary school teacher
FAMILY TIES? My brother Andrew plays in the North Yorkshire and Durham League
BEST ADVICE EVER RECEIVED? Always remember why you play cricket in the first place
'ROY OF THE ROVERS' MOMENT? My five-wicket haul in T20 cricket
BEST THING ABOUT YOUR HOME GROUND? The view from the new pavilion
BEST OPPOSING PLAYER IN COUNTY CRICKET? Ben Brown (Sus)
YOUNG OPPOSING PLAYER WHO HAS IMPRESSED YOU? Jofra Archer (Sus)
IF YOU WEREN'T A CRICKETER? I'd be playing left wing for Middlesbrough FC
SURPRISING FACT ABOUT YOU? I occasionally DJ for friends
SURPRISING FACT ABOUT A TEAMMATE? Craig Miles carries hand wipes at all times to clean any surface he may come in contact with
WHERE IS PARADISE? Cape Town
CRICKETING HERO? Ryan Sidebottom – not only was he a fine bowler, he's also a thoroughly nice guy
TWITTER: @chrisliddle11

Batting	Mat	Inns	NO	Runs	HS	Ave	SR	100	50	Ct	St
First-class	31	32	16	197	53	12.31	42.73	0	1	8	0
List A	69	29	9	125	18	6.25	70.22	0	0	18	0
T20s	83	17	9	54	16	6.75	69.23	0	0	21	0

Bowling	Mat	Balls	Runs	Wkts	BBI	BBM	Ave	Econ	SR	5w	10
First-class	31	3904	2204	44	3/42	4/82	50.09	3.38	88.7	0	0
List A	69	2669	2581	97	5/18	5/18	26.60	5.80	27.5	3	0
T20s	83	1558	2149	88	5/17	5/17	24.42	8.27	17.7	1	0

ARRON LILLEY

RHB / OB / R0 / W0

LANCASHIRE

FULL NAME: Arron Mark Lilley
BORN: April 1, 1991, Tameside, Lancashire
SQUAD NO: 19
HEIGHT: 6ft 2in
NICKNAME: The Bigshow, Lill, Azza
EDUCATION: Mossley Hollins High School, Tameside; Ashton Sixth Form
TEAMS: Lancashire
ROLE: Bowler
DEBUT: First-class: 2013; List A: 2012; T20: 2013

BEST BATTING: 63 Lancashire vs Derbyshire, Southport, 2015
BEST BOWLING: 5-23 Lancashire vs Derbyshire, Southport, 2015

WHAT GOT YOU INTO CRICKET? My grandads and my dad played at my local club, so I was there from a very young age
STRANGEST THING SEEN IN A GAME? Liam Livingstone trying to throw the stumps down from slip and hitting Steven Croft on the back of the knee
'ROY OF THE ROVERS' MOMENT? Winning the T20 Blast with Lancashire in 2015
HOW WOULD YOUR TEAMMATES DESCRIBE YOU IN THREE WORDS? Confident, loud, aggressive
CRICKETING HEROES? Shane Warne, Graeme Swann, Andrew Flintoff
NON-CRICKETING HEROES? Jim Carrey (funniest guy in the world), Paul Scholes (aka Sat Nav)
IF YOU WEREN'T A CRICKETER? I'd be a biomechanical scientist
UNUSUAL OBJECT AT HOME? A didgeridoo
TWITTER: @Arronlilley20

Batting	Mat	Inns	NO	Runs	HS	Ave	SR	100	50	Ct	St
First-class	13	17	5	398	63	33.16	94.31	0	2	4	0
List A	11	4	1	20	10	6.66	111.11	0	0	5	0
T20s	55	27	7	253	38	12.65	150.59	0	0	26	0

Bowling	Mat	Balls	Runs	Wkts	BBI	BBM	Ave	Econ	SR	5w	10
First-class	13	2454	1296	36	5/23	6/151	36.00	3.16	68.1	2	0
List A	11	372	321	15	4/30	4/30	21.40	5.17	24.8	0	0
T20s	55	861	1040	39	3/31	3/31	26.66	7.24	22.0	0	0

LIAM LIVINGSTONE

RHB / OB / R0 / W0 / MVP30

FULL NAME: Liam Stephen Livingstone
BORN: August 4, 1993, Barrow-in-Furness, Cumbria
SQUAD NO: 7
HEIGHT: 6ft 2in
NICKNAME: Livvy, Livvo
EDUCATION: Chetwynde School, Barrow-in-Furness
TEAMS: England, Lancashire
ROLE: Batsman
DEBUT: T20I: 2017; First-class: 2016; List A: 2015; T20: 2015

BEST BATTING: 224 Lancashire vs Warwickshire, Old Trafford, 2017
BEST BOWLING: 6-52 Lancashire vs Surrey, Old Trafford, 2017

WHAT GOT YOU INTO CRICKET? Playing on the outfield at Barrow CC from a very early age
FAMILY TIES? Father and brother played low-level club cricket
'ROY OF THE ROVERS' MOMENT? Winning the T20 Blast in 2015
HOW WOULD YOUR TEAMMATES DESCRIBE YOU IN THREE WORDS? Maverick, sociable, outgoing
SUPERSTITIONS? Left foot onto pitch first
BEST PLAYER IN COUNTY CRICKET? Joe Root (Yor)
YOUNG OPPOSING PLAYER WHO HAS IMPRESSED YOU? Mason Crane (Ham)
CRICKETING HEROES? Andrew Flintoff – so good to watch as a young kid. Shane Warne – I was a leg-spinner growing up
NON-CRICKETING HEROES? David Beckham
SURPRISING FACT? I scored 350 in a club game. I support Blackburn Rovers FC
TWITTER: @liaml4893

Batting	Mat	Inns	NO	Runs	HS	Ave	SR	100	50	Ct	St
T20Is	2	2	0	16	16	8.00	84.21	0	0	0	0
First-class	33	55	11	2020	224	45.90	58.01	6	10	46	0
List A	35	28	1	928	129	34.37	95.08	1	5	15	0
T20s	42	38	4	745	61	21.91	132.32	0	2	17	0

Bowling	Mat	Balls	Runs	Wkts	BBI	BBM	Ave	Econ	SR	5w	10
T20Is	2	-	-	-	-	-	-	-	-	-	-
First-class	33	1368	751	17	6/52	6/52	44.17	3.29	80.4	1	0
List A	35	718	633	17	3/51	3/51	37.23	5.28	42.2	0	0
T20s	42	51	59	4	2/11	2/11	14.75	6.94	12.7	0	0

DAVID LLOYD

RHB / OB / R0 / W0

FULL NAME: David Liam Lloyd
BORN: June 15, 1992, St Asaph, Denbighshire, Wales
SQUAD NO: 14
HEIGHT: 6ft
NICKNAME: Ram
EDUCATION: Darland High School, Wrexham; Shrewsbury School
TEAMS: Glamorgan
ROLE: Batsman
DEBUT: First-class: 2012; List A: 2014; T20: 2014

BEST BATTING: 107 Glamorgan vs Kent, Canterbury, 2016
BEST BOWLING: 3-36 Glamorgan vs Northamptonshire, Swansea, 2016

FAMILY TIES? My father and both of my uncles played local cricket and represented Wales Minor Counties
'ROY OF THE ROVERS' MOMENT? Scoring my maiden first-class hundred in 2016
BEST THING ABOUT YOUR HOME GROUND? Cardiff is a great city
BEST OPPOSING PLAYER IN COUNTY CRICKET? Darren Stevens (Ken)
YOUNG OPPOSING PLAYER WHO HAS IMPRESSED YOU? Joe Clarke (Wor)
IF YOU WEREN'T A CRICKETER? I'd be an actor
SURPRISING FACT ABOUT YOU? I support Wrexham FC and I have a degree in Economics
CRICKETING HERO? Jacques Kallis and Brendon McCullum – both liked to play attacking cricket and are great to watch
NON-CRICKETING HERO? Jamie Vardy (he's shown that it's never too late) and Usain Bolt (trained hard but always wore a smile on his face)
TWITTER: @lloyddl2010

Batting	Mat	Inns	NO	Runs	HS	Ave	SR	100	50	Ct	St
First-class	45	75	9	1797	107	27.22	61.03	3	6	15	0
List A	30	24	1	469	65	20.39	81.00	0	2	4	0
T20s	29	25	1	459	97*	19.12	120.47	0	2	9	0
Bowling	Mat	Balls	Runs	Wkts	BBI	BBM	Ave	Econ	SR	5w	10
First-class	45	2943	2032	42	3/36	3/53	48.38	4.14	70.0	0	0
List A	30	571	563	15	5/53	5/53	37.53	5.91	38.0	1	0
T20s	29	24	44	3	2/13	2/13	14.66	11.00	8.0	0	0

ADAM LYTH

LHB / OB / R3 / W0 / MVP26

FULL NAME: Adam Lyth
BORN: September 25, 1987, Whitby, Yorkshire
SQUAD NO: 9
HEIGHT: 5ft 9in
NICKNAME: Lythy, Budge, Peanut
EDUCATION: Caedmon School; Whitby Community School
TEAMS: England, Yorkshire
ROLE: Batsman
DEBUT: Test: 2015; First-class: 2007; List A: 2006; T20: 2008

YORKSHIRE

BEST BATTING: 251 Yorkshire vs Lancashire, Old Trafford, 2014
BEST BOWLING: 2-9 Yorkshire vs Middlesex, Scarborough, 2016
COUNTY CAP: 2010

FAMILY TIES? My brother and dad played for Scarborough and my grandad played for Whitby
CRICKETING HERO? Graham Thorpe – I just liked the way he batted
IF YOU WEREN'T A CRICKETER? I'd be playing football
SURPRISING FACT? I had trials with Manchester City before choosing cricket
TWITTER: @lythy09

Batting	Mat	Inns	NO	Runs	HS	Ave	SR	100	50	Ct	St
Tests	7	13	0	265	107	20.38	50.09	1	0	8	0
First-class	148	245	11	9202	251	39.32		22	48	188	0
List A	106	99	7	3131	136	34.03	92.33	3	16	51	0
T20s	88	79	2	1793	161	23.28	137.60	1	8	47	0

Bowling	Mat	Balls	Runs	Wkts	BBI	BBM	Ave	Econ	SR	5w	10
Tests	7	6	0	0	-	-	-	0.00	-	0	0
First-class	148	2111	1290	29	2/9	2/9	44.48	3.66	72.7	0	0
List A	106	252	260	3	1/6	1/6	86.66	6.19	84.0	0	0
T20s	88	78	88	4	2/5	2/5	22.00	6.76	19.5	0	0

CHARLIE MACDONELL

RHB / OB / R0 / W0

FULL NAME: Charles Michael Macdonell
BORN: February 23, 1995, Basingstoke, Hampshire
SQUAD NO: 3
HEIGHT: 5ft 9in
NICKNAME: Cmac
EDUCATION: Wellingborough School, Northampton; Durham University
TEAMS: Derbyshire
ROLE: Allrounder
DEBUT: First-class: 2015; List A: 2016

BEST BATTING: 91 Durham MCCU vs Gloucestershire, Bristol, 2016
BEST BOWLING: 2-57 Derbyshire vs West Indians, Derby, 2017

WHAT FIRST GOT YOU INTO CRICKET? It was on the TV and I was taken to Horton House CC aged six
STRANGEST THING SEEN IN A GAME? A drunk man coming on to the pitch to give advice to the players at a Durham MCCU game – he thought he was watching Durham CCC
'ROY OF THE ROVERS' MOMENT? Scoring a hundred for Durham MCCU against Warwickshire at Edgbaston in 2015
YOUNG OPPOSING PLAYER WHO HAS IMPRESSED YOU? Joe Clarke (Wor)
SURPRISING FACT? I was a model for the Collingwood College Fashion Show at university
CRICKETING HEROES? AB de Villiers, Ravi Ashwin
NON-CRICKETING HEROES? Roger Federer, Will Smith, Muhammad Ali
UNUSUAL OBJECT AT HOME? Some gravity boots

Batting	Mat	Inns	NO	Runs	HS	Ave	SR	100	50	Ct	St
First-class	6	10	3	325	91	46.42	46.96	0	2	1	0
List A	2	1	0	19	19	19.00	59.37	0	0	0	0

Bowling	Mat	Balls	Runs	Wkts	BBI	BBM	Ave	Econ	SR	5w	10
First-class	6	462	308	2	2/57	2/60	154.00	4.00	231.0	0	0
List A	2	-	-	-	-	-	-	-	-	-	-

WAYNE MADSEN

RHB / OB / R4 / W0 / MVP16

FULL NAME: Wayne Lee Madsen
BORN: January 2, 1984, Durban, South Africa
SQUAD NO: 77
HEIGHT: 5ft 11in
NICKNAME: Madders, Mads
EDUCATION: Highbury Preparatory School;
Kearsney College; University of South Africa
TEAMS: Derbyshire, KwaZulu-Natal
ROLE: Batsman
DEBUT: First-class: 2004; List A: 2004; T20: 2010

DERBYSHIRE

BEST BATTING: 231* Derbyshire vs Northamptonshire, Northampton, 2012
BEST BOWLING: 3-45 KwaZulu-Natal vs Eastern Province, Port Elizabeth, 2008
COUNTY CAP: 2011

FAMILY TIES? My uncles Trevor Madsen and Henry Fotheringham represented South Africa. My other uncle Mike Madsen played for Natal and so did my cousin Greg Fotheringham
STRANGEST THING SEEN IN A GAME? Snow stopped play, Derbyshire vs Glamorgan, Derby, 2016
'ROY OF THE ROVERS' MOMENT? Lifting the Division Two trophy with Derbyshire in 2012. We were tipped to finish bottom at the start of the season
YOUNG OPPOSING PLAYER WHO HAS IMPRESSED YOU? Callum Parkinson (Lei)
CRICKETING HEROES? Jonty Rhodes (for his energy), Dale Benkenstein (my first professional captain)
IF YOU WEREN'T A CRICKETER? I'd be a hockey player
SURPRISING FACT? I hold the Guinness World Record for cricket's version of keepy-uppies: the most bat touches in one minute (282)
UNUSUAL OBJECT AT HOME? A biltong-maker
TWITTER: @waynemadsen2017

Batting	Mat	Inns	NO	Runs	HS	Ave	SR	100	50	Ct	St
First-class	156	277	22	10031	231*	39.33	50.03	26	51	138	0
List A	88	80	16	2638	138	41.21	87.40	4	16	59	0
T20s	86	84	14	2014	86*	28.77	130.18	0	12	28	0

Bowling	Mat	Balls	Runs	Wkts	BBI	BBM	Ave	Econ	SR	5w	10
First-class	156	2469	1368	25	3/45	3/60	54.72	3.32	98.7	0	0
List A	88	272	218	11	3/27	3/27	19.81	4.80	24.7	0	0
T20s	86	342	419	16	2/20	2/20	26.18	7.35	21.3	0	0

STEVE MAGOFFIN

LHB / RFM / RO / W5

WORCESTERSHIRE

FULL NAME: Steven James Magoffin
BORN: December 17, 1979, Corinda, Queensland, Australia
SQUAD NO: 64
HEIGHT: 6ft 4in
NICKNAME: Mal
EDUCATION: Indooroopilly High School; Curtin University, Perth
TEAMS: Worcestershire, Queensland, Surrey, Sussex, Western Australia
ROLE: Bowler
DEBUT: First-class: 2004; List A: 2004; T20: 2006

BEST BATTING: 79 Western Australia vs Tasmania, Perth, 2008
BEST BOWLING: 8-20 Sussex vs Somerset, Horsham, 2013
COUNTY CAP: 2013 (Sussex)

FAMILY TIES? My older brother Chris played grade cricket in Brisbane
ROY OF THE ROVERS' MOMENT? Hitting the winning runs in the 2011/12 Sheffield Shield final for the Queensland Bulls
BEST OPPOSING PLAYER IN COUNTY CRICKET? Samit Patel (Not)
YOUNG OPPOSING PLAYER WHO HAS IMPRESSED YOU? Jofra Archer (Sus) – effortless pace, and he is becoming more skilful and smarter with every game. He gives the ball a good whack as well
SURPRISING FACT ABOUT YOU? I have dual citizenship
SURPRISING FACT ABOUT A TEAMMATE? Not sure yet – they're all new to me!
WHERE IS PARADISE? Rainbow Bay, Gold Coast, Australia
CRICKETING HERO? Curtly Ambrose – I grew up watching him dominate international cricket. He was so skilful and intimidating
NON-CRICKETING HERO? My kids George and Holly
TWITTER: @magsy64

Batting	Mat	Inns	NO	Runs	HS	Ave	SR	100	50	Ct	St
First-class	154	207	54	2592	79	16.94	47.56	0	5	35	0
List A	53	31	20	228	24*	20.72	76.25	0	0	12	0
T20s	12	3	1	21	11*	10.50	116.66	0	0	3	0

Bowling	Mat	Balls	Runs	Wkts	BBI	BBM	Ave	Econ	SR	5w	10
First-class	154	30547	13498	581	8/20	12/31	23.23	2.65	52.5	27	4
List A	53	2646	2084	66	4/58	4/58	31.57	4.72	40.0	0	0
T20s	12	246	364	9	2/15	2/15	40.44	8.87	27.3	0	0

SAQIB MAHMOOD

RHB / RFM / R0 / W0

FULL NAME: Saqib Mahmood
BORN: February 25, 1997, Birmingham
SQUAD NO: 25
HEIGHT: 6ft 3in
NICKNAME: Saq
EDUCATION: Matthew Moss High School, Rochdale
TEAMS: Lancashire, England Lions
ROLE: Bowler
DEBUT: First-class: 2016; List A: 2016; T20: 2015

BEST BATTING: 9 England Lions vs West Indies A, North Sound, Antigua, 2018
BEST BOWLING: 4-50 Lancashire vs Surrey, Old Trafford, 2017

TWITTER: @SaqMahmood25
NOTES: Pace bowler Mahmood joined the Lancashire Academy four years ago. He made his England U19 debut in 2015, taking 3-12 to help rout South Africa for 77 at Northampton. He was part of the Lancashire U17 side that won the One-Day Cup and shared the two-day Championship in 2014. Made his full Lancashire debut in 2015, playing three T20s. Impressed for England at the 2016 U19 World Cup and was a regular member of Lancashire's 50-over side that summer. Took 12 wickets at 21.33 in three Championship matches in 2017 but did not feature in the short formats. Made his England Lions debut in 2016 and was on this winter's tour of the West Indies

Batting	Mat	Inns	NO	Runs	HS	Ave	SR	100	50	Ct	St
First-class	5	7	5	18	9	9.00	29.03	0	0	1	0
List A	11	4	4	38	27*	-	77.55	0	0	4	0
T20s	6	-	-	-	-	-	-	-	-	0	0

Bowling	Mat	Balls	Runs	Wkts	BBI	BBM	Ave	Econ	SR	5w	10
First-class	5	735	444	16	4/50	5/120	27.75	3.62	45.9	0	0
List A	11	444	459	8	3/55	3/55	57.37	6.20	55.5	0	0
T20s	6	98	125	8	3/12	3/12	15.62	7.65	12.2	0	0

GAVIN MAIN

RHB / RFM / R0 / W0

FULL NAME: Gavin Thomas Main
BORN: February 28, 1995, Lanark, Scotland
SQUAD NO: 20
HEIGHT: 6ft 1in
NICKNAME: Gav
EDUCATION: The High School of Glasgow; University of Strathclyde
TEAMS: Scotland, Durham
ROLE: Bowler
DEBUT: T20I: 2015; First-class: 2014; List A: 2015; T20: 2015

BEST BATTING: 13 Durham vs Northamptonshire, Chester-le-Street, 2017
BEST BOWLING: 3-72 Durham vs Nottinghamshire, Trent Bridge, 2014

'ROY OF THE ROVERS' MOMENT? Taking a wicket with my first ball on my T20I debut
BEST THING ABOUT YOUR HOME GROUND? The large boundaries – a bowler's best friend
BEST OPPOSING PLAYER IN COUNTY CRICKET? Sam Northeast (Ham)
YOUNG OPPOSING PLAYER WHO HAS IMPRESSED YOU? Jofra Archer (Sus) – he took us apart last summer
IF YOU WEREN'T A CRICKETER? I'd be working in finance
SURPRISING FACT ABOUT YOU? I was the Scotland U8 swimming champion
SURPRISING FACT ABOUT A TEAMMATE? George Harding competed in the national flag twirling championships when he was 12
WHERE IS PARADISE? Banff, Canada
CRICKETING HERO? Brett Lee
NON-CRICKETING HERO? David Beckham – he has completed life
TWITTER: @gmain95

Batting	Mat	Inns	NO	Runs	HS	Ave	SR	100	50	Ct	St
T20Is	4	-	-	-	-	-	-	-	-	1	0
First-class	4	4	2	13	13	6.50	40.62	0	0	1	0
List A	2	-	-	-	-	-	-	-	-	0	0
T20s	4	-	-	-	-	-	-	-	-	1	0

Bowling	Mat	Balls	Runs	Wkts	BBI	BBM	Ave	Econ	SR	5w	10
T20Is	4	24	34	2	1/13	1/13	17.00	8.50	12.0	0	0
First-class	4	402	319	8	3/72	3/72	39.87	4.76	50.2	0	0
List A	2	102	74	4	2/35	2/35	18.50	4.35	25.5	0	0
T20s	4	24	34	2	1/13	1/13	17.00	8.50	12.0	0	0

DAWID MALAN

LHB / LB / R2 / W0

FULL NAME: Dawid Johannes Malan
BORN: September 3, 1987, Roehampton
SQUAD NO: 29
HEIGHT: 6ft
NICKNAME: Mal, Mala
EDUCATION: Paarl Boys' High School; University of South Africa
TEAMS: England, Middlesex, Barisal Bulls, Boland, Peshawar Zalmi, Prime Doleshwar Sporting Club
ROLE: Batsman
DEBUT: Test: 2017; T20I: 2017; First-class: 2006; List A: 2006; T20: 2006

BEST BATTING: 182* Middlesex vs Nottinghamshire, Trent Bridge, 2015
BEST BOWLING: 5-61 Middlesex vs Lancashire, Liverpool, 2012
COUNTY CAP: 2010

FAMILY TIES? My dad Dawid played for Transvaal B and Western Province B and my brother Charl played for MCC Young Cricketers and Loughborough MCCU
SUPERSTITIONS? Too many to write down
CRICKETING HEROES? Gary Kirsten, Matthew Hayden, Mike Hussey – all fellow left-handers
NON-CRICKETING HEROES? My dad – he's always there supporting and helping when needed
IF YOU WEREN'T A CRICKETER? I would like to have gone into sports psychology
SURPRISING FACT? I love to go to the cinema by myself
TWITTER: @DJMalan29

Batting	Mat	Inns	NO	Runs	HS	Ave	SR	100	50	Ct	St
Tests	10	17	0	572	140	33.64	41.26	1	5	4	0
T20Is	5	5	0	250	78	50.00	150.60	0	4	1	0
First-class	156	265	19	9275	182*	37.70	51.91	20	49	160	0
List A	142	138	21	4928	185*	42.11	83.61	10	24	47	0
T20s	144	139	26	3841	115*	33.99	126.26	2	23	52	0

Bowling	Mat	Balls	Runs	Wkts	BBI	BBM	Ave	Econ	SR	5w	10
Tests	10	132	61	0	-	-	-	2.77	-	0	0
T20Is	5	12	27	1	1/27	1/27	27.00	13.50	12.0	0	0
First-class	156	3463	2138	52	5/61	5/61	41.11	3.70	66.5	1	0
List A	142	1203	1150	38	4/25	4/25	30.26	5.73	31.6	0	0
T20s	144	430	530	22	2/10	2/10	24.09	7.39	19.5	0	0

AIDEN MARKRAM

RHB / OB / R0 / W0

DURHAM

FULL NAME: Aiden Kyle Markram
BORN: October 4, 1994, Centurion, South Africa
SQUAD NO: 4
TEAMS: South Africa, Durham, Northerns, Titans
ROLE: Batsman
DEBUT: Test: 2017; ODI: 2017; First-class: 2014; List A: 2014; T20: 2014

BEST BATTING: 182 Northerns vs Western Province, Cape Town, 2016
BEST BOWLING: 1-2 Titans vs Dolphins, Pietermaritzburg, 2017

TWITTER: @AidzMarkram
NOTES: Markram is set to be available for Durham's first four County Championship games of the campaign before handing overseas duties to New Zealand's Tom Latham. The 23-year-old was included in South Africa's Test squad which toured England last summer but had to wait until last September to make his debut, scoring 97 against Bangladesh. Centuries followed in his next two Tests before he hit an impressive 94 against India in Centurion. Markram led South Africa to victory at the 2014 Under-19 World Cup and he has already been fast-tracked into the role at senior level, deputising for the injured Faf du Plessis during the ODI series against India earlier this year. "Aiden offers confidence and maturity at the top of the batting order and, despite being just 23 years old, he has already been recognised by South Africa as a leader in the dressing room," said Durham chairman Sir Ian Botham

Batting	Mat	Inns	NO	Runs	HS	Ave	SR	100	50	Ct	St
Tests	6	10	0	520	143	52.00	65.40	2	2	6	0
ODIs	7	7	0	193	66	27.57	88.12	0	1	4	0
First-class	42	70	5	3103	182	47.73	60.34	8	16	42	0
List A	33	32	1	1200	183	38.70	93.75	4	2	16	0
T20s	30	27	5	781	82	35.50	125.56	0	7	9	0

Bowling	Mat	Balls	Runs	Wkts	BBI	BBM	Ave	Econ	SR	5w	10
Tests	6	12	13	0	-	-	-	6.50	-	0	0
ODIs	7	30	38	2	2/18	2/18	19.00	7.60	15.0	0	0
First-class	42	364	187	2	1/2	1/2	93.50	3.08	182.0	0	0
List A	33	372	332	14	4/45	4/45	23.71	5.35	26.5	0	0
T20s	30	213	217	7	3/21	3/21	31.00	6.11	30.4	0	0

MITCHELL MARSH

RHB / RFM / R0 / W0

FULL NAME: Mitchell Ross Marsh
BORN: October 20, 1991, Perth, Australia
SQUAD NO: 8
TEAMS: Australia, Surrey, Deccan Chargers, Fremantle, Perth Scorchers, Pune Warriors, Rising Pune Supergiants, Western Australia
ROLE: Allrounder
DEBUT: Test: 2014; ODI: 2011; T20I: 2011; First-class: 2009; List A: 2009; T20: 2009

BEST BATTING: 211 Australia A vs India A, Allan Border Field, Sydney, 2014
BEST BOWLING: 6-84 Western Australia vs Queensland, Perth, 2011

TWITTER: @mitchmarsh235
NOTES: The Australian allrounder turned down the possible opportunity of IPL riches to take up a full-season contract across all formats for Surrey, subject to international commitments. Marsh arrives in England off the back of a superb 2017/18 Ashes campaign. In Perth he scored 181 in an innings victory, registering his first Test century in the process. A second hundred followed in the fifth and final Test of the series in Sydney, as he combined with his older brother Shaun – who will be representing Glamorgan this season – in a fifth-wicket partnership of 169. A three-time winner of the Big Bash League with Perth Scorchers, Marsh will be hoping he can help Surrey reach a first T20 Blast Finals Day since 2014

Batting	Mat	Inns	NO	Runs	HS	Ave	SR	100	50	Ct	St
Tests	24	39	5	994	181	29.23	53.78	2	2	11	0
ODIs	53	49	9	1428	102*	35.70	93.08	1	11	25	0
T20Is	9	9	3	133	36	22.16	127.88	0	0	2	0
First-class	80	135	12	3873	211	31.48	56.39	7	18	38	0
List A	102	95	18	2875	124	37.33	92.29	3	20	52	0
T20s	65	58	16	1323	77*	31.50	123.99	0	6	26	0

Bowling	Mat	Balls	Runs	Wkts	BBI	BBM	Ave	Econ	SR	5w	10
Tests	24	2089	1219	29	4/61	5/86	42.03	3.50	72.0	0	0
ODIs	53	1700	1564	44	5/33	5/33	35.54	5.52	38.6	1	0
T20Is	9	102	145	4	1/17	1/17	36.25	8.52	25.5	0	0
First-class	80	6380	3656	124	6/84	9/156	29.48	3.43	51.4	1	0
List A	102	2804	2525	84	5/33	5/33	30.05	5.40	33.3	2	0
T20s	65	791	1106	40	4/6	4/6	27.65	8.38	19.7	0	0

SHAUN MARSH
LHB / SLA / R0 / W0

GLAMORGAN

FULL NAME: Shaun Edward Marsh
BORN: July 9, 1983, Narrogin, Western Australia
SQUAD NO: 43
HEIGHT: 6ft
NICKNAME: Sos
TEAMS: Australia, Glamorgan, Kings XI Punjab, Perth Scorchers, Western Australia, Yorkshire
ROLE: Batsman
DEBUT: Test: 2011; ODI: 2008; T20I: 2008; First-class: 2001; List A: 2002; T20: 2006

BEST BATTING: 182 Australia vs West Indies, Hobart, 2015
BEST BOWLING: 2-20 Western Australia vs New South Wales, Sydney, 2003

TWITTER: @shaunmarsh9
NOTES: Marsh is an established Australian Test batsman who scored a hundred on debut against Sri Lanka in 2011 and starred in the 2017/18 Ashes series, scoring two centuries. The son of former Australia opener Geoff and brother of Mitchell, who will be playing for Surrey this season, Shaun had a first taste of the County Championship last year, averaging 112.50 in his two games for Yorkshire. He has signed a two-year deal with Glamorgan, whom he played T20 cricket for in 2012, topping their averages in that campaign with 209 runs at 52.25. Glamorgan captain Michael Hogan said: "I think he can adapt to any conditions. He's got a good defence and he can be attacking when he needs to be, but one thing that excites me is that he's really tough and has got a lot of presence out in the middle"

Batting	Mat	Inns	NO	Runs	HS	Ave	SR	100	50	Ct	St
Tests	28	49	2	1921	182	40.87	44.96	6	9	19	0
ODIs	53	52	2	1896	151	37.92	77.64	3	12	13	0
T20Is	15	15	1	255	47*	18.21	102.82	0	0	3	0
First-class	139	244	27	9073	182	41.81	47.93	24	44	129	0
List A	137	133	8	5377	186	43.01	79.31	13	30	46	0
T20s	164	161	23	5466	115	39.60	129.00	2	42	57	0

Bowling	Mat	Balls	Runs	Wkts	BBI	BBM	Ave	Econ	SR	5w	10
Tests	28	-	-	-	-	-	-	-	-	-	-
ODIs	53	-	-	-	-	-	-	-	-	-	-
T20Is	15	-	-	-	-	-	-	-	-	-	-
First-class	139	216	155	2	2/20	2/20	77.50	4.30	108.0	0	0
List A	137	36	31	1	1/14	1/14	31.00	5.16	36.0	0	0
T20s	164	12	13	0	-	-	-	6.50	-	0	0

BARRY MCCARTHY — RHB / RMF / R0 / W0

FULL NAME: Barry John McCarthy
BORN: September 13, 1992, Dublin
SQUAD NO: 60
HEIGHT: 6ft 1in
NICKNAME: Baz, Gordon Ramsay
EDUCATION: St Michaels Catholic Boys College, Dublin; University College Dublin
TEAMS: Ireland, Durham
ROLE: Bowler
DEBUT: ODI: 2016; First-class: 2015; List A: 2016; T20: 2016

DURHAM

BEST BATTING: 51* Durham vs Hampshire, Chester-le-Street, 2016
BEST BOWLING: 6-63 Durham vs Kent, Canterbury, 2017

FAMILY TIES? My sister Louise plays for Ireland and has significantly more caps than me
'ROY OF THE ROVERS' MOMENT? Playing against England at Lord's in May 2017
BEST THING ABOUT YOUR HOME GROUND? The lovely warm weather
BEST OPPOSING PLAYER IN COUNTY CRICKET? Samit Patel (Not)
YOUNG OPPOSING PLAYER WHO HAS IMPRESSED YOU? Josh Tongue (Wor)
SURPRISING FACT ABOUT YOU? I'm the best footballer on the Durham staff
SURPRISING FACT ABOUT A TEAMMATE? Graham Clark is a magician
WHERE IS PARADISE? Anywhere warm
CRICKETING HERO? Shane Watson – I've always been told I look like him. Both of us have blonde hair and are lbw candidates
NON-CRICKETING HERO? All my heroes are cricketers
TWITTER: @barrymccarthy2

Batting	Mat	Inns	NO	Runs	HS	Ave	SR	100	50	Ct	St
ODIs	19	11	2	75	16*	8.33	51.72	0	0	6	0
T20Is	2	2	0	0	0	0.00	0.00	0	0	0	0
First-class	14	20	6	360	51*	25.71	53.33	0	1	7	0
List A	23	15	3	147	39	12.25	72.41	0	0	6	0
T20s	14	6	1	3	2*	0.60	27.27	0	0	1	0

Bowling	Mat	Balls	Runs	Wkts	BBI	BBM	Ave	Econ	SR	5w	10
ODIs	19	986	970	41	5/46	5/46	23.65	5.90	24.0	1	0
T20Is	2	48	102	4	4/33	4/33	25.50	12.75	12.0	0	0
First-class	14	2283	1439	48	6/63	7/120	29.97	3.78	47.5	2	0
List A	23	1115	1101	47	5/46	5/46	23.42	5.92	23.7	1	0
T20s	14	255	407	17	4/33	4/33	23.94	9.57	15.0	0	0

CONOR MCKERR

RHB / RFM / R0 / W0

SURREY

FULL NAME: Conor McKerr
BORN: January 19, 1998, Johannesburg, South Africa
SQUAD NO: 83
HEIGHT: 6ft 5in
NICKNAME: Drago
EDUCATION: St John's College, Johannesburg
TEAMS: Surrey, Derbyshire
ROLE: Bowler
DEBUT: First-class: 2017

BEST BATTING: 17 Derbyshire vs Northamptonshire, Northampton, 2017
BEST BOWLING: 5-54 Derbyshire vs Northamptonshire, Northampton, 2017

WHAT GOT YOU INTO CRICKET? Watching Graeme Smith captain South Africa
BEST ADVICE EVER RECEIVED? Train harder than everyone so you can have more fun than everyone when you play
'ROY OF THE ROVERS' MOMENT? Taking my first 10-wicket haul in a match at Northampton while I was on loan at Derbyshire last season
BEST THING ABOUT YOUR HOME GROUND? It's The Oval – need I say more?
YOUNG OPPOSING PLAYER WHO HAS IMPRESSED YOU? Max Holden (Mid)
IF YOU WEREN'T A CRICKETER? I'd be going to university in Johannesburg
SURPRISING FACT ABOUT YOU? My favourite subject at school was drama
WHERE IS PARADISE? A house on a beach
CRICKETING HERO? Dale Steyn – the best bowler of our generation
NON-CRICKETING HERO? Adrian Norris – former Eastern Transvaal cricketer who has been a mentor and legend for me
TWITTER: @cemckerr83

Batting	Mat	Inns	NO	Runs	HS	Ave	SR	100	50	Ct	St
First-class	4	4	1	34	17	11.33	33.00	0	0	0	0

Bowling	Mat	Balls	Runs	Wkts	BBI	BBM	Ave	Econ	SR	5w	10
First-class	4	665	392	15	5/54	10/141	26.13	3.53	44.3	2	1

LEWIS MCMANUS

RHB / WK / R0 / W0

FULL NAME: Lewis David McManus
BORN: October 9, 1994, Poole, Dorset
SQUAD NO: 18
HEIGHT: 5ft 8in
NICKNAME: Lewy, King
EDUCATION: Clayesmore School, Bournemouth; University of Exeter
TEAMS: Hampshire
ROLE: Wicketkeeper
DEBUT: First-class: 2015; List A: 2016; T20: 2016

HAMPSHIRE

BEST BATTING: 132* Hampshire vs Surrey, Southampton, 2016

WHAT GOT YOU INTO CRICKET? It was a sport to play during the football off-season
STRANGEST THING SEEN IN A GAME? James Tomlinson's one-handed catch at fine-leg while holding a banana in the other hand during a first-class game
'ROY OF THE ROVERS' MOMENT? My maiden first-class century in 2016
HOW WOULD YOUR TEAMMATES DESCRIBE YOU IN THREE WORDS? Can't count
CRICKETING HEROES? Ricky Ponting, Andrew Flintoff
NON-CRICKETING HEROES? Floyd Mayweather, Usain Bolt, Rick Ross, my family
IF YOU WEREN'T A CRICKETER? I'd be a gym junkie
SURPRISING FACT? I play in the same team as Batman
UNUSUAL OBJECT AT HOME? A golf putter
TWITTER: @lewis_mcmanus

Batting	Mat	Inns	NO	Runs	HS	Ave	SR	100	50	Ct	St
First-class	24	34	4	936	132*	31.20	49.41	1	4	54	9
List A	23	17	2	290	47	19.33	81.92	0	0	18	6
T20s	19	15	2	206	59	15.84	124.09	0	1	7	4

Bowling	Mat	Balls	Runs	Wkts	BBI	BBM	Ave	Econ	SR	5w	10
First-class	24	-	-	-	-	-	-	-	-	-	-
List A	23	-	-	-	-	-	-	-	-	-	-
T20s	19	-	-	-	-	-	-	-	-	-	-

STUART MEAKER

RHB / RF / R0 / W1

SURREY

FULL NAME: Stuart Christopher Meaker
BORN: January 21, 1989, Pietermaritzburg, South Africa
SQUAD NO: 18
HEIGHT: 5ft 11in
NICKNAME: Meaks, Ten Bears
EDUCATION: Cranleigh Senior School, Surrey
TEAMS: England, Surrey, Auckland
ROLE: Bowler
DEBUT: ODI: 2011; T20I: 2012; First-class: 2008; List A: 2008; T20: 2010

BEST BATTING: 94 Surrey vs Bangladeshis, The Oval, 2010
BEST BOWLING: 8-52 Surrey vs Somerset, The Oval, 2012
COUNTY CAP: 2012

BEST THING ABOUT YOUR HOME GROUND? The Oval has the best T20 crowds in the country
BEST OPPOSING PLAYER IN COUNTY CRICKET? Samit Patel (Not)
YOUNG OPPOSING PLAYER WHO HAS IMPRESSED YOU? Jamie Porter (Ess) – just keeps taking poles
IF YOU WEREN'T A CRICKETER? I'd be a McDonald's manager
SURPRISING FACT ABOUT YOU? I have a certificate in corporate governance but still don't know what it means
CRICKETING HERO? Allan Donald
NON-CRICKETING HERO? My grandfather
TWITTER: @SMeaker18

Batting	Mat	Inns	NO	Runs	HS	Ave	SR	100	50	Ct	St
ODIs	2	2	0	2	1	1.00	12.50	0	0	0	0
T20Is	2	-	-	-	-	-	-	-	-	1	0
First-class	84	111	23	1404	94	15.95	37.42	0	6	16	0
List A	67	33	17	97	21*	6.06	49.23	0	0	18	0
T20s	32	11	6	46	17	9.20	121.05	0	0	13	0

Bowling	Mat	Balls	Runs	Wkts	BBI	BBM	Ave	Econ	SR	5w	10
ODIs	2	114	110	2	1/45	1/45	55.00	5.78	57.0	0	0
T20Is	2	47	70	2	1/28	1/28	35.00	8.93	23.5	0	0
First-class	84	13084	8289	276	8/52	11/167	30.03	3.80	47.4	11	2
List A	67	2520	2575	75	4/37	4/37	34.33	6.13	33.6	0	0
T20s	32	519	774	26	4/30	4/30	29.76	8.94	19.9	0	0

ALEX MELLOR

LHB / WK / R0 / W0

FULL NAME: Alexander James Mellor
BORN: July 22, 1991, Stoke-on-Trent, Staffordshire
SQUAD NO: 15
HEIGHT: 5ft 10in
NICKNAME: Al, Mella
EDUCATION: Westwood College; Staffordshire University
TEAMS: Warwickshire, Derbyshire
ROLE: Wicketkeeper
DEBUT: First-class: 2016; List A: 2016; T20: 2016

BEST BATTING: 59 Warwickshire vs Oxford MCCU, Oxford, 2017

FAMILY TIES? Dad represented Staffordshire age-groups and the senior side. My brother represented Staffordshire age-groups
BEST THING ABOUT YOUR HOME GROUND? The atmosphere at Edgbaston is the best in the country
BEST OPPOSING PLAYER IN COUNTY CRICKET? Shivnarine Chanderpaul (Lan)
IF YOU WEREN'T A CRICKETER? I'd be a sports coach
SURPRISING FACT ABOUT YOU? I'm generally right-handed but I bat left-handed
WHERE IS PARADISE? The Maldives
CRICKETING HERO? Bob Taylor – fantastic person, brilliant keeper. Albie Morkel – I've known him since I was 10, clean striker of the ball, matchwinner. Brian Mellor (my dad) – he taught me love for the game. Andrew Flintoff – so passionate and a game-changer
NON-CRICKETING HERO? Conor McGregor – he has a presence and confidence everywhere he goes
TWITTER: @alexmellor22

Batting	Mat	Inns	NO	Runs	HS	Ave	SR	100	50	Ct	St
First-class	9	16	1	282	59	18.80	40.11	0	1	15	0
List A	2	-	-	-	-	-	-	-	-	0	0
T20s	9	6	3	38	18*	12.66	102.70	0	0	4	0

Bowling	Mat	Balls	Runs	Wkts	BBI	BBM	Ave	Econ	SR	5w	10
First-class	9	-	-	-	-	-	-	-	-	-	-
List A	2	-	-	-	-	-	-	-	-	-	-
T20s	9	-	-	-	-	-	-	-	-	-	-

JOE MENNIE

RHB / RFM / R0 / W0

FULL NAME: Joe Matthew Mennie
BORN: December 24, 1988, Coffs Harbour, New South Wales, Australia
SQUAD NO: 24
HEIGHT: 6ft 3in
TEAMS: Australia, Lancashire, Hobart Hurricanes, Melbourne Renegades, Perth Scorchers, South Australia, Sydney Sixers
ROLE: Bowler
DEBUT: Test: 2016; ODI: 2016; First-class: 2011; List A: 2011; T20: 2012

BEST BATTING: 79* South Australia vs Queensland, Brisbane, 2012
BEST BOWLING: 7-96 South Australia vs Western Australia, Perth, 2011

TWITTER: @Joe_Mennie
NOTES: The Australian international fast bowler has signed for Lancashire as an overseas player for 2018 and will be available in all three formats. Raised in New South Wales, Mennie moved to Adelaide in 2011 and won a contract with South Australia. In his first season he was the state's second-highest wicket-taker in the Sheffield Shield and followed that up with an impressive 33 wickets in the next campaign. Struggled in the next two years before returning to form and topping the charts with 51 wickets in the 2015/16 season. Played his only Test against South Africa in 2016, also making two ODI appearances. He has played for four different sides in the Big Bash, most recently the Melbourne Renegades. Australia and Lancashire teammate James Faulkner said: "To average 26 or so in first-class cricket in Australia is very impressive. I'm sure he will do very well in English conditions, especially when it reverses like it did at Lancashire when I was there in 2015"

Batting	Mat	Inns	NO	Runs	HS	Ave	SR	100	50	Ct	St
Tests	1	2	0	10	10	5.00	41.66	0	0	0	0
ODIs	2	2	0	1	1	0.50	25.00	0	0	0	0
First-class	56	94	14	1368	79*	17.10	47.02	0	6	24	0
List A	34	27	7	266	43*	13.30	83.38	0	0	5	0
T20s	18	8	1	16	4	2.28	39.02	0	0	5	0

Bowling	Mat	Balls	Runs	Wkts	BBI	BBM	Ave	Econ	SR	5w	10
Tests	1	168	85	1	1/85	1/85	85.00	3.03	168.0	0	0
ODIs	2	120	131	3	3/49	3/49	43.66	6.55	40.0	0	0
First-class	56	11787	5564	209	7/96	9/88	26.62	2.83	56.3	6	0
List A	34	1725	1461	40	5/36	5/36	36.52	5.08	43.1	1	0
T20s	18	297	397	18	3/20	3/20	22.05	8.02	16.5	0	0

CRAIG MESCHEDE RHB / RMF / R0 / W0 / MVP82

FULL NAME: Craig Anthony Joseph Meschede
BORN: November 21, 1991, Johannesburg, South Africa
SQUAD NO: 44
HEIGHT: 6ft 1in
NICKNAME: Mesh, Meshy
EDUCATION: King's College, Taunton
TEAMS: Glamorgan, Somerset
ROLE: Allrounder
DEBUT: First-class: 2011; List A: 2011; T20: 2011

BEST BATTING: 107 Glamorgan vs Northamptonshire, Cardiff, 2015
BEST BOWLING: 5-84 Glamorgan vs Essex, Chelmsford, 2016

BEST ADVICE EVER RECEIVED? Talent only goes so far
'ROY OF THE ROVERS' MOMENT? My maiden first-class wicket – Sachin Tendulkar – and my maiden first-class century against Surrey
BEST THING ABOUT YOUR HOME GROUND? The international atmosphere
YOUNG OPPOSING PLAYER WHO HAS IMPRESSED YOU? Tom Curran (Sur) – performs under pressure
IF YOU WEREN'T A CRICKETER? I'd be a pro tennis player
SURPRISING FACT ABOUT YOU? I'm big into my wildlife – would love to be involved in conservation
WHERE IS PARADISE? Barbados
CRICKETING HERO? Jacques Kallis – the best allrounder and someone I aspire to be like
NON-CRICKETING HERO? Roger Federer – he's stayed at the top for so long
TWITTER: @cmeschy

Batting	Mat	Inns	NO	Runs	HS	Ave	SR	100	50	Ct	St
First-class	66	93	12	2099	107	25.91	65.43	2	11	23	0
List A	52	36	5	462	45	14.90	92.95	0	0	11	0
T20s	79	56	15	585	53	14.26	122.38	0	1	15	0

Bowling	Mat	Balls	Runs	Wkts	BBI	BBM	Ave	Econ	SR	5w	10
First-class	66	8410	4983	133	5/84	7/80	37.46	3.55	63.2	1	0
List A	52	1905	1763	51	4/5	4/5	34.56	5.55	37.3	0	0
T20s	79	884	1261	48	3/9	3/9	26.27	8.55	18.4	0	0

GLOUCESTERSHIRE

CRAIG MILES — RHB / RFM / R0 / W2

FULL NAME: Craig Neil Miles
BORN: July 20, 1994, Swindon, Wiltshire
SQUAD NO: 34
HEIGHT: 6ft 4in
NICKNAME: Milo, Miler
EDUCATION: Bradon Forest School, Purton, Wiltshire; Filton College, Bristol
TEAMS: Gloucestershire
ROLE: Bowler
DEBUT: First-class: 2011; List A: 2011; T20: 2013

BEST BATTING: 62* Gloucestershire vs Worcestershire, Cheltenham, 2014
BEST BOWLING: 6-63 Gloucestershire vs Northamptonshire, Northampton, 2015
COUNTY CAP: 2011

WHAT GOT YOU INTO CRICKET? Learning to be a scorer at Purton CC
FAMILY TIES? My older brother Adam has played for Cardiff MCCU and for New Zealand side Otago in the Plunket Shield
BEST ADVICE EVER RECEIVED? If you always do what you've always done, you'll always get what you've already got
'ROY OF THE ROVERS' MOMENT? Winning the One-Day Cup final against Surrey in 2015
BEST THING ABOUT YOUR HOME GROUND? It's located in Bristol – top city!
BEST OPPOSING PLAYER IN COUNTY CRICKET? Samit Patel (Not)
YOUNG OPPOSING PLAYER WHO HAS IMPRESSED YOU? Josh Tongue (Wor) – young fast bowler with good skills, pace and control
SURPRISING FACT ABOUT YOU? I played football for Swindon Town Academy until I was 13
SURPRISING FACT ABOUT A TEAMMATE? Graeme van Buuren folds his dirty washing
WHERE IS PARADISE? The Kendleshire Golf Club, South Gloucestershire
TWITTER: @cmiles34

Batting	Mat	Inns	NO	Runs	HS	Ave	SR	100	50	Ct	St
First-class	54	74	9	1142	62*	17.56	48.65	0	5	13	0
List A	32	12	2	76	16	7.60	64.95	0	0	4	0
T20s	13	5	2	13	8	4.33	92.85	0	0	4	0

Bowling	Mat	Balls	Runs	Wkts	BBI	BBM	Ave	Econ	SR	5w	10
First-class	54	8958	5592	197	6/63	10/121	28.38	3.74	45.4	11	1
List A	32	1306	1327	37	4/29	4/29	35.86	6.09	35.2	0	0
T20s	13	265	351	15	3/25	3/25	23.40	7.94	17.6	0	0

TYMAL MILLS

RHB / LF / RO / WO

FULL NAME: Tymal Solomon Mills
BORN: August 12, 1992, Dewsbury, Yorkshire
SQUAD NO: 7
HEIGHT: 6ft 2in
NICKNAME: T, Tyrone
EDUCATION: Mildenhall College of Technology; University of East London
TEAMS: England, Sussex, Auckland, Brisbane Heat, Chittagong Vikings, Essex, Karachi Kings, Quetta Gladiators
ROLE: Bowler
DEBUT: T20I: 2016; First-class: 2011; List A: 2011; T20: 2012

SUSSEX

BEST BATTING: 31* England Lions vs Sri Lanka Emerging Players, Colombo, 2014
BEST BOWLING: 4-25 Essex vs Glamorgan, Cardiff, 2012

WHAT GOT YOU INTO CRICKET? My friend's team were short when I was 14 and he asked me to help them out
BEST ADVICE EVER RECEIVED? Find out what your strengths are and then back them
'ROY OF THE ROVERS' MOMENT? Making my England debut in 2016
BEST THING ABOUT YOUR HOME GROUND? Hove is the best non-Test ground in the country
BEST OPPOSING PLAYER IN COUNTY CRICKET? Michael Klinger (Glo)
YOUNG OPPOSING PLAYER WHO HAS IMPRESSED YOU? Sam Curran (Sur)
IF YOU WEREN'T A CRICKETER? I'd be a journo
SURPRISING FACT ABOUT YOU? I bowl with my left but throw with my right
WHERE IS PARADISE? A sunny day-off in Brighton having a coffee and brekkie with the lads
CRICKETING HERO? Don't have one!
NON-CRICKETING HERO? My mum – she did so much for me when I was growing up
TWITTER: @tmills15

Batting	Mat	Inns	NO	Runs	HS	Ave	SR	100	50	Ct	St
T20Is	4	1	0	0	0	0.00	0.00	0	0	1	0
First-class	32	38	15	260	31*	11.30	57.77	0	0	9	0
List A	23	9	5	7	3*	1.75	31.81	0	0	3	0
T20s	80	20	9	45	8*	4.09	84.90	0	0	15	0

Bowling	Mat	Balls	Runs	Wkts	BBI	BBM	Ave	Econ	SR	5w	10
T20Is	4	96	116	3	1/27	1/27	38.66	7.25	32.0	0	0
First-class	32	3531	2008	55	4/25	5/79	36.50	3.41	64.2	0	0
List A	23	790	787	22	3/23	3/23	35.77	5.97	35.9	0	0
T20s	80	1697	2213	90	4/22	4/22	24.58	7.82	18.8	0	0

MATT MILNES

RHB / RFM / R0 / W0

NOTTINGHAMSHIRE

FULL NAME: Matthew Edward Milnes
BORN: July 29, 1994, Nottingham
SQUAD NO: 16
HEIGHT: 6ft 1in
NICKNAME: Milnesy, Milner, Milno
EDUCATION: West Bridgford School; Durham University
TEAMS: Nottinghamshire
ROLE: Bowler
DEBUT: First-class: 2014

BEST BATTING: 9 Durham MCCU vs Durham, Chester-le-Street, 2014
BEST BOWLING: 2-37 Durham MCCU vs Durham, Chester-le-Street, 2014

WHAT GOT YOU INTO CRICKET? Having to bowl at my brother for hours on end in the garden
BEST ADVICE EVER RECEIVED? Fail to prepare, prepare to fail
'ROY OF THE ROVERS' MOMENT? Taking a six-for on my Durham MCCU debut having been asked to come down to bowl in the nets for a trial that morning
BEST THING ABOUT YOUR HOME GROUND? I used to play on the Trent Bridge outfield as a kid, so it's pretty special that it is now my home ground
BEST OPPOSING PLAYER IN COUNTY CRICKET? Shivnarine Chanderpaul (Lan) – the best batsman I've bowled at. He's an absolute wall
YOUNG OPPOSING PLAYER WHO HAS IMPRESSED YOU? Cameron Steel (Dur) – he had an amazing breakthrough season last year and is a good friend from our university days
IF YOU WEREN'T A CRICKETER? I'd be a teacher
SURPRISING FACT ABOUT YOU? I once scored a goal for Manchester United. It was a horror own goal when I was playing against them at U14 level, but I'm counting it
SURPRISING FACT ABOUT A TEAMMATE? Jake Libby has played in a pro golf competition
WHERE IS PARADISE? Loveshack Wednesdays (nightclub in Durham)
CRICKETING HERO? Jimmy Anderson – so skilful and makes it look so easy
NON-CRICKETING HERO? Lionel Messi – the best sportsman ever
TWITTER: @mmilnes84

Batting	Mat	Inns	NO	Runs	HS	Ave	SR	100	50	Ct	St
First-class	2	2	0	9	9	4.50	34.61	0	0	2	0

Bowling	Mat	Balls	Runs	Wkts	BBI	BBM	Ave	Econ	SR	5w	10
First-class	2	240	108	3	2/37	2/37	36.00	2.70	80.0	0	0

ALEX MILTON

RHB / WK / R0 / W0

FULL NAME: Alexander Geoffrey Milton
BORN: May 19, 1996, Redhill, Surrey
SQUAD NO: 12
HEIGHT: 5ft 7in
NICKNAME: Milts
EDUCATION: Malvern College; Cardiff Metropolitan University
TEAMS: Worcestershire
ROLE: Wicketkeeper/batsman
DEBUT: First-class: 2016

WORCESTERSHIRE

BEST BATTING: 12 Cardiff MCCU vs Hampshire, Southampton, 2016

WHAT GOT YOU INTO CRICKET? Watching my dad play
BEST ADVICE EVER RECEIVED? Play the ball, not the player
'ROY OF THE ROVERS' MOMENT? Contributing with the bat and being part of a winning team with Cardiff MCCU at Lord's
BEST THING ABOUT YOUR HOME GROUND? The view from the changing rooms
BEST OPPOSING PLAYER IN COUNTY CRICKET? James Foster (Ess)
YOUNG OPPOSING PLAYER WHO HAS IMPRESSED YOU? Haseeb Hameed (Lan)
IF YOU WEREN'T A CRICKETER? I'd be a musician
SURPRISING FACT ABOUT YOU? I played a drum solo blindfolded in my school unplugged concert
SURPRISING FACT ABOUT A TEAMMATE? Ben Twohig played drag in a theatre performance
WHERE IS PARADISE? Cape Town
CRICKETING HERO? Virat Kohli – an unbelievable batsman with an incredible will to win every game he plays
NON-CRICKETING HERO? Chad Smith – drummer of Red Hot Chili Peppers
TWITTER: @alex_milton12

Batting	Mat	Inns	NO	Runs	HS	Ave	SR	100	50	Ct	St
First-class	1	1	0	12	12	12.00	28.57	0	0	0	0

Bowling	Mat	Balls	Runs	Wkts	BBI	BBM	Ave	Econ	SR	5w	10
First-class	1	-	-	-	-	-	-	-	-	-	-

DARYL MITCHELL

RHB / RM / R6 / W0 / MVP17

WORCESTERSHIRE

FULL NAME: Daryl Keith Henry Mitchell
BORN: November 25, 1983, Badsey, Worcestershire
SQUAD NO: 27
HEIGHT: 6ft 2in
NICKNAME: Mitch
EDUCATION: Prince Henry's High School, Evesham; University of Worcester
TEAMS: Worcestershire, Mountaineers
ROLE: Allrounder
DEBUT: First-class: 2005; List A: 2005; T20: 2005

BEST BATTING: 298 Worcestershire vs Somerset, Taunton, 2009
BEST BOWLING: 4-49 Worcestershire vs Yorkshire, Headingley, 2009
BENEFIT: 2016

BEST ADVICE EVER RECEIVED? Things are never as good or as bad as they seem
'ROY OF THE ROVERS' MOMENT? Taking 5-28 against Northants in the T20 Blast in 2014
BEST THING ABOUT YOUR HOME GROUND? The view from my spot in the dressing room
BEST OPPOSING PLAYER IN COUNTY CRICKET? Wayne Madsen (Der)
YOUNG OPPOSING PLAYER WHO HAS IMPRESSED YOU? Jofra Archer (Sus) – rapid
IF YOU WEREN'T A CRICKETER? I'd be a professional darts player
SURPRISING FACT ABOUT YOU? I was in the Aston Villa Academy
SURPRISING FACT ABOUT A TEAMMATE? You can play table tennis on Ben Cox's forehead
WHERE IS PARADISE? Cape Town
CRICKETING HERO? Ian Botham and Graeme Hick – Worcester legends I grew up watching at New Road
NON-CRICKETING HERO? Paul McGrath – Villa legend
TWITTER: @mitchwccc

Batting	Mat	Inns	NO	Runs	HS	Ave	SR	100	50	Ct	St
First-class	178	321	37	11550	298	40.66	46.03	31	47	242	0
List A	119	105	16	3037	107	34.12	81.22	2	20	46	0
T20s	134	110	25	2080	68*	24.47	119.26	0	7	57	0

Bowling	Mat	Balls	Runs	Wkts	BBI	BBM	Ave	Econ	SR	5w	10
First-class	178	1964	1016	23	4/49	4/49	44.17	3.10	85.3	0	0
List A	119	2632	2440	70	4/19	4/19	34.85	5.56	37.6	0	0
T20s	134	1693	2204	75	5/28	5/28	29.38	7.81	22.5	1	0

TOM MOORES

LHB / WK / RO / WO

FULL NAME: Thomas James Moores
BORN: September 4, 1996, Brighton, Sussex
SQUAD NO: 23
HEIGHT: 5ft 10in
NICKNAME: Mooresy
EDUCATION: Loughborough Grammar School; Millfield School, Somerset
TEAMS: Nottinghamshire, Lancashire
ROLE: Wicketkeeper
DEBUT: First-class: 2016; List A: 2016; T20: 2016

BEST BATTING: 41 Nottinghamshire vs Yorkshire, Scarborough, 2016

FAMILY TIES? My father Peter played for Sussex and was England head coach. He's now my coach at Nottinghamshire
BEST ADVICE EVER RECEIVED? Be your own man
YOUNG OPPOSING PLAYER WHO HAS IMPRESSED YOU? Haseeb Hameed (Lan) – a very mature cricketer for his age
IF YOU WEREN'T A CRICKETER? I'd be a DJ
WHERE IS PARADISE? Mykonos, Greece
CRICKETING HERO? Adam Gilchrist – the way he changed the keeper-batter role inspired me
NON-CRICKETING HERO? Conor McGregor
TWITTER: @tommoores23

Batting	Mat	Inns	NO	Runs	HS	Ave	SR	100	50	Ct	St
First-class	7	12	0	202	41	16.83	40.48	0	0	7	0
List A	4	3	1	22	10	11.00	81.48	0	0	2	1
T20s	22	17	5	253	57	21.08	134.57	0	1	17	2

Bowling	Mat	Balls	Runs	Wkts	BBI	BBM	Ave	Econ	SR	5w	10
First-class	7	-	-	-	-	-	-	-	-	-	-
List A	4	-	-	-	-	-	-	-	-	-	-
T20s	22	-	-	-	-	-	-	-	-	-	-

EOIN MORGAN

LHB / RM / R1 / W0

FULL NAME: Eoin Joseph Gerard Morgan
BORN: September 10, 1986, Dublin
SQUAD NO: 16
HEIGHT: 5ft 9in
NICKNAME: Moggie, Morgs, Iceman
EDUCATION: Catholic University School, Dublin; Dulwich College, London
TEAMS: England, Ireland, Middlesex, Kolkata Knight Riders, Peshawar Zalmi, RC Bangalore, Sunrisers Hyderabad, Sydney Thunder
ROLE: Batsman
DEBUT: Test: 2010; ODI: 2006; T20I: 2009; First-class: 2004; List A: 2003; T20: 2006

BEST BATTING: 209* Ireland vs UAE, Abu Dhabi, 2007
BEST BOWLING: 2-24 Middlesex vs Nottinghamshire, Lord's, 2007
COUNTY CAP: 2008

TWITTER: @Eoin16
NOTES: An Irishman by birth, Morgan switched his allegiance to England after he was named in England's provisional squad for the 2009 World T20. Made his ODI debut for his adopted nation against West Indies in 2009 and his T20I debut a month later in a shock defeat to Netherlands at Lord's. His Test debut followed against Bangladesh in May 2010. After a lean 2013, Morgan rediscovered his form in the ODI series against Australia in January 2014. Handed the ODI captaincy ahead of the 2015 World Cup and has turned England into a 50-over force. Also leads the T20I side. Has not played a first-class match since 2015 but says he is keen to return to red-ball cricket this summer to hone his technique

Batting	Mat	Inns	NO	Runs	HS	Ave	SR	100	50	Ct	St
Tests	16	24	1	700	130	30.43	54.77	2	3	11	0
ODIs	197	184	25	5970	124*	37.54	88.23	11	35	73	0
T20Is	72	70	14	1678	85*	29.96	132.33	0	9	32	0
First-class	93	153	16	4791	209*	34.97	51.35	11	22	71	1
List A	317	292	39	9433	161	37.28	88.74	18	53	111	0
T20s	241	227	31	5175	85*	26.40	127.65	0	26	116	0

Bowling	Mat	Balls	Runs	Wkts	BBI	BBM	Ave	Econ	SR	5w	10
Tests	16	-	-	-	-	-	-	-	-	-	-
ODIs	197	-	-	-	-	-	-	-	-	-	-
T20Is	72	-	-	-	-	-	-	-	-	-	-
First-class	93	102	90	2	2/24	2/24	45.00	5.29	51.0	0	0
List A	317	42	49	0	-	-	-	7.00	-	0	0
T20s	241	-	-	-	-	-	-	-	-	-	-

OWEN MORGAN

RHB / SLA / RO / WO

FULL NAME: Alan Owen Morgan
BORN: April 14, 1994, Swansea
SQUAD NO: 29
HEIGHT: 5ft 11in
NICKNAME: Morgs, Ows, Strawbs
EDUCATION: Ysgol Gyfun Y Strade, Llanelli; Cardiff University
TEAMS: Glamorgan
ROLE: Allrounder
DEBUT: First-class: 2014; List A: 2016

GLAMORGAN

BEST BATTING: 103* Glamorgan vs Worcestershire, Worcester, 2016
BEST BOWLING: 2-37 Glamorgan vs Northamptonshire, Northampton, 2016

WHAT GOT YOU INTO CRICKET? A local volunteer came into primary school to start a local village side which I joined
'ROY OF THE ROVERS' MOMENT? My maiden first-class hundred – as a nightwatchman – against Worcestershire in 2016
BEST THING ABOUT YOUR HOME GROUND? It's an international venue
BEST OPPOSING PLAYER IN COUNTY CRICKET? Samit Patel (Not)
YOUNG OPPOSING PLAYER WHO HAS IMPRESSED YOU? Ben Duckett (Nor)
IF YOU WEREN'T A CRICKETER? I'd be working in finance
SURPRISING FACT ABOUT YOU? I'm fluent in Welsh, grew up on a farm, and have a degree in Accounting and Finance
CRICKETING HERO? Ricky Ponting
NON-CRICKETING HERO? My grandfather – he had the greatest influence on me as I was growing up and taught me a lot
UNUSUAL OBJECT AT HOME? A tractor
TWITTER: @owenmorgan14

Batting	Mat	Inns	NO	Runs	HS	Ave	SR	100	50	Ct	St
First-class	14	25	5	467	103*	23.35	40.75	1	1	4	0
List A	3	2	0	32	29	16.00	76.19	0	0	0	0

Bowling	Mat	Balls	Runs	Wkts	BBI	BBM	Ave	Econ	SR	5w	10
First-class	14	1626	849	15	2/37	3/57	56.60	3.13	108.4	0	0
List A	3	84	81	2	2/49	2/49	40.50	5.78	42.0	0	0

CHARLIE MORRIS RHB / RMF / RO / W2

WORCESTERSHIRE

FULL NAME: Charles Andrew John Morris
BORN: July 6, 1992, Hereford
SQUAD NO: 31
HEIGHT: 6ft
NICKNAME: Moz, Tim, Dug, Mr Beige, Tintin
EDUCATION: Kingswood School, Bath; King's College, Taunton; Oxford Brookes University
TEAMS: Worcestershire
ROLE: Bowler
DEBUT: First-class: 2012; List A: 2013; T20: 2013

BEST BATTING: 33* Oxford MCCU vs Warwickshire, Oxford, 2013
BEST BOWLING: 5-54 Worcestershire vs Derbyshire, Derby, 2014

WHAT GOT YOU INTO CRICKET? I saw a Test match on TV for the first time and then went with my dad to Toys R Us to buy a cricket set
BEST ADVICE EVER RECEIVED? Anything can be achieved with planning and preparation
'ROY OF THE ROVERS' MOMENT? Beating Surrey in 2014 to gain Championship promotion
BEST THING ABOUT YOUR HOME GROUND? The iconic view – there are few grounds in the world which have the character of New Road
YOUNG OPPOSING PLAYER WHO HAS IMPRESSED YOU? Adam Hose (War) – he strikes the ball cleanly and has a 360-degree game
IF YOU WEREN'T A CRICKETER? My ambition would be to join the Royal Marines
SURPRISING FACT ABOUT YOU? I enjoy the cold more than the warmth
WHERE IS PARADISE? Anywhere with family
CRICKETING HERO? Dale Steyn – passionate, quick, skilful and humble
UNUSUAL OBJECT AT HOME? A late Victorian, classic fusee-movement Post Office clock
TWITTER: @morris_9

Batting	Mat	Inns	NO	Runs	HS	Ave	SR	100	50	Ct	St
First-class	44	60	33	274	33*	10.14	28.39	0	0	12	0
List A	17	11	8	43	16*	14.33	68.25	0	0	2	0
T20s	4	2	1	5	3	5.00	83.33	0	0	1	0

Bowling	Mat	Balls	Runs	Wkts	BBI	BBM	Ave	Econ	SR	5w	10
First-class	44	7942	4057	127	5/54	9/109	31.94	3.06	62.5	2	0
List A	17	719	694	18	3/46	3/46	38.55	5.79	39.9	0	0
T20s	4	84	126	4	2/30	2/30	31.50	9.00	21.0	0	0

STEVEN MULLANEY

RHB / RM / R1 / W0 / MVP22

FULL NAME: Steven John Mullaney
BORN: November 19, 1986, Warrington, Cheshire
SQUAD NO: 5
HEIGHT: 5ft 7in
NICKNAME: Mull, Tev
EDUCATION: St Mary's Catholic High School, Greater Manchester
TEAMS: Nottinghamshire, Khelaghar Samaj Kallyan Samity, Lancashire
ROLE: Allrounder
DEBUT: First-class: 2006; List A: 2006; T20: 2006

BEST BATTING: 168 Nottinghamshire vs Kent, Trent Bridge, 2017
BEST BOWLING: 5-32 Nottinghamshire vs Gloucestershire, Trent Bridge, 2017
COUNTY CAP: 2013 (Nottinghamshire)

'ROY OF THE ROVERS' MOMENT? All the finals which we have won
BEST THING ABOUT YOUR HOME GROUND? When Trent Bridge is packed for the T20 matches – the atmosphere is amazing
BEST OPPOSING PLAYER IN COUNTY CRICKET? Marcus Trescothick (Som)
YOUNG OPPOSING PLAYER WHO HAS IMPRESSED YOU? Josh Tongue (Wor) – good pace and accuracy
IF YOU WEREN'T A CRICKETER? I did a three-month apprenticeship as an electrician
SURPRISING FACT ABOUT YOU? I played England schoolboy rugby league
SURPRISING FACT ABOUT A TEAMMATE? Jake Libby does 'Face Mask Fridays' with his partner
WHERE IS PARADISE? Barbados
CRICKETING HERO? Luke Fletcher
NON-CRICKETING HERO? Conor McGregor
TWITTER: @mull05

Batting	Mat	Inns	NO	Runs	HS	Ave	SR	100	50	Ct	St
First-class	111	184	8	6001	168	34.09	58.11	12	32	106	0
List A	95	67	14	1585	111	29.90	100.76	1	9	47	0
T20s	110	74	22	887	53	17.05	139.02	0	1	52	0
Bowling	Mat	Balls	Runs	Wkts	BBI	BBM	Ave	Econ	SR	5w	10
First-class	111	5541	2862	84	5/32	7/46	34.07	3.09	65.9	1	0
List A	95	3147	2732	86	4/29	4/29	31.76	5.20	36.5	0	0
T20s	110	1844	2393	79	4/19	4/19	30.29	7.78	23.3	0	0

JACK MURPHY

LHB / LFM / RO / WO

FULL NAME: Jack Roger Murphy
BORN: July 15, 1995, Haverfordwest, Pembrokeshire
SQUAD NO: 7
HEIGHT: 6ft 7in
NICKNAME: Pepe, J Rock
EDUCATION: Ysgol Greenhill School, Pembrokeshire; Cardiff Metropolitan University
TEAMS: Glamorgan
ROLE: Allrounder
DEBUT: First-class: 2015; List A: 2016

BEST BATTING: 27 Glamorgan vs Sussex, Colwyn Bay, 2017
BEST BOWLING: 2-90 Cardiff MCCU vs Glamorgan, Cardiff, 2015

WHAT GOT YOU INTO CRICKET? Playing garden cricket with my dad aged five
FAMILY TIES? My dad likes to think he used to be pretty good because he went on a tour to the West Indies but quite frankly he was rubbish
BEST ADVICE EVER RECEIVED? The only person stopping you from achieving your dreams is yourself
'ROY OF THE ROVERS' MOMENT? Taking four wickets in four balls for my old club Cresselly in Pembrokeshire
BEST THING ABOUT YOUR HOME GROUND? The changing rooms at Cardiff are massive and they have good sofas
BEST OPPOSING PLAYER IN COUNTY CRICKET? Samit Patel (Not)
IF YOU WEREN'T A CRICKETER? I would like to be in the Royal Air Force
SURPRISING FACT ABOUT YOU? I'm very tall
CRICKETING HERO? Simon Jones and Andrew Flintoff – they were both awesome to watch in the 2005 Ashes
NON-CRICKETING HERO? My dad – always there for me
TWITTER: @Jrock6ft7

Batting	Mat	Inns	NO	Runs	HS	Ave	SR	100	50	Ct	St
First-class	6	9	0	136	27	15.11	39.65	0	0	2	0
List A	1	1	0	6	6	6.00	35.29	0	0	0	0

Bowling	Mat	Balls	Runs	Wkts	BBI	BBM	Ave	Econ	SR	5w	10
First-class	6	240	135	2	2/90	2/90	67.50	3.37	120.0	0	0
List A	1	60	64	0	-	-	-	6.40	-	0	0

TIM MURTAGH

LHB / RFM / R0 / W6

FULL NAME: Timothy James Murtagh
BORN: August 2, 1981, Lambeth, London
SQUAD NO: 34
HEIGHT: 6ft
NICKNAME: Murts, Jack, Brow
EDUCATION: The John Fisher School, London; St Mary's College, Twickenham
TEAMS: Ireland, Middlesex, Surrey
ROLE: Bowler
DEBUT: ODI: 2012; T20I: 2012; First-class: 2000; List A: 2000; T20: 2003

BEST BATTING: 74* Surrey vs Middlesex, The Oval, 2004
BEST BOWLING: 7-82 Middlesex vs Derbyshire, Derby, 2009
COUNTY CAP: 2008 (Middlesex); **BENEFIT:** 2015 (Middlesex)

FAMILY TIES? My brother Chris played for Surrey and my uncle Andrew played for Hampshire
'ROY OF THE ROVERS' MOMENT? Winning the 2016 County Championship
SUPERSTITIONS? I bat with my lucky horseshoe inside my box
HOW WOULD YOUR TEAMMATES DESCRIBE YOU IN THREE WORDS? Tall, dark, handsome
BEST OPPOSING PLAYER IN COUNTY CRICKET? Ben Stokes (Dur)
CRICKETING HERO? My dad
NON-CRICKETING HEROES? Jürgen Klopp, followed closely by my wife
IF YOU WEREN'T A CRICKETER? I'd be spotting trains, emptying bins
SURPRISING FACT? I have a famous cousin who is a jockey
TWITTER: @tjmurtagh

Batting	Mat	Inns	NO	Runs	HS	Ave	SR	100	50	Ct	St
ODIs	36	24	7	148	23*	8.70	71.49	0	0	9	0
T20Is	14	5	3	26	12*	13.00	104.00	0	0	3	0
First-class	205	268	78	3713	74*	19.54		0	10	59	0
List A	184	113	40	779	35*	10.67		0	0	46	0
T20s	102	38	14	227	40*	9.45	106.57	0	0	22	0

Bowling	Mat	Balls	Runs	Wkts	BBI	BBM	Ave	Econ	SR	5w	10
ODIs	36	1824	1396	39	4/32	4/32	35.79	4.59	46.7	0	0
T20Is	14	268	324	13	3/23	3/23	24.92	7.25	20.6	0	0
First-class	205	35903	18625	696	7/82	10/77	26.76	3.11	51.5	28	4
List A	184	8300	7069	230	4/14	4/14	30.73	5.11	36.0	0	0
T20s	102	1984	2727	106	6/24	6/24	25.72	8.24	18.7	1	0

LHB / LB / WK / R0 / W0

GLOUCESTERSHIRE

FULL NAME: Philip Mustard
BORN: October 8, 1982, Sunderland
SQUAD NO: 19
HEIGHT: 5ft 10in
NICKNAME: Colonel
EDUCATION: Usworth Comprehensive, County Durham
TEAMS: England, Gloucestershire, Auckland, Barisal Burners, Durham, Lancashire, Mountaineers
ROLE: Wicketkeeper
DEBUT: ODI: 2007; T20I: 2008; First-class: 2002; List A: 2000; T20: 2003

BEST BATTING: 130 Durham vs Kent, Canterbury, 2006
BEST BOWLING: 1-9 Durham vs Sussex, Hove, 2013
BENEFIT: 2016 (Durham)

FAMILY TIES? My brother played for Sunderland and Chester-le-Street in the North East Premier League and my cousin is my former Durham teammate Chris Rushworth
BEST THING ABOUT YOUR HOME GROUND? My comfortable spot in the dressing room
BEST OPPOSING PLAYER IN COUNTY CRICKET? Samit Patel (Not)
IF YOU WEREN'T A CRICKETER? I'd be a wheeler-dealer
SURPRISING FACT ABOUT YOU? I'm very self-motivated
WHERE IS PARADISE? Bed
CRICKETING HERO? Adam Gilchrist – he's a spot-on bloke and has a fantastic knowledge of cricket
NON-CRICKETING HERO? Peter Kay – he makes me giggle
TWITTER: @colonel19

Batting	Mat	Inns	NO	Runs	HS	Ave	SR	100	50	Ct	St
ODIs	10	10	0	233	83	23.30	92.46	0	1	9	2
T20Is	2	2	0	60	40	30.00	162.16	0	0	0	0
First-class	210	322	36	8700	130	30.41	59.13	7	52	670	19
List A	205	188	9	5484	143	30.63		7	34	214	48
T20s	192	181	8	4229	97*	24.44	122.40	0	22	94	38

Bowling	Mat	Balls	Runs	Wkts	BBI	BBM	Ave	Econ	SR	5w	10
ODIs	10	-	-	-	-	-	-	-	-	-	-
T20Is	2	-	-	-	-	-	-	-	-	-	-
First-class	210	127	150	1	1/9	1/9	150.00	7.08	127.0	0	0
List A	205	-	-	-	-	-	-	-	-	-	-
T20s	192	-	-	-	-	-	-	-	-	-	-

JOHANN MYBURGH

RHB / OB / RO / WO

FULL NAME: Johann Gerhardus Myburgh
BORN: October 22, 1980, Pretoria, South Africa
SQUAD NO: 9
HEIGHT: 5ft 7in
NICKNAME: Mybs, Santi
EDUCATION: Pretoria Boys High School
TEAMS: Somerset, Auckland, Canterbury, Durham, Hampshire, Northerns, Titans
ROLE: Batsman
DEBUT: First-class: 1997; List A: 1999; T20: 2005

BEST BATTING: 203 Northerns B vs Easterns, Pretoria, 1998
BEST BOWLING: 4-56 Canterbury vs Northern Districts, Hamilton, 2008

FAMILY TIES? My brother Stephan is a Dutch international
ROY OF THE ROVERS' MOMENT? Sharing a hundred-run partnership with my brother
HOW WOULD YOUR TEAMMATES DESCRIBE YOU IN THREE WORDS? Short, easy-going, competitive
CRICKETING HEROES? Eric Simons, Brian Lara
NON-CRICKETING HEROES? Boris Becker, Dennis Bergkamp
IF YOU WEREN'T A CRICKETER? Ah, that's easy, I'd be a pro-golfer of course!
SURPRISING FACT? I might be taller than you think…

Batting	Mat	Inns	NO	Runs	HS	Ave	SR	100	50	Ct	St
First-class	108	190	23	6841	203	40.96		16	39	61	0
List A	110	103	10	2731	112	29.36		1	17	24	0
T20s	76	68	10	1684	88	29.03	125.11	0	10	17	0

Bowling	Mat	Balls	Runs	Wkts	BBI	BBM	Ave	Econ	SR	5w	10
First-class	108	4345	2160	45	4/56	4/80	48.00	2.98	96.5	0	0
List A	110	1790	1525	25	2/22	2/22	61.00	5.11	71.6	0	0
T20s	76	374	461	10	3/16	3/16	46.10	7.39	37.4	0	0

MOHAMMAD NABI

LEICESTERSHIRE

FULL NAME: Mohammad Nabi
BORN: January 1, 1985, Loger, Afghanistan
SQUAD NO: 7
TEAMS: Afghanistan, Leicestershire, Chittagong Vikings, Melbourne Renegades, Quetta Gladiators, St Kitts and Nevis Patriots, Sunrisers Hyderabad, Sylhet Royals
ROLE: Allrounder
DEBUT: ODI: 2009; T20I: 2010; First-class: 2007; List A: 2008; T20: 2010

BEST BATTING: 117 Afghanistan vs UAE, Sharjah, 2011
BEST BOWLING: 6-33 Afghanistan vs Namibia, Windhoek, 2013

TWITTER: @MohammadNabi007
NOTES: Nabi joins his compatriot Rashid Khan, who has been signed by Sussex, as the first Afghan cricketers to play county cricket. Leicestershire have signed the veteran off-spinning allrounder as an overseas player for the T20 Blast. Nabi has been a mainstay of the Afghanistan side which has shot to prominence over the last decade. He is his country's leading run-scorer in ODIs and leading wicket-taker in T20Is, and has played in some of the most prestigious T20 leagues around the world, including the IPL and the Big Bash. Leicestershire head coach Paul Nixon said: "He can make a huge impact in our middle order and is an off-break bowler who operates with great control and skill. Nabi has a brilliant white-ball record for Afghanistan and in T20 competitions around the world. He is exactly the type of player that we were looking for and is somebody who will fit in beautifully here"

Batting	Mat	Inns	NO	Runs	HS	Ave	SR	100	50	Ct	St
ODIs	93	83	10	2173	116	29.76	88.33	1	11	48	0
T20Is	60	55	8	961	89	20.44	139.88	0	2	32	0
First-class	32	51	4	1251	117	26.61	51.80	2	5	18	0
List A	127	115	13	3143	146	30.81	90.89	3	14	63	0
T20s	160	126	26	2191	89	21.91	139.28	0	6	76	0

Bowling	Mat	Balls	Runs	Wkts	BBI	BBM	Ave	Econ	SR	5w	10
ODIs	93	4326	3082	96	4/30	4/30	32.10	4.27	45.0	0	0
T20Is	60	1258	1513	61	4/10	4/10	24.80	7.21	20.6	0	0
First-class	32	4302	1924	86	6/33	8/85	22.37	2.68	50.0	3	0
List A	127	6067	4289	140	5/12	5/12	30.63	4.24	43.3	1	0
T20s	160	3293	3747	182	4/10	4/10	20.58	6.82	18.0	0	0

CHRIS NASH RHB / OB / R4 / W0 / MVP45

FULL NAME: Christopher David Nash
BORN: May 19, 1983, Cuckfield, Sussex
SQUAD NO: 3
HEIGHT: 6ft
NICKNAME: Nashy, Knocker, Beaut, Wig
EDUCATION: Collyer's Sixth Form College;
Loughborough University
TEAMS: Nottinghamshire, Auckland, England
Lions, Otago, Prime Doleshwar Sporting
Club, Sussex
ROLE: Allrounder
DEBUT: First-class: 2002; List A: 2006; T20:
2006

BEST BATTING: 184 Sussex vs Leicestershire, Leicester, 2010
BEST BOWLING: 4-12 Sussex vs Glamorgan, Cardiff, 2010
COUNTY CAP: 2008 (Sussex)

WHAT GOT YOU INTO CRICKET? I was watching my brother hit a ball against a wall when a great man called Dr John Dew got me out on the pitch at the age of two
BEST ADVICE EVER RECEIVED? See it, hit it (Luke Marshall, 2001)
'ROY OF THE ROVERS' MOMENT? My T20 hundred for Sussex against Somerset on Sky in 2016
BEST THING ABOUT YOUR HOME GROUND? It's big
BEST OPPOSING PLAYER IN COUNTY CRICKET? Luke Wright (Sus)
SURPRISING FACT ABOUT A TEAMMATE? Alex Hales is a better tennis player than me and eats at a David Lloyd gym twice a day
CRICKETING HERO? Michael Slater – he tried to whack the first over for as many as possible and that's what made me want to open the batting
NON-CRICKETING HERO? Eric Clapton – to stand in front of 100,000 people and entertain them with a guitar and microphone is cool
TWITTER: @chrisnash23

Batting	Mat	Inns	NO	Runs	HS	Ave	SR	100	50	Ct	St
First-class	184	314	19	11424	184	38.72	58.23	23	59	114	0
List A	116	109	5	3222	124*	30.98	89.87	2	20	27	0
T20s	154	146	19	3396	112*	26.74	125.54	1	20	47	0
Bowling	Mat	Balls	Runs	Wkts	BBI	BBM	Ave	Econ	SR	5w	10
First-class	184	5665	3205	75	4/12	5/67	42.73	3.39	75.5	0	0
List A	116	1537	1415	43	4/40	4/40	32.90	5.52	35.7	0	0
T20s	154	1022	1222	49	4/7	4/7	24.93	7.17	20.8	0	0

ROB NEWTON

RHB / LB / R1 / W0

NORTHAMPTONSHIRE

FULL NAME: Robert Irving Newton
BORN: January 18, 1990, Taunton
SQUAD NO: 10
HEIGHT: 5ft 8in
NICKNAME: Ewok, KOTL, Newts
EDUCATION: Framlingham College, Suffolk
TEAMS: Northamptonshire
ROLE: Batsman
DEBUT: First-class: 2010; List A: 2009; T20: 2010

BEST BATTING: 202* Northamptonshire vs Leicestershire, Northampton, 2016
BEST BOWLING: 1-82 Northamptonshire vs Derbyshire, Derby, 2017

BEST ADVICE EVER RECEIVED? Don't touch that – it's hot!
'ROY OF THE ROVERS' MOMENT? Every game of warm-up football. Or winning the 'stump game' at Northamptonshire's end-of-season celebrations
BEST THING ABOUT YOUR HOME GROUND? There's a pub attached
BEST OPPOSING PLAYER IN COUNTY CRICKET? Samit Patel (Not)
YOUNG OPPOSING PLAYER WHO HAS IMPRESSED YOU? Olly Stone (War) – bowls rockets and has the biggest ears in the game
IF YOU WEREN'T A CRICKETER? I'd be a pub landlord
WHERE IS PARADISE? My couch
CRICKETING HERO? Ajaz Akhtar
NON-CRICKETING HERO? Gazza
TWITTER: @robbienewts77

Batting	Mat	Inns	NO	Runs	HS	Ave	SR	100	50	Ct	St
First-class	82	143	11	4825	202*	36.55	58.09	12	23	24	0
List A	38	35	2	986	107	29.87	93.19	1	4	7	0
T20s	21	18	1	214	38	12.58	102.88	0	0	0	0

Bowling	Mat	Balls	Runs	Wkts	BBI	BBM	Ave	Econ	SR	5w	10
First-class	82	73	107	1	1/82	1/82	107.00	8.79	73.0	0	0
List A	38	-	-	-	-	-	-	-	-	-	-
T20s	21	-	-	-	-	-	-	-	-	-	-

ARON NIJJAR

LHB / SLA / R0 / W0

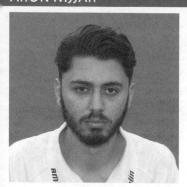

FULL NAME: Aron Stuart Singh Nijjar
BORN: September 24, 1994, Goodmayes, Essex
SQUAD NO: 24
EDUCATION: Ilford County High School
TEAMS: Essex
ROLE: Bowler
DEBUT: First-class: 2015; List A: 2015

ESSEX

BEST BATTING: 53 Essex vs Northamptonshire, Chelmsford, 2015
BEST BOWLING: 2-33 Essex vs Lancashire, Chelmsford, 2015

TWITTER: @aronnijjar
NOTES: A left-arm orthodox spinner and a fluent left-handed strokemaker, Nijjar has yet to establish himself at his hometown club and, despite having debuted in 2015, hasn't featured in any of the three competitions over the last two seasons. But Nijjar, who plays for the hugely successful Wanstead and Snaresbrook club, is highly regarded at Essex and is expected to have more opportunities soon – although it won't be easy to break into a side that was so successful last year. He spent most of 2017 in the second XI, also turning out for Cardiff MCCU. Made a pretty 30 against a strong West Indies attack in the tour match at Chelmsford last season

Batting	Mat	Inns	NO	Runs	HS	Ave	SR	100	50	Ct	St
First-class	10	12	5	185	53	26.42	46.13	0	1	1	0
List A	3	1	0	21	21	21.00	70.00	0	0	4	0

Bowling	Mat	Balls	Runs	Wkts	BBI	BBM	Ave	Econ	SR	5w	10
First-class	10	1017	691	15	2/33	3/48	46.06	4.07	67.8	0	0
List A	3	126	107	1	1/39	1/39	107.00	5.09	126.0	0	0

KIERAN NOEMA-BARNETT   LHB / RM / RO / WO

GLOUCESTERSHIRE

FULL NAME: Kieran Noema-Barnett
BORN: June 4, 1987, Dunedin, New Zealand
SQUAD NO: 11
HEIGHT: 6ft 1in
NICKNAME: Barney, Bear
EDUCATION: Kavanagh College, Dunedin;
Massey University, Palmerston North
TEAMS: Gloucestershire, Central Districts,
Otago
ROLE: Allrounder
DEBUT: First-class: 2009; List A: 2008; T20:
2007

BEST BATTING: 107 Central Districts vs Auckland, Auckland, 2011
BEST BOWLING: 4-20 Central Districts vs Otago, Dunedin, 2011

FAMILY TIES? Like me, my younger brother Arana has played for New Zealand U19, and my sister Molly also plays at a high level
'ROY OF THE ROVERS' MOMENT? I've been involved in winning three championships in New Zealand with the Central Stags. Captaining the side to the four-day title was unreal. A 43-ball hundred and a 14-ball fifty in T20 cricket would also be in there, as well as a first-class hat-trick
SUPERSTITIONS? No breakfast on game days – I need to be hungry
CRICKETING HEROES? Brian Lara – he made it look easy
NON-CRICKETING HEROES? My parents for raising my siblings and me. Manny Pacquiao – he does it all: boxer, congressman, basketball player. His fights are always good to watch
IF YOU WEREN'T A CRICKETER? I'd be working in a bank and looking forward to the weekend
SURPRISING FACT? I have an unusual laugh, according to some

Batting	Mat	Inns	NO	Runs	HS	Ave	SR	100	50	Ct	St
First-class	73	107	13	2566	107	27.29	52.56	2	15	35	0
List A	75	59	7	1171	74	22.51	95.28	0	6	34	0
T20s	100	86	16	1186	57*	16.94	132.95	0	3	20	0

Bowling	Mat	Balls	Runs	Wkts	BBI	BBM	Ave	Econ	SR	5w	10
First-class	73	8949	4066	120	4/20	6/29	33.88	2.72	74.5	0	0
List A	75	2370	2017	47	3/42	3/42	42.91	5.10	50.4	0	0
T20s	100	897	1365	32	2/13	2/13	42.65	9.13	28.0	0	0

SAM NORTHEAST

RHB / OB / R3 / W0 / MVP46

FULL NAME: Sam Alexander Northeast
BORN: October 16, 1989, Ashford, Kent
SQUAD NO: 17
HEIGHT: 5ft 11in
NICKNAME: North, Bam, Nick Knight
EDUCATION: Harrow School, London
TEAMS: Hampshire, England Lions, Kent
ROLE: Batsman
DEBUT: First-class: 2007; List A: 2007; T20: 2010

HAMPSHIRE

BEST BATTING: 191 Kent vs Derbyshire, Canterbury, 2016
BEST BOWLING: 1-60 Kent vs Gloucestershire, Cheltenham, 2013
COUNTY CAP: 2012 (Kent)

TWITTER: @sanortheast

NOTES: Northeast made a much publicised move to Hampshire in February 2018 after relations with Kent deteriorated before Christmas. He is being closely monitored by the England selectors, and Division One cricket may be the platform he needs to gain international recognition. Hotly tipped from the moment he was selected for the Harrow first team at the age of 14. Scored his maiden first-class hundred for Kent in 2009 and hit three Championship centuries in 2012, finishing just short of 1,400 runs in all forms of cricket. Struggled in 2013 and was dropped in 2014 but soon returned to the side and made four Championship centuries. Has scored 1,000 first-class runs in each of the last three seasons and has also been dominant in the short formats. Was handed the Championship captaincy at the end of 2015 after impressing as leader of the limited-overs teams. He leaves Kent after 10 years at the club

Batting	Mat	Inns	NO	Runs	HS	Ave	SR	100	50	Ct	St
First-class	137	235	18	8537	191	39.34	56.40	19	45	71	0
List A	88	80	5	2462	132	32.82	76.50	3	13	28	0
T20s	90	82	11	2282	114	32.14	137.13	1	17	22	0
Bowling	Mat	Balls	Runs	Wkts	BBI	BBM	Ave	Econ	SR	5w	10
First-class	137	178	147	1	1/60	1/60	147.00	4.95	178.0	0	0
List A	88	-	-	-	-	-	-	-	-	-	-
T20s	90	-	-	-	-	-	-	-	-	-	-

LIAM NORWELL RHB / RMF / RO / W2 / MVP67

GLOUCESTERSHIRE

FULL NAME: Liam Connor Norwell
BORN: December 27, 1991, Bournemouth
SQUAD NO: 24
HEIGHT: 6ft 3in
NICKNAME: Pasty
EDUCATION: Redruth School, Cornwall
TEAMS: Gloucestershire
ROLE: Bowler
DEBUT: First-class: 2011; List A: 2012; T20: 2012

BEST BATTING: 102 Gloucestershire vs Derbyshire, Bristol, 2016
BEST BOWLING: 8-43 Gloucestershire vs Leicestershire, Leicester, 2017
COUNTY CAP: 2011

WHAT GOT YOU INTO CRICKET? Watching my dad play in Bournemouth and then Plymouth and being able to have a day off school to play Kwik Cricket
'ROY OF THE ROVERS' MOMENT? Scoring a Championship hundred as a nightwatchman at Bristol in 2016
BEST THING ABOUT YOUR HOME GROUND? The Boston Tea Party café is at the end of the road
BEST OPPOSING PLAYER IN COUNTY CRICKET? Ben Duckett (Nor)
YOUNG OPPOSING PLAYER WHO HAS IMPRESSED YOU? Ed Barnard (Wor)
IF YOU WEREN'T A CRICKETER? I'd be still working at Card Factory
SURPRISING FACT ABOUT YOU? I was born in Bournemouth but everyone thinks I was born in Cornwall because that's where I grew up
CRICKETING HERO? Andrew Flintoff – because of his performances in the 2005 Ashes
NON-CRICKETING HERO? Richie McCaw – a great leader and competitor
TWITTER: @icnorwell24

Batting	Mat	Inns	NO	Runs	HS	Ave	SR	100	50	Ct	St
First-class	67	84	34	700	102	14.00	41.94	1	1	15	0
List A	17	10	2	47	16	5.87	69.11	0	0	2	0
T20s	23	5	5	5	2*	-	71.42	0	0	10	0

Bowling	Mat	Balls	Runs	Wkts	BBI	BBM	Ave	Econ	SR	5w	10
First-class	67	11868	6670	248	8/43	10/65	26.89	3.37	47.8	10	3
List A	17	780	716	23	6/52	6/52	31.13	5.50	33.9	2	0
T20s	23	413	631	12	3/27	3/27	52.58	9.16	34.4	0	0

DUANNE OLIVIER

RHB / RFM / R0 / W0

FULL NAME: Duanne Olivier
BORN: May 9, 1992, Groblersdal
SQUAD NO: TBC
TEAMS: South Africa, Derbyshire, Free State, Knights
ROLE: Bowler
DEBUT: Test: 2017; First-class: 2011; List A: 2011; T20: 2011

DERBYSHIRE

BEST BATTING: 72 Free State vs Namibia, Bloemfontein, 2014
BEST BOWLING: 6-60 Knights vs Titans, Centurion, 2016

TWITTER: @Duanne992
NOTES: Derbyshire have signed the South African fast bowler as an overseas player for the first half of the season, with Mitchell Santner filling in for the rest of the summer. Olivier is available for the first seven Championship matches and hopes to take part in the One-Day Cup. He has claimed 290 first-class wickets at the impressive average of 21.96 (as of March 2018). He was the highest wicket-taker in South Africa's four-day competition during the 2016/17 season (52 wickets), helping his Knights team to the domestic title. Made his Test debut in January 2017, with two appearances coming in the Test series against England last summer

Batting	Mat	Inns	NO	Runs	HS	Ave	SR	100	50	Ct	St
Tests	5	4	1	7	4	2.33	18.42	0	0	0	0
First-class	73	91	25	875	72	13.25	45.24	0	3	23	0
List A	34	17	4	149	25*	11.46	68.98	0	0	4	0
T20s	24	8	5	42	11*	14.00	87.50	0	0	4	0

Bowling	Mat	Balls	Runs	Wkts	BBI	BBM	Ave	Econ	SR	5w	10
Tests	5	606	393	17	3/38	5/57	23.11	3.89	35.6	0	0
First-class	73	12447	6371	290	6/60	11/149	21.96	3.07	42.9	16	2
List A	34	1347	1144	45	4/34	4/34	25.42	5.09	29.9	0	0
T20s	24	464	598	18	4/28	4/28	33.22	7.73	25.7	0	0

LANCASHIRE

FULL NAME: Graham Onions
BORN: September 9, 1982, Gateshead, County Durham
SQUAD NO: 99
HEIGHT: 6ft 2in
NICKNAME: Bunny, Wills
EDUCATION: St Thomas More Roman Catholic School, Blaydon, Gateshead
TEAMS: England, Lancashire, Dolphins, Durham, Unicorns
ROLE: Bowler
DEBUT: Test: 2009; ODI: 2009; First-class: 2004; List A: 2003; T20: 2004

BEST BATTING: 65 Durham vs Nottinghamshire, Chester-le-Street, 2016
BEST BOWLING: 9-67 Durham vs Nottinghamshire, Trent Bridge, 2012
BENEFIT: 2015 (Durham)

'ROY OF THE ROVERS' MOMENT? My Test debut, taking nine wickets against Nottinghamshire and returning to Test cricket against West Indies in 2012 after my serious back injury
SUPERSTITIONS? I lick my fingers before I bowl
CRICKETING HEROES? Darren Gough, Dale Steyn
IF YOU WEREN'T A CRICKETER? I'd be struggling! Maybe a PE teacher
TWITTER: @BunnyOnions
NOTES: The veteran former England fast bowler, plagued by injury throughout his career, returned to form at the end of last summer with 32 Championship wickets at 22.66. After 14 seasons at Durham, Onions moved to Lancashire in September 2017 along with Keaton Jennings

Batting	Mat	Inns	NO	Runs	HS	Ave	SR	100	50	Ct	St
Tests	9	10	7	30	17*	10.00	30.92	0	0	0	0
ODIs	4	1	0	1	1	1.00	50.00	0	0	1	0
First-class	169	219	81	1900	65	13.76	51.11	0	1	33	0
List A	87	32	10	130	19	5.90	68.78	0	0	13	0
T20s	44	13	6	61	31	8.71	107.01	0	0	10	0

Bowling	Mat	Balls	Runs	Wkts	BBI	BBM	Ave	Econ	SR	5w	10
Tests	9	1606	957	32	5/38	7/102	29.90	3.57	50.1	1	0
ODIs	4	204	185	4	2/58	2/58	46.25	5.44	51.0	0	0
First-class	169	29246	16427	619	9/67	11/95	26.53	3.37	47.2	26	3
List A	87	3616	3073	99	4/45	4/45	31.04	5.09	36.5	0	0
T20s	44	936	1034	35	3/15	3/15	29.54	6.62	26.7	0	0

CRAIG OVERTON   RHB / RFM / R0 / W0 / MVP4

FULL NAME: Craig Overton
BORN: April 10, 1994, Barnstaple, Devon
SQUAD NO: 12
HEIGHT: 6ft 5in
NICKNAME: Goober
EDUCATION: West Buckland School
TEAMS: England, Somerset
ROLE: Allrounder
DEBUT: Test: 2017; First-class: 2012; List A: 2012; T20: 2014

SOMERSET

BEST BATTING: 138 Somerset vs Hampshire, Taunton, 2016
BEST BOWLING: 6-74 Somerset vs Warwickshire, Edgbaston, 2015
COUNTY CAP: 2016

WHAT GOT YOU INTO CRICKET? Spending summers down our local cricket club watching my dad play
FAMILY TIES? My father played Minor County cricket and my twin brother Jamie also plays for Somerset
STRANGEST THING SEEN IN A GAME? Someone trying to go for a run-out and ending up kicking the ball for four overthrows
'ROY OF THE ROVERS' MOMENT? Scoring my maiden first-class hundred for Somerset in 2016
CRICKETING HERO? Andrew Flintoff
SURPRISING FACT? Me and brother don't live with each other
UNUSUAL OBJECT AT HOME? A toy putter which you can use while on the toilet
TWITTER: @craigoverton12

Batting	Mat	Inns	NO	Runs	HS	Ave	SR	100	50	Ct	St
Tests	2	4	1	62	41*	20.66	43.97	0	0	1	0
First-class	64	91	13	1707	138	21.88	65.07	1	7	37	0
List A	51	36	8	484	60*	17.28	111.00	0	1	20	0
T20s	29	16	7	194	35*	21.55	121.25	0	0	15	0

Bowling	Mat	Balls	Runs	Wkts	BBI	BBM	Ave	Econ	SR	5w	10
Tests	2	354	226	6	3/105	4/116	37.66	3.83	59.0	0	0
First-class	64	10190	5318	201	6/74	9/134	26.45	3.13	50.6	4	0
List A	51	2300	2027	58	3/21	3/21	34.94	5.28	39.6	0	0
T20s	29	534	826	22	3/17	3/17	37.54	9.28	24.2	0	0

JAMIE OVERTON

RHB / RFM / R0 / W0

SOMERSET

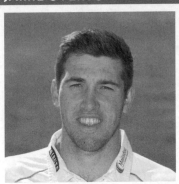

FULL NAME: Jamie Overton
BORN: April 10, 1994, Barnstaple, Devon
SQUAD NO: 8
HEIGHT: 6ft 5in
NICKNAME: Goober, J
EDUCATION: West Buckland School
TEAMS: Somerset, England Lions
ROLE: Bowler
DEBUT: First-class: 2012; List A: 2012; T20: 2015

BEST BATTING: 56 Somerset vs Warwickshire, Edgbaston, 2014
BEST BOWLING: 6-95 Somerset vs Middlesex, Taunton, 2013

FAMILY TIES? My dad played for Devon and my twin brother Craig plays for Somerset too
'ROY OF THE ROVERS' MOMENT? The run-chase against Gloucestershire in the 2016 One-Day Cup
CRICKETING HERO? James Anderson – growing up I felt we bowled in similar ways
NON-CRICKETING HEROES? Muhammad Ali – he was just a genius. Rory McIlroy – he makes it look so easy
SURPRISING FACT? I was in a film when I was younger
TWITTER: @JamieOverton

Batting	Mat	Inns	NO	Runs	HS	Ave	SR	100	50	Ct	St
First-class	45	61	17	766	56	17.40	80.88	0	4	4	0
List A	24	16	6	230	40*	23.00	126.37	0	0	13	0
T20s	26	14	6	95	31	11.87	148.43	0	0	11	0

Bowling	Mat	Balls	Runs	Wkts	BBI	BBM	Ave	Econ	SR	5w	10
First-class	45	5959	3604	103	6/95	7/134	34.99	3.62	57.8	2	0
List A	24	953	1032	37	4/42	4/42	27.89	6.49	25.7	0	0
T20s	26	525	786	28	4/22	4/22	28.07	8.98	18.7	0	0

FULL NAME: Antonio Paul Palladino
BORN: June 29, 1983, Tower Hamlets, London
SQUAD NO: 28
HEIGHT: 6ft 4in
NICKNAME: Battler, Pallas, Dino
EDUCATION: Cardinal Pole Sixth Form, London; Anglia Polytechnic University
TEAMS: Namibia, Derbyshire, Essex
ROLE: Bowler
DEBUT: First-class: 2003; List A: 2003; T20: 2005

DERBYSHIRE

BEST BATTING: 106 Derbyshire vs Australia A, Derby, 2012
BEST BOWLING: 7-53 Derbyshire vs Kent, Derby, 2012
COUNTY CAP: 2012 (Derbyshire)

FAMILY TIES? My dad played in the Kent league
'ROY OF THE ROVERS' MOMENT? Winning Division Two of the County Championship in 2012
BEST THING ABOUT YOUR HOME GROUND? It's normally got a bit in it for the seamers
BEST OPPOSING PLAYER IN COUNTY CRICKET? Darren Stevens (Ken)
YOUNG OPPOSING PLAYER WHO HAS IMPRESSED YOU? Josh Tongue (Wor) – he's tall, has good pace and swings it
SURPRISING FACT ABOUT YOU? I like classical music and I sometimes wear a Batman underarmour when I bowl
SURPRISING FACT ABOUT A TEAMMATE? Alex Hughes has toenails that could cut a man's head off
CRICKETING HERO? Ian Botham
UNUSUAL OBJECT AT HOME? The complete Sherlock Holmes collectors' hardback
TWITTER: @apalladino28

Batting	Mat	Inns	NO	Runs	HS	Ave	SR	100	50	Ct	St
First-class	143	200	41	2464	106	15.49	49.82	1	7	39	0
List A	56	32	7	267	31	10.68	92.06	0	0	6	0
T20s	26	12	5	48	14*	6.85	81.35	0	0	5	0

Bowling	Mat	Balls	Runs	Wkts	BBI	BBM	Ave	Econ	SR	5w	10
First-class	143	23380	11563	386	7/53	9/118	29.95	2.96	60.5	13	0
List A	56	2231	1998	54	5/49	5/49	37.00	5.37	41.3	1	0
T20s	26	490	614	28	4/21	4/21	21.92	7.51	17.5	0	0

GEORGE PANAYI

RHB / RFM / RO / WO

WARWICKSHIRE

FULL NAME: George David Panayi
BORN: September 23, 1997, Enfield, Middlesex
SQUAD NO: 33
HEIGHT: 6ft 3in
NICKNAME: Poon
EDUCATION: Shrewsbury School
TEAMS: Warwickshire
ROLE: Bowler
DEBUT: First-class: 2017

BEST BATTING: 16 Warwickshire vs Lancashire, Edgbaston, 2017
BEST BOWLING: 3-41 Warwickshire vs Lancashire, Edgbaston, 2017

WHAT GOT YOU INTO CRICKET? After failing at football it was the next sport on the list
FAMILY TIES? Dad played village cricket
'ROY OF THE ROVERS' MOMENT? Making my first-class debut in 2017
BEST THING ABOUT YOUR HOME GROUND? The Hollies Stand
BEST OPPOSING PLAYER IN COUNTY CRICKET? Samit Patel (Not)
YOUNG OPPOSING PLAYER WHO HAS IMPRESSED YOU? Ollie Pope (Sur) – he has every shot in the book
IF YOU WEREN'T A CRICKETER? I'd be a musician
SURPRISING FACT ABOUT YOU? I'm a big fan of jazz and I have a diploma in saxophone performance. I sing my favourite song of the day in my head as I walk out to bat
SURPRISING FACT ABOUT A TEAMMATE? Josh Poysden has an obsession with sausage dogs
WHERE IS PARADISE? Hogwarts
CRICKETING HERO? Andrew Flintoff – for sheer entertainment
NON-CRICKETING HERO? Derek Trotter – for his ability to sell rubbish from a suitcase
UNUSUAL OBJECT AT HOME? A fish graveyard
TWITTER: @Gpanayi

Batting	Mat	Inns	NO	Runs	HS	Ave	SR	100	50	Ct	St
First-class	2	3	0	17	16	5.66	29.31	0	0	0	0

Bowling	Mat	Balls	Runs	Wkts	BBI	BBM	Ave	Econ	SR	5w	10
First-class	2	231	141	4	3/41	3/75	35.25	3.66	57.7	0	0

CALLUM PARKINSON

RHB / SLA / R0 / W0

FULL NAME: Callum Francis Parkinson
BORN: October 24, 1996, Bolton, Lancashire
SQUAD NO: 10
HEIGHT: 5ft 9in
NICKNAME: Parko
EDUCATION: Bolton School; Canon Slade, Bolton
TEAMS: Leicestershire, Derbyshire
ROLE: Bowler
DEBUT: First-class: 2016; List A: 2017; T20: 2017

LEICESTERSHIRE

BEST BATTING: 75 Leicestershire vs Kent, Canterbury, 2017
BEST BOWLING: 8-148 Leicestershire vs Worcestershire, Worcester, 2017

WHAT GOT YOU INTO CRICKET? My dad took me to our local club Heaton CC when I was six
FAMILY TIES? My dad played in the Bolton league. My twin brother Matt is at Lancashire
BEST ADVICE EVER RECEIVED? Get your head down and give it a crack
'ROY OF THE ROVERS' MOMENT? Receiving abuse from the Yorkshire crowd on my List A debut after a misfield – I couldn't stop laughing
BEST THING ABOUT YOUR HOME GROUND? The food. And Harry the media intern
IF YOU WEREN'T A CRICKETER? I'd be a history teacher
SURPRISING FACT ABOUT YOU? I'm going bald
CRICKETING HERO? Daniel Vettori – a lovely bloke and great to watch as a bowler. And he scored useful lower-order runs, which I'm passionate about
NON-CRICKETING HERO? Roy Marland – my old mentor who sadly passed away a few years ago
TWITTER: @cal_parky

Batting	Mat	Inns	NO	Runs	HS	Ave	SR	100	50	Ct	St
First-class	9	13	6	183	75	26.14	54.30	0	1	3	0
List A	1	1	0	3	3	3.00	37.50	0	0	0	0
T20s	15	5	4	15	8*	15.00	75.00	0	0	3	0

Bowling	Mat	Balls	Runs	Wkts	BBI	BBM	Ave	Econ	SR	5w	10
First-class	9	1908	1087	31	8/148	10/185	35.06	3.41	61.5	1	1
List A	1	54	44	1	1/44	1/44	44.00	4.88	54.0	0	0
T20s	15	282	377	15	3/20	3/20	25.13	8.02	18.8	0	0

MATTHEW PARKINSON

RHB / LB / RO / WO

LANCASHIRE

FULL NAME: Matthew William Parkinson
BORN: October 24, 1996, Bolton, Lancashire
SQUAD NO: 28
HEIGHT: 5ft 9in
NICKNAME: Parky
EDUCATION: Canon Slade School, Bolton
TEAMS: Lancashire, England Lions
ROLE: Bowler
DEBUT: First-class: 2016; T20: 2017

BEST BATTING: 13 Lancashire vs Middlesex, Lord's, 2017
BEST BOWLING: 5-49 Lancashire vs Warwickshire, Old Trafford, 2016

WHAT GOT YOU INTO CRICKET? My dad got me into cricket at my local club Heaton CC
FAMILY TIES? Dad played for Lancashire Federation U19 and league cricket in Bolton. My
twin Callum plays for Leicestershire
'ROY OF THE ROVERS' MOMENT? Taking a five-for on my Lancashire debut against
Warwickshire at Old Trafford in 2016
BEST THING ABOUT YOUR HOME GROUND? The history and the heritage – it makes me
proud to be playing there
YOUNG OPPOSING PLAYER WHO HAS IMPRESSED YOU? Jamie Porter (Ess)
SURPRISING FACT ABOUT YOU? I lost my front four teeth in a cricket accident when I was 12
and recently underwent implant surgery
WHERE IS PARADISE? Whitehaven Beach, Australia
CRICKETING HERO? Stuart MacGill
NON-CRICKETING HERO? Nelson Mandela
TWITTER: @mattyparky96

Batting	Mat	Inns	NO	Runs	HS	Ave	SR	100	50	Ct	St
First-class	9	11	4	36	13	5.14	23.37	0	0	2	0
T20s	9	4	4	10	7*	-	111.11	0	0	1	0

Bowling	Mat	Balls	Runs	Wkts	BBI	BBM	Ave	Econ	SR	5w	10
First-class	9	1145	671	24	5/49	7/105	27.95	3.51	47.7	1	0
T20s	9	192	194	14	4/23	4/23	13.85	6.06	13.7	0	0

STEPHEN PARRY   RHB / SLA / R0 / W0 / MVP91

FULL NAME: Stephen David Parry
BORN: January 12, 1986, Manchester
SQUAD NO: 4
HEIGHT: 6ft
NICKNAME: Pazza
EDUCATION: Audenshaw High School, Manchester
TEAMS: England, Lancashire, Brisbane Heat
ROLE: Bowler
DEBUT: ODI: 2014; T20I: 2014; First-class: 2007; List A: 2009; T20: 2009

LANCASHIRE

BEST BATTING: 44 Lancashire vs Somerset, Old Trafford, 2017
BEST BOWLING: 5-23 Lancashire vs Durham UCCE, Durham University, 2007
COUNTY CAP: 2015

NON-CRICKETING HERO? Muhammad Ali
IF YOU WEREN'T A CRICKETER? I'd be fishing
SURPRISING FACT? I'm an elite table-tennis player
TWITTER: @SDParry86
NOTES: Left-arm spinner known as a white-ball specialist, Parry played a handful of limited-overs matches for England in 2014 and 2015. Has well over 200 wickets in List A and T20 cricket combined. After not playing a first-class match for nearly three years, Parry made a return to Championship action last summer, taking 25 wickets at 31.08 in 13 games

Batting	Mat	Inns	NO	Runs	HS	Ave	SR	100	50	Ct	St
ODIs	2	-	-	-	-	-	-	-	-	0	0
T20Is	5	1	0	1	1	1.00	100.00	0	0	2	0
First-class	23	28	2	445	44	17.11	45.92	0	0	7	0
List A	89	44	19	318	31	12.72	77.37	0	0	29	0
T20s	121	34	21	133	15*	10.23	104.72	0	0	27	0

Bowling	Mat	Balls	Runs	Wkts	BBI	BBM	Ave	Econ	SR	5w	10
ODIs	2	114	92	4	3/32	3/32	23.00	4.84	28.5	0	0
T20Is	5	96	138	3	2/33	2/33	46.00	8.62	32.0	0	0
First-class	23	3281	1442	47	5/23	6/101	30.68	2.63	69.8	2	0
List A	89	3879	3253	108	5/17	5/17	30.12	5.03	35.9	1	0
T20s	121	2526	3039	119	5/13	5/13	25.53	7.21	21.2	1	0

JEETAN PATEL

RHB / OB / RO / W5 / MVP2

WARWICKSHIRE

FULL NAME: Jeetan Shashi Patel
BORN: May 7, 1980, Wellington, New Zealand
SQUAD NO: 5
HEIGHT: 5ft 8in
NICKNAME: Dave
TEAMS: New Zealand, Warwickshire, North Island, Wellington
ROLE: Bowler
DEBUT: Test: 2006; ODI: 2005; T20I: 2005; First-class: 1999; List A: 1999; T20: 2005

BEST BATTING: 120 Warwickshire vs Yorkshire, Edgbaston, 2014
BEST BOWLING: 7-38 Warwickshire vs Somerset, Taunton, 2015
COUNTY CAP: 2012

WHAT GOT YOU INTO CRICKET? My old man – he's a cricket badger
BEST THING ABOUT YOUR HOME GROUND? Edgbaston has the best dressing rooms in the country
YOUNG OPPOSING PLAYER WHO HAS IMPRESSED YOU? Tom Abell (Som) – he has been excellent as captain
WHERE IS PARADISE? Any golf course
CRICKETING HERO? Sir Richard Hadlee, Saqlain Mushtaq
NON-CRICKETING HERO? Tiger Woods, Jim Furyk
UNUSUAL OBJECT AT HOME? A lot of shoe horns

Batting	Mat	Inns	NO	Runs	HS	Ave	SR	100	50	Ct	St
Tests	24	38	8	381	47	12.70	51.62	0	0	13	0
ODIs	43	15	8	95	34	13.57	58.64	0	0	13	0
T20Is	11	4	1	9	5	3.00	64.28	0	0	4	0
First-class	254	335	72	5894	120	22.41		3	26	130	0
List A	210	111	34	734	50	9.53		0	1	86	0
T20s	195	79	25	369	34*	6.83	126.80	0	0	70	0

Bowling	Mat	Balls	Runs	Wkts	BBI	BBM	Ave	Econ	SR	5w	10
Tests	24	5833	3078	65	5/110	6/151	47.35	3.16	89.7	1	0
ODIs	43	2014	1691	49	3/11	3/11	34.51	5.03	41.1	0	0
T20Is	11	199	269	16	3/20	3/20	16.81	8.11	12.4	0	0
First-class	254	51927	25028	731	7/38	10/123	34.23	2.89	71.0	26	2
List A	210	10149	7869	257	5/43	5/43	30.61	4.65	39.4	1	0
T20s	195	3953	4562	196	4/11	4/11	23.27	6.92	20.1	0	0

RAVI PATEL

RHB / SLA / RO / WO

FULL NAME: Ravi Hasmukh Patel
BORN: August 4, 1991, Harrow, Middlesex
SQUAD NO: 36
HEIGHT: 5ft 9in
NICKNAME: Rav, Ravster
EDUCATION: Merchant Taylors' School, London; Loughborough University
TEAMS: Middlesex, England Lions, Essex
ROLE: Bowler
DEBUT: First-class: 2010; List A: 2010; T20: 2013

MIDDLESEX

BEST BATTING: 26* Middlesex vs Warwickshire, Uxbridge, 2013
BEST BOWLING: 7-81 Middlesex vs Somerset, Taunton, 2017

WHAT GOT YOU INTO CRICKET? My dad pushed me to play when I was four
FAMILY TIES? My dad played university cricket in India
'ROY OF THE ROVERS' MOMENT? Taking the last Lancashire wicket to send them down in 2012
BEST THING ABOUT YOUR HOME GROUND? The history
BEST OPPOSING PLAYER IN COUNTY CRICKET? Ravi Bopara (Ess)
YOUNG OPPOSING PLAYER WHO HAS IMPRESSED YOU? Jack Leach (Som) – amazing accuracy for a left-arm spinner
IF YOU WEREN'T A CRICKETER? I'd be working in the property business
SURPRISING FACT ABOUT YOU? I can speak a little bit of German
WHERE IS PARADISE? Dubai
CRICKETING HERO? Pragyan Ojha – he's got the best action for a left-arm spinner that I've ever seen and I love watching him bowl
NON-CRICKETING HERO? Cristiano Ronaldo
TWITTER: @ravi36patel

Batting	Mat	Inns	NO	Runs	HS	Ave	SR	100	50	Ct	St
First-class	24	34	17	187	26*	11.00	38.87	0	0	6	0
List A	17	7	4	39	18	13.00	68.42	0	0	1	0
T20s	29	5	3	14	11*	7.00	70.00	0	0	5	0

Bowling	Mat	Balls	Runs	Wkts	BBI	BBM	Ave	Econ	SR	5w	10
First-class	24	4496	2372	75	7/81	12/173	31.62	3.16	59.9	3	1
List A	17	810	697	17	3/71	3/71	41.00	5.16	47.6	0	0
T20s	29	648	761	31	4/18	4/18	24.54	7.04	20.9	0	0

RYAN PATEL

LHB / RFM / RO / WO

FULL NAME: Ryan Patel
BORN: October 26, 1997, Sutton, Surrey
SQUAD NO: 26
HEIGHT: 5ft 10in
NICKNAME: Pat
EDUCATION: Whitgift School, Croydon
TEAMS: Surrey
ROLE: Allrounder
DEBUT: First-class: 2017

BEST BATTING: 81 Surrey vs Hampshire, Southampton, 2017
BEST BOWLING: 1-11 Surrey vs Somerset, The Oval, 2017

WHAT GOT YOU INTO CRICKET? Prep school
BEST ADVICE EVER RECEIVED? Keep things simple
'ROY OF THE ROVERS' MOMENT? Making my first-class debut against Middlesex
BEST THING ABOUT YOUR HOME GROUND? The atmosphere when a big crowd is in
BEST OPPOSING PLAYER IN COUNTY CRICKET? Marcus Trescothick (Som)
YOUNG OPPOSING PLAYER WHO HAS IMPRESSED YOU? Olly Stone (War)
IF YOU WEREN'T A CRICKETER? I'd be working in Arun Harinath's BP garage
SURPRISING FACT ABOUT YOU? I was an opening bowler who batted down the order until I was 15 but have since become an opening batsman who bowls
SURPRISING FACT ABOUT A TEAMMATE? Matt Dunn used to live in Norway
WHERE IS PARADISE? The Maldives
CRICKETING HERO? Jacques Kallis – the best allrounder ever
NON-CRICKETING HERO? My dad – he's shown me how to get through the difficult times

Batting	Mat	Inns	NO	Runs	HS	Ave	SR	100	50	Ct	St
First-class	4	6	0	170	81	28.33	43.36	0	1	2	0

Bowling	Mat	Balls	Runs	Wkts	BBI	BBM	Ave	Econ	SR	5w	10
First-class	4	252	128	2	1/11	1/28	64.00	3.04	126.0	0	0

SAMIT PATEL

RHB / SLA / R4 / W0 / MVP1

FULL NAME: Samit Rohit Patel
BORN: November 30, 1984, Leicester
SQUAD NO: 21
HEIGHT: 5ft 8in
NICKNAME: Sarnie, Slippery
EDUCATION: Worksop College, Nottinghamshire
TEAMS: England, Nottinghamshire, Islamabad United, Mohammedan Sporting Club, Rajshahi Kings, Warriors, Wellington
ROLE: Allrounder
DEBUT: Test: 2012; ODI: 2008; T20I: 2011; First-class: 2002; List A: 2002; T20: 2003

BEST BATTING: 257* Nottinghamshire vs Gloucestershire, Bristol, 2017
BEST BOWLING: 7-68 Nottinghamshire vs Hampshire, Southampton, 2011
COUNTY CAP: 2008; **BENEFIT:** 2017

FAMILY TIES? My dad played league cricket and my brother Akhil played for Notts for two years
'ROY OF THE ROVERS' MOMENT? Taking five wickets against South Africa at The Oval and scoring 70 off 40 balls at Chandigarh against India
SUPERSTITIONS? I always touch the floor before I cross the line as I am walking out to bat
CRICKETING HEROES? Sachin Tendulkar, Stephen Fleming
NON-CRICKETING HERO? Tiger Woods
IF YOU WEREN'T A CRICKETER? I'd be a sales rep
SURPRISING FACT? I bowl left-handed but throw right-handed

Batting	Mat	Inns	NO	Runs	HS	Ave	SR	100	50	Ct	St
Tests	6	9	0	151	42	16.77	44.67	0	0	3	0
ODIs	36	22	7	482	70*	32.13	93.23	0	1	7	0
T20Is	18	14	2	189	67	15.75	109.24	0	1	3	0
First-class	198	319	17	11337	257*	37.53	63.39	26	53	129	0
List A	228	198	32	5852	129*	35.25	85.09	6	33	67	0
T20s	215	192	32	4197	90*	26.23	125.73	0	27	63	0

Bowling	Mat	Balls	Runs	Wkts	BBI	BBM	Ave	Econ	SR	5w	10
Tests	6	858	421	7	2/27	3/164	60.14	2.94	122.5	0	0
ODIs	36	1187	1091	24	5/41	5/41	45.45	5.51	49.4	1	0
T20Is	18	252	321	7	2/6	2/6	45.85	7.64	36.0	0	0
First-class	198	22630	11662	303	7/68	11/111	38.48	3.09	74.6	4	1
List A	228	7495	6755	207	6/13	6/13	32.63	5.40	36.2	2	0
T20s	215	3906	4669	179	4/20	4/20	26.08	7.17	21.8	0	0

STEVEN PATTERSON RHB / RMF / RO / W2

YORKSHIRE

FULL NAME: Steven Andrew Patterson
BORN: October 3, 1983, Beverley, Yorkshire
SQUAD NO: 17
HEIGHT: 6ft 4in
NICKNAME: Dead Man, Patto
EDUCATION: Malet Lambert School, Hull; St Mary's Sixth Form College, Hull; University of Leeds
TEAMS: Yorkshire
ROLE: Bowler
DEBUT: First-class: 2005; List A: 2003; T20: 2009

BEST BATTING: 63* Yorkshire vs Warwickshire, Edgbaston, 2016
BEST BOWLING: 6-56 Yorkshire vs Durham, Chester-le-Street, 2016
COUNTY CAP: 2012

FAMILY TIES? My grandad played for Durham before the Second World War
'ROY OF THE ROVERS' MOMENT? Making my Championship debut at Scarborough, receiving my first XI cap, playing in the Champions League T20, winning the County Championship
CRICKETING HEROES? Glenn McGrath, Shaun Pollock
NON-CRICKETING HERO? My grandad
IF YOU WEREN'T A CRICKETER? I'd be working in finance
SURPRISING FACT? I love my golf

Batting	Mat	Inns	NO	Runs	HS	Ave	SR	100	50	Ct	St
First-class	132	152	39	1839	63*	16.27	37.44	0	3	23	0
List A	81	34	20	207	25*	14.78		0	0	12	0
T20s	50	7	4	9	3*	3.00	50.00	0	0	5	0

Bowling	Mat	Balls	Runs	Wkts	BBI	BBM	Ave	Econ	SR	5w	10
First-class	132	21143	9765	348	6/56	8/94	28.06	2.77	60.7	6	0
List A	81	3416	2852	101	6/32	6/32	28.23	5.00	33.8	2	0
T20s	50	1002	1401	49	4/30	4/30	28.59	8.38	20.4	0	0

DAVID PAYNE

RHB / LFM / R0 / W0

FULL NAME: David Alan Payne
BORN: February 15, 1991, Poole, Dorset
SQUAD NO: 14
HEIGHT: 6ft 2in
NICKNAME: Sid, Payney
EDUCATION: Lytchett Minster Secondary and Sixth Form, Poole, Dorset
TEAMS: Gloucestershire
ROLE: Bowler
DEBUT: First-class: 2011; List A: 2009; T20: 2010

GLOUCESTERSHIRE

BEST BATTING: 67* Gloucestershire vs Glamorgan, Cardiff, 2016
BEST BOWLING: 6-26 Gloucestershire vs Leicestershire, Bristol, 2011
COUNTY CAP: 2011

'ROY OF THE ROVERS' MOMENT? Bowling the final over of the 2015 One-Day Cup final against Surrey at Lord's with seven needed and taking the last two wickets
BEST THING ABOUT YOUR HOME GROUND? The enclosure when the temporary stands are up and there is a packed house
BEST OPPOSING PLAYER IN COUNTY CRICKET? Samit Patel (Not)
YOUNG OPPOSING PLAYER WHO HAS IMPRESSED YOU? Ed Barnard (Wor) – talented allrounder
IF YOU WEREN'T A CRICKETER? I'd be working in the media
SURPRISING FACT ABOUT YOU? I cut my own hair
SURPRISING FACT ABOUT A TEAMMATE? Ollie Currill and Callum Gregory are not brothers
CRICKETING HERO? Andrew Flintoff – for the way he played the game on and off the field
NON-CRICKETING HERO? David Beckham
TWITTER: @sidpayne7

Batting	Mat	Inns	NO	Runs	HS	Ave	SR	100	50	Ct	St
First-class	76	91	28	1337	67*	21.22	48.45	0	6	26	0
List A	58	23	14	102	23	11.33	69.38	0	0	16	0
T20s	55	17	9	46	10	5.75	90.19	0	0	11	0

Bowling	Mat	Balls	Runs	Wkts	BBI	BBM	Ave	Econ	SR	5w	10
First-class	76	11944	6528	198	6/26	9/96	32.96	3.27	60.3	3	0
List A	58	2441	2299	101	7/29	7/29	22.76	5.65	24.1	3	0
T20s	55	1022	1469	65	5/24	5/24	22.60	8.62	15.7	1	0

MARK PETTINI

RHB / RM / R1 / W0

LEICESTERSHIRE

FULL NAME: Mark Lewis Pettini
BORN: August 7, 1983, Brighton
SQUAD NO: 6
HEIGHT: 5ft 11in
NICKNAME: Swampy
EDUCATION: Hills Road Sixth Form College, Cambridge; Cardiff University
TEAMS: Leicestershire, Essex, Kala Bagan Krira Chakra, Mashonaland Eagles, Mountaineers
ROLE: Batsman
DEBUT: First-class: 2001; List A: 2001; T20: 2003

BEST BATTING: 209 Mountaineers vs Matabeleland Tuskers, Bulawayo, 2014
BEST BOWLING: 1-72 Essex vs Leicestershire, Leicester, 2012
COUNTY CAP: 2006 (Essex)

'ROY OF THE ROVERS' MOMENT? Winning two Pro40 titles with Essex, being made Essex captain in 2007 and winning the Friends Provident Trophy in 2008
CRICKETING HEROES? Graham Gooch, Andy Flower, Ronnie Irani
NOTES: Scored 208* against Derbyshire in 2006. Made England's inaugural 30-man squad for the 2007 World T20, the same month he replaced Ronnie Irani as Essex captain. Led Essex to victory in the 2008 FP Trophy final. Hit his highest score of 209* in 2014 for Mountaineers in Zimbabwe's Logan Cup. Took over the one-day and T20 captaincy when he joined Leicestershire in September 2015 but was replaced as limited-overs skipper by Clint McKay ahead of the 2017 season. Scored one hundred in the Championship last summer but was more consistent in 50-over cricket, finishing as Leicestershire's leading run-scorer in the One-Day Cup

Batting	Mat	Inns	NO	Runs	HS	Ave	SR	100	50	Ct	St
First-class	178	296	42	8933	209	35.16	47.90	15	49	120	0
List A	188	173	12	4811	159	29.88	84.19	9	30	69	0
T20s	135	131	10	3284	95*	27.14	127.83	0	21	43	0

Bowling	Mat	Balls	Runs	Wkts	BBI	BBM	Ave	Econ	SR	5w	10
First-class	178	132	263	1	1/72	1/72	263.00	11.95	132.0	0	0
List A	188	-	-	-	-	-	-	-	-	-	-
T20s	135	-	-	-	-	-	-	-	-	-	-

FULL NAME: Mathew William Pillans
BORN: July 4, 1991, Pretoria, South Africa
SQUAD NO: 47
HEIGHT: 6ft 4in
NICKNAME: Matty P
EDUCATION: Pretoria Boys High School
TEAMS: Surrey, Dolphins, KwaZulu-Natal, Leicestershire, Northerns
ROLE: Bowler
DEBUT: First-class: 2012; List A: 2013; T20: 2014

SURREY

BEST BATTING: 56 Leicestershire vs Northamptonshire, Northampton, 2017
BEST BOWLING: 6-67 Dolphins vs Knights, Durban, 2015

FAMILY TIES? My mum played for the Springbok hockey team for 13 years and my dad played rugby in Zimbabwe and represented the World XV
BEST ADVICE EVER RECEIVED? Just express yourself and your skills
'ROY OF THE ROVERS' MOMENT? Bowling the final over for Leicestershire against Notts in the T20 Blast last summer and defending eight runs
BEST OPPOSING PLAYER IN COUNTY CRICKET? Dan Christian (Not)
YOUNG OPPOSING PLAYER WHO HAS IMPRESSED YOU? Callum Parkinson (Lei) – he is an economic T20 bowler and had a great T20 Blast in 2017
IF YOU WEREN'T A CRICKETER? I'd be a fly-fisherman
SURPRISING FACT ABOUT YOU? I had open-heart surgery when I was 12
CRICKETING HERO? Brett Lee. He is an amazingly dedicated cricketer and a great man both on and off the field to anyone he meets
NON-CRICKETING HERO? Nelson Mandela – he put aside the wrongdoings he suffered and strived for a better, unified country
TWITTER: @matwilpil

Batting	Mat	Inns	NO	Runs	HS	Ave	SR	100	50	Ct	St
First-class	39	56	5	709	56	13.90	64.86	0	1	20	0
List A	12	8	4	79	20*	19.75	91.86	0	0	3	0
T20s	25	15	8	161	34*	23.00	106.62	0	0	6	0

Bowling	Mat	Balls	Runs	Wkts	BBI	BBM	Ave	Econ	SR	5w	10
First-class	39	6127	3453	126	6/67	10/129	27.40	3.38	48.6	3	1
List A	12	420	344	16	3/14	3/14	21.50	4.91	26.2	0	0
T20s	25	499	666	25	3/15	3/15	26.64	8.00	19.9	0	0

LIAM PLUNKETT

RHB / RFM / RO / W3

YORKSHIRE

FULL NAME: Liam Edward Plunkett
BORN: April 6, 1985, Middlesbrough
SQUAD NO: 28
HEIGHT: 6ft 3in
NICKNAME: Pudsy
EDUCATION: Nunthorpe Comprehensive School, Middlesbrough; Teesside Tertiary College
TEAMS: England, Yorkshire, Dolphins, Durham
ROLE: Bowler
DEBUT: Test: 2005; ODI: 2005; T20I: 2006; First-class: 2003; List A: 2003; T20: 2003

BEST BATTING: 126 Yorkshire vs Hampshire, Headingley, 2016
BEST BOWLING: 6-33 Durham vs Leeds/Bradford MCCU, Headingley, 2013
COUNTY CAP: 2013 (Yorkshire)

TWITTER: @Liam628
NOTES: Only the second player to record a five-wicket haul on his Championship debut for Durham, 5-53 vs Yorkshire at Headingley in 2003. Made his England Test debut in November 2005 against Pakistan at Lahore. Signed for Yorkshire in October 2012 and claimed 42 first-class wickets at 25.35 the following season. In 2014 he played his first Test for England since 2007 and picked up 18 wickets in four Tests before injury ended his summer. Has not played a Test since but continues to be a regular in England's limited-overs teams. Niggling injuries and England duty restricted Plunkett to just 10 appearances across all three competitions last summer

Batting	Mat	Inns	NO	Runs	HS	Ave	SR	100	50	Ct	St
Tests	13	20	5	238	55*	15.86	46.75	0	1	3	0
ODIs	65	38	13	516	56	20.64	101.97	0	1	22	0
T20Is	15	8	2	23	18	3.83	109.52	0	0	5	0
First-class	155	213	39	4376	126	25.14		3	22	86	0
List A	184	115	41	1509	72	20.39	101.61	0	3	57	0
T20s	119	74	29	697	41	15.48	132.00	0	0	34	0

Bowling	Mat	Balls	Runs	Wkts	BBI	BBM	Ave	Econ	SR	5w	10
Tests	13	2659	1536	41	5/64	9/176	37.46	3.46	64.8	1	0
ODIs	65	3122	3022	100	5/52	5/52	30.22	5.80	31.2	1	0
T20Is	15	335	416	19	3/21	3/21	21.89	7.45	17.6	0	0
First-class	155	23711	14273	452	6/33	11/119	31.57	3.61	52.4	11	1
List A	184	7931	7210	239	5/52	5/52	30.16	5.45	33.1	1	0
T20s	119	2229	2938	110	5/31	5/31	26.70	7.90	20.2	1	0

HARRY PODMORE

RHB / RMF / R0 / W0

FULL NAME: Harry William Podmore
BORN: July 23, 1994, Hammersmith, Middlesex
SQUAD NO: 23
HEIGHT: 6ft 3in
NICKNAME: Podders, Pods, Pongo, Chav
EDUCATION: Twyford CofE High School, London
TEAMS: Middlesex, Derbyshire, Glamorgan
ROLE: Bowler
DEBUT: First-class: 2016; List A: 2014; T20: 2014

MIDDLESEX

BEST BATTING: 66* Derbyshire vs Sussex, Hove, 2017
BEST BOWLING: 4-54 Middlesex vs Somerset, Taunton, 2016

WHAT GOT YOU INTO CRICKET? Ealing CC
STRANGEST THING SEEN IN A GAME? Ryan Higgins hit a bird out of the sky
'ROY OF THE ROVERS' MOMENT? Playing at Lord's for the first time (on TV!), signing for Middlesex, getting on the England fast-bowling programme
SUPERSTITIONS? The volume has to be on 23 on any electrical device
CRICKETING HEROES? Ian Botham, Andrew Flintoff
SURPRISING FACT? I have my family crest tattooed on my chest
TWITTER: @harrypod16

Batting	Mat	Inns	NO	Runs	HS	Ave	SR	100	50	Ct	St
First-class	12	18	4	209	66*	14.92	46.03	0	1	4	0
List A	6	1	1	1	1*	-	50.00	0	0	0	0
T20s	20	8	3	32	9	6.40	57.14	0	0	8	0

Bowling	Mat	Balls	Runs	Wkts	BBI	BBM	Ave	Econ	SR	5w	10
First-class	12	1693	968	31	4/54	7/143	31.22	3.43	54.6	0	0
List A	6	236	272	4	2/46	2/46	68.00	6.91	59.0	0	0
T20s	20	355	535	18	3/13	3/13	29.72	9.04	19.7	0	0

ED POLLOCK
LHB / OB / R0 / W0

FULL NAME: Edward John Pollock
BORN: July 10, 1995, High Wycombe, Buckinghamshire
SQUAD NO: 28
HEIGHT: 5ft 10in
EDUCATION: Royal Grammar School, Worcester; Shrewsbury School; Durham University
TEAMS: Warwickshire
ROLE: Batsman
DEBUT: First-class: 2015; T20: 2017

BEST BATTING: 52 Durham MCCU vs Gloucestershire, Bristol, 2017

WHAT GOT YOU INTO CRICKET? Playing in the back garden with my dad and brother
FAMILY TIES? My dad and brother have both captained Cambridge University
BEST ADVICE EVER RECEIVED? Keep it simple
BEST THING ABOUT YOUR HOME GROUND? The atmosphere in the Eric Hollies Stand
YOUNG OPPOSING PLAYER WHO HAS IMPRESSED YOU? Tom Kohler-Cadmore (Yor)
IF YOU WEREN'T A CRICKETER? I'd be an accountant
SURPRISING FACT ABOUT YOU? I am a published poet
SURPRISING FACT ABOUT A TEAMMATE? Josh Poysden's nickname is 'Dobby'
WHERE IS PARADISE? The Caribbean
CRICKETING HERO? Brian Lara – he played the game with such flair
NON-CRICKETING HERO? My parents – for all the sacrifices they've made for me
UNUSUAL OBJECT AT HOME? My first bat – a size three-quarters from Hunts County Bats
TWITTER: @kcollopde

Batting	Mat	Inns	NO	Runs	HS	Ave	SR	100	50	Ct	St
First-class	5	7	1	184	52	30.66	50.13	0	1	1	0
T20s	9	9	0	283	66	31.44	174.69	0	3	3	0

Bowling	Mat	Balls	Runs	Wkts	BBI	BBM	Ave	Econ	SR	5w	10
First-class	5	-	-	-	-	-	-	-	-	-	-
T20s	9	-	-	-	-	-	-	-	-	-	-

OLLIE POPE

RHB / WK / R0 / W0

FULL NAME: Oliver John Douglas Pope
BORN: January 2, 1998, Chelsea, Middlesex
SQUAD NO: 32
HEIGHT: 5ft 10in
NICKNAME: Pope-dog
EDUCATION: Cranleigh School, Surrey
TEAMS: Surrey
ROLE: Batsman/wicketkeeper
DEBUT: First-class: 2017; List A: 2016; T20: 2017

SURREY

BEST BATTING: 100* Surrey vs Hampshire, Southampton, 2017

'ROY OF THE ROVERS' MOMENT? My maiden first-class hundred for Surrey against Hampshire at Southampton in 2017
BEST THING ABOUT YOUR HOME GROUND? The crowd at The Oval for T20 matches
BEST OPPOSING PLAYER IN COUNTY CRICKET? Kyle Abbott (Ham)
YOUNG OPPOSING PLAYER WHO HAS IMPRESSED YOU? Eddie Byrom (Som) – he's not phased by much and has a solid technique
IF YOU WEREN'T A CRICKETER? I'd be a footballer
SURPRISING FACT ABOUT A TEAMMATE? Sam Curran is a useless footballer
WHERE IS PARADISE? The Oval
CRICKETING HERO? My former teammate Kumar Sangakkara – he just didn't stop scoring runs and was amazing to watch
NON-CRICKETING HERO? Dan Carter – rugby legend
TWITTER: @opope32

Batting	Mat	Inns	NO	Runs	HS	Ave	SR	100	50	Ct	St
First-class	6	10	3	270	100*	38.57	60.00	1	1	3	0
List A	6	5	0	138	55	27.60	102.98	0	1	2	0
T20s	13	13	3	253	46	25.30	124.63	0	0	3	0
Bowling	Mat	Balls	Runs	Wkts	BBI	BBM	Ave	Econ	SR	5w	10
First-class	6	-	-	-	-	-	-	-	-	-	-
List A	6	-	-	-	-	-	-	-	-	-	-
T20s	13	-	-	-	-	-	-	-	-	-	-

JAMIE PORTER — RHB / RMF / R0 / W3 / MVP8

ESSEX

FULL NAME: James Alexander Porter
BORN: May 25, 1993, Leytonstone, Essex
SQUAD NO: 44
HEIGHT: 6ft 1in
NICKNAME: Ports
EDUCATION: Oaks Park High School, Ilford; Epping Forest College, Essex
TEAMS: Essex, England Lions
ROLE: Bowler
DEBUT: First-class: 2014; List A: 2015; T20: 2017

BEST BATTING: 34 Essex vs Glamorgan, Cardiff, 2015
BEST BOWLING: 7-55 Essex vs Somerset, Chelmsford, 2017
COUNTY CAP: 2015

WHAT GOT YOU INTO CRICKET? Getting out of lessons at school! The 2005 Ashes got me hooked
STRANGEST THING SEEN IN A GAME? Teammate Ashar Zaidi blaze it with his black bat in a T20 against Middlesex in 2016
'ROY OF THE ROVERS' MOMENT? Winning the Championship in 2017
SUPERSTITIONS? I always sit close to the door in the dressing room
CRICKETING HEROES? Andrew Flintoff, James Anderson, Dale Steyn
NON-CRICKETING HEROES? James Bay (singer)
IF YOU WEREN'T A CRICKETER? I'd be selling caravans
SURPRISING FACT? I can cook minute-rice in 59 seconds
UNUSUAL OBJECT AT HOME? My black fridge
TWITTER: @jamieporter93

Batting	Mat	Inns	NO	Runs	HS	Ave	SR	100	50	Ct	St
First-class	51	58	24	216	34	6.35	25.47	0	0	18	0
List A	14	3	3	5	5*	-	125.00	0	0	0	0
T20s	8	1	1	1	1*	-	100.00	0	0	3	0

Bowling	Mat	Balls	Runs	Wkts	BBI	BBM	Ave	Econ	SR	5w	10
First-class	51	8574	4888	208	7/55	12/95	23.50	3.42	41.2	7	1
List A	14	567	497	15	4/40	4/40	33.13	5.25	37.8	0	0
T20s	8	114	183	6	4/20	4/20	30.50	9.63	19.0	0	0

MATTHEW POTTS

RHB / RFM / R0 / W0

FULL NAME: Matthew James Potts
BORN: October 29, 1998, Sunderland, County Durham
SQUAD NO: 35
HEIGHT: 6ft 2in
NICKNAME: Harry, Junior, Pottsy
EDUCATION: St Robert of Newminster Catholic School, Sunderland
TEAMS: Durham
ROLE: Allrounder
DEBUT: First-class: 2017

BEST BATTING: 53* Durham vs Derbyshire, Chester-le-Street, 2017
BEST BOWLING: 3-48 Durham vs Glamorgan, Chester-le-Street, 2017

WHAT GOT YOU INTO CRICKET? My family
BEST ADVICE EVER RECEIVED? Bowl at three wooden things
BEST THING ABOUT YOUR HOME GROUND? The lovely, warm temperatures in April
BEST OPPOSING PLAYER IN COUNTY CRICKET? Jofra Archer (Sus)
YOUNG OPPOSING PLAYER WHO HAS IMPRESSED YOU? Hamidullah Qadri (Der) – at the age of 16 he took a five-for on his first-class debut to bowl Derbyshire to a Championship victory against Glamorgan in 2017
IF YOU WEREN'T A CRICKETER? I'd be a PE teacher
SURPRISING FACT ABOUT A TEAMMATE? Ryan Pringle is a great chef
WHERE IS PARADISE? Wherever there is a gym
CRICKETING HERO? Kevin Pietersen – for the switch-hit
NON-CRICKETING HERO? Big Shaq
TWITTER: @mattyjpotts

Batting	Mat	Inns	NO	Runs	HS	Ave	SR	100	50	Ct	St
First-class	5	6	2	69	53*	17.25	46.00	0	1	0	0

Bowling	Mat	Balls	Runs	Wkts	BBI	BBM	Ave	Econ	SR	5w	10
First-class	5	978	465	14	3/48	5/106	33.21	2.85	69.8	0	0

STUART POYNTER

RHB / WK / R0 / W0

DURHAM

FULL NAME: Stuart William Poynter
BORN: October 18, 1990, Hammersmith, London
SQUAD NO: 90
HEIGHT: 5ft 8in
NICKNAME: Stuey, Points
EDUCATION: Teddington School, London
TEAMS: Ireland, Durham, Middlesex, Warwickshire
ROLE: Wicketkeeper
DEBUT: ODI: 2014; T20I: 2015; First-class: 2010; List A: 2012; T20: 2015

BEST BATTING: 125 Ireland vs Zimbabwe A, Harare, 2015

FAMILY TIES? My uncle Deryck and brother Andrew both played for Ireland
BEST ADVICE EVER RECEIVED? Play with a smile on your face
'ROY OF THE ROVERS' MOMENT? Making my debut for Ireland
BEST THING ABOUT YOUR HOME GROUND? Playing T20 under the lights at the Riverside
BEST OPPOSING PLAYER IN COUNTY CRICKET? Samit Patel (Not)
IF YOU WEREN'T A CRICKETER? I'd be working at Tesco
SURPRISING FACT ABOUT YOU? I'm a massive West Life fan and play the ukulele
SURPRISING FACT ABOUT A TEAMMATE? Graham Clark is a massive West Life fan too
WHERE IS PARADISE? At home on the sofa with my family watching Harry Potter
CRICKETING HERO? Jack Russell – the best keeper I have ever seen and one of the first I saw standing up to pace bowling
TWITTER: @spoynter_90

Batting	Mat	Inns	NO	Runs	HS	Ave	SR	100	50	Ct	St
ODIs	16	15	4	170	36	15.45	69.38	0	0	17	0
T20Is	14	12	0	152	39	12.66	111.76	0	0	6	1
First-class	25	36	1	806	125	23.02	63.26	1	2	69	2
List A	34	28	8	456	109	22.80	90.29	1	0	31	1
T20s	30	23	5	378	61*	21.00	125.16	0	1	14	4

Bowling	Mat	Balls	Runs	Wkts	BBI	BBM	Ave	Econ	SR	5w	10
ODIs	16	-	-	-	-	-	-	-	-	-	-
T20Is	14	-	-	-	-	-	-	-	-	-	-
First-class	25	-	-	-	-	-	-	-	-	-	-
List A	34	-	-	-	-	-	-	-	-	-	-
T20s	30	-	-	-	-	-	-	-	-	-	-

JOSH POYSDEN

LHB / LB / RO / WO

FULL NAME: Joshua Edward Poysden
BORN: August 8, 1991, Shoreham-by-Sea, Sussex
SQUAD NO: 14
HEIGHT: 5ft 10in
NICKNAME: Dobby, Bendicii, Nips like Stu's Eyes
EDUCATION: Cardinal Newman School, Hove; Anglia Ruskin University
TEAMS: Warwickshire, England Lions
ROLE: Bowler
DEBUT: First-class: 2011; List A: 2013; T20: 2014

WARWICKSHIRE

BEST BATTING: 47 Cambridge MCCU vs Surrey, Cambridge, 2011
BEST BOWLING: 5-53 Warwickshire vs Middlesex, Edgbaston, 2016

WHAT GOT YOU INTO CRICKET? Going to watch my dad when I was a youngster. Then playing at Brighton and Hove CC, coached by the great man Dick Roberts
'ROY OF THE ROVERS' MOMENT? Taking a catch in the 2015 Ashes as 12th man
BEST THING ABOUT YOUR HOME GROUND? The dressing-room attendant
BEST OPPOSING PLAYER IN COUNTY CRICKET? Marcus Trescothick (Som)
YOUNG OPPOSING PLAYER WHO HAS IMPRESSED YOU? Paul Coughlin (Not) – good allrounder and the quickest bloke in county cricket. Massive run-thief
SURPRISING FACT ABOUT YOU? I have a mild obsession with sausage dogs – I can't walk past one in the street without stroking it, and one day I hope to have one called Frank
SURPRISING FACT ABOUT A TEAMMATE? Ollie Hannon-Dalby rarely talks about it but he did the Big Bike Ride for the PCA
CRICKETING HERO? Shane Warne – he absolutely ragged it, had great control, and dated Liz Hurley
NON-CRICKETING HERO? Rory McIlroy – I'd do anything to have his golf swing
TWITTER: @JoshPoysden14

Batting	Mat	Inns	NO	Runs	HS	Ave	SR	100	50	Ct	St
First-class	10	8	2	71	47	11.83	42.01	0	0	2	0
List A	23	12	5	33	10*	4.71	60.00	0	0	6	0
T20s	21	9	8	13	9*	13.00	130.00	0	0	5	0

Bowling	Mat	Balls	Runs	Wkts	BBI	BBM	Ave	Econ	SR	5w	10
First-class	10	1095	752	21	5/53	8/133	35.80	4.12	52.1	1	0
List A	23	921	910	24	3/33	3/33	37.91	5.92	38.3	0	0
T20s	21	354	442	14	4/51	4/51	31.57	7.49	25.2	0	0

SEEKKUGE PRASANNA

RHB / LB / RO / WO

NORTHAMPTONSHIRE

FULL NAME: Seekkuge Prasanna
BORN: June 27, 1985, Balapitiya, Sri Lanka
SQUAD NO: 41
HEIGHT: 5ft 9in
EDUCATION: Rewatha College, Balapitiya
TEAMS: Sri Lanka, Northamptonshire, Barisal Bulls, Dhaka Dynamites, Hambantota Troopers, Kandurata, Southern Express, Uva Next
ROLE: Bowler
DEBUT: Test: 2011; ODI: 2011; T20I: 2013; First-class: 2006; List A: 2006; T20: 2009

BEST BATTING: 81 Sri Lanka Army vs Colts Cricket Club, Panagoda, 2013
BEST BOWLING: 8-59 Sri Lanka Army vs Bloomfield Cricket Club, Panagoda, 2009

NOTES: Northamptonshire re-signed Prasanna for the last year's T20 Blast but the Sri Lanka leg-spinner ultimately missed the entire competition with a hamstring injury. He is due to play throughout this summer's competition. Played 11 times for Northants in their victorious 2016 T20 campaign, taking 12 wickets. Useful lower-order batsman. Made a solitary Test appearance in 2011 but has been a regular member of Sri Lanka's ODI and T20I sides. "We know he's capable of boundary hitting – he's an archetypal T20 cricketer," said head coach David Ripley. "He gives it a whack, is a nice fielder and obviously brings wicket-taking potential for us in those middle overs"

Batting	Mat	Inns	NO	Runs	HS	Ave	SR	100	50	Ct	St
Tests	1	1	0	5	5	5.00	41.66	0	0	0	0
ODIs	38	35	3	405	95	12.65	94.84	0	2	6	0
T20Is	20	20	6	214	37*	15.28	132.91	0	0	4	0
First-class	102	163	7	3437	81	22.03	98.20	0	20	74	0
List A	136	116	12	1613	95	15.50	103.66	0	7	43	0
T20s	110	92	23	1192	53	17.27	161.73	0	2	37	0

Bowling	Mat	Balls	Runs	Wkts	BBI	BBM	Ave	Econ	SR	5w	10
Tests	1	138	80	0	-	-	-	3.47	-	0	0
ODIs	38	1855	1673	32	3/32	3/32	52.28	5.41	57.9	0	0
T20Is	20	300	359	10	2/45	2/45	35.90	7.18	30.0	0	0
First-class	102	19463	10953	502	8/59	14/181	21.81	3.37	38.7	38	8
List A	136	6182	4586	185	6/23	6/23	24.78	4.45	33.4	4	0
T20s	110	1940	2241	86	4/19	4/19	26.05	6.93	22.5	0	0

RYAN PRINGLE

RHB / OB / R0 / W0

FULL NAME: Ryan David Pringle
BORN: April 17, 1992, Sunderland
SQUAD NO: 17
HEIGHT: 6ft 1in
NICKNAME: Rhino
EDUCATION: Hetton Comprehensive School, Sunderland; Durham Sixth Form Centre; University of Sunderland
TEAMS: Durham
ROLE: Allrounder
DEBUT: First-class: 2014; List A: 2012; T20: 2013

DURHAM

BEST BATTING: 99 Durham vs Hampshire, Chester-le-Street, 2015
BEST BOWLING: 7-107 Durham vs Hampshire, Southampton, 2016

WHAT GOT YOU INTO CRICKET? My next-door neighbour made me my first bat, plus the tuck shop at my local club had great mix-up bags
BEST ADVICE EVER RECEIVED? Fours and sixes, no risks
'ROY OF THE ROVERS' MOMENT? The ton I scored in the 2016 One-Day Cup – my first for Durham
BEST THING ABOUT YOUR HOME GROUND? The view of the castle when you walk out onto the field
BEST OPPOSING PLAYER IN COUNTY CRICKET? Sam Northeast (Ham)
YOUNG OPPOSING PLAYER WHO HAS IMPRESSED YOU? Max Holden (Mid) – seems to have the ability to bat for long periods of time
SURPRISING FACT ABOUT YOU? I've never seen Titanic
SURPRISING FACT ABOUT A TEAMMATE? Gavin Main has 0% body fat
WHERE IS PARADISE? Filthy's Newcastle (pub)
NON-CRICKETING HERO? My grandad Geoff Pringle
UNUSUAL OBJECT AT HOME? A goat in my downstairs toilet
TWITTER: @RyanPringle

Batting	Mat	Inns	NO	Runs	HS	Ave	SR	100	50	Ct	St
First-class	36	56	8	1255	99	26.14	52.53	0	8	21	0
List A	32	23	0	415	125	18.04	106.41	1	0	10	0
T20s	64	45	5	388	33	9.70	119.38	0	0	21	0

Bowling	Mat	Balls	Runs	Wkts	BBI	BBM	Ave	Econ	SR	5w	10
First-class	36	3734	2286	58	7/107	10/260	39.41	3.67	64.3	2	1
List A	32	669	683	10	2/39	2/39	68.30	6.12	66.9	0	0
T20s	64	708	1004	27	3/30	3/30	37.18	8.50	26.2	0	0

FULL NAME: Luke Anthony Procter
BORN: June 24, 1988, Oldham, Lancashire
SQUAD NO: 2
HEIGHT: 5ft 11in
NICKNAME: Proccy
EDUCATION: Counthill School, Oldham
TEAMS: Northamptonshire, Lancashire
ROLE: Batsman
DEBUT: First-class: 2010; List A: 2009; T20: 2011

BEST BATTING: 137 Lancashire vs Hampshire, Old Trafford, 2016
BEST BOWLING: 7-71 Lancashire vs Surrey, Liverpool, 2012

BEST ADVICE EVER RECEIVED? Never settle for second-best
'ROY OF THE ROVERS' MOMENT? Winning the County Championship in 2011
BEST OPPOSING PLAYER IN COUNTY CRICKET? Samit Patel (Not)
YOUNG OPPOSING PLAYER WHO HAS IMPRESSED YOU? Alex Davies (Lan) – hard-working player
IF YOU WEREN'T A CRICKETER? I'd be single and on the dole
SURPRISING FACT ABOUT YOU? I'm a Level Two umpire
SURPRISING FACT ABOUT A TEAMMATE? Ben Duckett is tall – it's just that people look at him from far away
WHERE IS PARADISE? Oldham
CRICKETING HERO? Shiv Chanderpaul – he has grit, determination and class to go with it
TWITTER: @vvsprocter

Batting	Mat	Inns	NO	Runs	HS	Ave	SR	100	50	Ct	St
First-class	68	104	6	3105	137	31.68	43.12	3	17	17	0
List A	31	22	6	481	97	30.06	85.73	0	4	4	0
T20s	25	13	5	122	25*	15.25	96.06	0	0	7	0

Bowling	Mat	Balls	Runs	Wkts	BBI	BBM	Ave	Econ	SR	5w	10
First-class	68	4656	2686	75	7/71	8/79	35.81	3.46	62.0	2	0
List A	31	540	582	13	3/29	3/29	44.76	6.46	41.5	0	0
T20s	25	116	176	8	3/22	3/22	22.00	9.10	14.5	0	0

CHETESHWAR PUJARA

RHB / LB / RO / WO

FULL NAME: Cheteshwar Arvind Pujara
BORN: January 25, 1988, Rajkot, Gujarat
SQUAD NO: 27
TEAMS: India, Yorkshire, Derbyshire, India Green, Kings XI Punjab, Kolkata Knight Riders, Nottinghamshire, Royal Challengers Bangalore, Saurashtra
ROLE: Batsman
DEBUT: Test: 2010; ODI: 2013; First-class: 2005; List A: 2006; T20: 2007

BEST BATTING: 352 Saurashtra vs Karnataka, Rajkot, 2013
BEST BOWLING: 2-4 Saurashtra vs Rajasthan, Jaipur, 2007

TWITTER: @cheteshwar1
NOTES: Pujara returns for a second spell at Yorkshire, having played four Championship matches during their title-winning campaign of 2015, when he averaged 52.80. The right-handed batsman will be Yorkshire's overseas player for the first part of the summer before handing over to New Zealand captain Kane Williamson when India's Test series against England begins. Pujara is accustomed to county cricket having previously represented Derbyshire and Nottinghamshire. "Each time I've played county cricket it has improved me as a player. That's the plan again in 2018," he said. "It's an honour for me to play for the same county as Yuvraj Singh and Sachin Tendulkar." Pujara will arrive at Headingley in good form, having scored 1,140 runs in Test cricket in 2017, a figure surpassed only by Steve Smith

Batting	Mat	Inns	NO	Runs	HS	Ave	SR	100	50	Ct	St
Tests	57	96	7	4496	206*	50.51	47.45	14	17	40	0
ODIs	5	5	0	51	27	10.20	39.23	0	0	0	0
First-class	166	270	34	13316	352	56.42		44	45	116	0
List A	91	90	17	3955	158*	54.17		10	25	34	0
T20s	58	50	7	1096	81	25.48	105.18	0	6	30	0

Bowling	Mat	Balls	Runs	Wkts	BBI	BBM	Ave	Econ	SR	5w	10
Tests	57	6	2	0	-	-	-	2.00	-	0	0
ODIs	5	-	-	-	-	-	-	-	-	-	-
First-class	166	237	146	5	2/4	2/4	29.20	3.69	47.4	0	0
List A	91	6	8	0	-	-	-	8.00	-	0	0
T20s	58	-	-	-	-	-	-	-	-	-	-

HAMIDULLAH QADRI

DERBYSHIRE

FULL NAME: Hamidullah Qadri
BORN: December 5, 2000, Kandahar, Afghanistan
SQUAD NO: 75
HEIGHT: 5ft 5in
NICKNAME: Hammy
EDUCATION: Chellaston Academy, Derby
TEAMS: Derbyshire
ROLE: Bowler
DEBUT: First-class: 2017; List A: 2017; T20: 2017

BEST BATTING: 11* Derbyshire vs Glamorgan, Cardiff, 2017
BEST BOWLING: 5-60 Derbyshire vs Glamorgan, Cardiff, 2017

WHAT GOT YOU INTO CRICKET? My school
BEST ADVICE EVER RECEIVED? The team comes before you
'ROY OF THE ROVERS' MOMENT? My five-wicket haul on my Derbyshire first-class debut against Glamorgan in 2017
BEST THING ABOUT YOUR HOME GROUND? The changing room is close to the pitch and is a decent size
BEST OPPOSING PLAYER IN COUNTY CRICKET? Simon Harmer (Ess)
YOUNG OPPOSING PLAYER WHO HAS IMPRESSED YOU? Haseeb Hameed (Lan)
IF YOU WEREN'T A CRICKETER? I'd be a biologist or a chemist
SURPRISING FACT ABOUT YOU? I learnt the art of off-spin through watching YouTube clips
CRICKETING HERO? Saqlain Mushtaq – the inventor of the doosra
NON-CRICKETING HERO? My father – he never gives up

Batting	Mat	Inns	NO	Runs	HS	Ave	SR	100	50	Ct	St
First-class	3	6	4	20	11*	10.00	35.08	0	0	2	0
List A	1	-	-	-	-	-	-	-	-	0	0
T20s	1	-	-	-	-	-	-	-	-	0	0

Bowling	Mat	Balls	Runs	Wkts	BBI	BBM	Ave	Econ	SR	5w	10
First-class	3	609	288	10	5/60	6/76	28.80	2.83	60.9	1	0
List A	1	1	1	0	-	-	-	6.00	-	0	0
T20s	1	6	12	0	-	-	-	12.00	-	0	0

IMRAN QAYYUM

RHB / SLA / R0 / W0

FULL NAME: Imran Qayyum
BORN: May 23, 1993, Ealing, Middlesex
SQUAD NO: 11
HEIGHT: 5ft 11in
NICKNAME: Imy, IQ
EDUCATION: Villiers High School, Ealing; Greenford High School, Ealing; City University of London
TEAMS: Kent
ROLE: Bowler
DEBUT: First-class: 2016; List A: 2017; T20: 2017

KENT

BEST BATTING: 39 Kent vs Leicestershire, Canterbury, 2017
BEST BOWLING: 3-158 Kent vs Northamptonshire, Northampton, 2016

FAMILY TIES? Dad played in Pakistan, my brother plays club cricket in Hertfordshire
BEST ADVICE EVER RECEIVED? Try coffee
'ROY OF THE ROVERS' MOMENT? Playing alongside Geraint Jones
BEST THING ABOUT YOUR HOME GROUND? It's less than a mile away from my bed
BEST OPPOSING PLAYER IN COUNTY CRICKET? Varun Chopra (Ess)
YOUNG OPPOSING PLAYER WHO HAS IMPRESSED YOU? Jofra Archer (Sus) – he bowls rockets and is very accurate
IF YOU WEREN'T A CRICKETER? I'd be a finance analyst
SURPRISING FACT ABOUT YOU? I talk in my sleep
SURPRISING FACT ABOUT A TEAMMATE? Ivan Thomas eats two dinners every night
WHERE IS PARADISE? Heaven
CRICKETING HERO? Virat Kohli – he gives his all in every aspect of the game
NON-CRICKETING HERO? J Hus – check out the track 'Spirit'
TWITTER: @ImranQC

Batting	Mat	Inns	NO	Runs	HS	Ave	SR	100	50	Ct	St
First-class	5	7	2	40	39	8.00	42.55	0	0	3	0
List A	11	7	2	27	18	5.40	79.41	0	0	3	0
T20s	10	2	0	6	6	3.00	150.00	0	0	4	0

Bowling	Mat	Balls	Runs	Wkts	BBI	BBM	Ave	Econ	SR	5w	10
First-class	5	775	481	12	3/158	3/46	40.08	3.72	64.5	0	0
List A	11	576	448	14	4/33	4/33	32.00	4.66	41.1	0	0
T20s	10	198	274	7	2/19	2/19	39.14	8.30	28.2	0	0

MATT QUINN

RHB / RMF / RO / WO

ESSEX

FULL NAME: Matthew Richard Quinn
BORN: February 28, 1993, Auckland, New Zealand
SQUAD NO: 94
HEIGHT: 6ft 5in
NICKNAME: Quinny, Giraffe
EDUCATION: Sacred Heart College, Auckland; Auckland University of Technology
TEAMS: Essex, Auckland
ROLE: Bowler
DEBUT: First-class: 2013; List A: 2013; T20: 2012

BEST BATTING: 50 Auckland vs Canterbury, Auckland, 2013
BEST BOWLING: 7-76 Essex vs Gloucestershire, Cheltenham, 2016

FAMILY TIES? My great grandad played social cricket in Yorkshire
BEST ADVICE EVER RECEIVED? Just enjoy it
BEST THING ABOUT YOUR HOME GROUND? The crowd and their support
IF YOU WEREN'T A CRICKETER? I'd be driving a forklift
SURPRISING FACT ABOUT YOU? I was once attacked by a goose
WHERE IS PARADISE? Taupo, New Zealand
CRICKETING HERO? Martin Crowe – a fantastic player and even better man
NON-CRICKETING HERO? My dad – he always tries to be positive
TWITTER: @quinny_cricket

Batting	Mat	Inns	NO	Runs	HS	Ave	SR	100	50	Ct	St
First-class	27	34	5	298	50	10.27	56.76	0	1	5	0
List A	32	18	11	124	36	17.71	72.94	0	0	3	0
T20s	39	8	7	23	8*	23.00	135.29	0	0	8	0

Bowling	Mat	Balls	Runs	Wkts	BBI	BBM	Ave	Econ	SR	5w	10
First-class	27	5178	2869	101	7/76	11/163	28.40	3.32	51.2	1	1
List A	32	1606	1538	44	4/71	4/71	34.95	5.74	36.5	0	0
T20s	39	790	1178	39	4/35	4/35	30.20	8.94	20.2	0	0

AZEEM RAFIQ

RHB / OB / RO / WO

FULL NAME: Azeem Rafiq
BORN: February 27, 1991, Karachi, Pakistan
SQUAD NO: 30
NICKNAME: Rafa
EDUCATION: Holgate School, Barnsley;
Barnsley College
TEAMS: Yorkshire, Derbyshire
ROLE: Bowler
DEBUT: First-class: 2009; List A: 2009; T20:
2008

YORKSHIRE

BEST BATTING: 100 Yorkshire vs Worcestershire, Worcester, 2009
BEST BOWLING: 5-50 Yorkshire vs Essex, Chelmsford, 2012
COUNTY CAP: 2016 (Yorkshire)

TWITTER: @AzeemRafiq30
NOTES: Former captain of England age-group sides – U15, U17 and U19 – and the first player of Asian heritage to captain Yorkshire when he was T20 skipper in 2012. Released by the county in 2014 after struggling to build on notable early showings. Re-joined Yorkshire in 2016 after almost two years away from the professional game and impressed in one-day cricket with his intelligent off-breaks and canny batting. He was Yorkshire's joint-leading wicket-taker in the T20 Blast last summer (17 wickets) and top of the pile in the One-Day Cup (18 wickets)

Batting	Mat	Inns	NO	Runs	HS	Ave	SR	100	50	Ct	St
First-class	38	45	5	866	100	21.65	56.08	1	4	14	0
List A	35	24	10	252	52*	18.00	94.73	0	1	15	0
T20s	83	32	20	148	21*	12.33	95.48	0	0	34	0

Bowling	Mat	Balls	Runs	Wkts	BBI	BBM	Ave	Econ	SR	5w	10
First-class	38	5301	2804	71	5/50	8/115	39.49	3.17	74.6	1	0
List A	35	1353	1275	43	5/30	5/30	29.65	5.65	31.4	1	0
T20s	83	1715	2155	94	5/19	5/19	22.92	7.53	18.2	1	0

BEN RAINE

LHB / RMF / RO / W1

LEICESTERSHIRE

FULL NAME: Benjamin Alexander Raine
BORN: September 14, 1991, Sunderland
SQUAD NO: 44
HEIGHT: 6ft
NICKNAME: Rainger
EDUCATION: St Aidan's Catholic Academy, Sunderland
TEAMS: Leicestershire, Durham
ROLE: Bowler
DEBUT: First-class: 2011; List A: 2011; T20: 2014

BEST BATTING: 72 Leicestershire vs Lancashire, Old Trafford, 2013
BEST BOWLING: 6-66 Leicestershire vs Nottinghamshire, Leicester, 2017

WHAT GOT YOU INTO CRICKET? Watching my dad play local league cricket
'ROY OF THE ROVERS' MOMENT? Watching Charlie Shreck take his 500th wicket
HOW WOULD YOUR TEAMMATES DESCRIBE YOU IN THREE WORDS? Reserved, dependable, relaxed
IF YOU WEREN'T A CRICKETER? I'd be working at the Nissan factory
SURPRISING FACT? I'm not a Newcastle fan, as many seem to think I am
CRICKETING HERO? Matthew Hayden – he just destroyed bowlers
NON-CRICKETING HEROES? Mike Tyson and Tiger Woods – they're the best ever in their respective sports
TWITTER: @BenRaine88

Batting	Mat	Inns	NO	Runs	HS	Ave	SR	100	50	Ct	St
First-class	53	88	9	1608	72	20.35	46.86	0	7	10	0
List A	14	10	0	164	43	16.40	110.06	0	0	3	0
T20s	34	22	8	273	48	19.50	109.20	0	0	8	0

Bowling	Mat	Balls	Runs	Wkts	BBI	BBM	Ave	Econ	SR	5w	10
First-class	53	8573	4595	156	6/66	8/107	29.45	3.21	54.9	5	0
List A	14	624	656	13	3/62	3/62	50.46	6.30	48.0	0	0
T20s	34	698	957	42	3/7	3/7	22.78	8.22	16.6	0	0

RAVI RAMPAUL

LHB / RFM / RO / WO

FULL NAME: Ravindranath Rampaul
BORN: October 15, 1984, Preysal, Trinidad
SQUAD NO: 41
NICKNAME: Frisco Kid
EDUCATION: Presentation College, Trinidad
TEAMS: West Indies, Derbyshire, Barbados
Tridents, Ireland, Royal Challengers
Bangalore, Surrey, Trinidad and Tobago
ROLE: Bowler
DEBUT: Test: 2009; ODI: 2003; T20I: 2007;
First-class: 2002; List A: 2003; T20: 2007

BEST BATTING: 64* West Indies A vs Sri Lanka A, Basseterre, 2006
BEST BOWLING: 7-51 Trinidad and Tobago vs Barbados, Point-a-Pierre, 2007

TWITTER: @RaviRampaul14
NOTES: Veteran former West Indies seamer who joined Derbyshire over the winter
after spending two seasons at Surrey as a Kolpak. Rampaul is available to play in all
formats, adding consistency and experience to the county's seam attack. Took 21 wickets
at 24.28 in six Championship matches in 2016, and was also impressive in his fleeting
appearances in the short formats. Less effective at The Oval last summer, playing just two
Championship matches. Rampaul made his international debut in 2003 and last played
for West Indies in 2015

Batting	Mat	Inns	NO	Runs	HS	Ave	SR	100	50	Ct	St
Tests	18	31	8	335	40*	14.56	53.25	0	0	3	0
ODIs	92	40	11	362	86*	12.48	76.69	0	1	14	0
T20Is	23	6	5	12	8	12.00	57.14	0	0	2	0
First-class	69	102	22	1068	64*	13.35		0	2	20	0
List A	170	81	27	628	86*	11.62		0	1	30	0
T20s	126	40	22	161	23*	8.94	100.62	0	0	21	0

Bowling	Mat	Balls	Runs	Wkts	BBI	BBM	Ave	Econ	SR	5w	10
Tests	18	3440	1705	49	4/48	7/75	34.79	2.97	70.2	0	0
ODIs	92	4033	3434	117	5/49	5/49	29.35	5.10	34.4	2	0
T20Is	23	497	705	29	3/16	3/16	24.31	8.51	17.1	0	0
First-class	69	11005	6188	206	7/51	11/125	30.03	3.37	53.4	9	1
List A	170	7772	6222	255	5/49	5/49	24.40	4.80	30.4	2	0
T20s	126	2699	3414	155	5/9	5/9	22.02	7.58	17.4	1	0

BOYD RANKIN

LHB / RFM / R0 / W1

FULL NAME: William Boyd Rankin
BORN: July 5, 1984, Londonderry, Ireland
SQUAD NO: 30
HEIGHT: 6ft 8in
NICKNAME: Boydo
EDUCATION: Strabane Grammar School; Harper Adams University College
TEAMS: England, Ireland, Warwickshire, Derbyshire
ROLE: Bowler
DEBUT: Test: 2014; ODI: 2007; T20I: 2009; First-class: 2007; List A: 2006; T20: 2009

BEST BATTING: 56* Warwickshire vs Worcestershire, Edgbaston, 2015
BEST BOWLING: 6-55 Warwickshire vs Yorkshire, Headingley, 2015
COUNTY CAP: 2013 (Warwickshire)

FAMILY TIES? My dad played club cricket and my brothers Robert and David have played for Ireland at U19 level. My sister plays for my home club Bready
'ROY OF THE ROVERS' MOMENT? Beating Pakistan in the 2007 World Cup with Ireland on St Paddy's Day
HOW WOULD YOUR TEAMMATES DESCRIBE YOU IN THREE WORDS? Big friendly giant
CRICKETING HEROES? I watched Curtly Ambrose and Glenn McGrath while I was growing up and have tried to emulate them
IF YOU WEREN'T A CRICKETER? I would be back home in Ireland on the family farm
TWITTER: @boydrankin

Batting	Mat	Inns	NO	Runs	HS	Ave	SR	100	50	Ct	St
Tests	1	2	0	13	13	6.50	54.16	0	0	0	0
ODIs	51	21	14	59	18*	8.42	42.75	0	0	11	0
T20Is	26	6	4	31	16*	15.50	96.87	0	0	9	0
First-class	104	123	51	653	56*	9.06	40.81	0	1	27	0
List A	110	38	20	123	18*	6.83	48.80	0	0	22	0
T20s	64	15	9	53	16*	8.83	91.37	0	0	13	0

Bowling	Mat	Balls	Runs	Wkts	BBI	BBM	Ave	Econ	SR	5w	10
Tests	1	125	81	1	1/47	1/81	81.00	3.88	125.0	0	0
ODIs	51	2439	1962	67	4/44	4/44	29.28	4.82	36.4	0	0
T20Is	26	522	537	28	3/16	3/16	19.17	6.17	18.6	0	0
First-class	104	15028	8959	340	6/55	8/115	26.35	3.57	44.2	9	0
List A	110	4712	3857	140	4/34	4/34	27.55	4.91	33.6	0	0
T20s	64	1290	1470	73	4/9	4/9	20.13	6.83	17.6	0	0

ADIL RASHID

RHB / LB / RO / W2

FULL NAME: Adil Usman Rashid
BORN: February 17, 1988, Bradford, Yorkshire
SQUAD NO: 3
HEIGHT: 5ft 8in
NICKNAME: Dilly, Dilo, Rash
EDUCATION: Heaton School, Bradford; Bellevue Sixth Form College, Bradford
TEAMS: England, Yorkshire, Adelaide Strikers, South Australia
ROLE: Allrounder
DEBUT: Test: 2015; ODI: 2009; T20I: 2009; First-class: 2006; List A: 2006; T20: 2008

YORKSHIRE

BEST BATTING: 180 Yorkshire vs Somerset, Headingley, 2013
BEST BOWLING: 7-107 Yorkshire vs Hampshire, Southampton, 2008
COUNTY CAP: 2008

'ROY OF THE ROVERS' MOMENT? Playing for England
CRICKETING HEROES? Sachin Tendulkar, Shane Warne
NON-CRICKETING HERO? Muhammad Ali
IF YOU WEREN'T A CRICKETER? I'd be a taxi driver
SURPRISING FACT? I have a big FIFA video game rivalry with Moeen Ali
TWITTER: @AdilRashid03
NOTES: Made the decision not to play Championship cricket in 2018

Batting	Mat	Inns	NO	Runs	HS	Ave	SR	100	50	Ct	St
Tests	10	18	2	295	61	18.43	35.28	0	2	3	0
ODIs	61	26	7	422	69	22.21	109.04	0	1	20	0
T20Is	28	12	7	38	9*	7.60	77.55	0	0	9	0
First-class	166	236	38	6577	180	33.21		10	37	78	0
List A	168	102	30	1477	71	20.51	90.11	0	2	52	0
T20s	152	81	30	672	36*	13.17	105.16	0	0	46	0

Bowling	Mat	Balls	Runs	Wkts	BBI	BBM	Ave	Econ	SR	5w	10
Tests	10	2544	1626	38	5/64	7/178	42.78	3.83	66.9	1	0
ODIs	61	3082	2852	88	5/27	5/27	32.40	5.55	35.0	1	0
T20Is	28	534	694	23	3/25	3/25	30.17	7.79	23.2	0	0
First-class	166	28629	17185	490	7/107	11/114	35.07	3.60	58.4	19	1
List A	168	7611	6771	217	5/27	5/27	31.20	5.33	35.0	2	0
T20s	152	3087	3835	170	4/19	4/19	22.55	7.45	18.1	0	0

DELRAY RAWLINS

LHB / SLA / RO / WO

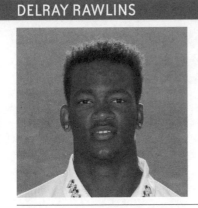

FULL NAME: Delray Millard Wendell Rawlins
BORN: September 14, 1997, Bermuda
SQUAD NO: 9
HEIGHT: 6ft 2in
NICKNAME: Del
EDUCATION: St Bede's School, East Sussex
TEAMS: Sussex
ROLE: Allrounder
DEBUT: First-class: 2017; List A: 2017

BEST BATTING: 96 Sussex vs South Africa A, Arundel, 2017
BEST BOWLING: 1-46 Sussex vs Kent, Hove, 2017

WHAT GOT YOU INTO CRICKET? Watching my dad play local league cricket
BEST ADVICE EVER RECEIVED? If it's in the arc, it's out the park!
'ROY OF THE ROVERS' MOMENT? Making a hundred against India U19 on my England U19 ODI debut in 2017
BEST THING ABOUT YOUR HOME GROUND? The atmosphere for the T20 Blast
BEST OPPOSING PLAYER IN COUNTY CRICKET? Mark Stoneman (Sur)
YOUNG OPPOSING PLAYER WHO HAS IMPRESSED YOU? Ollie Pope (Sur) – he's fearless
IF YOU WEREN'T A CRICKETER? I'd be a university student
SURPRISING FACT ABOUT YOU? I eat pineapple slices out of the tin
WHERE IS PARADISE? Bermuda
CRICKETING HERO? Brian Lara
NON-CRICKETING HERO? LeBron James – he's a machine
TWITTER: @Delraw09

Batting	Mat	Inns	NO	Runs	HS	Ave	SR	100	50	Ct	St
First-class	5	9	0	217	96	24.11	41.57	0	2	0	0
List A	1	1	0	41	41	41.00	136.66	0	0	0	0

Bowling	Mat	Balls	Runs	Wkts	BBI	BBM	Ave	Econ	SR	5w	10
First-class	5	240	161	1	1/46	1/46	161.00	4.02	240.0	0	0
List A	1	24	30	0	-	-	-	7.50	-	0	0

OLLIE RAYNER

RHB / OB / RO / W1

FULL NAME: Oliver Philip Rayner
BORN: November 1, 1985, Bad Fallingbostel, Lower Saxony, Germany
SQUAD NO: 2
HEIGHT: 6ft 6in
NICKNAME: Draynes, Vaynes, Great Raynes, Ashton Kutcher
EDUCATION: St Bede's School, East Sussex
TEAMS: Middlesex, England Lions, Mid West Rhinos, Sussex
ROLE: Bowler
DEBUT: First-class: 2006; List A: 2006; T20: 2006

BEST BATTING: 143* Middlesex vs Nottinghamshire, Trent Bridge, 2012
BEST BOWLING: 8-46 Middlesex vs Surrey, The Oval, 2013
COUNTY CAP: 2015 (Middlesex)

WHAT GOT YOU INTO CRICKET? Playing with my family on the beach when the tide went out in Eastbourne. And Mr Duckett
'ROY OF THE ROVERS' MOMENT? Winning the Championship in 2016
YOUNG OPPOSING PLAYER WHO HAS IMPRESSED YOU? Sam Curran (Sur) – a good boy and a great allrounder
IF YOU WEREN'T A CRICKETER? I'd be a water-slide tester
SURPRISING FACT ABOUT YOU? Online gamers call me "the dentist"
SURPRISING FACT ABOUT A TEAMMATE? Tim Murtagh has a bath every morning
WHERE IS PARADISE? Harry Potter World, Orlando, Florida
CRICKETING HERO? Richard Smith – he took me under his wing when I was a youngster
NON-CRICKETING HERO? Professor Dumbledore – the most powerful wizard in the world
UNUSUAL OBJECT AT HOME? Some interesting art prints and a longboard collection
TWITTER: @ollie2rayner

Batting	Mat	Inns	NO	Runs	HS	Ave	SR	100	50	Ct	St
First-class	129	170	28	3079	143*	21.68	51.63	2	13	173	0
List A	61	42	19	508	61	22.08	90.07	0	1	32	0
T20s	71	43	16	343	41*	12.70	103.00	0	0	17	0

Bowling	Mat	Balls	Runs	Wkts	BBI	BBM	Ave	Econ	SR	5w	10
First-class	129	19765	9406	286	8/46	15/118	32.88	2.85	69.1	10	1
List A	61	2346	2017	53	4/35	4/35	38.05	5.15	44.2	0	0
T20s	71	1323	1620	41	5/18	5/18	39.51	7.34	32.2	1	0

LUIS REECE

LHB / LM / RO / WO / MVP69

DERBYSHIRE

FULL NAME: Luis Michael Reece
BORN: August 4, 1990, Taunton
SQUAD NO: 10
HEIGHT: 6ft 1in
NICKNAME: Reecey, Rexy, Red Rum
EDUCATION: St Michael's School;
Myerscough College; Leeds Metropolitan
University
TEAMS: Derbyshire, Lancashire
ROLE: Batsman
DEBUT: First-class: 2012; List A: 2011; T20:
2016

BEST BATTING: 168 Derbyshire vs Northamptonshire, Derby, 2017
BEST BOWLING: 4-28 Leeds/Bradford MCCU vs Leicestershire, Leicester, 2013

BEST ADVICE EVER RECEIVED? Control the controllables and enjoy the journey
'ROY OF THE ROVERS' MOMENT? Scoring 97 not out in a T20 match in 2017 to beat my old club Lancashire
BEST THING ABOUT YOUR HOME GROUND? The homely feel created by the staff and players
BEST OPPOSING PLAYER IN COUNTY CRICKET? Darren Stevens (Ken)
YOUNG OPPOSING PLAYER WHO HAS IMPRESSED YOU? Jofra Archer (Sus) – bowls at a good pace and is a handy batsman too
SURPRISING FACT ABOUT YOU? I played chess at national level as a kid
SURPRISING FACT ABOUT A TEAMMATE? Matt Critchley went to the same school as me
WHERE IS PARADISE? Mooloolaba Beach, Queensland
CRICKETING HERO? AB de Villiers
NON-CRICKETING HERO? My dad – he's been in my corner no matter what
TWITTER: @lreece17

Batting	Mat	Inns	NO	Runs	HS	Ave	SR	100	50	Ct	St
First-class	41	72	6	2235	168	33.86	49.66	3	17	21	0
List A	27	23	4	424	59	22.31	82.97	0	2	6	0
T20s	26	25	4	622	97*	29.61	130.67	0	5	9	0

Bowling	Mat	Balls	Runs	Wkts	BBI	BBM	Ave	Econ	SR	5w	10
First-class	41	1653	1015	22	4/28	6/67	46.13	3.68	75.1	0	0
List A	27	452	486	6	4/35	4/35	81.00	6.45	75.3	0	0
T20s	26	192	255	10	3/33	3/33	25.50	7.96	19.2	0	0

GEORGE RHODES

RHB / OB / R0 / W0

FULL NAME: George Harry Rhodes
BORN: October 26, 1993, Birmingham
SQUAD NO: 34
HEIGHT: 6ft
NICKNAME: Rhodesy, Gnomey, Big Sword
EDUCATION: The Chase School, Malvern;
University of Worcester
TEAMS: Worcestershire
ROLE: Allrounder
DEBUT: First-class: 2016; List A: 2016; T20:
2016

BEST BATTING: 59 Worcestershire vs Essex, Chelmsford, 2016
BEST BOWLING: 2-83 Worcestershire vs Kent, Canterbury, 2016

FAMILY TIES? My father Steve played for Worcestershire for 20 years and played 11
Tests and nine ODIs for England. My grandfather William played first-class cricket for
Nottinghamshire in the 1960s
BEST ADVICE EVER RECEIVED? Never trust a man with two first names
'ROY OF THE ROVERS' MOMENT? Winning Division Two of the County Championship in 2017
BEST THING ABOUT YOUR HOME GROUND? The teas and cakes in the Ladies Pavilion
BEST OPPOSING PLAYER IN COUNTY CRICKET? Tom Kohler-Cadmore (Yor)
YOUNG OPPOSING PLAYER WHO HAS IMPRESSED YOU? Sam Curran (Sur)
IF YOU WEREN'T A CRICKETER? I'd be an astronaut
SURPRISING FACT ABOUT YOU? I'm a skydive survivor
WHERE IS PARADISE? Barbados
TWITTER: @Ghrhodes

Batting	Mat	Inns	NO	Runs	HS	Ave	SR	100	50	Ct	St
First-class	14	26	4	653	59	29.68	42.65	0	4	7	0
List A	5	2	1	5	5*	5.00	71.42	0	0	3	0
T20s	10	7	2	43	17*	8.60	102.38	0	0	3	0

Bowling	Mat	Balls	Runs	Wkts	BBI	BBM	Ave	Econ	SR	5w	10
First-class	14	617	465	6	2/83	2/83	77.50	4.52	102.8	0	0
List A	5	168	162	5	2/34	2/34	32.40	5.78	33.6	0	0
T20s	10	60	77	5	4/13	4/13	15.40	7.70	12.0	0	0

WILL RHODES

LHB / RMF / RO / WO

WARWICKSHIRE

FULL NAME: William Michael Harry Rhodes
BORN: March 2, 1995, Nottingham
SQUAD NO: 35
HEIGHT: 6ft 2in
NICKNAME: Codhead, Besty
EDUCATION: Cottingham High School, Hull
TEAMS: Warwickshire, Essex, Yorkshire
ROLE: Allrounder
DEBUT: First-class: 2015; List A: 2013; T20: 2013

BEST BATTING: 95 Yorkshire vs MCC, Abu Dhabi, 2016
BEST BOWLING: 3-42 Yorkshire vs Middlesex, Headingley, 2015

FAMILY TIES? My dad played a bit of Nottinghamshire junior cricket
BEST ADVICE EVER RECEIVED? Always hit the middle of the ball
'ROY OF THE ROVERS' MOMENT? 150 not out for a school in a Twenty20 match
BEST THING ABOUT YOUR HOME GROUND? The changing rooms are massive
BEST OPPOSING PLAYER IN COUNTY CRICKET? Jamie Porter (Ess)
YOUNG OPPOSING PLAYER WHO HAS IMPRESSED YOU? Dan Lawrence (Ess)
IF YOU WEREN'T A CRICKETER? I'd be a professional footballer
SURPRISING FACT ABOUT YOU? I once did one million keepie-uppies with a balloon
SURPRISING FACT ABOUT A TEAMMATE? Don't know them well enough yet!
WHERE IS PARADISE? The Cheese Room at Pryzm nightclub, Leeds
CRICKETING HERO? My brother Dom Rhodes – he hits it miles
NON-CRICKETING HERO? Levi Towell – king of the lads
TWITTER: @willrhodes_152

Batting	Mat	Inns	NO	Runs	HS	Ave	SR	100	50	Ct	St
First-class	19	28	2	693	95	26.65	42.51	0	3	9	0
List A	21	17	2	252	46	16.80	72.62	0	0	8	0
T20s	18	16	3	128	45	9.84	105.78	0	0	2	0

Bowling	Mat	Balls	Runs	Wkts	BBI	BBM	Ave	Econ	SR	5w	10
First-class	19	1559	829	25	3/42	4/114	33.16	3.19	62.3	0	0
List A	21	415	364	11	2/22	2/22	33.09	5.26	37.7	0	0
T20s	18	187	283	13	3/27	3/27	21.76	9.08	14.3	0	0

MICHAEL RICHARDSON

RHB / WK / R2 / W0

FULL NAME: Michael John Richardson
BORN: October 4, 1986, Port Elizabeth, SA
SQUAD NO: 10
HEIGHT: 5ft 11in
NICKNAME: Richie, Rory, Chelsea
EDUCATION: Rondebosch Boys High School, South Africa; Stonyhurst College, Lancashire; University of Nottingham
TEAMS: Durham, Badureliya Sports Club, Colombo
ROLE: Wicketkeeper/batsman
DEBUT: First-class: 2010; List A: 2012; T20: 2013

DURHAM

BEST BATTING: 148 Durham vs Yorkshire, Chester-le-Street, 2014

FAMILY TIES? My father David played for South Africa, my grandfather John played for Northern Transvaal, my cousin Matthew played for Border, my uncle Ralph played for Western Province
'ROY OF THE ROVERS' MOMENT? Beating Yorkshire in the 2016 T20 semi-final or winning the County Championship in 2013
BEST THING ABOUT YOUR HOME GROUND? It's cold do it's tough for away teams
YOUNG OPPOSING PLAYER WHO HAS IMPRESSED YOU? Joe Clarke (Wor)
IF YOU WEREN'T A CRICKETER? I'd be Del Boy
WHERE IS PARADISE? Indonesia
CRICKETING HERO? Sachin Tendulkar – loved watching him as a kid
NON-CRICKETING HERO? Rafa Nadal – he's very humble and has a great work ethic
UNUSUAL OBJECT AT HOME? An egg boiler
TWITTER: @richo18howu

Batting	Mat	Inns	NO	Runs	HS	Ave	SR	100	50	Ct	St
First-class	92	156	11	4439	148	30.61	53.57	5	25	178	5
List A	17	15	3	697	100*	58.08	87.01	1	7	8	0
T20s	46	34	10	514	53	21.41	115.76	0	1	23	0

Bowling	Mat	Balls	Runs	Wkts	BBI	BBM	Ave	Econ	SR	5w	10
First-class	92	24	13	0	-	-	-	3.25	-	0	0
List A	17	-	-	-	-	-	-	-	-	-	-
T20s	46	-	-	-	-	-	-	-	-	-	-

ADAM RILEY

RHB / OB / RO / W1

KENT

FULL NAME: Adam Edward Nicholas Riley
BORN: March 23, 1992, Sidcup, Kent
SQUAD NO: 33
HEIGHT: 6ft 2in
NICKNAME: MadDog, General, Riles, Gen
EDUCATION: Beths Grammar School, Bexley, London; Loughborough University
TEAMS: Kent, England Lions
ROLE: Bowler
DEBUT: First-class: 2011; List A: 2011; T20: 2011

BEST BATTING: 34 Kent vs Derbyshire, Canterbury, 2015
BEST BOWLING: 7-150 Kent vs Hampshire, Southampton, 2013

WHAT GOT YOU INTO CRICKET? Learning to be a scorer at my dad's club
BEST ADVICE EVER RECEIVED? If you can't be good, be lucky
'ROY OF THE ROVERS' MOMENT? Zinging a 25-yarder into the top corner at The Oval during a T20 five-a-side warm-up and receiving a ripple of applause from the crowd
BEST THING ABOUT YOUR HOME GROUND? The car park and the dressing rooms are based in two different postcodes
BEST OPPOSING PLAYER IN COUNTY CRICKET? Jeetan Patel (War)
YOUNG OPPOSING PLAYER WHO HAS IMPRESSED YOU? Sam Curran (Sur)
IF YOU WEREN'T A CRICKETER? I'd be a full-time supporter of Charlton Athletic FC
SURPRISING FACT ABOUT YOU? I've never been for a sunbed
SURPRISING FACT ABOUT A TEAMMATE? Alex Blake regularly goes for a sunbed
WHERE IS PARADISE? The Valley
CRICKETING HERO? Shane Warne – he was a good bowler
UNUSUAL OBJECT AT HOME? A small home for my two resident tortoises
TWITTER: @AdamRiley92

Batting	Mat	Inns	NO	Runs	HS	Ave	SR	100	50	Ct	St
First-class	52	66	23	429	34	9.97	27.18	0	0	27	0
List A	33	12	5	61	21*	8.71	62.24	0	0	11	0
T20s	29	8	5	18	5*	6.00	85.71	0	0	5	0

Bowling	Mat	Balls	Runs	Wkts	BBI	BBM	Ave	Econ	SR	5w	10
First-class	52	6883	4245	117	7/150	9/123	36.28	3.70	58.8	5	0
List A	33	1284	1098	32	4/40	4/40	34.31	5.13	40.1	0	0
T20s	29	532	687	23	4/22	4/22	29.86	7.74	23.1	0	0

NATHAN RIMMINGTON

RHB / RFM / R0 / W0

FULL NAME: Nathan John Rimmington
BORN: November 11, 1982, Redcliffe, Queensland, Australia
SQUAD NO: 11
HEIGHT: 5ft 9in
NICKNAME: Rimmo
EDUCATION: Wellington College, Berkshire
TEAMS: Durham, Derbyshire, Hampshire, Kings XI Punjab, Melbourne Renegades, Perth Scorchers, Queensland, Western Australia
ROLE: Bowler
DEBUT: First-class: 2006; List A: 2006; T20: 2006

DURHAM

BEST BATTING: 102* Western Australia vs New South Wales, Sydney, 2011
BEST BOWLING: 5-27 Western Australia vs Queensland, Perth, 2014

TWITTER: @nrimmo11
NOTES: The 35-year-old Australian fast bowler has signed a two-year deal with Durham to play in all formats until the end of the 2019 season. "I feel like I have a lot to offer in terms of experience and leadership," he said. "I've always enjoyed playing in the UK and believe the conditions at Emirates Riverside will suit me." Rimmington broke into Queensland's first-class side during the 2005/06 season and has since proved himself capable with both red and white ball. He has featured for Kings XI Punjab in the IPL and has taken 45 wickets in 46 appearances for Melbourne Renegades and Perth Scorchers in the Big Bash, establishing himself as a death bowler. After six seasons with Western Australia he returned to his native Queensland for the 2017/18 season. He played one T20 for Hampshire in 2014 and 11 for Derbyshire the following year, taking 10 wickets

Batting	Mat	Inns	NO	Runs	HS	Ave	SR	100	50	Ct	St
First-class	39	53	13	734	102*	18.35	50.44	1	1	11	0
List A	50	33	6	462	55	17.11	91.48	0	1	8	0
T20s	81	30	14	171	26	10.68	104.90	0	0	20	0

Bowling	Mat	Balls	Runs	Wkts	BBI	BBM	Ave	Econ	SR	5w	10
First-class	39	6476	3183	105	5/27	7/90	30.31	2.94	61.6	3	0
List A	50	2652	2042	65	4/34	4/34	31.41	4.61	40.8	0	0
T20s	81	1608	2132	86	5/27	5/27	24.79	7.95	18.6	1	0

OLIVER ROBINSON

RHB / WK / R0 / W0

KENT

FULL NAME: Oliver Graham Robinson
BORN: December 1, 1998, Sidcup, Kent
SQUAD NO: 21
HEIGHT: 5ft 9in
NICKNAME: Robbo
EDUCATION: Hurstmere School; Chislehurst and Sidcup Grammar
TEAMS: Kent
ROLE: Wicketkeeper
DEBUT: List A: 2017

WHAT GOT YOU INTO CRICKET? My parents and grandparents
STRANGEST THING SEEN IN A GAME? A swarm of bees stop play
'ROY OF THE ROVERS' MOMENT? Scoring 271 for Kent U17
SUPERSTITIONS? I have to put on everything on the left first – including my contact lenses
IF YOU WEREN'T A CRICKETER? I'd be playing darts
SURPRISING FACT ABOUT YOU? I have a very small head
CRICKETING HEROES? AB de Villiers, Adam Gilchrist
NON-CRICKETING HERO? Jack Whitehall
UNUSUAL OBJECT AT HOME? A harp
TWITTER: @ollierobinson7

Batting	Mat	Inns	NO	Runs	HS	Ave	SR	100	50	Ct	St
List A	1	-	-	-	-	-	-	-	-	1	0

Bowling	Mat	Balls	Runs	Wkts	BBI	BBM	Ave	Econ	SR	5w	10
List A	1	-	-	-	-	-	-	-	-	-	-

OLLIE ROBINSON
RHB / RMF / R0 / W0

FULL NAME: Oliver Edward Robinson
BORN: December 1, 1993, Margate, Kent
SQUAD NO: 25
HEIGHT: 6ft 5in
NICKNAME: Robbo, Rig, Riggy, Ols
EDUCATION: King's School, Canterbury
TEAMS: Sussex, Hampshire, Yorkshire
ROLE: Allrounder
DEBUT: First-class: 2015; List A: 2013; T20: 2014

SUSSEX

BEST BATTING: 110 Sussex vs Durham, Chester-le-Street, 2015
BEST BOWLING: 6-33 Sussex vs Warwickshire, Hove, 2015

WHAT GOT YOU INTO CRICKET? I started with a wind ball in my grandparents' garden at the age of two. I played my first hard-ball game aged six, taking 5-5 (including a hat-trick)
'ROY OF THE ROVERS' MOMENT? Scoring a hundred against Durham on my first-class debut in 2015
BEST THING ABOUT YOUR HOME GROUND? The location – it's a great place to celebrate a win
SURPRISING FACT ABOUT YOU? I was county champion at discus and shot put at the age of 13 and came fourth at the nationals
SURPRISING FACT ABOUT A TEAMMATE? Stuart Whittingham loves a musical
WHERE IS PARADISE? Hamilton Island, Australia
UNUSUAL OBJECT AT HOME? A dressmakers' mannequin (my girlfriend is a fashion designer)
TWITTER: @ollierobinson25

Batting	Mat	Inns	NO	Runs	HS	Ave	SR	100	50	Ct	St
First-class	27	39	8	787	110	25.38	68.49	1	3	9	0
List A	8	6	3	75	30	25.00	82.41	0	0	5	0
T20s	20	9	3	29	10	4.83	67.44	0	0	9	0

Bowling	Mat	Balls	Runs	Wkts	BBI	BBM	Ave	Econ	SR	5w	10
First-class	27	4513	2500	84	6/33	8/108	29.76	3.32	53.7	2	0
List A	8	252	259	4	2/61	2/61	64.75	6.16	63.0	0	0
T20s	20	338	516	20	3/16	3/16	25.80	9.15	16.9	0	0

SAM ROBSON

RHB / LB / R2 / W0

FULL NAME: Samuel David Robson
BORN: July 1, 1989, Sydney, Australia
SQUAD NO: 12
HEIGHT: 6ft
NICKNAME: Robbo, Chum, Jar-counter, Mick, Guru
EDUCATION: Marcellin College, Sydney
TEAMS: England, Middlesex
ROLE: Batsman
DEBUT: Test: 2014; First-class: 2009; List A: 2008; T20: 2011

BEST BATTING: 231 Middlesex vs Warwickshire, Lord's, 2016
BEST BOWLING: 1-4 England Lions vs Sri Lanka A, Dambulla, 2014
COUNTY CAP: 2013

FAMILY TIES? My brother Angus played for Leicestershire, father Jim played grade cricket in Australia and for Worcestershire Second XI
BEST ADVICE EVER RECEIVED? Always wear flip-flops in public showers
'ROY OF THE ROVERS' MOMENT? My maiden Test century vs Sri Lanka at Headingley in 2014
BEST OPPOSING PLAYER IN COUNTY CRICKET? Gary Ballance (Yor)
YOUNG OPPOSING PLAYER WHO HAS IMPRESSED YOU? Dan Lawrence (Ess) – very talented, well-organised and scores lots of runs
SURPRISING FACT ABOUT YOU? I like drawing
SURPRISING FACT ABOUT A TEAMMATE? Tim Murtagh is a nudist
WHERE IS PARADISE? The Anglesea Arms beer terrace in South Kensington on a sunny Friday evening in midsummer
CRICKETING HEROES? Michael Slater, Michael Vaughan

Batting	Mat	Inns	NO	Runs	HS	Ave	SR	100	50	Ct	St
Tests	7	11	0	336	127	30.54	44.50	1	1	5	0
First-class	128	226	16	8082	231	38.48	51.66	19	33	127	0
List A	16	14	0	407	88	29.07	68.17	0	2	5	0
T20s	4	4	2	53	28*	26.50	103.92	0	0	2	0

Bowling	Mat	Balls	Runs	Wkts	BBI	BBM	Ave	Econ	SR	5w	10
Tests	7	-	-	-	-	-	-	-	-	-	-
First-class	128	140	110	2	1/4	1/4	55.00	4.71	70.0	0	0
List A	16	-	-	-	-	-	-	-	-	-	-
T20s	4	-	-	-	-	-	-	-	-	-	-

GARETH RODERICK

RHB / WK / R0 / W0

FULL NAME: Gareth Hugh Roderick
BORN: August 29, 1991, Durban, South Africa
SQUAD NO: 27
HEIGHT: 6ft
NICKNAME: Roders, Pear
EDUCATION: Maritzburg College, South Africa
TEAMS: Gloucestershire, KwaZulu-Natal
ROLE: Batsman/wicketkeeper
DEBUT: First-class: 2011; List A: 2011; T20: 2011

BEST BATTING: 171 Gloucestershire vs Leicestershire, Bristol, 2014
COUNTY CAP: 2013

WHAT GOT YOU INTO CRICKET? School started us playing at six years old
STRANGEST THING SEEN IN A GAME? During a club game in South Africa two gun shots went off in the field next to us
'ROY OF THE ROVERS' MOMENT? The One-Day Cup win in 2015
HOW WOULD YOUR TEAMMATES DESCRIBE YOU IN THREE WORDS? Saffa, stubborn, pear
BEST OPPOSING PLAYER IN COUNTY CRICKET? Chris Woakes (War)
CRICKETING HEROES? Steve Waugh – best Test captain and played cricket the way it should be played. Ruthless
IF YOU WEREN'T A CRICKETER? I'd be working with my father in South Africa
SURPRISING FACT? I'm an avid golfer
UNUSUAL OBJECT AT HOME? A shisha pipe
TWITTER: @Roders369

Batting	Mat	Inns	NO	Runs	HS	Ave	SR	100	50	Ct	St
First-class	69	109	15	3562	171	37.89	52.36	5	25	175	4
List A	37	28	3	727	104	29.08	79.28	1	5	37	4
T20s	27	14	5	124	32	13.77	113.76	0	0	9	1

Bowling	Mat	Balls	Runs	Wkts	BBI	BBM	Ave	Econ	SR	5w	10
First-class	69	-	-	-	-	-	-	-	-	-	-
List A	37	-	-	-	-	-	-	-	-	-	-
T20s	27	-	-	-	-	-	-	-	-	-	-

TOBY ROLAND-JONES · RHB / RMF / R0 / W2 / MVP59

MIDDLESEX

FULL NAME: Tobias Skelton Roland-Jones
BORN: January 29, 1988, Ashford, Middlesex
SQUAD NO: 21
HEIGHT: 6ft 3in
NICKNAME: Rojo, TRJ
EDUCATION: Hampton School, Greater London; University of Leeds
TEAMS: England, Middlesex
ROLE: Bowler
DEBUT: Test: 2017; ODI: 2017; First-class: 2010; List A: 2010; T20: 2011

BEST BATTING: 103* Middlesex vs Yorkshire, Lord's, 2015
BEST BOWLING: 6-50 Middlesex vs Northamptonshire, Northampton, 2014
COUNTY CAP: 2012

FAMILY TIES? My older brother Olly played for Leeds/Bradford MCCU and Middlesex Second XI. My dad is a coach
'ROY OF THE ROVERS' MOMENT? Winning the 2016 County Championship in the final session of the season will take some beating
CRICKETING HERO? Ian Botham
NON-CRICKETING HEROES? Ricky Gervais, Alan Partridge, Paul Scholes
IF YOU WEREN'T A CRICKETER? I'd be working in my friends' wine-investment company
SURPRISING FACT? I actually live in Surrey
UNUSUAL OBJECT AT HOME? A stuffed panda
TWITTER: @tobyrj21

Batting	Mat	Inns	NO	Runs	HS	Ave	SR	100	50	Ct	St
Tests	4	6	2	82	25	20.50	69.49	0	0	0	0
ODIs	1	1	1	37	37*	-	100.00	0	0	0	0
First-class	99	137	26	2409	103*	21.70	58.79	1	9	30	0
List A	71	42	13	553	65	19.06	90.35	0	1	12	0
T20s	40	24	10	196	30	14.00	130.66	0	0	8	0

Bowling	Mat	Balls	Runs	Wkts	BBI	BBM	Ave	Econ	SR	5w	10
Tests	4	536	334	17	5/57	8/129	19.64	3.73	31.5	1	0
ODIs	1	42	34	1	1/34	1/34	34.00	4.85	42.0	0	0
First-class	99	17498	9245	364	6/50	12/105	25.39	3.17	48.0	16	3
List A	71	3230	2745	113	4/10	4/10	24.29	5.09	28.5	0	0
T20s	40	800	1171	45	4/25	4/25	26.02	8.78	17.7	0	0

BILLY ROOT

LHB / OB / R0 / W0

FULL NAME: William Thomas Root
BORN: August 5, 1992, Sheffield
SQUAD NO: 66
HEIGHT: 5ft 10in
NICKNAME: Rooty
EDUCATION: Worksop College, Nottinghamshire; Leeds Metropolitan University
TEAMS: Nottinghamshire
ROLE: Batsman
DEBUT: First-class: 2015; List A: 2017; T20: 2017

NOTTINGHAMSHIRE

BEST BATTING: 133 Leeds/Bradford MCCU vs Sussex, Hove, 2016
BEST BOWLING: 3-29 Nottinghamshire vs Sussex, Hove, 2017

WHAT GOT YOU INTO CRICKET? Watching my dad Matt play on the weekends for Sheffield Collegiate
FAMILY TIES? My dad was a good cricketer and my brother plays the occasional game
'ROY OF THE ROVERS' MOMENT? Winning the One-Day Cup and T20 Blast with Notts last season
BEST THING ABOUT YOUR HOME GROUND? Everything
BEST OPPOSING PLAYER IN COUNTY CRICKET? Darren Stevens (Ken)
YOUNG OPPOSING PLAYER WHO HAS IMPRESSED YOU? Adam Hose (War) – hits it like a golf ball
IF YOU WEREN'T A CRICKETER? I'd be a golf caddy
SURPRISING FACT ABOUT YOU? I am right-handed but bat left-handed
SURPRISING FACT ABOUT A TEAMMATE? Luke Wood's hair is a wig
WHERE IS PARADISE? Sheffield
CRICKETING HERO? My dad – great to watch
NON-CRICKETING HERO? Andrew 'Beef' Johnston (golfer)
TWITTER: @Rootdog22

Batting	Mat	Inns	NO	Runs	HS	Ave	SR	100	50	Ct	St
First-class	8	12	1	501	133	45.54	60.80	2	2	0	0
List A	9	7	3	259	107*	64.75	92.17	1	1	1	0
T20s	10	4	3	78	37	78.00	130.00	0	0	1	0

Bowling	Mat	Balls	Runs	Wkts	BBI	BBM	Ave	Econ	SR	5w	10
First-class	8	98	52	3	3/29	3/29	17.33	3.18	32.6	0	0
List A	9	46	42	0	-	-	-	5.47	-	0	0
T20s	10	6	17	0	-	-	-	17.00	-	0	0

JOE ROOT

RHB / OB / R3 / W0

YORKSHIRE

FULL NAME: Joseph Edward Root
BORN: December 30, 1990, Sheffield
SQUAD NO: 66
HEIGHT: 6ft
NICKNAME: Rooty, Roota, Rootfish
EDUCATION: King Ecgbert School, Sheffield; Worksop College, Nottinghamshire
TEAMS: England, Yorkshire
ROLE: Batsman
DEBUT: Test: 2012; ODI: 2013; T20I: 2012; First-class: 2010; List A: 2009; T20: 2011

BEST BATTING: 254 England vs Pakistan, Old Trafford, 2016
BEST BOWLING: 3-33 Yorkshire vs Warwickshire, Headingley, 2011
COUNTY CAP: 2012

FAMILY TIES? My dad played club cricket and represented Nottinghamshire Second XI and Colts. My brother Billy is at Notts
'ROY OF THE ROVERS' MOMENT? Winning the Ashes in 2015
CRICKETING HERO? Michael Vaughan
NON-CRICKETING HEROES? Seve Ballesteros, Alan Shearer
IF YOU WEREN'T A CRICKETER? I'd be studying art and design at college or university
SURPRISING FACT? I taught myself to play the ukulele on tour with England
TWITTER: @root66

Batting	Mat	Inns	NO	Runs	HS	Ave	SR	100	50	Ct	St
Tests	65	119	12	5701	254	53.28	55.76	13	37	76	0
ODIs	104	98	13	4306	133*	50.65	86.77	10	27	50	0
T20Is	25	23	4	743	90*	39.10	128.76	0	4	14	0
First-class	119	205	22	9393	254	51.32	56.63	22	52	111	0
List A	141	134	18	5482	133*	47.25	85.24	11	35	62	0
T20s	57	51	10	1325	92*	32.31	125.59	0	7	24	0

Bowling	Mat	Balls	Runs	Wkts	BBI	BBM	Ave	Econ	SR	5w	10
Tests	65	1628	817	17	2/9	2/9	48.05	3.01	95.7	0	0
ODIs	104	1186	1129	20	3/52	3/52	56.45	5.71	59.3	0	0
T20Is	25	84	139	6	2/9	2/9	23.16	9.92	14.0	0	0
First-class	119	3149	1634	32	3/33	3/33	51.06	3.11	98.4	0	0
List A	141	1695	1556	33	3/52	3/52	47.15	5.50	51.3	0	0
T20s	57	258	408	10	2/9	2/9	40.80	9.48	25.8	0	0

ADAM ROSSINGTON

FULL NAME: Adam Matthew Rossington
BORN: May 5, 1993, Edgware, Middlesex
SQUAD NO: 7
HEIGHT: 6ft
NICKNAME: Rosso
EDUCATION: Belmont Preparatory School, Surrey; Mill Hill School, London
TEAMS: Northamptonshire, Middlesex
ROLE: Wicketkeeper/batsman
DEBUT: First-class: 2010; List A: 2012; T20: 2011

NORTHAMPTONSHIRE

BEST BATTING: 138* Northamptonshire vs Sussex, Arundel, 2016

WHAT GOT YOU INTO CRICKET? My dad and two brothers
BEST ADVICE EVER RECEIVED? Watch the ball
'ROY OF THE ROVERS' MOMENT? Winning the T20 Blast in 2016
BEST THING ABOUT YOUR HOME GROUND? The fans
BEST OPPOSING PLAYER IN COUNTY CRICKET? Jeetan Patel (War)
YOUNG OPPOSING PLAYER WHO HAS IMPRESSED YOU? Max Holden (Mid) – talented batsman who has a very good temperament
IF YOU WEREN'T A CRICKETER? I'd try to be a pro golfer or else a property developer
SURPRISING FACT ABOUT YOU? I can't ride a bicycle. I support Barnet FC
SURPRISING FACT ABOUT A TEAMMATE? Nathan Buck gets dressed in the dark
WHERE IS PARADISE? Cottesloe Beach Hotel, Perth, Australia
CRICKETING HERO? Alec Stewart
NON-CRICKETING HERO? Roger Federer
UNUSUAL OBJECT AT HOME? A dartboard
TWITTER: @rossington17

Batting	Mat	Inns	NO	Runs	HS	Ave	SR	100	50	Ct	St
First-class	51	81	9	2549	138*	35.40	73.43	6	16	99	9
List A	36	31	6	926	97	37.04	99.03	0	7	20	4
T20s	65	61	5	1153	85	20.58	143.05	0	6	33	10

Bowling	Mat	Balls	Runs	Wkts	BBI	BBM	Ave	Econ	SR	5w	10
First-class	51	90	66	0	-	-	-	4.40	-	0	0
List A	36	-	-	-	-	-	-	-	-	-	-
T20s	65	-	-	-	-	-	-	-	-	-	-

RILEE ROSSOUW LHB / OB / R0 / W0

FULL NAME: Rilee Roscoe Rossouw
BORN: October 9, 1989, Bloemfontein, South Africa
SQUAD NO: 30
NICKNAME: Rudi
EDUCATION: Grey College, Bloemfontein
TEAMS: South Africa, Hampshire, Basnahira Cricket Dundee, Eagles, Free State, Knights, Quetta Gladiators, Royal Challengers Bangalore
ROLE: Batsman
DEBUT: ODI: 2014; T20I: 2014; First-class: 2007; List A: 2007; T20: 2008

BEST BATTING: 319 Eagles vs Titans, Centurion, 2010
BEST BOWLING: 1-1 Knights vs Cape Cobras, Cape Town, 2013

TWITTER: @Rileerr
NOTES: A top-order batsman, Rossouw quit international cricket ahead of the 2017 season to take up a three-year Kolpak deal with Hampshire to play in all formats. He struggled in his first season with the club, scoring one fifty in 13 Championship innings, although a hundred in the One-Day Cup served notice of his qualities. The left-hander's South Africa career got off to a shaky start in 2014, with ducks in four of his first six ODI innings, but he soon established himself as one of his country's most consistent white-ball performers. His highest first-class score, a 291-ball innings of 319 which included 47 fours and eight sixes, is more indicative of his pedigree in the longer format

Batting	Mat	Inns	NO	Runs	HS	Ave	SR	100	50	Ct	St
ODIs	36	35	3	1239	132	38.71	94.36	3	7	22	0
T20Is	15	14	3	327	78	29.72	137.97	0	2	9	0
First-class	87	153	6	6193	319	42.12	63.73	18	26	109	0
List A	133	131	7	4864	156	39.22	94.59	10	29	73	0
T20s	117	113	9	2841	78	27.31	129.90	0	15	47	0

Bowling	Mat	Balls	Runs	Wkts	BBI	BBM	Ave	Econ	SR	5w	10
ODIs	36	45	44	1	1/17	1/17	44.00	5.86	45.0	0	0
T20Is	15	-	-	-	-	-	-	-	-	-	-
First-class	87	78	70	3	1/1	1/1	23.33	5.38	26.0	0	0
List A	133	45	44	1	1/17	1/17	44.00	5.86	45.0	0	0
T20s	117	11	13	1	1/8	1/8	13.00	7.09	11.0	0	0

FULL NAME: Adam Paul Rouse
BORN: June 30, 1992, Harare, Zimbabwe
SQUAD NO: 12
EDUCATION: Perins Community Sports College, Hampshire; Peter Symonds College, Winchester
TEAMS: Kent, Gloucestershire, Hampshire
ROLE: Wicketkeeper/batsman
DEBUT: First-class: 2013; List A: 2013; T20: 2014

BEST BATTING: 95* Kent vs Derbyshire, Canterbury, 2017

TWITTER: @Rousie20

NOTES: A former England U19 wicketkeeper/batsman, Zimbabwean-born Rouse had a trial with Kent in 2015 and also played for their second XI the previous summer. He has had brief spells with Gloucestershire and Hampshire. Agreed a deal with Kent ahead of the 2016 season, in which he played six Championship matches but only one game of white-ball cricket. Last summer he played 10 Championship matches, making his highest first-class score of 95 not out

Batting	Mat	Inns	NO	Runs	HS	Ave	SR	100	50	Ct	St
First-class	24	34	2	828	95*	25.87	51.33	0	4	78	4
List A	26	23	7	437	75*	27.31	68.17	0	2	26	2
T20s	8	7	2	61	35*	12.20	117.30	0	0	4	4

Bowling	Mat	Balls	Runs	Wkts	BBI	BBM	Ave	Econ	SR	5w	10
First-class	24	-	-	-	-	-	-	-	-	-	-
List A	26	-	-	-	-	-	-	-	-	-	-
T20s	8	-	-	-	-	-	-	-	-	-	-

SOMERSET

FULL NAME: Timothy David Rouse
BORN: April 9, 1996, Sheffield
SQUAD NO: 44
HEIGHT: 6ft
NICKNAME: Rousey, Chunk
EDUCATION: Kingswood School, Bath; Cardiff University
TEAMS: Somerset
ROLE: Allrounder
DEBUT: First-class: 2015; T20: 2016

BEST BATTING: 69 Somerset vs Yorkshire, Scarborough, 2017
BEST BOWLING: 2-31 Cardiff MCCU vs Glamorgan, Cardiff, 2017

FAMILY TIES? My older brother Harry has played first-class cricket for Leeds/Bradford MCCU and represented Somerset Second XI
BEST ADVICE EVER RECEIVED? Smile
BEST THING ABOUT YOUR HOME GROUND? The supporters
YOUNG OPPOSING PLAYER WHO HAS IMPRESSED YOU? Jamie Porter (Ess) – bowls 'areas'
IF YOU WEREN'T A CRICKETER? I'd hopefully be a lawyer
SURPRISING FACT ABOUT YOU? I'm 21 but am yet to attempt a driving test
SURPRISING FACT ABOUT A TEAMMATE? Ollie Sale has kept the hair from his shorn mullet
WHERE IS PARADISE? Taunton
CRICKETING HERO? Marcus Trescothick – well, it had to be, didn't it? Legend of the 2005 Ashes and still loves the game
NON-CRICKETING HERO? Christopher Hitchens – great speaker
TWITTER: @tim_rouse

Batting	Mat	Inns	NO	Runs	HS	Ave	SR	100	50	Ct	St
First-class	9	13	1	205	69	17.08	40.83	0	1	5	0
T20s	1	1	0	9	9	9.00	90.00	0	0	1	0

Bowling	Mat	Balls	Runs	Wkts	BBI	BBM	Ave	Econ	SR	5w	10
First-class	9	228	185	5	2/31	2/31	37.00	4.86	45.6	0	0
T20s	1	-	-	-	-	-	-	-	-	-	-

JASON ROY

RHB / RM / R1 / W0

FULL NAME: Jason Jonathan Roy
BORN: July 21, 1990, Durban, South Africa
SQUAD NO: 20
HEIGHT: 6ft
NICKNAME: JRoy, Roy the Boy
EDUCATION: Whitgift School, Croydon
TEAMS: England, Surrey, Chittagong Kings, Delhi Daredevils, Sydney Sixers, Sydney Thunder
ROLE: Batsman
DEBUT: ODI: 2015; T20I: 2014; First-class: 2010; List A: 2008; T20: 2008

SURREY

BEST BATTING: 143 Surrey vs Lancashire, The Oval, 2015
BEST BOWLING: 3-9 Surrey vs Gloucestershire, Bristol, 2014
COUNTY CAP: 2014

'ROY OF THE ROVERS' MOMENT? Getting promoted with Surrey, my England T20I and ODI debuts and my first century for England in ODI cricket
HOW WOULD YOUR TEAMMATES DESCRIBE YOU IN THREE WORDS? Charismatic, confident, loyal
CRICKETING HERO? Jacques Kallis
NON-CRICKETING HERO? I don't really have any heroes but if I did it would be Superman
IF YOU WEREN'T A CRICKETER? I'd be a professional surfer and living on a beach
TWITTER: @JasonRoy20

Batting	Mat	Inns	NO	Runs	HS	Ave	SR	100	50	Ct	St
ODIs	55	54	2	1949	180	37.48	103.23	4	11	21	0
T20Is	27	27	0	518	78	19.18	133.85	0	2	3	0
First-class	78	127	11	4376	143	37.72	82.22	8	20	72	0
List A	141	136	7	4738	180	36.72	105.42	11	25	53	0
T20s	165	162	8	4205	122*	27.30	144.80	4	27	68	0

Bowling	Mat	Balls	Runs	Wkts	BBI	BBM	Ave	Econ	SR	5w	10
ODIs	55	-	-	-	-	-	-	-	-	-	-
T20Is	27	-	-	-	-	-	-	-	-	-	-
First-class	78	712	495	14	3/9	4/47	35.35	4.17	50.8	0	0
List A	141	6	12	0	-	-	-	12.00	-	0	0
T20s	165	18	39	1	1/23	1/23	39.00	13.00	18.0	0	0

CHRIS RUSHWORTH RHB / RFM / R0 / W3 / MVP66

DURHAM

FULL NAME: Christopher Rushworth
BORN: July 11, 1986, Sunderland
SQUAD NO: 22
HEIGHT: 6ft 2in
NICKNAME: Rushy, Sponge
EDUCATION: Castle View Comprehensive School, Sunderland
TEAMS: Durham
ROLE: Bowler
DEBUT: First-class: 2010; List A: 2004; T20: 2011

BEST BATTING: 57 Durham vs Kent, Canterbury, 2017
BEST BOWLING: 9-52 Durham vs Northamptonshire, Chester-le-Street, 2014

FAMILY TIES? My father Joe played local cricket, my brother Lee played county age-groups and represented England U17 and U19. My cousin Phil Mustard is now at Gloucestershire
'ROY OF THE ROVERS' MOMENT? Winning a Lord's final in the 2014 One-Day Cup, followed closely by taking 15 wickets in a day against Northants in the same season
BEST THING ABOUT YOUR HOME GROUND? It takes me three minutes to drive there
BEST OPPOSING PLAYER IN COUNTY CRICKET? Riki Wessels (Not)
YOUNG OPPOSING PLAYER WHO HAS IMPRESSED YOU? Ed Barnard (Wor) – picks up wickets, capable of scoring runs and a brilliant fielder
IF YOU WEREN'T A CRICKETER? I'd be some kind of tradesman
SURPRISING FACT ABOUT YOU? I love wearing slippers
SURPRISING FACT ABOUT A TEAMMATE? James Weighell's fringe starts at the back of his head
WHERE IS PARADISE? Any beach where it's sunny and warm
CRICKETING HERO? Shaun Pollock and Glenn McGrath – watched them both as I was growing up. Their skill level and accuracy at the highest level inspired me to become a fast bowler. Well, a medium-fast bowler at least

Batting	Mat	Inns	NO	Runs	HS	Ave	SR	100	50	Ct	St
First-class	100	137	36	1322	57	13.08	65.93	0	1	22	0
List A	67	26	13	153	38*	11.76	85.95	0	0	15	0
T20s	71	14	9	18	5	3.60	51.42	0	0	16	0

Bowling	Mat	Balls	Runs	Wkts	BBI	BBM	Ave	Econ	SR	5w	10
First-class	100	17343	8758	359	9/52	15/95	24.39	3.02	48.3	18	2
List A	67	2866	2563	102	5/31	5/31	25.12	5.36	28.0	2	0
T20s	71	1353	1776	67	3/14	3/14	26.50	7.87	20.1	0	0

ABI SAKANDE

RHB / RFM / R0 / W0

FULL NAME: Abidine Sakande
BORN: September 22, 1994, Chester, Cheshire
SQUAD NO: 11
HEIGHT: 6ft 4in
EDUCATION: Ardingly College; St John's College, Oxford University
TEAMS: Sussex
ROLE: Bowler
DEBUT: First-class: 2014; List A: 2016

SUSSEX

BEST BATTING: 33 Oxford MCCU vs Cambridge MCCU, Cambridge, 2015
BEST BOWLING: 5-43 Sussex vs South Africa A, Arundel, 2017

WHAT GOT YOU INTO CRICKET? The 2005 Ashes
BEST ADVICE EVER RECEIVED? Treat every meal as an opportunity
'ROY OF THE ROVERS' MOMENT? Taking my maiden first-class five-for against South Africa A at Arundel in 2017
BEST THING ABOUT YOUR HOME GROUND? The boundaries are small so the crowd feel very close to the action
BEST OPPOSING PLAYER IN COUNTY CRICKET? Your own mind can be a better opponent than any player
YOUNG OPPOSING PLAYER WHO HAS IMPRESSED YOU? Cameron Steel (Dur) – coming from nowhere to score 899 Championship runs last season is a great effort
SURPRISING FACT ABOUT A TEAMMATE? Michael Burgess is as vanilla as they come
CRICKETING HERO? Michael Holding – just love his action
NON-CRICKETING HERO? Barack Obama – for his belief and positive attitude to making change happen
UNUSUAL OBJECT AT HOME? A tub of peanut butter made by grandmother in Burkina Faso
TWITTER: @AbiSakande

Batting	Mat	Inns	NO	Runs	HS	Ave	SR	100	50	Ct	St
First-class	9	11	3	103	33	12.87	32.08	0	0	4	0
List A	2	1	1	7	7*	-	58.33	0	0	0	0

Bowling	Mat	Balls	Runs	Wkts	BBI	BBM	Ave	Econ	SR	5w	10
First-class	9	1290	728	23	5/43	6/87	31.65	3.38	56.0	1	0
List A	2	83	108	3	2/62	2/62	36.00	7.80	27.6	0	0

OLLIE SALE

RHB / RFM / R0 / W0

FULL NAME: Oliver Richard Trethowan Sale
BORN: September 30, 1995, Newcastle-under-Lyme, Staffordshire
SQUAD NO: 82
HEIGHT: 6ft 2in
NICKNAME: Saler, Salo, Salestorm
EDUCATION: Sherborne School, Dorset; Newcastle University
TEAMS: Somerset
ROLE: Allrounder
DEBUT: T20: 2016

WHAT GOT YOU INTO CRICKET? I taught myself to bowl by watching it on TV
BEST ADVICE EVER RECEIVED? Aim for the stars and you might hit the moon
BEST THING ABOUT YOUR HOME GROUND? That the Somerset faithfuls always pack out the ground
YOUNG OPPOSING PLAYER WHO HAS IMPRESSED YOU? Jofra Archer (Sus) – bowls rockets and whacks it
IF YOU WEREN'T A CRICKETER? I'd be a Premier League footballer (maybe)
SURPRISING FACT ABOUT YOU? I'm scared of sponges… when I say 'scared' I mean I literally cannot deal with the feel of them
SURPRISING FACT ABOUT A TEAMMATE? Tim Rouse has the biggest chest in the world
WHERE IS PARADISE? The Toon
CRICKETING HERO? Andrew Flintoff – what an entertainer
NON-CRICKETING HERO? Steve Jobs
UNUSUAL OBJECT AT HOME? No sponges, that's for sure
TWITTER: @olliesale1

Batting	Mat	Inns	NO	Runs	HS	Ave	SR	100	50	Ct	St
T20s	1	1	0	1	1	1.00	33.33	0	0	0	0

Bowling	Mat	Balls	Runs	Wkts	BBI	BBM	Ave	Econ	SR	5w	10
T20s	1	18	40	0	-	-	-	13.33	-	0	0

PHIL SALT

RHB / OB / R0 / W0

FULL NAME: Philip Dean Salt
BORN: August 28, 1996, Bodelwyddan, Denbighshire, Wales
SQUAD NO: 28
HEIGHT: 6ft
NICKNAME: Salty
EDUCATION: Harrison College, Barbados; Reed's School, Surrey
TEAMS: Sussex
ROLE: Batsman
DEBUT: First-class: 2016; List A: 2015; T20: 2016

BEST BATTING: 72 Sussex vs Durham, Chester-le-Street, 2017

WHAT GOT YOU INTO CRICKET? Playing Kwik Cricket at school
STRANGEST THING SEEN IN A GAME? When a streaker ran on in a T20 game against Kent a couple of years ago and took out all three stumps with a diving headbutt
'ROY OF THE ROVERS' MOMENT? Scoring a double hundred for Sussex Academy
CRICKETING HERO? Growing up in Barbados, I didn't look past Sir Garry Sobers
NON-CRICKETING HERO? Anyone in the emergency services and armed forces
IF YOU WEREN'T A CRICKETER? I'd be in the NBA
SURPRISING FACT? I once picked up Sir Garry Sobers' Indian takeaway by accident
UNUSUAL OBJECT AT HOME? The head of a WW1 bomb
TWITTER: @PhilSalt1

Batting	Mat	Inns	NO	Runs	HS	Ave	SR	100	50	Ct	St
First-class	7	10	1	203	72	22.55	54.42	0	1	2	0
List A	7	7	0	186	81	26.57	92.07	0	1	2	0
T20s	11	10	2	179	33	22.37	125.17	0	0	3	0

Bowling	Mat	Balls	Runs	Wkts	BBI	BBM	Ave	Econ	SR	5w	10
First-class	7	-	-	-	-	-	-	-	-	-	-
List A	7	-	-	-	-	-	-	-	-	-	-
T20s	11	-	-	-	-	-	-	-	-	-	-

ANDREW SALTER

RHB / OB / R0 / W0

FULL NAME: Andrew Graham Salter
BORN: June 1, 1993, Haverfordwest, Pembrokeshire
SQUAD NO: 21
HEIGHT: 5ft 10in
NICKNAME: Beak, Salty
EDUCATION: Milford Haven School, Pembrokeshire; Cardiff Metropolitan University
TEAMS: Glamorgan
ROLE: Bowler
DEBUT: First-class: 2012; List A: 2012; T20: 2014

BEST BATTING: 88 Glamorgan vs Gloucestershire, Cardiff, 2017
BEST BOWLING: 3-5 Glamorgan vs Northamptonshire, Cardiff, 2015

WHAT GOT YOU INTO CRICKET? Trying to bowl my brother out in the garden
FAMILY TIES? Father and brother both played, mum made teas and scored
'ROY OF THE ROVERS' MOMENT? Hitting six sixes in an over for St Ishmaels U15
BEST THING ABOUT YOUR HOME GROUND? The warm Welsh welcome
YOUNG OPPOSING PLAYER WHO HAS IMPRESSED YOU? Alex Davies (Lan)
IF YOU WEREN'T A CRICKETER? I'd be a Steve McQueen wannabe
SURPRISING FACT ABOUT YOU? I co-manage a motorcycle initiative called Baffle Culture which aims at "seizing the opportunity to bring like-minded riders together"
SURPRISING FACT ABOUT A TEAMMATE? Kiran Carlson can't reach the sweet jar in the kitchen
WHERE IS PARADISE? Pembrokeshire
CRICKETING HERO? Nathan Lyon – appreciation from one off-spinner to another
NON-CRICKETING HERO? Charley Boorman (TV presenter and motorbike enthusiast)
TWITTER: @AndySalts

Batting	Mat	Inns	NO	Runs	HS	Ave	SR	100	50	Ct	St
First-class	44	67	14	1378	88	26.00	43.08	0	7	20	0
List A	28	21	9	282	51	23.50	84.93	0	1	7	0
T20s	43	23	13	175	37*	17.50	114.37	0	0	13	0

Bowling	Mat	Balls	Runs	Wkts	BBI	BBM	Ave	Econ	SR	5w	10
First-class	44	5437	3268	64	3/5	6/69	51.06	3.60	84.9	0	0
List A	28	910	797	11	2/41	2/41	72.45	5.25	82.7	0	0
T20s	43	480	671	18	2/19	2/19	37.27	8.38	26.6	0	0

BEN SANDERSON

RHB / RMF / R0 / W1 / MVP76

FULL NAME: Ben William Sanderson
BORN: January 3, 1989, Sheffield
SQUAD NO: 26
HEIGHT: 6ft
NICKNAME: Sando
EDUCATION: Ecclesfield School, Sheffield;
Sheffield College
TEAMS: Northamptonshire, Yorkshire
ROLE: Bowler
DEBUT: First-class: 2008; List A: 2010; T20:
2010

BEST BATTING: 42 Northamptonshire vs Kent, Canterbury, 2015
BEST BOWLING: 8-73 Northamptonshire vs Gloucestershire, Northampton, 2016

WHAT GOT YOU INTO CRICKET? Watching my dad play for Whiteley Hall CC
BEST ADVICE EVER RECEIVED? Bite the apple and brush your ear when bowling
'ROY OF THE ROVERS' MOMENT? Rory Kleinveldt getting the last wicket with three runs
required against Leicestershire in the Championship in 2017
BEST THING ABOUT YOUR HOME GROUND? The ice-cream truck
BEST OPPOSING PLAYER IN COUNTY CRICKET? Simon Kerrigan (Lan)
IF YOU WEREN'T A CRICKETER? I'd be a plumber
SURPRISING FACT ABOUT YOU? My nose has been broken
SURPRISING FACT ABOUT A TEAMMATE? Josh Cobb's teeth once belonged to Frankel
the racehorse
WHERE IS PARADISE? Anywhere that doesn't involve bowling
CRICKETING HERO? Darren Gough
NON-CRICKETING HERO? Chris Waddle, Kevin Pressman
UNUSUAL OBJECT AT HOME? Cannonballs
TWITTER: @sando567

Batting	Mat	Inns	NO	Runs	HS	Ave	SR	100	50	Ct	St
First-class	32	39	11	187	42	6.67	40.38	0	0	6	0
List A	18	6	4	43	19*	21.50	76.78	0	0	7	0
T20s	17	5	4	21	12*	21.00	116.66	0	0	0	0

Bowling	Mat	Balls	Runs	Wkts	BBI	BBM	Ave	Econ	SR	5w	10
First-class	32	5328	2477	112	8/73	10/89	22.11	2.78	47.5	7	1
List A	18	576	580	17	3/36	3/36	34.11	6.04	33.8	0	0
T20s	17	323	463	21	4/21	4/21	22.04	8.60	15.3	0	0

MITCHELL SANTNER

LHB / SLA / RO / WO

FULL NAME: Mitchell Josef Santner
BORN: February 5, 1992, Hamilton, New Zealand
SQUAD NO: TBC
NICKNAME: Flatline
TEAMS: New Zealand, Derbyshire, Northern Districts, Worcestershire
ROLE: Allrounder
DEBUT: Test: 2015; ODI: 2015; T20I: 2015; First-class: 2011; List A: 2014; T20: 2014

BEST BATTING: 118 Northern Districts vs Canterbury, Gisborne, 2014
BEST BOWLING: 3-51 Northern Districts vs Auckland, Whangarei, 2014

TWITTER: @MitchellSantner
NOTES: The New Zealander has been signed by Derbyshire for the Blast after two T20 campaigns with Worcestershire. He was restricted to just two appearances in 2016 because of a fractured finger but took 13 wickets in 13 matches last summer, with an economy-rate of well under seven. Persistent, parsimonious and accurate with the ball, and more than useful with the bat, the left-arm spinner has three years of international cricket under his belt after making his ODI debut against England in 2015. Impressed in the 2016 World T20 and was until recently the No.1 T20I bowler in the ICC rankings

Batting	Mat	Inns	NO	Runs	HS	Ave	SR	100	50	Ct	St
Tests	17	21	0	535	73	25.47	42.49	0	2	7	0
ODIs	50	40	15	663	63*	26.52	91.95	0	1	20	0
T20Is	27	17	6	170	37	15.45	128.78	0	0	12	0
First-class	41	60	4	1651	118	29.48	47.21	2	10	32	0
List A	74	62	16	1290	86	28.04	89.45	0	5	34	0
T20s	54	41	11	609	45*	20.30	128.21	0	0	24	0

Bowling	Mat	Balls	Runs	Wkts	BBI	BBM	Ave	Econ	SR	5w	10
Tests	17	2702	1260	34	3/60	5/173	37.05	2.79	79.4	0	0
ODIs	50	2317	1888	58	5/50	5/50	32.55	4.88	39.9	1	0
T20Is	27	521	620	29	4/11	4/11	21.37	7.14	17.9	0	0
First-class	41	5445	2725	59	3/51	5/173	46.18	3.00	92.2	0	0
List A	74	3447	2692	88	5/50	5/50	30.59	4.68	39.1	1	0
T20s	54	1097	1280	51	4/11	4/11	25.09	7.00	21.5	0	0

ROB SAYER

RHB / OB / RO / WO

FULL NAME: Robert John Sayer
BORN: January 25, 1995, Huntingdon, Cambridgeshire
SQUAD NO: 12
HEIGHT: 6ft 2in
NICKNAME: Leo
EDUCATION: Abbey College, Cambridgeshire; Leeds Metropolitan University
TEAMS: Leicestershire
ROLE: Bowler
DEBUT: First-class: 2015; List A: 2015; T20: 2015

LEICESTERSHIRE

BEST BATTING: 34 Leicestershire vs Gloucestershire, Leicester, 2015
BEST BOWLING: 2-41 Leicestershire vs Sri Lankans, Leicester, 2016

WHAT GOT YOU INTO CRICKET? Indoor cricket with my best mate
'ROY OF THE ROVERS' MOMENT? Winning on my first-class debut vs Derbyshire
SUPERSTITIONS? Do everything in twos when I bat
HOW WOULD YOUR TEAMMATES DESCRIBE YOU IN THREE WORDS? Very, very messy
BEST OPPOSING PLAYER IN COUNTY CRICKET? Tim Bresnan (Yor)
CRICKETING HEROES? Andrew Flintoff – could change a game in minutes. Graeme Swann – an off-spinner like me
NON-CRICKETING HERO? Muhammad Ali – for his ruthlessness and self-confidence
IF YOU WEREN'T A CRICKETER? I'd be failing uni, hacking around golf courses and playing Sunday league football
SURPRISING FACT? I played football for Peterborough Centre of Excellence
UNUSUAL OBJECT AT HOME? An elliptical trainer
TWITTER: @Sayer1995

Batting	Mat	Inns	NO	Runs	HS	Ave	SR	100	50	Ct	St
First-class	11	13	2	152	34	13.81	36.71	0	0	3	0
List A	15	13	2	138	26	12.54	80.70	0	0	4	0
T20s	8	3	1	14	9	7.00	87.50	0	0	1	0

Bowling	Mat	Balls	Runs	Wkts	BBI	BBM	Ave	Econ	SR	5w	10
First-class	11	1778	1123	14	2/41	3/88	80.21	3.78	127.0	0	0
List A	15	714	663	11	2/65	2/65	60.27	5.57	64.9	0	0
T20s	8	108	185	6	2/16	2/16	30.83	10.27	18.0	0	0

GEORGE SCOTT

RHB / RM / R0 / W0

FULL NAME: George Frederick Buchan Scott
BORN: November 6, 1995, Hemel Hempstead, Hertfordshire
SQUAD NO: 17
HEIGHT: 6ft 2in
NICKNAME: Scotty
EDUCATION: Beechwood Park School, St Albans; St Albans School; University of Leeds
TEAMS: Middlesex
ROLE: Allrounder
DEBUT: First-class: 2015; List A: 2015; T20: 2015

BEST BATTING: 16* Leeds/Bradford MCCU vs Sussex, Hove, 2016
BEST BOWLING: 2-67 Leeds/Bradford MCCU vs Sussex, Hove, 2015

FAMILY TIES? I have an older brother and younger brother who play Minor Counties cricket for Hertfordshire, and another younger brother in the Middlesex Academy
BEST ADVICE EVER RECEIVED? The stiller you are, the easier it is to see
'ROY OF THE ROVERS' MOMENT? Playing in front of a full house of 28,000 at Lord's
BEST OPPOSING PLAYER IN COUNTY CRICKET? Kane Williamson (Yor)
YOUNG OPPOSING PLAYER WHO HAS IMPRESSED YOU? Jofra Archer (Sus) – he bowls swinging thunderbolts
SURPRISING FACT ABOUT YOU? I was a music scholar at St Albans School, playing the piano and the bassoon
WHERE IS PARADISE? The Maldives
CRICKETING HERO? Kumar Sangakarra – having a degree in Law and being one of the best cricketers ever shows he must be a very intelligent and well-rounded individual
NON-CRICKETING HEROES? My brothers
TWITTER: @georgefbscott

Batting	Mat	Inns	NO	Runs	HS	Ave	SR	100	50	Ct	St
First-class	4	5	2	37	16*	12.33	22.56	0	0	2	0
List A	1	1	0	4	4	4.00	36.36	0	0	0	0
T20s	9	8	3	159	38*	31.80	100.63	0	0	2	0

Bowling	Mat	Balls	Runs	Wkts	BBI	BBM	Ave	Econ	SR	5w	10
First-class	4	126	121	2	2/67	2/67	60.50	5.76	63.0	0	0
List A	1	18	28	0	-	-	-	9.33	-	0	0
T20s	9	12	22	1	1/22	1/22	22.00	11.00	12.0	0	0

GEORGE SCRIMSHAW

RHB / RMF / R0 / W0

FULL NAME: George Louis Sheridan Scrimshaw
BORN: February 10, 1998, Burton-on-Trent, Staffordshire
SQUAD NO: 9
HEIGHT: 6ft 6in
NICKNAME: Scrim, Scrimmy, Groot
EDUCATION: Thomas Russel Junior School; John Taylor High School, Burton-on-Trent
TEAMS: Worcestershire
ROLE: Bowler
DEBUT: T20: 2017

FAMILY TIES? My dad and grandad both played county age-group cricket

'ROY OF THE ROVERS' MOMENT? Taking 5-12 in a second XI T20 match for Worcestershire against Yorkshire in 2017

BEST THING ABOUT YOUR HOME GROUND? The balcony at New Road

BEST OPPOSING PLAYER IN COUNTY CRICKET? Alastair Cook (Ess)

YOUNG OPPOSING PLAYER WHO HAS IMPRESSED YOU? Tom Barber (Mid) – exciting young fast bowler who can reach 90mph

SURPRISING FACT ABOUT YOU? I once hit 16 sixes in a row in Kwik Cricket. My favourite footballer is Steve Morison – the former Norwich and Leeds United player who is currently at Millwall

WHERE IS PARADISE? Dunstall Cricket Club, Staffordshire

CRICKETING HERO? Dale Steyn – he has been a great player for a long time and I love his aggression. For a fast bowler like myself, he is a role model

NON-CRICKETING HERO? My dad – he got me into cricket in the first place and has supported me all the way

UNUSUAL OBJECT AT HOME? A glass-spinning globe

TWITTER: @Gscrimshaw98

Batting	Mat	Inns	NO	Runs	HS	Ave	SR	100	50	Ct	St
T20s	4	1	1	1	1*	-	50.00	0	0	0	0

Bowling	Mat	Balls	Runs	Wkts	BBI	BBM	Ave	Econ	SR	5w	10
T20s	4	60	90	3	1/20	1/20	30.00	9.00	20.0	0	0

NICK SELMAN

RHB / RM / RO / WO

FULL NAME: Nicholas James Selman
BORN: October 18, 1995, Brisbane, Australia
SQUAD NO: 9
HEIGHT: 6ft 3in
NICKNAME: Salmon
EDUCATION: Matthew Flinders Anglican College, Queensland, Australia
TEAMS: Glamorgan
ROLE: Batsman
DEBUT: First-class: 2016; List A: 2016; T20: 2016

BEST BATTING: 142* Glamorgan vs Gloucestershire, Cardiff, 2017

WHAT GOT YOU INTO CRICKET? Playing in the backyard with my mum and dad
BEST ADVICE EVER RECEIVED? Play straight, leave well
'ROY OF THE ROVERS' MOMENT? Hitting 14 off the last over to beat Durham in a Championship game last season
BEST THING ABOUT YOUR HOME GROUND? The all-you-can-eat lunches
BEST OPPOSING PLAYER IN COUNTY CRICKET? Steve Magoffin (Wor)
YOUNG OPPOSING PLAYER WHO HAS IMPRESSED YOU? Haseeb Hameed (Lan) – good technique and temperament against the new ball
IF YOU WEREN'T A CRICKETER? I'd be a groundsman
SURPRISING FACT ABOUT YOU? I name my bats after greyhounds
WHERE IS PARADISE? Coogee Beach
CRICKETING HERO? Virat Kohli – he's on a different level when it comes to batting. Works extremely hard on and off the field
NON-CRICKETING HERO? Hugh Bowman (horse jockey) – always finds a way to win
TWITTER: @nickselman22

Batting	Mat	Inns	NO	Runs	HS	Ave	SR	100	50	Ct	St
First-class	25	46	4	1372	142*	32.66	47.78	6	5	23	0
List A	1	1	0	6	6	6.00	42.85	0	0	1	0
T20s	5	3	0	99	66	33.00	128.57	0	1	2	0

Bowling	Mat	Balls	Runs	Wkts	BBI	BBM	Ave	Econ	SR	5w	10
First-class	25	18	8	0	-	-	-	2.66	-	0	0
List A	1	-	-	-	-	-	-	-	-	-	-
T20s	5	-	-	-	-	-	-	-	-	-	-

JACK SHANTRY

LHB / LM / R0 / W2

FULL NAME: Jack David Shantry
BORN: January 29, 1988, Shrewsbury
SQUAD NO: 11
HEIGHT: 6ft 4in
NICKNAME: Shants
EDUCATION: Shrewsbury Sixth Form College; University of Manchester
TEAMS: Worcestershire
ROLE: Bowler
DEBUT: First-class: 2009; List A: 2009; T20: 2010

WORCESTERSHIRE

BEST BATTING: 106 Worcestershire vs Gloucestershire, Worcester, 2016
BEST BOWLING: 7-60 Worcestershire vs Oxford MCCU, Oxford, 2013

FAMILY TIES? My brother (Adam) played for Glamorgan, Warwickshire and Northants. My dad (Brian) played for Gloucestershire
BEST ADVICE EVER RECEIVED? Do not seek refuge in the false security of the consensus – Hitchens. Do not bowl short and wide – Rhodes
'ROY OF THE ROVERS' MOMENT? Taking 10 wickets and scoring a hundred against Surrey to help achieve promotion in 2014. I also once ate six desserts during a batting day at Taunton
BEST THING ABOUT YOUR HOME GROUND? The cakes in the Ladies Pavilion
YOUNG OPPOSING PLAYER WHO HAS IMPRESSED YOU? Sam Curran (Sur) – good skills with both red and white ball, and he has the batting potential to become a genuine allrounder
SURPRISING FACT ABOUT YOU? According to the Beaufort scale, hurricane-force wind is classed as 73mph and above. So it's a fact that I bowl faster than a hurricane
WHERE IS PARADISE? A tropical beach with white sand and excellent Wi-Fi
CRICKETING HERO? Wasim Akram – left-arm fast, swung it both ways, fantastically skilful
NON-CRICKETING HERO? Christopher Hitchens – gifted writer and orator
TWITTER: @JackShantry

Batting	Mat	Inns	NO	Runs	HS	Ave	SR	100	50	Ct	St
First-class	92	118	32	1640	106	19.06	55.38	2	2	30	0
List A	73	33	16	188	31	11.05	70.41	0	0	18	0
T20s	90	23	11	87	12*	7.25	95.60	0	0	20	0

Bowling	Mat	Balls	Runs	Wkts	BBI	BBM	Ave	Econ	SR	5w	10
First-class	92	16197	7783	266	7/60	10/26	29.25	2.88	60.8	12	2
List A	73	2999	2800	92	4/29	4/29	30.43	5.60	32.5	0	0
T20s	90	1930	2596	92	4/33	4/33	28.21	8.07	20.9	0	0

ISHANT SHARMA

RHB / RFM / R0 / W0

FULL NAME: Ishant Sharma
BORN: September 2, 1988, Delhi, India
SQUAD NO: 97
TEAMS: India, Sussex, Deccan Chargers, Delhi, India Red, Kings XI Punjab, Kolkata Knight Riders, North Zone, Rising Pune Supergiants, Sunrisers Hyderabad
ROLE: Bowler
DEBUT: Test: 2007; ODI: 2007; T20I: 2008; First-class: 2006; List A: 2006; T20: 2007

BEST BATTING: 31* India vs Sri Lanka, Galle, 2010
BEST BOWLING: 7-24 Delhi vs Orissa, Delhi, 2008

TWITTER: @ImIshant
NOTES: The experienced Indian seamer has joined Sussex for the first two months of the season and is set to be available for five Championship matches and the One-Day Cup group stages. Ishant has been a familiar face on the international circuit for more than a decade. At the time of writing he is the ninth-highest Test wicket-taker among Indian bowlers. He returned career-best Test figures of 7-74 at Lord's during India's tour of England in 2014 and is expected to feature in this summer's series following his stint at Sussex. "Securing Ishant's services has been very important to us," said Sussex's director of cricket Keith Greenfield. "Once Jofra [Archer] and CJ [Chris Jordan] were picked up in the IPL draft, it became crucial to sign an experienced international-quality seam bowler who could provide valuable support and know-how to the rest of the seamers"

Batting	Mat	Inns	NO	Runs	HS	Ave	SR	100	50	Ct	St
Tests	81	110	42	572	31*	8.41	28.33	0	0	16	0
ODIs	80	28	13	72	13	4.80	35.46	0	0	19	0
T20Is	14	3	2	8	5*	8.00	88.88	0	0	4	0
First-class	118	147	59	732	31*	8.31	28.72	0	0	25	0
List A	117	43	19	163	31	6.79	45.53	0	0	26	0
T20s	113	29	21	55	9	6.87	74.32	0	0	22	0

Bowling	Mat	Balls	Runs	Wkts	BBI	BBM	Ave	Econ	SR	5w	10
Tests	81	15600	8411	234	7/74	10/108	35.94	3.23	66.6	7	1
ODIs	80	3733	3563	115	4/34	4/34	30.98	5.72	32.4	0	0
T20Is	14	278	400	8	2/34	2/34	50.00	8.63	34.7	0	0
First-class	118	22117	11385	374	7/24	11/51	30.44	3.08	59.1	12	2
List A	117	5570	4942	170	5/21	5/21	29.07	5.32	32.7	1	0
T20s	113	2437	3189	88	5/12	5/12	36.23	7.85	27.6	1	0

JOSH SHAW

RHB / RMF / R0 / W0

FULL NAME: Joshua Shaw
BORN: January 3, 1996, Wakefield, Yorkshire
SQUAD NO: 25
HEIGHT: 6ft 1in
NICKNAME: Shawy
EDUCATION: Crofton Academy Wakefield; Skills Exchange College, Wakefield
TEAMS: Yorkshire, Gloucestershire
ROLE: Bowler
DEBUT: First-class: 2016; T20: 2015

YORKSHIRE

BEST BATTING: 29 Gloucestershire vs Leicestershire, Cheltenham, 2016
BEST BOWLING: 5-79 Gloucestershire vs Sussex, Bristol, 2016

WHAT GOT YOU INTO CRICKET? My father Chris played for Yorkshire. We also lived on the back of Streethouse CC so I was always around cricket from a young age
BEST ADVICE EVER RECEIVED? Be myself
'ROY OF THE ROVERS' MOMENT? Taking a hat-trick for Yorkshire Academy in the Yorkshire League Cup final in 2014
BEST THING ABOUT YOUR HOME GROUND? It's so homely
YOUNG OPPOSING PLAYER WHO HAS IMPRESSED YOU? George Hankins (Glo)
IF YOU WEREN'T A CRICKETER? I'd be working in the joinery trade
SURPRISING FACT ABOUT YOU? I passed my driving test with no minors
WHERE IS PARADISE? Home
CRICKETING HERO? Andrew Flintoff – for his ability to perform with bat and ball when it mattered most
NON-CRICKETING HERO? Tiger Woods – for his natural ability but also his willingness to work hard to improve his game
TWITTER: @joshuashaw1

Batting	Mat	Inns	NO	Runs	HS	Ave	SR	100	50	Ct	St
First-class	21	26	6	194	29	9.70	36.32	0	0	5	0
T20s	3	2	1	1	1	1.00	50.00	0	0	1	0

Bowling	Mat	Balls	Runs	Wkts	BBI	BBM	Ave	Econ	SR	5w	10
First-class	21	3291	2131	55	5/79	5/79	38.74	3.88	59.8	2	0
T20s	3	36	71	0	-	-	-	11.83	-	0	0

DOMINIC SIBLEY

WARWICKSHIRE

FULL NAME: Dominic Peter Sibley
BORN: September 5, 1995, Epsom, Surrey
SQUAD NO: 45
HEIGHT: 6ft 3in
NICKNAME: Frocko, Big Tree
EDUCATION: Whitgift School, Croydon
TEAMS: Warwickshire, Surrey
ROLE: Batsman
DEBUT: First-class: 2013; List A: 2013; T20: 2016

BEST BATTING: 242 Surrey vs Yorkshire, The Oval, 2013
BEST BOWLING: 2-103 Surrey vs Hampshire, Southampton, 2016

'ROY OF THE ROVERS' MOMENT? Making 242 against Yorkshire at The Oval in 2013 in my third first-class match
BEST OPPOSING PLAYER IN COUNTY CRICKET? Jamie Porter (Ess)
YOUNG OPPOSING PLAYER WHO HAS IMPRESSED YOU? Sam Curran (Sur) – he has a big head on his shoulders
IF YOU WEREN'T A CRICKETER? I'd be a footballer
SURPRISING FACT ABOUT YOU? I am half-French
WHERE IS PARADISE? Cape Town
CRICKETING HERO? Virat Kohli – he churns out runs
NON-CRICKETING HERO? Muhammad Ali
TWITTER: @DomSibley

Batting	Mat	Inns	NO	Runs	HS	Ave	SR	100	50	Ct	St
First-class	36	63	7	1843	242	32.91	40.11	2	13	25	0
List A	12	10	2	164	37	20.50	71.92	0	0	5	0
T20s	21	19	2	579	74*	34.05	120.87	0	5	8	0

Bowling	Mat	Balls	Runs	Wkts	BBI	BBM	Ave	Econ	SR	5w	10
First-class	36	374	264	4	2/103	2/117	66.00	4.23	93.5	0	0
List A	12	48	53	1	1/20	1/20	53.00	6.62	48.0	0	0
T20s	21	186	268	4	2/33	2/33	67.00	8.64	46.5	0	0

PETER SIDDLE

RHB / RFM / R0 / W0

FULL NAME: Peter Matthew Siddle
BORN: November 25, 1984, Traralgon, Victoria, Australia
SQUAD NO: TBC
HEIGHT: 6ft 2in
NICKNAME: Vicious, Dermie
TEAMS: Australia, Essex, Adelaide Strikers, Lancashire, Melbourne Renegades, Nottinghamshire, Victoria
ROLE: Bowler
DEBUT: Test: 2008; ODI: 2009; T20I: 2009; First-class: 2005; List A: 2005; T20: 2006

ESSEX

BEST BATTING: 103* Australia A vs Scotland, Edinburgh, 2013
BEST BOWLING: 8-54 Victoria vs South Australia, Adelaide, 2015

TWITTER: @petersiddle403
NOTES: Siddle made his Test debut against India in 2008 and famously took a Test hat-trick on his birthday on the opening day of the 2010/11 Ashes at The Gabba. The right-arm paceman also played all five Tests during Australia's 5-0 whitewash of England in 2013/14. Essex first signed Siddle for their T20 campaign in 2012 but he pulled out with injury. He then played county cricket for Nottinghamshire in 2014 before switching to Lancashire in 2015, and has taken 55 Championship wickets at an average of 27.91. He has been signed to play Essex's first five Championship games this season. Siddle was a junior wood-chopping champion before giving up the pursuit because he feared that slicing off a toe could end his cricket career. He is a vegan and has said he eats "between 15-20 bananas a day"

Batting	Mat	Inns	NO	Runs	HS	Ave	SR	100	50	Ct	St
Tests	62	86	14	1063	51	14.76	47.18	0	2	16	0
ODIs	17	4	2	21	9*	10.50	116.66	0	0	1	0
T20Is	2	1	1	1	1*	-	100.00	0	0	0	0
First-class	141	184	33	2582	103*	17.09	50.86	1	5	46	0
List A	52	27	9	230	62	12.77	100.00	0	1	6	0
T20s	34	10	7	24	9*	8.00	75.00	0	0	7	0

Bowling	Mat	Balls	Runs	Wkts	BBI	BBM	Ave	Econ	SR	5w	10
Tests	62	12941	6314	211	6/54	9/104	29.92	2.92	61.3	8	0
ODIs	17	751	581	15	3/55	3/55	38.73	4.64	50.0	0	0
T20Is	2	48	58	3	2/24	2/24	19.33	7.25	16.0	0	0
First-class	141	26967	13279	466	8/54	9/77	28.49	2.95	57.8	17	0
List A	52	2614	1978	57	4/27	4/27	34.70	4.54	45.8	0	0
T20s	34	725	842	31	4/29	4/29	27.16	6.96	23.3	0	0

WARWICKSHIRE

FULL NAME: Ryan Nathan Sidebottom
BORN: August 14, 1989, Shepparton, Victoria, Australia
SQUAD NO: 22
HEIGHT: 6ft 2in
NICKNAME: Sidey
TEAMS: Warwickshire, Victoria
ROLE: Bowler
DEBUT: First-class: 2013

BEST BATTING: 13 Warwickshire vs Hampshire, Edgbaston, 2017
BEST BOWLING: 4-29 Warwickshire vs Middlesex, Lord's, 2017

WHAT GOT YOU INTO CRICKET? My brothers
BEST ADVICE EVER RECEIVED? Never give up
'ROY OF THE ROVERS' MOMENT? Making my Warwickshire debut against Middlesex – at Lord's! Had to pinch myself
BEST THING ABOUT YOUR HOME GROUND? It doesn't get much better than Edgbaston
IF YOU WEREN'T A CRICKETER? I would be extremely bored
SURPRISING FACT ABOUT YOU? I've got four brothers, one of whom plays Aussie rules for Collingwood. We grew up in Tallygaroopna near Melbourne, but I have a British passport because my mum moved to Devon
WHERE IS PARADISE? Australia
CRICKETING HERO? Glenn McGrath – he was so consistent with his line and length
TWITTER: @ryansidebottom2

Batting	Mat	Inns	NO	Runs	HS	Ave	SR	100	50	Ct	St
First-class	7	14	6	26	13	3.25	22.80	0	0	0	0

Bowling	Mat	Balls	Runs	Wkts	BBI	BBM	Ave	Econ	SR	5w	10
First-class	7	929	603	24	4/29	6/70	25.12	3.89	38.7	0	0

JOHN SIMPSON

LHB / WK / R0 / W0 / MVP57

FULL NAME: John Andrew Simpson
BORN: July 13, 1988, Bury, Lancashire
SQUAD NO: 20
HEIGHT: 5ft 11in
NICKNAME: Simmo
EDUCATION: St Gabriel's RC High School, Bury; Holy Cross College, Bury
TEAMS: Middlesex
ROLE: Wicketkeeper
DEBUT: First-class: 2009; List A: 2009; T20: 2009

BEST BATTING: 143 Middlesex vs Surrey, Lord's, 2011
COUNTY CAP: 2011

FAMILY TIES? Dad played for England Amateurs and Lancashire Cricket Board and holds club and league records in Lancashire/Central Lancashire leagues. Grandad captained the Army XI. My uncle plays for Woodbank CC. Two cousins play for Lancashire Second XI
BEST ADVICE EVER RECEIVED? There are no fielders in the air
'ROY OF THE ROVERS' MOMENT? Nearly getting hit by an arrow at The Oval in 2017
BEST THING ABOUT YOUR HOME GROUND? The food
IF YOU WEREN'T A CRICKETER? I'd be a wheeler-dealer
SURPRISING FACT ABOUT YOU? I don't drink tea or coffee
SURPRISING FACT ABOUT A TEAMMATE? Tim Murtagh bowls outswing
WHERE IS PARADISE? Dhaka
CRICKETING HERO? Adam Gilchrist
NON-CRICKETING HERO? Roger Federer
UNUSUAL OBJECT AT HOME? A Don Bradman porcelain given to me by my grandad
TWITTER: @johnsimpson_88

Batting	Mat	Inns	NO	Runs	HS	Ave	SR	100	50	Ct	St
First-class	130	205	32	5471	143	31.62	47.26	5	33	403	20
List A	75	55	9	1157	82*	25.15	83.84	0	6	60	12
T20s	83	71	14	1311	84*	23.00	128.27	0	6	42	15

Bowling	Mat	Balls	Runs	Wkts	BBI	BBM	Ave	Econ	SR	5w	10
First-class	130	12	21	0	-	-	-	10.50	-	0	0
List A	75	-	-	-	-	-	-	-	-	-	-
T20s	83	-	-	-	-	-	-	-	-	-	-

SUNNY SINGH

LHB / SLA / R0 / W0

FULL NAME: Sukhjit Singh
BORN: March 30, 1993, Punjab, India
SQUAD NO: 58
HEIGHT: 6ft
NICKNAME: Sunny
EDUCATION: George Dixon International School, Birmingham; South and City College
TEAMS: Warwickshire
ROLE: Bowler
DEBUT: First-class: 2017

BEST BATTING: 16* Warwickshire vs Hampshire, Southampton, 2017
BEST BOWLING: 6-144 Warwickshire vs Hampshire, Southampton, 2017

WHAT GOT YOU INTO CRICKET? Watching Suresh Raina bat
BEST ADVICE EVER RECEIVED? One day you can play for England – if you work hard, do everything right, and concentrate
'ROY OF THE ROVERS' MOMENT? Opening the bowling in the second innings on my Championship debut
BEST OPPOSING PLAYER IN COUNTY CRICKET? Liam Livingstone (Lan)
YOUNG OPPOSING PLAYER WHO HAS IMPRESSED YOU? Dom Bess (Som) – he's taken plenty of wickets at a young age, and his batting is better than he has shown so far
IF YOU WEREN'T A CRICKETER? I'd be working at a supermarket
SURPRISING FACT ABOUT YOU? I'm a big Liverpool fan and love bhangra music
SURPRISING FACT ABOUT A TEAMMATE? Matt Lamb supports West Brom
WHERE IS PARADISE? India
CRICKETING HERO? Suresh Raina – his batting and fielding inspires me to give it my best to be like him. And Eaten Gordon – he helped me a lot when I started playing cricket at the age of 13 for Handsworth CC
NON-CRICKETING HERO? My mum – she helped me a lot with my early cricket career when I was struggling financially
TWITTER: @sunnyy58

Batting	Mat	Inns	NO	Runs	HS	Ave	SR	100	50	Ct	St
First-class	5	8	2	18	16*	3.00	18.18	0	0	1	0

Bowling	Mat	Balls	Runs	Wkts	BBI	BBM	Ave	Econ	SR	5w	10
First-class	5	916	452	17	6/144	6/144	26.58	2.96	53.8	2	0

BEN SLATER

LHB / OB / R0 / W0

FULL NAME: Benjamin Thomas Slater
BORN: August 26, 1991, Chesterfield, Derbyshire
SQUAD NO: 26
HEIGHT: 5ft 11in
NICKNAME: BennySlats, Slats, Slatsy
EDUCATION: Netherthorpe School, Staveley; Leeds Metropolitan University
TEAMS: Derbyshire, Southern Rocks
ROLE: Batsman
DEBUT: First-class: 2012; List A: 2012; T20: 2012

DERBYSHIRE

BEST BATTING: 119 Derbyshire vs Leicestershire, Derby, 2014

FAMILY TIES? Both dad and grandad played to a good standard of league cricket. My sister also used to play for Derbyshire Ladies
STRANGEST THING SEEN IN A GAME? My team in Zimbabwe (Southern Rocks) bowling a side out for 26 when they were set 66 to win in a first-class game which was over in two days. The wicket wasn't even that bad
'ROY OF THE ROVERS' MOMENT? Making 148* against Northants in 2016 to break Derbyshire's List A record score against a county side, or scoring back-to-back hundreds in the last game of the 2014 County Championship
HOW WOULD YOUR TEAMMATES DESCRIBE YOU IN THREE WORDS? Charismatic, charming, calm
CRICKETING HEROES? Brian Lara, Marcus Trescothick, Matthew Hayden, my grandad (all left-handed batsmen)
TWITTER: @BennySlats

Batting	Mat	Inns	NO	Runs	HS	Ave	SR	100	50	Ct	St
First-class	56	104	5	2978	119	30.08	43.97	3	17	20	0
List A	23	20	3	873	148*	51.35	81.13	3	4	1	0
T20s	6	6	0	183	57	30.50	101.10	0	1	0	0

Bowling	Mat	Balls	Runs	Wkts	BBI	BBM	Ave	Econ	SR	5w	10
First-class	56	105	113	0	-	-	-	6.45	-	0	0
List A	23	-	-	-	-	-	-	-	-	-	-
T20s	6	-	-	-	-	-	-	-	-	-	-

DARYN SMIT

RHB / LB / WK / RO / WO

FULL NAME: Daryn Smit
BORN: January 28, 1984, Durban, South Africa
SQUAD NO: 11
HEIGHT: 6ft 1in
NICKNAME: Smitty, Speech, Dazza
EDUCATION: Northwood School, Durban; University of South Africa
TEAMS: Derbyshire, Dolphins, KwaZulu-Natal
ROLE: Batsman/wicketkeeper
DEBUT: First-class: 2004; List A: 2004; T20: 2004

BEST BATTING: 156* KwaZulu-Natal vs North West, Durban, 2015
BEST BOWLING: 7-27 KwaZulu-Natal vs South Western Districts, Durban, 2014

BEST ADVICE EVER RECEIVED? If you believe you can or can't, you are right
BEST THING ABOUT YOUR HOME GROUND? It's close to home so I can sleep in my own bed – I hate hotels!
BEST OPPOSING PLAYER IN COUNTY CRICKET? Darren Stevens (Ken)
YOUNG OPPOSING PLAYER WHO HAS IMPRESSED YOU? Josh Tongue (Wor) – he has raw pace
IF YOU WEREN'T A CRICKETER? I'd be a golfer
SURPRISING FACT ABOUT YOU? I've represented South Africa at football
SURPRISING FACT ABOUT A TEAMMATE? There's nothing Wayne Madsen can't do
WHERE IS PARADISE? Mauritius
CRICKETING HERO? Mark Boucher – a tenacious cricketer who I'd far rather have on my side
NON-CRICKETING HERO? My wife – for putting up with me
TWITTER: @darynsmit

Batting	Mat	Inns	NO	Runs	HS	Ave	SR	100	50	Ct	St
First-class	133	200	35	5948	156*	36.04	46.87	9	33	350	22
List A	115	86	24	2040	109	32.90	78.37	1	11	101	13
T20s	94	55	22	842	57	25.51	123.64	0	2	52	10

Bowling	Mat	Balls	Runs	Wkts	BBI	BBM	Ave	Econ	SR	5w	10
First-class	133	6749	3501	106	7/27	8/30	33.02	3.11	63.6	3	0
List A	115	2107	1718	45	4/39	4/39	38.17	4.89	46.8	0	0
T20s	94	630	721	28	3/19	3/19	25.75	6.86	22.5	0	0

RUAIDHRI SMITH RHB / RM / RO / WO

FULL NAME: Ruaidhri Alexander James Smith
BORN: August 5, 1994, Glasgow
SQUAD NO: 20
HEIGHT: 6ft 2in
NICKNAME: Trigger
EDUCATION: The Cathedral School, Llandaff; Shrewsbury School; University of Bristol
TEAMS: Scotland, Glamorgan
ROLE: Allrounder
DEBUT: ODI: 2016; First-class: 2013; List A: 2013; T20: 2014

GLAMORGAN

BEST BATTING: 57* Glamorgan vs Gloucestershire, Bristol, 2014
BEST BOWLING: 3-23 Glamorgan vs Derbyshire, Chesterfield, 2015

FAMILY TIES? My dad used to play club cricket and he introduced me to the game
'ROY OF THE ROVERS' MOMENT? Taking a wicket with my first ball for Glamorgan
BEST THING ABOUT YOUR HOME GROUND? The food
BEST OPPOSING PLAYER IN COUNTY CRICKET? Darren Stevens (Ken)
YOUNG OPPOSING PLAYER WHO HAS IMPRESSED YOU? Jamie Porter (Ess)
IF YOU WEREN'T A CRICKETER? I'd try to be a rugby player
SURPRISING FACT ABOUT YOU? Born in Scotland, Irish mother, English father, raised in Wales
SURPRISING FACT ABOUT A TEAMMATE? Kieran Bull was a tennis prodigy
WHERE IS PARADISE? Antigua
CRICKETING HERO? Andrew Flintoff in the 2005 Ashes
NON-CRICKETING HERO? Jonny Wilkinson
TWITTER: @ruaidhrismith

Batting	Mat	Inns	NO	Runs	HS	Ave	SR	100	50	Ct	St
ODIs	2	1	0	10	10	10.00	166.66	0	0	0	0
First-class	19	23	4	374	57*	19.68	54.75	0	1	3	0
List A	13	7	2	33	10	6.60	82.50	0	0	2	0
T20s	4	3	2	29	16*	29.00	116.00	0	0	1	0

Bowling	Mat	Balls	Runs	Wkts	BBI	BBM	Ave	Econ	SR	5w	10
ODIs	2	90	97	1	1/34	1/34	97.00	6.46	90.0	0	0
First-class	19	2157	1471	38	3/23	5/87	38.71	4.09	56.7	0	0
List A	13	402	460	12	4/76	4/76	38.33	6.86	33.5	0	0
T20s	4	16	35	1	1/11	1/11	35.00	13.12	16.0	0	0

TOM SMITH

RHB / SLA / R0 / W0

GLOUCESTERSHIRE

FULL NAME: Thomas Michael John Smith
BORN: August 29, 1987, Eastbourne, Sussex
SQUAD NO: 6
HEIGHT: 5ft 9in
NICKNAME: Smudge
EDUCATION: Seaford Head Community College, East Sussex; Sussex Downs College
TEAMS: Gloucestershire, Middlesex, Surrey, Sussex
ROLE: Bowler
DEBUT: First-class: 2007; List A: 2006; T20: 2007

BEST BATTING: 80 Gloucestershire vs Surrey, Bristol, 2014
BEST BOWLING: 4-35 Gloucestershire vs Kent, Canterbury, 2014
COUNTY CAP: 2013 (Gloucestershire)

WHAT GOT YOU INTO CRICKET? I found a bat at my nan's house when I was three and asked my dad what it was
BEST ADVICE EVER RECEIVED? Peel ginger with a teaspoon
'ROY OF THE ROVERS' MOMENT? Winning the One-Day Cup in 2015 (especially after Michael Klinger was out for 0)
BEST OPPOSING PLAYER IN COUNTY CRICKET? Johann Myburgh (Som) – he whacks me every time!
YOUNG OPPOSING PLAYER WHO HAS IMPRESSED YOU? Max Holden (Mid) – I've seen his game progress since he was 12
SURPRISING FACT ABOUT YOU? I'm a qualified plumber
SURPRISING FACT ABOUT A TEAMMATE? Benny Howell has 17 different types of delivery
CRICKETING HERO? Daniel Vettori
NON-CRICKETING HERO? My parents Mike and Claudine – they have been a huge support in my career

Batting	Mat	Inns	NO	Runs	HS	Ave	SR	100	50	Ct	St
First-class	43	59	12	1055	80	22.44	39.04	0	2	12	0
List A	68	33	14	445	65	23.42	74.41	0	1	31	0
T20s	104	41	27	274	36*	19.57	113.22	0	0	35	0

Bowling	Mat	Balls	Runs	Wkts	BBI	BBM	Ave	Econ	SR	5w	10
First-class	43	6359	3641	74	4/35	6/155	49.20	3.43	85.9	0	0
List A	68	2392	2180	55	4/26	4/26	39.63	5.46	43.4	0	0
T20s	104	1951	2378	106	5/24	5/24	22.43	7.31	18.4	2	0

WILL SMITH

RHB / OB / R1 / W0

FULL NAME: William Rew Smith
BORN: September 28, 1982, Luton
SQUAD NO: 2
HEIGHT: 5ft 9in
NICKNAME: Smudger, Jiggy
EDUCATION: Bedford School; Durham University
TEAMS: Durham, Hampshire, Nottinghamshire
ROLE: Batsman
DEBUT: First-class: 2002; List A: 2002; T20: 2003

BEST BATTING: 210 Hampshire vs Lancashire, Southampton, 2016
BEST BOWLING: 3-34 Durham UCCE vs Leicestershire, Leicester, 2005
COUNTY CAP: 2015 (Hampshire)

WHAT GOT YOU INTO CRICKET? My brother Ben hurling balls at my head at the tender age of six
BEST ADVICE EVER RECEIVED? Control the controllables – everything else is not worth worrying about
'ROY OF THE ROVERS' MOMENT? Scoring 120 not out off 79 balls in my final one-day innings of my previous stint at Durham in 2013
BEST OPPOSING PLAYER IN COUNTY CRICKET? Marcus Trescothick (Som)
YOUNG OPPOSING PLAYER WHO HAS IMPRESSED YOU? Tom Curran (Sur) – he executes his skills under pressure
IF YOU WEREN'T A CRICKETER? Professional gambler/bloodstock trader in horse-racing
WHERE IS PARADISE? Sani Resort in Thessaloniki, Greece
CRICKETING HERO? Graeme Fowler – he was my mentor at university and has a brilliant outlook on cricket and life
TWITTER: @WillSmith_2

Batting	Mat	Inns	NO	Runs	HS	Ave	SR	100	50	Ct	St
First-class	172	292	21	8986	210	33.15	42.63	17	35	109	0
List A	110	94	8	2516	120*	29.25	75.82	2	20	37	0
T20s	105	83	21	1006	55	16.22	117.38	0	3	44	0
Bowling	Mat	Balls	Runs	Wkts	BBI	BBM	Ave	Econ	SR	5w	10
First-class	172	2377	1394	28	3/34	3/68	49.78	3.51	84.8	0	0
List A	110	443	427	12	2/19	2/19	35.58	5.78	36.9	0	0
T20s	105	899	1085	42	3/15	3/15	25.83	7.24	21.4	0	0

ISH SODHI

RHB / LB / R0 / W0

FULL NAME: Inderbir Singh Sodhi
BORN: October 31, 1992, Ludhiana, India
SQUAD NO: 61
TEAMS: New Zealand, Nottinghamshire, Adelaide Strikers, Northern Districts
ROLE: Bowler
DEBUT: Test: 2013; ODI: 2015; T20I: 2014; First-class: 2012; List A: 2013; T20: 2013

BEST BATTING: 82* Northern Districts vs Otago, Dunedin, 2014
BEST BOWLING: 7-59 Northern Districts vs Otago, Dunedin, 2017

TWITTER: @ish_sodhi
NOTES: Nottinghamshire re-signed the New Zealand leg-spinner for the duration of the T20 Blast campaign after he played an integral part in the team which won the competition last year. He played in all 16 games in 2017. "I can't wait to come back as it was such an amazing experience playing in a winning team last year," said Sodhi. "We had such a great bond as a team, as well as some very talented players." Sodhi impressed during a brief spell with Adelaide Strikers in the 2016/17 Big Bash, taking 6-11 against Sydney Thunder. He was a standout player at the 2016 World T20, claiming 10 wickets at an average of 12, and was the No.1 ranked T20I bowler in the world at the beginning of 2018

Batting	Mat	Inns	NO	Runs	HS	Ave	SR	100	50	Ct	St
Tests	14	19	3	365	63	22.81	58.87	0	2	8	0
ODIs	19	5	0	6	5	1.20	19.35	0	0	2	0
T20Is	26	5	2	39	15	13.00	97.50	0	0	8	0
First-class	59	90	13	1664	82*	21.61	56.90	0	8	25	0
List A	67	32	7	265	44*	10.60	90.75	0	0	15	0
T20s	92	25	12	157	51	12.07	113.76	0	1	15	0

Bowling	Mat	Balls	Runs	Wkts	BBI	BBM	Ave	Econ	SR	5w	10
Tests	14	2826	1774	38	4/60	7/79	46.68	3.76	74.3	0	0
ODIs	19	928	836	21	3/38	3/38	39.80	5.40	44.1	0	0
T20Is	26	562	696	36	3/18	3/18	19.33	7.43	15.6	0	0
First-class	59	11023	6930	184	7/59	11/189	37.66	3.77	59.9	9	1
List A	67	3341	2770	92	4/10	4/10	30.10	4.97	36.3	0	0
T20s	92	1845	2356	102	6/11	6/11	23.09	7.66	18.0	1	0

CHRIS SOLE

RHB / RM / RO / WO

FULL NAME: Christopher Barclay Sole
BORN: February 24, 1994, Edinburgh
SQUAD NO: 71
HEIGHT: 6ft 1in
NICKNAME: Soley, Elos, Oh Soooooley (in a deep Scottish accent), anything Scottish-related
EDUCATION: Merchiston Castle School, Edinburgh
TEAMS: Scotland, Hampshire
ROLE: Bowler
DEBUT: ODI: 2016; T20I: 2017; First-class: 2016; List A: 2016; T20: 2017

BEST BATTING: 21 Scotland vs Papua New Guinea, Port Moresby, 2017
BEST BOWLING: 3-79 Scotland vs Ireland, Dubai, 2017

BEST ADVICE EVER RECEIVED? Always bowl as fast as you can
'ROY OF THE ROVERS' MOMENT? The 2016 season – from not playing cricket at all to making my international debut for Scotland and signing for Hampshire
IF YOU WEREN'T A CRICKETER? I'd be a javelin thrower
SURPRISING FACT ABOUT YOU? I used to be a rare-pig breeder
WHERE IS PARADISE? Glenbuchat, Aberdeenshire
CRICKETING HERO? Allan Donald
NON-CRICKETING HERO? My dad David, the former Scotland rugby captain
TWITTER: @chris_868

Batting	Mat	Inns	NO	Runs	HS	Ave	SR	100	50	Ct	St
ODIs	8	4	0	9	4	2.25	32.14	0	0	3	0
T20Is	1	-	-	-	-	-	-	-	-	0	0
First-class	3	3	0	33	21	11.00	35.48	0	0	0	0
List A	12	6	2	21	10*	5.25	50.00	0	0	3	0
T20s	1	-	-	-	-	-	-	-	-	0	0

Bowling	Mat	Balls	Runs	Wkts	BBI	BBM	Ave	Econ	SR	5w	10
ODIs	8	378	282	13	4/28	4/28	21.69	4.47	29.0	0	0
T20Is	1	24	22	0	-	-	-	5.50	-	0	0
First-class	3	432	285	5	3/79	4/138	57.00	3.95	86.4	0	0
List A	12	594	432	21	4/24	4/24	20.57	4.36	28.2	0	0
T20s	1	24	22	0	-	-	-	5.50	-	0	0

TOM SOLE

RHB / OB / RO / WO

FULL NAME: Thomas Barclay Sole
BORN: June 21, 1996, Edinburgh
SQUAD NO: 90
HEIGHT: 5ft 11in
NICKNAME: Soley, Stollers
EDUCATION: Merchiston Castle School, Edinburgh
TEAMS: Scotland, Northamptonshire
ROLE: Allrounder
DEBUT: ODI: 2018; List A: 2017

WHAT GOT YOU INTO CRICKET? Playing backyard cricket with my brothers
FAMILY TIES? My older brother Chris plays for Scotland and Hampshire. My uncle Christopher Trembath played for Wiltshire and Gloucestershire
BEST ADVICE EVER RECEIVED? Do what you enjoy
'ROY OF THE ROVERS' MOMENT? Getting 7-11 at U11 level – including six wickets in six balls – or nearly getting Northants over the line against South Africa on my 50-over debut in 2017
BEST THING ABOUT YOUR HOME GROUND? The step through the sliding door into the changing rooms – our coach David Ripley frequently trips over it
YOUNG OPPOSING PLAYER WHO HAS IMPRESSED YOU? Max Holden (Mid) – he's a gun
IF YOU WEREN'T A CRICKETER? I'd be a physiotherapist
SURPRISING FACT ABOUT YOU? I still have a baby tooth
SURPRISING FACT ABOUT A TEAMMATE? One of my teammates has had plastic surgery
WHERE IS PARADISE? Queenstown, New Zealand
CRICKETING HERO? My brother Chris
NON-CRICKETING HERO? My dad David – for winning the 1990 rugby union Grand Slam as Scotland captain and inspiring me to chase my dreams
TWITTER: @TomSole1

Batting	Mat	Inns	NO	Runs	HS	Ave	SR	100	50	Ct	St
ODIs	1	1	0	20	20	20.00	142.85	0	0	0	0
List A	2	2	0	74	54	37.00	129.82	0	1	0	0

Bowling	Mat	Balls	Runs	Wkts	BBI	BBM	Ave	Econ	SR	5w	10
ODIs	1	36	44	2	2/44	2/44	22.00	7.33	18.0	0	0
List A	2	96	113	3	2/44	2/44	37.66	7.06	32.0	0	0

FULL NAME: Nathan Adam Sowter
BORN: October 12, 1992, Penrith, New South Wales, Australia
SQUAD NO: 72
HEIGHT: 5ft 10in
NICKNAME: Sowts, Racing Snake, Goblin
EDUCATION: Hills Sport High School, New South Wales
TEAMS: Middlesex
ROLE: Bowler
DEBUT: First-class: 2017; List A: 2016; T20: 2015

MIDDLESEX

BEST BATTING: 37 Middlesex vs Warwickshire, Lord's, 2017
BEST BOWLING: 1-23 Middlesex vs Warwickshire, Lord's, 2017

WHAT GOT YOU INTO CRICKET? Playing with my dad in the backyard
'ROY OF THE ROVERS' MOMENT? Playing at Lord's and being part of the Middlesex squad that won the Championship in 2016
BEST THING ABOUT YOUR HOME GROUND? It's the most iconic ground in the world
BEST OPPOSING PLAYER IN COUNTY CRICKET? Jonny Bairstow (Yor)
YOUNG OPPOSING PLAYER WHO HAS IMPRESSED YOU? Ollie Pope (Sur)
IF YOU WEREN'T A CRICKETER? I'd be a groundsman
SURPRISING FACT ABOUT YOU? I have a girlfriend. And I'm also a glazier by trade
SURPRISING FACT ABOUT A TEAMMATE? Steve Eskinazi doesn't wash his bedsheets – he just buys new ones when needed
WHERE IS PARADISE? Anywhere with my family
CRICKETING HERO? Shane Warne
NON-CRICKETING HERO? Roger Federer
UNUSUAL OBJECT AT HOME? A red chicken
TWITTER: @nsowter

Batting	Mat	Inns	NO	Runs	HS	Ave	SR	100	50	Ct	St
First-class	1	2	0	37	37	18.50	148.00	0	0	0	0
List A	2	1	0	0	0	0.00	0.00	0	0	3	0
T20s	31	8	4	39	12	9.75	114.70	0	0	9	0

Bowling	Mat	Balls	Runs	Wkts	BBI	BBM	Ave	Econ	SR	5w	10
First-class	1	61	25	1	1/23	1/25	25.00	2.45	61.0	0	0
List A	2	48	62	0	-	-	-	7.75	-	0	0
T20s	31	526	689	27	4/23	4/23	25.51	7.85	19.4	0	0

BILLY STANLAKE

LHB / RF / RO / WO

YORKSHIRE

FULL NAME: Billy Stanlake
BORN: November 4, 1994, Hervey Bay, Australia
SQUAD NO: TBC
HEIGHT: 6ft 8in
ROLE: Bowler
DEBUT: ODI: 2017; T20I: 2017; First-class: 2015; List A: 2015; T20: 2015

BEST BATTING: 1* Queensland vs South Australia, Brisbane, 2015
BEST BOWLING: 3-50 Queensland vs South Australia, Brisbane, 2015

TWITTER: @BillyJS94
NOTES: Yorkshire have signed the 6ft 8in Australian fast bowler for the T20 Blast. Stanlake plays for Queensland in Australia and Adelaide Strikers in the Big Bash League. Made his domestic debuts in 2015 but suffered back injuries which kept him out for 10 months. Was a surprise selection by Australia in January 2017 for ODI fixtures against Pakistan and his T20I debut followed against Sri Lanka a month later. Played two matches in the 2017 IPL for Royal Challengers Bangalore before helping Adelaide Strikers to their first Big Bash title in the 2017/18 campaign. Stanlake impressed when Australia won the T20I tri-series against England and New Zealand earlier this year, taking eight wickets in five matches

Batting	Mat	Inns	NO	Runs	HS	Ave	SR	100	50	Ct	St
ODIs	2	1	1	1	1*	-	16.66	0	0	0	0
T20Is	6	-	-	-	-	-	-	-	-	0	0
First-class	2	2	2	1	1*	-	14.28	0	0	0	0
List A	6	5	3	2	1*	-	8.69	0	0	3	0
T20s	25	4	4	8	4*	-	72.72	0	0	5	0

Bowling	Mat	Balls	Runs	Wkts	BBI	BBM	Ave	Econ	SR	5w	10
ODIs	2	78	68	1	1/55	1/55	68.00	5.23	78.0	0	0
T20Is	6	138	208	8	3/15	3/15	26.00	9.04	17.2	0	0
First-class	2	371	151	7	3/50	6/103	21.57	2.44	53.0	0	0
List A	6	288	246	8	4/37	4/37	30.75	5.12	36.0	0	0
T20s	25	566	707	29	3/15	3/15	24.37	7.49	19.5	0	0

CAMERON STEEL

RHB / LB / RO / WO

FULL NAME: Cameron Tate Steel
BORN: September 13, 1995, Greenbrae, California, USA
SQUAD NO: 14
HEIGHT: 5ft 10in
NICKNAME: Steely, Lex
EDUCATION: Millfield Prep School, Somerset; Scotch College, Perth, Australia; Durham University
TEAMS: Durham
ROLE: Batsman
DEBUT: First-class: 2014; List A: 2017; T20: 2017

DURHAM

BEST BATTING: 224 Durham vs Leicestershire, Leicester, 2017
BEST BOWLING: 2-24 Durham vs Derbyshire, Chester-le-Street, 2017

WHAT GOT YOU INTO CRICKET? My dad and my neighbour in Somerset
FAMILY TIES? My sister played youth cricket for Somerset and Western Australia
'ROY OF THE ROVERS' MOMENT? Scoring my maiden first-class double hundred against Leicestershire in 2017
BEST THING ABOUT YOUR HOME GROUND? It's location at the greatest town on earth: Chester-le-Street
BEST OPPOSING PLAYER IN COUNTY CRICKET? Sam Northeast (Ham)
YOUNG OPPOSING PLAYER WHO HAS IMPRESSED YOU? Joe Clarke (Wor) – he does seriously well across all formats on a consistent basis
IF YOU WEREN'T A CRICKETER? I'd be free on weekends
SURPRISING FACT ABOUT YOU? I was the U9 West of England chess champion
WHERE IS PARADISE? Can Can Karaoke Bar in South Shields, Tyneside
CRICKETING HERO? Tom Latham – just look at that smile
NON-CRICKETING HERO? Prince Harry
TWITTER: @CameronSteel2

Batting	Mat	Inns	NO	Runs	HS	Ave	SR	100	50	Ct	St
First-class	19	33	2	1214	224	39.16	42.65	2	7	7	0
List A	7	6	1	132	77	26.40	72.92	0	1	0	0
T20s	6	6	0	93	37	15.50	125.67	0	0	2	0

Bowling	Mat	Balls	Runs	Wkts	BBI	BBM	Ave	Econ	SR	5w	10
First-class	19	506	393	9	2/24	2/24	43.66	4.66	56.2	0	0
List A	7	30	47	0	-	-	-	9.40	-	0	0
T20s	6	48	88	2	2/60	2/60	44.00	11.00	24.0	0	0

DARREN STEVENS   RHB / RM / R3 / W3 / MVP5

FULL NAME: Darren Ian Stevens
BORN: April 30, 1976, Leicester
SQUAD NO: 3
HEIGHT: 5ft 11in
NICKNAME: Stevo
EDUCATION: John Cleveland College, Hinckley; Charles Keene College, Leicester
TEAMS: Kent, Comilla Victorians, Dhaka Gladiators, Leicestershire, Mid West Rhinos, Otago
ROLE: Allrounder
DEBUT: First-class: 1997; List A: 1997; T20: 2003

BEST BATTING: 208 Kent vs Middlesex, Canterbury, 2009
BEST BOWLING: 8-75 Kent vs Leicestershire, Canterbury, 2017
COUNTY CAP: 2002 (Leicestershire); 2005 (Kent); **BENEFIT:** 2016 (Kent)

WHAT GOT YOU INTO CRICKET? My dad pestered me to play. I preferred football but gave in after a year
CRICKETING HERO? Sir Viv Richards
NON-CRICKETING HEROES? Roger Federer, Fred Couples, Arnold Palmer
IF YOU WEREN'T A CRICKETER? I'd be a professional golfer
SURPRISING FACT? I am colour blind with browns, reds and greens. I struggled when I was with Otago in New Zealand because there were no sightscreens!
TWITTER: @Stevo208

Batting	Mat	Inns	NO	Runs	HS	Ave	SR	100	50	Ct	St
First-class	278	437	26	14721	208	35.81		33	75	192	0
List A	300	278	30	7476	147	30.14		7	46	125	0
T20s	208	187	39	3970	90	26.82	136.66	0	17	65	0

Bowling	Mat	Balls	Runs	Wkts	BBI	BBM	Ave	Econ	SR	5w	10
First-class	278	23419	11284	421	8/75	11/70	26.80	2.89	55.6	19	1
List A	300	5668	4563	141	5/32	5/32	32.36	4.83	40.1	2	0
T20s	208	2224	2925	114	4/14	4/14	25.65	7.89	19.5	0	0

FULL NAME: Ryan Anthony Stevenson
BORN: April 2, 1992, Torquay
SQUAD NO: 47
HEIGHT: 6ft 2in
NICKNAME: Raz, Stevo
EDUCATION: King Edward VI Community College, Devon
TEAMS: Hampshire
ROLE: Bowler
DEBUT: First-class: 2015; List A: 2016; T20: 2016

HAMPSHIRE

BEST BATTING: 30 Hampshire vs Durham, Chester-le-Street, 2015
BEST BOWLING: 1-15 Hampshire vs Nottinghamshire, Trent Bridge, 2015

WHAT GOT YOU INTO CRICKET? My dad taking me to nets
FAMILY TIES? My dad has played for Devon Over-50s
ROY OF THE ROVERS' MOMENT? My first-class debut in 2015 – I was absolutely clueless about what I was doing!
BEST THING ABOUT YOUR HOME GROUND? The facilities: hotel, golf course and two cricket pitches. Plus a curry house on site!
BEST OPPOSING PLAYER IN COUNTY CRICKET? Moeen Ali (Wor)
YOUNG OPPOSING PLAYER WHO HAS IMPRESSED YOU? Dom Bess (Som) – he has adapted to first-class cricket amazingly and is a great bloke
IF YOU WEREN'T A CRICKETER? I'd be a farmer
SURPRISING FACT ABOUT YOU? I gave up cricket for a year as a teenager to do other things
WHERE IS PARADISE? Devon – nowhere else comes close
CRICKETING HERO? Shaun Pollock – an unbelievable bowler and one of the first cricketers I saw playing live
TWITTER: @ryanstevenson47

Batting	Mat	Inns	NO	Runs	HS	Ave	SR	100	50	Ct	St
First-class	4	5	1	73	30	18.25	57.48	0	0	0	0
List A	3	1	0	0	0	0.00	0.00	0	0	0	0
T20s	1	1	0	3	3	3.00	60.00	0	0	1	0

Bowling	Mat	Balls	Runs	Wkts	BBI	BBM	Ave	Econ	SR	5w	10
First-class	4	431	270	3	1/15	1/46	90.00	3.75	143.6	0	0
List A	3	120	142	2	1/28	1/28	71.00	7.10	60.0	0	0
T20s	1	24	40	2	2/40	2/40	20.00	10.00	12.0	0	0

GRANT STEWART

RHB / RFM / RO / WO

KENT

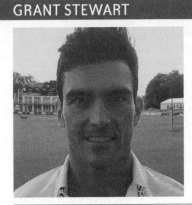

FULL NAME: Grant Stewart
BORN: February 19, 1994, Kalgoorlie, Western Australia, Australia
SQUAD NO: 9
HEIGHT: 6ft 3in
NICKNAME: Stewie
EDUCATION: All Saints College, New South Wales; University of Newcastle, NSW
TEAMS: Kent
ROLE: Allrounder
DEBUT: First-class: 2017; List A: 2018

BEST BATTING: 15* Kent vs Glamorgan, Canterbury, 2017
BEST BOWLING: 2-52 Kent vs Glamorgan, Canterbury, 2017

WHAT GOT YOU INTO CRICKET? My older brothers
BEST ADVICE EVER RECEIVED? Work hard
'ROY OF THE ROVERS' MOMENT? My first-class debut for Kent against Glamorgan at Canterbury in 2017
BEST THING ABOUT YOUR HOME GROUND? The slope at Canterbury really adds to the home advantage we get there
BEST OPPOSING PLAYER IN COUNTY CRICKET? Ben Stokes (Dur)
YOUNG OPPOSING PLAYER WHO HAS IMPRESSED YOU? Ollie Pope (Sur)
IF YOU WEREN'T A CRICKETER? I'd be a civil engineer
SURPRISING FACT ABOUT YOU? I was a wicketkeeper until I was 16
WHERE IS PARADISE? Barcelona
CRICKETING HERO? Steve Waugh
NON-CRICKETING HERO? Hugh Jackman
TWITTER: @GStewart195

Batting	Mat	Inns	NO	Runs	HS	Ave	SR	100	50	Ct	St
First-class	1	2	1	15	15*	15.00	45.45	0	0	0	0
List A	5	4	1	69	44	23.00	62.72	0	0	1	0

Bowling	Mat	Balls	Runs	Wkts	BBI	BBM	Ave	Econ	SR	5w	10
First-class	1	120	89	2	2/52	2/89	44.50	4.45	60.0	0	0
List A	5	242	152	8	3/17	3/17	19.00	3.76	30.2	0	0

PAUL STIRLING

RHB / OB / RO / WO

FULL NAME: Paul Robert Stirling
BORN: September 3, 1990, Belfast, Northern Ireland
SQUAD NO: 39
HEIGHT: 5ft 9in
NICKNAME: Stirlo
EDUCATION: Belfast High School
TEAMS: Ireland, Middlesex, Sylhet Royals
ROLE: Allrounder
DEBUT: ODI: 2008; T20I: 2009; First-class: 2008; List A: 2008; T20: 2008

BEST BATTING: 146 Ireland vs UAE, Malahide, 2015
BEST BOWLING: 2-27 Ireland vs Namibia, Windhoek, 2015
COUNTY CAP: 2016

FAMILY TIES? My brother Richard played for Ireland in the 2006 U19 World Cup in Sri Lanka
STRANGEST THING SEEN IN A GAME? A pigeon hit out of the sky
ROY OF THE ROVERS' MOMENT? Getting a first-class wicket with a flipper while bowling leg-spin, and scoring a century at Lord's
SUPERSTITIONS? Don't walk in shadows
HOW WOULD YOUR TEAMMATES DESCRIBE YOU IN THREE WORDS? Poor man's Inzi
CRICKETING HERO? Damien Martyn – pleasing to watch
NON-CRICKETING HERO? George Best – a Belfast legend
SURPRISING FACT? My father is an ex-international rugby referee
TWITTER: @stirlo90

Batting	Mat	Inns	NO	Runs	HS	Ave	SR	100	50	Ct	St
ODIs	91	89	2	3028	177	34.80	90.87	6	15	34	0
T20Is	44	43	4	975	79	25.00	133.37	0	6	13	0
First-class	58	89	4	2479	146	29.16	62.87	5	13	30	0
List A	162	157	7	5116	177	34.10	93.68	11	23	59	0
T20s	144	143	7	3419	90	25.13	141.39	0	22	40	0

Bowling	Mat	Balls	Runs	Wkts	BBI	BBM	Ave	Econ	SR	5w	10
ODIs	91	2266	1803	39	6/55	6/55	46.23	4.77	58.1	1	0
T20Is	44	354	413	13	3/21	3/21	31.76	7.00	27.2	0	0
First-class	58	2134	997	23	2/27	3/31	43.34	2.80	92.7	0	0
List A	162	3002	2485	62	6/55	6/55	40.08	4.96	48.4	1	0
T20s	144	1164	1334	54	4/10	4/10	24.70	6.87	21.5	0	0

BEN STOKES

LHB / RFM / RO / WO

FULL NAME: Benjamin Andrew Stokes
BORN: June 4, 1991, Christchurch, New Zealand
SQUAD NO: 38
HEIGHT: 6ft 2in
NICKNAME: Stokesy, Benji, Stoker
EDUCATION: Cockermouth School, Cumbria
TEAMS: England, Durham, Canterbury, Melbourne Renegades, Rajasthan Royals, Rising Pune Supergiant
ROLE: Allrounder
DEBUT: Test: 2013; ODI: 2011; T20I: 2011; First-class: 2010; List A: 2009; T20: 2010

BEST BATTING: 258 England vs South Africa, Cape Town, 2016
BEST BOWLING: 7-67 Durham vs Sussex, Chester-le-Street, 2014

SUPERSTITIONS? Swiping my bat across the crease at the end of every over
CRICKETING HEROES? Herschelle Gibbs
IF YOU WEREN'T A CRICKETER? I'd be on the dole
SURPRISING FACT? My father played one Test match for New Zealand at rugby league. I was a right-handed batsman when I was younger
TWITTER: @benstokes38

Batting	Mat	Inns	NO	Runs	HS	Ave	SR	100	50	Ct	St
Tests	39	69	1	2429	258	35.72	63.77	6	12	38	0
ODIs	64	56	8	1725	102*	35.93	97.62	3	11	28	0
T20Is	21	18	5	192	38	14.76	136.17	0	0	8	0
First-class	113	187	9	6207	258	34.87		14	31	77	0
List A	134	120	17	3626	164	35.20	99.12	7	18	58	0
T20s	92	82	13	1721	103*	24.94	138.12	1	7	37	0

Bowling	Mat	Balls	Runs	Wkts	BBI	BBM	Ave	Econ	SR	5w	10
Tests	39	5734	3224	95	6/22	8/161	33.93	3.37	60.3	4	0
ODIs	64	2079	2110	57	5/61	5/61	37.01	6.08	36.4	1	0
T20Is	21	322	485	10	3/26	3/26	48.50	9.03	32.2	0	0
First-class	113	13249	7771	256	7/67	10/121	30.35	3.51	51.7	6	1
List A	134	3724	3564	119	5/61	5/61	29.94	5.74	31.2	1	0
T20s	92	1124	1562	46	3/18	3/18	33.95	8.33	24.4	0	0

OLLY STONE

RHB / RFM / R0 / W0

FULL NAME: Oliver Peter Stone
BORN: October 9, 1993, Norwich
SQUAD NO: 6
HEIGHT: 6ft 2in
NICKNAME: Stoney
EDUCATION: Thorpe St Andrew High School, Norwich; Moulton College
TEAMS: Warwickshire, Northamptonshire
ROLE: Bowler
DEBUT: First-class: 2012; List A: 2012; T20: 2011

WARWICKSHIRE

BEST BATTING: 60 Northamptonshire vs Kent, Northampton, 2016
BEST BOWLING: 5-44 Northamptonshire vs Kent, Northampton, 2015

WHAT GOT YOU INTO CRICKET? Playing down the driveway with my brother
BEST ADVICE EVER RECEIVED? Don't celebrate your wickets
'ROY OF THE ROVERS' MOMENT? Making my first-class debut and taking my first wicket
BEST THING ABOUT YOUR HOME GROUND? The physio – gets me back on the park
BEST OPPOSING PLAYER IN COUNTY CRICKET? Richard Gleeson (Nor)
YOUNG OPPOSING PLAYER WHO HAS IMPRESSED YOU? Max Holden (Mid)
IF YOU WEREN'T A CRICKETER? I'd be a farmer or a butcher
SURPRISING FACT ABOUT YOU? My great-grandad created the Twix chocolate bar
SURPRISING FACT ABOUT A TEAMMATE? Sam Hain never showers
WHERE IS PARADISE? Nerja, Costa del Sol
CRICKETING HERO? Paul Bradshaw – always gets wickets
NON-CRICKETING HERO? Peter Lewis – a good, solid bloke
UNUSUAL OBJECT AT HOME? A wand
TWITTER: @ollystone2

Batting	Mat	Inns	NO	Runs	HS	Ave	SR	100	50	Ct	St
First-class	26	34	8	446	60	17.15	46.36	0	1	14	0
List A	17	11	7	90	24*	22.50	65.69	0	0	7	0
T20s	37	10	6	23	8*	5.75	109.52	0	0	7	0

Bowling	Mat	Balls	Runs	Wkts	BBI	BBM	Ave	Econ	SR	5w	10
First-class	26	4157	2280	73	5/44	6/90	31.23	3.29	56.9	2	0
List A	17	634	556	11	3/34	3/34	50.54	5.26	57.6	0	0
T20s	37	642	968	26	3/29	3/29	37.23	9.04	24.6	0	0

MARK STONEMAN
LHB / OB / R5 / W0 / MVP28

FULL NAME: Mark Daniel Stoneman
BORN: June 26, 1987, Newcastle
SQUAD NO: 23
HEIGHT: 5ft 10in
NICKNAME: Rocky
EDUCATION: Whickham Comprehensive School, Newcastle Upon Tyne
TEAMS: England, Surrey, Durham
ROLE: Batsman
DEBUT: Test: 2017; First-class: 2007; List A: 2008; T20: 2010

BEST BATTING: 197 Surrey vs Sussex, Guildford, 2017

WHAT GOT YOU INTO CRICKET? Following my dad everywhere as soon as I could, carrying my little plastic bat along with me
FAMILY TIES? Grandfather played and umpired locally for many years. Dad played all over the north-east as a local pro
'ROY OF THE ROVERS' MOMENT? Captaining the Durham side which won the 2014 One-Day Cup at Lord's
SUPERSTITIONS? Nervous wee box goes on first
CRICKETING HEROES? Dad – he got me into the game and gave me every opportunity to be successful. Michael Di Venuto – the best role model a young county cricketer could have
IF YOU WEREN'T A CRICKETER? I'd be a fisherman
SURPRISING FACT? The Lion King makes me cry
TWITTER: @mark23stone

Batting	Mat	Inns	NO	Runs	HS	Ave	SR	100	50	Ct	St
Tests	8	14	1	352	56	27.07	45.71	0	3	0	0
First-class	159	278	7	9595	197	35.40	58.27	21	48	77	0
List A	70	67	5	2575	144*	41.53	93.97	6	16	21	0
T20s	62	59	4	1140	89*	20.72	121.14	0	6	26	0

Bowling	Mat	Balls	Runs	Wkts	BBI	BBM	Ave	Econ	SR	5w	10
Tests	8	-	-	-	-	-	-	-	-	-	-
First-class	159	204	150	0	-	-	-	4.41	-	0	0
List A	70	4	8	1	1/8	1/8	8.00	12.00	4.0	0	0
T20s	62	-	-	-	-	-	-	-	-	-	-

HARRY SWINDELLS

RHB / WK / R0 / W0

FULL NAME: Harry John Swindells
BORN: February 21, 1999, Leicester
SQUAD NO: 28
HEIGHT: 5ft 8in
NICKNAME: Dumbo
EDUCATION: Brockington College,
Leicestershire; Lutterworth College;
Loughborough College
TEAMS: Leicestershire, England U19
ROLE: Wicketkeeper

WHAT GOT YOU INTO CRICKET? The 2005 Ashes
BEST ADVICE EVER RECEIVED? Be the hardest worker
'ROY OF THE ROVERS' MOMENT? Playing for England in an U19 Test match against India. Or playing against West Indies in a tour match
BEST THING ABOUT YOUR HOME GROUND? The great atmosphere – especially for the T20 Blast games
BEST OPPOSING PLAYER IN COUNTY CRICKET? Darren Stevens (Ken)
YOUNG OPPOSING PLAYER WHO HAS IMPRESSED YOU? Max Holden (Mid) – great temperament for such a young player. Knows his game so well and plays to his strengths
IF YOU WEREN'T A CRICKETER? I'd be a sports coach
SURPRISING FACT ABOUT YOU? I'm a Leicester City FC supporter and go to both the home and away matches
SURPRISING FACT ABOUT A TEAMMATE? I've played with Sam Evans since we were 10
WHERE IS PARADISE? Phillip Island, Australia
CRICKETING HERO? Adam Gilchrist – the best wicketkeeper-batsman of all time
NON-CRICKETING HERO? Muhammad Ali – so charismatic. He overcame adversity and stuck to what he believed in, as well as being one of the greatest boxers
TWITTER: @harryswindells1

JONNY TATTERSALL

RHB / LB / R0 / W0

YORKSHIRE

FULL NAME: Jonathan Andrew Tattersall
BORN: December 15, 1994, Harrogate, Yorkshire
SQUAD NO: 12
HEIGHT: 5ft 8in
NICKNAME: Tatts
EDUCATION: King James' School, Knaresborough
TEAMS: Yorkshire
ROLE: Batsman
DEBUT: List A: 2013

WHAT GOT YOU INTO CRICKET? My dad and brother
BEST ADVICE EVER RECEIVED? Always remember why you played the game in the first place
'ROY OF THE ROVERS' MOMENT? Being released from Yorkshire and then getting another contract with the county
BEST THING ABOUT YOUR HOME GROUND? The Western Terrace – for the atmosphere it generates
BEST OPPOSING PLAYER IN COUNTY CRICKET? Alastair Cook (Ess)
YOUNG OPPOSING PLAYER WHO HAS IMPRESSED YOU? Joe Clarke (Wor) – I played with him for England U19 and he has gone from strength to strength
IF YOU WEREN'T A CRICKETER? I'd be a coach
SURPRISING FACT ABOUT YOU? I have a handicap of nine in golf
SURPRISING FACT ABOUT A TEAMMATE? Eddie Barnes loves a glass of rosé
WHERE IS PARADISE? South Africa
CRICKETING HERO? Rahul Dravid – for his temperament
NON-CRICKETING HERO? Steve Coogan – for his impressions and for being Alan Partridge
TWITTER: @JonnyTatts

Batting	Mat	Inns	NO	Runs	HS	Ave	SR	100	50	Ct	St
List A	2	1	0	0	0	0.00	0.00	0	0	1	0

Bowling	Mat	Balls	Runs	Wkts	BBI	BBM	Ave	Econ	SR	5w	10
List A	2	-	-	-	-	-	-	-	-	-	-

WILL TAVARÉ

RHB / RMF / R1 / W0

FULL NAME: William Andrew Tavaré
BORN: January 1, 1990, Bristol
SQUAD NO: 4
HEIGHT: 6ft 1in
NICKNAME: Tav, Tekkers, Postman, Mezut, Zukkers
EDUCATION: Bristol Grammar School; Loughborough University
TEAMS: Gloucestershire, Tamil Union Cricket and Athletic Club
ROLE: Batsman
DEBUT: First-class: 2010; List A 2014

BEST BATTING: 139 Gloucestershire vs Hampshire, Bristol, 2014

FAMILY TIES? My dad played for Gloucestershire Second XI and my uncle Chris played for England
BEST ADVICE EVER RECEIVED? Enjoy it
'ROY OF THE ROVERS' MOMENT? Winning the One-Day Cup in 2015
BEST THING ABOUT YOUR HOME GROUND? It's located in Bristol, which is my home town
BEST OPPOSING PLAYER IN COUNTY CRICKET? Jofra Archer (Sus)
YOUNG OPPOSING PLAYER WHO HAS IMPRESSED YOU? Jamie Porter (Ess)
SURPRISING FACT ABOUT YOU? I lived in Dallas, Texas
SURPRISING FACT ABOUT A TEAMMATE? David Payne is in love with David Beckham
WHERE IS PARADISE? Melbourne
CRICKETING HERO? Mike Hussey – class
NON-CRICKETING HERO? Jonny Wilkinson – I loved how determined he was and I will never forget his drop goal to win the World Cup
UNUSUAL OBJECT AT HOME? Lots of mould
TWITTER: @wtav90

Batting	Mat	Inns	NO	Runs	HS	Ave	SR	100	50	Ct	St
First-class	54	92	6	2721	139	31.63	45.17	6	14	36	0
List A	8	8	0	221	77	27.62	72.22	0	2	1	0

Bowling	Mat	Balls	Runs	Wkts	BBI	BBM	Ave	Econ	SR	5w	10
First-class	54	102	82	0	-	-	-	4.82	-	0	0
List A	8	-	-	-	-	-	-	-	-	-	-

BRAD TAYLOR

RHB / OB / RO / WO

HAMPSHIRE

FULL NAME: Bradley Jacob Taylor
BORN: March 14, 1997, Winchester, Hampshire
SQUAD NO: 93
HEIGHT: 6ft
NICKNAME: Bradders
EDUCATION: Alton College, Hampshire
TEAMS: Hampshire
ROLE: Bowler
DEBUT: First-class: 2013; List A: 2013; T20: 2014

BEST BATTING: 36 Hampshire vs Cardiff MCCU, Southampton, 2016
BEST BOWLING: 4-64 Hampshire vs Lancashire, Southport, 2013

FAMILY TIES? My dad is a Level 3 coach
'ROY OF THE ROVERS' MOMENT? Taking four wickets on my first-class debut, getting Simon Katich on my one-day debut and being Man of the Match for England U19 against South Africa U19 on TV
CRICKETING HEROES? Daniel Vettori, Graeme Swann
NON-CRICKETING HERO? LeBron James – he works hard and is always motivated to become better even though he is the best in the world at his sport
SURPRISING FACT? I'm a massive Southampton fan and go to the home games whenever possible
TWITTER: @bradtay93

Batting	Mat	Inns	NO	Runs	HS	Ave	SR	100	50	Ct	St
First-class	5	8	3	112	36	22.40	43.41	0	0	2	0
List A	10	8	3	200	69	40.00	63.49	0	1	3	0
T20s	6	3	1	21	9*	10.50	84.00	0	0	2	0

Bowling	Mat	Balls	Runs	Wkts	BBI	BBM	Ave	Econ	SR	5w	10
First-class	5	702	494	11	4/64	4/106	44.90	4.22	63.8	0	0
List A	10	468	341	9	4/26	4/26	37.88	4.37	52.0	0	0
T20s	6	68	84	3	2/20	2/20	28.00	7.41	22.6	0	0

FULL NAME: Callum John Taylor
BORN: June 26, 1997, Norwich
SQUAD NO: 67
HEIGHT: 5ft 10in
NICKNAME: Chappy
EDUCATION: Cromer Academy, Norfolk;
Eastern College, Norwich
TEAMS: Essex
ROLE: Allrounder
DEBUT: First-class: 2015; T20: 2015

ESSEX

BEST BATTING: 26 Essex vs Glamorgan, Cardiff, 2015
BEST BOWLING: 2-20 Essex vs West Indians, Chelmsford, 2016

WHAT GOT YOU INTO CRICKET? Playing in the back garden with my brothers
'ROY OF THE ROVERS' MOMENT? Scoring 212 runs and taking six wickets in one day for Mount Lawley District CC in Australian grade cricket in December 2016
SUPERSTITIONS? I mark my guard by dragging my bat five times down and then three times across
HOW WOULD YOUR TEAMMATES DESCRIBE YOU IN THREE WORDS? Aggressive, fun, sociable
YOUNG OPPOSING PLAYER WHO HAS IMPRESSED YOU? George Garton (Sus)
CRICKETING HEROES? Andrew Flintoff, Jacques Kallis
NON-CRICKETING HEROES? Dad, Ryan Giggs
SURPRISING FACT? I always shave the day before a game
UNUSUAL OBJECT AT HOME? A cocktail shaker
TWITTER: @Callumjtaylor12

Batting	Mat	Inns	NO	Runs	HS	Ave	SR	100	50	Ct	St
First-class	3	4	0	62	26	15.50	45.92	0	0	1	0
T20s	10	6	1	24	14	4.80	68.57	0	0	1	0

Bowling	Mat	Balls	Runs	Wkts	BBI	BBM	Ave	Econ	SR	5w	10
First-class	3	129	70	5	2/20	4/64	14.00	3.25	25.8	0	0
T20s	10	6	19	0	-	-	-	19.00	-	0	0

JACK TAYLOR RHB / OB / R0 / W0 / MVP56

GLOUCESTERSHIRE

FULL NAME: Jack Martin Robert Taylor
BORN: November 12, 1991, Banbury, Oxfordshire
SQUAD NO: 10
HEIGHT: 6ft
NICKNAME: Tails, Tringale, Jacko
EDUCATION: Chipping Norton School, Oxfordshire
TEAMS: Gloucestershire
ROLE: Allrounder
DEBUT: First-class: 2010; List A: 2011; T20: 2011

BEST BATTING: 156 Gloucestershire vs Northamptonshire, Cheltenham, 2015
BEST BOWLING: 4-16 Gloucestershire vs Glamorgan, Bristol, 2016
COUNTY CAP: 2010

FAMILY TIES? My grandad and dad both played Minor Counties for Oxfordshire. My younger brother Matt also plays for Gloucestershire
BEST ADVICE EVER RECEIVED? It's not how, it's how many
'ROY OF THE ROVERS' MOMENT? Winning the 2015 One-Day Cup and being Man of the Match in the Lord's final
BEST OPPOSING PLAYER IN COUNTY CRICKET? Michael Hogan (Gla)
YOUNG OPPOSING PLAYER WHO HAS IMPRESSED YOU? Josh Tongue (Wor) – he has all the attributes to play at the highest level
SURPRISING FACT ABOUT YOU? I do everything left-handed – apart from batting and bowling
SURPRISING FACT ABOUT A TEAMMATE? Benny Howell will be my brother-in-law in 2018
WHERE IS PARADISE? Playing cards by the pool in Port Douglas, Australia
CRICKETING HERO? Jacques Kallis – the ultimate three-dimensional cricketer
TWITTER: @jacktaylor141

Batting	Mat	Inns	NO	Runs	HS	Ave	SR	100	50	Ct	St
First-class	57	85	8	2498	156	32.44	72.23	6	8	32	0
List A	36	28	5	690	68	30.00	129.69	0	5	14	0
T20s	54	39	10	488	80	16.82	136.31	0	1	14	0

Bowling	Mat	Balls	Runs	Wkts	BBI	BBM	Ave	Econ	SR	5w	10
First-class	57	5661	3290	75	4/16	5/140	43.86	3.48	75.4	0	0
List A	36	1184	1021	29	4/38	4/38	35.20	5.17	40.8	0	0
T20s	54	634	862	26	4/16	4/16	33.15	8.15	24.3	0	0

JAMES TAYLOR

RHB / RM / R0 / W0

FULL NAME: James Philip Arthur Taylor
BORN: January 19, 2001, Stoke-on-Trent, Staffordshire
SQUAD NO: 32
HEIGHT: 6ft 3in
NICKNAME: JT
EDUCATION: Trentham High School, Stoke-on-Trent
TEAMS: Derbyshire
ROLE: Bowler
DEBUT: First-class: 2017

DERBYSHIRE

BEST BOWLING: 1-14 Derbyshire vs West Indians, Derby, 2017

WHAT GOT YOU INTO CRICKET? My dad
BEST ADVICE EVER RECEIVED? Play late, straight and be great
'ROY OF THE ROVERS' MOMENT? Making 105 not out as a nine-year-old for Staffordshire in the Malvern Cricket Festival
BEST THING ABOUT YOUR HOME GROUND? The changing rooms
BEST OPPOSING PLAYER IN COUNTY CRICKET? Richard Levi (Nor)
YOUNG OPPOSING PLAYER WHO HAS IMPRESSED YOU? Fin Trenouth (Som) – he hits the ball clean and very far
IF YOU WEREN'T A CRICKETER? I'd be a drummer in a band
SURPRISING FACT ABOUT YOU? I'm not very surprising
WHERE IS PARADISE? Home
CRICKETING HERO? Andrew Flintoff in the 2005 Ashes
NON-CRICKETING HERO? Superman – he saves lives
TWITTER: @_Jamestaylor19

Batting	Mat	Inns	NO	Runs	HS	Ave	SR	100	50	Ct	St
First-class	1	1	1	0	0*	-	0.00	0	0	0	0

Bowling	Mat	Balls	Runs	Wkts	BBI	BBM	Ave	Econ	SR	5w	10
First-class	1	102	77	1	1/14	1/77	77.00	4.52	102.0	0	0

MATT TAYLOR

RHB / LMF / RO / WO

FULL NAME: Matthew David Taylor
BORN: July 8, 1994, Banbury, Oxfordshire
SQUAD NO: 36
HEIGHT: 6ft 2in
NICKNAME: MT, Tayls, Melon, Swede, Balloon
EDUCATION: Chipping Norton Secondary School, Oxfordshire
TEAMS: Gloucestershire
ROLE: Bowler
DEBUT: First-class: 2013; List A: 2011; T20: 2015

BEST BATTING: 36 Gloucestershire vs Kent, Bristol, 2017
BEST BOWLING: 5-75 Gloucestershire vs Hampshire, Bristol, 2014
COUNTY CAP: 2013

WHAT GOT YOU INTO CRICKET? My dad and grandad played so I was around cricket from an early age
FAMILY TIES? My older brother Jack also plays for Gloucestershire. My dad and grandad played Minor Counties for Oxfordshire
'ROY OF THE ROVERS' MOMENT? Taking my maiden first-class wicket in 2013
BEST THING ABOUT YOUR HOME GROUND? The showers
YOUNG OPPOSING PLAYER WHO HAS IMPRESSED YOU? Jofra Archer (Sus) – quick and accurate
WHERE IS PARADISE? Barcelona
CRICKETING HERO? Darren Gough – he was a fiery cricketer and bowled great yorkers
NON-CRICKETING HERO? Cristiano Ronaldo – for his drive to be the best
TWITTER: @matt_taylor94

Batting	Mat	Inns	NO	Runs	HS	Ave	SR	100	50	Ct	St
First-class	28	38	18	270	36	13.50	39.88	0	0	3	0
List A	17	7	5	37	16	18.50	90.24	0	0	2	0
T20s	26	7	4	21	9*	7.00	87.50	0	0	5	0

Bowling	Mat	Balls	Runs	Wkts	BBI	BBM	Ave	Econ	SR	5w	10
First-class	28	4407	2788	62	5/75	6/101	44.96	3.79	71.0	2	0
List A	17	749	737	14	3/48	3/48	52.64	5.90	53.5	0	0
T20s	26	444	620	22	3/16	3/16	28.18	8.37	20.1	0	0

ROSS TAYLOR

RHB / OB / RO / WO

FULL NAME: Luteru Ross Poutoa Lote Taylor
BORN: March 8, 1984, Lower Hutt, Wellington, NZ
SQUAD NO: TBC
HEIGHT: 6ft 1in
NICKNAME: Rosco
EDUCATION: Wairarapa College, Masterton
TEAMS: NZ, Nottinghamshire, Central
Districts, Delhi Daredevils, Durham, Pune
Warriors, Rajasthan Royals, RC Bangalore, St
Lucia Zouks, Sussex, Victoria
ROLE: Batsman
DEBUT: Test: 2007; ODI: 2006; T20I: 2006;
First-class: 2003; List A: 2003; T20: 2006

NOTTINGHAMSHIRE

BEST BATTING: 290 New Zealand vs Australia, Perth, 2015
BEST BOWLING: 2-4 New Zealand vs India, Ahmedabad, 2010

TWITTER: @RossLTaylor
NOTES: The New Zealand batsman has joined Nottinghamshire as their overseas player until the end of June, making him available for eight Championship matches and eight One-Day Cup fixtures. Taylor arrives in superb form, having excelled in the ODI series against England in March, including a career-best 181 not out to see his side to victory in Dunedin. He is New Zealand's second-highest run-scorer in ODI cricket and in February 2017 he became only the sixth player to score a century in the 50-over format against all Full Member nations (before Ireland and Afghanistan joined the top table). He is also his country's third-highest run-scorer in Tests. His innings of 290 in Perth in 2015 was the highest score by a Kiwi away from home in Test cricket and a record for an overseas batsman in Australia. Notts will be Taylor's third county, with the 34-year-old previously representing Durham and Sussex

Batting	Mat	Inns	NO	Runs	HS	Ave	SR	100	50	Ct	St
Tests	83	149	19	6246	290	48.04	59.42	17	28	125	0
ODIs	204	190	33	7267	181*	46.28	82.87	19	41	130	0
T20Is	81	73	17	1415	63	25.26	121.04	0	5	44	0
First-class	149	251	22	10152	290	44.33		24	52	186	0
List A	256	242	37	9246	181*	45.10		23	57	161	0
T20s	245	229	54	5426	111*	31.00	133.48	1	27	111	0

Bowling	Mat	Balls	Runs	Wkts	BBI	BBM	Ave	Econ	SR	5w	10
Tests	83	96	48	2	2/4	2/4	24.00	3.00	48.0	0	0
ODIs	204	42	35	0	-	-	-	5.00	-	0	0
T20Is	81	-	-	-	-	-	-	-	-	-	-
First-class	149	684	378	6	2/4	2/4	63.00	3.31	114.0	0	0
List A	256	318	242	3	1/13	1/13	80.66	4.56	106.0	0	0
T20s	245	186	280	8	3/28	3/28	35.00	9.03	23.2	0	0

TOM TAYLOR

RHB / RMF / R0 / W0

LEICESTERSHIRE

FULL NAME: Thomas Alexander Ian Taylor
BORN: December 21, 1994, Stoke-on-Trent, Staffordshire
SQUAD NO: 16
HEIGHT: 6ft 3in
NICKNAME: Audi, Anne Robinson
EDUCATION: Trentham High School, Stoke-on-Trent; Newcastle-under-Lyme College; Leeds Metropolitan University
TEAMS: Leicestershire, Derbyshire
ROLE: Bowler
DEBUT: First-class: 2014; List A 2014

BEST BATTING: 80 Derbyshire vs Kent, Derby, 2016
BEST BOWLING: 6-61 Derbyshire vs Lancashire, Derby, 2015

FAMILY TIES? Father, cousins, uncles all play cricket; other family members used to run my home club
'ROY OF THE ROVERS' MOMENT? Probably my maiden first-class five-wicket haul against Lancashire. Getting Hashim Amla as my maiden first-class wicket wasn't bad either
STRANGEST THING SEEN IN A GAME? Match abandoned because all the balls were lost
HOW WOULD YOUR TEAMMATES DESCRIBE YOU IN THREE WORDS? Surprisingly strong legs
BEST OPPOSING PLAYER IN COUNTY CRICKET? Jeetan Patel (War)
CRICKETING HEROES? Shane Warne, Andrew Flintoff, Brett Lee, James Anderson
SURPRISING FACT? I drink a lot of milk
TWITTER: @TomTaylor43

Batting	Mat	Inns	NO	Runs	HS	Ave	SR	100	50	Ct	St	
First-class	25	39	6	587	80	17.78	41.98	0	2	5		0
List A	5	-	-	-	-	-	-	-	-	0		0

Bowling	Mat	Balls	Runs	Wkts	BBI	BBM	Ave	Econ	SR	5w	10	
First-class	25	3716	2335	64	6/61	8/116	36.48	3.77	58.0	2		0
List A	5	218	225	5	3/48	3/48	45.00	6.19	43.6	0		0

RYAN TEN DOESCHATE   RHB / RMF / R1 / W0 / MVP43

FULL NAME: Ryan Neil ten Doeschate
BORN: June 30, 1980, Port Elizabeth, SA
SQUAD NO: 27
HEIGHT: 5ft 11in
EDUCATION: University of Cape Town
TEAMS: Netherlands, Essex, Adelaide Strikers, Canterbury, Chittagong Kings, Comilla Victorians, Dhaka Dynamites, Impi, Kolkata Knight Riders, Mashonaland Eagles, Otago, Tasmania, Western Province
ROLE: Allrounder
DEBUT: ODI: 2006; T20I: 2008; First-class: 2003; List A: 2003; T20: 2003

BEST BATTING: 259* Netherlands vs Canada, Pretoria, 2006
BEST BOWLING: 6-20 Netherlands vs Canada, Pretoria, 2006
COUNTY CAP: 2006

TWITTER: @rtendo27
NOTES: Netherlands allrounder who led Essex to the Championship title in 2017. Took on the captaincy in all formats following the 2016 season. This will be his 16th season at Chelmsford. Has played T20 cricket all over the globe, including for Kolkata Knight Riders in the IPL. For Netherlands he scored 686 runs at an average of 228.66 in the ICC Intercontinental Cup in 2006, recording four consecutive hundreds, including a competition record 259* vs Canada in Pretoria. Made a century (119) against England at Nagpur in the World Cup 2011, becoming the first batsman from the Netherlands to make a hundred in the World Cup finals, and scored a second century against Ireland at Kolkata

Batting	Mat	Inns	NO	Runs	HS	Ave	SR	100	50	Ct	St
ODIs	33	32	9	1541	119	67.00	87.70	5	9	13	0
T20Is	9	9	4	214	56	42.80	128.91	0	1	3	0
First-class	160	233	35	9581	259*	48.38		26	44	97	0
List A	207	172	52	5587	180	46.55		11	29	62	0
T20s	298	261	59	5888	121*	29.14	135.54	2	25	115	0

Bowling	Mat	Balls	Runs	Wkts	BBI	BBM	Ave	Econ	SR	5w	10
ODIs	33	1580	1327	55	4/31	4/31	24.12	5.03	28.7	0	0
T20Is	9	204	241	12	3/23	3/23	20.08	7.08	17.0	0	0
First-class	160	10892	7165	212	6/20	9/112	33.79	3.94	51.3	7	0
List A	207	5367	5163	170	5/50	5/50	30.37	5.77	31.5	1	0
T20s	298	2077	2817	109	4/24	4/24	25.84	8.13	19.0	0	0

IVAN THOMAS

RHB / RMF / RO / WO

FULL NAME: Ivan Alfred Astley Thomas
BORN: September 25, 1991, Greenwich, Kent
SQUAD NO: 5
HEIGHT: 6ft 4in
NICKNAME: Blade, Big Iv, Big Red, Backpacker, The Viking, Goober
EDUCATION: The John Roan School, Greenwich; University of Leeds
TEAMS: Kent
ROLE: Bowler
DEBUT: First-class: 2012; List A: 2014; T20: 2015

BEST BATTING: 13 Kent vs Australians, Canterbury, 2015
BEST BOWLING: 4-48 Kent vs Leicestershire, Canterbury, 2015

WHAT GOT YOU INTO CRICKET? A Kwik Cricket tournament in primary school
'ROY OF THE ROVERS' MOMENT? Knuckleballing Jesse Ryder on my T20 debut
CRICKETING HERO? Andrew Flintoff
NON-CRICKETING HEROES? Sean Conway and Mark Beaumont – both are fantastic adventurers
IF YOU WEREN'T A CRICKETER? I'd be struggling
SURPRISING FACT? I have clicking bones, and I can tear an apple in half
TWITTER: @ivanthomas_5

Batting	Mat	Inns	NO	Runs	HS	Ave	SR	100	50	Ct	St
First-class	20	30	14	97	13	6.06	26.72	0	0	3	0
List A	21	8	5	18	6	6.00	37.50	0	0	8	0
T20s	8	3	2	3	3*	3.00	60.00	0	0	1	0

Bowling	Mat	Balls	Runs	Wkts	BBI	BBM	Ave	Econ	SR	5w	10
First-class	20	2983	1462	45	4/48	6/75	32.48	2.94	66.2	0	0
List A	21	1036	964	31	4/30	4/30	31.09	5.58	33.4	0	0
T20s	8	168	245	7	2/42	2/42	35.00	8.75	24.0	0	0

AARON THOMASON

RHB / RFM / R0 / W0

FULL NAME: Aaron Dean Thomason
BORN: June 26, 1997, Birmingham
SQUAD NO: 26
HEIGHT: 5ft 10in
NICKNAME: Thomo
EDUCATION: Barr Beacon School, Walsall
TEAMS: Warwickshire
ROLE: Allrounder
DEBUT: List A: 2014; T20: 2016

WARWICKSHIRE

FAMILY TIES? We are members of Sutton Coldfield CC, where my brother plays and my whole family go and watch each Saturday
'ROY OF THE ROVERS' MOMENT? Making my Warwickshire debut at Lord's
HOW WOULD YOUR TEAMMATES DESCRIBE YOU IN THREE WORDS? Childish, determined, demanding
BEST OPPOSING PLAYER IN COUNTY CRICKET? Joe Root (Yor)
CRICKETING HERO? Andrew Flintoff – bats, bowls, fields well and has a great laugh off the field
NON-CRICKETING HERO? My great-grandad watched us all the time. He left me some medals he was awarded for service in the war which I treasure
IF YOU WEREN'T A CRICKETER? I'd be window-cleaning with my dad
SURPRISING FACT? Me and Chris Woakes went to the same school – a non-cricket-playing school

Batting	Mat	Inns	NO	Runs	HS	Ave	SR	100	50	Ct	St
List A	9	8	3	105	28	21.00	92.92	0	0	4	0
T20s	20	15	4	212	42	19.27	140.39	0	0	6	0

Bowling	Mat	Balls	Runs	Wkts	BBI	BBM	Ave	Econ	SR	5w	10
List A	9	120	170	4	4/64	4/64	42.50	8.50	30.0	0	0
T20s	20	192	320	12	3/33	3/33	26.66	10.00	16.0	0	0

JORDAN THOMPSON

LHB / RM / RO / WO

YORKSHIRE

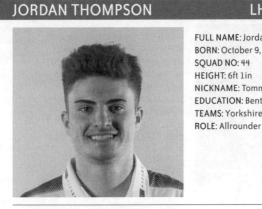

FULL NAME: Jordan Aaron Thompson
BORN: October 9, 1996, Leeds, Yorkshire
SQUAD NO: 44
HEIGHT: 6ft 1in
NICKNAME: Tommo, Lizard
EDUCATION: Benton Park School, Leeds
TEAMS: Yorkshire
ROLE: Allrounder

WHAT GOT YOU INTO CRICKET? My family
'ROY OF THE ROVERS' MOMENT? Scoring 146 not out in a Second XI Championship match for Yorkshire against Worcestershire at Scarborough in 2016
BEST THING ABOUT YOUR HOME GROUND? On a Friday night under the lights the Western Terrace is electric
YOUNG OPPOSING PLAYER WHO HAS IMPRESSED YOU? Haseeb Hameed (Lan) – I've played against him since I was 10 and he has scored runs every time
IF YOU WEREN'T A CRICKETER? I'd be a professional goalkeeper
SURPRISING FACT ABOUT YOU? I'm a Type 1 diabetic
SURPRISING FACT ABOUT A TEAMMATE? Matthew Waite has the nickname 'Pingu' because we all think he walks like a penguin
WHERE IS PARADISE? Dover Beach, Barbados
CRICKETING HERO? Ben Stokes – because of his aggressive style on the field
NON-CRICKETING HERO? Pontus Jansson – Leeds United footballer. Love his aggression and passion on the football field
TWITTER: @Tommo455

ALEX THOMSON

RHB / OB / R0 / W0

FULL NAME: Alexander Thomas Thomson
BORN: October 30, 1993, Stoke-on-Trent, Staffordshire
SQUAD NO: 29
HEIGHT: 6ft 5in
NICKNAME: Tommo, Big Al
EDUCATION: Denstone College; Cardiff Metropolitan University
TEAMS: Warwickshire
ROLE: Allrounder
DEBUT: First-class: 2014

BEST BATTING: 26 Warwickshire vs Hampshire, Edgbaston, 2017
BEST BOWLING: 6-138 Cardiff MCCU vs Hampshire, Southampton, 2017

BEST ADVICE EVER RECEIVED? Stay disciplined and aim high
'ROY OF THE ROVERS' MOMENT? Taking five wickets at Lord's for Cardiff MCCU in 2017
BEST THING ABOUT YOUR HOME GROUND? There's a bar located under every section of the ground
BEST OPPOSING PLAYER IN COUNTY CRICKET? Alastair Cook (Ess)
YOUNG OPPOSING PLAYER WHO HAS IMPRESSED YOU? Mason Crane (Ham) – he has the ability to consistently challenge your defence and has multiple variations
IF YOU WEREN'T A CRICKETER? I'd be a teacher
SURPRISING FACT ABOUT YOU? I'm an avid angler
SURPRISING FACT ABOUT A TEAMMATE? Alex Mellor can't spell his own name
WHERE IS PARADISE? Bora Bora island, Tahiti
CRICKETING HERO? Jacques Kallis – he mastered all three disciplines and demonstrated unbelievable composure over a number of years
NON-CRICKETING HERO? David McGuigan – he proves that not all heroes wear capes
TWITTER: @ tommo1039

Batting	Mat	Inns	NO	Runs	HS	Ave	SR	100	50	Ct	St
First-class	6	7	0	113	26	16.14	43.29	0	0	2	0

Bowling	Mat	Balls	Runs	Wkts	BBI	BBM	Ave	Econ	SR	5w	10
First-class	6	475	326	9	6/138	7/176	36.22	4.11	52.7	1	0

JOSH TONGUE

RHB / RFM / RO / WO

FULL NAME: Joshua Charles Tongue
BORN: November 15, 1997, Redditch, Worcestershire
SQUAD NO: 24
HEIGHT: 6ft 4in
NICKNAME: Tonguey
EDUCATION: King's School, Worcester; Christopher Whitehead Language College, Worcester
TEAMS: Worcestershire
ROLE: Bowler
DEBUT: First-class: 2016; List A: 2017; T20: 2017

BEST BATTING: 41 Worcestershire vs Glamorgan, Worcester, 2017
BEST BOWLING: 6-97 Worcestershire vs Glamorgan, Worcester, 2017

WHAT GOT YOU INTO CRICKET? Watching my dad play for his club and playing back-garden cricket with my brother
FAMILY TIES? My dad is a coach and my mum used to be manager for different age-groups in Worcester
BEST ADVICE EVER RECEIVED? Don't change who you are
BEST THING ABOUT YOUR HOME GROUND? The view from the players' balcony
BEST OPPOSING PLAYER IN COUNTY CRICKET? Last year in Division Two it was Joe Denly (Ken)
YOUNG OPPOSING PLAYER WHO HAS IMPRESSED YOU? Ollie Pope (Sur)
IF YOU WEREN'T A CRICKETER? I'd be a footballer
WHERE IS PARADISE? America
CRICKETING HERO? Andrew Flintoff – he took the game away from the opposition with bat and ball
NON-CRICKETING HERO? Cristiano Ronaldo
TWITTER: @Josh Tongue

Batting	Mat	Inns	NO	Runs	HS	Ave	SR	100	50	Ct	St
First-class	15	18	3	138	41	9.20	41.56	0	0	2	0
List A	4	3	2	12	11*	12.00	66.66	0	0	0	0
T20s	5	2	2	3	2*	-	150.00	0	0	2	0

Bowling	Mat	Balls	Runs	Wkts	BBI	BBM	Ave	Econ	SR	5w	10
First-class	15	2152	1261	51	6/97	6/97	24.72	3.51	42.1	2	0
List A	4	141	162	4	2/46	2/46	40.50	6.89	35.2	0	0
T20s	5	84	122	3	2/32	2/32	40.66	8.71	28.0	0	0

REECE TOPLEY

RHB / LFM / R0 / W0

FULL NAME: Reece James William Topley
BORN: February 21, 1994, Ipswich
SQUAD NO: 6
HEIGHT: 6ft 6in
NICKNAME: Toppers, Smash, Neil, Zlatan
EDUCATION: Royal Hospital School, Suffolk
TEAMS: England, Hampshire, Essex
ROLE: Bowler
DEBUT: ODI: 2015; T20I: 2015; First-class: 2011; List A: 2011; T20: 2012

BEST BATTING: 16 Hampshire vs Yorkshire, Southampton, 2017
BEST BOWLING: 6-29 Essex vs Worcestershire, Chelmsford, 2013
COUNTY CAP: 2013 (Essex)

FAMILY TIES? My father Don played for Essex and Surrey and also coached Zimbabwe. My uncle Peter played for Kent
'ROY OF THE ROVERS' MOMENT? Taking 4-50 for England in an ODI against South Africa in Port Elizabeth
CRICKETING HERO? Wasim Akram – best left-arm bowler ever
IF YOU WEREN'T A CRICKETER? I'd be an actor
SURPRISING FACT? I speak Spanish to a very good standard
UNUSUAL OBJECT AT HOME? Mike Tyson's boxing glove
TWITTER: @reece_topley
NOTES: Ongoing injury problems led Topley to sign a contract to play only white-ball cricket in 2018

Batting	Mat	Inns	NO	Runs	HS	Ave	SR	100	50	Ct	St
ODIs	10	5	4	7	6	7.00	17.50	0	0	2	0
T20Is	6	1	1	1	1*	-	50.00	0	0	1	0
First-class	34	41	19	94	16	4.27	19.26	0	0	8	0
List A	45	14	8	41	19	6.83	41.83	0	0	10	0
T20s	63	12	7	15	5*	3.00	50.00	0	0	16	0

Bowling	Mat	Balls	Runs	Wkts	BBI	BBM	Ave	Econ	SR	5w	10
ODIs	10	463	410	16	4/50	4/50	25.62	5.31	28.9	0	0
T20Is	6	103	173	5	3/24	3/24	34.60	10.07	20.6	0	0
First-class	34	5966	3401	127	6/29	11/85	26.77	3.42	46.9	7	2
List A	45	2074	1937	78	4/26	4/26	24.83	5.60	26.5	0	0
T20s	63	1323	1827	84	4/26	4/26	21.75	8.28	15.7	0	0

FULL NAME: James Cullum Tredwell
BORN: February 27, 1982, Ashford, Kent
SQUAD NO: 15
HEIGHT: 5ft 11in
NICKNAME: Tredders, Treddy, Pingu, Chad
EDUCATION: Dymchurch Primary School, Kent; Southlands Community Comprehensive, Kent
TEAMS: England, Kent, Sussex
ROLE: Bowler
DEBUT: Test: 2010; ODI: 2010; T20I: 2012; First-class: 2001; List A: 2000; T20: 2003

BEST BATTING: 124 Kent vs Essex, Chelmsford, 2016
BEST BOWLING: 8-66 Kent vs Glamorgan, Canterbury, 2009
COUNTY CAP: 2007 (Kent); **TESTIMONIAL:** 2018 (Kent)

FAMILY TIES? Dad played to a good club level for Ashford and then Folkestone in the Kent league
'ROY OF THE ROVERS' MOMENT? Receiving my cap to play for England
HOW WOULD YOUR TEAMMATES DESCRIBE YOU IN THREE WORDS? Quiet, solid, committed
SURPRISING FACT? I enjoy growing my own fruit and veg, and make my own chutney/jam
CRICKETING HEROES? Shane Warne, David Gower

Batting	Mat	Inns	NO	Runs	HS	Ave	SR	100	50	Ct	St
Tests	2	2	0	45	37	22.50	51.72	0	0	2	0
ODIs	45	25	11	163	30	11.64	67.35	0	0	14	0
T20Is	17	6	3	32	22	10.66	160.00	0	0	2	0
First-class	177	247	31	4728	124	21.88	43.90	4	17	196	0
List A	270	174	63	1917	88	17.27		0	4	110	0
T20s	166	74	27	519	34*	11.04	106.13	0	0	48	0

Bowling	Mat	Balls	Runs	Wkts	BBI	BBM	Ave	Econ	SR	5w	10
Tests	2	786	321	11	4/47	6/181	29.18	2.45	71.4	0	0
ODIs	45	2104	1666	60	4/41	4/41	27.76	4.75	35.0	0	0
T20Is	17	317	416	7	1/16	1/16	59.42	7.87	45.2	0	0
First-class	177	30574	15439	426	8/66	11/120	36.24	3.02	71.7	12	3
List A	270	11606	9076	276	6/27	6/27	32.88	4.69	42.0	1	0
T20s	166	3242	3964	128	4/21	4/21	30.96	7.33	25.3	0	0

PETER TREGO

RHB / RM / R1 / W1

FULL NAME: Peter David Trego
BORN: June 12, 1981, Weston-super-Mare
SQUAD NO: 7
HEIGHT: 6ft
NICKNAME: Tregs, Pirate, Big Tone
EDUCATION: Wyvern School, Weston-super-Mare
TEAMS: Somerset, Central Districts, England Lions, Kent, Mashonaland Eagles, Middlesex, Sylhet Royals
ROLE: Allrounder
DEBUT: First-class: 2000; List A: 1999; T20: 2003

BEST BATTING: 154* Somerset vs Lancashire, Old Trafford, 2016
BEST BOWLING: 7-84 Somerset vs Yorkshire, Headingley, 2014
COUNTY CAP: 2007 (Somerset)

'ROY OF THE ROVERS' MOMENT? Winning the PCA MVP award, all of my England Lions appearances and playing in the Hong Kong Sixes
HOW WOULD YOUR TEAMMATES DESCRIBE YOU IN THREE WORDS? Pain in arse
CRICKETING HEROES? Graham Rose, Ian Botham, Justin Langer
IF YOU WEREN'T A CRICKETER? I'd be doing something manual and dominating Sunday football
SURPRISING FACT? My house is full of pets – it's like a bloody zoo and it drives me crackers
TWITTER: @tregs140

Batting	Mat	Inns	NO	Runs	HS	Ave	SR	100	50	Ct	St
First-class	215	318	37	9464	154*	33.67		15	54	86	0
List A	179	157	25	4197	147	31.79		8	21	54	0
T20s	181	167	20	3527	94*	23.99	124.62	0	18	51	0

Bowling	Mat	Balls	Runs	Wkts	BBI	BBM	Ave	Econ	SR	5w	10
First-class	215	24055	13827	379	7/84	11/153	36.48	3.44	63.4	5	1
List A	179	5701	5320	164	5/40	5/40	32.43	5.59	34.7	2	0
T20s	181	1704	2404	77	4/27	4/27	31.22	8.46	22.1	0	0

FIN TRENOUTH

RHB / WK / R0 / W0

FULL NAME: Finlay Robert Trenouth
BORN: September 22, 1998, London
SQUAD NO: TBC
HEIGHT: 6ft 2in
NICKNAME: Sparta
EDUCATION: Clifton College, Bristol; Millfield School
TEAMS: Somerset, England U19
ROLE: Batsman

WHAT GOT YOU INTO CRICKET? Playing in the back garden with my dad and my brothers
BEST ADVICE EVER RECEIVED? It doesn't matter how many runs you have scored, it will never be enough
'ROY OF THE ROVERS' MOMENT? Playing for England in the U19 World Cup in New Zealand
BEST THING ABOUT YOUR HOME GROUND? The atmosphere and the support from all the fans at Taunton is terrific
BEST OPPOSING PLAYER IN COUNTY CRICKET? Jofra Archer (Sus)
YOUNG OPPOSING PLAYER WHO HAS IMPRESSED YOU? Harry Brook (Yor) – he is simply a run-machine
IF YOU WEREN'T A CRICKETER? I'd be a professional footballer
WHERE IS PARADISE? Queenstown, New Zealand
CRICKETING HERO? Jason Roy – he is very aggressive and innovative, and he never lets a bowler get on top of him
NON-CRICKETING HERO? Anthony Joshua – he's the best in the world and a complete champion
TWITTER: @trenouth_fin

MARCUS TRESCOTHICK

LHB / RM / R8 / W0

FULL NAME: Marcus Edward Trescothick
BORN: December 25, 1975, Keynsham, Somerset
SQUAD NO: 2
HEIGHT: 6ft 3in
NICKNAME: Banger, Tresco
EDUCATION: Sir Bernard Lovell School, Bristol
TEAMS: England, Somerset
ROLE: Batsman
DEBUT: Test: 2000; ODI: 2000; T20I: 2005; First-class: 1993; List A: 1993; T20: 2004

BEST BATTING: 284 Somerset vs Northamptonshire, Northampton, 2007
BEST BOWLING: 4-36 Somerset vs Young Australia, Taunton, 1995
COUNTY CAP: 1999; **BENEFIT:** 2008

TWITTER: @Trescricket
NOTES: Trescothick's maiden Test appearance came against West Indies at Old Trafford in 2000. His highest Test score was 219 against South Africa in a decisive nine-wicket victory at The Oval. Played his last Test against Pakistan at the same ground in 2006. Wisden Cricketer of the Year in 2005 and PCA Player of the Year in 2000, 2009 and 2011. Has the English record for ODI hundreds, scoring 12 of them. Passed 1,000 runs five years in a row between 2007 and 2011 and then for three successive seasons between 2014 and 2016. Had a modest 2017 by his own high standards. Stood down as captain in January 2016 after six years in charge. Now plays Championship cricket only. This summer is his 26th as a Somerset player

Batting	Mat	Inns	NO	Runs	HS	Ave	SR	100	50	Ct	St
Tests	76	143	10	5825	219	43.79	54.51	14	29	95	0
ODIs	123	122	6	4335	137	37.37	85.21	12	21	49	0
T20Is	3	3	0	166	72	55.33	126.71	0	2	2	0
First-class	375	647	36	25598	284	41.89		65	123	534	0
List A	372	357	29	12229	184	37.28		28	63	149	0
T20s	89	87	5	2363	108*	28.81	150.60	2	17	29	0

Bowling	Mat	Balls	Runs	Wkts	BBI	BBM	Ave	Econ	SR	5w	10
Tests	76	300	155	1	1/34	1/34	155.00	3.10	300.0	0	0
ODIs	123	232	219	4	2/7	2/7	54.75	5.66	58.0	0	0
T20Is	3	-	-	-	-	-	-	-	-	-	-
First-class	375	2704	1551	36	4/36	7/106	43.08	3.44	75.1	0	0
List A	372	2010	1644	57	4/50	4/50	28.84	4.90	35.2	0	0
T20s	89	-	-	-	-	-	-	-	-	-	-

LIAM TREVASKIS

LHB / SLA / RO / WO

FULL NAME: Liam Trevaskis
BORN: April 18, 1999, Carlisle, Cumberland
SQUAD NO: 80
HEIGHT: 5ft 11in
NICKNAME: Trev, Trav, Trevor
EDUCATION: Queen Elizabeth Grammar School, Penrith, Cumbria
TEAMS: Durham
ROLE: Allrounder
DEBUT: First-class: 2017; T20: 2017

BEST BATTING: 9 Durham vs Worcestershire, Worcester, 2017
BEST BOWLING: 1-69 Durham vs Worcestershire, Worcester, 2017

WHAT GOT YOU INTO CRICKET? My friend invited me to the local cricket club for training after school one day
BEST ADVICE EVER RECEIVED? Do what you love and you will never have to work a day in your life
BEST THING ABOUT YOUR HOME GROUND? That Lumley Castle appears in the background
BEST OPPOSING PLAYER IN COUNTY CRICKET? Samit Patel (Not)
YOUNG OPPOSING PLAYER WHO HAS IMPRESSED YOU? Josh Tongue (Wor)
IF YOU WEREN'T A CRICKETER? I'd be a PE teacher
SURPRISING FACT ABOUT YOU? I've never seen an episode of Game of Thrones
WHERE IS PARADISE? Lilli Pilli Beach, Bateman's Bay, New South Wales
CRICKETING HERO? Steve Waugh – because he changed his game for the good of the team
NON-CRICKETING HERO? Alan Sugar – because he has worked so hard for everything that he has achieved
TWITTER: @LiamTrevaskis

Batting	Mat	Inns	NO	Runs	HS	Ave	SR	100	50	Ct	St
First-class	1	2	0	14	9	7.00	18.91	0	0	0	0
T20s	1	1	1	13	13*	-	76.47	0	0	0	0

Bowling	Mat	Balls	Runs	Wkts	BBI	BBM	Ave	Econ	SR	5w	10
First-class	1	156	126	1	1/69	1/126	126.00	4.84	156.0	0	0
T20s	1	24	33	1	1/33	1/33	33.00	8.25	24.0	0	0

JONATHAN TROTT   RHB / RM / R8 / W0 / MVP72

FULL NAME: Ian Jonathan Leonard Trott
BORN: April 22, 1981, Cape Town, South Africa
SQUAD NO: 9
HEIGHT: 6ft
NICKNAME: Booger, Trotters
EDUCATION: Rondebosch Boys High School; Stellenbosch University
TEAMS: England, Warwickshire, Boland, Otago, Western Province
ROLE: Batsman
DEBUT: Test: 2009; ODI: 2009; T20I: 2007; First-class: 2000; List A: 2000; T20: 2003

BEST BATTING: 226 England vs Bangladesh, Lord's, 2010
BEST BOWLING: 7-39 Warwickshire vs Kent, Canterbury, 2003
COUNTY CAP: 2005; **BENEFIT:** 2014

CRICKETING HEROES? Sachin Tendulkar, Adam Hollioake, Steve Waugh, Jacques Kallis
SURPRISING FACT? I'm a San Francisco 49ers fan
TWITTER: @Trotty
NOTES: Scored 245 on debut for Warwickshire Second XI, 134 on his Championship debut in 2003, and 119 on Test debut for England in the deciding match of the 2009 Ashes at The Oval. Played in three Ashes-winning England sides. Quit international cricket in 2015 following stress-related problems. Returned to his best form in 2016, averaging 44.31 in the Championship and scoring 515 runs at 85.83 to guide Warwickshire to the One-Day Cup trophy, making 82* in the final. Passed 1,000 first-class runs last summer despite the turmoil affecting the rest of the Warwickshire top order

Batting	Mat	Inns	NO	Runs	HS	Ave	SR	100	50	Ct	St
Tests	52	93	6	3835	226	44.08	47.18	9	19	29	0
ODIs	68	65	10	2819	137	51.25	77.06	4	22	14	0
T20Is	7	7	1	138	51	23.00	95.83	0	1	0	0
First-class	266	444	43	17616	226	43.93		43	86	212	0
List A	266	247	43	9785	137	47.96		21	66	74	0
T20s	79	74	16	2122	86*	36.58	114.27	0	13	18	0

Bowling	Mat	Balls	Runs	Wkts	BBI	BBM	Ave	Econ	SR	5w	10
Tests	52	708	400	5	1/5	1/5	80.00	3.38	141.6	0	0
ODIs	68	183	166	2	2/31	2/31	83.00	5.44	91.5	0	0
T20Is	7	-	-	-	-	-	-	-	-	-	-
First-class	266	6206	3487	70	7/39		49.81	3.37	88.6	1	0
List A	266	1684	1582	54	4/55	4/55	29.29	5.63	31.1	0	0
T20s	79	144	234	8	2/19	2/19	29.25	9.75	18.0	0	0

BEN TWOHIG

WORCESTERSHIRE

FULL NAME: Benjamin Jake Twohig
BORN: April 13, 1998, Dewsbury, Yorkshire
SQUAD NO: 42
HEIGHT: 5ft 9in
NICKNAME: Twiggy, The Owl, Twiglet
EDUCATION: Malvern College
TEAMS: Worcestershire, England U19
ROLE: Bowler

WHAT GOT YOU INTO CRICKET? It was a big part of my life at a young age as I grew up five minutes away from the local cricket club
FAMILY TIES? My dad played a lot of club cricket when I was younger and so did my brother
BEST ADVICE EVER RECEIVED? Fours and sixes, and don't get out
'ROY OF THE ROVERS' MOMENT? Representing England U19
BEST THING ABOUT YOUR HOME GROUND? The view at New Road
BEST OPPOSING PLAYER IN COUNTY CRICKET? Samit Patel (Not)
YOUNG OPPOSING PLAYER WHO HAS IMPRESSED YOU? Jofra Archer (Sus)
IF YOU WEREN'T A CRICKETER? I'd be an actor
SURPRISING FACT ABOUT YOU? I played Dorothy in The Wizard of Oz for a school play
SURPRISING FACT ABOUT A TEAMMATE? Ed Barnard is a terrible golfer
WHERE IS PARADISE? Cape Town
CRICKETING HERO? Kevin Pietersen – for the way he played his cricket without any fear. Daniel Vettori – someone I look up to as a fellow slow left-armer
NON-CRICKETING HERO? Muhammad Ali – he stood up for what he believed in
UNUSUAL OBJECT AT HOME? A circular saw
TWITTER: @Ben_Twohig

RHB / RFM / R0 / W0

FULL NAME: Andrew James Tye
BORN: December 12, 1986, Perth, Australia
SQUAD NO: 68
HEIGHT: 6ft 3in
NICKNAME: AJ
EDUCATION: Padbury Senior High School, Western Australia
TEAMS: Australia, Gloucestershire, Gujarat Lions, Perth Scorchers, Sydney Thunder, Western Australia
ROLE: Bowler
DEBUT: ODI: 2018; T20I: 2016; First-class: 2014; List A: 2013; T20: 2014

BEST BATTING: 10 Western Australia vs Tasmania, Hobart, 2014
BEST BOWLING: 3-47 Western Australia vs Queensland, Brisbane, 2015

TWITTER: @aj191
NOTES: A teammate of Michael Klinger for the Perth Scorchers, Tye was a key component of the team's Big Bash wins in 2015 and 2016. He took 16 wickets in just six games in the 2017/18 edition. Now he is returning for his second T20 stint at Gloucestershire, having taken 18 wickets in 2016. Was due to play for the county in last season's competition but was sidelined with a shoulder injury. A late developer, he made his Australia T20I debut in January 2016 aged 29 and his ODI debut two years later. Has had second XI stints in England with Durham, Northamptonshire and Somerset

Batting	Mat	Inns	NO	Runs	HS	Ave	SR	100	50	Ct	St
ODIs	4	4	2	23	8	11.50	135.29	0	0	1	0
T20Is	12	4	2	4	4	2.00	50.00	0	0	3	0
First-class	9	10	0	52	10	5.20	46.42	0	0	1	0
List A	28	19	8	158	28*	14.36	112.05	0	0	9	0
T20s	70	24	10	197	42	14.07	115.88	0	0	13	0

Bowling	Mat	Balls	Runs	Wkts	BBI	BBM	Ave	Econ	SR	5w	10
ODIs	4	219	169	8	5/46	5/46	21.12	4.63	27.3	1	0
T20Is	12	260	402	16	4/23	4/23	25.12	9.27	16.2	0	0
First-class	9	1699	991	27	3/47	6/159	36.70	3.49	62.9	0	0
List A	28	1409	1235	58	5/46	5/46	21.29	5.25	24.2	2	0
T20s	70	1543	2000	101	5/17	5/17	19.80	7.77	15.2	2	0

ANDY UMEED

RHB / LB / R0 / W0

WARWICKSHIRE

FULL NAME: Andrew Robert Isaac Umeed
BORN: April 19, 1996, Glasgow
SQUAD NO: 23
HEIGHT: 6ft 1in
EDUCATION: The High School of Glasgow
TEAMS: Scotland, Warwickshire
ROLE: Batsman
DEBUT: First-class: 2015

BEST BATTING: 113 Warwickshire vs Lancashire, Edgbaston, 2017
BEST BOWLING: 1-19 Warwickshire vs Lancashire, Old Trafford, 2017

WHAT GOT YOU INTO CRICKET? My father's passion for the game
BEST ADVICE EVER RECEIVED? Play late, play straight
'ROY OF THE ROVERS' MOMENT? Scoring a hundred on my Championship debut against Durham at Edgbaston in 2016
BEST THING ABOUT YOUR HOME GROUND? The food
IF YOU WEREN'T A CRICKETER? I'd be a stunt man
SURPRISING FACT ABOUT YOU? I can juggle
SURPRISING FACT ABOUT A TEAMMATE? Matt Lamb has the largest head in the history of county cricket
WHERE IS PARADISE? Hawaii
CRICKETING HERO? Sachin Tendulkar
NON-CRICKETING HERO? Michael Jordan
TWITTER: @andyumeed

Batting	Mat	Inns	NO	Runs	HS	Ave	SR	100	50	Ct	St
First-class	15	25	1	497	113	20.70	34.92	2	0	13	0

Bowling	Mat	Balls	Runs	Wkts	BBI	BBM	Ave	Econ	SR	5w	10
First-class	15	84	73	2	1/19	1/19	36.50	5.21	42.0	0	0

GRAEME VAN BUUREN

RHB / SLA / RO / WO

FULL NAME: Graeme Lourens van Buuren
BORN: August 22, 1990, Pretoria, South Africa
SQUAD NO: 12
NICKNAME: GVB
EDUCATION: Pretoria Boys High School, South Africa
TEAMS: Gloucestershire, Northerns, Titans
ROLE: Allrounder
DEBUT: First-class: 2010; List A: 2010; T20: 2011

BEST BATTING: 235 Northerns vs Eastern Province, Centurion, 2015
BEST BOWLING: 4-12 Northerns vs South Western Districts, Oudtshoorn, 2013

'ROY OF THE ROVERS' MOMENT? Scoring 172 not out for Gloucestershire in 2016 – my maiden first-class century for the club
HOW WOULD YOUR TEAMMATES DESCRIBE YOU IN THREE WORDS? Energetic, fun, laugh
CRICKETING HEROES? AB de Villiers
NON-CRICKETING HEROES? Novak Djokovic
IF YOU WEREN'T A CRICKETER? I'd be a golfer
UNUSUAL OBJECT AT HOME? A hippopotamus on the dinning-room table
TWITTER: @GraemeGVB

Batting	Mat	Inns	NO	Runs	HS	Ave	SR	100	50	Ct	St
First-class	67	104	17	4021	235	46.21	63.97	10	23	40	0
List A	62	55	11	1309	119*	29.75	81.20	1	6	16	0
T20s	44	34	10	540	64	22.50	108.87	0	3	23	0

Bowling	Mat	Balls	Runs	Wkts	BBI	BBM	Ave	Econ	SR	5w	10
First-class	67	4739	2223	80	4/12	6/87	27.78	2.81	59.2	0	0
List A	62	1872	1457	48	5/35	5/35	30.35	4.66	39.0	1	0
T20s	44	601	632	27	5/8	5/8	23.40	6.30	22.2	1	0

FREDDIE VAN DEN BERGH

RHB / SLA / RO / WO

SURREY

FULL NAME: Freddie Oliver Edward van den Bergh
BORN: June 14, 1992, Bickley, Kent
SQUAD NO: 5
HEIGHT: 6ft 4in
NICKNAME: Vanders, Fruba(e)
EDUCATION: Whitgift School, Croydon; Durham University
TEAMS: Surrey
ROLE: Bowler
DEBUT: First-class: 2011; List A 2014

BEST BATTING: 34 Surrey vs Nottinghamshire, Trent Bridge, 2013
BEST BOWLING: 4-84 Surrey vs Nottinghamshire, Trent Bridge, 2013

WHAT GOT YOU INTO CRICKET? My dad taking me down to the local cricket club
FAMILY TIES? My dad used to work for the ECB
BEST ADVICE EVER RECEIVED? Keep it simple and natural – don't force things
'ROY OF THE ROVERS' MOMENT? Dismissing Shaun Marsh on my Championship debut
BEST THING ABOUT YOUR HOME GROUND? Playing in front of big crowds – the atmosphere is amazing
BEST OPPOSING PLAYER IN COUNTY CRICKET? Jeetan Patel (War)
IF YOU WEREN'T A CRICKETER? Hopefully I'd be putting my university degree to good use in the City
WHERE IS PARADISE? Canada – exploring the great lakes in Ontario and camping in the wilderness
CRICKETING HERO? Andrew Flintoff – watching him in the 2005 Ashes was inspiring
NON-CRICKETING HERO? Tiger Woods – for the way he dominated golf and changed the way the sport was played
TWITTER: @freddievdb15

Batting	Mat	Inns	NO	Runs	HS	Ave	SR	100	50	Ct	St
First-class	7	9	1	62	34	7.75	48.06	0	0	1	0
List A	3	1	1	29	29*	-	107.40	0	0	0	0

Bowling	Mat	Balls	Runs	Wkts	BBI	BBM	Ave	Econ	SR	5w	10
First-class	7	1159	667	15	4/84	5/145	44.46	3.45	77.2	0	0
List A	3	156	122	0	-	-	-	4.69	-	0	0

TIMM VAN DER GUGTEN   RHB / RFM / RO / W1

FULL NAME: Timm van der Gugten
BORN: February 25, 1991, Sydney, Australia
SQUAD NO: 64
HEIGHT: 6ft 1in
NICKNAME: Sock, Bull
EDUCATION: St Pius X College, Sydney;
Swinburn University
TEAMS: Netherlands, Glamorgan, Hobart
Hurricanes, New South Wales, Northern
Districts, Tasmania
ROLE: Bowler
DEBUT: ODI: 2012; T20I: 2012; First-class:
2011; List A: 2011; T20: 2012

GLAMORGAN

BEST BATTING: 57 Netherlands vs Papua New Guinea, Amstelveen, 2015
BEST BOWLING: 7-68 Netherlands vs Namibia, Windhoek, 2013

WHAT GOT YOU INTO CRICKET? My uncle was a good cricketer, and I fell in love with the game playing in the backyard with him and my cousins
BEST THING ABOUT YOUR HOME GROUND? Everything about it: the crowd, the facilities, the people who make it run the way it does, the city
BEST OPPOSING PLAYER IN COUNTY CRICKET? Chris Nash (Not)
YOUNG OPPOSING PLAYER WHO HAS IMPRESSED YOU? Jofra Archer (Sus)
IF YOU WEREN'T A CRICKETER? I'd be living out of a suitcase
SURPRISING FACT ABOUT YOU? I'm quite superstitious about cricket
SURPRISING FACT ABOUT A TEAMMATE? Andrew Salter can do the Keith Lemon dance
WHERE IS PARADISE? On a beach with no phone signal
CRICKETING HERO? Brett Lee – serious athlete and very competitive

Batting	Mat	Inns	NO	Runs	HS	Ave	SR	100	50	Ct	St
ODIs	4	2	0	4	2	2.00	66.66	0	0	0	0
T20Is	25	7	3	45	12*	11.25	102.27	0	0	2	0
First-class	25	34	6	300	57	10.71	42.43	0	1	4	0
List A	41	21	7	246	36	17.57	90.10	0	0	5	0
T20s	61	21	6	111	16	7.40	101.83	0	0	9	0

Bowling	Mat	Balls	Runs	Wkts	BBI	BBM	Ave	Econ	SR	5w	10
ODIs	4	126	85	8	5/24	5/24	10.62	4.04	15.7	1	0
T20Is	25	455	529	25	3/18	3/18	21.16	6.97	18.2	0	0
First-class	25	4615	2463	95	7/68	10/121	25.92	3.20	48.5	8	1
List A	41	1827	1691	52	5/24	5/24	32.51	5.55	35.1	1	0
T20s	61	1081	1336	66	5/21	5/21	20.24	7.41	16.3	1	0

ROELOF VAN DER MERWE RHB/SLA/R0/W0/MVP60

SOMERSET

FULL NAME: Roelof Erasmus van der Merwe
BORN: December 31, 1984, Johannesburg, South Africa
SQUAD NO: 52
HEIGHT: 5ft 8in
NICKNAME: Roela
EDUCATION: Pretoria High School
TEAMS: Netherlands, South Africa, Somerset, Brisbane Heat, Delhi Daredevils, Northerns, RC Bangalore, St Lucia Zouks, Titans
ROLE: Allrounder
DEBUT: ODI: 2009; T20I: 2009; First-class: 2006; List A: 2006; T20: 2008

BEST BATTING: 205* Titans vs Warriors, Benoni, 2014
BEST BOWLING: 4-22 Somerset vs Middlesex, Taunton, 2017

BEST ADVICE EVER RECEIVED? There are no fielders in the air
'ROY OF THE ROVERS' MOMENT? My debut for South Africa on my home ground, Centurion
BEST THING ABOUT YOUR HOME GROUND? The Somerset fans. And the fridge in the dressing room
IF YOU WEREN'T A CRICKETER? I'd be a caravan salesman
SURPRISING FACT ABOUT YOU? I hate vegetables
SURPRISING FACT ABOUT A TEAMMATE? Max Waller loves losing to me
CRICKETING HERO? Jonty Rhodes – electrifying fielder and batter
NON-CRICKETING HERO? Usain Bolt
TWITTER: @Roela52

Batting	Mat	Inns	NO	Runs	HS	Ave	SR	100	50	Ct	St
ODIs	13	7	3	39	12	9.75	95.12	0	0	3	0
T20Is	24	15	6	174	48	19.33	131.81	0	0	12	0
First-class	62	101	14	3053	205*	35.09	70.11	6	18	46	0
List A	159	129	40	2359	165*	26.50	101.50	1	8	60	0
T20s	172	129	35	1954	89*	20.78	130.00	0	8	68	0

Bowling	Mat	Balls	Runs	Wkts	BBI	BBM	Ave	Econ	SR	5w	10
ODIs	13	705	561	17	3/27	3/27	33.00	4.77	41.4	0	0
T20Is	24	480	546	29	2/3	2/3	18.82	6.82	16.5	0	0
First-class	62	8432	4199	118	4/22	8/104	35.58	2.98	71.4	0	0
List A	159	7035	5653	214	5/26	5/26	26.41	4.82	32.8	4	0
T20s	172	3324	3926	160	3/13	3/13	24.53	7.08	20.7	0	0

PAUL VAN MEEKEREN

RHB / RFM / RO / WO

FULL NAME: Paul Adriaan van Meekeren
BORN: January 15, 1993, Amsterdam, Netherlands
SQUAD NO: 47
HEIGHT: 6ft 4in
NICKNAME: Meerkat, Smacky, Meeks
TEAMS: Netherlands, Somerset
ROLE: Bowler
DEBUT: ODI: 2013; T20I: 2013; First-class: 2013; List A: 2013; T20: 2013

BEST BATTING: 34 Netherlands vs Papua New Guinea, Amstelveen, 2015
BEST BOWLING: 4-60 Somerset vs Essex, Chelmsford, 2017

WHAT GOT YOU INTO CRICKET? My dad dragged me around to the cricket every weekend, made me watch all the old men play. I was convinced I was better than them
BEST ADVICE EVER RECEIVED? Control the controllable
'ROY OF THE ROVERS' MOMENT? Taking 4-11 against Ireland at the 2016 World Twenty20
IF YOU WEREN'T A CRICKETER? I'd be Superman
SURPRISING FACT ABOUT YOU? I'm single (that was my brother's immediate response)
WHERE IS PARADISE? Amsterdam
CRICKETING HEROES? The first-team players at my club in Holland. It was hard to watch cricket at home, so I always looked up to those guys
NON-CRICKETING HERO? Dennis Bergkamp
TWITTER: @paulvanmeekeren

Batting	Mat	Inns	NO	Runs	HS	Ave	SR	100	50	Ct	St
ODIs	2	1	1	15	15*	-	88.23	0	0	0	0
T20Is	18	4	0	21	18	5.25	110.52	0	0	4	0
First-class	7	12	2	100	34	10.00	33.89	0	0	2	0
List A	34	18	7	72	15*	6.54	58.53	0	0	8	0
T20s	32	12	3	39	18	4.33	97.50	0	0	11	0

Bowling	Mat	Balls	Runs	Wkts	BBI	BBM	Ave	Econ	SR	5w	10
ODIs	2	66	79	1	1/54	1/54	79.00	7.18	66.0	0	0
T20Is	18	324	330	18	4/11	4/11	18.33	6.11	18.0	0	0
First-class	7	1226	718	20	4/60	5/75	35.90	3.51	61.3	0	0
List A	34	1162	960	33	3/21	3/21	29.09	4.95	35.2	0	0
T20s	32	560	681	23	4/11	4/11	29.60	7.29	24.3	0	0

STIAAN VAN ZYL

LHB / RM / R1 / W0 / MVP70

SUSSEX

FULL NAME: Stiaan van Zyl
BORN: September 19, 1987, Cape Town, South Africa
SQUAD NO: 74
HEIGHT: 5ft 11in
NICKNAME: Stigo
EDUCATION: Kenridge Primary School, Western Cape; Boland Agricultural School
TEAMS: South Africa, Sussex, Boland, Cape Cobras, Western Province
ROLE: Allrounder
DEBUT: Test: 2014; First-class: 2006; List A: 2006; T20: 2008

BEST BATTING: 228 Cape Cobras vs Lions, Paarl, 2018
BEST BOWLING: 5-32 Boland vs Northerns, Paarl, 2011

BEST ADVICE EVER RECEIVED? Play with a smile on your face
'ROY OF THE ROVERS' MOMENT? Making 101 not out on my Test debut for South Africa against West Indies at Centurion in 2014
BEST THING ABOUT YOUR HOME GROUND? The crowd – they come even in terrible weather
BEST OPPOSING PLAYER IN COUNTY CRICKET? Darren Stevens (Ken)
YOUNG OPPOSING PLAYER WHO HAS IMPRESSED YOU? Joe Clarke (Wor)
IF YOU WEREN'T A CRICKETER? I'd be a pilot
SURPRISING FACT ABOUT A TEAMMATE? Can't name him, but there is a player who won't enjoy a beer with the lads because he wants to look good for his wife
WHERE IS PARADISE? Cape Town
CRICKETING HERO? Kumar Sangakkara – a legend and a leftie
TWITTER: @laggies74

Batting	Mat	Inns	NO	Runs	HS	Ave	SR	100	50	Ct	St
Tests	12	17	2	395	101*	26.33	50.77	1	0	6	0
First-class	154	257	37	9715	228	44.15	52.08	24	43	92	0
List A	116	106	12	3350	114*	35.63	74.76	5	18	32	0
T20s	68	61	7	1434	86*	26.55	119.59	0	9	20	0
Bowling	Mat	Balls	Runs	Wkts	BBI	BBM	Ave	Econ	SR	5w	10
Tests	12	403	148	6	3/20	3/22	24.66	2.20	67.1	0	0
First-class	154	5114	2346	63	5/32	7/82	37.23	2.75	81.1	1	0
List A	116	1056	927	20	4/24	4/24	46.35	5.26	52.8	0	0
T20s	68	120	160	7	2/14	2/14	22.85	8.00	17.1	0	0

RICARDO VASCONCELOS

LHB / WK / R0 / W0

FULL NAME: Ricardo Vasconcelos
BORN: October 27, 1997, Johannesburg, South Africa
SQUAD NO: TBC
TEAMS: Boland
ROLE: Wicketkeeper/batsman
DEBUT: First-class: 2016; List A: 2016; T20: 2017

BEST BATTING: 140 Boland vs Namibia, Windhoek, 2017

NOTES: Northamptonshire signed South African wicketkeeper Ricardo Vasconcelos shortly before the start of the new season. As a Portuguese passport-holder, he qualifies as a domestic player and will act as cover for first-choice keeper Adam Rossington. "I am looking forward to working with and learning from some of the more experienced players so that I can accelerate my growth as a player as quickly as possible," said Vasconcelos. The 20-year-old made his debut for Boland in 2016 and is a more than capable left-handed batsman, having registered two hundreds in 11 first-class matches before he joined Northants. "He's a young, hungry cricketer who's able to provide wicketkeeper cover and push the guys for batting spots," said Northants head coach David Ripley

Batting	Mat	Inns	NO	Runs	HS	Ave	SR	100	50	Ct	St
First-class	11	21	2	644	140	33.89	62.28	2	4	13	3
List A	16	16	0	409	56	25.56	73.16	0	2	14	2
T20s	2	2	2	53	45*	-	155.88	0	0	4	0

Bowling	Mat	Balls	Runs	Wkts	BBI	BBM	Ave	Econ	SR	5w	10
First-class	11	-	-	-	-	-	-	-	-	-	-
List A	16	-	-	-	-	-	-	-	-	-	-
T20s	2	-	-	-	-	-	-	-	-	-	-

DANE VILAS

RHB / WK / R0 / W0 / MVP75

FULL NAME: Dane James Vilas
BORN: June 10, 1985, Johannesburg, South Africa
SQUAD NO: 33
HEIGHT: 6ft
NICKNAME: Vili
EDUCATION: King Edward VII School, Johannesburg
TEAMS: South Africa, Lancashire, Cape Cobras, Dolphins, Gauteng, Lions, South Western Districts, Western Province
ROLE: Wicketkeeper/batsman
DEBUT: Test: 2015; T20I: 2012; First-class: 2006; List A: 2006; T20: 2009

BEST BATTING: 244 Lancashire vs Hampshire, Old Trafford, 2017

TWITTER: @DaneVilas

NOTES: The former Test wicketkeeper was another South African cricketer to announce his international retirement in early 2017 to take up a two-year Kolpak deal with Lancashire to play across all formats. The highlights of his first season at Old Trafford were a career-best 244 against Hampshire in the Championship and a brace of hundreds in the One-Day Cup. He appeared in every game across all three formats. The last of his six Tests came against England in 2016, with his final innings ended by James Taylor's miraculous catch at short-leg. The emergence of Quinton de Kock had pushed him down the pecking order

Batting	Mat	Inns	NO	Runs	HS	Ave	SR	100	50	Ct	St
Tests	6	9	0	94	26	10.44	44.76	0	0	13	0
T20Is	1	-	-	-	-	-	-	-	-	0	0
First-class	120	185	23	6451	244	39.82	66.83	15	30	310	15
List A	142	132	20	3964	120	35.39	97.18	8	18	146	24
T20s	105	88	20	2076	71*	30.52	124.46	0	11	55	17

Bowling	Mat	Balls	Runs	Wkts	BBI	BBM	Ave	Econ	SR	5w	10
Tests	6	-	-	-	-	-	-	-	-	-	-
T20Is	1	-	-	-	-	-	-	-	-	-	-
First-class	120	6	3	0	-	-	-	3.00	-	0	0
List A	142	-	-	-	-	-	-	-	-	-	-
T20s	105	-	-	-	-	-	-	-	-	-	-

HARDUS VILJOEN

RHB / RF / RO / WO

FULL NAME: GC Viljoen
BORN: March 6, 1989, Witbank, South Africa
SQUAD NO: 7
HEIGHT: 6ft 2in
NICKNAME: H'ie, H
EDUCATION: Waterkloof High School, Pretoria, South Africa
TEAMS: South Africa, Derbyshire, Easterns, Kent, Lions, Multan Sultans, Titans
ROLE: Bowler
DEBUT: Test: 2016; First-class: 2008; List A: 2009; T20: 2011

BEST BATTING: 72 Lions vs Titans, Centurion, 2016
BEST BOWLING: 8-90 Derbyshire vs Sussex, Hove, 2017

BEST ADVICE EVER RECEIVED? Do what got you to where you are – don't change to please people
ROY OF THE ROVERS' MOMENT? Taking 15 wickets at Hove in 2017
BEST THING ABOUT YOUR HOME GROUND? Our beloved fans – they always get behind us whether we are losing or winning
IF YOU WEREN'T A CRICKETER? I'd be a lawyer. Or a Navy Seal
SURPRISING FACT ABOUT YOU? I love big, fast cars. Anyone feel like sponsoring a Nissan GT-R?
CRICKETING HERO? I look up to Andrew Flintoff and Malcolm Marshall – I have a similar action to both of them. They never backed down
NON-CRICKETING HERO? Tiger Woods – as a non-white golfer, he faced some considerable challenges early in his career and went on to dominate the game for so long
TWITTER: @Hardus_Vijl

Batting	Mat	Inns	NO	Runs	HS	Ave	SR	100	50	Ct	St
Tests	1	2	1	26	20*	26.00	83.87	0	0	0	0
First-class	101	138	17	1713	72	14.15	56.79	0	6	30	0
List A	85	52	18	573	54*	16.85	82.68	0	2	19	0
T20s	76	39	21	318	41*	17.66	121.37	0	0	17	0

Bowling	Mat	Balls	Runs	Wkts	BBI	BBM	Ave	Econ	SR	5w	10
Tests	1	114	94	1	1/79	1/94	94.00	4.94	114.0	0	0
First-class	101	17610	10528	400	8/90	15/170	26.32	3.58	44.0	25	5
List A	85	3894	3838	123	6/19	6/19	31.20	5.91	31.6	1	0
T20s	76	1628	2107	83	5/16	5/16	25.38	7.76	19.6	1	0

JAMES VINCE

RHB / RM / R2 / W0 / MVP18

HAMPSHIRE

FULL NAME: James Michael Vince
BORN: March 14, 1991, Cuckfield, Sussex
SQUAD NO: 14
HEIGHT: 6ft 2in
NICKNAME: Vincey
EDUCATION: Warminster School, Wiltshire
TEAMS: England, Hampshire, Karachi Kings, Sydney Thunder
ROLE: Batsman
DEBUT: Test: 2016; ODI: 2015; T20I: 2015; First-class: 2009; List A: 2009; T20: 2010

BEST BATTING: 240 Hampshire vs Essex, Southampton, 2014
BEST BOWLING: 5-41 Hampshire vs Loughborough MCCU, Southampton, 2013
COUNTY CAP: 2013

WHAT GOT YOU INTO CRICKET? Kwik Cricket day at school
STRANGEST THING SEEN IN A GAME? James Tomlinson taking a one-handed diving catch while eating a banana at fine-leg
'ROY OF THE ROVERS' MOMENT? Winning the Lord's one-day final in 2012
SUPERSTITIONS? Don't eat duck, calamari or onion rings the day before a game (blame Neil McKenzie)
CRICKETING HEROES? Growing up I used to love watching Andrew Flintoff. More recently, AB de Villiers – he's the best player across all three formats
TWITTER: @vincey14

Batting	Mat	Inns	NO	Runs	HS	Ave	SR	100	50	Ct	St
Tests	12	20	0	454	83	22.70	48.76	0	2	6	0
ODIs	5	4	0	104	51	26.00	84.55	0	1	4	0
T20Is	7	7	0	194	46	27.71	117.57	0	0	0	0
First-class	140	231	18	8132	240	38.17	62.17	20	32	126	0
List A	112	104	7	3651	178	37.63	95.35	6	18	38	0
T20s	142	137	13	3716	107*	29.96	132.28	1	24	77	0

Bowling	Mat	Balls	Runs	Wkts	BBI	BBM	Ave	Econ	SR	5w	10
Tests	12	24	13	0	-	-	-	3.25	-	0	0
ODIs	5	-	-	-	-	-	-	-	-	-	-
T20Is	7	-	-	-	-	-	-	-	-	-	-
First-class	140	1603	997	22	5/41	6/56	45.31	3.73	72.8	1	0
List A	112	84	84	1	1/18	1/18	84.00	6.00	84.0	0	0
T20s	142	72	81	3	1/5	1/5	27.00	6.75	24.0	0	0

AMAR VIRDI

RHB / OB / R0 / W0

FULL NAME: Guramar Singh Virdi
BORN: July 19, 1998, Chiswick, Middlesex
SQUAD NO: 19
HEIGHT: 5ft 10in
NICKNAME: Virds
EDUCATION: Guru Nanak Sikh Academy, Middlesex
TEAMS: Surrey
ROLE: Bowler
DEBUT: First-class: 2017

SURREY

BEST BATTING: 8* Surrey vs Essex, Chelmsford, 2017
BEST BOWLING: 3-82 Surrey vs Essex, Chelmsford, 2017

WHAT GOT YOU INTO CRICKET? My brother
BEST ADVICE EVER RECEIVED? Treat everyone the way you wish to be treated
'ROY OF THE ROVERS' MOMENT? Making my first-team debut for Surrey and my five-for on debut for England U19 against Sri Lanka U19
BEST THING ABOUT YOUR HOME GROUND? The Oval is just the best place to play in the whole world
YOUNG OPPOSING PLAYER WHO HAS IMPRESSED YOU? Dan Lawrence (Ess) – he plays very freely and is tough to bowl at
IF YOU WEREN'T A CRICKETER? I'd be a businessman
SURPRISING FACT ABOUT YOU? I have the longest beard of any 19-year-old who is playing county cricket
WHERE IS PARADISE? Cape Town
CRICKETING HERO? Saqlain Mushtaq – he changed the world of spin bowling and was the best spinner to watch
NON-CRICKETING HERO? My dad – he taught me how to get through hard times
UNUSUAL OBJECT AT HOME? A dartboard
TWITTER: @amarsinghvirdi

Batting	Mat	Inns	NO	Runs	HS	Ave	SR	100	50	Ct	St
First-class	3	4	1	18	8*	6.00	40.90	0	0	0	0

Bowling	Mat	Balls	Runs	Wkts	BBI	BBM	Ave	Econ	SR	5w	10
First-class	3	528	271	6	3/82	3/82	45.16	3.07	88.0	0	0

GARETH WADE

RHB / RMF / R0 / W0

NORTHAMPTONSHIRE

FULL NAME: Gareth Wade
BORN: January 11, 1991, Hexham, Northumberland
SQUAD NO: 9
HEIGHT: 6ft 2in
NICKNAME: Gwade, Wadey
EDUCATION: Prudhoe Community High School, Northumberland; Sunderland University
TEAMS: Northamptonshire
ROLE: Bowler
DEBUT: First-class: 2017

BEST BOWLING: 1-100 Northamptonshire vs Loughborough MCCU, Northampton, 2017

WHAT GOT YOU INTO CRICKET? It was a good way to meet people
BEST ADVICE EVER RECEIVED? You'll never make it
'ROY OF THE ROVERS' MOMENT? Playing at Trent Bridge
BEST OPPOSING PLAYER IN COUNTY CRICKET? Ben Stokes (Dur)
YOUNG OPPOSING PLAYER WHO HAS IMPRESSED YOU? Max Holden (Mid) – a thing of beauty
IF YOU WEREN'T A CRICKETER? I'd be a skydiving instructor or a policeman living in Australia or New Zealand
SURPRISING FACT ABOUT YOU? I won the community award in the Northamptonshire CCC awards at the end of last season. My first Minor Counties season was in 2015 for Northumberland under Geoff Cook, Stewart Tiffin and Jacques du Toit
SURPRISING FACT ABOUT A TEAMMATE? Steven Crook starred in Harry Potter as the Sorting Hat
WHERE IS PARADISE? Queenstown, New Zealand
CRICKETING HERO? Mitchell Johnson – he doesn't care how good you are or who you are: he will back himself 100% to win the battle
NON-CRICKETING HERO? My family – they have backed me 100% all the time. And Alan Shearer
TWITTER: @gareth_wade

Batting	Mat	Inns	NO	Runs	HS	Ave	SR	100	50	Ct	St
First-class	1	-	-	-	-	-	-	-	-	0	0

Bowling	Mat	Balls	Runs	Wkts	BBI	BBM	Ave	Econ	SR	5w	10
First-class	1	108	100	1	1/100	1/100	100.00	5.55	108.0	0	0

GRAHAM WAGG

RHB / LM / R0 / W2

FULL NAME: Graham Grant Wagg
BORN: April 28, 1983, Rugby, Warwickshire
SQUAD NO: 8
HEIGHT: 6ft
NICKNAME: Waggy
EDUCATION: Ashlawn School, Rugby
TEAMS: Glamorgan, Derbyshire, Warwickshire
ROLE: Allrounder
DEBUT: First-class: 2002; List A: 2000; T20: 2003

GLAMORGAN

BEST BATTING: 200 Glamorgan vs Surrey, Guildford, 2015
BEST BOWLING: 6-29 Glamorgan vs Surrey, The Oval, 2014
COUNTY CAP: 2007 (Derbyshire); 2013 (Glamorgan)

FAMILY TIES? My dad played second XI cricket, Minor Counties and a good standard of Premier League cricket – he could bowl a heavy ball and hit a long ball. My little man Brayden Wagg is just learning, so watch out for his name
'ROY OF THE ROVERS' MOMENT? Getting my first contract at Warwickshire and playing for England Schools in all the age groups
CRICKETING HEROES? Ian Botham, Allan Donald, Viv Richards
IF YOU WEREN'T A CRICKETER? I'd be a full-time dad
SURPRISING FACT? I'm a dark horse on the snooker table
TWITTER: @GGWagg

Batting	Mat	Inns	NO	Runs	HS	Ave	SR	100	50	Ct	St
First-class	147	216	22	5284	200	27.23	65.16	4	31	49	0
List A	124	102	15	1643	62*	18.88		0	3	42	0
T20s	116	87	29	1144	62	19.72	123.54	0	3	33	0

Bowling	Mat	Balls	Runs	Wkts	BBI	BBM	Ave	Econ	SR	5w	10
First-class	147	25244	14717	429	6/29	10/133	34.30	3.49	58.8	12	1
List A	124	4760	4706	138	4/35	4/35	34.10	5.93	34.4	0	0
T20s	116	1954	2710	107	5/14	5/14	25.32	8.32	18.2	1	0

ESSEX

FULL NAME: Neil Wagner
BORN: March 13, 1986, Pretoria, South Africa
SQUAD NO: 13
HEIGHT: 5ft 9in
NICKNAME: Wags
EDUCATION: Afrikaans Boys High School,
Pretoria, South Africa
TEAMS: New Zealand, Essex, Lancashire,
Northerns, Otago
ROLE: Bowler
DEBUT: Test: 2012; First-class: 2006; List A:
2006; T20: 2009

BEST BATTING: 70 Otago vs Wellington, Queenstown, 2009
BEST BOWLING: 7-39 New Zealand vs West Indies, Wellington, 2017

WHAT GOT YOU INTO CRICKET? Playing with family and friends in the backyard
STRANGEST THING SEEN IN A GAME? My run-out against Bangladesh at Christchurch in
2017. I grounded my bat in time and was well inside the crease, but was given out because
my whole body and bat were in mid-air when the bails came off
'ROY OF THE ROVERS' MOMENT? Taking five wickets in one over for Otago against
Wellington in 2011
YOUNG OPPOSING PLAYER WHO HAS IMPRESSED YOU? Liam Livingstone (Lan)
CRICKETING HEROES? Allan Donald, Brett Lee, Brian Lara, Jacques Kallis, Shane Bond
NON-CRICKETING HEROES? Richie McCaw, Dan Carter, Usain Bolt
IF YOU WEREN'T A CRICKETER? I'd be a rugby player
SURPRISING FACT? I play golf right-handed
TWITTER: @NeilWagner13

Batting	Mat	Inns	NO	Runs	HS	Ave	SR	100	50	Ct	St
Tests	34	44	11	402	37	12.18	42.72	0	0	8	0
First-class	146	194	41	2542	70	16.61	51.35	0	7	40	0
List A	96	52	10	499	42	11.88	80.09	0	0	15	0
T20s	68	32	12	143	14	7.15	111.71	0	0	11	0

Bowling	Mat	Balls	Runs	Wkts	BBI	BBM	Ave	Econ	SR	5w	10
Tests	34	7445	4014	144	7/39	9/141	27.87	3.23	51.7	5	0
First-class	146	29960	16307	607	7/39	11/111	26.86	3.26	49.3	29	2
List A	96	4634	4148	151	5/34	5/34	27.47	5.37	30.6	2	0
T20s	68	1370	1999	73	4/33	4/33	27.38	8.75	18.7	0	0

JAMES WAINMAN   RHB / LM / R0 / W0

FULL NAME: James Charles Wainman
BORN: January 25, 1993, Harrogate, Yorkshire
SQUAD NO: 15
HEIGHT: 6ft 4in
NICKNAME: Wainers
EDUCATION: Leeds Grammar School
TEAMS: Yorkshire
ROLE: Bowler
DEBUT: List A: 2014; T20: 2016

FAMILY TIES? My dad played a good standard of club cricket and coached me as a junior
'ROY OF THE ROVERS' MOMENT? My first List A game against Sri Lanka A, taking 3-51 and scoring 33 runs
CRICKETING HERO? Glenn McGrath
NON-CRICKETING HERO? Leonardo DiCaprio
TWITTER: @jcwainman
NOTES: Left-arm seamer with a reputation for putting a squeeze on the run-rate. Claimed 42 wickets from 24 appearances in all forms of second XI cricket in 2016, including two five-wicket hauls in the three-day Championship. Made his List A debut in 2014 and played two matches in the 2016 T20 Blast but did not feature in any format last season

Batting	Mat	Inns	NO	Runs	HS	Ave	SR	100	50	Ct	St
List A	1	1	0	33	33	33.00	122.22	0	0	1	0
T20s	2	1	1	12	12*	-	100.00	0	0	0	0

Bowling	Mat	Balls	Runs	Wkts	BBI	BBM	Ave	Econ	SR	5w	10
List A	1	48	51	3	3/51	3/51	17.00	6.37	16.0	0	0
T20s	2	30	49	1	1/27	1/27	49.00	9.80	30.0	0	0

MATTHEW WAITE

RHB / RFM / R0 / W0

YORKSHIRE

FULL NAME: Matthew James Waite
BORN: December 24, 1995, Leeds
SQUAD NO: 6
NICKNAME: Pingu
EDUCATION: Brigshaw High School, West Yorkshire
TEAMS: Yorkshire
ROLE: Allrounder
DEBUT: First-class: 2017; List A: 2014; T20: 2015

BEST BATTING: 18 Yorkshire vs Somerset, Taunton, 2017
BEST BOWLING: 2-41 Yorkshire vs Somerset, Taunton, 2017

TWITTER: @mat_waite

NOTES: A seam-bowling allrounder, Waite signed a two-year junior professional contract with Yorkshire at the end of 2015. He made his senior debut in the One-Day Cup in 2014, and played his first T20 Blast game the following year. In 2016 he made two appearances for Yorkshire in white-ball cricket, impressing on both occasions. He hit 19* and took 1-6 from two overs in the T20 quarter-final against Glamorgan at Cardiff, and then 38 and 3-48 from 10 overs in the One-Day Cup semi-final against Surrey at Headingley. Made his Championship debut against Somerset at Taunton last summer, and took 10 wickets in seven 50-over games as well as scoring a fifty

Batting	Mat	Inns	NO	Runs	HS	Ave	SR	100	50	Ct	St
First-class	1	2	0	22	18	11.00	41.50	0	0	0	0
List A	11	9	2	246	71	35.14	90.44	0	1	0	0
T20s	5	3	3	34	19*	-	147.82	0	0	3	0

Bowling	Mat	Balls	Runs	Wkts	BBI	BBM	Ave	Econ	SR	5w	10
First-class	1	96	70	3	2/41	3/70	23.33	4.37	32.0	0	0
List A	11	411	424	13	4/65	4/65	32.61	6.18	31.6	0	0
T20s	5	48	67	2	1/6	1/6	33.50	8.37	24.0	0	0

ALEX WAKELY

RHB / RM / R0 / W0 / MVP82

FULL NAME: Alex George Wakely
BORN: November 3, 1988, London
SQUAD NO: 8
HEIGHT: 6ft 2in
NICKNAME: Wakers, Baby Seal
EDUCATION: Bedford School
TEAMS: Northamptonshire
ROLE: Batsman
DEBUT: First-class: 2007; List A: 2005; T20: 2009

BEST BATTING: 123 Northamptonshire vs Leicestershire, Northampton, 2015
BEST BOWLING: 2-62 Northamptonshire vs Somerset, Taunton, 2007
COUNTY CAP: 2012

WHAT GOT YOU INTO CRICKET? My grandad made me a bat when I was five. Then watching my dad play for Ampthill Town CC for many years
'ROY OF THE ROVERS' MOMENT? Winning the T20 Cup in 2013
BEST THING ABOUT YOUR HOME GROUND? It's my hometown and I am proud to be associated with Northampton
BEST OPPOSING PLAYER IN COUNTY CRICKET? Joe Leach (Wor)
YOUNG OPPOSING PLAYER WHO HAS IMPRESSED YOU? Max Holden (Mid) – mature beyond his years and a great kid
SURPRISING FACT ABOUT YOU? I play the piano
WHERE IS PARADISE? Anywhere with my family
CRICKETING HERO? David Sales – he was captain when I made my debut and took me under his wing. Best batsman I have watched
UNUSUAL OBJECT AT HOME? A gekko
TWITTER: @AlexWakely1

Batting	Mat	Inns	NO	Runs	HS	Ave	SR	100	50	Ct	St
First-class	122	195	14	5717	123	31.58	47.58	7	31	80	0
List A	73	69	8	1911	109*	31.32	84.78	2	12	24	0
T20s	100	93	19	2026	64	27.37	119.17	0	12	33	0

Bowling	Mat	Balls	Runs	Wkts	BBI	BBM	Ave	Econ	SR	5w	10
First-class	122	509	426	6	2/62	2/62	71.00	5.02	84.8	0	0
List A	73	136	131	5	2/14	2/14	26.20	5.77	27.2	0	0
T20s	100	12	29	0	-	-	-	14.50	-	0	0

MAX WALLER

RHB / LB / RO / WO

SOMERSET

FULL NAME: Maximilian Thomas Charles Waller
BORN: March 3, 1988, Salisbury, Wiltshire
SQUAD NO: 10
HEIGHT: 6ft
NICKNAME: Goose, Jun Jun, Maxy
EDUCATION: Millfield School, Somerset; Bournemouth University
TEAMS: Somerset
ROLE: Bowler
DEBUT: First-class: 2009; List A: 2009; T20: 2009

BEST BATTING: 28 Somerset vs Hampshire, Southampton, 2009
BEST BOWLING: 3-33 Somerset vs Cambridge MCCU, Taunton, 2012

WHAT GOT YOU INTO CRICKET? My grandad took me to cricket camps at Lord's
BEST ADVICE EVER RECEIVED? Nothing good comes easy
BEST THING ABOUT YOUR HOME GROUND? The atmosphere and the knowledgeable crowd
YOUNG OPPOSING PLAYER WHO HAS IMPRESSED YOU? Jofra Archer (Sus) – bowls quick and whacks it!
IF YOU WEREN'T A CRICKETER? I'd be an artist
SURPRISING FACT ABOUT YOU? I've sold paintings in an art shop
SURPRISING FACT ABOUT A TEAMMATE? Lewis Gregory is a black belt in judo but couldn't hurt a fly
WHERE IS PARADISE? Barbados
CRICKETING HERO? Shane Warne – the greatest-ever bowler and fun to watch
NON-CRICKETING HERO? Tiger Woods – he changed the game of golf
UNUSUAL OBJECT AT HOME? An ostrich egg-shell lamp
TWITTER: @MaxTCWaller – if you're not following me, why not?!

Batting	Mat	Inns	NO	Runs	HS	Ave	SR	100	50	Ct	St
First-class	8	9	1	91	28	11.37	42.92	0	0	5	0
List A	54	20	14	97	25*	16.16	69.78	0	0	25	0
T20s	95	28	18	79	17	7.90	74.52	0	0	52	0

Bowling	Mat	Balls	Runs	Wkts	BBI	BBM	Ave	Econ	SR	5w	10
First-class	8	840	493	10	3/33	3/57	49.30	3.52	84.0	0	0
List A	54	1711	1598	42	3/37	3/37	38.04	5.60	40.7	0	0
T20s	95	1767	2187	95	4/16	4/16	23.02	7.42	18.6	0	0

PAUL WALTER

LHB / LFM / R0 / W0

FULL NAME: Paul Ian Walter
BORN: May 28, 1994, Basildon, Essex
SQUAD NO: 22
HEIGHT: 6ft 7in
EDUCATION: Billericay School, Essex
TEAMS: Essex
ROLE: Allrounder
DEBUT: First-class: 2016; List A: 2017; T20: 2016

ESSEX

BEST BATTING: 68* Essex vs West Indians, Chelmsford, 2017
BEST BOWLING: 3-44 Essex vs Derbyshire, Derby, 2016

TWITTER: @PWalter_22
NOTES: Walter signed a professional contract with his hometown club midway through the 2016 season after impressing in club cricket for Hornchurch and for Essex Second XI. An allrounder with Premier League hundreds under his belt allied to a series of thrusting spells of high-quality pace bowling, Walter offers Essex options, especially in one-day cricket. At 6ft 7in, he brings considerable physical presence to the Essex attack. Played five Championship matches in the second half of last season as Essex romped to the Championship title, and took 15 wickets in 13 games in the T20 Blast

Batting	Mat	Inns	NO	Runs	HS	Ave	SR	100	50	Ct	St
First-class	8	8	3	219	68*	43.80	56.01	0	1	0	0
List A	4	2	2	15	11*	-	166.66	0	0	2	0
T20s	20	13	8	107	20*	21.40	128.91	0	0	6	0

Bowling	Mat	Balls	Runs	Wkts	BBI	BBM	Ave	Econ	SR	5w	10
First-class	8	858	501	11	3/44	4/68	45.54	3.50	78.0	0	0
List A	4	160	155	7	4/37	4/37	22.14	5.81	22.8	0	0
T20s	20	372	584	19	3/24	3/24	30.73	9.41	19.5	0	0

JARED WARNER RHB / RFM / RO / WO

FULL NAME: Jared David Warner
BORN: November 14, 1996, Wakefield, Yorkshire
SQUAD NO: 45
HEIGHT: 6ft 1in
NICKNAME: Jazz
EDUCATION: Silcoates School, West Yorkshire; Kettlethorpe High School, Wakefield
TEAMS: Yorkshire, England U19
ROLE: Bowler

WHAT GOT YOU INTO CRICKET? Wakefield Thornes CC
BEST ADVICE EVER RECEIVED? Have no fear
'ROY OF THE ROVERS' MOMENT? Winning the double with Yorkshire Academy. Taking figures of 9-19 from 10.2 overs for Yorkshire Academy against Castleford in a Yorkshire Premier League North match in 2016. Representing England U19
BEST THING ABOUT YOUR HOME GROUND? It has a great atmosphere
BEST OPPOSING PLAYER IN COUNTY CRICKET? Jamie Porter (Ess)
YOUNG OPPOSING PLAYER WHO HAS IMPRESSED YOU? Sam Curran (Sur) – he has great skills and a lot of confidence
IF YOU WEREN'T A CRICKETER? I'd be involved in sport in some capacity
SURPRISING FACT ABOUT YOU? I'm a big Sheffield United fan
WHERE IS PARADISE? Top of the Kop at Bramall Lane
CRICKETING HERO? Andrew Flintoff – my first memories of watching cricket are of him winning the Ashes in 2005
NON-CRICKETING HERO? Michael Owen – he got me into football
TWITTER: @JaredWarner96

JOE WEATHERLEY

RHB / OB / RO / WO

FULL NAME: Joe James Weatherley
BORN: January 19, 1997, Winchester, Hampshire
SQUAD NO: 5
HEIGHT: 6ft 2in
NICKNAME: Lord, Weathers
EDUCATION: King Edward VI School, Southampton
TEAMS: Hampshire, Kent
ROLE: Batsman
DEBUT: First-class: 2016; List A: 2016; T20: 2016

HAMPSHIRE

BEST BATTING: 83 Hampshire vs Cardiff MCCU, Southampton, 2016
BEST BOWLING: 1-46 Hampshire vs Surrey, Southampton, 2017

WHAT GOT YOU INTO CRICKET? Driving past my local cricket club
BEST ADVICE EVER RECEIVED? The small things are the big things and humour is essential because it's a funny old game
'ROY OF THE ROVERS' MOMENT? Captaining England U19
BEST THING ABOUT YOUR HOME GROUND? It has a golf course on site
YOUNG OPPOSING PLAYER WHO HAS IMPRESSED YOU? Jamie Porter (Ess) – he's very impressive with the new ball
IF YOU WEREN'T A CRICKETER? Not a clue!
SURPRISING FACT ABOUT YOU? My dad Ken was a tennis player and played at Wimbledon in 1972
SURPRISING FACT ABOUT A TEAMMATE? Mason Crane has pet tortoises
WHERE IS PARADISE? Crane Beach, Barbados
CRICKETING HERO? Marcus Trescothick
NON-CRICKETING HERO? Roger Federer – the greatest sportsman of all time
TWITTER: @Joe_Weatherley

Batting	Mat	Inns	NO	Runs	HS	Ave	SR	100	50	Ct	St
First-class	10	15	0	331	83	22.06	45.52	0	1	1	0
List A	10	10	2	247	56*	30.87	68.61	0	3	2	0
T20s	5	4	0	81	43	20.25	132.78	0	0	3	0

Bowling	Mat	Balls	Runs	Wkts	BBI	BBM	Ave	Econ	SR	5w	10
First-class	10	114	96	1	1/46	1/46	96.00	5.05	114.0	0	0
List A	10	327	221	8	4/25	4/25	27.62	4.05	40.8	0	0
T20s	5	6	9	0	-	-	-	9.00	-	0	0

JAMES WEIGHELL

LHB / RMF / RO / WO

FULL NAME: William James Weighell
BORN: January 28, 1994, Middlesbrough, Yorkshire
SQUAD NO: 28
HEIGHT: 6ft 3in
EDUCATION: Stokesley School, North Yorkshire
TEAMS: Durham
ROLE: Bowler
DEBUT: First-class: 2015; List A: 2017; T20: 2017

BEST BATTING: 58 Durham vs Sussex, Hove, 2017
BEST BOWLING: 5-33 Durham vs Warwickshire, Edgbaston, 2016

WHAT GOT YOU INTO CRICKET? Watching my dad and older brothers play club cricket when I was a kid
'ROY OF THE ROVERS' MOMENT? My maiden first-class five-wicket haul in 2016 against Warwickshire at Edgbaston
BEST OPPOSING PLAYER IN COUNTY CRICKET? Graham Onions (Lan)
SURPRISING FACT ABOUT A TEAMMATE? Graham Clark can fit 26 grapes in his mouth at once
WHERE IS PARADISE? Filthy's Newcastle (pub)
CRICKETING HERO? Andrew Flintoff – I loved the way he played the game
TWITTER: @jamesweighell

Batting	Mat	Inns	NO	Runs	HS	Ave	SR	100	50	Ct	St
First-class	9	15	4	284	58	25.81	69.60	0	2	2	0
List A	8	3	1	22	14	11.00	73.33	0	0	3	0
T20s	13	4	4	14	6*	-	140.00	0	0	7	0

Bowling	Mat	Balls	Runs	Wkts	BBI	BBM	Ave	Econ	SR	5w	10
First-class	9	1465	946	28	5/33	9/130	33.78	3.87	52.3	1	0
List A	8	396	416	18	5/57	5/57	23.11	6.30	22.0	1	0
T20s	13	225	350	9	3/28	3/28	38.88	9.33	25.0	0	0

LUKE WELLS

LHB / OB / R2 / W0

FULL NAME: Luke William Peter Wells
BORN: December 29, 1990, Eastbourne, Sussex
SQUAD NO: 31
HEIGHT: 6ft 4in
NICKNAME: Dave, Rinser
EDUCATION: St Bede's, Hailsham; Loughborough University
TEAMS: Sussex, Colombo Cricket Club
ROLE: Batsman
DEBUT: First-class: 2010; List A: 2010; T20: 2011

SUSSEX

BEST BATTING: 258 Sussex vs Durham, Hove, 2017
BEST BOWLING: 3-35 Sussex vs Durham, Arundel, 2015

FAMILY TIES? My dad Alan played for Sussex, Kent and England. My uncle Colin played for Sussex, Derbyshire and England
'ROY OF THE ROVERS' MOMENT? Scoring a match-winning hundred against Surrey in 2012 and a double hundred in 2013
BEST OPPOSING PLAYER IN COUNTY CRICKET? Darren Stevens (Ken)
YOUNG OPPOSING PLAYER WHO HAS IMPRESSED YOU? Zak Chappell (Lei)
SURPRISING FACT ABOUT YOU? I can speak French
SURPRISING FACT ABOUT A TEAMMATE? Despite his tough persona on the pitch, Ben Brown has a massive phobia of spiders
WHERE IS PARADISE? Home with my family. Or the south of France in a seafront restaurant with a glass of wine
CRICKETING HERO? Matthew Hayden – loved the way he played at the top of the order as a left-hander
NON-CRICKETING HERO? Jeremy Clarkson and Ricky Gervais
TWITTER: @luke_wells07

Batting	Mat	Inns	NO	Runs	HS	Ave	SR	100	50	Ct	St
First-class	110	183	11	6546	258	38.05	47.14	17	26	54	0
List A	18	13	0	110	23	8.46	59.78	0	0	1	0
T20s	5	5	0	18	11	3.60	66.66	0	0	1	0

Bowling	Mat	Balls	Runs	Wkts	BBI	BBM	Ave	Econ	SR	5w	10
First-class	110	3574	2202	46	3/35	5/119	47.86	3.69	77.6	0	0
List A	18	209	178	6	3/19	3/19	29.66	5.11	34.8	0	0
T20s	5	1	4	0	-	-	-	24.00	-	0	0

TOM WELLS

RHB / RMF / RO / WO

FULL NAME: Thomas Joshua Wells
BORN: March 15, 1993, Grantham, Lincolnshire
SQUAD NO: 48
HEIGHT: 6ft 2in
NICKNAME: Wellsy
EDUCATION: Gartree High School, Leicester; Beauchamp College, Leicester
TEAMS: Leicestershire
ROLE: Allrounder
DEBUT: First-class: 2013; List A: 2012; T20: 2013

BEST BATTING: 87* Leicestershire vs Sri Lankans, Leicester, 2016
BEST BOWLING: 4-46 Leicestershire vs Loughborough MCCU, Leicester, 2017

WHAT GOT YOU INTO CRICKET? Paul Nixon was my next-door neighbour!
'ROY OF THE ROVERS' MOMENT? Playing in the Championship win over Essex a couple of years ago
STRANGEST THING SEEN IN A GAME? The batsman hits the ball to short extra-cover, hits him flush on the head, and mid-off takes a catch diving forward
HOW WOULD YOUR TEAMMATES DESCRIBE YOU IN THREE WORDS? Very large head
IF YOU WEREN'T A CRICKETER? I'd be an ice-road trucker or a gardener
SURPRISING FACT? I hate flying
CRICKETING HEROES? Paul Nixon, Andrew Flintoff
NON-CRICKETING HERO? My old man was the Leicester Tigers rugby captain and coach, and he has been a big influence on my career
TWITTER: @t_wells15

Batting	Mat	Inns	NO	Runs	HS	Ave	SR	100	50	Ct	St
First-class	17	27	2	522	87*	20.88	56.06	0	2	8	0
List A	24	21	6	387	67	25.80	91.48	0	1	7	0
T20s	54	40	11	572	64*	19.72	127.11	0	2	31	0

Bowling	Mat	Balls	Runs	Wkts	BBI	BBM	Ave	Econ	SR	5w	10
First-class	17	1168	858	19	4/46	4/46	45.15	4.40	61.4	0	0
List A	24	586	667	15	3/44	3/44	44.46	6.82	39.0	0	0
T20s	54	142	240	4	1/5	1/5	60.00	10.14	35.5	0	0

RIKI WESSELS

RHB / WK / R2 / W0 / MVP23

FULL NAME: Mattheus Hendrik Wessels
BORN: November 12, 1985, Australia
SQUAD NO: 9
HEIGHT: 5ft 11in
NICKNAME: Blood, Weasel, Bobby
EDUCATION: Woodridge College, Port Elizabeth; University of Northampton
TEAMS: Nottinghamshire, Karachi Kings, Mid West Rhinos, Nondescripts, Northamptonshire, Sydney Sixers
ROLE: Batsman/wicketkeeper
DEBUT: First-class: 2004; List A: 2005; T20: 2005

BEST BATTING: 202* Nottinghamshire vs Sussex, Trent Bridge, 2017
BEST BOWLING: 1-10 Mid West Rhinos vs Matabeleland Tuskers, Bulawayo, 2009

'ROY OF THE ROVERS' MOMENT? That has to be my maiden first-class hundred, and also the finals I've taken part in
CRICKETING HEROES? Michael Slater, Justin Langer
NON-CRICKETING HEROES? All the soldiers fighting currently, having lost a few friends to war myself
IF YOU WEREN'T A CRICKETER? I'd probably be in the army on the front line
SURPRISING FACT? I've bungee-jumped at Victoria Falls, I lived in Colombo for six months and I love hunting
TWITTER: @rikiwessels

Batting	Mat	Inns	NO	Runs	HS	Ave	SR	100	50	Ct	St
First-class	185	304	26	10172	202*	36.58	63.64	22	51	297	16
List A	162	151	14	4179	146	30.50	98.60	4	22	111	0
T20s	180	167	23	4314	110	29.95	137.08	1	20	70	15
Bowling	Mat	Balls	Runs	Wkts	BBI	BBM	Ave	Econ	SR	5w	10
First-class	185	240	130	3	1/10	1/10	43.33	3.25	80.0	0	0
List A	162	49	48	1	1/0	1/0	48.00	5.87	49.0	0	0
T20s	180	-	-	-	-	-	-	-	-	-	-

OLLIE WESTBURY

RHB / OB / R0 / W0

FULL NAME: Oliver Edward Westbury
BORN: July 2, 1997, Dudley, West Midlands
SQUAD NO: 19
HEIGHT: 5ft 11in
NICKNAME: Wes, Westy
EDUCATION: Ellowes Hall Sports College, Dudley; Shrewsbury School
TEAMS: Worcestershire, England U19
ROLE: Batsman

WHAT GOT YOU INTO CRICKET? The 2005 Ashes
'ROY OF THE ROVERS' MOMENT? Scoring a century on my England U19 debut against Sri Lanka U19 in 2016
BEST THING ABOUT YOUR HOME GROUND? The scenery
BEST OPPOSING PLAYER IN COUNTY CRICKET? Samit Patel (Not)
YOUNG OPPOSING PLAYER WHO HAS IMPRESSED YOU? Max Holden (Mid)
IF YOU WEREN'T A CRICKETER? I'd be on a ski season somewhere in Europe, working in a bar or restaurant by night and skiing during the day
SURPRISING FACT ABOUT YOU? I know all the lyrics to 'We Didn't Start The Fire' by Billy Joel
WHERE IS PARADISE? The French Alps
CRICKETING HERO? Andrew Flintoff
NON-CRICKETING HERO? Morgan Freeman
UNUSUAL OBJECT AT HOME? A turbo trainer
TWITTER: @ollywestbury

TOM WESTLEY — RHB / OB / R1 / W0 / MVP100

FULL NAME: Thomas Westley
BORN: March 13, 1989, Cambridge
SQUAD NO: 21
HEIGHT: 6ft 2in
NICKNAME: Westie, Shellsy, Wezzo
EDUCATION: Linton Valley College, South Cambridgeshire; Hills Road College, Cambridge; Durham University
TEAMS: England, Essex, Bloomfield Cricket and Athletic Club
ROLE: Batsman
DEBUT: Test: 2017; First-class: 2007; List A: 2006; T20: 2010

BEST BATTING: 254 Essex vs Worcestershire, Chelmsford, 2016
BEST BOWLING: 4-55 Durham MCCU vs Durham, Durham University, 2010
COUNTY CAP: 2013

FAMILY TIES? My dad, uncle and brother all play for Weston Colville Cricket Club. My dad also harbours ambitions to play for England Over-50s
CRICKETING HEROES? Jacques Kallis, Sachin Tendulkar, Ben Matthews, Max Nolan, Dave Babbage, James Bunbury, Ben Lawrence
NON-CRICKETING HERO? Giovanni Colussi
SURPRISING FACT? I was part of the first group of students to study Harry Potter academically
TWITTER: @Westley21

Batting	Mat	Inns	NO	Runs	HS	Ave	SR	100	50	Ct	St
Tests	5	9	1	193	59	24.12	42.60	0	1	1	0
First-class	149	246	19	8326	254	36.67	52.67	18	41	102	0
List A	71	65	3	2093	111*	33.75	85.39	4	15	16	0
T20s	59	53	6	1487	109*	31.63	130.43	2	5	23	0

Bowling	Mat	Balls	Runs	Wkts	BBI	BBM	Ave	Econ	SR	5w	10
Tests	5	24	12	0	-	-	-	3.00	-	0	0
First-class	149	4825	2567	55	4/55	5/122	46.67	3.19	87.7	0	0
List A	71	1006	830	20	4/60	4/60	41.50	4.95	50.3	0	0
T20s	59	246	311	7	2/27	2/27	44.42	7.58	35.1	0	0

BRAD WHEAL

HAMPSHIRE

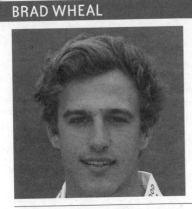

FULL NAME: Bradley Thomas James Wheal
BORN: August 28, 1996, Durban, South Africa
SQUAD NO: 58
EDUCATION: Clifton School, Durban
TEAMS: Scotland, Hampshire
ROLE: Bowler
DEBUT: ODI: 2016; T20I: 2016; First-class: 2015; List A: 2016; T20: 2016

BEST BATTING: 18 Hampshire vs Yorkshire, Headingley, 2017
BEST BOWLING: 6-51 Hampshire vs Nottinghamshire, Trent Bridge, 2016

TWITTER: @Brad_wheal
NOTES: Born in South Africa, Wheal's mother is Scottish and he holds a British passport. Made his Hampshire debut in 2015 and is contracted to the county until the end of the 2019 season. Made his Scotland debut in January 2016, aged 19. The fast bowler chipped in with key contributions with the ball in one-day and Championship cricket for Hampshire during the 2016 summer, taking a career-best 6-51 against Nottinghamshire. With strong competition for places in the bowling attack, Wheal played just four Championship games last season, taking 11 wickets at 32.00

Batting	Mat	Inns	NO	Runs	HS	Ave	SR	100	50	Ct	St
ODIs	5	4	3	2	2*	2.00	10.00	0	0	0	0
T20Is	5	2	2	2	2*	-	100.00	0	0	1	0
First-class	19	22	7	94	18	6.26	20.98	0	0	4	0
List A	16	11	6	46	18*	9.20	60.52	0	0	2	0
T20s	12	5	3	22	16	11.00	95.65	0	0	1	0

Bowling	Mat	Balls	Runs	Wkts	BBI	BBM	Ave	Econ	SR	5w	10
ODIs	5	259	218	7	2/31	2/31	31.14	5.05	37.0	0	0
T20Is	5	104	143	5	3/20	3/20	28.60	8.25	20.8	0	0
First-class	19	2663	1618	45	6/51	7/71	35.95	3.64	59.1	1	0
List A	16	718	631	24	4/38	4/38	26.29	5.27	29.9	0	0
T20s	12	224	317	11	3/20	3/20	28.81	8.49	20.3	0	0

ADAM WHEATER

RHB / WK / R0 / W0

FULL NAME: Adam Jack Aubrey Wheater
BORN: February 13, 1990, Whipps Cross Hospital, London
SQUAD NO: 31
EDUCATION: Millfield School, Somerset; Anglia Ruskin University
TEAMS: Essex, Badureliya Sports Club, Hampshire, Matabeleland Tuskers
ROLE: Batsman/wicketkeeper
DEBUT: First-class: 2008; List A: 2010; T20: 2009

BEST BATTING: 204* Hampshire vs Warwickshire, Edgbaston, 2016
BEST BOWLING: 1-86 Essex vs Leicestershire, Leicester, 2012

'ROY OF THE ROVERS' MOMENT? On a broader scale, having the opportunity to see the world through cricket
CRICKETING HEROES? Alec Stewart, Nasser Hussain, Adam Gilchrist
IF YOU WEREN'T A CRICKETER? I'd find myself a very wealthy girlfriend I could sponge off

Batting	Mat	Inns	NO	Runs	HS	Ave	SR	100	50	Ct	St
First-class	117	173	20	5646	204*	36.90	66.72	11	31	184	10
List A	71	56	5	1323	135	25.94	97.42	2	5	29	11
T20s	86	65	13	964	78	18.53	119.75	0	3	32	18

Bowling	Mat	Balls	Runs	Wkts	BBI	BBM	Ave	Econ	SR	5w	10
First-class	117	24	86	1	1/86	1/86	86.00	21.50	24.0	0	0
List A	71	-	-	-	-	-	-	-	-	-	-
T20s	86	-	-	-	-	-	-	-	-	-	-

FULL NAME: Graeme Geoffrey White
BORN: April 18, 1987, Milton Keynes, Buckinghamshire
SQUAD NO: 87
HEIGHT: 5ft 10in
NICKNAME: Whitey, G
EDUCATION: Royal Latin School, Buckinghamshire; Stowe School
TEAMS: Northamptonshire, Nottinghamshire
ROLE: Bowler
DEBUT: First-class: 2006; List A: 2007; T20: 2007

BEST BATTING: 65 Northamptonshire vs Glamorgan, Colwyn Bay, 2007
BEST BOWLING: 6-44 Northamptonshire vs Glamorgan, Northampton, 2016

WHAT GOT YOU INTO CRICKET? Playing on a beach in France
BEST ADVICE EVER RECEIVED? You need a steak and a Guiness to fill out lad (told to me by Nick Cook when I was 13)
'ROY OF THE ROVERS' MOMENT? Winning the T20 Blast in 2016
BEST OPPOSING PLAYER IN COUNTY CRICKET? Ben Stokes (Dur)
YOUNG OPPOSING PLAYER WHO HAS IMPRESSED YOU? Harry Gurney (Not) – best fine-leg fielder around
IF YOU WEREN'T A CRICKETER? I'd be a farmer
SURPRISING FACT ABOUT YOU? I have 35 tattoos
SURPRISING FACT ABOUT A TEAMMATE? Josh Cobb's teeth are stolen from Frankel the racehorse
WHERE IS PARADISE? Wantage Road
NON-CRICKETING HERO? Zlatan Ibrahimovic
UNUSUAL OBJECT AT HOME? A Nintendo 64

Batting	Mat	Inns	NO	Runs	HS	Ave	SR	100	50	Ct	St
First-class	39	55	5	659	65	13.18	48.85	0	2	12	0
List A	76	44	15	420	40	14.48	84.84	0	0	29	0
T20s	86	29	14	188	34	12.53	134.28	0	0	33	0

Bowling	Mat	Balls	Runs	Wkts	BBI	BBM	Ave	Econ	SR	5w	10
First-class	39	4776	2730	65	6/44	7/89	42.00	3.42	73.4	1	0
List A	76	2778	2331	84	6/37	6/37	27.75	5.03	33.0	2	0
T20s	86	1265	1690	67	5/22	5/22	25.22	8.01	18.8	1	0

ROBBIE WHITE

RHB / WK / R0 / W0

FULL NAME: Robert George White
BORN: September 15, 1995, Ealing, London
SQUAD NO: 14
HEIGHT: 5ft 10in
NICKNAME: Whitey
EDUCATION: Harrow School, London;
Loughborough University
TEAMS: Middlesex
ROLE: Batsman/wicketkeeper
DEBUT: First-class: 2015

BEST BATTING: 69 Loughborough MCCU vs Northamptonshire, Northampton, 2017

WHAT GOT YOU INTO CRICKET? Playing in the garden (and lounge) with my brother
BEST ADVICE EVER RECEIVED? Stay level
'ROY OF THE ROVERS' MOMENT? Taking figures of 3-1-3-3 against Norfolk U10
BEST THING ABOUT YOUR HOME GROUND? The lunches
BEST OPPOSING PLAYER IN COUNTY CRICKET? Sam Northeast (Ham)
YOUNG OPPOSING PLAYER WHO HAS IMPRESSED YOU? Cameron Steel (Dur) – he scores runs in tough situations
IF YOU WEREN'T A CRICKETER? I'd be a professional golfer
SURPRISING FACT ABOUT YOU? I like my custard cold
SURPRISING FACT ABOUT A TEAMMATE? Harry Podmore is taking a degree
WHERE IS PARADISE? Radlett CC (on a nice day)
CRICKETING HERO? AB de Villiers – a humble genius
NON-CRICKETING HERO? Ian Poulter – a team player who stands up to be counted when the pressure is on
UNUSUAL OBJECT AT HOME? A putting-rebounder machine
TWITTER: @rwhitey15

Batting	Mat	Inns	NO	Runs	HS	Ave	SR	100	50	Ct	St
First-class	6	6	0	110	69	18.33	55.55	0	1	6	0

Bowling	Mat	Balls	Runs	Wkts	BBI	BBM	Ave	Econ	SR	5w	10
First-class	6	-	-	-	-	-	-	-	-	-	-

ROSS WHITELEY

WORCESTERSHIRE

FULL NAME: Ross Andrew Whiteley
BORN: September 13, 1988, Sheffield
SQUAD NO: 44
HEIGHT: 6ft 2in
NICKNAME: Rossco, Pico, Shaggy
EDUCATION: Repton School, Derbyshire;
Leeds Metropolitan University
TEAMS: Worcestershire, Derbyshire, England Lions
ROLE: Batsman
DEBUT: First-class: 2008; List A: 2008; T20: 2011

BEST BATTING: 130* Derbyshire vs Kent, Derby, 2011
BEST BOWLING: 2-6 Derbyshire vs Hampshire, Derby, 2012
COUNTY CAP: 2013 (Worcestershire)

FAMILY TIES? My brother played for Derbyshire Academy and a handful of second XI games
BEST ADVICE EVER RECEIVED? Don't try to impress anyone other than yourself
'ROY OF THE ROVERS' MOMENT? Hitting six sixes in the T20 Blast against Yorkshire in 2017 – one of five times that has happened in the history of cricket!
BEST THING ABOUT YOUR HOME GROUND? The Ladies Pavilion – they serve incredible cakes
BEST OPPOSING PLAYER IN COUNTY CRICKET? Even though he has retired now, I've got to say Kumar Sangakkara – he still deserves that title
YOUNG OPPOSING PLAYER WHO HAS IMPRESSED YOU? Jofra Archer (Sus) – he bowls 90-plus effortlessly
SURPRISING FACT ABOUT YOU? I have 11 sheep with each squad number of the Derbyshire side which won Division Two shaved onto them
WHERE IS PARADISE? In my workshop with my tools, building things
TWITTER: @rosswhiteley44

Batting	Mat	Inns	NO	Runs	HS	Ave	SR	100	50	Ct	St
First-class	71	115	12	2788	130*	27.06	48.42	3	14	47	0
List A	61	52	8	1054	77	23.95	89.24	0	6	17	0
T20s	86	80	23	1540	91*	27.01	143.25	0	3	28	0

Bowling	Mat	Balls	Runs	Wkts	BBI	BBM	Ave	Econ	SR	5w	10
First-class	71	2257	1646	29	2/6	4/43	56.75	4.37	77.8	0	0
List A	61	381	423	8	1/17	1/17	52.87	6.66	47.6	0	0
T20s	86	78	123	4	1/10	1/10	30.75	9.46	19.5	0	0

STUART WHITTINGHAM

RHB / RFM / R0 / W0

FULL NAME: Stuart Gordon Whittingham
BORN: February 10, 1994, Derby
SQUAD NO: 29
HEIGHT: 6ft 2in
NICKNAME: The Jug
EDUCATION: Christ's Hospital, Horsham; Loughborough University
TEAMS: Scotland, Sussex
ROLE: Bowler
DEBUT: ODI: 2017; First-class: 2015; List A: 2017

SUSSEX

BEST BATTING: 22 Sussex vs Nottinghamshire, Hove, 2017
BEST BOWLING: 5-70 Scotland vs Ireland, Dubai, 2017

BEST ADVICE EVER RECEIVED? Respect the game and it will look after you (Russell Cobb)
ROY OF THE ROVERS' MOMENT? My first Championship five-for against Derbyshire
BEST THING ABOUT YOUR HOME GROUND? The slope – it gives you an extra couple of yards as a bowler
YOUNG OPPOSING PLAYER WHO HAS IMPRESSED YOU? Josh Tongue (Wor)
IF YOU WEREN'T A CRICKETER? I'd be a scientist
SURPRISING FACT ABOUT YOU? I have a brother who is a celebrity in South Korea
SURPRISING FACT ABOUT A TEAMMATE? Phi Salt has a YouTube channel where he uploads covers of songs
WHERE IS PARADISE? On a beach
CRICKETING HERO? Dale Steyn – the complete fast bowler
NON-CRICKETING HERO? Bradley Wiggins
TWITTER: @Stuartwhitt10

Batting	Mat	Inns	NO	Runs	HS	Ave	SR	100	50	Ct	St
ODIs	4	3	2	6	3*	6.00	66.66	0	0	3	0
First-class	13	15	5	68	22	6.80	39.76	0	0	3	0
List A	4	3	2	6	3*	6.00	66.66	0	0	3	0

Bowling	Mat	Balls	Runs	Wkts	BBI	BBM	Ave	Econ	SR	5w	10
ODIs	4	203	174	7	3/58	3/58	24.85	5.14	29.0	0	0
First-class	13	1843	1272	42	5/70	8/93	30.28	4.14	43.8	2	0
List A	4	203	174	7	3/58	3/58	24.85	5.14	29.0	0	0

DAVID WIESE

RHB / RMF / R0 / W0 / MVP79

SUSSEX

FULL NAME: David Wiese
BORN: May 18, 1985, Roodepoort, Transvaal, South Africa
SQUAD NO: 96
HEIGHT: 6ft 3in
NICKNAME: Weez
EDUCATION: Witbank High School, SA
TEAMS: South Africa, Sussex, Barbados Tridents, Easterns, Guyana Amazon Warriors, Royal Challengers Bangalore, Titans
ROLE: Allrounder
DEBUT: ODI: 2015; T20I: 2013; First-class: 2005; List A: 2005; T20: 2008

BEST BATTING: 208 Easterns vs Griqualand West, Benoni, 2008
BEST BOWLING: 6-58 Titans vs Knights, Centurion, 2015

BEST ADVICE EVER RECEIVED? Your performance on the field doesn't dictate the person you are off the field
BEST OPPOSING PLAYER IN COUNTY CRICKET? Jason Roy (Sur)
YOUNG OPPOSING PLAYER WHO HAS IMPRESSED YOU? Sam Curran (Sur) – very talented and skilful allrounder, and seems hard-working and eager to learn
IF YOU WEREN'T A CRICKETER? I'd probably be a forensic auditor because that's what I studied
SURPRISING FACT ABOUT YOU? I'm a huge fan of the theatre and musicals
SURPRISING FACT ABOUT A TEAMMATE? Stiaan van Zyl can in fact speak English
CRICKETING HERO? Hansie Cronje – he was an amazing competitor and leader and really knew how to get the best out of his players
TWITTER: @David_Wiese

Batting	Mat	Inns	NO	Runs	HS	Ave	SR	100	50	Ct	St
ODIs	6	6	1	102	41*	20.40	88.69	0	0	0	0
T20Is	20	11	4	92	28	13.14	122.66	0	0	9	0
First-class	95	151	16	4549	208	33.69	70.17	9	24	66	0
List A	132	112	23	2967	106	33.33	115.17	1	15	43	0
T20s	158	103	43	1272	71*	21.20	148.25	0	3	46	0

Bowling	Mat	Balls	Runs	Wkts	BBI	BBM	Ave	Econ	SR	5w	10
ODIs	6	294	316	9	3/50	3/50	35.11	6.44	32.6	0	0
T20Is	20	392	497	24	5/23	5/23	20.70	7.60	16.3	1	0
First-class	95	13881	7488	271	6/58	10/111	27.63	3.23	51.2	7	1
List A	132	4824	4290	121	5/25	5/25	35.45	5.33	39.8	1	0
T20s	158	2257	3102	130	5/19	5/19	23.86	8.24	17.3	3	0

DAVID WILLEY

LHB / LFM / R0 / W0 / MVP92

FULL NAME: David Jonathan Willey
BORN: February 28, 1990, Northampton
SQUAD NO: 72
HEIGHT: 6ft 1in
NICKNAME: Will, Wills, Wildman
EDUCATION: Northampton School For Boys
TEAMS: England, Yorkshire, Northamptonshire, Perth Scorchers
ROLE: Allrounder
DEBUT: ODI: 2015; T20I: 2015; First-class: 2009; List A: 2009; T20: 2009

BEST BATTING: 104* Northamptonshire vs Gloucestershire, Northampton, 2015
BEST BOWLING: 5-29 Northamptonshire vs Gloucestershire, Northampton, 2011
COUNTY CAP: 2013 (Northamptonshire); 2016 (Yorkshire)

FAMILY TIES? My dad Peter played for England, Northamptonshire and Leicestershire
BEST ADVICE EVER RECEIVED? Hard to pick one, but most of it came from my dad
'ROY OF THE ROVERS' MOMENT? Making my England debut in 2015
YOUNG OPPOSING PLAYER WHO HAS IMPRESSED YOU? Olly Stone (War)
SURPRISING FACT ABOUT YOU? My wife Carolynne is a country singer and was a two-time X Factor contestant
CRICKETING HERO? My dad – I always wanted to follow in his footsteps
NON-CRICKETING HERO? Karl Pilkington
TWITTER: @david_willey

Batting	Mat	Inns	NO	Runs	HS	Ave	SR	100	50	Ct	St
ODIs	34	19	10	140	26	15.55	70.35	0	0	17	0
T20Is	20	14	3	119	21	10.81	130.76	0	0	9	0
First-class	64	89	10	2137	104*	27.05	64.50	2	14	14	0
List A	110	77	17	1299	167	21.65	92.65	2	3	40	0
T20s	147	111	21	2097	118	23.30	142.55	2	7	59	0

Bowling	Mat	Balls	Runs	Wkts	BBI	BBM	Ave	Econ	SR	5w	10
ODIs	34	1383	1300	36	4/34	4/34	36.11	5.63	38.4	0	0
T20Is	20	401	575	24	3/20	3/20	23.95	8.60	16.7	0	0
First-class	64	8920	4883	161	5/29	10/75	30.32	3.28	55.4	5	1
List A	110	3875	3650	108	5/62	5/62	33.79	5.65	35.8	1	0
T20s	147	2394	3122	143	4/9	4/9	21.83	7.82	16.7	0	0

YORKSHIRE

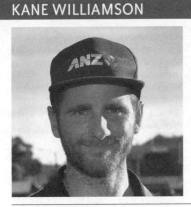

FULL NAME: Kane Stuart Williamson
BORN: August 8, 1990, Tauranga, New Zealand
SQUAD NO: 8
TEAMS: New Zealand, Yorkshire, Barbados Tridents, Gloucestershire, Northern Districts, Sunrisers Hyderabad
ROLE: Batsman
DEBUT: Test: 2010; ODI: 2010; T20I: 2011; First-class: 2007; List A: 2007; T20: 2009

BEST BATTING: 284* Northern Districts vs Wellington, Lincoln, 2011
BEST BOWLING: 5-75 Northern Districts vs Canterbury, Christchurch, 2009

NOTES: The New Zealand captain returns for a fourth stint with Yorkshire and is available from July for four Championship matches and 11 T20 Blast fixtures. Scored 2,633 international runs for New Zealand in 2015, including his first Test double hundred. Has scored well over 17,000 runs in international cricket. In 2016 he took over from Brendon McCullum as New Zealand captain across all formats. Played two seasons with Gloucestershire in 2011 and 2012. Has scored more than 1,000 runs for Yorkshire in 16 first-class matches

Batting	Mat	Inns	NO	Runs	HS	Ave	SR	100	50	Ct	St
Tests	63	113	10	5214	242*	50.62	50.51	17	26	56	0
ODIs	124	118	10	4985	145*	46.15	83.37	10	33	51	0
T20Is	51	49	7	1316	73*	31.33	120.95	0	8	24	0
First-class	126	217	17	9697	284*	48.48	51.37	27	49	117	0
List A	185	175	18	7106	145*	45.26	82.41	14	45	78	0
T20s	136	128	13	3073	101*	26.72	118.01	1	17	58	0

Bowling	Mat	Balls	Runs	Wkts	BBI	BBM	Ave	Econ	SR	5w	10
Tests	63	2031	1129	29	4/44	4/44	38.93	3.33	70.0	0	0
ODIs	124	1329	1207	35	4/22	4/22	34.48	5.44	37.9	0	0
T20Is	51	118	164	6	2/16	2/16	27.33	8.33	19.6	0	0
First-class	126	6480	3634	85	5/75	5/59	42.75	3.36	76.2	1	0
List A	185	2618	2280	65	5/51	5/51	35.07	5.22	40.2	1	0
T20s	136	758	885	30	3/33	3/33	29.50	7.00	25.2	0	0

GARY WILSON

RHB / WK / R0 / W0

FULL NAME: Gary Craig Wilson
BORN: February 5, 1986, Dundonald, Northern Ireland
SQUAD NO: 14
HEIGHT: 5ft 9in
NICKNAME: Wils
EDUCATION: Methodist College, Belfast
TEAMS: Ireland, Derbyshire, Surrey
ROLE: Wicketkeeper/batsman
DEBUT: ODI: 2007; T20I: 2008; First-class: 2005; List A: 2006; T20: 2008

DERBYSHIRE

BEST BATTING: 160* Surrey vs Leicestershire, The Oval, 2014
COUNTY CAP: 2014 (Surrey)

WHAT FIRST GOT YOU INTO CRICKET? My dad was an umpire
FAMILY TIES? Dad played league cricket
STRANGEST THING SEEN IN A GAME? William Porterfield and Andre Botha involved in a mix-up against Scotland. Google it
BEST MOMENT IN CRICKET? Beating England in the 2011 World Cup
YOUNG OPPOSING PLAYER WHO HAS IMPRESSED YOU? Sam Curran (Sur)
CRICKETING HEROES? Alec Stewart
NON-CRICKETING HEROES? AP McCoy, Brian O'Driscoll – any Irish sportsperson doing well
IF YOU WEREN'T A CRICKETER? I'd be a policeman or fireman
SURPRISING FACT? I like numbers
TWITTER: @gwilson14

Batting	Mat	Inns	NO	Runs	HS	Ave	SR	100	50	Ct	St
ODIs	91	85	10	1850	113	24.66	72.89	1	12	62	10
T20Is	53	46	6	891	65*	22.27	104.57	0	2	28	4
First-class	94	145	20	4359	160*	34.87		3	27	173	5
List A	187	167	18	3465	113	23.25	70.94	1	21	133	27
T20s	156	136	31	2635	65*	25.09	114.56	0	9	84	19

Bowling	Mat	Balls	Runs	Wkts	BBI	BBM	Ave	Econ	SR	5w	10
ODIs	91	-	-	-	-	-	-	-	-	-	-
T20Is	53	-	-	-	-	-	-	-	-	-	-
First-class	94	108	89	0	-	-	-	4.94	-	0	0
List A	187	-	-	-	-	-	-	-	-	-	-
T20s	156	-	-	-	-	-	-	-	-	-	-

CHRIS WOAKES   RHB / RFM / R0 / W3

WARWICKSHIRE

FULL NAME: Christopher Roger Woakes
BORN: March 2, 1989, Birmingham
SQUAD NO: 19
HEIGHT: 6ft 1in
NICKNAME: Woaksy, Woako, Wiz, GB
EDUCATION: Barr Beacon Language College
TEAMS: England, Warwickshire, Sydney Thunder, Wellington
ROLE: Allrounder
DEBUT: Test: 2013; ODI: 2011; T20I: 2011; First-class: 2006; List A: 2007; T20: 2008

BEST BATTING: 152* Warwickshire vs Derbyshire, Derby, 2013
BEST BOWLING: 9-36 Warwickshire vs Durham, Edgbaston, 2016
COUNTY CAP: 2009

FAMILY TIES? My brothers played Birmingham League cricket
STRANGEST THING SEEN IN A GAME? Jonathan Trott catching a ball in his pocket (not on purpose)
'ROY OF THE ROVERS' MOMENT? Receiving my first England cap
SUPERSTITIONS? Only one: always turn off my left shoulder at the end of my run-up
CRICKETING HERO? Jacques Kallis
NON-CRICKETING HERO? Paul 'God' McGrath
SURPRISING FACT? I won a keep-uppy competition when I was 10 (70 keepy-ups)
TWITTER: @chriswoakes

Batting	Mat	Inns	NO	Runs	HS	Ave	SR	100	50	Ct	St
Tests	22	37	9	789	66	28.17	47.02	0	3	9	0
ODIs	73	53	18	1015	95*	29.00	91.03	0	4	30	0
T20Is	8	7	4	91	37	30.33	144.44	0	0	1	0
First-class	133	196	46	5268	152*	35.12		9	21	55	0
List A	149	101	34	1664	95*	24.83	89.99	0	4	43	0
T20s	102	63	33	708	55*	23.60	134.34	0	1	37	0

Bowling	Mat	Balls	Runs	Wkts	BBI	BBM	Ave	Econ	SR	5w	10
Tests	22	3952	2025	60	6/70	11/102	33.75	3.07	65.8	2	1
ODIs	73	3486	3241	103	6/45	6/45	31.46	5.57	33.8	2	0
T20Is	8	162	253	7	2/40	2/40	36.14	9.37	23.1	0	0
First-class	133	22589	11560	455	9/36	11/97	25.40	3.07	49.6	19	4
List A	149	6456	5945	176	6/45	6/45	33.77	5.52	36.6	2	0
T20s	102	1972	2700	109	4/21	4/21	24.77	8.21	18.0	0	0

CHRIS WOOD

RHB / LMF / R0 / W0

FULL NAME: Christopher Philip Wood
BORN: June 27, 1990, Basingstoke, Hampshire
SQUAD NO: 25
HEIGHT: 6ft 3in
NICKNAME: Woody, Nuts
EDUCATION: St Lawrence CE Primary School; Amery Hill School; Alton College, Hampshire
TEAMS: Hampshire
ROLE: Bowler
DEBUT: First-class: 2010; List A: 2010; T20: 2010

HAMPSHIRE

BEST BATTING: 105* Hampshire vs Leicestershire, Leicester, 2012
BEST BOWLING: 5-39 Hampshire vs Kent, Canterbury, 2014

STRANGEST THING SEEN IN A GAME? The final over of the 2010 T20 final
'ROY OF THE ROVERS' MOMENT? Winning the 2012 One-Day Cup at Lord's
HOW WOULD YOUR TEAMMATES DESCRIBE YOU IN THREE WORDS? Loud, mad, competitive
YOUNG OPPOSING PLAYER WHO HAS IMPRESSED YOU? Saqib Mahmood (Lan)
CRICKETING HEROES? Nathan Bracken, Andrew Flintoff
NON-CRICKETING HERO? Novak Djokovic
SURPRISING FACT? I played football at semi-professional level
TWITTER: @CWoody27

Batting	Mat	Inns	NO	Runs	HS	Ave	SR	100	50	Ct	St
First-class	40	57	5	1270	105*	24.42	66.28	1	6	12	0
List A	68	40	13	368	41	13.62	93.63	0	0	23	0
T20s	95	31	13	219	27	12.16	103.30	0	0	30	0

Bowling	Mat	Balls	Runs	Wkts	BBI	BBM	Ave	Econ	SR	5w	10
First-class	40	5737	2906	99	5/39	7/49	29.35	3.03	57.9	3	0
List A	68	2750	2472	97	5/22	5/22	25.48	5.39	28.3	2	0
T20s	95	1922	2705	98	4/16	4/16	27.60	8.44	19.6	0	0

LUKE WOOD

LHB / LMF / RO / WO

FULL NAME: Luke Wood
BORN: August 2, 1995, Sheffield
SQUAD NO: 14
HEIGHT: 5ft 9in
NICKNAME: Biscuit
EDUCATION: Portland Comprehensive School, Worksop; Outwood Post 16 Centre Worksop
TEAMS: Nottinghamshire
ROLE: Bowler
DEBUT: First-class: 2014; List A: 2016; T20: 2016

BEST BATTING: 100 Nottinghamshire vs Sussex, Trent Bridge, 2015
BEST BOWLING: 5-40 Nottinghamshire vs Cambridge MCCU, Cambridge, 2016

WHAT GOT YOU INTO CRICKET? My neighbour took me down to the local club
BEST ADVICE EVER RECEIVED? Do what you do because that's what got you here in the first place
'ROY OF THE ROVERS' MOMENT? My maiden first-class century against Sussex in 2015
BEST THING ABOUT YOUR HOME GROUND? The atmosphere on T20 Friday nights – gives you a 12th player
BEST OPPOSING PLAYER IN COUNTY CRICKET? Jofra Archer (Sus)
YOUNG OPPOSING PLAYER WHO HAS IMPRESSED YOU? Jamie Porter (Ess)
IF YOU WEREN'T A CRICKETER? I'd be a PE teacher
SURPRISING FACT ABOUT YOU? I like grime/hip-hop
SURPRISING FACT ABOUT A TEAMMATE? Jake Libby is ridiculously good at golf
WHERE IS PARADISE? South Africa
CRICKETING HERO? Ryan Sidebottom – a fellow left-arm bowler who I always looked up to as a kid
TWITTER: @lwood_95

Batting	Mat	Inns	NO	Runs	HS	Ave	SR	100	50	Ct	St
First-class	23	35	8	774	100	28.66	66.43	1	2	6	0
List A	3	2	1	56	52	56.00	160.00	0	1	0	0
T20s	7	3	1	1	1*	0.50	25.00	0	0	2	0

Bowling	Mat	Balls	Runs	Wkts	BBI	BBM	Ave	Econ	SR	5w	10
First-class	23	3147	1977	62	5/40	8/83	31.88	3.76	50.7	1	0
List A	3	96	89	3	2/44	2/44	29.66	5.56	32.0	0	0
T20s	7	90	168	5	2/15	2/15	33.60	11.20	18.0	0	0

MARK WOOD

RHB / RF / RO / WO

FULL NAME: Mark Andrew Wood
BORN: January 11, 1990, Ashington, Northumberland
SQUAD NO: 33
HEIGHT: 6ft
NICKNAME: Woody
EDUCATION: Ashington High School; Newcastle College
TEAMS: England, Durham
ROLE: Bowler
DEBUT: Test: 2015; ODI: 2015; List A: 2015; First-class: 2011; List A: 2011; T20: 2013

DURHAM

BEST BATTING: 72* Durham vs Kent, Chester-le-Street, 2017
BEST BOWLING: 5-32 England Lions vs Sri Lanka A Emerging Players, Colombo, 2014

FAMILY TIES? My dad Derek and uncle Neil played for Ashington CC and Minor Counties for Northumberland
CRICKETING HEROES? Graham Onions, Stephen Harmison, Ben Harmison, Michael Holding, Ian Botham
NON-CRICKETING HEROES? Lennox Lewis, David Beckham, Jonny Wilkinson
SURPRISING FACT? I was in the Newcastle United FC Academy
TWITTER: @MAWood33

Batting	Mat	Inns	NO	Runs	HS	Ave	SR	100	50	Ct	St
Tests	10	18	5	219	32*	16.84	55.30	0	0	3	0
ODIs	23	7	4	39	13	13.00	97.50	0	0	5	0
T20Is	4	2	2	10	5*	-	83.33	0	0	0	0
First-class	43	70	14	1182	72*	21.10	55.44	0	3	10	0
List A	49	18	9	68	15*	7.55	85.00	0	0	14	0
T20s	18	7	4	39	12	13.00	95.12	0	0	2	0

Bowling	Mat	Balls	Runs	Wkts	BBI	BBM	Ave	Econ	SR	5w	10
Tests	10	1863	1057	26	3/39	5/83	40.65	3.40	71.6	0	0
ODIs	23	1225	1104	25	4/33	4/33	44.16	5.40	49.0	0	0
T20Is	4	87	139	8	3/26	3/26	17.37	9.58	10.8	0	0
First-class	43	6636	3731	130	5/32	6/47	28.70	3.37	51.0	6	0
List A	49	2268	1967	63	4/33	4/33	31.22	5.20	36.0	0	0
T20s	18	351	490	20	4/25	4/25	24.50	8.37	17.5	0	0

DANIEL WORRALL

RHB / RFM / R0 / W0

GLOUCESTERSHIRE

FULL NAME: Daniel James Worrall
BORN: July 10, 1991, Melbourne, Australia
SQUAD NO: 41
TEAMS: Australia, Gloucestershire, Melbourne Stars, South Australia
ROLE: Bowler
DEBUT: ODI: 2016; First-class: 2012; List A: 2012; T20: 2014

BEST BATTING: 26 South Australia vs Tasmania, Adelaide, 2016
BEST BOWLING: 6-96 South Australia vs Victoria, Adelaide, 2016

NOTES: Worrall is an Australian pace bowler who plays for South Australia in the Sheffield Shield and for the Melbourne Stars in the Big Bash. He has signed for Gloucestershire as an overseas player and will be available for the Championship and the One-Day Cup from the start of the season until the beginning of July. Worrall made his first-class debut in 2012 but his career really took off after good performances during the 2015/16 season, when he finished as the second-highest wicket-taker in the Sheffield Shield with 44 dismissals at an average of 26.18. He played three ODIs for Australia in 2016. "He bowls a full length with decent pace and has good one-day skills," said Gloucestershire head coach Richard Dawson. "He will add depth and experience to our bowling attack for the start of the season"

Batting	Mat	Inns	NO	Runs	HS	Ave	SR	100	50	Ct	St
ODIs	3	1	1	6	6*	-	150.00	0	0	1	0
First-class	33	49	20	250	26	8.62	40.58	0	0	11	0
List A	24	11	8	43	16	14.33	72.88	0	0	7	0
T20s	14	6	3	48	16	16.00	126.31	0	0	4	0

Bowling	Mat	Balls	Runs	Wkts	BBI	BBM	Ave	Econ	SR	5w	10
ODIs	3	158	171	1	1/43	1/43	171.00	6.49	158.0	0	0
First-class	33	7122	3820	125	6/96	8/113	30.56	3.21	56.9	4	0
List A	24	1244	1098	28	5/62	5/62	39.21	5.29	44.4	1	0
T20s	14	297	447	13	3/11	3/11	34.38	9.03	22.8	0	0

CHRIS WRIGHT

RHB / RFM / RO / W1

FULL NAME: Christopher Julian Clement Wright
BORN: July 14, 1985, Chipping Norton, Oxfordshire
SQUAD NO: 31
HEIGHT: 6ft 3in
NICKNAME: Wrighty, Dog, Wrightdog
EDUCATION: Eggars Grammar School, Alton
TEAMS: Warwickshire, England Lions, Essex, Middlesex, Tamil Union
ROLE: Bowler
DEBUT: First-class: 2004; List A: 2004; T20: 2004

BEST BATTING: 77 Essex vs Cambridge MCCU, Cambridge, 2011
BEST BOWLING: 6-22 Essex vs Leicestershire, Leicester, 2008
COUNTY CAP: 2013 (Warwickshire)

WHAT GOT YOU INTO CRICKET? Watching my father play for Liphook and Ripsley CC
STRANGEST THING SEEN IN A GAME? Instead of doing a traditional coin toss the two coach/ captains decided to play a game of tossing various objects closest to the stumps at the other end. It lasted 15 minutes
'ROY OF THE ROVERS' MOMENT? Bowling out Worcestershire in a morning session. Keith Barker and I each got five wickets in the session and effectively sealed the title for Warwickshire in 2012. Our figures were 5-24 and 5-36. 60 all out!
CRICKETING HEROES? Jason Gillespie – amazing action, quick, moved it away, long hair. Mark Ramprakash – my favourite batter to watch as a boy. Great technique
NON-CRICKETING HEROES? James Richardson – former presenter of Gazzetta Football Italia
SURPRISING FACT? I once (a long time ago but as a professional) missed a pre-season game to play in the Irish Open Poker tournament. I got knocked out on day one of the four-day event and as a result got very drunk! I then overslept and missed my flight home. I was £10,000 poorer and very ill but a good life experience. The captain and coach of the club didn't think so
TWITTER: @chriswright1985

Batting	Mat	Inns	NO	Runs	HS	Ave	SR	100	50	Ct	St
First-class	131	169	40	2357	77	18.27	50.61	0	9	22	0
List A	99	39	18	229	42	10.90	77.36	0	0	17	0
T20s	58	14	9	28	6*	5.60	103.70	0	0	13	0

Bowling	Mat	Balls	Runs	Wkts	BBI	BBM	Ave	Econ	SR	5w	10
First-class	131	20858	12316	365	6/22	9/89	33.74	3.54	57.1	10	0
List A	99	3833	3568	100	4/20	4/20	35.68	5.58	38.3	0	0
T20s	58	1167	1739	52	4/24	4/24	33.44	8.94	22.4	0	0

LUKE WRIGHT

RHB / RM / R1 / W0 / MVP90

SUSSEX

FULL NAME: Luke James Wright
BORN: March 7, 1985, Grantham, Lincolnshire
SQUAD NO: 10
HEIGHT: 5ft 10in
NICKNAME: Bammers, Bam Bam
EDUCATION: Loughborough University
TEAMS: England, Sussex, Abhani Limited, Auckland, Dhaka Gladiators, Impi, Leicestershire, Melbourne Stars, Pune Warriors, Quetta Gladiators, Wellington
ROLE: Batsman
DEBUT: ODI: 2007; T20I: 2007; First-class: 2003; List A 2002; T20: 2004

BEST BATTING: 226* Sussex vs Worcestershire, Worcester, 2015
BEST BOWLING: 5-65 Sussex vs Derbyshire, Derby, 2010
COUNTY CAP: 2007

FAMILY TIES? My brother Ashley was a pro at Leicestershire
BEST ADVICE EVER RECEIVED? Don't get too down on the bad days – everything can change with your next innings
'ROY OF THE ROVERS' MOMENT? Scoring a T20 hundred to win the local derby for the Melbourne Stars against the Renegades in front of 86,000 at the MCG
BEST THING ABOUT YOUR HOME GROUND? The deckchairs
YOUNG OPPOSING PLAYER WHO HAS IMPRESSED YOU? Joe Clarke (Wor) – best young batsman I have seen. Destined to play for England
SURPRISING FACT ABOUT YOU? I don't bowl anymore
WHERE IS PARADISE? Melbourne with my wife and three kids
TWITTER: @lukewright204

Batting	Mat	Inns	NO	Runs	HS	Ave	SR	100	50	Ct	St
ODIs	50	39	4	707	52	20.20	86.21	0	2	18	0
T20Is	51	45	5	759	99*	18.97	137.00	0	4	14	0
First-class	134	206	23	7273	226*	39.74	65.82	17	37	57	0
List A	198	164	21	4488	143*	31.38		9	16	62	0
T20s	287	267	26	6747	153*	27.99	143.64	7	33	92	0

Bowling	Mat	Balls	Runs	Wkts	BBI	BBM	Ave	Econ	SR	5w	10
ODIs	50	1038	884	15	2/34	2/34	58.93	5.10	69.2	0	0
T20Is	51	330	465	18	2/24	2/24	25.83	8.45	18.3	0	0
First-class	134	8264	4862	120	5/65	7/127	40.51	3.53	68.8	3	0
List A	198	4752	4231	111	4/12	4/12	38.11	5.34	42.8	0	0
T20s	287	1799	2563	79	3/17	3/17	32.44	8.54	22.7	0	0

SAIF ZAIB

LHB / SLA / RO / WO

FULL NAME: Saif Ali Zaib
BORN: May 22, 1998, High Wycombe, Buckinghamshire
SQUAD NO: 5
HEIGHT: 5ft 9in
NICKNAME: Saify, Zaiby
EDUCATION: Royal Grammar School, High Wycombe
TEAMS: Northamptonshire
ROLE: Allrounder
DEBUT: First-class: 2015; List A: 2014; T20: 2017

BEST BATTING: 65* Northamptonshire vs Glamorgan, Swansea, 2016
BEST BOWLING: 6-115 Northamptonshire vs Loughborough MCCU, Northampton, 2017

FAMILY TIES? My dad played Minor Counties
BEST ADVICE EVER RECEIVED? Relax and enjoy the moment
'ROY OF THE ROVERS' MOMENT? Playing against the Aussies in 2015
BEST THING ABOUT YOUR HOME GROUND? The atmosphere is electric for T20s
YOUNG OPPOSING PLAYER WHO HAS IMPRESSED YOU? Josh Tongue (Wor) – tall fast bowler with a bright future
IF YOU WEREN'T A CRICKETER? I'd be a businessman
SURPRISING FACT ABOUT YOU? I'm scared of swimming in open water due to my fear of sharks and crocodiles
SURPRISING FACT ABOUT A TEAMMATE? Alex Wakely has OCD when it comes to his kit
WHERE IS PARADISE? Home
CRICKETING HERO? Brian Lara – for the way he could turn a game in half an hour
TWITTER: @zaib_05

Batting	Mat	Inns	NO	Runs	HS	Ave	SR	100	50	Ct	St
First-class	6	8	2	168	65*	28.00	49.70	0	1	3	0
List A	6	3	0	44	17	14.66	83.01	0	0	0	0
T20s	5	2	0	7	6	3.50	50.00	0	0	2	0

Bowling	Mat	Balls	Runs	Wkts	BBI	BBM	Ave	Econ	SR	5w	10
First-class	6	477	345	11	6/115	6/115	31.36	4.33	43.3	2	0
List A	6	36	52	2	2/22	2/22	26.00	8.66	18.0	0	0
T20s	5	48	76	0	-	-	-	9.50	-	0	0

ESSEX

FULL NAME: Syed Ashar Ahmed Zaidi
BORN: July 13, 1981, Karachi, Pakistan
SQUAD NO: 99
HEIGHT: 5ft 7in
NICKNAME: Ashi
TEAMS: Essex, Islamabad, Pakistan Telecommunication Company Limited, Rawalpindi, Khan Research Laboratories, Federal Areas, Sussex, Gazi Tank Cricketers, Comilla Victorians
ROLE: Allrounder
DEBUT: First-class: 1999; List A: 1999; T20: 2006

BEST BATTING: 202 Islamabad vs Sialkot, Sialkot, 2009
BEST BOWLING: 4-50 Islamabad vs Hyderabad, Hyderabad, 2009

'ROY OF THE ROVERS' MOMENT? Representing Pakistan U19 and Pakistan A, and playing county cricket in England
YOUNG OPPOSING PLAYER WHO HAS IMPRESSED YOU? Harry Finch (Sus)
CRICKETING HEROES? Saeed Anwar, Brian Lara
IF YOU WEREN'T A CRICKETER? I'd be an air-force pilot
TWITTER: @Asharzaidi1981

Batting	Mat	Inns	NO	Runs	HS	Ave	SR	100	50	Ct	St
First-class	112	179	13	6015	202	36.23		12	29	84	0
List A	100	94	11	2780	141	33.49		4	12	34	0
T20s	61	50	10	970	59*	24.25	134.53	0	4	16	0

Bowling	Mat	Balls	Runs	Wkts	BBI	BBM	Ave	Econ	SR	5w	10
First-class	112	6023	2803	94	4/50	5/81	29.81	2.79	64.0	0	0
List A	100	3187	2330	75	4/39	4/39	31.06	4.38	42.4	0	0
T20s	61	810	969	38	4/11	4/11	25.50	7.17	21.3	0	0

ADAM ZAMPA

RHB / LB / RO / WO

FULL NAME: Adam Zampa
BORN: March 31, 1992, Shellharbour, New South Wales, Australia
SQUAD NO: TBC
TEAMS: Australia, Essex, Adelaide Strikers, Guyana Amazon Warriors, Melbourne Stars, New South Wales, Rising Pune Supergiant, South Australia, Sydney Thunder
ROLE: Bowler
DEBUT: ODI: 2016; T20I: 2016; First-class: 2012; List A: 2012; T20: 2012

BEST BATTING: 74 South Australia vs Western Australia, Adelaide, 2015
BEST BOWLING: 6-62 South Australia vs Queensland, Adelaide, 2017

NOTES: An Australian leg-spinner, Zampa has played in multiple T20 leagues around the world, including the IPL, the Caribbean Premier League and the Big Bash League, having represented four different teams in the latter. In 2016 he claimed the second-best figures in IPL history – 6-19 for Rising Pune Supergiant against Sunrisers Hyderabad. He made his Australia T20I debut against South Africa in 2016, and took five wickets in the 2016 World T20 at an economy of 6.27. He has been signed to play the entirety of Essex's T20 Blast campaign. Essex's new head coach Anthony McGrath said: "He has the ability to spin the ball both ways and that mystery in the middle overs is something that we have been missing from our T20 side"

Batting	Mat	Inns	NO	Runs	HS	Ave	SR	100	50	Ct	St
ODIs	31	14	4	67	12	6.70	59.29	0	0	7	0
T20Is	13	3	3	11	5*	-	122.22	0	0	0	0
First-class	35	58	7	1111	74	21.78	71.44	0	6	9	0
List A	59	36	9	465	66	17.22	96.07	0	3	12	0
T20s	74	25	8	91	15	5.35	90.09	0	0	6	0

Bowling	Mat	Balls	Runs	Wkts	BBI	BBM	Ave	Econ	SR	5w	10
ODIs	31	1540	1459	42	3/16	3/16	34.73	5.68	36.6	0	0
T20Is	13	258	258	17	3/16	3/16	15.17	6.00	15.1	0	0
First-class	35	7066	4629	100	6/62	10/119	46.29	3.93	70.6	2	1
List A	59	3071	2761	83	4/18	4/18	33.26	5.39	37.0	0	0
T20s	74	1518	1785	86	6/19	6/19	20.75	7.05	17.6	1	0

England
Women

FIXTURES

CAPTAIN: Heather Knight
HEAD COACH: Mark Robinson

2018 SUMMER FIXTURES

June 9
England vs South Africa
1st ODI
Worcester

June 12
England vs South Africa
2nd ODI
Hove

June 15
England vs South Africa
3rd ODI
Canterbury

June 20
England vs South Africa
T20I Tri-Series
Taunton

June 23
England vs South Africa
T20I Tri-Series
Taunton

June 23
England vs New Zealand
T20I Tri-Series
Taunton

June 28
England vs New Zealand
T20I Tri-Series
Bristol

July 7
England vs New Zealand
1st ODI
Headingley

July 10
England vs New Zealand
2nd ODI
Derby

July 13
England vs New Zealand
3rd ODI
Leicester

TAMMY BEAUMONT

RHB / WK

FULL NAME: Tamsin Tilley Beaumont
BORN: March 11, 1991, Dover, Kent
SQUAD NO: 12
HEIGHT: 5ft 3in
NICKNAME: Tambeau, Little Mitts
EDUCATION: Sir Roger Manwood's School;
Loughborough University
TEAMS: England, Kent, Southern Vipers,
Adelaide Strikers, Diamonds, Emeralds,
Sapphires, Surrey Stars
ROLE: Batsman
DEBUT: Test: 2013; ODI: 2009; T20I: 2009

ENGLAND WOMEN

BEST ODI BATTING: 168* England vs Pakistan, Taunton, 2016

WHAT GOT YOU INTO CRICKET? My older brother and dad used to play for Sandwich Town CC every weekend when I was growing up. I soon got bored of just watching

'ROY OF THE ROVERS' MOMENT? Diving in to get my first ODI hundred at Worcester (I'm still relieved the fielder missed the stumps)

BEST OPPOSING PLAYER IN COUNTY CRICKET? Suzie Bates (NZ) or Ellyse Perry (Aus)

YOUNG OPPOSING PLAYER WHO HAS IMPRESSED YOU? Alice Davidson-Richards (Ken) – contributes with bat and ball

IF YOU WEREN'T A CRICKETER? I'd be a scientist

SURPRISING FACT ABOUT YOU? I won a national school gymnastics competition as a kid and wanted to be in the Olympics before becoming a cricketer

SURPRISING FACT ABOUT A TEAMMATE? Katherine Brunt is a big softie off the pitch

CRICKETING HERO? My dad may not have played to a high standard but I always looked up at him and tried to bat like him

NON-CRICKETING HERO? My grandad – who doesn't think their grandad is a superhero when you're growing up?

TWITTER: @Tammy_Beaumont

Batting	Mat	Inns	NO	Runs	HS	Ave	SR	100	50	Ct	St
Tests	3	5	0	132	70	26.40	40.74	0	1	1	0
ODIs	47	40	5	1334	168*	38.11	70.84	3	5	12	4
T20Is	47	33	4	453	82	15.62	92.63	0	2	7	4

Bowling	Mat	Balls	Runs	Wkts	BBI	BBM	Ave	Econ	SR	5w	10
Tests	3	-	-	-	-	-	-	-	-	-	-
ODIs	47	-	-	-	-	-	-	-	-	-	-
T20Is	47	-	-	-	-	-	-	-	-	-	-

KATHERINE BRUNT

RHB / RFM

ENGLAND WOMEN

FULL NAME: Katherine Helen Brunt
BORN: July 2, 1985, Barnsley
SQUAD NO: 26
HEIGHT: 5ft 5in
NICKNAME: Brunty, Nunny, Ethel
EDUCATION: Penistone Grammar School
TEAMS: England, Yorkshire, Yorkshire Diamonds, Braves, Knight Riders, Perth Scorchers, Sapphires
ROLE: Bowler
DEBUT: Test: 2004; ODI: 2005; T20I: 2005

BEST ODI BATTING: 52 England vs Australia, Coffs Harbour, 2017
BEST ODI BOWLING: 5-18 England vs Australia, Wormsley, 2011

WHAT GOT YOU INTO CRICKET? My brother and my father. My brother Daniel is nearly four years older than me and he would make me watch cricket videos of Darren Gough and Curtly Ambrose and then bowl at him outside in the garden
'ROY OF THE ROVERS' MOMENT? My first Ashes Test match – I top-scored at No.10 and took nine wickets (had a couple dropped too!)
BEST THING ABOUT YOUR HOME GROUND? Headingley attracts the loudest supporters and the best in fancy dress! And the wicket produces results
BEST OPPOSING PLAYER IN COUNTY CRICKET? Nat Sciver (Sur)
YOUNG OPPOSING PLAYER WHO HAS IMPRESSED YOU? Katie Levick (Yor) – bowls unorthodox leg-spin and takes bags of wickets
IF YOU WEREN'T A CRICKETER? I'd be a rugby 7s player
SURPRISING FACT ABOUT YOU? I have dates of all my major career achievements tattooed on my ribs. The last one was "23rd July 2017" to mark the day we won the World Cup
NON-CRICKETING HERO? My dad – taught me to be tough and never give up
TWITTER: @KBrunt26

Batting	Mat	Inns	NO	Runs	HS	Ave	SR	100	50	Ct	St
Tests	11	14	4	156	52	15.60	30.83	0	1	3	0
ODIs	106	55	13	602	52	14.33	79.73	0	1	30	0
T20Is	60	31	15	234	35	14.62	98.73	0	0	19	0

Bowling	Mat	Balls	Runs	Wkts	BBI	BBM	Ave	Econ	SR	5w	10
Tests	11	2082	852	39	6/69	9/111	21.84	2.45	53.3	2	0
ODIs	106	5231	3023	127	5/18	5/18	23.80	3.46	41.1	4	0
T20Is	60	1314	1110	55	3/6	3/6	20.18	5.06	23.8	0	0

KATE CROSS RHB / RMF

FULL NAME: Kathryn Laura Cross
BORN: October 3, 1991, Manchester
SQUAD NO: 16
HEIGHT: 5ft 8in
NICKNAME: Crossy, Sunny
EDUCATION: Bury Grammar School;
University of Leeds
TEAMS: England, Lancashire, Lancashire
Thunder, Brisbane Heat, Emeralds,
Sapphires, Western Australia
ROLE: Bowler
DEBUT: Test: 2014; ODI: 2013; T20I: 2013

ENGLAND WOMEN

BEST ODI BATTING: 4* England vs India, Scarborough, 2014
BEST ODI BOWLING: 5-24 England vs New Zealand, Lincoln, 2015

FAMILY TIES? My uncle was the U11 coach at Heywood CC, where I first played boys' cricket.
My brother had a year on the books at Lancashire and my sister played for Lancashire
BEST ADVICE EVER RECEIVED? Don't get too high when you do well, don't get too low when
you don't
'ROY OF THE ROVERS' MOMENT? My Test debut at the WACA – I took a wicket in my first
over and ended the game with 3-35 in both innings
BEST THING ABOUT YOUR HOME GROUND? The new Hilton Hotel at Old Trafford has four
outdoor beds with a view on the game – perfect for a cold Manchester evening
BEST OPPOSING PLAYER IN COUNTY CRICKET? Nat Sciver (Sur)
YOUNG OPPOSING PLAYER WHO HAS IMPRESSED YOU? Sophia Dunkley (Mid)
IF YOU WEREN'T A CRICKETER? I'd be a criminal psychologist
SURPRISING FACT ABOUT YOU? I can make my tongue into the shape of a three-leaf clover
CRICKETING HERO? Andrew Flintoff – a fellow Lancastrian I loved watching in the 2005 Ashes
UNUSUAL OBJECT AT HOME? A few lucky pigs
TWITTER: @katecross16

Batting	Mat	Inns	NO	Runs	HS	Ave	SR	100	50	Ct	St
Tests	3	6	3	15	4*	5.00	24.19	0	0	0	0
ODIs	14	4	2	7	4*	3.50	33.33	0	0	3	0
T20Is	4	-	-	-	-	-	-	-	-	-	0

Bowling	Mat	Balls	Runs	Wkts	BBI	BBM	Ave	Econ	SR	5w	10
Tests	3	554	209	14	3/29	6/70	14.92	2.26	39.5	0	0
ODIs	14	636	476	16	5/24	5/24	29.75	4.49	39.7	1	0
T20Is	4	72	83	3	2/27	2/27	27.66	6.91	24.0	0	0

SOPHIE ECCLESTONE

RHB / SLA

FULL NAME: Sophie Ecclestone
BORN: May 6, 1999, Chester, Cheshire
SQUAD NO: 71
HEIGHT: 5ft 10in
NICKNAME: Ecclescake
EDUCATION: Helsby High School
TEAMS: England, Lancashire, Lancashire Thunder, Cheshire
ROLE: Bowler
DEBUT: Test: 2017; ODI: 2016; T20I: 2016

BEST ODI BATTING: 3 England vs West Indies, Florence Hall, 2016
BEST ODI BOWLING: 2-28 England vs West Indies, Florence Hall, 2016

WHAT GOT YOU INTO CRICKET? My brother and my dad played at my local club and they taught me all I know
FAMILY TIES? I play in the same team as my brother on Saturdays
'ROY OF THE ROVERS' MOMENT? Making my Test debut in Australia
BEST THING ABOUT YOUR HOME GROUND? Alvanley CC is my home club and my favourite ground. Great view of the surroundings
BEST OPPOSING PLAYER IN COUNTY CRICKET? It's got to be my mum's favourite player: Katherine Brunt (Yor)
YOUNG OPPOSING PLAYER WHO HAS IMPRESSED YOU? Sophia Dunkley (Mid) – just class
IF YOU WEREN'T A CRICKETER? I'd be a zookeeper looking after koalas or kangaroos
SURPRISING FACT ABOUT YOU? I love playing crown green bowls competitively
WHERE IS PARADISE? Cheshire Oaks Factory Outlet centre
UNUSUAL OBJECT AT HOME? My mum still has my brownie outfit – with my sash and all my badges on it
TWITTER: @sophecc19

Batting	Mat	Inns	NO	Runs	HS	Ave	SR	100	50	Ct	St
Tests	1	1	1	8	8*	-	42.10	0	0	0	0
ODIs	4	4	1	7	3	2.33	31.81	0	0	1	0
T20Is	5	1	0	6	6	6.00	300.00	0	0	0	0

Bowling	Mat	Balls	Runs	Wkts	BBI	BBM	Ave	Econ	SR	5w	10
Tests	1	222	107	3	3/107	3/107	35.66	2.89	74.0	0	0
ODIs	4	174	135	5	2/28	2/28	27.00	4.65	34.8	0	0
T20Is	5	119	131	7	2/24	2/24	18.71	6.60	17.0	0	0

GEORGIA ELWISS

RHB / RMF

FULL NAME: Georgia Amanda Elwiss
BORN: May 31, 1991, Wolverhampton
SQUAD NO: 34
HEIGHT: 5ft 7in
NICKNAME: G, George, G Dog
EDUCATION: Wolverhampton Girls High School; Loughborough University
TEAMS: England, Sussex, Loughborough Lightning, Diamonds, Emeralds, Knight Riders, Melbourne Stars, Rubies, Staffordshire, Sapphires
ROLE: Allrounder
DEBUT: Test: 2015; ODI: 2011; T20I: 2011

BEST ODI BATTING: 77 England vs Pakistan, Taunton, 2016
BEST ODI BOWLING: 3-17 England vs India, Wormsley, 2012

WHAT GOT YOU INTO CRICKET? My grandparents
'ROY OF THE ROVERS' MOMENT? Winning the World Cup final at Lord's
BEST THING ABOUT YOUR HOME GROUND? The fans
BEST OPPOSING PLAYER IN COUNTY CRICKET? Heather Knight (Ber)
YOUNG OPPOSING PLAYER WHO HAS IMPRESSED YOU? Ashleigh Gardner (Aus) – she hits it far
IF YOU WEREN'T A CRICKETER? I'd be a nutritionist
SURPRISING FACT ABOUT YOU? I learnt Russian at school
SURPRISING FACT ABOUT A TEAMMATE? Danni Wyatt is older than me
WHERE IS PARADISE? Phuket, Thailand
CRICKETING HERO? AB de Villiers
NON-CRICKETING HERO? My parents – for all the sacrifices they've made for me
UNUSUAL OBJECT AT HOME? A model tuk-tuk
TWITTER: @gelwiss

Batting	Mat	Inns	NO	Runs	HS	Ave	SR	100	50	Ct	St
Tests	2	4	1	131	46	43.66	28.60	0	0	0	0
ODIs	25	17	3	308	77	22.00	78.77	0	2	7	0
T20Is	13	4	2	24	18	12.00	100.00	0	0	3	0

Bowling	Mat	Balls	Runs	Wkts	BBI	BBM	Ave	Econ	SR	5w	10
Tests	2	96	51	1	1/40	1/40	51.00	3.18	96.0	0	0
ODIs	25	688	389	16	3/17	3/17	24.31	3.39	43.0	0	0
T20Is	13	151	139	8	2/9	2/9	17.37	5.52	18.8	0	0

TASH FARRANT
LHB / LM

ENGLAND WOMEN

FULL NAME: Natasha Eleni Farrant
BORN: May 29, 1996, Athens, Greece
SQUAD NO: 53
HEIGHT: 5ft 5in
NICKNAME: Faz
EDUCATION: Sevenoaks School;
Loughborough University
TEAMS: England, Kent, Southern Vipers,
Sapphires, Western Australia
ROLE: Bowler
DEBUT: ODI: 2013; T20I: 2013

BEST ODI BATTING: 1* England vs West Indies, Port of Spain, 2013
BEST ODI BOWLING: 1-14 England vs West Indies, Port of Spain, 2013

WHAT GOT YOU INTO CRICKET? Playing in the garden with my two brothers. Then playing for Kent U11 when I was eight
BEST ADVICE EVER RECEIVED? Bowl it at the stumps (from my mum)
'ROY OF THE ROVERS' MOMENT? Running out West Indies' Stafanie Taylor off my own bowling and being mauled by most of the team
BEST THING ABOUT YOUR HOME GROUND? I love the balcony of the home dressing room at Canterbury
BEST OPPOSING PLAYER IN COUNTY CRICKET? Nat Sciver (Sur)
YOUNG OPPOSING PLAYER WHO HAS IMPRESSED YOU? Sophia Dunkley (Mid) – she's a great allrounder and her leggies are really useful
IF YOU WEREN'T A CRICKETER? I'd be a hockey player
SURPRISING FACT ABOUT YOU? I have lived in four countries (Greece, Italy, Singapore, England)
SURPRISING FACT ABOUT A TEAMMATE? Laura Marsh is a DIY extraordinaire
WHERE IS PARADISE? Krabi, Thailand
CRICKETING HERO? Andrew Flintoff – an entertainer who knew how to win big games for England
NON-CRICKETING HERO? Jessica Ennis-Hill
TWITTER: @tashfarrant

Batting	Mat	Inns	NO	Runs	HS	Ave	SR	100	50	Ct	St
ODIs	1	1	1	1	1*	-	12.50	0	0	0	0
T20Is	9	1	1	1	1*	-	100.00	0	0	1	0

Bowling	Mat	Balls	Runs	Wkts	BBI	BBM	Ave	Econ	SR	5w	10
ODIs	1	42	14	1	1/14	1/14	14.00	2.00	42.0	0	0
T20Is	9	209	174	6	2/15	2/15	29.00	4.99	34.8	0	0

JENNY GUNN

RHB / RMF

FULL NAME: Jennifer Louise Gunn
BORN: May 9, 1986, Nottingham
SQUAD NO: 24
HEIGHT: 5ft 10in
NICKNAME: Chuckie
EDUCATION: South Nottingham College
TEAMS: England, Warwickshire, Loughborough Lightning, Diamonds, Emeralds, Knight Riders, Nottinghamshire, Rubies, South Australia, Super Strikers, Western Australia, Yorkshire Diamonds
ROLE: Allrounder
DEBUT: Test: 2004; ODI: 2004; T20I: 2004

BEST ODI BATTING: 73 England vs New Zealand, Taunton, 2007
BEST ODI BOWLING: 5-22 England vs Pakistan, Louth, 2013

WHAT GOT YOU INTO CRICKET? My family played so I wanted to give it a go
FAMILY TIES? Dad was a professional footballer and, no, I'm not related to the Gunns that played for Notts years ago
'ROY OF THE ROVERS' MOMENT? Taking my first five-wicket haul in a Test match and making my maiden Test fifty in the same match
BEST THING ABOUT YOUR HOME GROUND? It's close to home
BEST OPPOSING PLAYER IN COUNTY CRICKET? Nat Sciver (Sur)
IF YOU WEREN'T A CRICKETER? I'd be a chef or a PE teacher
SURPRISING FACT ABOUT A TEAMMATE? Heather Knight has webbed feet
WHERE IS PARADISE? Australia
CRICKETING HERO? Glenn McGrath – because he was medium pace but excelled nevertheless
NON-CRICKETING HERO? I looked up to Alan Shearer as I wanted to play football for England
TWITTER: @GunnJenny

Batting	Mat	Inns	NO	Runs	HS	Ave	SR	100	50	Ct	St
Tests	11	19	2	391	62*	23.00	30.38	0	1	6	0
ODIs	142	110	28	1625	73	19.81	57.89	0	5	48	0
T20Is	98	65	18	665	69	14.14	100.60	0	1	55	0

Bowling	Mat	Balls	Runs	Wkts	BBI	BBM	Ave	Econ	SR	5w	10
Tests	11	2189	645	29	5/19	5/59	22.24	1.76	75.4	1	0
ODIs	142	5828	3749	135	5/22	5/22	27.77	3.85	43.1	2	0
T20Is	98	1265	1304	70	5/18	5/18	18.62	6.18	18.0	1	0

ALEX HARTLEY
RHB / SLA

FULL NAME: Alexandra Hartley
BORN: September 26, 1993, Blackburn, Lancashire
SQUAD NO: 65
HEIGHT: 5ft 4in
NICKNAME: Hartley (boring)
EDUCATION: Ribbledale High School; Loughborough College
TEAMS: England, Lancashire, Lancashire Thunder, Emeralds, Middlesex, Rubies, Surrey Stars
ROLE: Bowler
DEBUT: ODI: 2016; T20I: 2016

BEST ODI BATTING: 2* England vs West Indies, Florence Hall, 2016
BEST ODI BOWLING: 4-24 England vs West Indies, Kingston, 2016

WHAT GOT YOU INTO CRICKET? The lads on my estate all started going up to the local club on a Friday evening so I asked my mum if I could join them as there was no one to play football with after school on a Friday
'ROY OF THE ROVERS' MOMENT? During a club game a few years ago when a team was giving me grief about being a girl and being rubbish – I went on to take seven wickets!
BEST OPPOSING PLAYER IN COUNTY CRICKET? Katherine Brunt (Yor)
YOUNG OPPOSING PLAYER WHO HAS IMPRESSED YOU? Rachel Dickinson (Lan) – a hard worker behind the scenes and really impressed with the ball last year
IF YOU WEREN'T A CRICKETER? I'd be a zookeeper
SURPRISING FACT ABOUT YOU? I was an extra in Made in Chelsea
SURPRISING FACT ABOUT A TEAMMATE? Fran Wilson is always up for a debate/argument
WHERE IS PARADISE? In the sunshine somewhere – anywhere!
CRICKETING HERO? Monty Panesar – I can relate to the highs and lows of his career – he had to work so hard on all aspects of his game to stay in the England team
NON-CRICKETING HERO? My grandad – I didn't believe him when he told me that I would represent my country but it inspired me to work hard
TWITTER: @alexhartley93

Batting	Mat	Inns	NO	Runs	HS	Ave	SR	100	50	Ct	St
ODIs	20	9	9	7	2*	-	26.92	0	0	3	0
T20Is	2	-	-	-	-	-	-	-	-	0	0

Bowling	Mat	Balls	Runs	Wkts	BBI	BBM	Ave	Econ	SR	5w	10
ODIs	20	1044	703	33	4/24	4/24	21.30	4.04	31.6	0	0
T20Is	2	30	43	3	2/19	2/19	14.33	8.60	10.0	0	0

DANIELLE HAZELL

RHB / OB

FULL NAME: Danielle Hazell
BORN: May 13, 1988, Durham
SQUAD NO: 17
HEIGHT: 5ft 3in
NICKNAME: Pet
EDUCATION: Deerness Valley School
TEAMS: England, Yorkshire, Lancashire Thunder, Diamonds, Durham, Emeralds, Melbourne Stars, Sapphires, Yorkshire Diamonds
ROLE: Bowler
DEBUT: Test: 2011; ODI: 2009; T20I: 2009

BEST ODI BATTING: 45 England vs Sri Lanka, Colombo, 2016
BEST ODI BOWLING: 3-21 England vs Sri Lanka, Colombo, 2016

WHAT GOT YOU INTO CRICKET? Watching my dad play village cricket
FAMILY TIES? Dad coaches at Durham City and my mum does the scoring for the first team
BEST ADVICE EVER RECEIVED? Be yourself
'ROY OF THE ROVERS' MOMENT? Winning the Ashes in 2013 and 2014
BEST THING ABOUT YOUR HOME GROUND? My home ground is Durham City CC – my mam does the teas on Saturdays!
IF YOU WEREN'T A CRICKETER? I'd be a rally driver
SURPRISING FACT ABOUT YOU? I have a dog called Maverick
WHERE IS PARADISE? County Durham
CRICKETING HERO? Ricky Ponting – such a great competitor
NON-CRICKETING HERO? Alan Shearer – I'm a massive Newcastle United fan
TWITTER: @dhazell17

Batting	Mat	Inns	NO	Runs	HS	Ave	SR	100	50	Ct	St
Tests	3	5	1	28	15	7.00	17.17	0	0	1	0
ODIs	50	24	5	313	45	16.47	85.05	0	0	9	0
T20Is	73	26	8	166	18*	9.22	84.69	0	0	11	0

Bowling	Mat	Balls	Runs	Wkts	BBI	BBM	Ave	Econ	SR	5w	10
Tests	3	390	204	2	2/32	2/52	102.00	3.13	195.0	0	0
ODIs	50	2433	1611	53	3/21	3/21	30.39	3.97	45.9	0	0
T20Is	73	1656	1453	75	4/12	4/12	19.37	5.26	22.0	0	0

J

AMY JONES   RHB / WK

ENGLAND WOMEN

FULL NAME: Amy Ellen Jones
BORN: June 13, 1993, Solihull, Warwickshire
SQUAD NO: 40
HEIGHT: 5ft 9in
NICKNAME: Jonesy
EDUCATION: John Willmott School;
Loughborough College
TEAMS: England, Warwickshire,
Loughborough Lightning, Diamonds,
Emeralds, Rubies, Sydney Sixers, Western
Australia
ROLE: Wicketkeeper/batsman
DEBUT: ODI: 2013; T20I: 2013

BEST ODI BATTING: 41 England vs Sri Lanka, Mumbai, 2013

WHAT GOT YOU INTO CRICKET? I played in a local football team and a lot of the boys played cricket so I went along with them to Walmley CC
FAMILY TIES? My younger sister played for Warwickshire U13. My mum played two games for Walmley when we were short
'ROY OF THE ROVERS' MOMENT? Scoring 155 not out for England Academy against Australia
BEST THING ABOUT YOUR HOME GROUND? The quick outfield and short boundaries
BEST OPPOSING PLAYER IN COUNTY CRICKET? Katherine Brunt (Yor)
YOUNG OPPOSING PLAYER WHO HAS IMPRESSED YOU? Ellie Threlkeld (Lan) – a great young wicketkeeper with a lot of talent
SURPRISING FACT ABOUT YOU? I used to play football for Aston Villa
SURPRISING FACT ABOUT A TEAMMATE? Beth Langston ate 47 chicken wings in one sitting as a challenge
WHERE IS PARADISE? Anywhere with family and friends
CRICKETING HERO? AB de Villiers
NON-CRICKETING HERO? My parents. My dad taught me to catch and mum drove me to all my games
TWITTER: @amyjones313

Batting	Mat	Inns	NO	Runs	HS	Ave	SR	100	50	Ct	St
ODIs	20	14	2	185	41	15.41	68.51	0	0	12	5
T20Is	15	9	0	60	14	6.66	89.55	0	0	7	1

Bowling	Mat	Balls	Runs	Wkts	BBI	BBM	Ave	Econ	SR	5w	10
ODIs	20	-	-	-	-	-	-	-	-	-	-
T20Is	15	-	-	-	-	-	-	-	-	-	-

HEATHER KNIGHT   RHB / OB

FULL NAME: Heather Clare Knight
BORN: December 26, 1990, Plymouth
SQUAD NO: 5
HEIGHT: 5ft 7in
NICKNAME: Trev
EDUCATION: Plymstock School; Cardiff University
TEAMS: England, Berkshire, Western Storm, Devon, Emeralds, Hobart Hurricanes, Rubies, Sapphires, Tasmania
ROLE: Allrounder
DEBUT: Test: 2011; ODI: 2010; T20I: 2010

BEST ODI BATTING: 106 England vs Pakistan, Leicester, 2017
BEST ODI BOWLING: 5-26 England vs Pakistan, Leicester, 2016

WHAT GOT YOU INTO CRICKET? My brother – I always had to bat because if I bowled he would whack me over the fence and we'd lose the ball
FAMILY TIES? My brother played for Devon
BEST ADVICE EVER RECEIVED? Fashion advice from Kate Cross
'ROY OF THE ROVERS' MOMENT? Scoring my first Test hundred
BEST OPPOSING PLAYER IN COUNTY CRICKET? Katherine Brunt (Yor)
YOUNG OPPOSING PLAYER WHO HAS IMPRESSED YOU? Katie Levick (Yor) – very funny on Twitter
SURPRISING FACT ABOUT YOU? I played in the match which set the record for the highest-altitude game of cricket (Mount Kilimanjaro, Tanzania, 2014)
SURPRISING FACT ABOUT A TEAMMATE? Laura Marsh likes mushroom sandwiches
WHERE IS PARADISE? The view from a high place
CRICKETING HERO? Marcus Trescothick – a west country legend
NON-CRICKETING HERO? Julie Walters
TWITTER: @heatherknight55

Batting	Mat	Inns	NO	Runs	HS	Ave	SR	100	50	Ct	St
Tests	6	12	1	358	157	32.54	41.38	1	2	6	0
ODIs	78	74	16	2067	106	35.63	67.92	1	14	28	0
T20Is	39	34	5	418	51	14.41	106.36	0	1	13	0

Bowling	Mat	Balls	Runs	Wkts	BBI	BBM	Ave	Econ	SR	5w	10
Tests	6	179	80	2	1/7	1/7	40.00	2.68	89.5	0	0
ODIs	78	1331	957	43	5/26	5/26	22.25	4.31	30.9	1	0
T20Is	39	303	279	12	3/10	3/10	23.25	5.52	25.2	0	0

ENGLAND WOMEN

FULL NAME: Bethany Alicia Langston
BORN: September 6, 1992, Harold Wood, Essex
SQUAD NO: 42
HEIGHT: 5ft 7in
NICKNAME: Langers
EDUCATION: Coopers' Company and Coborn School; Loughborough University
TEAMS: England, Yorkshire, Yorkshire Diamonds, Diamonds, Emeralds, Essex, Loughborough Lightning, Otago
ROLE: Bowler
DEBUT: ODI: 2016; T20I: 2013

BEST ODI BATTING: 21 England vs Sri Lanka, Colombo, 2016
BEST ODI BOWLING: 1-23 England vs Sri Lanka, Colombo, 2016

WHAT GOT YOU INTO CRICKET? My dad and my three older brothers played at our local club Upminster CC

BEST THING ABOUT YOUR HOME GROUND? There's usually a buzz at the Haslegrave ground at Loughborough even with only a few hundred spectators because it's a small ground

BEST OPPOSING PLAYER IN COUNTY CRICKET? Nat Sciver (Sur)

YOUNG OPPOSING PLAYER WHO HAS IMPRESSED YOU? Sophia Dunkley (Mid) – hits the ball cleanly and in unorthodox places. Also bowls handy leg-spin

IF YOU WEREN'T A CRICKETER? I'd be a professional dog-walker

SURPRISING FACT ABOUT YOU? I can play the bass guitar on expert level in the video game Rock Band

SURPRISING FACT ABOUT A TEAMMATE? Katherine Brunt has a tattoo of the dates of all her cricketing milestones

WHERE IS PARADISE? New Zealand

NON-CRICKETING HERO? JK Rowling – for creating Harry Potter, doing lots of charity work and also being a sass queen on Twitter

UNUSUAL OBJECT AT HOME? A pair of onion-chopping glasses that wouldn't look out of place on Dame Edna Everage

TWITTER: @B_Langers92

Batting	Mat	Inns	NO	Runs	HS	Ave	SR	100	50	Ct	St
ODIs	4	2	1	21	21	21.00	100.00	0	0	2	0
T20Is	2	-	-	-	-	-	-	-	-	1	0

Bowling	Mat	Balls	Runs	Wkts	BBI	BBM	Ave	Econ	SR	5w	10
ODIs	4	186	94	2	1/23	1/23	47.00	3.03	93.0	0	0
T20Is	2	48	44	1	1/16	1/16	44.00	5.50	48.0	0	0

LAURA MARSH   RHB / OB

FULL NAME: Laura Alexandra Marsh
BORN: December 5, 1986, Pembury, Kent
SQUAD NO: 7
HEIGHT: 5ft 5in
NICKNAME: Boggy, Marshy
EDUCATION: Brighton College;
Loughborough University
TEAMS: England, Kent, Surrey Stars, Braves,
Emeralds, New South Wales, Otago, Rubies,
Sapphires, Sussex, Sydney Sixers
ROLE: Bowler
DEBUT: Test: 2006; ODI: 2006; T20I: 2007

BEST ODI BATTING: 67 England vs Ireland, Kibworth, 2010
BEST ODI BOWLING: 5-15 England vs Pakistan, Sydney, 2009

WHAT GOT YOU INTO CRICKET? My brother
'ROY OF THE ROVERS' MOMENT? Winning the World Cup at Lord's in 2017
BEST OPPOSING PLAYER IN COUNTY CRICKET? Nat Sciver (Sur)
YOUNG OPPOSING PLAYER WHO HAS IMPRESSED YOU? Katie George (Ham) – natural talent
IF YOU WEREN'T A CRICKETER? I'd be a golfer or hockey player
SURPRISING FACT ABOUT YOU? I was the U13 national javelin champion
WHERE IS PARADISE? Barbados
CRICKETING HERO? AB de Villiers – so creative and skilful
NON-CRICKETING HERO? Andy Murray – I admire his work ethic and modesty
UNUSUAL OBJECT AT HOME? A workbench and tools – I like to make things like wine racks
and coffee tables when I have time
TWITTER: @lauramarsh7

Batting	Mat	Inns	NO	Runs	HS	Ave	SR	100	50	Ct	St
Tests	8	11	0	123	55	11.18	22.61	0	1	4	0
ODIs	89	54	11	603	67	14.02	67.60	0	1	21	0
T20Is	60	51	6	729	54	16.20	99.31	0	1	6	0

Bowling	Mat	Balls	Runs	Wkts	BBI	BBM	Ave	Econ	SR	5w	10
Tests	8	1763	679	20	3/44	4/83	33.95	2.31	88.1	0	0
ODIs	89	4618	2936	109	5/15	5/15	26.93	3.81	42.3	1	0
T20Is	60	1347	1169	60	3/12	3/12	19.48	5.20	22.4	0	0

NATALIE SCIVER

RHB / RM

FULL NAME: Natalie Ruth Sciver
BORN: August 20, 1992, Tokyo
SQUAD NO: 39
HEIGHT: 5ft 10in
NICKNAME: Sciv
EDUCATION: Epsom College; Loughborough University
TEAMS: England, Surrey, Surrey Stars, Emeralds, Melbourne Stars, Perth Scorchers, Rubies
ROLE: Allrounder
DEBUT: Test: 2014; ODI: 2013; T20I: 2013

BEST ODI BATTING: 137 England vs Pakistan, Leicester, 2017
BEST ODI BOWLING: 3-3 England vs West Indies, Bristol, 2017

WHAT GOT YOU INTO CRICKET? It was one of many family garden sports
BEST ADVICE EVER RECEIVED? Work hard enough and you can achieve anything
'ROY OF THE ROVERS' MOMENT? Making my maiden ODI hundred against Pakistan in the 2017 World Cup. It was a day when everything went right
BEST THING ABOUT YOUR HOME GROUND? The crowd – they're always on your side!
BEST OPPOSING PLAYER IN COUNTY CRICKET? Emma Lamb (Lan)
YOUNG OPPOSING PLAYER WHO HAS IMPRESSED YOU? Hollie Armitage (Yor) – a hard-hitting batsman who bowls leg-spin and is difficult to face when she gets it right
IF YOU WEREN'T A CRICKETER? I'd pursue a career in dance
SURPRISING FACT ABOUT YOU? I played rugby 7s when I was at school
SURPRISING FACT ABOUT A TEAMMATE? Beth Langston can fit her whole fist in her mouth
WHERE IS PARADISE? The mountains
NON-CRICKETING HERO? David Beckham – I played a lot of football in midfield and wanted to be like him
TWITTER: @natsciver

Batting	Mat	Inns	NO	Runs	HS	Ave	SR	100	50	Ct	St
Tests	4	7	0	140	49	20.00	30.97	0	0	3	0
ODIs	44	38	8	1254	137	41.80	101.86	2	9	22	0
T20Is	40	37	7	543	47	18.10	96.96	0	0	20	0

Bowling	Mat	Balls	Runs	Wkts	BBI	BBM	Ave	Econ	SR	5w	10
Tests	4	269	130	1	1/30	1/30	130.00	2.89	269.0	0	0
ODIs	44	1102	812	32	3/3	3/3	25.37	4.42	34.4	0	0
T20Is	40	569	615	35	4/15	4/15	17.57	6.48	16.2	0	0

ANYA SHRUBSOLE

RHB / RFM

FULL NAME: Anya Shrubsole
BORN: December 7, 1991, Bath
SQUAD NO: 41
HEIGHT: 5ft 10in
NICKNAME: Hoof
EDUCATION: Hayesfield School;
Loughborough University
TEAMS: England, Somerset, Western Storm,
Braves, Emeralds, Perth Scorchers, Rubies
ROLE: Bowler
DEBUT: Test: 2013; ODI: 2008; T20I: 2008

BEST ODI BATTING: 29 England vs New Zealand, Mount Maunganui, 2015
BEST ODI BOWLING: 6-46 England vs India, Lord's, 2017

FAMILY TIES? Dad played for Bath CC for many years and a bit of Minor Counties
BEST ADVICE EVER RECEIVED? Move on quickly when things don't go well
'ROY OF THE ROVERS' MOMENT? My last spell at the 2017 World Cup final
BEST THING ABOUT YOUR HOME GROUND? The familiarity of the surroundings
BEST OPPOSING PLAYER IN COUNTY CRICKET? Heather Knight (Ber)
YOUNG OPPOSING PLAYER WHO HAS IMPRESSED YOU? Katie George (Ham) – can bat, bowl
and field. She has the all-round game to play international cricket
IF YOU WEREN'T A CRICKETER? I'd have tried any other sport I could
SURPRISING FACT ABOUT YOU? I have a cat that I trained to sit and do paw high-fives like a
dog would
WHERE IS PARADISE? Home in Bath
CRICKETING HERO? Michael Holding – for the way he bowled with seemingly minimal effort
NON-CRICKETING HERO? Sir Steve Redgrave – for what he achieved in adversity
TWITTER: @anya_shrubsole

Batting	Mat	Inns	NO	Runs	HS	Ave	SR	100	50	Ct	St
Tests	5	8	0	51	20	6.37	25.12	0	0	3	0
ODIs	49	20	8	169	29	14.08	105.62	0	0	13	0
T20Is	49	10	5	33	10*	6.60	97.05	0	0	15	0

Bowling	Mat	Balls	Runs	Wkts	BBI	BBM	Ave	Econ	SR	5w	10
Tests	5	1098	417	17	4/51	7/99	24.52	2.27	64.5	0	0
ODIs	49	2350	1663	62	6/46	6/46	26.82	4.24	37.9	2	0
T20Is	49	993	929	68	5/11	5/11	13.66	5.61	14.6	1	0

FULL NAME: Sarah Jane Taylor
BORN: May 20, 1989, London
SQUAD NO: 30
HEIGHT: 5ft 8in
NICKNAME: Sezzie, Squirt, Staylor
EDUCATION: St Bede's School; Brighton College
TEAMS: England, Sussex, Surrey Stars, Adelaide Strikers, Emeralds, Lancashire Thunder, Rubies, South Australia, Super Strikers, Wellington
ROLE: Wicketkeeper/batsman
DEBUT: Test: 2006; ODI: 2006; T20I: 2006

BEST ODI BATTING: 129 England vs South Africa, Lord's, 2008

WHAT GOT YOU INTO CRICKET? It was an after-school club at my primary school and, seeing as I used to play football at lunch with the boys, I was convinced to give cricket a go
FAMILY TIES? None. My dad caught a ball once. Apparently
'ROY OF THE ROVERS' MOMENT? Keeping next to Mark Cosgrove at first slip for Northern Districts in the men's A-Grade in Australia
BEST THING ABOUT YOUR HOME GROUND? The burger stand
BEST OPPOSING PLAYER IN COUNTY CRICKET? Tammy Beaumont (Ken)
YOUNG OPPOSING PLAYER WHO HAS IMPRESSED YOU? Sophie Ecclestone (Lan) – she has a brilliant cricket brain for someone so young
IF YOU WEREN'T A CRICKETER? I'd be an archaeologist
SURPRISING FACT ABOUT YOU? I travel with a teddy bear called Bephy
WHERE IS PARADISE? My bed
CRICKETING HERO? Graham Thorpe – he kept the game simple
NON-CRICKETING HERO? Steffi Graf – I loved watching her fight
TWITTER: @sarah_taylor30

Batting	Mat	Inns	NO	Runs	HS	Ave	SR	100	50	Ct	St
Tests	9	16	1	295	40	19.66	49.74	0	0	18	2
ODIs	113	106	13	3786	147	40.70	81.89	6	19	80	45
T20Is	84	82	11	2091	77	29.45	109.76	0	15	22	47

Bowling	Mat	Balls	Runs	Wkts	BBI	BBM	Ave	Econ	SR	5w	10
Tests	9	-	-	-	-	-	-	-	-	-	-
ODIs	113	-	-	-	-	-	-	-	-	-	-
T20Is	84	-	-	-	-	-	-	-	-	-	-

FRAN WILSON

RHB / OB

FULL NAME: Frances Claire Wilson
BORN: November 7, 1991, Farnham, Surrey
SQUAD NO: 35
HEIGHT: 5ft 4in
EDUCATION: University of Bath;
Loughborough University
TEAMS: England, Middlesex, Western Storm,
Diamonds, Emeralds, Rubies, Somerset,
Sydney Thunder, Wellington
ROLE: Batsman
DEBUT: Test: 2017; ODI: 2010; T20I: 2010

ENGLAND WOMEN

BEST ODI BATTING: 81 England vs India, Derby, 2017

WHAT GOT YOU INTO CRICKET? My family and the neighbours next door
'ROY OF THE ROVERS' MOMENT? Being Player of the Match against Pakistan in 2016 after a
five-year absence from international cricket
BEST OPPOSING PLAYER IN COUNTY CRICKET? Heather Knight (Ber)
YOUNG OPPOSING PLAYER WHO HAS IMPRESSED YOU? Sophie Ecclestone (Lan) – she is a
true allrounder
IF YOU WEREN'T A CRICKETER? I'd be a teacher or a coach
SURPRISING FACT ABOUT YOU? I didn't play international cricket for five years after my
England debut. I have an MSc in Sport and Exercise Nutrition and run a business delivering
nutrition workshops in schools
WHERE IS PARADISE? Home
CRICKETING HERO? Brett Lee – always competing and smiling
NON-CRICKETING HEROES? My mum and dad
UNUSUAL OBJECT AT HOME? A violin from year three (I stopped playing in year four)
TWITTER: @fwilson07

Batting	Mat	Inns	NO	Runs	HS	Ave	SR	100	50	Ct	St
Tests	1	1	0	13	13	13.00	24.52	0	0	0	0
ODIs	17	13	0	263	81	20.23	93.26	0	1	7	0
T20Is	10	9	5	115	43*	28.75	102.67	0	0	3	0

Bowling	Mat	Balls	Runs	Wkts	BBI	BBM	Ave	Econ	SR	5w	10
Tests	1	-	-	-	-	-	-	-	-	-	-
ODIs	17	-	-	-	-	-	-	-	-	-	-
T20Is	10	-	-	-	-	-	-	-	-	-	-

LAUREN WINFIELD RHB / WK

FULL NAME: Lauren Winfield
BORN: August 16, 1990, York
SQUAD NO: 58
HEIGHT: 5ft 7in
NICKNAME: Loz
EDUCATION: Lougborough University
TEAMS: England, Yorkshire, Yorkshire
Diamonds, Brisbane Heat, Diamonds, Hobart
Hurricanes, Rubies, Sapphires
ROLE: Batsman/wicketkeeper
DEBUT: Tests: 2014; ODI: 2013; T20I: 2013

BEST ODI BATTING: 123 England vs Pakistan, Worcester, 2016

WHAT GOT YOU INTO CRICKET? My dad plays and we spent many a Saturday afternoon
down at my local club Stamford Bridge
BEST ADVICE EVER RECEIVED? Nothing is a given
'ROY OF THE ROVERS' MOMENT? Winning the World Cup at Lord's in 2017 was pretty
great. Also sharing the highest opening-partnership stand for England – 235 – with Tammy
Beaumont and making my first international hundred in the same game
BEST THING ABOUT YOUR HOME GROUND? The support from the home fans
BEST OPPOSING PLAYER IN COUNTY CRICKET? Sophia Dunkley (Mid)
IF YOU WEREN'T A CRICKETER? I think I'd be in the police force
SURPRISING FACT ABOUT YOU? I love classical music
WHERE IS PARADISE? The Maldives
CRICKETING HERO? Graham Dilley – my former coach at Loughborough, my mentor and a
good friend
NON-CRICKETING HERO? My mum
UNUSUAL OBJECT AT HOME? A ukulele
TWITTER: @Lozwinfield

Batting	Mat	Inns	NO	Runs	HS	Ave	SR	100	50	Ct	St
Tests	3	6	0	94	35	15.66	25.06	0	0	1	0
ODIs	35	35	2	773	123	23.42	64.95	1	3	13	0
T20Is	18	18	1	404	74	23.76	112.53	0	3	6	0
Bowling	Mat	Balls	Runs	Wkts	BBI	BBM	Ave	Econ	SR	5w	10
Tests	3	-	-	-	-	-	-	-	-	-	-
ODIs	35	-	-	-	-	-	-	-	-	-	-
T20Is	18	-	-	-	-	-	-	-	-	-	-

DANIELLE WYATT

RHB / OB

FULL NAME: Danielle Nicole Wyatt
BORN: April 22, 1991, Stoke-on-Trent, Staffordshire
SQUAD NO: 28
HEIGHT: 5ft 4in
NICKNAME: Chesney, Waggy
EDUCATION: St Peter's High School; Stoke-on-Trent Sixth Form College
TEAMS: England, Sussex, Southern Vipers, Lancashire Thunder, Melbourne Renegades, Nottinghamshire, Sapphires, Staffordshire
ROLE: Allrounder
DEBUT: ODI: 2010; T20I: 2010

ENGLAND WOMEN

BEST ODI BATTING: 44 England vs West Indies, Florence Hall, 2016
BEST ODI BOWLING: 3-7 England vs South Africa, Cuttack, 2013

FAMILY TIES? My older brother Ryan played but then he quit when I got better than him – whoops! Dad still rolls them over on a Sunday for the mighty Whitmore Third XI
BEST ADVICE EVER RECEIVED? Block the good 'uns, hit the bad 'uns (Charlotte Edwards, 2012)
'ROY OF THE ROVERS' MOMENT? Scoring a hundred for the men's Whitmore team – the opposition complained to the league that I should not have been allowed to play. Ha!
BEST THING ABOUT YOUR HOME GROUND? Whitmore CC is home. I'll be visiting it till the day I die. It's my happiness
BEST OPPOSING PLAYER IN COUNTY CRICKET? Tash Farrant (Ken)
YOUNG OPPOSING PLAYER WHO HAS IMPRESSED YOU? Katie George (Ham) – left-arm seamer with good pace, athletic fielder, and not short of confidence!
IF YOU WEREN'T A CRICKETER? I'd be a vet, or a zookeeper who looks after dolphins
SURPRISING FACT ABOUT YOU? I fell out of a tree aged 10. Broke my wrist and foot
WHERE IS PARADISE? Watching the sun go down at St Kilda, Melbourne, with a burrito and a cup of tea and some chocolate
NON-CRICKETING HERO? My grandad Baggaley, who sadly passed away in November. I've never been so broke in all my life. He ran marathons until he was 70
TWITTER: @Danni_wyatt

Batting	Mat	Inns	NO	Runs	HS	Ave	SR	100	50	Ct	St
ODIs	53	42	7	602	44	17.20	73.50	0	0	10	0
T20Is	73	52	8	657	100	14.93	114.26	1	1	16	0

Bowling	Mat	Balls	Runs	Wkts	BBI	BBM	Ave	Econ	SR	5w	10
ODIs	53	864	718	27	3/7	3/7	26.59	4.98	32.0	0	0
T20Is	73	711	671	46	4/11	4/11	14.58	5.66	15.4	0	0

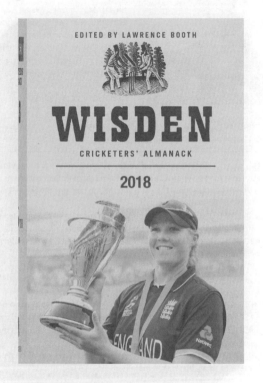

The
Umpires

ROB BAILEY

NAME: Robert John Bailey
BORN: October 28, 1963,
Biddulph, Staffordshire
HEIGHT: 6ft 3in
NICKNAME: Bailers
APPOINTED TO FIRST-CLASS
LIST: 2006
INTERNATIONAL PANEL: 2011-
ELITE PANEL: 2014
TESTS UMPIRED: 1 (1 as TV)

ODIS UMPIRED: 24 (4 as TV)
T20IS UMPIRED: 23 (8 as TV)
COUNTIES AS PLAYER:
Northamptonshire, Derbyshire
ROLE: Batsman; RHB OB
COUNTY DEBUT: 1982
(Northamptonshire), 2000
(Derbyshire)
TEST DEBUT: 1988
ODI DEBUT: 1985

Batting	Mat	Inns	NO	Runs	HS	Ave	SR	100	50	Ct	St
Tests	4	8	0	119	43	14.87	36.50	0	0	0	0
ODIs	4	4	2	137	43*	68.50	69.89	0	0	1	0
First-class	374	628	89	21844	224*	40.52		47	111	272	0
List A	396	376	65	12076	153*	38.82		10	79	111	0

Bowling	Mat	Balls	Runs	Wkts	BBI	BBM	Ave	Econ	SR	5w	10
Tests	4	-	-	-	-	-	-	-	-	-	-
ODIs	4	36	25	0	-	-	-	4.16	-	0	0
First-class	374	9713	5144	121	5/54	5/59	42.51	3.17	80.2	2	0
List A	396	3092	2564	72	5/45	5/45	35.61	4.97	42.9	1	0

NEIL BAINTON

NAME: Neil Laurence Bainton
BORN: October 2, 1970,
Romford, Essex
HEIGHT: 5ft 8in
APPOINTED TO FIRST-CLASS
LIST: 2006

FAVOURITE OUTGROUND? Colwyn Bay. Lovely little ground, great pitch, friendly people
TRICKS TO MAINTAIN CONCENTRATION? Split sessions into 15-minute segments
STRANGEST LOCATION WHERE UMPIRED? I'm lucky to have umpired in Mozambique and
Uganda on MCC tours
FAVOURITE UMPIRE AS A PLAYER? As a non-player, I always looked up to Nigel Plews – he
was a great help to recreational umpires
HIGHLIGHT OF YOUR PLAYING CAREER? I kept wicket for South of England U15 at the
England Schools Festival in 1986
FAVOURITE PASTIMES OUTSIDE OF CRICKET? Playing golf badly
SURPRISING FACT? I still work for the Royal Mail as a postman during the winter months

PAUL BALDWIN

NAME: Paul Kerr Baldwin
BORN: July 18, 1973, Epsom, Surrey
APPOINTED TO FIRST-CLASS LIST: 2015
ODIS UMPIRED: 20 (2 as TV umpire)
T20IS UMPIRED: 9

UNUSUAL ITEM RECEIVED FROM A BOWLER? Teeth
HIGHLIGHT OF YOUR PLAYING CAREER? Being selected to captain RAF Brüggen, my club side in Germany in 1996, which I captained for the next four years
FAVOURITE PASTIMES OUTSIDE OF CRICKET? Equestrian photography – mostly when our horses compete. And walking with our two black labs in the Lincolnshire countryside
SURPRISING FACT? I was the English voice on BFBS Forces radio of DJ Ötzi who sung 'Hey Baby!' in the '90s
UNUSUAL OBJECT AT HOME? A trophy for winning an episode of Fifteen to One (on Channel 4). It belongs to my partner Emma – she's incredibly intelligent and even more competitive than I am

IAN BLACKWELL

NAME: Ian David Blackwell
BORN: June 10, 1978, Chesterfield, Derbyshire
HEIGHT: 6ft 2in
NICKNAME: Blackdog
APPOINTED TO FIRST-CLASS LIST: 2014
COUNTIES AS PLAYER: Derbyshire, Somerset, Durham, Warwickshire

ROLE: Allrounder; LHB SLA
COUNTY DEBUT: 1997 (Derbyshire), 2000 (Somerset), 2009 (Durham), 2012 (Warwickshire)
TEST DEBUT: 2006
ODI DEBUT: 2002

Batting	Mat	Inns	NO	Runs	HS	Ave	SR	100	50	Ct	St
Tests	1	1	0	4	4	4.00	25.00	0	0	0	0
ODIs	34	29	2	403	82	14.92	86.66	0	1	8	0
First-class	210	319	26	11595	247*	39.57		27	64	66	0
List A	254	233	21	5765	134*	27.19		3	34	64	0
T20s	77	69	9	1281	82	21.35	131.79	0	5	17	0

Bowling	Mat	Balls	Runs	Wkts	BBI	BBM	Ave	Econ	SR	5w	10
Tests	1	114	71	0	-	-	-	3.73		0	0
ODIs	34	1230	877	24	3/26	3/26	36.54	4.27	51.2	0	0
First-class	210	31618	14295	398	7/52	9/154	35.91	2.71	79.4	14	0
List A	254	8885	7102	207	5/26	5/26	34.30	4.79	42.9	1	0
T20s	77	1273	1508	50	4/26	4/26	30.16	7.10	25.4	0	0

MIKE BURNS

NAME: Mike Burns
BORN: February 6, 1969,
Barrow-in- Furness,
Lancashire
**APPOINTED TO FIRST-CLASS
LIST:** 2016
COUNTIES AS PLAYER:
Warwickshire, Somerset
ROLE: Allrounder; RHB RM
WK

COUNTY DEBUT: 1992
(Warwickshire), 1997
(Somerset)

Batting	Mat	Inns	NO	Runs	HS	Ave	SR	100	50	Ct	St
First-class	154	248	14	7648	221	32.68		8	51	142	7
List A	221	207	21	4802	115*	25.81		3	31	101	15
T20s	9	7	0	108	36	15.42	108.00	0	0	3	0

Bowling	Mat	Balls	Runs	Wkts	BBI	BBM	Ave	Econ	SR	5w	10
First-class	154	4751	2885	68	6/54	6/120	42.42	3.64	69.8	1	0
List A	221	1844	1769	58	4/39	4/39	30.50	5.75	31.7	0	0
T20s	9	36	55	2	1/15	1/15	27.50	9.16	18.0	0	0

NICK COOK

NAME: Nicholas Grant Billson
Cook
HEIGHT: 6ft
NICKNAME: Beast
**APPOINTED TO FIRST-CLASS
LIST:** 2009
COUNTIES AS PLAYER:
Leicestershire,
Northamptonshire

ROLE: Bowler; RHB SLA
COUNTY DEBUT: 1978
(Leicestershire), 1986
(Northamptonshire)
TEST DEBUT: 1983
ODI DEBUT: 1984

Batting	Mat	Inns	NO	Runs	HS	Ave	SR	100	50	Ct	St
Tests	15	25	4	179	31	8.52	23.58	0	0	5	0
ODIs	3	-	-	-	-	-	-	-	-	2	0
First-class	356	365	96	3137	75	11.66		0	4	197	0
List A	223	89	36	491	23	9.26		0	0	74	0

Bowling	Mat	Balls	Runs	Wkts	BBI	BBM	Ave	Econ	SR	5w	10
Tests	15	4174	1689	52	6/65	11/83	32.48	2.42	80.2	4	1
ODIs	3	144	95	5	2/18	2/18	19.00	3.95	28.8	0	0
First-class	356	64460	25507	879	7/34	12/130	29.01	2.37	73.3	31	4
List A	223	10077	6812	200	4/22	4/22	34.06	4.05	50.3	0	0

BEN DEBENHAM

NAME: Benjamin John Debenham
BORN: October 11, 1967, Chelmsford, Essex
APPOINTED TO FIRST-CLASS LIST: 2012

FAVOURITE OUTGROUND? Radlett CC – a good ground, great food and only 45 minutes from home
TRICKS TO MAINTAIN CONCENTRATION? Enjoying the cricket helps to retain focus
UNUSUAL ITEM RECEIVED FROM A BOWLER? A mobile phone – the bowler's friends were saying he was bowling rubbish on Snapchat
STRANGEST LOCATION WHERE UMPIRED? At a coffee plantation in Arusha, North Tanzania
FAVOURITE UMPIRE AS A PLAYER? Neil Bainton – he made me look fit even when I was past it
HIGHLIGHT OF YOUR PLAYING CAREER? Captaining MCC against Melbourne CC at the MCG
UNUSUAL OBJECT AT HOME? A dog from Madagascar

JEFF EVANS

NAME: Jeffrey Howard Evans
BORN: August 7, 1954, Llanelli, Carmarthenshire, Wales
HEIGHT: 5ft 8in
APPOINTED TO FIRST-CLASS LIST: 2001

FAVOURITE OUTGROUND? Scarborough – for its atmosphere and excellent support
TRICKS TO MAINTAIN CONCENTRATION? Healthy body, healthy mind
FUNNIEST THING HEARD IN THE MIDDLE? "Bowl him a piano and see if he can play that" (after a batsman had continually played and missed)
MOST MEMORABLE DISMISSAL? Giving Brian Lara out first ball in the Indian Cricket League. Thankfully the replays showed the decision was correct
FUNNIEST MOMENT AS AN UMPIRE? Watching the band of the Royal Gurkha Regiment march towards the boundary in Canterbury only for them to immediately turn around and march towards the pitch. At this point my colleague Vanburn Holder called "play" with the band situated at mid-off

MICHAEL GOUGH

NAME: Michael Andrew Gough
BORN: December 18, 1978, Hartlepool
HEIGHT: 6ft 5in
NICKNAME: Goughy
APPOINTED TO FIRST-CLASS LIST: 2009
INTERNATIONAL PANEL: 2013-
ELITE PANEL: 2014
TESTS UMPIRED: 9 (3 as TV)

ODIS UMPIRED: 55 (16 as TV)
T20IS UMPIRED: 16 (5 as TV)
COUNTY AS PLAYER: Durham
ROLE: Batsman; RHB OB
COUNTY DEBUT: 1998

FAVOURITE OUTGROUND? Colchester – I scored my first Championship hundred and umpired my first Championship match at the ground
SURPRISING FACT? I'm a qualified football ref and season-ticket holder at Hartlepool United FC
UNUSUAL OBJECT AT HOME? U19 World Cup winner's medal from South Africa, 1998

Batting	Mat	Inns	NO	Runs	HS	Ave	SR	100	50	Ct	St
First-class	67	119	3	2952	123	25.44		2	15	57	0
List A	49	45	4	974	132	23.75		1	3	14	0

Bowling	Mat	Balls	Runs	Wkts	BBI	BBM	Ave	Econ	SR	5w	10
First-class	67	2486	1350	30	5/66	5/104	45.00	3.25	82.8	1	0
List A	49	1136	947	21	3/26	3/26	45.09	5.00	54.0	0	0

IAN GOULD

NAME: Ian James Gould
BORN: August 19, 1957, Taplow, Buckinghamshire
HEIGHT: 5ft 7in
NICKNAME: Gunner
APPOINTED TO FIRST-CLASS LIST: 2002
INTERNATIONAL PANEL: 2006-
ELITE PANEL: 2009-
TESTS UMPIRED: 85 (21 as TV)

ODIS UMPIRED: 166 (41 as TV)
T20IS UMPIRED: 55 (18 as TV)
COUNTIES AS PLAYER: Middlesex, Sussex
ROLE: Wicketkeeper; LHB
COUNTY DEBUT: 1975 (Middlesex), 1981 (Sussex)
ODI DEBUT: 1983

Batting	Mat	Inns	NO	Runs	HS	Ave	SR	100	50	Ct	St
ODIs	18	14	2	155	42	12.91	63.78	0	0	15	3
First-class	298	399	63	8756	128	26.05		4	47	536	67
List A	315	270	41	4377	88	19.11		0	20	242	37

Bowling	Mat	Balls	Runs	Wkts	BBI	BBM	Ave	Econ	SR	5w	10
ODIs	18	-	-	-	-	-	-	-	-	-	-
First-class	298	478	365	7	3/10	3/10	52.14	4.58	68.2	0	0
List A	315	20	16	1	1/0	1/0	16.00	4.80	20.0	0	0

PETER HARTLEY

NAME: Peter John Hartley
BORN: April 18, 1960, Keighley, Yorkshire
HEIGHT: 6ft
NICKNAME: Jack
APPOINTED TO FIRST-CLASS LIST: 2003
INTERNATIONAL PANEL: 2006-2009
TESTS UMPIRED: 9 (9 as TV)

ODIS UMPIRED: 16 (10 as TV)
T20IS UMPIRED: 7 (4 as TV)
COUNTIES AS PLAYER: Warwickshire, Yorkshire, Hampshire
ROLE: Bowler; RHB RFM
COUNTY DEBUT: 1982 (Warwickshire), 1985 (Yorkshire), 1998 (Hampshire)

STRANGEST LOCATION WHERE UMPIRED? An army camp in Kuala Lumpur
CAREER HIGHLIGHT AS AN UMPIRE? Standing in T20 Finals Day
IF YOU COULD CHANGE ONE RULE ABOUT CRICKET, WHAT WOULD IT BE? Any ball that passes above the height of the stumps (without bouncing) should be a no-ball

Batting	Mat	Inns	NO	Runs	HS	Ave	SR	100	50	Ct	St
First-class	232	283	66	4321	127*	19.91		2	14	68	0
List A	269	170	62	1765	83	16.34		0	4	46	0

Bowling	Mat	Balls	Runs	Wkts	BBI	BBM	Ave	Econ	SR	5w	10
First-class	232	37108	20635	683	9/41	11/168	30.21	3.33	54.3	23	3
List A	269	12636	9069	356	5/20	5/20	25.47	4.30	35.4	5	0

RICHARD ILLINGWORTH

NAME: Richard Keith Illingworth
HEIGHT: 5ft 11in
NICKNAME: Harry, Lucy
APPOINTED TO FIRST-CLASS LIST: 2006
INTERNATIONAL PANEL: 2009-
ELITE PANEL: 2013-
TESTS UMPIRED: 44 (13 as TV)
ODIS UMPIRED: 102 (45 as TV)

T20IS UMPIRED: 23 (7 as TV)
COUNTIES AS PLAYER: Worcestershire, Derbyshire
ROLE: Bowler; RHB SLA
COUNTY DEBUT: 1982 (Worcestershire), 2001 (Derbyshire)
TEST DEBUT: 1991
ODI DEBUT: 1991

Batting	Mat	Inns	NO	Runs	HS	Ave	SR	100	50	Ct	St
Tests	9	14	7	128	28	18.28	32.08	0	0	5	0
ODIs	25	11	5	68	14	11.33	57.14	0	0	8	0
First-class	376	435	122	7027	120*	22.45		4	21	161	0
List A	381	185	87	1458	53*	14.87		0	1	93	0

Bowling	Mat	Balls	Runs	Wkts	BBI	BBM	Ave	Econ	SR	5w	10
Tests	9	1485	615	19	4/96	6/150	32.36	2.48	78.1	0	0
ODIs	25	1501	1059	30	3/33	3/33	35.30	4.23	50.0	0	0
First-class	376	65868	26213	831	7/50	13/159	31.54	2.38	79.2	27	6
List A	381	16918	11157	412	5/24	5/24	27.08	3.95	41.0	2	0

RICHARD KETTLEBOROUGH

NAME: Richard Allan Kettleborough
HEIGHT: 5ft 10in
NICKNAME: Ketts
APPOINTED TO FIRST-CLASS LIST: 2006
INTERNATIONAL PANEL: 2008-
ELITE PANEL: 2011-
TESTS UMPIRED: 67 (17 as TV)
ODIS UMPIRED: 108 (34 as TV)

T20IS UMPIRED: 31 (9 as TV)
COUNTIES AS PLAYER: Yorkshire, Middlesex
ROLE: Batsman; LHB RM
COUNTY DEBUT: 1994 (Yorkshire), 1998 (Middlesex)

CAREER HIGHLIGHT AS AN UMPIRE? Standing in the World Cup final at the MCG in front of 95,000 people and in Sachin Tendulkar's final Test match in Mumbai
RITUALS OR QUIRKS? I always take a picture of my children out to the middle with me

Batting	Mat	Inns	NO	Runs	HS	Ave	SR	100	50	Ct	St
First-class	33	56	6	1258	108	25.16		1	7	20	0
List A	21	16	4	290	58	24.16		0	1	6	0

Bowling	Mat	Balls	Runs	Wkts	BBI	BBM	Ave	Econ	SR	5w	10
First-class	33	378	243	3	2/26	2/26	81.00	3.85	126.0	0	0
List A	21	270	230	6	2/43	2/43	38.33	5.11	45.0	0	0

NIGEL LLONG

NAME: Nigel James Llong
BORN: February 11, 1969, Ashford, Kent
HEIGHT: 6ft
NICKNAME: Nidge
APPOINTED TO FIRST-CLASS LIST: 2002
INTERNATIONAL PANEL: 2004-2006 (TV umpire), 2006-present (full member)

ELITE PANEL: 2012-
TESTS UMPIRED: 72 (23 as TV)
ODIS UMPIRED: 178 (66 as TV)
T20IS UMPIRED: 44 (12 as TV)
COUNTY AS PLAYER: Kent
ROLE: Allrounder; LHB OB
COUNTY DEBUT: 1990

FAVOURITE OUTGROUND? Tunbridge Wells – beautiful with the rhododendrons in flower
STRANGEST LOCATION WHERE UMPIRED? Dharamsala under the Himalayas in India
HIGHLIGHT OF YOUR PLAYING CAREER? Kent v Glamorgan at Canterbury in 1995. One-day match to decide the league champions. Best atmosphere I've played in

Batting	Mat	Inns	NO	Runs	HS	Ave	SR	100	50	Ct	St
First-class	68	108	11	3024	130	31.17		6	16	59	0
List A	136	115	24	2302	123	25.29		2	8	41	0

Bowling	Mat	Balls	Runs	Wkts	BBI	BBM	Ave	Econ	SR	5w	10
First-class	68	2273	1259	35	5/21	6/76	35.97	3.32	64.9	2	0
List A	136	1317	1210	40	4/24	4/24	30.25	5.51	32.9	0	0

GRAHAM LLOYD

NAME: Graham David Lloyd
BORN: July 1, 1969, Accrington, Lancashire
APPOINTED TO FIRST-CLASS LIST: 2014
COUNTY AS PLAYER: Lancashire
ROLE: Batsman; RHB RM
COUNTY DEBUT: 1988
ODI DEBUT: 1996

Batting	Mat	Inns	NO	Runs	HS	Ave	SR	100	50	Ct	St
ODIs	6	5	1	39	22	9.75	48.75	0	0	2	0
First-class	203	323	28	11279	241	38.23		24	64	140	0
List A	295	258	48	6117	134	29.12		4	29	67	0

Bowling	Mat	Balls	Runs	Wkts	BBI	BBM	Ave	Econ	SR	5w	10
ODIs	6	-	-	-	-	-	-	-	-	-	-
First-class	203	339	440	2	1/4	1/4	220.00	7.78	169.5	0	0
List A	295	72	103	1	1/23	1/23	103.00	8.58	72.0	0	0

JEREMY LLOYDS

NAME: Jeremy William Lloyds
BORN: November 17, 1954, Penang, Malaysia
HEIGHT: 5ft 11in
NICKNAME: Jerry
APPOINTED TO FIRST-CLASS LIST: 1998
INTERNATIONAL PANEL: 2002-2004 (TV umpire); 2004-2006 (full member)

TESTS UMPIRED: 15 (10 as TV)
ODIS UMPIRED: 40 (22 as TV)
T20IS UMPIRED: 1
COUNTIES AS PLAYER: Somerset, Gloucestershire
ROLE: Allrounder; LHB OB
COUNTY DEBUT: 1979 (Somerset), 1985 (Gloucestershire)

FAVOURITE OUTGROUND? Scarborough, Chesterfield, Cheltenham or Southport
HIGHLIGHT OF YOUR PLAYING CAREER? Winning the NatWest Trophy final in 1983 with Somerset
SURPRISING FACT? I'm probably a better rugby player than a cricketer, or so my friends at Taunton RFC tell me

Batting	Mat	Inns	NO	Runs	HS	Ave	SR	100	50	Ct	St
First-class	267	408	64	10679	132*	31.04		10	62	229	0
List A	177	150	26	1982	73*	15.98		0	5	58	0

Bowling	Mat	Balls	Runs	Wkts	BBI	BBM	Ave	Econ	SR	5w	10
First-class	267	24175	12943	333	7/88	11/95	38.86	3.21	72.5	13	1
List A	177	1522	1129	26	3/14	3/14	43.42	4.45	58.5	0	0

NEIL MALLENDER

NAME: Neil Alan Mallender
BORN: August 13, 1961, Kirk Sandall, Yorkshire
HEIGHT: 6ft
NICKNAME: Ghostie
APPOINTED TO FIRST-CLASS LIST: 1999
INTERNATIONAL PANEL: 2002-2004
TESTS UMPIRED: 8 (5 as TV)

ODIS UMPIRED: 32 (10 as TV)
COUNTIES AS PLAYER: Northamptonshire, Somerset
ROLE: Bowler; RHB RFM
COUNTY DEBUT: 1980 (Northamptonshire), 1987 (Somerset)
TEST DEBUT: 1992

Batting	Mat	Inns	NO	Runs	HS	Ave	SR	100	50	Ct	St
Tests	2	3	0	8	4	2.66	36.36	0	0	0	0
First-class	345	396	122	4709	100*	17.18		1	10	111	0
List A	325	163	75	1146	38*	13.02		0	0	60	0

Bowling	Mat	Balls	Runs	Wkts	BBI	BBM	Ave	Econ	SR	5w	10
Tests	2	449	215	10	5/50	8/122	21.50	2.87	44.9	1	0
First-class	345	53215	24654	937	7/27	12/92	26.31	2.77	56.7	36	5
List A	325	15488	9849	387	7/37	7/37	25.44	3.81	40.0	3	0

DAVID MILLNS

NAME: David James Millns
BORN: February 7, 1965, Clipstone, Nottinghamshire
HEIGHT: 6ft 3in
NICKNAME: Rocket Man
APPOINTED TO FIRST-CLASS LIST: 2009
COUNTIES AS A PLAYER: Nottinghamshire, Leicestershire

ROLE: Bowler; LHB RF
COUNTY DEBUT: 1988 (Nottinghamshire), 1990 (Leicestershire)

UNUSUAL ITEM RECEIVED FROM A BOWLER? Tino Best gave me his gold chain to hold in Barbados when the clasp broke – must have weighed at least two pounds. Proper bling
STRANGEST LOCATION WHERE UMPIRED? Palam Station Air Force Base in Delhi, India
HIGHLIGHT OF YOUR PLAYING CAREER? Winning two Championships with Leicestershire

Batting	Mat	Inns	NO	Runs	HS	Ave	SR	100	50	Ct	St
First-class	171	203	63	3082	121	22.01		3	8	76	0
List A	91	49	26	338	39*	14.69		0	0	18	0

Bowling	Mat	Balls	Runs	Wkts	BBI	BBM	Ave	Econ	SR	5w	10
First-class	171	26571	15129	553	9/37	12/91	27.35	3.41	48.0	23	4
List A	91	3931	3144	83	4/26	4/26	37.87	4.79	47.3	0	0

STEVE O'SHAUGHNESSY

NAME: Steven Joseph O'Shaughnessy
BORN: September 9, 1961, Bury, Lancashire
APPOINTED TO FIRST-CLASS LIST: 2011
COUNTIES AS PLAYER: Lancashire, Worcestershire
ROLE: Allrounder; RHB RM

COUNTY DEBUT: 1980 (Lancashire), 1988 (Worcestershire)

UMPIRES

NOTES: O'Shaughnessy started umpiring in 2007 and was appointed to the full list for the 2011 season. He has officiated in four women's ODIs, including in the 2013 Ashes series. As a player he won the Walter Lawrence Trophy for the fastest hundred of the 1983 season – a 35-minute blitz for Lancashire against Leicestershire at Old Trafford

Batting	Mat	Inns	NO	Runs	HS	Ave	SR	100	50	Ct	St
First-class	112	181	28	3720	159*	24.31		5	16	57	0
List A	176	151	23	2999	101*	23.42		1	15	44	0

Bowling	Mat	Balls	Runs	Wkts	BBI	BBM	Ave	Econ	SR	5w	10
First-class	112	7179	4108	114	4/66	5/94	36.03	3.43	62.9	0	0
List A	176	5389	4184	115	4/17	4/17	36.38	4.65	46.8	0	0

PAUL POLLARD

NAME: Paul Raymond Pollard
BORN: September 24, 1968, Nottingham
APPOINTED TO FIRST-CLASS LIST: 2018
COUNTIES AS PLAYER: Nottinghamshire, Worcestershire
ROLE: Batsman; LHB RM

COUNTY DEBUT: 1987 (Nottinghamshire), 2004 (Worcestershire)

STRANGEST LOCATION WHERE UMPIRED? Mumbles CC in the Gower Pensinula, South Wales – 40mph winds on a huge slope at the side of a cliff
HIGHLIGHT OF YOUR PLAYING CAREER? Being in a meeting with Ken Taylor (then Notts manager) and Clive Rice in which I was told that I could play for Notts

Batting	Mat	Inns	NO	Runs	HS	Ave	SR	100	50	Ct	St
First-class	192	332	24	9685	180	31.44		15	48	158	0
List A	187	173	17	5233	132*	33.54		5	33	66	0

Bowling	Mat	Balls	Runs	Wkts	BBI	BBM	Ave	Econ	SR	5w	10
First-class	192	275	272	4	2/79	2/79	68.00	5.93	68.7	0	0
List A	187	18	9	0	-	-	-	3.00	-	0	0

UMPIRES

TIM ROBINSON

NAME: Robert Timothy Robinson
BORN: November 21, 1958, Sutton-in-Ashfield, Nottinghamshire
HEIGHT: 6ft
NICKNAME: Robbo, Chop
APPOINTED TO FIRST-CLASS LIST: 2007
INTERNATIONAL PANEL: 2013-

TESTS UMPIRED: 1 (1 as TV)
ODIS UMPIRED: 14 (1 as TV)
T20IS UMPIRED: 17 (7 as TV)
COUNTY AS PLAYER: Nottinghamshire
ROLE: Batsman; RHB RM
COUNTY DEBUT: 1978
TEST DEBUT: 1984
ODI DEBUT: 1984

Batting	Mat	Inns	NO	Runs	HS	Ave	SR	100	50	Ct	St
Tests	29	49	5	1601	175	36.38	41.62	4	6	8	0
ODIs	26	26	0	597	83	22.96	58.18	0	3	6	0
First-class	425	739	85	27571	220*	42.15		63	141	257	0
List A	397	386	40	11879	139	34.33		9	75	120	0

Bowling	Mat	Balls	Runs	Wkts	BBI	BBM	Ave	Econ	SR	5w	10
Tests	29	6	0	0	-	-	-	0.00	-	0	0
ODIs	26	-	-	-	-	-	-	-	-	-	-
First-class	425	259	289	4	1/22	1/22	72.25	6.69	64.7	0	0
List A	397	-	-	-	-	-	-	-	-	-	-

MARTIN SAGGERS

NAME: Martin John Saggers
BORN: May 23, 1972, King's Lynn, Norfolk
HEIGHT: 6ft 2in
NICKNAME: Saggs
APPOINTED TO FIRST-CLASS LIST: 2012
COUNTIES AS PLAYER: Durham, Kent
ROLE: Bowler; RHB RFM

COUNTY DEBUT: 1996 (Durham), 1999 (Kent)
TEST DEBUT: 2003

Batting	Mat	Inns	NO	Runs	HS	Ave	SR	100	50	Ct	St
Tests	3	3	0	1	1	0.33	3.33	0	0	1	0
First-class	119	147	43	1165	64	11.20		0	2	27	0
List A	124	68	34	313	34*	9.20		0	0	23	0
T20s	10	1	0	5	5	5.00	62.50	0	0	2	0

Bowling	Mat	Balls	Runs	Wkts	BBI	BBM	Ave	Econ	SR	5w	10
Tests	3	493	247	7	2/29	3/62	35.28	3.00	70.4	0	0
First-class	119	20676	10513	415	7/79	9/112	25.33	3.05	49.8	18	0
List A	124	5622	4229	166	5/22	5/22	25.47	4.51	33.8	2	0
T20s	10	186	256	6	2/14	2/14	42.66	8.25	31.0	0	0

BILLY TAYLOR

NAME: Billy Victor Taylor
BORN: January 11, 1977,
Southampton, Hampshire
**APPOINTED TO FIRST-CLASS
LIST:** 2016
COUNTIES AS PLAYER: Sussex,
Hampshire
ROLE: Bowler; LHB RMF
COUNTY DEBUT: 1999
(Sussex), 2004 (Hampshire)

Batting	Mat	Inns	NO	Runs	HS	Ave	SR	100	50	Ct	St
First-class	54	68	26	431	40	10.26		0	0	6	0
List A	142	58	28	191	21*	6.36		0	0	26	0
T20s	37	9	8	22	12*	22.00	84.61	0	0	3	0

Bowling	Mat	Balls	Runs	Wkts	BBI	BBM	Ave	Econ	SR	5w	10
First-class	54	8412	4535	136	6/32	9/83	33.34	3.23	61.8	4	0
List A	142	6311	4699	182	5/28	5/28	25.81	4.46	34.6	1	0
T20s	37	713	883	30	2/9	2/9	29.43	7.43	23.7	0	0

RUSSELL WARREN

NAME: Russell John Warren
BORN: September 10, 1971,
Northampton
HEIGHT: 6ft 2in
NICKNAME: Rabbit
**APPOINTED TO FIRST-CLASS
LIST:** 2014
COUNTIES AS PLAYER:
Northamptonshire,
Nottinghamshire

ROLE: Wicketkeeper/batsman;
RHB OB
COUNTY DEBUT: 1992
(Northamptonshire), 2003
(Nottinghamshire)

Batting	Mat	Inns	NO	Runs	HS	Ave	SR	100	50	Ct	St
First-class	146	238	26	7776	201*	36.67		15	41	128	5
List A	177	162	25	3363	100*	24.54		1	15	135	11
T20s	2	1	0	26	26	26.00	86.66	0	0	0	0

Bowling	Mat	Balls	Runs	Wkts	BBI	BBM	Ave	Econ	SR	5w	10
First-class	146	6	0	0	-	-	-	0.00	-	0	0
List A	177	-	-	-	-	-	-	-	-	-	-
T20s	2	-	-	-	-	-	-	-	-	-	-

ALEX WHARF

NAME: Alexander George Wharf
BORN: June 4, 1975, Bradford, Yorkshire
HEIGHT: 6ft 4in
NICKNAME: Gangster
APPOINTED TO FIRST-CLASS LIST: 2014
COUNTIES AS PLAYER: Yorkshire, Nottinghamshire, Glamorgan

ROLE: Allrounder; RHB RMF
COUNTY DEBUT: 1994 (Yorkshire), 1998 (Nottinghamshire), 2000 (Glamorgan)
ODI DEBUT: 2004

Batting	Mat	Inns	NO	Runs	HS	Ave	SR	100	50	Ct	St
ODIs	13	5	3	19	9	9.50	67.85	0	0	1	0
First-class	121	184	29	3570	128*	23.03		6	14	63	0
List A	155	109	22	1411	72	16.21		0	1	42	0
T20s	34	20	7	157	19	12.07	120.76	0	0	5	0

Bowling	Mat	Balls	Runs	Wkts	BBI	BBM	Ave	Econ	SR	5w	10
ODIs	13	584	428	18	4/24	4/24	23.77	4.39	32.4	0	0
First-class	121	16825	10941	293	6/59		37.34	3.90	57.4	5	1
List A	155	6497	5552	192	6/5	6/5	28.91	5.12	33.8	1	0
T20s	34	644	1028	39	4/39	4/39	26.35	9.57	16.5	0	0

Roll *of*
Honour

Division One

Team	Mat	Won	Lost	Tied	Draw	Aban	Pts
Essex	14	10	0	0	4	0	248
Lancashire	14	5	3	0	6	0	176
Surrey	14	2	2	0	10	0	163
Yorkshire	14	4	5	0	5	0	148
Hampshire	14	3	3	0	8	0	148
Somerset	14	4	6	0	4	0	147
Middlesex	14	3	4	0	7	0	146
Warwickshire	14	1	9	0	4	0	86

Division Two

Team	Mat	Won	Lost	Tied	Draw	Aban	Pts
Worcestershire	14	9	3	0	2	0	238
Nottinghamshire	14	7	2	0	5	0	222
Northamptonshire	14	9	3	0	2	0	217
Sussex	14	7	5	0	2	0	196
Kent	14	4	2	0	7	1	175
Gloucestershire	14	3	4	0	7	0	147
Glamorgan	14	3	7	0	4	0	133
Derbyshire	14	3	7	0	3	1	127
Durham	14	3	6	0	5	0	98
Leicestershire	14	0	9	0	5	0	75

North Group

Team	Mat	Won	Lost	Tied	N/R	Pts	Net RR
Worcestershire	8	6	1	1	0	13	0.029
Yorkshire	8	6	2	0	0	12	0.865
Nottinghamshire	8	4	3	0	1	9	-0.05
Lancashire	8	4	4	0	0	8	0.198
Durham	8	4	3	0	1	7	0.24
Leicestershire	8	3	4	0	1	7	-0.001
Derbyshire	8	2	5	0	1	5	-0.339
Northamptonshire	8	1	4	1	2	5	-0.72
Warwickshire	8	2	6	0	0	4	-0.527

South Group

Team	Mat	Won	Lost	Tied	N/R	Pts	Net RR
Essex	8	7	1	0	0	14	0.882
Somerset	8	5	2	0	1	11	0.543
Surrey	8	4	3	0	1	9	0.101
Glamorgan	8	4	4	0	0	8	-0.66
Sussex	8	3	3	0	2	8	0.535
Hampshire	8	3	4	0	1	7	-0.109
Gloucestershire	8	3	4	0	1	7	-0.435
Middlesex	8	2	4	0	2	6	-0.243
Kent	8	1	7	0	0	2	-0.409

QUARTER-FINALS

Somerset v Nottinghamshire at Taunton
June 13 – *Nottinghamshire won by 24 runs*
Nottinghamshire 429-9 (50/50 ov); Somerset 405
(48/50 ov)

Yorkshire v Surrey at Headingley
June 13 – *Surrey won by 24 runs*
Surrey 313-7 (50/50 ov); Yorkshire 289-9 (50/50 ov)

*The two group winners progressed straight into
the semi-finals; the second- and third-placed
teams played two 'quarter-finals'*

SEMI-FINALS

Essex v Nottinghamshire at Chelmsford
June 16 – *Nottinghamshire won by 5 wickets*
Essex 370-5 (50/50 ov); Nottinghamshire 373-5
(49.3/50 ov)

Worcestershire v Surrey at Worcester
June 17 – *Surrey won by 153 runs*
Surrey 363-7 (50/50 ov); Worcestershire 210
(33.2/50 ov)

FINAL

Nottinghamshire v Surrey at Lord's
July 1 – *Nottinghamshire won by 4 wickets*
Surrey 297-9 (50/50 ov); Nottinghamshire 298-6
(47.5/50 ov)

North Group

Team	Mat	Won	Lost	Tied	N/R	Pts	Net RR
Nottinghamshire	14	8	4	0	2	18	0.484
Derbyshire	14	8	5	0	1	17	0.457
Warwickshire	14	8	5	0	1	17	0.23
Leicestershire	14	8	5	0	1	17	0.133
Yorkshire	14	6	5	1	2	15	1.127
Northamptonshire	14	6	5	0	3	15	-0.63
Lancashire	14	5	6	1	2	13	0.174
Worcestershire	14	3	10	0	1	7	-0.713
Durham	14	3	10	0	1	3	-1.206

South Group

Team	Mat	Won	Lost	Tied	N/R	Pts	Net RR
Glamorgan	14	7	3	0	4	18	0.045
Surrey	14	7	5	0	2	16	-0.13
Hampshire	14	7	6	0	1	15	-0.021
Somerset	14	6	6	0	2	14	0.491
Sussex	14	5	5	1	3	14	0.423
Kent	14	6	7	1	0	13	-0.158
Middlesex	14	5	7	1	1	12	0.221
Essex	14	5	7	0	2	12	-0.204
Gloucestershire	14	4	6	1	3	12	-0.648

QUARTER-FINALS

Derbyshire v Hampshire at Derby
August 22 – *Hampshire won by 101 runs*
Hampshire 249-8 (20/20 ov); Derbyshire 148 (19.5/20 ov)

Glamorgan v Leicestershire at Cardiff
August 23 – *Glamorgan won by 9 wickets*
Leicestershire 123 (19.2/20 ov); Glamorgan 126-1 (13.4/20 ov)

Nottinghamshire v Somerset at Trent Bridge
August 24 – *Nottinghamshire won by 5 wickets*
Somerset 151-6 (20/20 ov); Nottinghamshire 152-5 (18.3/20 ov)

Surrey v Warwickshire at The Oval
August 25 – *Warwickshire won by 6 wickets*
Surrey 204-5 (20/20 ov); Warwickshire 207-4 (19.4/20 ov)

SEMI-FINALS

Warwickshire v Glamorgan at Edgbaston
September 2 – *Warwickshire won by 11 runs*
Warwickshire 175-9 (20/20 ov); Glamorgan 164 (19.4/20 ov)

Hampshire v Nottinghamshire at Edgbaston
September 2 – *Nottinghamshire won by 23 runs*
Nottinghamshire 169-7 (20/20 ov); Hampshire 146 (18.4/20 ov)

FINAL

Warwickshire v Nottinghamshire at Edgbaston
September 2 – *Nottinghamshire won by 22 runs*
Nottinghamshire 190-4 (20/20 ov); Warwickshire 168-8 (20/20 ov)

FIRST-CLASS AVERAGES

Name	Mat	Inns	NO	Runs	HS	Ave	BF	SR	100	50	0	4s	6s
LWP Wells	12	22	2	1292	258	64.6	1995	64.76	4	4	2	185	15
GS Ballance	16	24	4	1164	203*	58.2	2266	51.36	3	6	0	153	4
JL Denly	14	24	2	1266	227	57.54	2060	61.45	5	5	3	157	19
DKH Mitchell	14	26	3	1266	161	55.04	2045	61.9	7	3	3	159	6
MD Stoneman	17	28	1	1481	197	54.85	2307	64.19	4	7	1	217	6
AN Cook	14	23	0	1239	243	53.86	2356	52.58	4	3	0	167	0
SA Northeast	13	23	3	1017	173*	50.85	1512	67.26	3	4	2	136	8
MH Wessels	15	20	2	913	202*	50.72	1296	70.44	3	3	2	119	16
BT Foakes	15	22	5	841	127*	49.47	1511	55.65	2	4	1	112	4
PD Collingwood	14	24	2	1087	177	49.4	1825	59.56	3	5	0	124	4
S van Zyl	13	22	1	1023	166*	48.71	1979	51.69	2	4	2	145	2
MJ Cosgrove	13	25	1	1161	188	48.37	1715	67.69	2	6	1	173	5
SR Patel	15	21	2	919	257*	48.36	1335	68.83	2	2	1	115	9
RJ Burns	15	24	1	1106	219*	48.08	2268	48.76	1	8	0	144	2
NLJ Browne	16	25	0	1147	221	45.88	2400	47.79	2	6	2	163	2
DI Stevens	13	21	3	822	115	45.66	1044	78.73	2	5	3	127	7
JC Archer	13	20	6	638	81*	45.57	725	88	0	5	2	72	21
CDJ Dent	14	25	3	978	135*	44.45	1994	49.04	2	8	0	127	4
JM Clarke	15	26	5	920	142	43.8	1293	71.15	2	3	1	129	2
AL Davies	15	26	2	1046	140*	43.58	1871	55.9	3	5	3	162	3
RI Newton	14	25	0	1060	166	42.4	1809	58.59	2	10	0	133	6
LS Livingstone	13	22	3	805	224	42.36	1391	57.87	2	3	1	100	11
AG Salter	13	20	5	623	88	41.53	1421	43.84	0	5	0	83	8
CB Cooke	13	22	5	705	113*	41.47	1317	53.53	1	4	2	97	9
JMR Taylor	15	21	4	697	143	41	1001	69.63	2	2	1	95	4
SR Dickson	14	24	0	982	318	40.91	1800	54.55	2	4	5	111	7
CT Steel	13	24	2	899	224	40.86	2040	44.06	2	4	1	110	4
D Elgar	11	21	1	813	158	40.65	1611	50.46	3	4	1	111	3
IJL Trott	15	27	4	1097	175	40.62	2095	52.36	4	5	4	139	4
CT Bancroft	11	21	4	685	206*	40.29	1395	49.1	1	4	2	91	2
DW Lawrence	16	26	4	880	141*	40	1870	47.05	3	3	3	111	4
AL Hughes	13	22	2	800	142	40	1542	51.88	2	3	0	107	2
BA Godleman	12	22	2	799	156*	39.95	1531	52.18	3	2	3	87	0
RN ten Doeschate	15	20	2	717	168*	39.83	1163	61.65	1	4	1	90	6
SD Robson	12	21	0	832	159	39.61	1482	56.14	2	4	3	123	0
T Westley	18	27	4	894	111	38.86	1824	49.01	3	3	1	149	1
DP Sibley	14	26	5	804	104*	38.28	1831	43.91	1	8	1	94	4
CA Ingram	12	20	2	672	155*	37.33	1394	48.2	2	1	2	89	5
LJ Wright	12	21	1	742	118	37.1	1019	72.81	1	4	1	109	8
G Clark	12	21	0	769	109	36.61	1235	62.26	1	6	1	101	10
LM Reece	12	21	1	732	168	36.6	1407	52.02	2	5	2	94	0
DJ Vilas	15	24	3	762	244	36.28	1260	60.47	1	3	1	83	4
EG Barnard	14	20	4	580	75	36.25	886	65.46	0	5	0	70	6
NJ Selman	15	27	2	902	142*	36.08	1864	48.39	4	3	4	110	3
BL D'Oliveira	14	25	0	891	150	35.64	1561	57.07	3	3	3	113	6
AG Wakely	14	26	4	776	112	35.27	1400	55.42	2	2	3	88	5
SM Davies	14	24	2	775	142	35.22	1427	54.3	2	3	1	93	1
JM Vince	13	21	0	738	147	35.14	1266	58.29	2	2	1	109	3
RS Bopara	15	22	2	690	192	34.5	1542	44.74	1	3	1	76	7
SS Eskinazi	14	25	2	793	179	34.47	1412	56.16	2	4	1	109	8

FIRST-CLASS BOWLING AVERAGES *Minimum of 2000 balls*

Player	Mat	Overs	Mdns	Runs	Wkts	BBI	BBM	Ave	Econ	SR	5	10
JM Anderson	13	415	125	938	60	7/42	9/73	15.63	2.26	41.5	4	0
JA Porter	15	459	108	1423	85	7/55	12/95	16.74	3.1	32.4	5	1
KJ Abbott	14	415.3	131	1092	60	7/41	9/105	18.2	2.62	41.5	4	0
DI Stevens	13	414.4	109	1157	63	8/75	9/110	18.36	2.79	39.4	7	0
SR Harmer	15	546.2	128	1429	74	9/95	14/128	19.31	2.61	44.2	4	2
J Leach	14	397.5	73	1338	69	5/32	10/122	19.39	3.36	34.5	4	1
BO Coad	13	386.4	108	1081	53	6/25	10/102	20.39	2.79	43.7	4	1
MG Hogan	13	383.4	88	1075	52	6/43	10/87	20.67	2.8	44.2	3	1
BW Sanderson	10	334.1	93	860	40	5/39	9/83	21.5	2.57	50.1	2	0
C Overton	13	373.5	106	1030	46	5/47	9/134	22.39	2.75	48.7	2	0
RK Kleinveldt	12	350.1	68	1153	50	9/65	13/98	23.06	3.29	42	2	1
R McLaren	15	389.1	91	1150	46	4/37	8/113	25	2.95	50.7	0	0
JC Archer	13	475.1	91	1543	61	7/67	11/137	25.29	3.24	46.7	4	1
JC Tongue	14	333.4	46	1212	47	6/97	6/97	25.78	3.63	42.5	2	0
C Rushworth	13	436.3	96	1217	47	5/52	8/111	25.89	2.78	55.7	1	0
MJ Leach	15	540.1	154	1403	53	6/78	9/111	26.47	2.59	61.1	4	0
GK Berg	14	391.5	103	987	37	4/28	7/45	26.67	2.51	63.5	0	0
TS Roland-Jones	13	366.4	86	1214	45	5/57	8/129	26.97	3.31	48.8	1	0
LA Dawson	13	395	102	1004	37	4/22	8/129	27.13	2.54	64	0	0
SD Parry	14	334.1	75	792	29	5/45	6/101	27.31	2.37	69.1	1	0
SCJ Broad	13	367.2	88	1038	38	3/34	5/78	27.31	2.82	58	0	0
TJ Murtagh	12	372	93	995	36	6/63	6/79	27.63	2.67	62	1	0
R Clarke	15	378	96	1095	38	7/55	9/83	28.81	2.89	59.6	1	0
JS Patel	13	482	149	1222	41	6/50	8/111	29.8	2.53	70.5	1	0
CJ Jordan	11	353.5	57	1182	36	5/46	8/128	32.83	3.34	58.9	1	0
M de Lange	11	345.5	47	1315	34	5/95	6/135	38.67	3.8	61	1	0
MT Coles	11	335	60	1313	32	6/84	6/125	41.03	3.91	62.8	1	0
SM Curran	15	388.5	74	1312	31	3/74	4/85	42.32	3.37	75.2	0	0

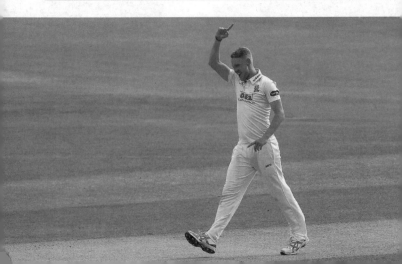

Name	Mat	Inns	Dis	Ct	St	Max Dis Inns	Dis/Inn
CMW Read	15	28	57	56	1	4 (4ct 0st)	2.035
JA Simpson	14	23	54	53	1	5 (5ct 0st)	2.347
AL Davies	15	26	53	46	7	6 (6ct 0st)	2.038
JS Foster	10	19	49	48	1	5 (5ct 0st)	2.578
SM Davies	14	25	46	39	7	4 (4ct 0st)	1.840
OB Cox	14	26	43	42	1	4 (4ct 0st)	1.653
CB Cooke	13	21	40	40	0	5 (5ct 0st)	1.904
AJ Hodd	13	22	40	39	1	4 (4ct 0st)	1.818
JM Bairstow	9	16	35	33	2	4 (4ct 0st)	2.187
AP Rouse	12	19	34	33	1	3 (3ct 0st)	1.789
BT Foakes	15	24	34	32	2	4 (4ct 0st)	1.416
LD McManus	11	20	32	29	3	4 (4ct 0st)	1.600
TR Ambrose	14	23	31	28	3	4 (4ct 0st)	1.347
SW Poynter	9	16	30	30	0	4 (4ct 0st)	1.875

FIRST-CLASS FIELDING *Minimum of 15 catches*

Name	Mat	Inns	Ct	Max	Ct/Inn
AN Cook	14	28	25	3	0.892
PD Collingwood	14	25	23	4	0.920
A Lyth	14	23	22	2	0.956
SG Borthwick	13	20	21	4	1.050
ME Trescothick	14	25	21	3	0.840
DKH Mitchell	14	26	21	3	0.807
GT Hankins	12	21	20	3	0.952
MH Wessels	15	28	20	2	0.714
V Chopra	11	21	18	3	0.857
BA Stokes	8	15	16	3	1.066
HZ Finch	12	22	16	5	0.727
NJ Selman	15	25	16	3	0.640
KK Jennings	17	31	16	3	0.516
OP Rayner	11	17	15	4	0.882
AL Hughes	13	22	15	3	0.681
SJ Mullaney	12	24	15	3	0.625
JHK Adams	13	25	15	3	0.600

#	Name	County	Batting	Bowling	Field	Capt.	Wins	Pld	Pts	Average
1	Patel, Samit	Notts	327.55	162.13	21	0	25.0	41	535	13.06
2	Patel, Jeetan	Warks	126.02	320.78	21	0	13.0	37	481	12.99
3	Abbott, Kyle	Hants	85.89	367.53	8	0	13.0	35	474	13.55
4	Overton, Craig	Somerset	78.48	355.87	22	0	15.0	35	471	13.47
5	Stevens, Darren	Kent	166.72	282.23	8	0	11.0	33	468	14.17
6	Harmer, Simon	Essex	58.82	362.26	21	0	22.0	36	464	12.89
7	Sangakkara, Kumar	Surrey	431.30	0.00	17	0	10.0	23	458	19.93
8	Porter, James	Essex	7.51	425.27	5	0	14.0	26	452	17.38
9	Archer, Jofra	Sussex	115.77	305.20	16	0	14.0	34	451	13.27
10	Ingram, Colin	Glamorgan	351.40	67.04	12	0	14.0	34	444	13.07
11	McLaren, Ryan	Lancs	171.48	241.59	10	1	12.0	31	436	14.07
12	Collingwood, Paul	Durham	293.67	89.76	28	3	10.0	33	425	12.87
13	Clarke, Rikki	Warks/Sur	118.46	277.56	20	0	8.0	31	424	13.68
14	Denly, Joe	Kent	346.58	44.58	15	0	11.0	34	417	12.28
15	Leach, Joe	Worcs	69.71	299.67	11	18	18.0	36	416	11.55
16	Madsen, Wayne	Derbyshire	263.15	100.87	26	0	13.0	35	403	11.52
17	Mitchell, Daryl	Worcs	302.08	60.97	23	0	16.0	33	402	12.18
18	Vince, James	Hants	345.71	2.69	28	12	13.0	34	401	11.81
19	Bopara, Ravi	Essex	202.46	139.27	15	0	21.0	35	378	10.79
20	Berg, Gareth	Hants	108.48	241.15	14	0	13.0	33	377	11.41
21	Curran, Sam	Surrey	99.94	240.49	11	0	15.0	36	366	10.18
22	Mullaney, Steven	Notts	178.42	145.43	21	0	21.0	35	366	10.45
23	Wessels, Riki	Notts	303.93	-0.24	31	0	25.0	41	359	8.77
24	Dawson, Liam	Hants	87.91	247.06	11	0	9.0	25	355	14.20
25	de Lange, Marchant	Glamorgan	46.62	280.45	12	0	13.0	33	352	10.67
26	Lyth, Adam	Yorks	289.65	3.52	36	0	16.0	34	345	10.15
27	Coughlin, Paul	Durham	141.81	180.95	7	3	10.0	30	343	11.44
28	Stoneman, Mark	Surrey	315.37	0.00	12	0	11.0	27	338	12.53
29	Cosgrove, Mark	Leics	316.44	4.54	6	0	11.0	35	338	9.65
30	Livingstone, Liam	Lancs	242.46	50.23	26	1	13.0	31	333	10.73
31	Kleinveldt, Rory	Northants	66.29	237.81	10	0	15.0	26	330	12.67
32	Hogan, Michael	Glamorgan	15.40	284.26	12	3	14.0	33	329	9.97
33	Barnard, Ed	Worcs	119.85	168.90	19	0	18.0	35	326	9.31
34	Hales, Alex	Notts	293.77	0.00	7	0	20.0	30	321	10.69
35	Bresnan, Tim	Yorks	72.90	211.13	16	5	14.0	31	319	10.29
36	Davies, Steven	Somerset	196.07	0.00	108	0	12.0	32	316	9.88
37	D'Oliveira, Brett	Worcs	197.98	77.88	18	0	18.0	36	312	8.66
38	Levi, Richard	Northants	289.58	0.00	11	0	11.0	26	311	11.97
39	Davies, Alex	Lancs	201.39	0.00	100	0	9.0	22	310	14.11
40	Cox, Ben	Worcs	193.17	0.00	97	0	18.0	36	308	8.55
41	Clarke, Joe	Worcs	278.22	0.00	12	0	17.0	35	307	8.78
42	Ballance, Gary	Yorks	274.37	0.00	6	11	11.0	22	302	13.74
43	ten Doeschate, Ryan	Essex	221.61	18.19	18	22	22.0	35	302	8.62
44	Bell-Drummond, Daniel	Kent	270.30	-0.80	21	0	11.0	35	302	8.61
45	Nash, Chris	Sussex	270.10	-0.90	15	2	14.0	33	300	9.09
46	Northeast, Sam	Kent	266.66	0.00	11	11	11.0	35	300	8.56
47	Barker, Keith	Warks	104.25	183.50	5	0	6.0	24	299	12.45
48	Coad, Ben	Yorks	22.56	264.03	4	0	7.0	18	298	16.53
49	Gregory, Lewis	Somerset	102.45	167.62	8	1	10.0	25	289	11.56
50	Cook, Alastair	Essex	260.78	0.00	16	0	12.0	16	289	18.05

#	Name	County	Batting	Bowling	Field	Capt.	Wins	Pld	Pts	Average
51	McKay, Clint	Leics	65.02	195.30	8	9	9.0	27	287	10.62
52	Hildreth, James	Somerset	252.36	0.00	19	0	15.0	35	286	8.18
53	Leach, Jack	Somerset	33.65	243.37	5	0	4.0	14	286	20.43
54	Batty, Gareth	Surrey	30.93	222.38	5	13	13.0	33	284	8.62
55	Chopra, Varun	Essex	244.52	0.00	20	0	19.0	31	284	9.15
56	Taylor, Jack	Gloucs	193.16	57.41	19	0	10.0	34	280	8.22
57	Simpson, John	Middx	181.58	-1.05	89	0	10.0	35	280	7.99
58	Bell, Ian	Warks	240.67	0.00	17	10	10.0	33	278	8.41
59	Roland-Jones, Toby	Middx	59.61	203.68	5	0	4.0	20	272	13.61
60	van der Merwe, Roelof	Somerset	99.23	144.86	16	0	12.0	25	272	10.88
61	Curran, Tom	Surrey	69.83	179.10	11	0	12.0	29	272	9.38
62	Bailey, George	Hants	243.34	-0.45	15	2	12.0	31	272	8.77
63	Finn, Steven	Middx	24.87	228.54	9	0	8.0	25	270	10.82
64	Hain, Sam	Warks	230.13	0.00	25	0	12.0	32	267	8.35
65	Howell, Benny	Gloucs	114.19	133.78	10	0	7.0	21	265	12.62
66	Rushworth, Chris	Durham	32.75	213.16	11	0	8.0	31	265	8.55
67	Norwell, Liam	Gloucs	15.98	238.81	5	0	5.0	17	265	15.58
68	Foakes, Ben	Surrey	193.37	0.00	62	0	9.0	29	264	9.12
69	Reece, Luis	Derbyshire	214.49	26.55	9	0	11.0	30	261	8.71
70	van Zyl, Stiaan	Sussex	211.65	26.67	9	0	14.0	29	261	9.00
71	Rudolph, Jacques	Glamorgan	228.18	0.00	6	12	14.0	33	261	7.90
72	Trott, Jonathan	Warks	242.83	1.67	11	0	3.0	22	259	11.75
73	Jordan, Chris	Sussex	57.59	173.45	15	0	12.0	25	258	10.34
74	Clark, Jordan	Lancs	119.82	123.18	3	0	12.0	28	258	9.21
75	Vilas, Dane	Lancs	224.12	0.00	18	0	14.0	34	256	7.53
76	Sanderson, Ben	Northants	14.93	224.70	3	0	13.0	24	256	10.67
77	Ball, Jake	Notts	23.99	204.59	8	0	19.0	27	255	9.45
78	Jennings, Keaton	Durham	168.00	58.10	19	4	6.0	23	255	11.08
79	Wiese, David	Sussex	78.42	155.98	6	0	13.0	31	254	8.19
80	Clark, Graham	Durham	220.21	0.00	19	0	9.0	34	248	7.30
81	Duckett, Ben	Northants	214.31	2.48	18	0	13.0	28	248	8.84
82	Wakely, Alex	Northants	194.65	-0.64	21	16	16.0	31	247	7.97
83	Coles, Matt	Kent	58.52	165.07	14	0	9.0	28	246	8.79
84	Cooke, Chris	Glamorgan	164.42	0.00	66	0	15.0	34	246	7.22
85	Handscomb, Peter	Yorks	193.08	0.00	39	0	13.0	25	245	9.80
86	Godleman, Billy	Derbyshire	215.60	0.00	12	4	12.0	34	244	7.18
87	Gurney, Harry	Notts	8.74	207.07	6	0	22.0	38	244	6.41
88	Hughes, Alex	Derbyshire	199.09	11.26	28	0	13.0	35	242	6.92
89	Lawrence, Dan	Essex	190.10	22.58	12	0	16.0	27	241	8.91
90	Wright, Luke	Sussex	209.71	0.00	10	4	12.0	29	236	8.12
91	Parry, Stephen	Lancs	46.89	157.68	14	0	14.0	33	233	7.05
92	Willey, David	Yorks	122.07	91.50	9	0	10.0	18	233	12.92
93	Crane, Mason	Hants	12.53	196.20	9	0	13.0	27	231	8.55
94	Groenewald, Tim	Somerset	30.70	182.65	4	0	12.0	27	229	8.49
95	Gleeson, Richard	Northants	9.52	196.83	8	0	11.0	25	225	9.01
96	Burns, Rory	Surrey	194.05	0.00	19	0	12.0	27	225	8.34
97	Hastings, John	Worcs	82.33	125.26	6	0	11.0	23	225	9.76
98	Elgar, Dean	Somerset	205.68	6.30	8	0	4.0	14	224	16.00
99	Wagner, Neil	Essex	32.70	168.95	6	0	12.0	17	220	12.92
100	Westley, Tom	Essex	179.95	11.69	12	0	16.0	25	220	8.79